P9-DBL-576

QuickBooks® 2009
The Official Guide

DISCARD

QuickBooks® 2009
The Official Guide

KATHY IVENS

New York   Chicago   San Francisco
Lisbon   London   Madrid   Mexico City   Milan
New Delhi   San Juan   Seoul   Singapore   Sydney   Toronto

The McGraw·Hill Companies

Cataloging-in-Publication Data is on file with the Library of Congress

McGraw-Hill books are available at special quantity discounts to use as premiums and sales promotions, or for use in corporate training programs. To contact a special sales representative, please visit the Contact Us page at www.mhprofessional.com.

QuickBooks® 2009 The Official Guide

Copyright © 2009 by The McGraw-Hill Companies. All rights reserved. Printed in the United States of America. Except as permitted under the Copyright Act of 1976, no part of this publication may be reproduced or distributed in any form or by any means, or stored in a database or retrieval system, without the prior written permission of publisher, with the exception that the program listings may be entered, stored, and executed in a computer system, but they may not be reproduced for publication.

1 2 3 4 5 6 7 8 9 0   FGR FGR   0 1 9 8

ISBN   978-0-07-159859-0
MHID   0-07-159859-6

Sponsoring Editor Megg Morin	**Copy Editor** Sally Engelfried	**Composition** International Typesetting and Composition
Editorial Supervisor Patty Mon	**Proofreader** LeeAnn Pickrell	**Illustration** International Typesetting and Composition
Project Editor LeeAnn Pickrell	**Indexer** Rebecca Plunkett	**Art Director, Cover** Jeff Weeks
Acquisitions Coordinator Carly Stapleton	**Production Supervisor** George Anderson	
Technical Editor Thomas E. Barich		

Information has been obtained by McGraw-Hill from sources believed to be reliable. However, because of the possibility of human or mechanical error by our sources, McGraw-Hill, or others, McGraw-Hill does not guarantee the accuracy, adequacy, or completeness of any information and is not responsible for any errors or omissions or the results obtained from the use of such information.

Contents at a Glance

Part One

Getting Started

Part Two

Bookkeeping with QuickBooks

Part Three
Financial Planning and Reporting

Part Four
Managing QuickBooks

Part Five
Appendix

Contents

Part Two
Bookkeeping with QuickBooks

• **Part Three**
Financial Planning and Reporting

Part Four
Managing QuickBooks

Part Five
Appendix

Acknowledgments

I want to express my appreciation to the people who worked hard to get this book into your hands. At McGraw-Hill, thanks to Megg Morin for the opportunity to continue to do this book for twelve years, kudos to Production Editor LeeAnn Pickrell for her skillful management of all the complicated processes involved in producing a book, and a grateful nod of appreciation to Carly Stapleton for tracking all the steps that take place as a book moves from manuscript to a bound volume.

I've been lucky enough to work with a team that includes wonderful independent freelancers. I'm always glad to have the opportunity to work with Sally Engelfried, who is an amazingly talented copy editor, and with technical editor Thomas E. Barich (www.infodesigning.com), who is the best!

Many people at Intuit provided information, support, and advice throughout the writing of this book, and I'm indebted to them for the time and knowledge they contributed. It's impossible to list everyone at Intuit who helped (it would take too many pages), but I want to extend my gratitude to some of the generous folks who were kind enough to go back and forth with me multiple times as I asked questions and then asked more and more questions. Alvin Lee, who was there 24/7, directing my questions to the appropriate experts within Intuit, has my everlasting appreciation. Abdenour Bezzouh, Jon Burt, Angela Cheung, Victoria Dolginsky, Pranay Kapadia, Puja Ramani, Mark Russell, Laurie Wood, and "Sam" from QuickBooks Beta Support have my thanks for the time and patience they expended, as well as my admiration for their knowledge and understanding of QuickBooks features.

Introduction

How to Use This Book

I tried to organize this book with a certain amount of logic connected to the way you'll probably use your QuickBooks software. You can consult the table of contents, where you'll notice that the topics start with the tasks you perform immediately after installing the software, move on to the tasks you perform often, and then cover the tasks you perform less frequently.

The index guides you to specific tasks and features, so when you absolutely must know immediately how to do something, it's easy to find the instructions.

However, there are some sections of this book you should read first, just because accounting software is much more complex than most other types of software. You should read Chapter 1 to learn what information to have at hand in order to set up your accounting system properly. Then, you should read the first two chapters so you can configure your system properly. After that, consult the index and head for the chapter or section you need.

What's Provided in This Book to Help You

There are some special elements in this book that you'll find extremely useful:

- **Tips**   Give you some additional insight about a subject or a task. Sometimes they're shortcuts, and sometimes they're tricks I've learned from working with clients.
- **Notes**   Provide extra information about a topic or a task. Sometimes they provide information about what happens behind the scenes when you perform a task, and sometimes they have additional information I think you might be curious about.

- **Cautions**   Are presented to help you avoid the traps you can fall into if a task has a danger zone.
- **FYI boxes**   Are filled with facts you don't necessarily need to perform a task, but the information may be helpful. Some FYI boxes help you understand the way QuickBooks "thinks" (all software applications have a predictable thinking pattern); others are designed to point out the way certain procedures help you run your business.

You and Your Accountant

One of the advantages of double-entry bookkeeping software like QuickBooks is that a great many simple bookkeeping tasks are performed automatically. If you've been keeping manual books or using a check-writing program such as Quicken, your accountant will probably have less work to do now that you're using QuickBooks.

Many accountants visit clients regularly or ask that copies of checkbook registers be sent to the accountants' offices. Then, using the data from the transactions, a general ledger is created, along with a trial balance and other reports based on the general ledger (Profit & Loss Statements and Balance Sheets).

If you've had such a relationship with your accountant, it ends with QuickBooks. Your accountant will only have to provide tax advice and business planning advice. All those bookkeeping chores are performed by QuickBooks, which keeps a general ledger and provides reports based on the data in the general ledger.

Throughout this book, I've provided information about general ledger postings as you create transactions in QuickBooks, and you'll also find I speak up about other information I believe is important to your accountant. Accountants tend to ask questions about how software handles certain issues (especially payroll, inventory, accounts receivable, and accounts payable), and I've had many years of experience working with accountants who asked me "why?" and "what's this?" as I set up bookkeeping software. There are also a number of places in this book where I advise you to call your accountant before making a decision about how to handle certain types of transactions.

Don't worry, your accountant won't complain about losing the day-to-day, boring bookkeeping tasks. Most accountants prefer to handle more professional chores, and they rarely protest when you tell them they no longer have to be bookkeepers. Their parents didn't spend all that money on their advanced, difficult education for that.

Part One

Getting Started

ongratulations on deciding to use QuickBooks to track your business finances. This is a big decision, and it's one that will change your business life for the better. However, working in QuickBooks isn't the same as working in most other software programs. For example, with a word processor you can open the program and dive right in, sending letters to your family or memos to your staff.

Accounting software such as QuickBooks, however, has to be set up, configured, and carefully tweaked before you can begin using it. If you don't do the preliminary work, the software won't work properly. In fact, the first time you use QuickBooks, you'll be asked to take part in an interview that's designed to help you configure your QuickBooks system properly.

In Part One of this book, you'll learn how to gather the information you need to get started, and then you'll learn how to create your company file. I'll explain what's really important, and what you can do all by yourself instead of using the automated interview wizard to set up your company file properly. I'll even explain when it's okay to lie and how to lie in a way that makes your QuickBooks company file accurate. Part One also includes chapters containing instructions and hints about putting all those boring, but vitally important, elements into your QuickBooks system, like customers, vendors, general ledger information, and a variety of lists that contain data to help you track your finances more assiduously. (Sorry, but these tasks are necessary; you cannot keep accurate books without them.)

Using QuickBooks for the First Time

*I*n *this chapter:*

- Things to do first

- Understand a general ledger

- Open QuickBooks

- Create a company file

- Get to know the QuickBooks window

The first time you launch QuickBooks, you have to introduce yourself and your company to the software by means of a rather substantial setup process. This process has a lot of tasks to wade through, but it's a one-time-only job.

Do This First

If you're new to QuickBooks, before you work in the software you have to do three things:

- Decide on the starting date for your QuickBooks system.
- Find all the detailed records, notes, memos, and other items that you've been using to track your financial numbers.
- Create an opening trial balance to enter into QuickBooks.

If you don't prepare your records properly, all the advantages of a computer-bookkeeping system will be lost to you. The information you enter when you first start using QuickBooks will follow you forever. If it's accurate, that's great! It means you have the right foundation for all the calculations that QuickBooks will perform for you and all the reports you generate to keep an eye on your business and file your tax returns.

If it's not accurate, that fact will haunt you. It's not that you can't change things in QuickBooks; it's that if you start with bad numbers you frequently can't figure out which numbers were bad. Your inability to trace the origin of a problem will be what makes the problem permanent.

So get out that shoebox, manila envelope, or a printout of the spreadsheet you've been using to keep numbers. We're going to organize your records in a way that makes it easy to get QuickBooks up and running—accurately.

Deciding on the Start Date

The *start date* is the date on which you begin entering your bookkeeping records into QuickBooks. Think of it as a conversion date. In the computer consulting field, we call this "the date we go live." Things went on before this date (these are historical records and some of them must be entered into QuickBooks), but from this date on, your transactions go through QuickBooks.

This is not a trivial decision. The date you select has an enormous impact on how much work it's going to be to set up QuickBooks. For example, if you choose a starting date in September, every transaction that occurred in your business prior to that date has to be entered into your QuickBooks system before you start entering September transactions. Okay, that's an exaggeration because you can enter some numbers in bulk instead of entering each individual transaction, but the principle is the same. If it's March, this decision is a lot easier because the work attached to your QuickBooks setup is less onerous.

Here's what to think about as you make this decision:

- The best way to start a new computer-accounting software system is to have every individual transaction in the system—every invoice you sent to customers, every check you wrote to vendors, every payroll check you gave an employee.
- The second best way to start a new computer-accounting software system is to enter running totals of categories (general ledger accounts) of the transactions that made up each total. Then enter any open transactions (unpaid customer invoices and vendor bills), up to a certain date (your starting date), and then after that every single transaction goes into the system.

There is no third best way, because any fudging on either of those choices makes your figures suspect.

If it's the first half of the year when you read this, make your start date the first day of the year and enter everything you've done so far this year. It sounds like a lot of work, but it really isn't. When you start entering transactions in QuickBooks, such as customer invoices, you just pick the customer, enter a little information, and move on to the next invoice. Of course, you have to enter all your customers, but you'd have to do that even if you weren't entering every transaction for the current year. (The next few chapters are all about entering lists: accounts, customers, vendors, and so on.)

If it's the middle of the year, toss a coin. Seriously, if you have gobs of transactions every month, you might want to enter large opening balances and then enter real transactions as they occur, beginning with the start date.

If it's late in the year as you read this, perhaps October or November or later, and you usually send a lot of invoices to customers, write a lot of checks, and do your own payroll, think about waiting until next year to start using QuickBooks.

Gathering the Information You Need

You have to have quite a bit of information available when you first start to use QuickBooks, and it's ridiculous to hunt it down as each particle of information is needed when you're sitting at your computer, using the software. It's much better to gather it all together now, before you start working in QuickBooks.

The work you have to do to create opening balances in QuickBooks is covered in Chapter 8 (which is devoted to technical instructions about entering all this information), so the discussions in this section are devoted to helping you assemble the information you need.

Cash Balances

You have to tell QuickBooks what the balance is for each bank account you use in your business. Don't glance at the checkbook stubs—that's not the balance I'm talking about. The balance is the *reconciled* balance. And it has to be a reconciled balance as of the starting date you're using in QuickBooks.

If you haven't balanced your checkbooks against the bank statements for a while, do it now. In addition to the reconciled balance, you need to have a list of the dates, customer/vendor, and amounts of the transactions that haven't yet cleared.

Customer Balances

If any customer owes you money as of your starting date, you have to tell QuickBooks about it. Enter each unpaid customer invoice, using the real, original dates for each invoice. Those dates must be earlier than your QuickBooks start date. This means you have to assemble all the information about unpaid customer invoices, including such details as how much of each invoice was for services, for items sold, for shipping, and for sales tax.

Vendor Balances

The vendor balances (the money you owe as of your start date) are treated like the customer balances. You have the same chores (and the same decisions) facing you regarding any unpaid bills you owe to vendors. If you have the financial wherewithal, it might be easiest to pay them, just to avoid the work of entering all that data.

Asset Balances

Besides your bank accounts, you have to know the balance of all your assets. You'll need to know the current value and accumulated depreciation for fixed assets. For the accounts receivable balance, as you enter your open customer balances QuickBooks will be creating that number automatically.

Liability Balances

Get all the information about your liabilities together. The open vendor bills you enter determine your accounts payable balance automatically. You'll need to know the current balance of any loans or mortgages. If there are unpaid withholding amounts from payroll, they must be entered (but this is definitely something that's smarter to pay instead of entering as an open liability).

Payroll Information

If you do the payroll instead of using a payroll service, you'll need to know everything about each employee: social security number, all the information that goes into determining tax status (federal, state, and local), and which deductions are taken for health or pension. You have all this information, of course; you just have to get it together. If your employees are on salary, you've probably been repeating the check information every payday, with no need to look up these items. Dig up the W-4 forms and all your notes about who's on what deduction plan.

You also need to know which payroll items you have to track: salary, wages, federal deductions, state deductions (tax, SUI, SDI), local income tax deductions, benefits, pension, and any other deductions (garnishments, for example). And that's not all—you also have to know the name of the vendor to whom these withholding amounts are remitted (government tax agencies, insurance companies, and so on).

Inventory Information

You need to know the name of every inventory item you carry, how much you paid for each item, and how many of each item you have in stock as of the starting date.

Understanding the General Ledger

The general ledger is a list of posting accounts, and in QuickBooks it's called the *chart of accounts*. This chart of accounts is a list of categories, called *accounts*, to which money is attached. When you link a transaction to a category, that's called *posting*. For instance, when you deposit money into your bank, there's an account named Bank (which you can name to match the name of your bank, such as BigFederal), and you post the money to that account. All of your postings to the chart of accounts make up your *general ledger*. You need to put together your categories, including assets, liabilities, income, and expenses.

Because QuickBooks is an accounting software application, you have to follow the rules of accounting, which means you must have an equal, offsetting posting to another account every time you enter a transaction. If the bank deposit is the result of a sale of goods, the offset posting for the bank deposit is to an income account (which you might name Income or Revenue).

All accounting software is based on a double-entry system of bookkeeping. This means that for every entry you make, there must be an equal and opposite entry made. Opposite refers to the other side of the ledger, and the ledger sides are labeled Debit and Credit.

DEBIT	CREDIT
ASSETS	
	LIABILITIES
	EQUITY
	REVENUE
EXPENSES	

Assets

An *asset* is something you own, such as

- Money in your bank accounts (sometimes called *cash on hand*)
- Money owed to you by your customers (called *accounts receivable*)
- Equipment, furniture, and so on (called *fixed assets*)
- The inventory you stock for resale if you are a distributor or manufacturer (called *inventory assets*)

Liabilities

A *liability* is something that you may be holding but does not belong to you. It is something you owe to someone else, such as

- Money you owe your vendors and suppliers (called *accounts payable*)
- Sales tax you have collected and must turn over to the state (called *current liabilities*)
- Money withheld from employees' pay that you must turn over to government agencies (also part of *current liabilities*)
- Outstanding loan balances (called *long term liabilities*)

Equity

Your *equity* is your net worth and is made up of the following:

- The capital invested in your business (called *capital*)
- The capital you've withdrawn from the business (if your business isn't a corporation)
- The profit (or loss) including accumulated earnings in prior years (called *retained earnings*)

Revenue

Revenue is income, which you can track using multiple categories in order to analyze where and how you are receiving funds, such as

- Money you collect when you sell products
- Fees you collect for services
- Income derived from interest

Expenses

Expenses are the monies you spend. You use the chart of accounts to divide your expenses by category (account) for the purpose of meeting requirements on tax returns and also for your own analysis. Generally, expenses are divided into two main categories: cost of goods sold (COGS), and general and administrative expenses.

Cost of goods sold is usually tracked for the following categories:

- Cost of raw materials for manufacturing
- Cost of goods you resell in a wholesale or retail business
- Cost of materials consumed/sold in a service business

General and administrative expenses include

- Overhead (utilities, rent, insurance, and so on)
- Office supplies
- Payroll
- Services you purchase
- Taxes

As you enter transactions in QuickBooks, you don't have to worry about the equal and opposite posting. QuickBooks takes care of the "other side" automatically. (QuickBooks knows what the other side is because you indicate that information when you set up your company file.)

For example, if you sell goods or services to a customer and send an invoice (you don't have the money yet), the invoice transaction screen asks you to fill in the name of the customer, the product or service you sold, and the amount you're charging. QuickBooks posts the amount to accounts receivable (on the Debit side of the ledger) and to Income (on the Credit side of the ledger) and also posts a record of the transaction in the customer's record. Later, when the customer pays the invoice, QuickBooks credits that amount to accounts receivable (washing away the original debited amount) and debits your bank account.

On the other hand, if you collect the cash at the time of the sale, the accounts receivable account isn't needed. Instead, your bank account receives a debit posting for the amount of the sale, and the income account receives a credit.

As you begin to use QuickBooks and read the chapters of this book, all of this will become clearer; I promise.

Other Useful Bits of Paper

Find last year's tax return. QuickBooks is going to want to know which tax forms you use. Also, there's usually other information on the tax forms you might need (such as depreciation amounts).

If you have a loan or mortgage, have the amortization schedule handy. You can figure out the year-to-date (the "date" is the QuickBooks starting date) principal and interest amounts.

Opening Trial Balance

Your opening trial balance, which probably should be prepared with the help of your accountant, almost creates itself during the setup process. If your QuickBooks start date is the beginning of the year, it's a snap. The opening trial balance for the first day of the year has no income or expenses. It should look something like this:

Account Type	Account	Debit	Credit
Assets	Bank	$10,000	
	Fixed Assets	$50,000	
	Accumulated Depreciation		$5,000
Liabilities	Loan from Bank		$15,000
Equity	Equity (Capital, Prior Retained Earnings, and so on)		$40,000

Notice that there is no inventory figure in this opening balance (even though inventory is an asset). You should receive the inventory into your system with QuickBooks transaction windows for receiving inventory, so there's a quantity available for each inventory item. As you bring the inventory in and assign it a value, your inventory asset will build its own worth. (Inventory is covered in Chapter 7.)

Also, notice there are no amounts for accounts receivable (an asset) or accounts payable (a liability). As you enter the open (unpaid) customer invoices and vendor bills, those postings will take care of filling in the totals for those accounts.

NOTE: Read Chapter 8 for detailed instructions on setting up all your opening account balances.

You're now ready to set up and configure your QuickBooks company file! Let's get started.

Launching the Software

The QuickBooks installation program places a shortcut to the software on your desktop, and that's the easiest way to open QuickBooks. If you have software windows covering the desktop, you can use the Start menu, where you'll find QuickBooks in the Programs menu. Place your pointer on the QuickBooks listing in the Programs menu and choose QuickBooks from the submenu.

 TIP: For even faster access to QuickBooks, copy or move the desktop shortcut to your Quick Launch toolbar, which requires only a single click to open software. Right-drag the shortcut icon onto the Quick Launch toolbar, and then choose Move Here (or Copy Here, if you want a shortcut in both places).

When QuickBooks opens for the first time, you see an explanation of the QuickBooks Update service (covered in Chapter 27), followed by the Welcome To QuickBooks Pro 2009 window, which offers several options for starting to work in QuickBooks.

Overview Tutorial   Select this option to view a tutorial on QuickBooks features.

Explore QuickBooks   Click this option to display a list of two sample companies you can explore and play with in order to get familiar with QuickBooks. One company is designed for product-based businesses, the other for service-based businesses.

Create A New Company File   Select this option to begin the process of creating a company file. All of the steps involved in this task are covered in this chapter.

Open An Existing Company File   Select this option if you're upgrading from a previous version of QuickBooks. Go through the windows in the Open Or Restore Company Wizard to select your company file. QuickBooks offers to upgrade the file to your new version, and after you type **Yes** and click OK to accept the offer, QuickBooks insists on making a backup of your file in its current version. When the backup is complete, the file is converted to QuickBooks 2009, and you can begin working.

CAUTION: If you're working in a network environment and you installed QuickBooks 2009 as an upgrade to a previous version, upgrade QuickBooks on the computer that holds the company data file first. Then upgrade QuickBooks on the other computers.

Creating Your Company File

For now, choose Create A New Company File, because that's what this chapter is all about. The EasyStep Interview window opens to begin the process of creating your company file (see Figure 1-1).

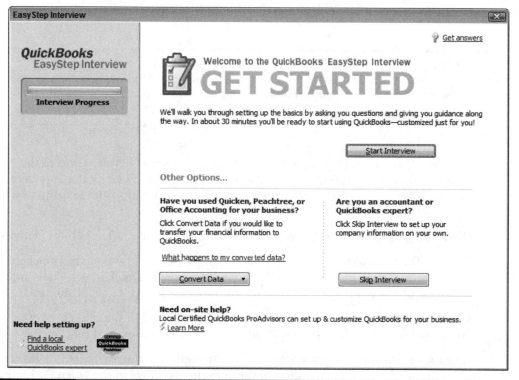

FIGURE 1-1 The EasyStep Interview takes you on a walk through the processes involved in setting up your company file.

QuickBooks offers two methods for creating this file:

- Use the EasyStep Interview (a wizard in which you move through the pages, answering questions and providing information).
- Create your company file manually.

I'll cover both methods in this chapter, starting with the EasyStep Interview.

Using the EasyStep Interview

Click Start Interview to begin the wizard that helps you create your company file. As with all wizards, you click Next to move through the windows.

Entering Company Information

To begin, QuickBooks needs basic information about your company (see Figure 1-2). Notice that the information about your company name has two entry fields. The first field is for the real company name, the one you do business as. The second field, for your company's legal name, is optional and is used only if the legal name of your company differs from the company name you use for doing business. For instance, your company may do business as WeAreWidgets, but your legal or corporate name might be WAW, Inc.

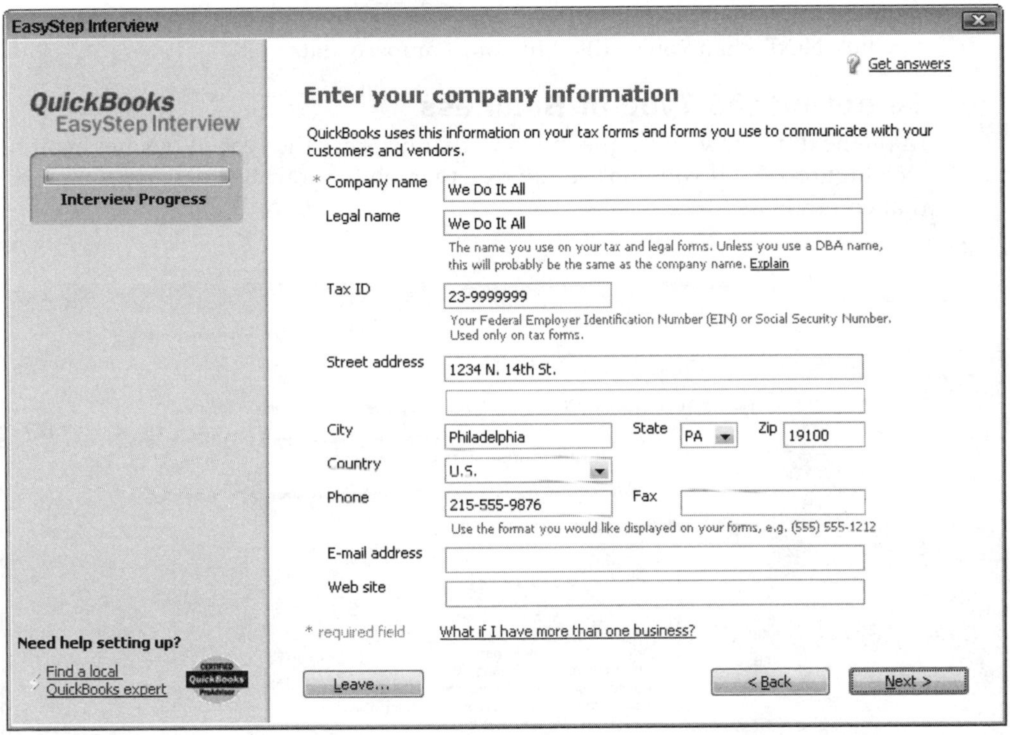

FIGURE 1-2   Enter basic information about your business.

Enter the company tax ID number. If you have a federal employer ID number (EIN), it's a nine-digit number in the format *XX-YYYYYYY*. If you don't have an EIN, enter your social security number.

You have a tax ID number if you have employees, and you may have one if you have a business bank account (many banks require this, although some banks merely ask for a copy of a fictitious name registration certificate and will accept your social security number instead of a federal ID).

If you are a sole proprietor, using your social security number for business purposes, you should apply for a federal ID number. This helps you separate your business and personal finances by using the EIN for business transactions and maintaining a separate bank account in your business name. Additionally, because you should be thinking in terms of business growth, you're going to need an EIN eventually to pay subcontractors, consultants, or employees. Get it now and avoid the rush.

Enter the contact information (address, telephone, and so on). This data is used on the transactions you print (such as invoices), so enter this data as you want those elements to appear on printed documents. For example, you may want to display your telephone number as AAA.BBB.CCCC or (AAA) BBB-CCCC.

Click Next when you've filled in your company data.

Selecting the Type of Business

In the next window, select the industry that matches the type of business you have (see Figure 1-3). If you don't see an exact match for your business type, choose one that comes close.

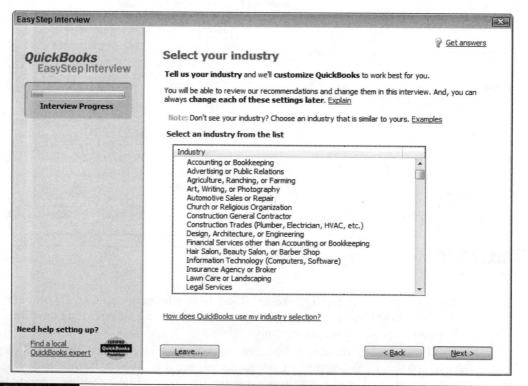

FIGURE 1-3 Find the type of business that matches yours.

Selecting Your Legal Entity Type

The next window displays the various types of legal entities for businesses, such as proprietorship, partnership, corporation, and so on. Select the one that matches the way your business is organized.

If you're not sure, ask your accountant, or find a copy of the business income tax you filed last year (unless this is your first year in business) and match the form number to the list in the window. If you can't find the information, select Other/ None. You can change it later in the Company Information dialog accessed from the Company menu.

In truth, it doesn't matter what you enter here unless you do your own taxes. QuickBooks uses this information to attach information to all your accounts that affect your taxes. The information includes the form and line number used by each account in your federal tax forms.

Configuring Your Fiscal Year

In the next window, enter the first month of your fiscal year. QuickBooks enters January as the default entry, but if you're not using a calendar year select the appropriate month from the drop-down list.

Setting Up the Administrator

The next window asks you for an administrator password. It's a good idea to create a password to limit access to your company file, and to prevent anyone who gets near your computer from spying on your financial information.

If multiple users will access the file simultaneously (on a network), user names are required (and each should have a password).

However, you can wait until after you've finished the EasyStep Interview and implement the feature later, when you can concentrate on the task and make notes about the passwords.

NOTE: User logins and passwords let you place restrictions on users and the types of transactions they can work on or the type of information they can see. Those features are covered in Chapter 26.

Saving Your Company File

The next window explains that you're about to save your company file. Click Next to see the Filename For New Company dialog, which is ready to save the file using a filename based on the company name you've entered. Just click Save to use that filename. Or, if you prefer, you can change the name of the file (especially if your company name is long or complicated). It takes a few seconds for QuickBooks to save the company file and set up all the files for the company.

TIP: It's a good idea to use a filename that hints at your company name, instead of choosing a filename such as Myfiles. Then, if you start another business, you can choose another specific filename for your new venture. Of course, you may end up using QuickBooks for your personal financial records, in which case you'll want a specific filename for that, too.

By default, QuickBooks saves your company file in a subfolder under the Documents subfolder for the computer user named All Users (which may be named Shared Documents, depending the version of Windows you're using).

Most experienced users find it better to create a folder on your hard drive for your QuickBooks data (for instance, C:\QBDataFiles). This makes it easier to find and back up your data.

CAUTION: If you run QuickBooks on a network, or another user works in QuickBooks on your computer, make sure the folder you create for your data has permissions set properly—the EVERYONE group must be given Full Control.

Customizing Your Company File

The ensuing wizard windows provide a series of choices and options about the way you do business. For example, you're asked what you sell (services, products, or both), whether you charge sales tax, whether you use estimates, and so on. The questions are clearly stated and easy to answer. You don't have to perform any setup tasks if you answer Yes; for example, if you answer Yes when you're asked if you have employees, you don't have to create employee information. You can do all of that later.

Essentially, the wizard is setting configuration options for you, but you can set any of those options for yourself at any time in the future. Information about the options you need to perform certain tasks is found throughout this book, in the appropriate chapters.

Some Wizard Questions to Consider Carefully

During the customization process the wizard covers three topics you need to consider carefully:

Your start date   For the wizard window on your start date, be sure to read the information found earlier in this chapter about this topic before you fill in your answer.

Your bank account   When the wizard asks if you want to set up a bank account, you can answer No, and set up your bank account later (which is my recommendation). If you answer Yes, the next window asks you to fill in the name of the account and indicate whether the account was established before the starting date you entered as your QuickBooks "go live" date, or on/after that date.

Your bank account was probably established before your QuickBooks start date, and if you select that option, in the next window the wizard asks for the date of the last reconciliation, and the bank balance as of that date.

Do *not* enter a balance for the bank account; it causes work for your accountant. QuickBooks posts the amount of the opening balance to an account named Opening Bal Equity, which is a QuickBooks invention to hold amounts that haven't yet been assigned to the correct category. Your accountant will have to empty that account and post the money that's already in your bank account to real accounts (and that task can be a time-consuming process).

Either leave the amount at zero, or go back to the question about when your account was established and lie to the wizard, indicating that your bank account was opened *after* your QuickBooks start date.

CAUTION: *Never* fill in an opening balance for any accounts you create, whether you create them during company file setup or later when you've begun using QuickBooks. Instead, work with your accountant (or your checkbook register) to enter all your opening balances by posting the information to real accounts instead of the Opening Bal Equity account. You learn how to create an opening trial balance in Chapter 8.

Enabling multiple currencies If you enable this option at this time, you can't disable it. If you decide not to track multiple currencies, and the feature is enabled, no harm results; however, all your customer/vendor names and most of the transaction windows you use will have currency fields.

Creating the Chart of Accounts

The Review Income And Expense Accounts Wizard window lets you set up the chart of accounts, which is a list of accounts you'll use to post transactions.

The wizard displays the income and expense accounts it has established for your company, based on the responses you made to the interview question regarding your type of business (see Figure 1-4).

You can select or deselect specific accounts if you know you need or don't need any of the accounts listed. However, it may be easier to go through that process later. You'll need additional accounts in your chart of accounts (assets, liabilities, and so on in addition to other income and expense accounts your accountant recommends), but it's easier to add them after you've finished this company setup task (setting up your chart of accounts is covered in Chapter 2).

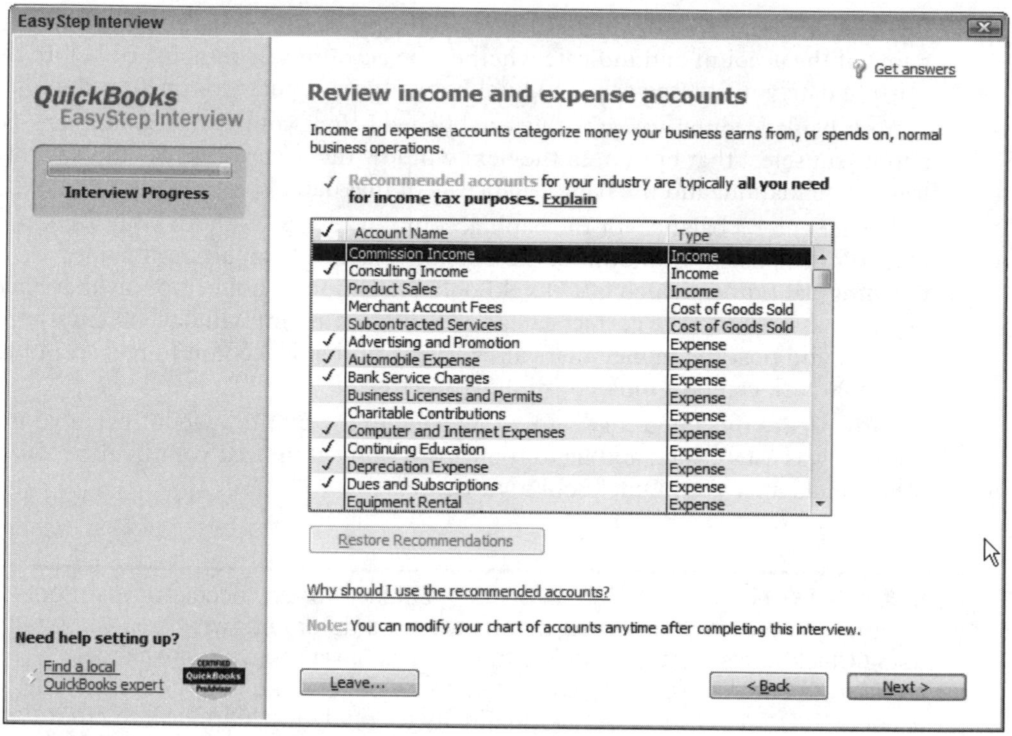

FIGURE 1-4 You can select or deselect accounts now, or wait until you've begun using QuickBooks.

CAUTION: At the bottom of the chart of accounts listed in the wizard window is an account named Political Contributions. Do *not* select it. It is absolutely illegal to declare political contributions in a business, and if you select that account and then enter a contribution, that entry affects your net profit and taxable income; until, of course, the IRS pays a visit.

Setting Up an Intuit Online Account

The wizard offers the opportunity to set up an online account with Intuit, which provides access to online features. If you're interested in creating this account (it's free), you can do so now or wait until you've begun using QuickBooks.

That's it; you're finished. QuickBooks opens your company's Home page. Later in this chapter, in the section "The QuickBooks Software Window," I'll explain how to begin learning about the QuickBooks Home page and other elements you see when you're using the software.

Performing a Manual Setup

If you click Skip Interview in the first EasyStep Interview window, the Skip Interview dialog opens, and you can enter the basic information quickly (see Figure 1-5).

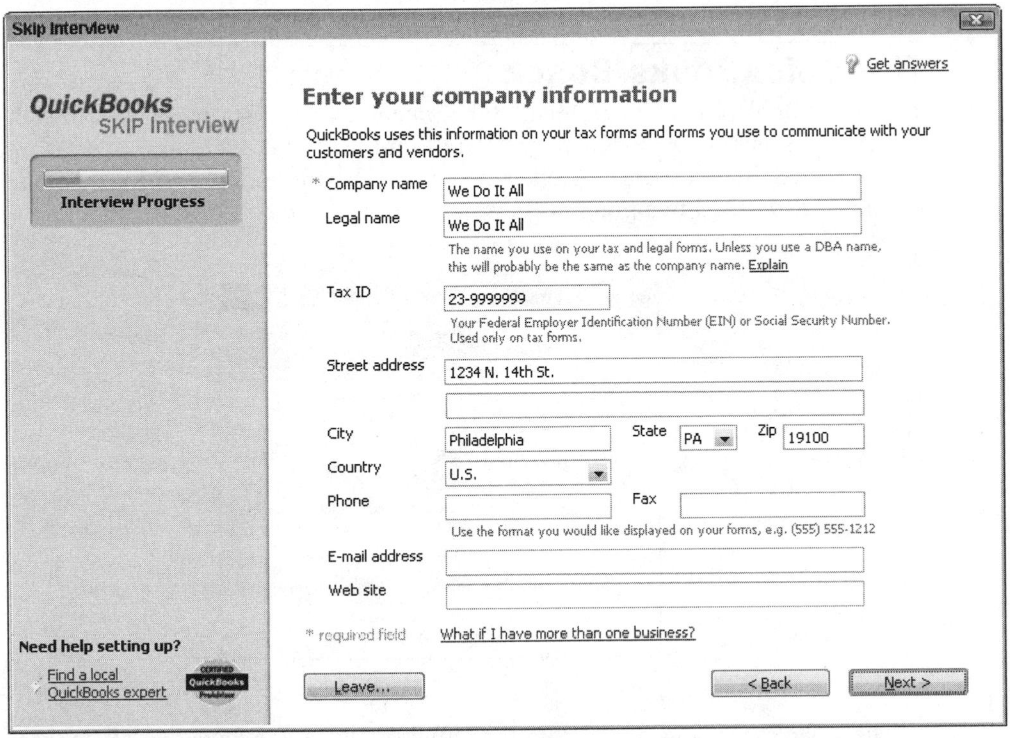

FIGURE 1-5 Enter company information in the Creating New Company dialog.

Click Next to select the type of business entity you used to create your company, which also tells QuickBooks the type of tax return you file. QuickBooks uses this information to attach information to all your accounts about tax lines on tax returns and to create the appropriate type of equity accounts.

In the next window, enter the first month of your fiscal year. Most small businesses use a calendar year, so the default selection of January is probably appropriate. If you operate on a noncalendar fiscal year, select the first month from the drop-down list.

In the next window, select the industry that comes closest to describing your business. QuickBooks uses this information to install some appropriate accounts in your chart of accounts.

Follow the prompts to save your company file and decide whether to sign up for an Intuit online account.

The QuickBooks Software Window

When the EasyStep Interview window closes, or when you save your company file after creating it manually, QuickBooks opens its software window, which I'll go over in the following sections.

The QuickBooks Coach

The QuickBooks Coach is designed to help new users get started. If you installed QuickBooks as a "new" installation (you did not install it over a recent version of QuickBooks), and you created a new company file (instead of opening a company file that was created in a previous version), you get to meet the QuickBooks Coach.

The Coach's window appears on the QuickBooks Home Page and offers three options:

- **View The Tutorial**   Select this feature to watch an animated tutorial that explains the basics of keeping accounting records in QuickBooks.
- **Use Intuit.com Services**   This is the option to create an Intuit online account, as described earlier in this chapter.
- **Start Working**   Select this feature to tell the Coach to explain all those icons on the Home page, so you understand the workflow as you create transactions in QuickBooks. Clicking the Coach's icon on any workflow section displays an explanation of what the first transaction in the workflow does and highlights the ensuing tasks involved in completing the task.

If you click the X in the upper-right corner of the Coach's window, the window doesn't close, it merely moves to the right side of the Home page, waiting for you to ask for help.

N O T E : The Coach resides on the Home page, so if you close the Home page the Coach leaves too. To open the Home page again, click the icon labeled Home in the Icon Bar.

Basic QuickBooks Window Elements

By default, the QuickBooks software window has the following elements:

- Title bar, which displays the name of your company
- Menu bar, which contains all the commands for working in QuickBooks
- Icon Bar, which contains buttons for quick access to oft-used functions (see the section "Customizing the Icon Bar," later in this chapter, to learn how to customize the Icon Bar)

Home Page

The Home page has links and icons you use to access the features and functions you need to run your business in QuickBooks. The Home page window is divided into sections to make it easy to find icons and see the workflow those icons represent.

The Home page is dynamic; that is, the icons and workflow arrows it contains change as you enable the various features available in QuickBooks. For example, if you enable inventory tracking, QuickBooks adds icons in the Vendors section for inventory-related tasks.

QuickBooks Centers

QuickBooks centers are windows in which information is displayed about specific areas of your company. You can see current data, analyze that data, and perform tasks. The following centers are available:

- Customer Center
- Vendor Center
- Employee Center
- Report Center

You can open any center by clicking its icon. In addition, the Home page sections for Vendors, Customers, and Employees have an icon on the left edge that opens the appropriate center when clicked.

Customer Center

The Customer Center holds everything you'd ever need to know about your customers. It's where QuickBooks stores the list of customers and all the information about each customer. You can choose the specific information you want to view by changing the options in the drop-down lists. You can also perform tasks, using the buttons at the top of the Customer Center window. Information about using and customizing the Customer Center is in Chapter 3.

Vendor Center

As with the Customer Center, the Vendor Center makes it easy to view detailed information about vendors. You can learn how to use and customize the Vendor Center in Chapter 4.

Employee Center

If you do your own payroll, open the Employee Center to see detailed information about each employee, your payroll liabilities, and your payroll items. Payroll is covered in Chapter 17.

Report Center

The Report Center, seen in Figure 1-6, is a user-friendly version of the Reports menu. Each major category of reports is displayed in the left pane, and clicking a

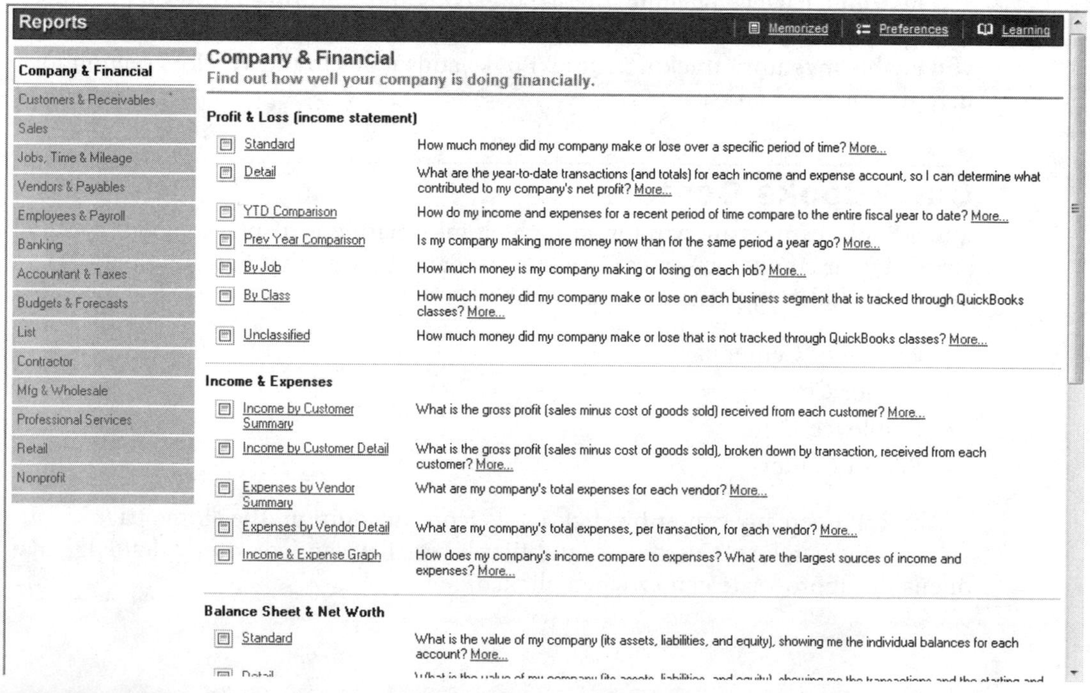

FIGURE 1-6   It's easier to choose the right report when you understand the contents.

category displays the list of reports for that category in the right pane, along with explanations of each report's contents. The Report Center even provides a visual representation of each report when you hover your mouse pointer over the icon to the left of the report.

Click a report name to open the report. In the report explanations, clicking the link labeled More opens a Help file page that offers additional explanations.

Customizing the Icon Bar

QuickBooks put icons on the Icon Bar, but the icons QuickBooks chose may not match the features you use most frequently. Putting your own icons on the Icon Bar makes using QuickBooks easier and faster.

To customize the Icon Bar, choose View | Customize Icon Bar to open the Customize Icon Bar dialog, which displays a list of the icons currently occupying your Icon Bar.

TIP: If you log into QuickBooks, either because a single computer is set up for multiple users, or because you're using QuickBooks on a network, the settings you establish are linked to your login name. You are not changing the Icon Bar for other users.

Changing the Order of Icons

You can change the order in which icons appear on the Icon Bar. The list of icons in the Customize Icon Bar dialog reads top to bottom, representing the left-to-right display on the Icon Bar. Therefore, moving an icon's listing up moves it to the left on the Icon Bar (and vice versa).

To move an icon, click the small diamond to the left of the icon's listing, hold down the left mouse button, and drag the listing to a new position.

Changing the Icon Bar Display

You can change the way the icons display in several ways, which are covered in this section.

Display Icons Without Title Text

By default, icons and text display on the Icon Bar. You can select Show Icons Only to remove the title text under the icons. As a result, the icons are much smaller (and you can fit more icons on the Icon Bar). Positioning your mouse pointer over a small icon displays the icon's description as a Tool Tip.

Change the Icon's Graphic, Text, or Description

To change an individual icon's appearance, select the icon's listing and click Edit. Then choose a different graphic (the currently selected graphic is enclosed in a box), change the Label (the title), or change the Description (the Tool Tip text).

Separate Icons

You can insert a separator between two icons, which is an effective way to create groups of icons (after you move icons into logical groups). The separator is a gray vertical line. In the Customize Icon Bar dialog, select the icon that should appear to the left of the separator bar and click Add Separator. QuickBooks inserts the separator on the icon bar and "(space)" in the listing to indicate the location of the separator.

Removing an Icon

If there are any icons you never use or use so infrequently that you'd rather use the space they take up for icons representing features you use a lot, remove them. Select the icon in the Customize Icon Bar dialog and click Delete. QuickBooks does not ask you to confirm the deletion; the icon is just zapped from the Icon Bar.

Adding an Icon

You can add an icon to the Icon Bar in either of two ways:

- Choose Add in the Customize Icon Bar dialog.
- Automatically add an icon for a window (transaction or report) you're currently using.

Using the Customize Icon Bar Dialog to Add an Icon

To add an icon from the Customize Icon Bar dialog, click Add. If you want to position your new icon at a specific place within the existing row of icons (instead of at the right end of the Icon Bar), first select the existing icon that you want to sit to the left of your new icon. Then click Add to display the Add Icon Bar Item dialog.

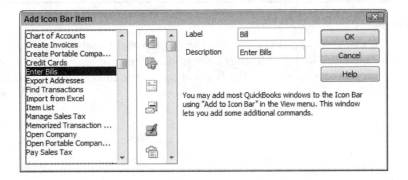

Scroll through the list to select the task you want to add to the Icon Bar. Then choose a graphic to represent the new icon. If you wish, you can change the label (the title that appears below the icon) or the description (the text that appears in the Tool Tip when you hold your mouse pointer over the icon).

Adding an Icon for the Current Window

If you're currently working in a QuickBooks window, and it strikes you that it would be handy to have an icon for fast access to this window, you can accomplish the deed quickly. While the window is active, choose View | Add *Name Of Window* To Icon Bar (substitute the name of the current window for *Name Of Window*). A dialog appears so you can choose a graphic, name, and description for the new icon.

Closing QuickBooks

To exit QuickBooks, click the X in the top-right corner of the QuickBooks window or choose File | Exit from the menu bar. The company file that's open at the time you exit the software is the file that opens the next time you launch QuickBooks.

The Chart of Accounts

In *this chapter:*

- Decide whether to use numbers for accounts

- Create accounts

- Create subaccounts

- Edit, delete, and merge accounts

The chart of accounts is your general ledger, where all the financial data you enter in transaction windows meets, categorized and totaled by category. You need to make sure you have a chart of accounts that will make it easy to enter transactions and understand reports about your financial health. QuickBooks created some accounts for you during the initial setup of your company, but you'll need additional accounts in order to keep books accurately. You create the chart of accounts first because some of the other QuickBooks lists you create require you to link the items in the list to accounts. For example, the items you sell are linked to income accounts.

Using Numbered Accounts

By default, QuickBooks uses account names only in the chart of accounts. However, you can change the default so that your accounts have numbers in addition to the names.

The advantage of using numbers is that you can arrange each section of the chart of accounts by category and subcategory, because within each type of account QuickBooks displays your chart of accounts in numerical order (without numbers, QuickBooks displays each section of your chart of accounts in alphabetical order).

For example, if accounts of the type Expense are arranged numerically instead of alphabetically, you can list related expense accounts contiguously. This means you can export reports to Excel and insert subtotals for related categories, which makes it easier to analyze where you're spending your money. If your related categories are numbered in a way that you can create subtotals that match the categories required on your company's tax return, this is also useful (especially to your accountant, who will spend less time on your tax return, which saves you money!).

You can also use numbered subaccounts to provide subtotals for related expenses (or income) right on your QuickBooks reports, without the need to export the report to Excel. See the section "Using Subaccounts" later in this chapter.

Many users tell me that a good argument for account numbers is the ability to arrange your bank accounts in a logical order, making sure your primary bank account is always at the top of the drop-down list users see when making bank deposits or writing checks. If your money market account is named for the bank (AlfaSavings), or even if you name the account Money Market, an alphabetic listing puts that account at the top of the bank account list when your operating account is named OperatingAccount, or it's named for the bank, which might be RiversideBank.

E-mail I receive from users tells me that the ability to manipulate the order in which bank accounts appear in drop-down lists becomes incredibly important if you add another bank account at a different bank, or you change banks. Suppose the people who enter data in your company file have gotten used to selecting the second account on the list (because that's where your general operating account sits in alphabetic order), and your new account is now the third account on a drop-down list (or the first account, depending on the alphabetical sort and whether you

➡➡ FYI

When You Need the Chart of Accounts Displayed in Alphabetical Order

As convenient as it is for you (and your accountant) to have numbered accounts so you can track your finances by category and subcategory, suppose you have to submit financial reports to a bank because that's part of the requirements of your line of credit? Your bankers have certain financial categories they look at first, and it's easier for them if your accounts, especially your expenses, are in alphabetical order.

To produce reports without account numbers, putting each account type list back into alphabetical order, turn off the account number feature by deselecting the option in the Preferences dialog. Print the reports, and then turn the feature on again. QuickBooks stores account numbers as part of the account name, so when you re-enable account numbers all your numbers appear exactly as you created them.

made the old bank account inactive so it doesn't appear at all). By the time everyone notices, figures out, and gets used to, the new bank list, you'll have a lot of transaction searching to do, followed by a lot of journal entries or changes to transaction records. You'll discover this when you try to reconcile your bank accounts. If you use numbered accounts, you can make sure the bank accounts always appear in the most convenient order. Even if your old bank was number 10000, and you want your new bank to use that number, it's a simple task to edit the original bank number to 14990 (moving it to the bottom of the list) and give the new bank the 10000 number to keep it at the top of the list.

Enabling Account Numbers

To switch to a number format for your accounts, you have to enable the account number feature. Choose Edit | Preferences from the menu bar to open the Preferences dialog, and select the Accounting icon in the left pane. Click the Company Preferences tab, and select the Use Account Numbers check box (see Figure 2-1).

If you chose a prebuilt chart of accounts when you set up your company file, those accounts are switched to numbered accounts automatically. However, the QuickBooks numbering scheme is designed to keep accounts in alphabetical order, especially in the Expenses section. This costs you some of the advantages and efficiencies that well-planned numbers bring, but all you have to do is create your own plan and then edit the accounts to change the numbers (see "Editing Accounts" later in this chapter).

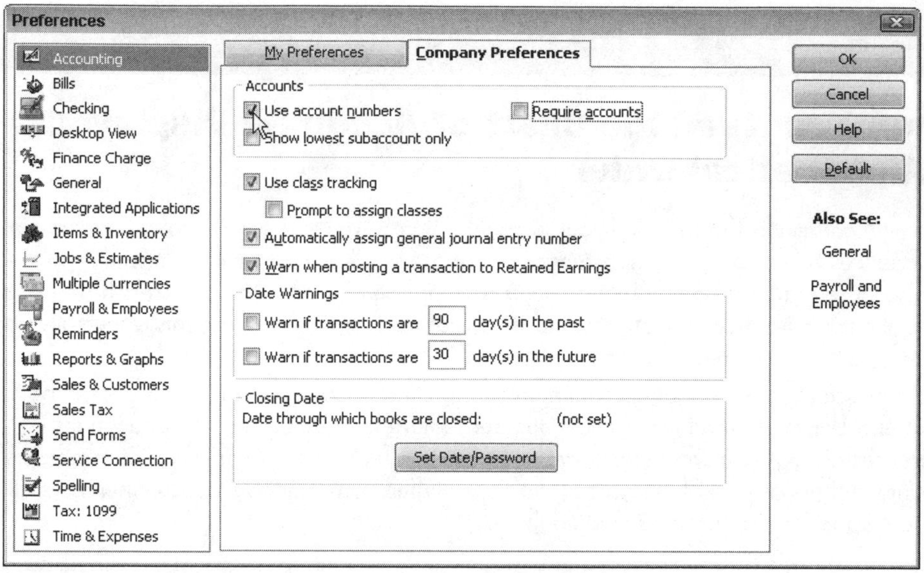

FIGURE 2-1 Enable numbers for your chart of accounts.

Accounts you added yourself (over and above the prebuilt accounts that were automatically brought into your company file) have to be edited to add numbers; QuickBooks doesn't automatically number them.

When you select the option to use account numbers, the option Show Lowest Subaccount Only becomes accessible (it's grayed out if you haven't opted for account numbers). This option tells QuickBooks to display only the subaccount on transaction windows instead of both the parent account and the subaccount, making it easier to see precisely which account is receiving the posting. (Subaccounts, and details about this feature to display them alone, are discussed later in the section "Using Subaccounts.")

If all your accounts aren't numbered and you select Show Lowest Subaccount Only, when you click OK, QuickBooks displays an error message that you cannot enable this option until all your accounts have numbers assigned. After you've edited existing accounts that need numbers (any accounts that QuickBooks didn't automatically number for you), you can return to the Preferences dialog and enable this subaccount option.

Creating a Numbering Scheme

After you've set up numbered accounts, you have a more efficient chart of accounts, so you, your bookkeeper, and your accountant will have an easier time. Numbers give you a quick clue about the type and category of the account you're working with.

As you create accounts, you must use the numbers intelligently, assigning ranges of numbers to account types. The most common approach to account numbering uses the following pattern:

- 1*xxxx* Assets
- 2*xxxx* Liabilities
- 3*xxxx* Equity
- 4*xxxx* Income
- 5*xxxx* Expenses
- 6*xxxx* Expenses
- 7*xxxx* Expenses
- 8*xxxx* Expenses
- 9*xxxx* Other Income and Expenses

I'm using five-digit numbers in my examples because QuickBooks uses five-digit account numbers. QuickBooks permits account numbers of up to seven digits, so you're not going to run out of numbers no matter how many accounts you need to run your business efficiently.

Creating Ranges of Numbers

Account types have subtypes, and you need to assign ranges of account numbers to match those subtypes. The starting number of each range has to be the same as the starting number for the account type (for instance, if you use numbers starting with a 1 for assets, all of the number ranges for different subtypes of assets must start with a 1). However, the ranges let you assign specific numbers to specific account types.

For example, thinking about the breakdown of assets, you can use 10000 through 10999 for bank accounts, 11000 through 11999 for receivables and other current assets, then use 12000 through 12999 for tracking fixed assets such as equipment, furniture, and so on. Follow the same pattern for liabilities, starting with current liabilities and moving to long term. It's also a good idea to keep all the payroll withholding liabilities accounts (they're current liabilities) together.

You can, if you wish, have a variety of expense types and reserve the starting number for specific types. Many companies, for example, use 5*xxxx* for sales expenses (they even separate the payroll postings between the salespeople and the rest of the employees), then use 60000 through 79999 for general operating expenses, then use 8*xxxx* and 9*xxxx* for other specific expenses that should appear together in reports (such as taxes, penalty fees, and so on).

Some companies use one range of expense accounts, such as 70000 through 79999 for expenses that fall into the "overhead" category. This is useful if you bid on work and need to know the total overhead expenses so you can apportion them to appropriate categories as you prepare your bid.

➡ FYI

How QuickBooks Sorts Accounts

You have to create a numbering scheme that conforms to the QuickBooks account subtypes because QuickBooks sorts your chart of accounts and your reports by those subtypes. If you have contiguous numbers that vary by account type, your reports won't appear in numerical order. QuickBooks uses the following sort order for the chart of accounts:

Assets
- Bank
- Accounts Receivable
- Other Current Asset
- Fixed Asset
- Other Asset

Liabilities
- Accounts Payable
- Credit Card
- Other Current Liability
- Long-Term Liability

Equity

Income

Cost Of Goods Sold

Expense

Other Income

Other Expense

Nonposting Accounts (Nonposting accounts are created automatically by QuickBooks when you enable features that use those account types, such as Estimates and Purchase Orders—they track transactions but do not affect financial data because no amounts are posted to any accounts.)

If you have inventory and you track cost of goods, you can reserve a section of the chart of accounts for those account types. Some companies use 43000 through 49999 for cost of goods, and some companies dedicate the numbers in the 5*xxxx* range to that purpose.

Usually, you should create new accounts by increasing the previous account number by 10 or 20 (or even 100 if you don't have a lot of accounts), so you have room to insert more accounts that belong in the same general area of your chart of accounts when they need to be added later.

Naming Accounts

Whether or not you choose to enable account numbers, you have to give each account a name. Here's an important rule about naming accounts: memorize it, print it out in big letters, and post it all over the office: *Design and Follow a Company Protocol for Naming and Using Accounts*.

The company protocol is a system you invent for naming accounts. Your protocol must be clear, so that when everyone follows the rules, the account naming convention is consistent. Why is this important? Because when I visit clients who haven't invented and enforced protocols, I find accounts with names such as the following:

- Telephone Exp
- Exps-Telephone
- Tele Expense
- Telephone
- Tele

You get the idea, and I'll bet you're not shocked to hear that every one of those accounts had amounts posted to them. That's because users "guess" at account names when they see a drop-down list, and they point and click on whatever they see that seems remotely related. If they don't find the account the way they would have entered the name, they invent a new account (using a name that seems logical to them). Avoid all of those errors by establishing protocols about creating account names, and then make sure everyone searches the account list before applying an account to a transaction.

Here are a few suggested protocols—you can amend them to fit your own situation or invent different protocols that you're more comfortable with. The important thing is consistency, absolute consistency.

- Avoid apostrophes.
- Set the number of characters for abbreviations. For example, if you permit four characters, telephone is abbreviated "tele"; a three-character rule produces "tel."
- Decide whether to use the ampersand (&) or a hyphen. For example, is it "Repairs & Maintenance" or "Repairs-Maintenance"?
- Make a rule about whether spaces are allowed. For example, would you have "Repairs & Maintenance" or "Repairs&Maintenance"?

Creating Accounts

After you've done your homework, made your decisions, invented your protocols, and planned your number scheme, creating accounts is a piece of cake:

1. Press CTRL-A to open the Chart Of Accounts window.
2. Press CTRL-N to enter a new account.
3. In the Add New Account: Choose Account Type dialog (see Figure 2-2), select the type of account you're creating. If the account type you need doesn't appear in the major category list on the dialog, select Other Account Types and choose an account type from the drop-down list.

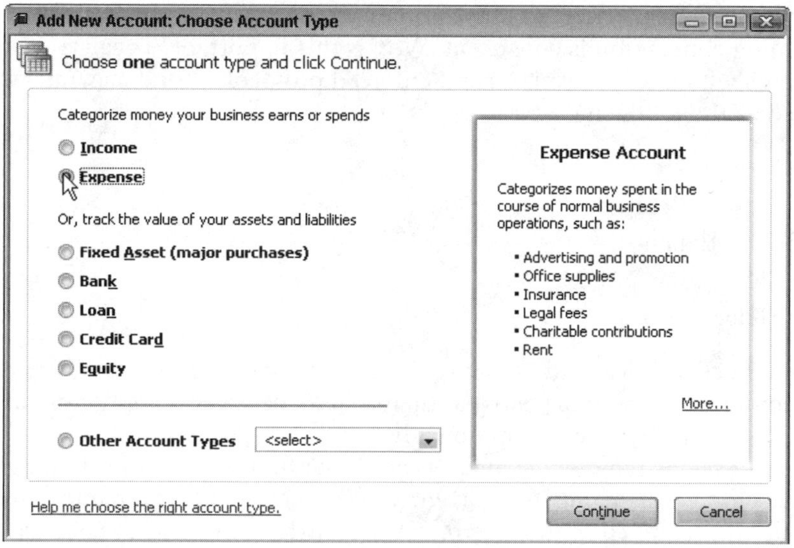

FIGURE 2-2   Start by selecting the type of account you want to add.

4. Click Continue to create the account.

The dialog you see when you fill out account information varies depending on the account type you chose, because different types of accounts require different information. In addition, if you've opted to use numbers for your accounts, there's a field for the account number. Figure 2-3 shows a blank Add New Account dialog for an Expense account.

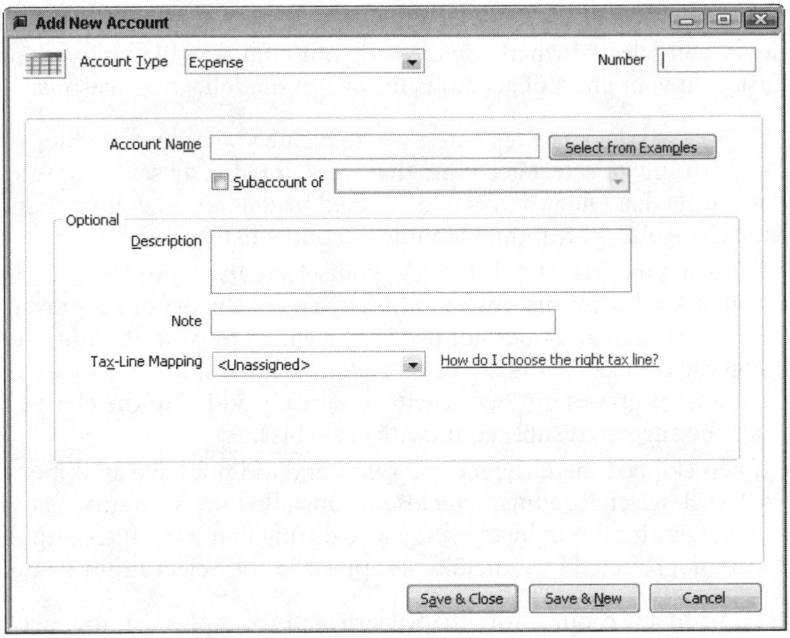

FIGURE 2-3 The only required entry for an account is a name (and number if you've enabled account numbers).

Select From Examples

If you created your company file in QuickBooks 2009 (instead of updating the file from a previous version of QuickBooks), some account types display a button labeled Select From Examples in the Add New Account dialog. Clicking the button produces a list of accounts that QuickBooks thinks you might want to consider adding to your chart of accounts. As you can see in Figure 2-4, the list of accounts matches the account type you selected when you started the process of adding an account.

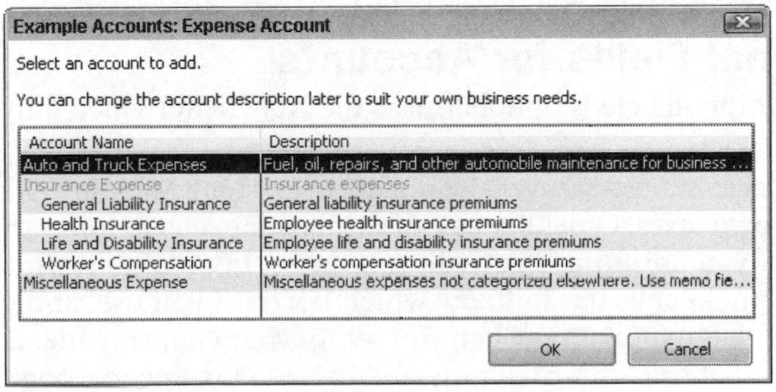

FIGURE 2-4 QuickBooks suggests accounts to add to your chart of accounts.

The accounts that are suggested are those accounts that were available for the industry you selected when you created your company file but were not selected for inclusion in your chart of accounts for one of the following reasons:

- If you used the EasyStep Interview to create your company file, you had an opportunity to select accounts that were not already selected or to deselect accounts that QuickBooks had selected by default. Accounts that remained unselected appear in the Example Accounts list.
- If, during the EasyStep Interview, you selected accounts for which QuickBooks suggests subaccounts, the account appears in the list but is grayed out (because it was selected and does not need to be added to your chart of accounts). The suggested subaccounts are listed (refer back to Figure 2-4 to see that Insurance Expense is grayed out because it was already added to the chart of accounts, but the suggested subaccounts are available).
- If you skipped the EasyStep Interview and did not have an opportunity to select/deselect accounts, QuickBooks installed the accounts that were selected by default for the industry you chose during company file setup. Accounts that were not selected by QuickBooks appear in the Select From Examples list.

If you add an account from the Select From Examples list, that account is removed from the list. If you delete the account from your chart of accounts, it is put back on the Select From Examples list.

If you did not select an industry during company file setup (instead, you selected None), the Select From Examples button is grayed out and inaccessible.

The following account types do *not* have the Select From Examples feature:

- Bank
- Credit Card
- Equity
- Account Receivable
- Accounts Payable
- Long Term Liability

Optional Fields for Accounts

The Description field is optional, as is the Note field (which only appears on some account types).

Some account types have a field named Tax-Line Mapping, which is useful if you do your own taxes. QuickBooks exports data for each account to the appropriate tax line if you use Turbo Tax to do your taxes. In order to perform this helpful action, QuickBooks has to know which tax form you use, and you probably provided that information when you set up your company file. If you didn't select a tax form, that field doesn't appear. You can add tax line information by opening the Company menu, selecting Company Information, and choosing the appropriate income tax form. When you click OK to save the new data, the Tax-Line Mapping field appears on the appropriate account records and you can use the drop-down list to insert the right line number for your tax form. (If you selected a tax form when you set up the company file, QuickBooks automatically inserts the right tax line. If you add the field later and use the drop-down list, you have to know which line each income/expense/asset account needs to be transferred to on the tax form, which may require some research.)

Some account types (assets, liabilities, and equity) have a button labeled Enter Opening Balance. Clicking it opens a dialog in which you can enter an opening balance. Do *not* enter opening balances when you're creating accounts, because it causes complications that your accountant won't appreciate. (See the FYI "Don't Enter Opening Balances for Accounts.")

As you finish creating each account, click Save & New to move to another blank Add New Account dialog. By default, the new dialog is configured for the same account type as the account you just created, but you can change the account type by selecting another type from the drop-down list at the top of the dialog.

When you're finished creating accounts, click Save & Close, and then close the Chart Of Accounts window by clicking the X in the upper-right corner.

➡ FYI

Don't Enter Opening Balances for Accounts

Unless you start your business the day you start using QuickBooks, and you haven't yet opened a bank account, and you also haven't purchased any equipment for your business, many accounts already have an existing balance. For example, you probably have money in your business bank account, either because your business has been operating for a long time and you're just getting around to using QuickBooks, or you provided startup money for your new business.

Never never enter any figures in the Opening Balance field of any account that has this option, because QuickBooks is a true double-entry accounting application and therefore makes an offsetting entry of the same amount you entered. Of course, QuickBooks has no way of knowing the source of that money, so it dumps it into an account named Opening Bal Equity, which is an account QuickBooks invented for just this purpose. This account is treated as if it were an account that shows previous profits, but that role should be reserved for the account named Retained Earnings. The money in your bank account may actually be the result of a loan you made your business, capital you invested in your business, or sales you made before you started keeping records in QuickBooks; it may very well *not* be existing previous profits.

Your accountant will want to get rid of the balance in Opening Bal Equity, and sometimes that's a difficult job because it's hard to tell how the balance was arrived at—was this opening balance the result of transactions in past years? If so, it needs to be moved to the Retained Earnings account. Is it from the current year? If so, what's the real source of the amount (because it has to be moved to the proper account)? Is it a combination of both? If so, you'll have to

---

➡ FYI (cont.)

remember every entry and explain it to your accountant so he or she can move the appropriate amounts to the appropriate accounts.

Ignore the Opening Balance when you create an account, and after you've created the account, create a transaction that accurately describes the source of this amount. Chapter 8 has information to help you enter opening balances and historical data correctly and efficiently. Ask your accountant to help you create the transactions that provide opening balances for accounts; believe me, your accountant will be happy to take the time to do this because I've never met an accountant who didn't groan at the sight of a balance in the Opening Bal Equity account.

Using Subaccounts

Subaccounts provide a way to post transactions more precisely by using subcategories for main account categories. For example, if you create an expense account for insurance expenses, you may want to have subaccounts for vehicle insurance, liability insurance, equipment insurance, and so on. (To create a subaccount, you must first create the parent account).

For example, suppose you have the following parent accounts:

- 60200 Utilities
- 60300 Travel

You can create the following subaccounts:

- 60210 Utilities:Heat
- 60220 Utilities:Electric
- 60310 Travel:Sales
- 60320 Travel:Seminars and Meetings

The colon in the account names listed here is added automatically by QuickBooks to indicate a *parentaccount:subaccount* relationship.

Viewing Subaccounts

When you have subaccounts, the Chart Of Accounts window displays them indented under their parent accounts (see Figure 2-5), as long as you've configured the window to display accounts in Hierarchical View.

If you know you created subaccounts, but you don't see any indented listings, your Chart Of Accounts window has been configured to display accounts in Flat View (a simple listing of accounts). To remedy this, click the Account button at the bottom of the window and select Hierarchical View.

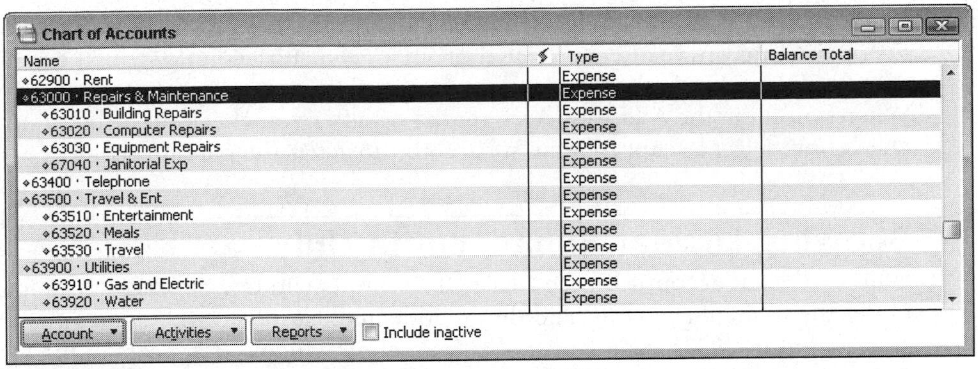

FIGURE 2-5 It's easy to see that the Repairs & Maintenance account has subaccounts to track expenses more specifically.

Creating Subaccounts

To create a subaccount, you must have already created the parent account. Then take these steps:

1. Open the Chart Of Accounts list.
2. Press CTRL-N to create a new account.
3. Select the appropriate account type.
4. Click Continue.
5. Enter a number (if you're using numbered accounts).
6. Name the account.
7. Click the Subaccount Of check box to place a check mark in it.
8. In the drop-down box next to the check box, select the parent account.
9. Click Save & New to create another account or Save & Close if you're finished creating accounts.

Multiple Levels of Subaccounts

You can have multiple levels of subaccounts. For example, you may want to track income in the following manner:

Income
    Income:Consulting
        Income:Consulting:Engineering
        Income:Consulting:Training
    Income:Products
        Income:Products:Technical
        Income:Products:Accessories
        Income:Products:Repairs

Creating the sub-subaccounts is as easy as creating the first level subaccounts; just make sure you've already created the first-level subaccounts (which become the parents of the sub-subaccounts; I guess we can call the sub-subaccounts grandchildren). When you fill in the Add New Account dialog, after you check the Subaccount Of check box, select the appropriate subaccount to act as the parent account.

Showing Lowest Subaccounts Only

When you view accounts in the Chart Of Accounts window, subaccounts appear under their parent accounts, and they're indented. However, when you view a subaccount in the drop-down list of a transaction window, it appears in the format: *ParentAccount:Subaccount.* (If you're using three levels, the list appears as *ParentAccount:Subaccount:Sub-subaccount.*)

For example, if you create a parent account named Income with a subaccount Consulting, the Account field drop-down list in transaction windows shows Income:Consulting. If you've used numbers, remember that the number is part of the account name, so the Account field shows the following:

```
40000-Income:40010-Consulting
```

Because many of the fields or columns in transaction windows are narrow, you may not be able to see the subaccount names without scrolling through each account. This can be annoying, and it's much easier to work if only the subaccount name is displayed. That's the point of enabling the preference Show Lowest Subaccount Only, discussed earlier in this chapter. When you enable that option, you see only the subaccounts in the drop-down list when you're working in a transaction window, which makes it much easier to select the account you need.

Posting to Subacccounts

Post transactions only to the subaccounts, never to the parent account. When you create reports, QuickBooks displays the individual totals for the subaccounts and displays the grand total for the parent account.

If, after you've been posting to the subaccounts, you post a transaction to the parent account, QuickBooks doesn't stop you from performing that action. However, to remind you to post only to subaccounts, when you create financial reports that include this account you'll see that postings to the parent account are displayed as if you'd posted to a subaccount named "Other."

To fix this, drill down by double-clicking the listing for "Other" and then double-clicking each transaction listing to open the original transaction window. Change the posting to a subaccount, and if you don't have an appropriate subaccount (which may be the reason you posted to the parent account), select <Add New> from the account drop-down list and create the subaccount you need.

Editing Accounts

If you need to make changes to any account information (including adding a number after you enable numbered accounts), select the account's listing in the Chart Of Accounts window and press CTRL-E. The Edit Account dialog appears, which looks like the account card you just filled out. Make your changes and click Save & Close to save them.

Deleting Accounts

It's not uncommon to clean up your chart of accounts to get rid of accounts you'll never use or to remove duplicate accounts. (You can't have two accounts with the same name or number because QuickBooks doesn't permit that, but it's certainly possible to end up with multiple accounts that are similar; for instance, Tele, Telephone.)

To delete an account, select its listing in the Chart Of Accounts window and press CTRL-D. QuickBooks asks you to confirm the fact that you want to delete the account. Click OK to remove the account.

You can delete any account that isn't in use, which means the account has never been used in a transaction, nor linked to a sales or payroll item. You don't have to search all your transactions to find out whether an account has been used in your system; you can just try to delete it and, if it's been assigned to a transaction or item, QuickBooks issues an error message explaining why you can't get rid of this account.

You cannot delete an account that has subaccounts unless you first delete the subaccounts (which can only be accomplished if the subaccounts have never been used or assigned). However, a workaround for saving the subaccounts and getting rid of the parent account is to turn the subaccounts into parent accounts. To accomplish this, either drag the subaccount listing to the left in the Chart Of Accounts window (be sure the window is displaying accounts in Hierarchical View), or edit the subaccount to remove the check mark in the Subaccount Of check box.

If you can't delete an account but you don't want anyone to use it, you can hide the account (make it inactive). If the account can't be deleted, and it's a duplicate account, you can merge it with the other account (the one you want to continue to use). Those topics are covered next.

Making Accounts Inactive (Hiding Accounts)

When you make an account inactive, you're hiding the account from users. When an account is inactive, it doesn't appear in drop-down lists in transaction windows, so users can't select it. The account continues to exist, and its history remains in the system; it just doesn't appear in drop-down lists during transaction entry.

To make an account inactive, right-click its listing in the Chart Of Accounts window and select Make Account Inactive. QuickBooks doesn't ask you to confirm your action. (You can also make an account inactive by selecting it and pressing CTRL-E to open the account record in Edit mode, then select the check box labeled Account Is Inactive to enter a check mark, but that's more work, and I always take the quickest, easiest route for any task.)

By default, inactive accounts aren't displayed in the Chart Of Accounts window, but if you've made any accounts inactive, the Include Inactive check box at the bottom of the window becomes accessible (it's grayed out if no inactive accounts exist). Select the check box to insert a check mark, and you can see your inactive accounts, which are displayed with an "X" to the left of the listing.

To return an inactive account to active status, click the "X" to toggle the account's status to Active (the Chart Of Accounts window must be displaying inactive accounts)

Merging Accounts

Sometimes you have two accounts that should be one. For instance, you may have accidentally created two accounts for the same purpose. As I discussed earlier in this chapter, I've been to client sites that had accounts named Telephone and Tele, with transactions posted to both accounts. Those accounts badly need merging. You can only merge accounts when the following conditions exist:

- Both accounts are of the same account type (for example, you cannot merge an Expense account with an Other Expense account).
- Both accounts are at the same level (you cannot merge a subaccount with a parent account).

Take the following steps to merge two accounts:

1. Open the Chart Of Accounts window.
2. Select (highlight) the account that has the name you *do not* want to use.
3. Press CTRL-E to open the Edit Account dialog.
4. Change the account name or number (or both) to match the account you want to keep.
5. Click Save & Close.
6. QuickBooks displays a dialog telling you that the account number or name you've entered already exists for another account and asks if you want to merge the accounts. Click Yes to confirm that you want to merge the two accounts.

Remember, the way to do this is to start with the "bad" account and rename it to match the "good" account.

Configuring Customers and Jobs

In this chapter:

- The Customer Center
- Create customers
- Create jobs
- Edit, delete, and merge customers and jobs
- Create custom fields for customers
- Set up security for customer credit card information

In QuickBooks, customers and jobs are handled together. You can create a customer and consider anything and everything you invoice to that customer a single job, or you can create multiple jobs for the same customer.

Some businesses don't worry about jobs; it's just the customer that's tracked. But if you're a building contractor or subcontractor, an interior decorator, a consultant, or some other kind of service provider who usually sends invoices based on a project, you should track jobs.

Jobs don't stand alone as an entity; they are attached to customers, and you can attach as many jobs to a single customer as you need to.

If you enter your existing customers and jobs when you're first starting to use QuickBooks, all the other work connected to the customer is much easier. It's bothersome to have to stop in the middle of every invoice you enter to create a new customer record.

The Customer Center

The QuickBooks Customer Center is where all your customers and jobs, and detailed information about those customers and jobs, are kept. It's also where you go to create, edit, and get reports about customers and jobs.

To open the Customer Center (seen in Figure 3-1), press CTRL-J.

NOTE: You can also open the Customer Center by choosing Customers | Customer Center, or by clicking the Customer Center icon on the Icon Bar.

The left pane of the Customer Center has two tabs: Customers & Jobs and Transactions. A customer is always selected in the Customers & Jobs list (by default, the first customer in the list when you first open the Customer Center), and the right pane of the Customer Center displays information about the selected customer or job.

The Transactions tab lists all your sales transactions (Invoices, Sales Receipts, and so on). Selecting a transaction type displays the current transactions of that type in the right pane. The display can be manipulated and filtered by choosing categories and sorting by column.

Customizing the Customers & Jobs List

You can customize the information displayed in the Customers & Jobs list. By default, the list has two columns: Name and Balance Total (and Currency, if you've enabled the Multicurrency feature). You don't even have to select a customer's listing to see the current balance because the balances for all your customers are right in front of you (except, of course, you may have to scroll down to get to the part of the list that has the customer or job you want to see).

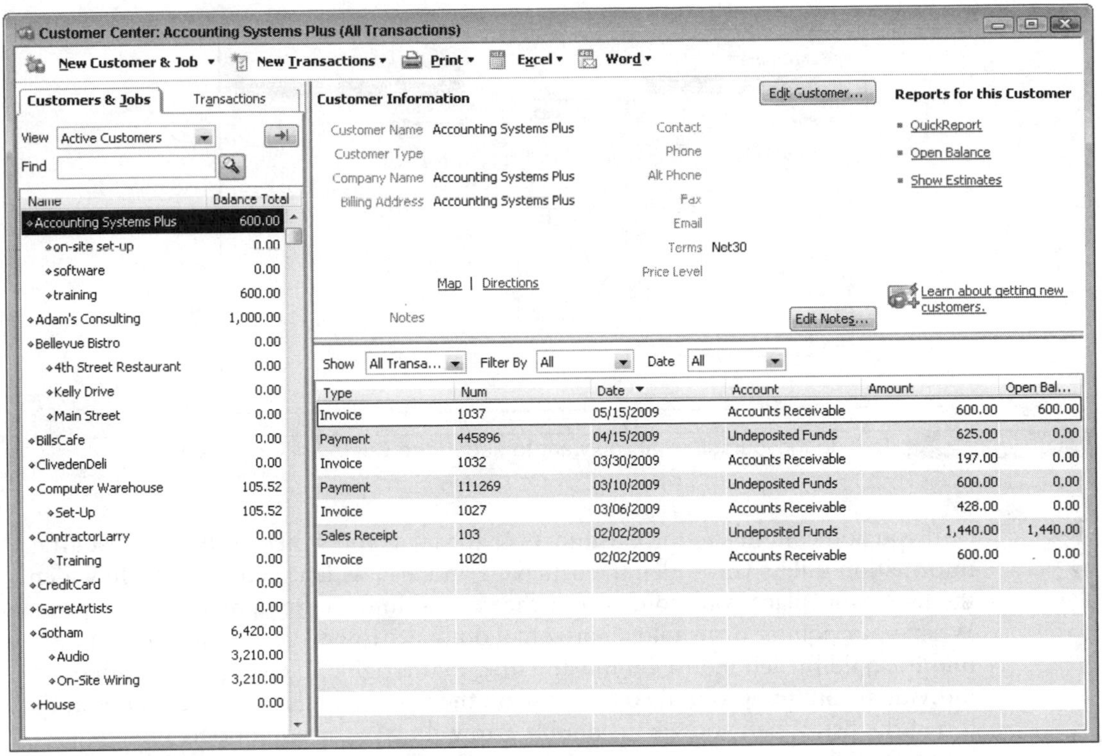

FIGURE 3-1 The Customer Center is a one-stop location for information about your customers and jobs.

You can add more columns to the Customers & Jobs list. To do so, right-click anywhere in the list and choose Customize Columns to open the Customize Columns dialog seen in Figure 3-2.

To add a column, select its label in the left pane and click Add. The information the column describes is displayed for each customer and job in the list. As long as the customer or job you're interested in is displayed on the portion of the list that's visible, the information is available—you don't have to select the listing or open the record.

Some users find it useful to add the Rep name to the display, so they know whom to call to discuss the customer without having to open the customer record. Another useful data display is the Terms category, which makes it easy to see that information without having to select the customer when you're talking about (or talking with) a customer who's overdue.

You can rearrange the left-to-right order of the columns by opening the Customize Columns dialog and selecting a column you want to move. Choose Move Up to move a column to the left or Move Down to move it to the right. The order of columns displayed in the Chosen Columns pane of the dialog translates as Top to Bottom = Left to Right.

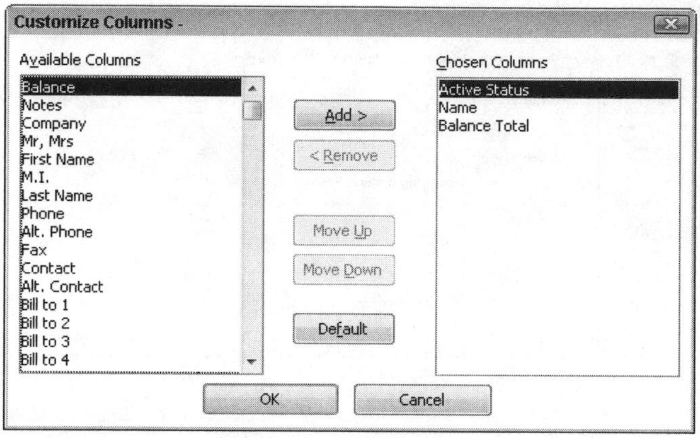

FIGURE 3-2   Decide for yourself what you want to see in the Customers & Jobs list.

If you add columns to the Customers & Jobs list, you won't be able to see all the information unless you widen the list's pane and also widen each column. To widen the list's pane, place your pointer over the vertical line on the right side of the pane. When your pointer turns into a horizontal double arrow with a vertical line in the middle, hold the left mouse button and drag to the right. To change the width of an individual column, position your mouse on the vertical line between columns at the top of the list. When you see the double arrow, drag in the appropriate direction.

Customizing the Customer Information Pane

You can filter the financial information in the right pane by choosing different categories from the drop-down lists in the column headings, and you can sort the information by selecting a column heading to sort by.

In addition, you can add and remove columns by clicking anywhere on or below the column headings and choosing Customize Columns. In the Customize Columns dialog (see Figure 3-3), add, remove, and change the order of columns.

> **TIP:** I find it helpful to display the memo field for transactions.

Creating a Customer

To create a new customer, click the New Customer & Job button at the top of the Customer Center window, and select New Customer from the submenu. This action opens the New Customer window (see Figure 3-4). Fill in the appropriate information using the guidelines in the following sections.

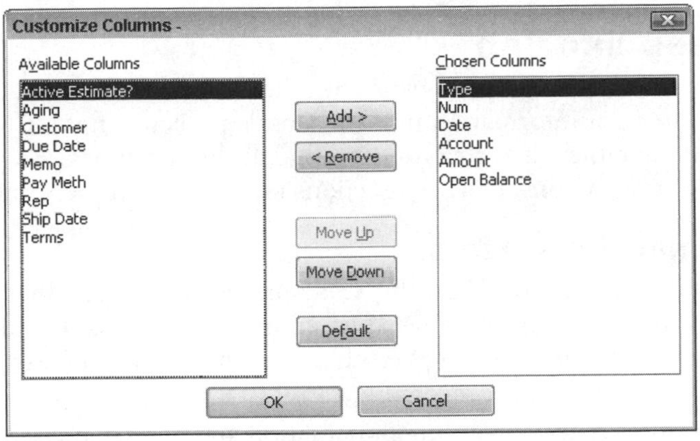

FIGURE 3-3 Display the information you need for each customer.

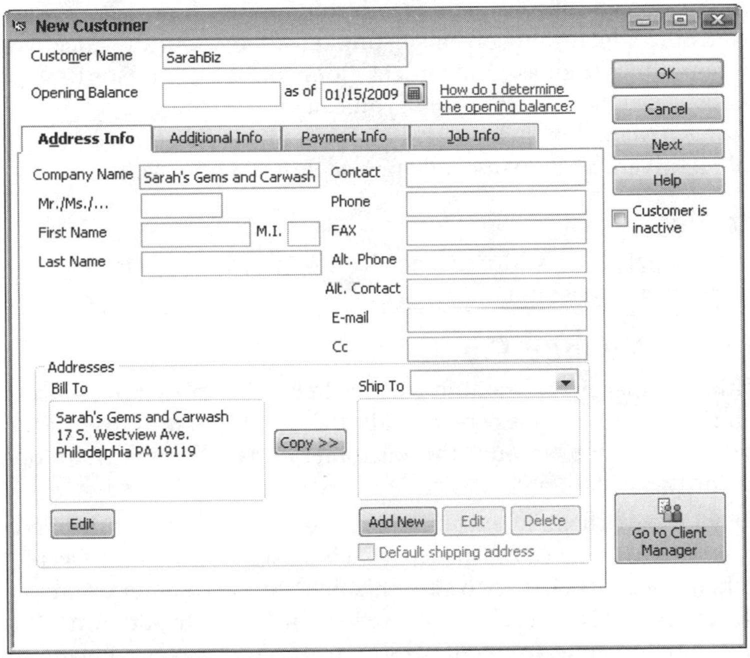

FIGURE 3-4 The customer record holds quite a lot of information.

Address Info Tab

The New Customer window opens with the Address Info tab in the foreground. The first field to enter information in is the Customer Name field. Consider this field an internal code rather than a customer name. It doesn't appear on your invoices or other sales transactions. (The transactions use the data in the Company Name field.)

Customer Name Field

You must invent a protocol for this Customer Name field so that you'll enter every customer in a consistent manner. If you don't you'll almost certainly end up with customers entered multiple times (each time with a slightly different Customer Name).

Notice the Customer Name field in Figure 3-4. This customer code entry has no punctuation or spaces. Avoiding punctuation and spaces in codes is a good protocol for filling in code fields. For example, names with apostrophes (such as O'Reilly) should be entered as Oreilly.

Each customer must have a unique entry in this field, so if you have a lot of customers named Johnson, you may want to enter them in a way that makes it easy to determine which Johnson this listing represents. For instance, you could have customer names such as JohnsonJack, JohnsonMary, JohnsonRestaurant, and so on. If you have several Jack Johnsons, you can use JohnsonJackMainSt for the Jack Johnson on Main Street. This field can contain up to 41 characters, so you should be able to invent a company code protocol that works well.

Currency

If you've enabled the Multicurrency feature, this field appears so you can select the currency for this customer.

Opening Balance Field

QuickBooks makes an Opening Balance field available, along with the date for which this balance applies (by default, the current date is inserted). The field is designed to hold the amount this customer currently owes (if an open balance exists for the customer).

Do *not* use this field. If you enter an amount, you'll have no detailed records on how the customer arrived at this balance, which makes it difficult to accept payments against specific invoices. It's better to skip this field and then enter an invoice or multiple invoices to post this customer's balance to your books. In addition, QuickBooks posts the amount you enter to Accounts Receivable and makes a balancing entry into an account named Opening Bal Equity. Your accountant will want to get rid of the balance in Opening Bal Equity, and sometimes that's a difficult job because it's hard to tell how the balance was arrived at—is this an opening balance you entered from past years? Is it from the current year? Is it a combination of both? Entering transactions that represent the way the customer's current status was reached is far more accurate than using the Opening Balance field.

Customer Address Info

In the Company and Addresses sections of the window, enter the company name, optionally enter a contact, and enter the billing address. Add any other contact information you want to track for this customer (telephone, e-mail, and so on).

Ship To Addresses

You can maintain multiple shipping addresses for your customers. Each shipping address has a name (title) you invent, so you can select it from a drop-down list when you're entering sales transactions. If the shipping address isn't different from the billing address (or if you have a service business and never ship products), you can ignore the shipping address field, or use the Copy button to copy the data from the Bill To field.

To create a shipping address, click the Add New button under the Ship To address block to open the Add Ship To Address Information dialog.

Give this Ship To address a name. QuickBooks automatically enters the name Ship To 1, but that's merely a placeholder. Replace that text with a name that reminds you of the address location (such as Chicago or MainStreet), to make it easier to select this address from a drop-down list when you have to ship goods to this customer.

NOTE: If you already entered a Ship To address, the default name of the next address is Ship To 2.

Enter the address information and specify whether this address should be the default Ship To address, then click OK. If needed, enter another Ship To address for this customer.

Additional Info Tab

The information you enter in the Additional Info tab of a customer card (see Figure 3-5) ranges from essential to convenient. Prepopulating the fields with information makes your work go faster when you're filling out transaction windows, and it makes it easier to create detailed reports (because you can design reports based on the data entered in the fields). It's worth spending the time to design some rules for the way data is entered. (Remember, making data entry rules ensures consistency, without which you'll have difficulty getting the reports you want.)

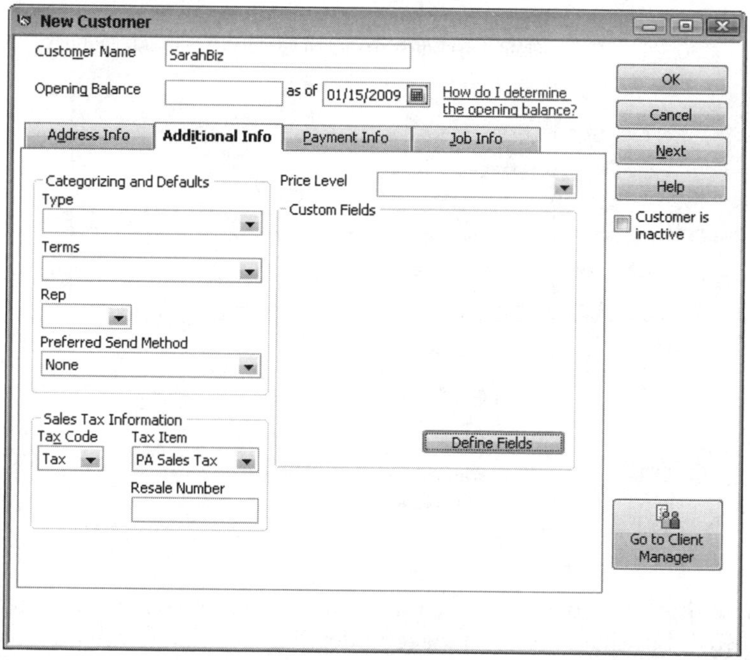

FIGURE 3-5 Entering additional information makes your work in QuickBooks go faster.

NOTE: The fields you see on the Additional Info tab may not be the same as the fields shown in Figure 3-5. The preferences you configure (for example, whether you track sales tax or have enabled multicurrency) determine the available fields.

Let's spend a minute going over the fields in this tab. Most of the fields are also QuickBooks lists, and if you haven't already entered items in those lists, you can do so as you fill out the fields in the customer card. With the exception of the Preferred Send Method list, each field that is also a list has an entry named <Add New>, and selecting that entry opens the appropriate new blank entry window.

Type

Use the Type field to sort your customers by a type you find important (or convenient) when you create reports. QuickBooks maintains a Customer Type List that you create (covered in detail in Chapter 5).

For example, you may want to use customer types to distinguish between wholesale and retail customers, or to track the source of referrals. To use the field, click the arrow to select a type that you already entered, or create a new type.

Terms

Terms, of course, refers to payment terms. Click the arrow to the right of the text box to see the terms that QuickBooks already defined, or choose <Add New> to define a new one.

The terms in the Terms List are for both customers and vendors, and you may need additional terms to meet your customers' and vendors' needs. See Chapter 5 to learn how to create different types of terms.

Rep

This field is the place to track a sales representative, and it's useful whether you pay commissions or you just want to know who is in charge of this customer. Sales reps can be employees, vendors, or "other names" (which means the name is entered in the Other Names List). Select a rep from the list of reps or add a new rep by choosing <Add New>. Chapter 5 has more information on populating this list.

Preferred Send Method

This field stores the default value for the way you want to send invoices, statements, or estimates to this customer (it does not refer to the method you use to send products to the customer). The choices are the following:

- **None** No special features are used to send the documents. You print them and you mail them (the old-fashioned way).
- **E-mail** You e-mail the documents. This feature lets you attach the documents as PDF files to an e-mail message. The processes involved are managed within QuickBooks, using a QuickBooks server for sending the e-mail. Chapter 9 has the details.
- **Mail** You use a QuickBooks service to mail the invoices. The data is reproduced on a form that has a tear-off your customers enclose with their payment. Regardless of the method you choose as your default, you can use any send method when you're creating a transaction. Chapter 25 has more information on using these methods.

Sales Tax Information

If you've configured QuickBooks to collect sales tax, the sales tax information uses several fields. If the customer is liable for sales tax, select the appropriate sales tax item for this customer, or create a new sales tax item. If the customer does not pay sales tax, select Non (for nontaxable customer) and enter the Resale Number provided by the customer (this is handy to have when the state tax investigators pop in for a surprise audit). See Chapter 6 for a complete discussion of sales tax codes and sales tax items.

Price Level

Price levels are a pricing scheme, usually involving special discounts that you want to use for this customer's purchases. Select an existing price level or create a new one. See Chapter 5 to learn about creating and assigning price levels.

Custom Fields

Custom fields provide an opportunity to invent fields for sorting and arranging your QuickBooks lists using data for which fields are not provided in the built-in customer record. See the section "Using Custom Fields" later in this chapter.

Payment Info Tab

This tab (see Figure 3-6) puts all the important information about customer finances in one place.

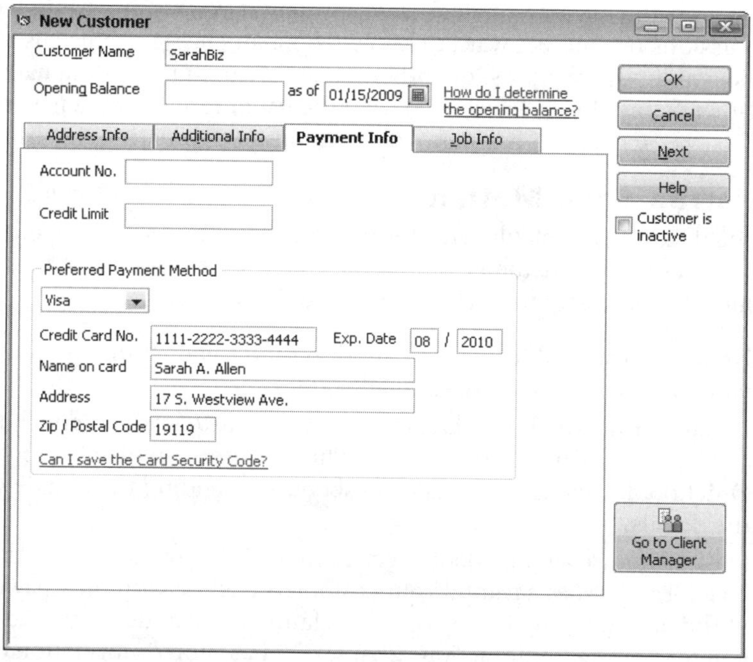

FIGURE 3-6 Use the Payment Info tab to track details needed for this customer's transactions.

Account No.

This is an optional field you can use if you assign account numbers to your customers.

Credit Limit

A credit limit is a way to set a threshold for the amount of money you'll extend to a customer's credit. If a customer places an order, and the new order combined with any unpaid invoices exceeds the threshold, QuickBooks displays a warning. QuickBooks won't prevent you from continuing to sell to and invoice the customer, but you should consider rejecting the order (or shipping it COD).

TIP: If you aren't going to enforce the credit limit, don't bother to use the field.

Preferred Payment Method

This means the customer's preferred method for payments, and a list of payment methods is offered in the drop-down list. You can select the appropriate item from the list or add a new one by selecting <Add New>. See Chapter 5 for more information on this list.

TIP: The payment method you select automatically appears on the Receive Payments window when you are using this customer in the transaction. You can change the payment method at that time, if necessary.

Credit Card No.

This field is intended to contain this customer's credit card number, if that's the customer's preferred payment method. Don't fill it in at all unless your computer and your QuickBooks file are protected with all sorts of security. For more information on credit card security issues and rules see the section, "Securing Customer Credit Card Information," later in this chapter.

Currency

If you've enabled the Multicurrency feature (discussed in Appendix A), select the appropriate currency for this customer. As you can see in Figure 3-7, this customer's currency is the Mexican Peso.

When you have finished filling out the fields (I'm skipping the Job Info tab because there's a full discussion on entering jobs later in this chapter), choose Next

| **FIGURE 3-7** | You can do business with a foreign customer in that customer's currency. |

to move to another blank customer card so you can enter the next customer. When you have finished entering all of your customers, click OK.

Editing Customer Records

You can make changes to the information in a customer record quite easily. Open the Customer Center and double-click the customer's listing in the Customers & Jobs list to open the customer card in Edit mode.

When you open the customer card, you can change any information or fill in data you didn't have when you first created the customer entry. In fact, you can fill in data you *did* have but didn't bother to enter. (Some people find it's faster to enter just the customer name and company name when they're creating their customer lists and then fill in the rest at their leisure or the first time they invoice the customer.)

However, there are several things to note about editing the customer card:

- Don't mess with the Customer Name field.
- There's a Notes button on the right side of the customer card.
- There is no opening balance field.

Unless you've reinvented the protocol you're using to enter data in the Customer Name field, don't change this data. Some high-end (translate that as "expensive and incredibly powerful") accounting software applications lock this field and never permit changes. QuickBooks lets you change it, so you have to impose controls on yourself.

Click the Notes button to open a Notepad window that's dedicated to this customer, as shown in Figure 3-8. This is a useful feature, and I bet you'll use it frequently. The notepad is a great sales and marketing tool because you can use it to follow up on a promised order, track a customer's special preferences, and notify the customer when something special is available.

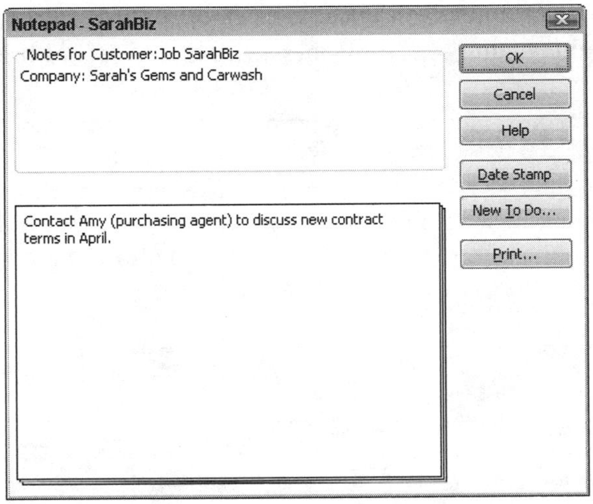

FIGURE 3-8   Each customer has a notepad.

Click the Date Stamp button to insert the current date automatically when you're adding text to the notepad.

Click the New To Do button to compose a reminder and specify the date on which you want to be reminded. QuickBooks adds this task to the Reminders List. (Choose Edit | Preferences and select the Reminders category to make sure you've enabled To Do Notes in your Reminders settings.) When the task is complete, open this reminder and click Done to remove the note from the Reminders list.

When you view the Customers & Jobs list, some of the text of your notes appears in the right pane if you've entered notes for the selected customer. For any customer you select, an Edit Notes icon appears in the right pane of the Customer Center. You can open the notepad for the selected customer by clicking the icon; you don't have to open the customer record to get to the note.

Using Jobs

If you plan to track jobs, you can enter the ones you know about during your QuickBooks setup phase, or enter them as they're needed in transactions. Jobs are attached to customers; they can't stand alone, so the customer for the job has to exist in your QuickBooks Customers & Jobs list before you can create the job.

When you create a job, you can track its progress and keep an eye on the promised end date. You can do the same thing for a customer without creating a job, because the customer record has a Job Info tab that matches the tab available in the job record (see the following sections about filling in job data). However, unless you're absolutely sure that this is the only job this customer is ever going to award to you, it's better to create a discrete job. (If you think the customer won't return to you for more business, you need to rethink your "attitude"; successful business owners should go after repeat business with a sense of confidence.)

Creating Jobs

To create a job, press CTRL-J to open the Customer Center and right-click the listing of the customer for whom you're creating a job. Choose Add Job to open the New Job window, shown in Figure 3-9. Create a name for the job (you can use up to

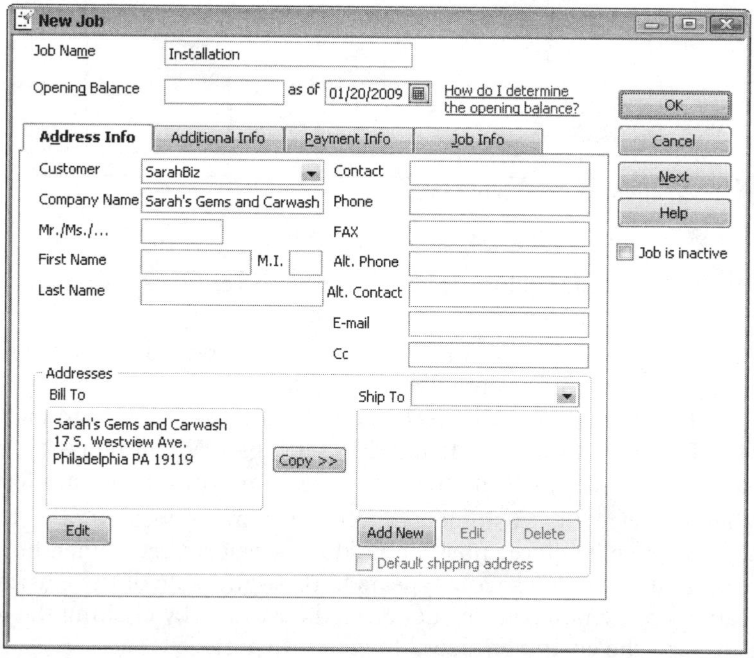

FIGURE 3-9 To create a new job, enter the job name—all the basic information about the customer is already filled in.

41 characters) and make it descriptive enough for both you and your customer to understand.

If this job requires you to bill the customer at an address that's different from the address you entered for this customer, or to ship goods to a different shipping address, make the appropriate changes in the job's Address Info tab. QuickBooks maintains this information only for this job and won't change the original shipping address in the customer record.

The Additional Info tab and the Payment Info tab are related to the customer rather than the job, so you can skip them.

Unfortunately, QuickBooks does not have a field on the Additional Info tab for Rep, so if you have different reps assigned to individual jobs for a customer (a common occurrence), you can't track them. As a workaround, use one of the following methods:

- Enter the rep's name on the Alt. Contact name on the Address Info tab.
- If you aren't using the Job Type field to categorize jobs, enter rep names in the Job Type list so you can use the data in the Job Type field.

Move to the Job Info tab (see Figure 3-10) to begin configuring this job. All of the information on the Job Info tab is optional.

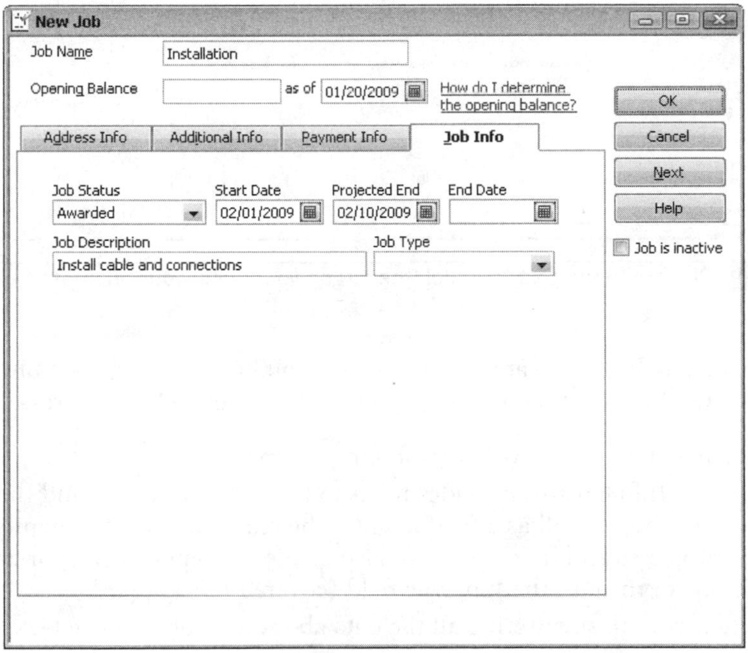

FIGURE 3-10 Track job details on the Job Info tab.

The Job Status drop-down list offers choices that you can change as the progress of the job moves along. You can change the default text that describes each progress level to suit your own business (and the jargon you use in-house), but the changes you make for the text are system wide and affect every job. Here's how to change the text you use to track job status:

1. Choose Edit | Preferences to open the Preferences dialog.
2. Click the Jobs & Estimates icon in the left pane, and click the Company Preferences tab in the right pane to see the current descriptive text for each status level (see Figure 3-11).

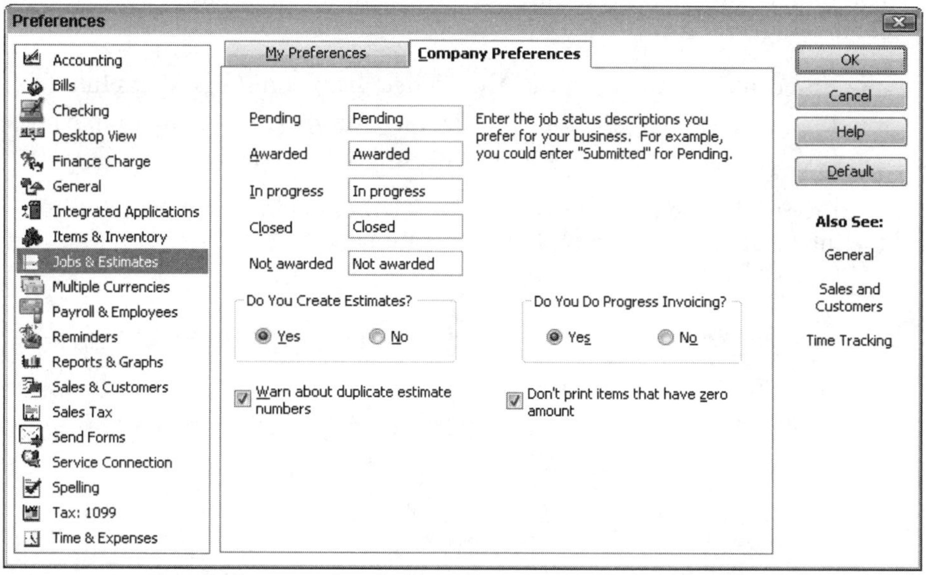

FIGURE 3-11 Customize the text to match the jargon you use in your business.

3. Change the text of any status levels if you have a descriptive phrase you like better. For example, you may prefer "Working" to "In Progress."

The new text is used on every job in your system.

The Job Info tab also provides fields to track the start date and the projected end date of the job, as well as a field to enter the real end date (frequently not the same as the projected end date). You can also create job types to categorize jobs and select one of them in the Job Type field (covered in Chapter 5).

When you finish entering all the data about this job, choose Next to create another job for the same customer. Otherwise, click OK to close the New Job window and return to the Customers & Jobs list. The jobs you create for a customer become part of the customer listing.

Editing Jobs

It's common to open a job record to make changes because most people track the current status (and occasionally change the projected end date). In addition, you may want to change some of the basic data you entered for a job.

To edit a job, double-click its listing in the Customers & Jobs list. You can make changes to any of the fields in any tab.

Deleting Customers & Jobs

It's not a common practice to delete a customer, although sometimes you create a customer and realize it's a duplicate record for a customer who already exists. Deleting a job is a bit more common, because sometimes users add a job when they pitch the client for the work and then delete the job if the customer turns down the offer.

You can only delete a customer or a job if it has never been used in a transaction. I hear from many users who complain that they can't remove a customer that is essentially "dead wood" on their Customers & Jobs list. The customer has a zero balance, and there hasn't been a sale to this customer for a long time (possibly years). Sorry, but a zero balance doesn't matter, the rule is that you can only delete a customer or a job if it has never been used in a transaction.

You cannot delete a customer who has jobs; instead you must first delete the jobs (if they can be deleted) and then delete the customer.

To delete a customer or job (if you find any that can be deleted), select its listing on the Customers & Jobs list and press CTRL-D. QuickBooks asks you to confirm the fact that you want to delete this customer or job. Click OK to remove the customer or job.

Making Customers & Jobs Inactive (Hiding)

If you have a customer who can't be deleted but is no longer active, you can prevent users from selecting this customer in transaction windows by making the customer inactive (hiding the customer so it doesn't appear in drop-down lists). You can do the same thing for any job.

To make a customer or job inactive, right-click its listing in the Customers & Jobs list and choose Make Customer:Job Inactive.

 N O T E : If you make a customer with jobs inactive, all of the jobs are automatically made inactive. You cannot hide a customer without hiding all the jobs associated with that customer.

If your Customers & Jobs list is configured to show Active Customers (the default view), inactive customers and jobs don't appear on the list. To see which customers and jobs are inactive, click the arrow to the right of the View field at the top of the list and select All Customers from the drop-down list. Inactive customers and jobs have an "X" to the left of their listings (see Figure 3-12).

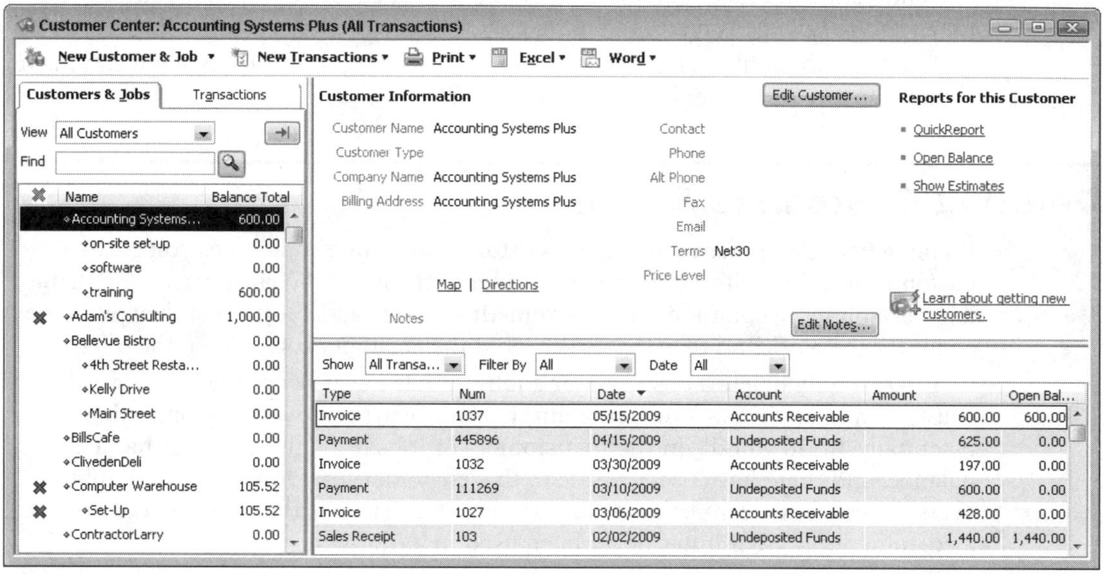

FIGURE 3-12 It's easy to spot hidden customers and jobs.

To make a customer or job active again, select All Customers as the view, and click the "X" next to the hidden customer or job to toggle the setting back to active. If you're reactivating a customer with jobs (which were automatically hidden when you made the customer inactive), QuickBooks asks if you also want to make all the jobs active. (The message actually says, "Do you want to activate the subs as well?") If you click Yes, the customer and all jobs are activated. If you click No, the customer is activated, and all the jobs remain inactive, and you can activate any of the jobs individually.

NOTE: Inactive customers and jobs are included in reports, so you can continue to get accurate information about customer activities.

Merging Customers or Jobs

Sometimes you create a customer or job and enter at least one transaction before you realize it's a duplicate of an existing customer or an existing job for the same customer. (Once you enter a transaction, you can't delete the customer or job to correct your error). To merge two customers or two jobs and move all the transaction history into one customer record, use the following steps:

1. Double-click the listing of the customer or job you do *not* want to keep to put its record in Edit mode.
2. Change the customer or job name to match the name of the customer or job you want to keep.
3. Click OK.
4. QuickBooks displays a message telling you that the name is in use and asks if you want to merge the names.
5. Click Yes.

   Merging customers only works when one of the following circumstances exists:
   • Neither customer has any jobs associated with it.
   • The customer name you want to get rid of has no jobs attached (it's OK if the customer name you want to keep has jobs).

   Merging jobs only works when both jobs are linked to the same customer.

Using Custom Fields

You can add your own fields to the Customer, Vendor, and Employee records (these are custom fields for names, and there are also custom fields you can create for items).

Custom fields for names are added to all names lists, but you can configure each custom field you create to limit its appearance to specific names lists. For example, you might create a custom field that you want to use in only the Customer & Jobs list or in both the Customer & Jobs and Vendors lists.

Custom fields are useful if there's information you want to track but QuickBooks doesn't provide a field for it. For example, if you want to track customer birthdays or annual renewals for a contract, you can add fields to track that information.

Adding a Custom Field for Names

To add one or more custom fields to names, follow these steps:

1. Open one of the names lists (Customers & Jobs, Vendor, or Employee).
2. Select any name on the list and press CTRL-E to put the record in Edit mode.

3. Move to the Additional Info tab.
4. Click the Define Fields button to open the Define Fields dialog, where you can name the field and indicate the list(s) in which you want to use the new field (see Figure 3-13).

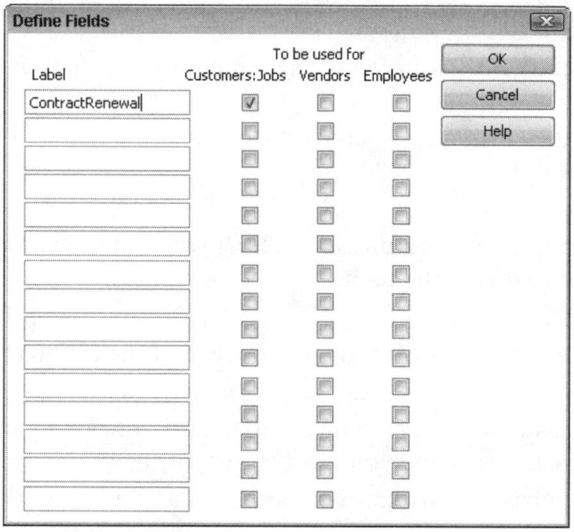

FIGURE 3-13   Custom fields appear on all the records of the list(s) you select.

That's all there is to it, except you must click OK to save the information. When you do, QuickBooks displays a message reminding you that if you customize your templates (forms for transactions, such as invoices or sales receipts), you can add these fields. Instructions for adding fields to transaction windows are found throughout this book in chapters covering invoices, estimates, purchase orders, and so on.

The Additional Info tab for every name in the list(s) you selected now shows those fields.

Adding Data to Custom Fields

To add data to the custom fields for each name on the list, select the name and press CTRL-E to put the record into Edit mode. Move to the Additional Info tab where the custom field you created appears (see Figure 3-14).

Be sure you enter data in a consistent manner for each customer, or you won't be able to get the information when you customize a report to include this information. For example, in the custom field data shown in Figure 3-14, the data

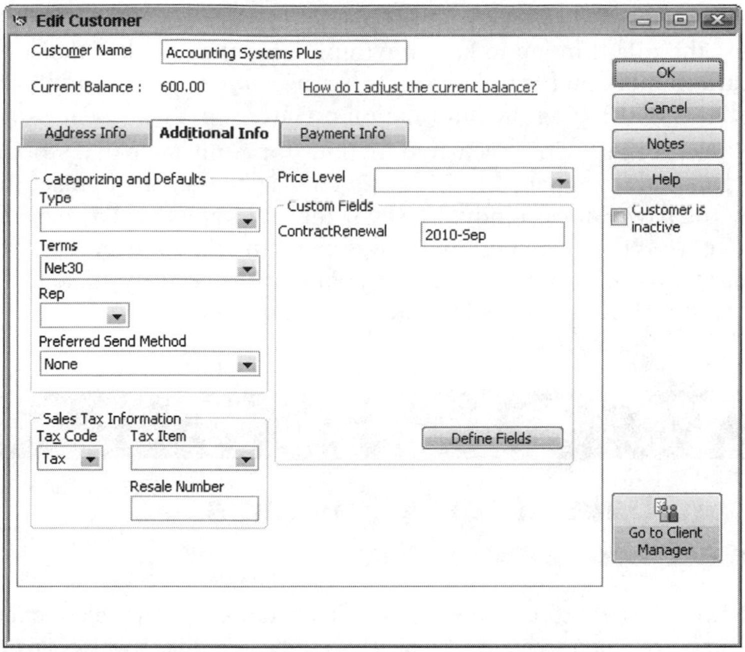

FIGURE 3-14 Add data to the custom field for each customer to which this custom field is relevant.

is a date. I entered the date in the format: Year-Month, using a four-digit year and a three-character month.

If I use that format for all customers who have contract expiration dates (such as 2010-Jun, or 2010-Jan) I can customize reports based on a question, "Who has a contract expiring 2010-Sep?" If I used Sept for some data entry, and Sep for other data entry, or if I forgot to enter a dash and used a space, I won't see all the customers with September contract dates.

> **TIP:** Another way to use custom fields for date-based data is to create two custom fields: a Month field and a Year field.

Securing Customer Credit Card Information

It's very convenient to maintain credit card information about customers because it's easy to take an order over the telephone or by a purchase order and process it quickly. However, keeping credit card information on your computer can be dangerous. In fact, the laws (both government and merchant-card providers) about keeping credit card numbers on file are getting stricter, and it's almost certainly against the rules for you to keep anything more than the last four or five digits of the card number on file unless you can prove you've set up strong security paradigms for keeping the information private.

QuickBooks provides security functions for companies that store customer credit card data in the company file. These functions are designed to meet the requirements set by the payment card industry (PCI) that are known as *Payment Application Best Practices* (*PABP*). If you configure your company file to meet the PABP security standards, you can meet PCI requirements for the security standards required for the handling and storage of credit card information.

⏩ FYI

Credit Card Data Security Problems Often Start with Employees

One serious breach in credit card security is the fact that a great many "information thefts" are committed by employees of merchants who accept credit cards. This is why online credit card purchases are often safer than physically providing your credit card to a sales clerk. Many online shopping carts are totally automated for credit card processing, so no human eyes ever see the data. In addition, a security log, similar to the security log QuickBooks initiates when you enable credit card protection, notes the name of any person who opens a file to view customer data. (I have to resist the urge to deliver a lecture when I hear people say, "I'd never enter my credit card information on a website," as I watch them hand a credit card to a person behind the cash register at a store, where, in addition to giving a human being a credit card number, they're also providing a signature for people to forge).

For many years, as I worked with small business clients to trace security breaches (including product theft, embezzlement, credit card data theft, and so on), I heard, "I'm sure the employee who has access to this information isn't the culprit, because he's my nephew" (substitute "son," "daughter," brother," "sister," or any other relative for the word "nephew"). Small business owners frequently hire relatives and assume that family loyalty will protect them from crimes of this type. Forget it! The number of internal business crimes committed by relatives of the owner is equal to the number of internal business crimes committed by "ordinary" employees.

Enabling the recommended security measures provides protection (or at least a viable defense) if the customer credit card information you store is used inappropriately. It won't be long before credit card companies will insist on this (and may even audit your security measures) if you want to continue to accept credit cards.

Summary of the QuickBooks Credit Card Protection Feature

The QuickBooks credit card protection feature is designed to secure customer credit card information with security safeguards that meet the Payment Application Best Practices standards of the Payment Card Industries. The following basic safeguards are implemented in QuickBooks:

- All users who have permission to view full credit card detail in the customer record must set up a *complex password* (see the next section, "Managing Complex Passwords").
- The password must be changed every 90 days. Users who don't change their password cannot open the file. If the Admin fails to change his or her password, the credit card protection feature is disabled (and you see messages about your failure to comply with the rules set for businesses that accept credit cards).
- You cannot reuse any of the last four passwords.
- If a user enters an incorrect password three times (users sometimes "guess different passwords when they can't remember their password), the company file closes for that user.
- Only the user named Admin can configure the functions in this feature.
- The QuickBooks credit card security audit log tracks all actions that involve credit cards (including viewing customer credit card information).

Managing Complex Passwords

Complex passwords (sometimes called *strong passwords*) are passwords that can't easily be discovered by hacker software that uses permutations and combinations of letters and numbers to break into password-protected files. This software "plays the odds" that it can break the password.

The more complex a password is, the higher the odds are against breaking in. For example, a password that contains seven characters and includes one uppercase letter and six lowercase letters is harder to break than a password that is entirely uppercase or lowercase (the odds are somewhere in the range of one in many millions). When you mix numbers with letters, and at least one letter is in a different case than the others, the odds grow even greater. If you add characters (such as insisting on a password that is at least nine characters long), and insist that at least two of those characters are numbers, and at least two of the letters are in a different case than the other letters, the odds of breaking in grow to astronomical levels (in the range of one in many billions).

Another hallmark of software (or an operating system) that requires strong passwords is the requirement to change the password periodically to limit access by an intruder in case another person learns the current password.

Of course, the more complicated a password is, the harder it is to remember. In fact, in a system that requires you to mix letters, numbers, and case and also requires you to invent a new password periodically, I'm confident that I'm right when I say that almost nobody could remember his/her password (I'd omit the word "almost" but if I do I'll get a lot of e-mail from readers who claim they have such excellent memories that this never happens to them).

Because these passwords are difficult to remember, users write them down and store them. Therefore, you have to apply some common sense rules in your company; and, you have to enforce those rules. (A breach of security that results in someone obtaining a customer's credit card number can result in an audit by your merchant card company, and failure to meet security standards for passwords can cost you the ability to take credit card payments. In addition, as merchant card companies begin to perform audits of standards and processes more frequently, even without the occurrence of a breach, you'll need to be able to pass the audit in order to keep your merchant account.)

A note pinned to a monitor or lying on a desk or placed in an unlocked desk draw that says "My QuickBooks password—MyNaMeiskathy99" is an obviously ludicrous way to make a password secret and secure. Nevertheless, I see this in more than half of the companies I visit.

Understanding the need to have a record of the password to refer to when logging in because of its complexity, in the following sections I offer some suggestions to maintain security.

Maintaining Passwords in Documents

Saving your password in a document is actually a nifty idea because when you have to log in you can open the document and copy and paste the password instead of typing it and risking a typo (because you can't see the characters you're typing in a Password field). However, you must use the following guidelines for a document that contains passwords:

- Save the password in a document with an innocuous and unexciting name (don't name it MyPasswords, choose something like Blood Pressure Test Results).
- Store the document in an encrypted folder (also named in a way that hides its purpose). Create a subfolder in another folder (such as My Documents) so that the folder is more difficult to spot, and configure the subfolder for encryption (see the Windows Help files for instructions on encryption).

 TIP: Use the same document for other important information that has to be secure, such as passwords and PINs for online secure sites, your own credit cards and their numbers/expiration dates, and so on. Use a Word document that's set up as a table, with the first column (the column that has the name of the entity) sorted alphabetically to make it easier to find data.

Maintaining Passwords on Paper

If users can't, or don't want to, store passwords in an electronic document and need a written record to refer to when logging in to QuickBooks, implement one or more of the following rules:

- Keep the paper in a drawer that's locked when you're not at your desk (and don't leave the keys on the desk).
- Don't put a "title" on the paper. Just enter the characters for your password, without a heading that says "QuickBooks Password" or any other title. You'll know what it is when you look at it, you don't need to announce what it is to every passerby.
- When you copy the password to paper, enter it backwards, and then read from right to left as you enter your password in the QuickBooks Login dialog. (Another method is to enter the characters one under another, creating a vertical list of characters, which won't be easily recognized as a password.)

Important Common Sense Rules for Passwords

Don't use anything that people can easily guess as your password. I've broken into locked files of employees who left my clients' companies by asking coworkers questions like, "What's the name of his dog?", "What are his children's' names?", "What is his wife's name?", "What's his home address?", "What's his car's license plate number?", and other similar questions.

It almost never failed. 'Nuff said.

Enabling Credit Card Protection

If you log in to your company file as Admin, you may see a reminder about enabling credit card protection when you open the file.

NOTE: If you're not sharing your company file with other users, and you didn't bother to set up an Admin password, nor to set up other users and permissions, you are inherently logging in as Admin (even though you never see a Login dialog).

You should enable the credit card protection feature as soon as possible, but if you don't respond to the reminder by selecting Enable Protection, you can perform the task by choosing Company | Customer Credit Card Protection and selecting Enable Protection.

CAUTION: You must be logged in as the user named Admin to configure credit card protection.

In the explanatory window that opens, select Enable Protection to begin setting up this feature. The first chore you face is changing your own Admin password so it matches the standards for complex passwords required by the credit card protection feature (see Figure 3-15).

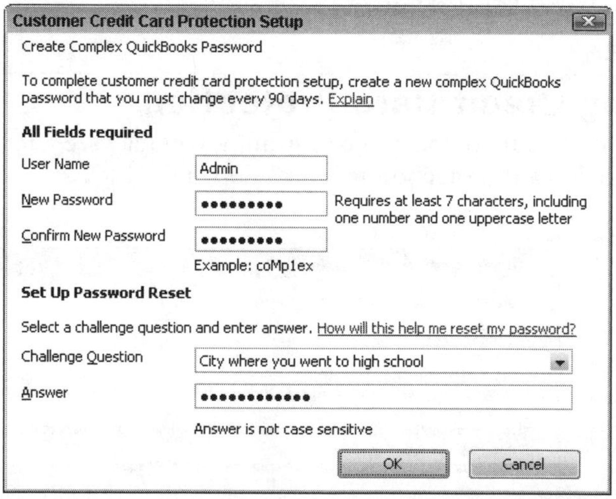

Customer Credit Card Protection Setup

Create Complex QuickBooks Password

To complete customer credit card protection setup, create a new complex QuickBooks password that you must change every 90 days. Explain

All Fields required

User Name	Admin	
New Password	•••••••••	Requires at least 7 characters, including one number and one uppercase letter
Confirm New Password	•••••••••	
	Example: coMp1ex	

Set Up Password Reset

Select a challenge question and enter answer. How will this help me reset my password?

Challenge Question	City where you went to high school ▼	
Answer	•••••••••••••	
	Answer is not case sensitive	

OK   Cancel

FIGURE 3-15   Start by setting a complex password for the QuickBooks Admin user account.

The Challenge Question section is optional, but I urge you to use it, especially for the Admin account. If you forget your password, you can click the Reset Password button on the Login dialog. When you answer the challenge question correctly, QuickBooks lets you change your password to a new complex password. Without the challenge question, you have to remove the Admin password, which involves either sending your file to Intuit or obtaining software from Intuit.

When you complete the dialog and click OK, QuickBooks confirms the fact that you've changed your password and informs you that you'll have to repeat this task every 90 days.

QuickBooks also displays a message to inform you that customer credit card protection has been enabled.

User Permissions for Viewing Credit Card Information

With credit card protection enabled, when you set up users and give them Full Access to the Sales and Accounts Receivable area, those users are not given permission to view customer credit card information unless you specifically select that option.

Users who do not have permission to view credit card information see only the last four numbers of the credit card when they open the Payment Information tab of a customer's record (see Figure 3-16).

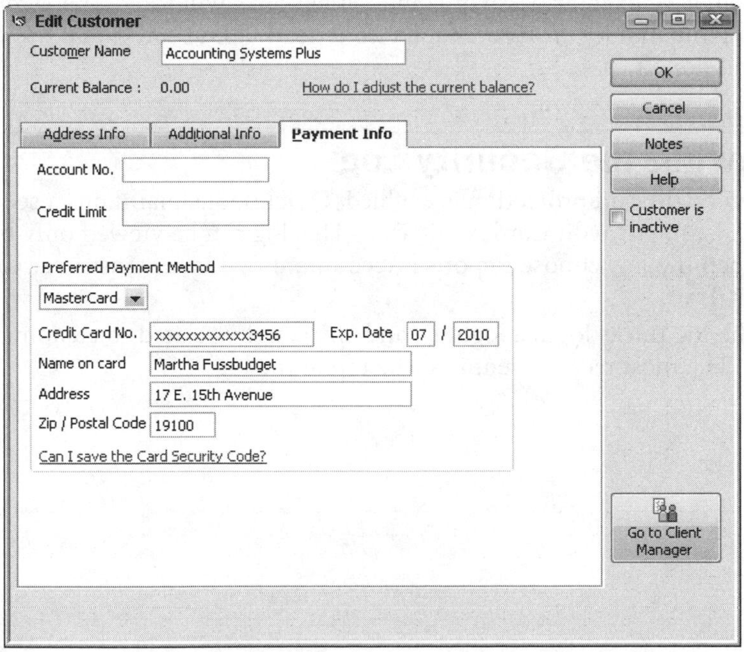

FIGURE 3-16 Users without the proper permissions can't see credit card numbers.

Users who have permission to view customer information are forced to create a complex password during their next login (see Figure 3-17).

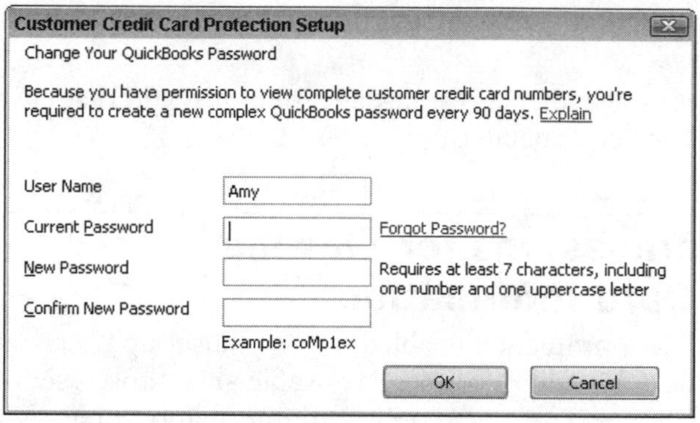

FIGURE 3-17 Any user with permission to view customer information must create a complex password.

When you set up new users and give them permission to access customer information, it's not necessary to set up a complex password for them. Provide a regular, easy to enter password, and QuickBooks will force a password change during the first login. (See Chapter 26 to learn about setting up users and permissions.)

Viewing the Security Log

When credit card protection is enabled, QuickBooks maintains a security log, called the Customer Credit Card Audit Trail. This log can be viewed only by the Admin. To open the log, choose Reports | Accountant & Taxes | Customer Credit Card Audit Trail.

The log tracks logins, logouts, and any activity related to customer credit card data. The most recent event is at the top of the log.

Configuring Vendors

In this chapter:

- The Vendor Center
- Creating vendors
- Editing vendors
- Deleting vendors
- Merging vendors
- Creating custom fields for vendor records

The vendors you purchase goods and services from have to be entered into your QuickBooks system, and it's far easier to do it before you start entering transactions. Otherwise, you'll have to go through the process of establishing the vendor and entering all the detailed information about that vendor at the moment you need to enter a vendor bill or write a check.

The Vendor Center

The Vendor Center is where your Vendors List is stored, along with all the information about each vendor's transactions. To open the vendor center, choose Vendors | Vendor Center from the menu bar (or click the Vendor Center icon on the Icon Bar. The Vendor Center displays your Vendors List along with a slew of functions and features (see Figure 4-1).

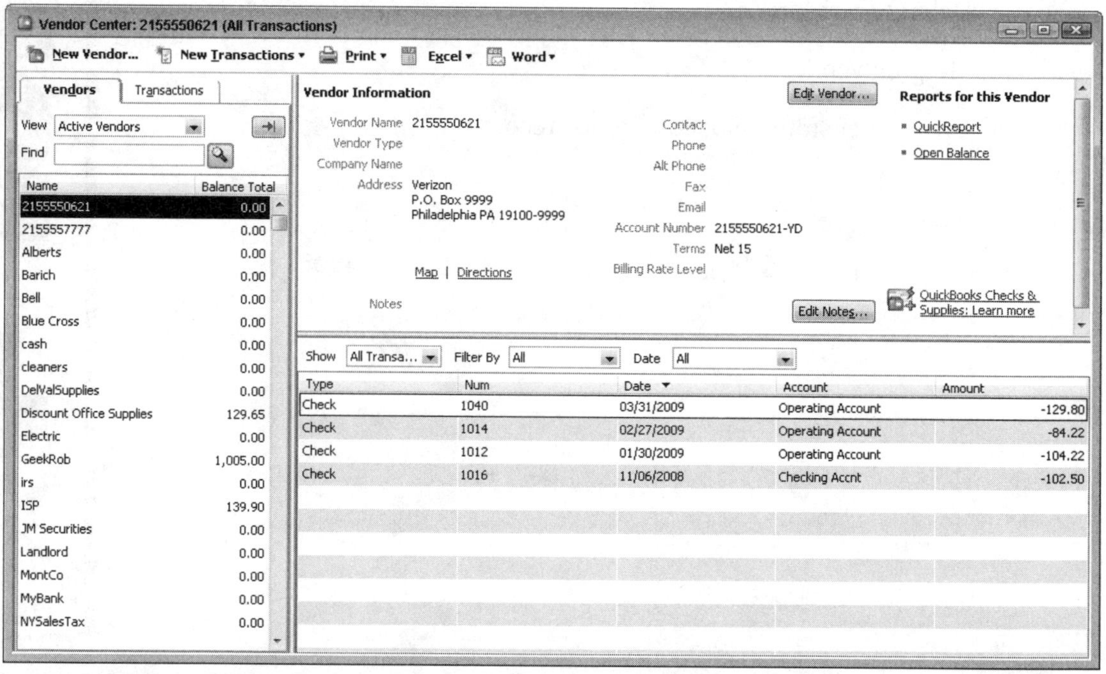

FIGURE 4-1   The Vendor Center is chock full of information about your spending.

The left pane of the Vendor Center has two tabs: Vendors (which is your Vendors List) and Transactions. A vendor is always selected in the list (by default, the first vendor in the list when you first open the Vendor Center), and the right pane of the Vendor Center displays information about the selected vendor.

The financial information in the bottom of the right pane can be filtered by choosing different categories in the drop-down lists and sorted by selecting a column heading. The Transactions tab lists all your transaction types. Selecting a transaction type displays the current transactions of that type in the right pane. The display can be manipulated and filtered by choosing categories and sorting by column.

Customizing the Vendor Center

You can customize the information displayed in the Vendors List (the Vendors tab in the left pane of the window), as well as the Vendor Information pane on the right side of the window.

Customize the Vendors List

By default, the list has two columns: Name and Balance Total. You don't even have to select a listing to see those two information items; they're right in front of you (except, of course, you may have to scroll down to get to the part of the list that has the vendor you want to see).

You can use the View drop-down list at the top of the Vendors tab to display your vendors in any of following ways:

- All Vendors
- Active Vendors
- Vendors With Open Balances
- Custom Filter

Use the Custom Filter to display only vendors that match the criteria you set in the Custom Filter dialog. The options in the dialog are easy to understand and use.

You can add more columns to the list by right-clicking anywhere in the list and choosing Customize Columns to open the Customize Columns dialog seen in Figure 4-2.

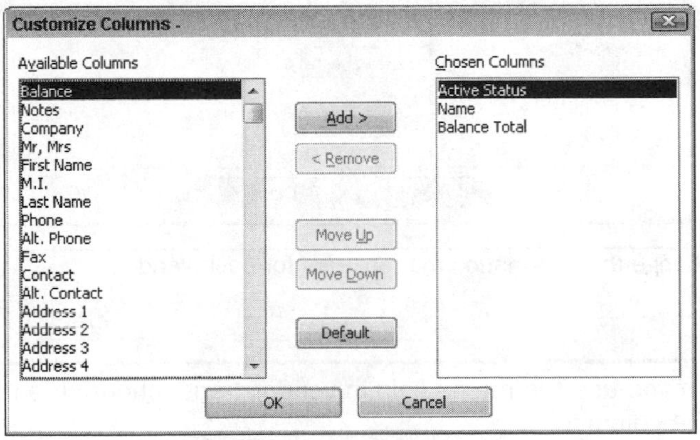

FIGURE 4-2   Decide for yourself what you want to see in the Vendors List.

To add a column, select its label in the left pane and click Add. The information the column describes is displayed for each vendor in the list. As long as the vendor you're interested in is displayed on the portion of the list that's visible, the information is available—you don't have to select the listing or open the record.

You can rearrange the left-to-right order of the columns by opening the Customize Columns dialog and selecting a column you want to move. Choose Move Up to move a column to the left or Move Down to move it to the right. The order of columns displayed in the Chosen Columns pane of the dialog translates as Top to Bottom = Left to Right.

If you add columns to the Vendors List, you won't be able to see all the information unless you widen the list's pane and also adjust the width of each column. To widen the list's pane, place your pointer over the vertical line on the right side of the pane. When your pointer turns into a horizontal double arrow with a vertical line in the middle, hold the left mouse button and drag to the right. To change the width of an individual column, position your mouse on the vertical line between columns at the top of the list. When you see the double arrow, drag in the appropriate direction.

Customize the Vendor Information Pane

You can filter the information that's displayed for each vendor by choosing different criteria for the three filters displayed above the columns. In addition, you can add and remove columns by clicking anywhere on or below the column headings and choosing Customize Columns. In the Customize Columns dialog (see Figure 4-3), add, remove, and change the order of columns.

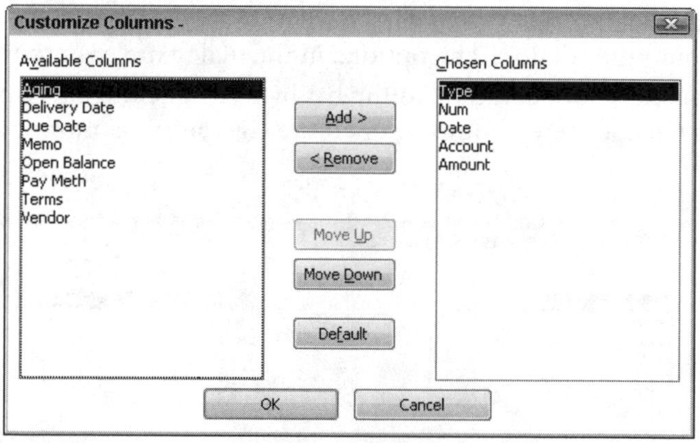

FIGURE 4-3 Change the information that appears for each vendor.

TIP: If you use the memo field in vendor transactions, it's useful to add that field to the columns.

Creating Vendors

To create a vendor, click the New Vendor icon above the Vendors List, which opens the New Vendor dialog seen in Figure 4-4.

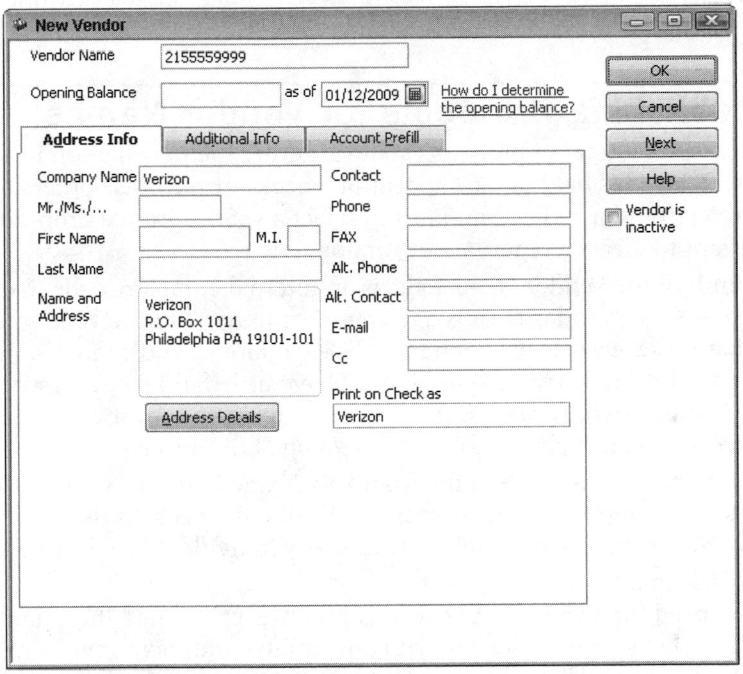

FIGURE 4-4 Vendor records are less complicated than customer records.

Start by filling in the Vendor Name field at the top of the dialog. (You may not want to use the real vendor name; to learn why, see the section "Establishing Protocols for Vendor Names.")

Do *not* enter anything in the Opening Balance field. Instead, separately enter historical data for vendors by inputting the existing vendor bills that represent the current open (unpaid) balances. See Chapter 8 to learn how get vendor history into your company file.

Currency

If you've enabled multicurrency, select the appropriate currency for this vendor if the vendor is in another country. See Appendix A for information about using the Multicurrency feature.

Vendor Address Info Tab

Fill in as much information about vendor names, contacts, telephone numbers, and so on, as you think you'll need. The Name and Address block is important if you're planning to print checks and the vendor doesn't enclose a return envelope. You can purchase window envelopes, and when you insert the check in the envelope, the vendor name and address block is in the right place.

Establishing Protocols for Vendor Names

You must have a set of protocols about entering the information in the Vendor Name field. This field doesn't appear on checks or purchase orders; it's used to sort and select vendors when you need to select a vendor from a drop-down list or when you want to create a report about vendor activity.

Think of the Vendor Name field as an internal company code. Notice that in Figure 4-4, the vendor code is a telephone number, but the vendor is the telephone company. I receive three telephone bills each month and cannot send one check to cover all three bills (well, I could, but I have little faith it would work properly in today's automated world). By creating a discrete vendor for each telephone line, I can create separate checks for each telephone bill I receive.

As soon as I enter data in the Company Name field (in this case, Verizon), QuickBooks duplicates that data in the Print On Check As field. By using codes in the Vendor Name field, I can create as many individual checks made out to Verizon as I need.

The need for protocols such as this becomes even more important (and more apparent) when you're dealing with government and tax agencies. How many checks do you send to your state or local governments for different reasons? In Pennsylvania, my checks for remitting sales tax, employee payroll withholding, corporate income tax, and several other items are made out to PA Department of Revenue. To avoid confusion, especially when multiple payments are made the same day (but the addresses on the enclosed envelopes or coupons are different for each type of payment), my Vendor Name entries are PASales (sales tax), PA501 (the form number for employee withholding remittances), PACorpTax, and so on. Every one of those vendor records has PA Department of Revenue as the data for the Print On Check As field.

Vendor Additional Info Tab

The Additional Info tab for vendors (see Figure 4-5) has several important categories:

- **Account No.** Enter your account number with this vendor (to the vendor, it's your customer number), and the number will appear in the memo field of printed checks.

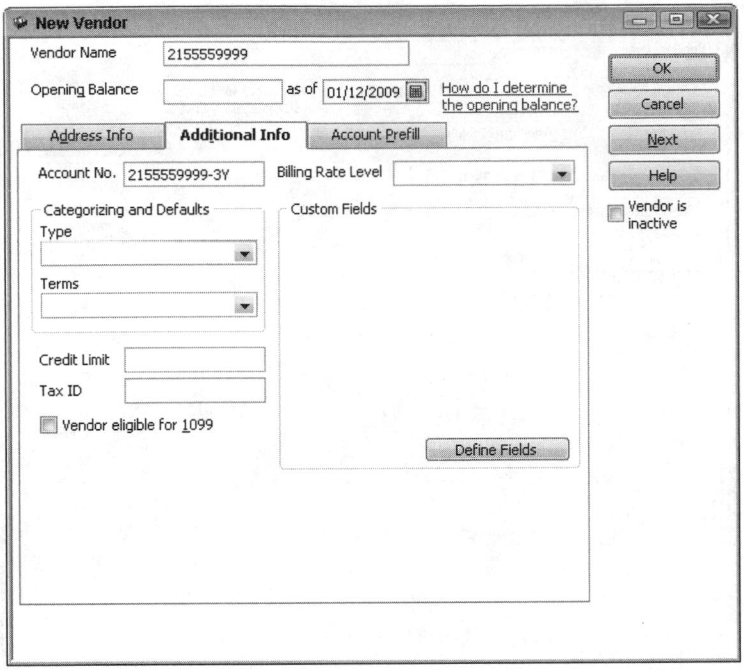

FIGURE 4-5 Add data to this tab to make it easier to print checks and produce detailed reports.

- **Type** Optionally, select a vendor type or create one. The Type field is handy if you want to sort vendors by type, which makes reports more efficient. For example, you can create vendor types for inventory suppliers, tax authorities, and so on.
- **Terms** Enter the terms for payment this vendor has assigned to you.
- **Credit Limit** Enter the credit limit this vendor has given you.
- **Tax ID** Use this field to enter the social security number or EIN if this vendor receives a Form 1099.
- **1099 status** If appropriate, select the check box for Vendor Eligible For 1099.
- **Custom Fields** You can create custom fields for vendors (see the section "Using Custom Fields in Vendor Records" later in this chapter).

Account Prefill Tab

This is a marvelous way to save time and ensure accuracy when filling out vendor bills or writing checks. You can prefill an account for this vendor (see Figure 4-6) and have the right account(s) appear automatically in the transaction window.

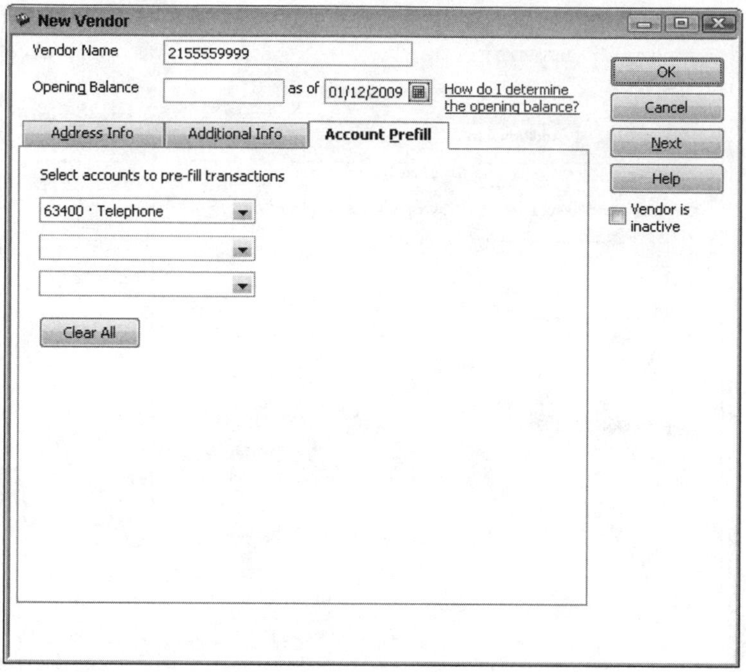

FIGURE 4-6 Prefill the usual posting account for a vendor to save time and avoid errors.

When you're using the vendor in a transaction, you can replace the prefilled account, if necessary.

You can prefill up to three accounts for a vendor, which is very useful for credit card vendors (for which you post accounts for each purchase), loan payments (which require postings to principal and interest), and other multi-account payments.

TIP: If you have a vendor that needs only one account, but you often split the amount due in order to assign parts of the bill to customers, enter the same account in all three fields of the Account Prefill tab. QuickBooks will list all the accounts in the transaction window. For example, parts of your telephone bill (usually long distance charges) may be charged to multiple clients as reimbursable expenses.

After you fill in the information on all the New Vendor tabs, choose Next to move to the next blank card and enter the next vendor. When you're finished, click OK.

Editing Vendor Information

You can edit a vendor's information by double-clicking the vendor's listing in the Vendors List. The vendor's record opens in Edit mode, as seen in Figure 4-7.

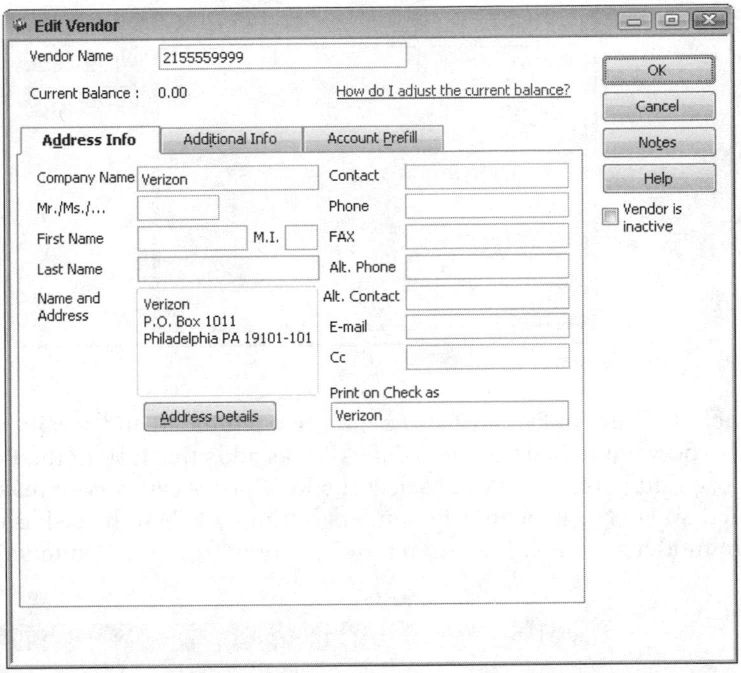

FIGURE 4-7 The Edit Vendor dialog is slightly different from the original dialog you used to create the vendor.

You can fill in data details you didn't enter when you first created the vendor. (Many QuickBooks users prefer to enter just the vendor name and company name when they set up vendors, so they can start entering historical transactions immediately. Later, when they have some time, they edit the record to fill in the missing data.)

You can change any data you've previously entered, but unless you've reinvented the protocol you're using to enter data in the Vendor Name field, don't change that data field.

Click the Notes button to open a Notepad window that's dedicated to this vendor. You can enter information, remarks, or track orders. Click the Date Stamp button to auto-insert the current date in front of any note you enter.

Click the New To Do button to compose a reminder, and specify the date on which you want to be reminded. QuickBooks adds this task to the Reminders List. (Choose Edit | Preferences and select the Reminders category to make sure you've enabled To Do Notes in your Reminders settings.) When the task is complete, open this reminder and click Done to remove the note from the Reminders list.

Deleting a Vendor

You can only remove a vendor from the list if that vendor has never been involved in a transaction. It doesn't matter if there's no open balance, or the last transaction was a long time ago; the fact that a vendor is in your transaction history means you cannot delete the vendor.

To delete a vendor, select its listing in the Vendors tab of the Vendor Center and press CTRL-D. QuickBooks asks you to confirm the fact that you want to delete the vendor; just click OK to finish the task. If the vendor has ever been involved in a transaction, QuickBooks issues an error message saying you can't delete this vendor.

If you can't delete a vendor but you don't want this vendor used in transactions, you can hide the vendor's listing (covered next).

Making a Vendor Inactive (Hiding a Vendor)

If you have a vendor who can't be deleted, but you don't want to use the vendor anymore, you can prevent users from selecting this vendor in transaction windows by making the vendor inactive (hiding the vendor name so it doesn't appear in drop-down lists).

To make a vendor inactive, right-click its listing in the Vendors List and choose Make Vendor Inactive.

If your Vendors List is configured to show Active Vendors (the default view), inactive vendors don't appear on the list. To see which vendors are inactive, click the arrow to the right of the View field at the top of the list and select All Vendors from the drop-down list. Inactive vendors have an "X" to the left of their listings.

To make a vendor active again, select All Vendors as the view, and click the "X" next to the hidden vendor or job to toggle the setting back to active.

NOTE: Inactive vendors are included in reports, so you can continue to get accurate reports on purchases and other vendor activity.

Merging Vendors

Sometimes you create a vendor and enter transactions for that vendor before you realize it's a duplicate of an existing vendor. This happens often if you haven't insisted on rigid protocols for entering data in the Vendor Name field when you create a vendor.

You need to merge the vendors to keep accurate records. To merge two vendors and move all the transaction history into one vendor record, use the following steps:

1. Double-click the listing of the vendor you do *not* want to keep, which opens its record in Edit mode.
2. Change the data in the Vendor Name field to match the name of the vendor you want to keep.
3. Click OK.
4. QuickBooks displays a message telling you that the name is in use and asks if you want to merge the names.
5. Click Yes.

Remember, the trick to merging is to start with the vendor name you *don't* want and merge into the vendor name you *do* want.

Using Custom Fields in Vendor Records

You can add your own fields to the Vendor, Customer, and Employee records. QuickBooks provides the ability to create custom fields for Names lists (and also offers custom fields for Items).

Custom fields for Names lists are added to all Names lists, but you can configure each custom field you create to limit its appearance to specific Names lists. For example, you might create a custom field that you want to use in only the Vendors List, or in both the Customers & Jobs and Vendors Lists.

Custom fields are useful if there's information you want to track but QuickBooks doesn't provide a field for it. For example, if you have vendors with whom you've signed contracts, you might want to add a field that will let you track contract renewal dates.

Adding a Custom Field for Names

To add one or more custom fields to a names list, follow these steps:

1. Open one of the Names lists (Vendors, Customers & Jobs, or Employee).
2. Select any name on the list and press CTRL-E to put the record in Edit mode.
3. Move to the Additional Info tab.
4. Click the Define Fields button to open the Define Fields dialog, where you can name the field and indicate the list(s) in which you want to use the new field (see Figure 4-8).

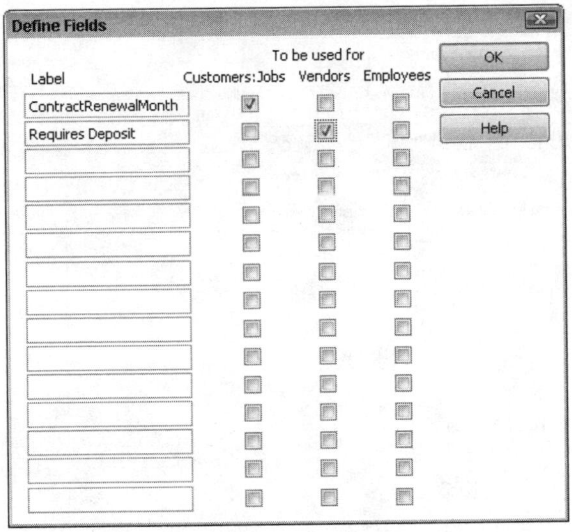

FIGURE 4-8 Design custom fields that you can use for one list or multiple lists.

That's all there is to it, except you must click OK to save the information. When you do, QuickBooks flashes a message reminding you that if you customize your templates (forms for transactions, such as bills or checks), you can add these fields. The Additional Info tab for every name in the list(s) you selected now shows those fields, and you can add data to any name for which these fields have relevance.

Adding Data to Custom Fields

To add data to the custom fields for each name on the list that needs the data, select the name and press CTRL-E to put the record into Edit mode. Move to the Additional Info tab where the custom field you created appears (see Figure 4-9).

Be sure that you enter data in a consistent manner for each vendor, or you won't be able to get the information when you customize a report to include this information.

For example, consider the data entered in the custom field shown in Figure 4-9. The protocol for this data is established as a single character. If you enter N for some vendors, and No for others, and then customize a report looking for N, all the No vendors will be missing from the report.

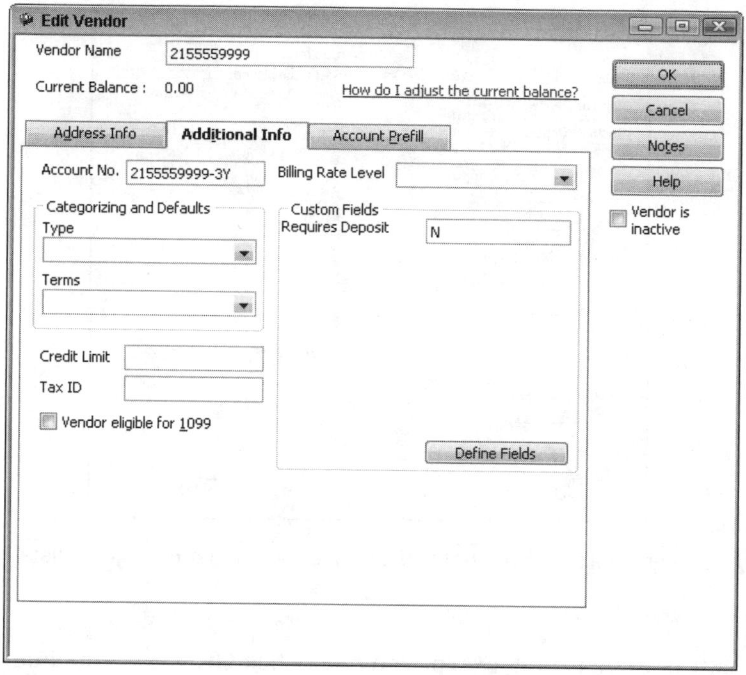

FIGURE 4-9 Add data to the custom field for each vendor to which this custom field is relevant.

Creating 1099 Vendors

If any vendors are eligible for 1099 forms, you need to configure 1099 settings for your system and then link the appropriate vendors to that configuration.

Configuring 1099 Options

To configure your 1099 settings, choose Edit | Preferences and select the Tax: 1099 icon in the left pane. Then click the Company Preferences tab to see the dialog shown in Figure 4-10.

You must assign an account to each category for which you'll be issuing Form 1099-MISC to vendors. You can assign multiple accounts to a 1099 category, but you cannot assign any accounts to more than one 1099 category.

For example, if you have an expense account "subcontractors" and an expense account "outside consultants," both of the accounts can be linked to the same 1099 category (Nonemployee Compensation). However, once you link those accounts to that category, you cannot use those same accounts in any other 1099 category.

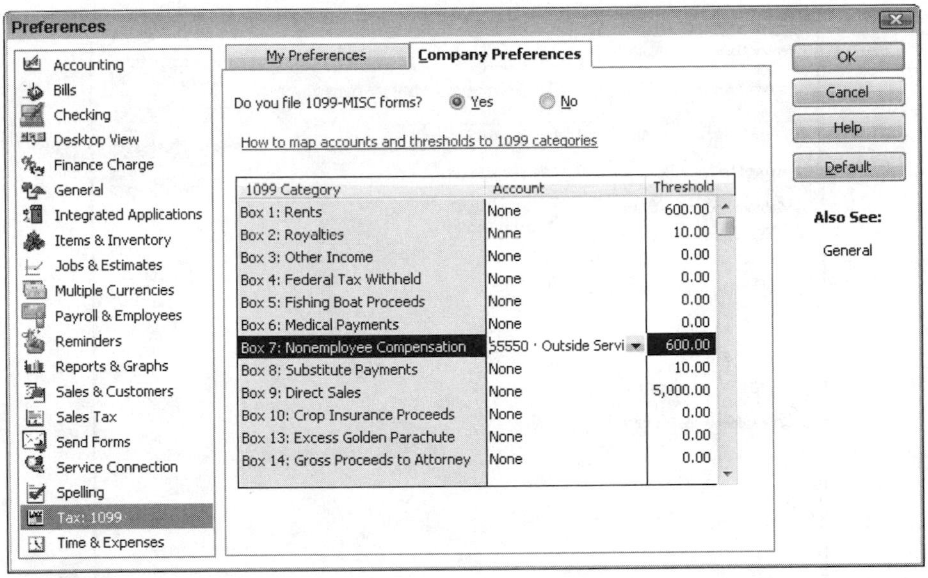

FIGURE 4-10 Set up your 1099 configuration options in order to send the forms to vendors who need them.

To assign a single account to a category, click the category to select it. Click the text in the account column (it probably says "None") and then click the arrow to select the account for this category.

To assign multiple accounts to a category, instead of selecting an account after you click the arrow, choose the Multiple Accounts option (at the top of the list). In the Select Account dialog, click each account to put a check mark next to its listing. Click OK to assign all the accounts you checked. Then click OK to close the Preferences dialog.

Marking Vendors as 1099 Recipients

You are required to issue Form 1099 at the end of the calendar year to any vendor who operates as a business, unless the vendor is a corporation. Business that are organized as LLCs can opt to be proprietorships, partnerships, or corporations for the purpose of filing tax returns, so ask any LLC vendors whether they are reporting as a corporation and are therefore exempt from Form 1099.

To issue Form 1099, you must have the vendor's federal Tax Identification Number (TIN), which can be a social security number or an Employer Identification Number (EIN).

Open each appropriate vendor listing and move to the Additional Info tab. Select the option labeled Vendor Eligible For 1099, and fill in the Tax ID as seen in Figure 4-11.

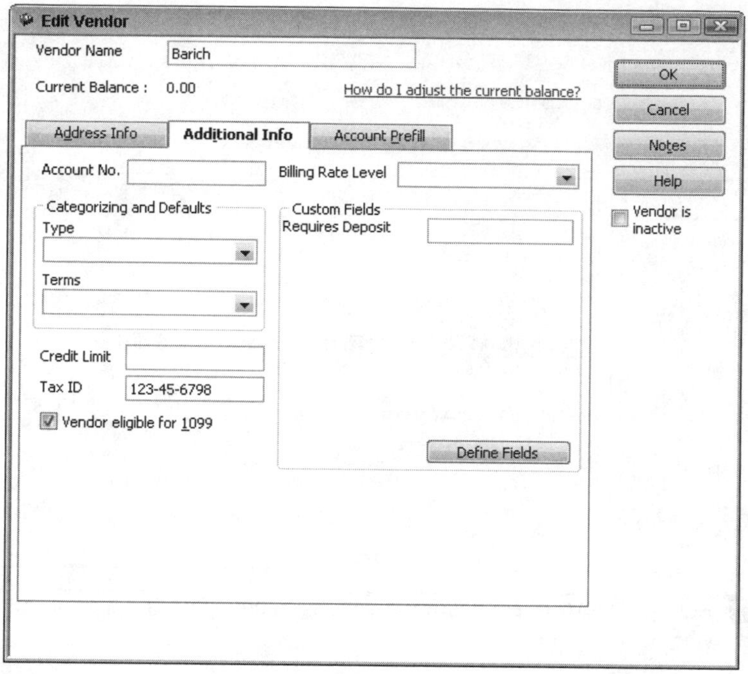

FIGURE 4-11 Mark each eligible vendor for 1099 reporting, and fill in the TIN.

Managing Transactions for 1099 Vendors

When you enter a bill or a direct disbursement check for a 1099 vendor, you must post all expenses to accounts that have been linked to your 1099 configuration options, as explained in this chapter. Otherwise, the total amount you pay the vendor won't be reflected in the Form 1099 you send.

NOTE: To learn how to print 1099 reports and issue Form 1099 to vendors, see Chapter 24.

Creating Other Lists You Need

In this chapter:

- Fixed Asset Item list

- Price Level list

- Currency list

- Class List

- Other Names list

- Profile lists

There are some lists in the Lists menu that you can set up to make your work in QuickBooks more efficient and to make it easier to create customized reports that contain details you find helpful.

These lists don't require extensive amounts of data, and you may not use all of them. Some of these items are in the Lists menu, and some of them are in a submenu of the Lists menu called Customer & Vendor Profile Lists.

> **NOTE:** Several lists aren't covered here. Some of them (customers, vendors, employees) are covered in their own chapters, and others (such as Templates and Memorized Transactions/Reports) are created automatically as you customize transaction windows and reports.

Fixed Asset Item List

Use the Fixed Asset Item list to store information about fixed assets. This list provides a way to track data about the assets you purchase and depreciate. As you can see in Figure 5-1, you can record detailed information about the asset.

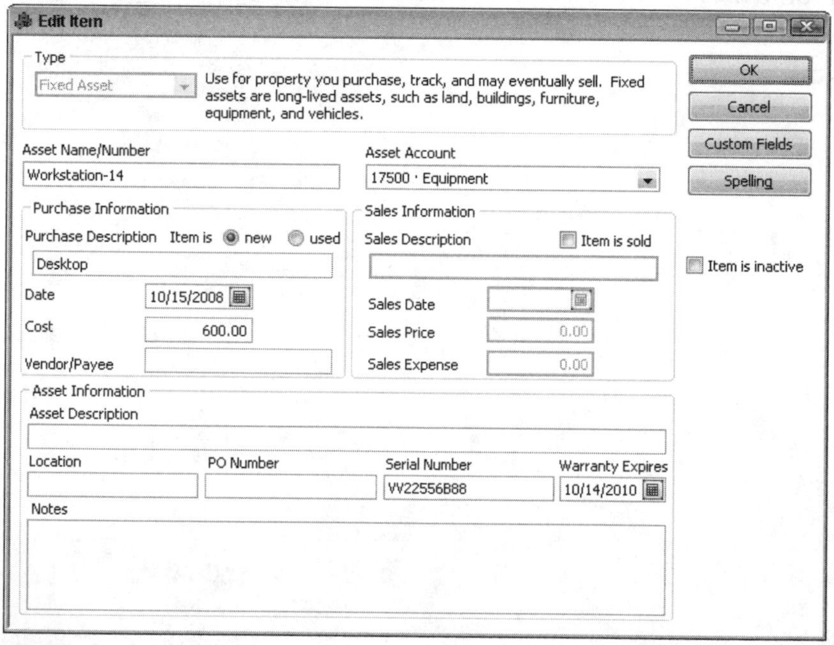

FIGURE 5-1   Keep information about fixed assets in the Fixed Asset Item list.

This is an inert list that doesn't provide any links to any financial data in your QuickBooks company file. It does not interact with the chart of accounts, so any values you enter in this list have to be entered in your Fixed Asset accounts separately.

This list does not add any financial information to your company file, nor does it perform any calculations. It's merely a way to use QuickBooks to catalog your fixed assets instead of whatever list you're keeping in Microsoft Word, Microsoft Excel, a legal pad, or a shoebox full of index cards.

CAUTION: Another fact to consider about the items you add to the Fixed Asset Item list is that those items show up in the drop-down list you see when you create a transaction that involves items, such as an invoice, cash sale, or a purchase order (the "regular" items you created to transact business, which are discussed in Chapter 6). If a user accidentally selects a fixed asset, your financial records can become confusing. If you choose to use the Fixed Asset Item list, consider making all the items in the list inactive to suppress their display in drop-down lists.

However, QuickBooks Premier Accountant Edition contains a program called Fixed Asset Manager (FAM), which uses the Fixed Asset Item list. If you send your file to your accountant (assuming your accountant is using Premier Accountant Edition), FAM reads the Fixed Asset Item list to populate the data needed to generate depreciation as part of the tax preparation chores for your company.

Price Level List

The Price Level list is a nifty, easy way to apply special pricing to customers and jobs. This list is only available if Price Levels are enabled in the Sales & Customers section of your Preferences. To accomplish this, use the following steps:

1. Choose Edit | Preferences, and select the Sales & Customers category in the left pane.
2. Move to the Company Preferences tab.
3. Select the option labeled Use Price Levels.
4. Click OK.

Creating a Price Level

To create a price level, open the Price Level list from the Lists menu and press CTRL-N to open the New Price Level dialog.

Each price level has two components: a name and a formula. The name can be anything you wish, and the formula is a percentage of the price you entered for the items in your Item List (the formula increases or reduces the price by the percentage you specify).

For example, you may want to give your favorite customers an excellent discount. Name the price level something like "Special" or "StarCustomer." Then enter a healthy percentage by which to reduce the price of items purchased by this customer. Or you may want to create a discount price level for customers that are nonprofit organizations.

On the other hand, you may want to keep your regular prices steady (assuming they're competitive) and increase them for certain customers (perhaps customers who don't pay in a timely fashion). It's probably politically incorrect to name the price level "Deadbeat," so choose something innocuous such as "DB," or "StandardPrice." You could also use numbers for the price-level names, perhaps making the highest numbers the highest prices.

Linking Price Levels to Customers

After you create price levels, you can apply a price level to customers. Open the Customers & Jobs list in the Customer Center and double-click the customer's listing. Enter a price level in the Price Level field of the Additional Info tab.

Once a price level is linked to a customer, sales transactions for that customer reflect the price level automatically. See Chapter 9 to learn how to create sales transactions with price levels.

> **TIP:** QuickBooks Premier editions have a price-level feature that's more robust—you can apply price levels to items in addition to customers, which makes it easier to provide discounts (or increases) while you're creating invoices. These per-item price levels let you set custom prices (using either a specific amount or a percentage) for items. If you've purchased a Premier edition of QuickBooks or are considering upgrading to a Premier edition, you can learn how to use price levels in *Running QuickBooks 2009 Premier Editions* from CPA911 Publishing (www.cpa911publishing.com). You can buy the book at your favorite bookstore.

Currency List

Available if you've enabled the QuickBooks Multicurrency feature (covered in Appendix A), this list specifies the currencies you want to work with (see Figure 5-2). By default, the majority of currencies are marked Inactive; open this list to activate the currencies you need so they appear in drop-down lists.

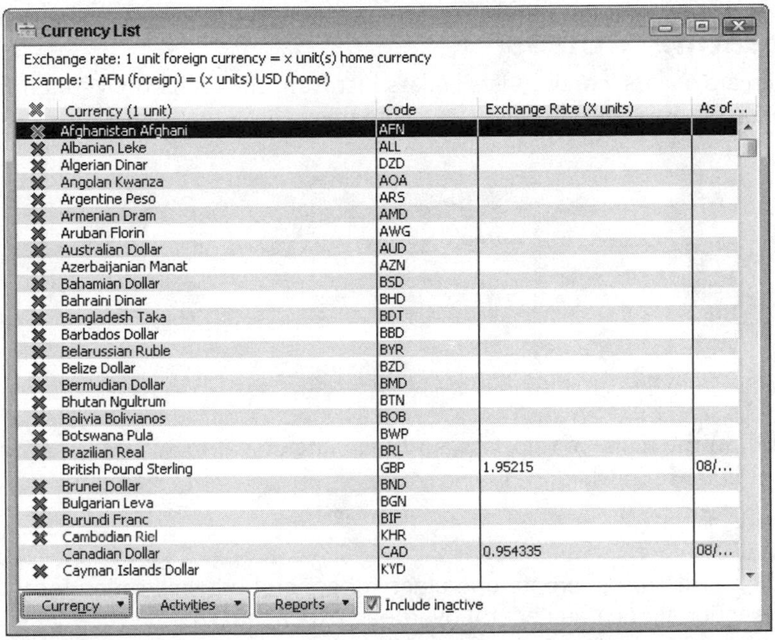

FIGURE 5-2 Activate the currency you need for your customers and vendors.

Class List

The Class List appears in the Lists menu only if you've enabled the Use ClassTracking feature (in the Accounting category of the Preferences dialog). Classes provide a method of organizing your income and disbursement activities to produce reports that let you see those activities on a per-class basis. Some of the common reasons to configure classes include

- Reporting by location if you have more than one office
- Reporting by division or department
- Reporting by business type (perhaps you have both retail and wholesale businesses under your company umbrella)

You should use classes for a single purpose; otherwise, the feature won't work properly. For example, you can use classes to separate your business into locations or by type of business, but don't try to do both. If you need to further define a class or narrow its definition, you can use subclasses.

When you enable classes, QuickBooks adds a Class field to transaction forms. For each transaction or each line of any transaction, you can assign one of the classes you created.

Creating a Class

To create a class, choose Lists | Class List from the QuickBooks menu bar to display the Class List window. Press CTRL-N to open the New Class dialog.

Fill in the name of the class, and then click Next to add another class, or click OK if you are finished.

TIP: Be sure to create one class for general administration for those transactions (such as general overhead expenses) that aren't specific to one of the classes you create in order to track divisions, departments, etc. You can allocate that overhead to other classes with a journal entry, and that subject is covered in Chapter 19.

Creating a Subclass

Subclasses let you post transactions to specific subcategories of classes, and they work similarly to subaccounts in your chart of accounts. If you set up a subclass, you must post transactions only to the subclass, never to the parent class. However, unlike the chart of accounts, classes have no option to force the display of only the subclass when you're working in a transaction window. As a result, if you're using subclasses you must keep the name of the parent class short, to lessen the need to scroll through the field to see the entire class name.

You create a subclass using the same steps required to create a class. After you enter a name for the subclass in the Class Name field, click the check box next to the option Subclass Of to insert a check mark. Then select the appropriate parent class from the drop-down list.

Other Names List

QuickBooks provides a list called Other Names, which is the list of people whose names are used when you write checks, but they don't fit the definition of vendor because you don't need to track payables and transactions the way you do for a vendor.

The names in the Other Names list appear in the drop-down list when you write checks but are unavailable when you're entering vendor bills, purchase orders, or any other regular QuickBooks transaction type.

The most common reason to add a name to the Other Names list is to be able to write checks to owners and partners. Strictly speaking, these people aren't vendors of your company, and they also aren't employees. You can also use the Other Names list for Cash and use that name when you write checks for cash to fill your petty cash box (covered in Chapter 13).

TIP: If you reimburse employees for expenses they incur, and you don't want to manage the reimbursement through their paychecks, create an Other Name listing for those employees and use that name for reimbursements. QuickBooks does not allow duplicate names, so you'll have to change the name you use in the Employee list slightly to create the Other Name listing (for instance, add or remove a middle initial).

To open the Other Names list, choose Lists | Other Names List. To create a new name for the list, press CTRL-N to open a New Name window.

The New Name window provides fields for the address (handy for printing checks you're going to place into window envelopes), telephone numbers, and other contact information.

> **TIP:** Many people overuse this category and end up having to move these names to the Vendor List because they find they *do* need to track the activity or issue a Form 1099. Only use this list for check payees you don't have to track as vendors.

Profile Lists

The Profile lists are those lists that appear in the submenu you see when you choose Customer & Vendor Profile Lists. Most of the lists in the submenu are designed to help you categorize and refine the information you keep about your customers and vendors. Other lists can contain data that is available when you create transactions.

Sales Rep List

By common definition, a *sales rep* is a person who is connected to a customer, usually because he or she receives a commission on sales to that customer. However, it's frequently advantageous to track sales reps who are not garnering commissions as a way to determine who is the primary contact for a customer (some people call this a *service rep*).

To create a sales rep, the rep's name has to exist in your QuickBooks system as a vendor, employee, or a member of the Other Names list.

To create a new sales rep from an existing name, open the Sales Rep list and press CTRL-N to open a New Sales Rep form. Select the person's name from the drop-down list. QuickBooks automatically fills in the Sales Rep Initials field (which is the data used in reports and transaction windows that have a Sales Rep field) and the Sales Rep Type (the list that contains this sales rep).

Customer Type List

When you create your customer list, you may decide to use the Customer Type field as a way to categorize your customers. This gives you the opportunity to sort and select customers in reports, so you can view the total income from specific types of customers.

For example, you may use the Customer Type list to track the source of referrals, or to separate wholesale and retail customers.

Vendor Type List

See the preceding paragraph and substitute the word "vendor" for the word "customer."

Job Type List

Use this list to set up categories for jobs. For example, if you're a plumber, you may want to separate new construction from repairs.

Terms List

QuickBooks keeps both customer and vendor payment terms in one list, so the terms you need are all available whether you're creating an invoice, entering a vendor bill, or creating a purchase order. To create a terms listing, open the Terms List window and press CTRL-N to open the New Terms window seen in Figure 5-3.

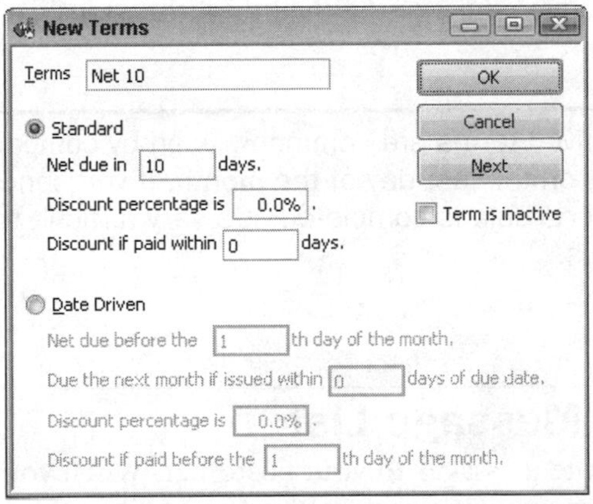

FIGURE 5-3   Set up the terms you need for customers and vendors.

Use the Standard section to create terms that are due at some elapsed time after the invoice date:

- Net Due In is the number of days allowed for payment after the invoice date.
- To create a discount for early payment, enter the discount percentage and the number of days after the invoice date that the discount is in effect. For example, if 30 days are allowed for payment, enter a discount percentage that is in effect for 10 days after the invoice date (such terms are usually referred to as "*X* percent 10, net 30," substituting the amount of the discount for *X*).

NOTE: Discounts for early payment are commonly found only in the manufacturing and wholesale distribution industries and are applied to product sales. It would be unusual to receive (or give) such discounts for ordinary business expenses, such as utilities, rent, services rendered, and so on.

Use the Date Driven section to describe terms that are due on a particular date, regardless of the invoice date:

- Enter the day of the month the invoice payment is due.
- Enter the number of days before the due date that invoices are considered payable on the following month (but it's not fair to insist that invoices be paid on the 10th of the month if you mail them to customers on the 8th of the month).
- To create a discount for early payment, enter the discount percentage and the day of the month at which the discount period ends. For example, if the standard due date is the 15th of the month, you may want to extend a discount to any customer who pays by the 8th of the month.

TIP: Date-driven terms are commonly used by companies that send invoices monthly, usually on the last day of the month. If you send invoices weekly, or immediately after a sale is completed, it's very difficult to track and enforce date-driven terms.

Customer Message List

If you like to write messages to your customers when you're creating a sales transaction (an invoice or a cash sales receipt), you can enter a bunch of appropriate messages ahead of time and then just select the one you want to use. For example, you may want to insert the message "Thanks for doing business with us" or "Pay on time or else."

Press CTRL-N to enter a new message to add to the list. You just have to type out the text (which can't be longer than 101 characters, counting spaces)—this is one of the easier lists to create.

Payment Method List

You can track the way payments arrive from customers. This not only provides some detail about those payments (in case you're having a conversation with a customer about invoices and payments), but also allows you to print reports on payments that are subtotaled by the method of payment, such as credit card, check, cash, and so on. (Your bank may use the same subtotaling method on your monthly statement, which makes it easier to reconcile the bank account.)

QuickBooks prepopulates the payment methods with common payment types. If you have a payment method that isn't listed, you can add that method to the list. To do so, press CTRL-N to open the New Payment Method window. Name the payment method and select the appropriate payment type.

Ship Via List

Use this list to add a description of your shipping method to your invoices (in the field named Via), which many customers appreciate. QuickBooks prepopulates the list with a variety of shipment methods, but you may need to add a shipping method. To do so, press CTRL-N to add a new Shipping Method entry to the list. All you need to do is enter the name, for example Our Truck, or Sam's Delivery Service.

If you use one shipping method more than any other, you can select a default Ship Via entry, which appears automatically on your invoices (you can change it on any invoice if the shipping method is different). The default entry is in the Sales & Customers category of the Preferences dialog, where you can select the Usual Shipping Method entry you want to appear by default on your sales transactions. You can also enter the FOB site you want to appear on invoices, if you wish to display this information.

FOB (Free On Board) is the site from which an order is shipped and is also the point at which transportation and other costs are the buyer's responsibility. (There are no financial implications for FOB—it's merely informational.)

Vehicle List

The Vehicle list lets you create vehicle records in which you track mileage for vehicles used in your business. You can use the mileage information for tax deductions for your vehicles and to bill customers for mileage expenses. However, even if you don't bill customers for mileage or your accountant uses a formula for tax deductions, the Vehicle list is a handy way to track information about the vehicles you use for business purposes. (You can learn how to track mileage and bill customers for mileage in Chapter 16.)

To add a vehicle to the list, press CTRL-N to open a New Vehicle dialog. The record has two fields:

- Vehicle, in which you enter a name or code for a specific vehicle. For example, you could enter BlueTruck, JudysToyota, FordMustangConvertible, or any other recognizable name.
- Description, in which you enter descriptive information about the vehicle.

While the Description field is handy for standard description terms (such as black or blue/white truck), take advantage of the field by entering information you really need. For example, the VIN, the license plate number, the expiration date for the plate, the insurance policy number, or other "official" pieces of information are good candidates for inclusion. You can enter up to 256 characters in the field.

Creating Items

In this chapter:

- Understand how items are used
- Learn about different types of items
- Create items
- Set up sales tax items

In QuickBooks, *items* are the components you use when you create sales. An item can be a product (that you may or may not be tracking as inventory), a service, or another necessary entry in a sales transaction.

What other necessary entries could there be besides products and services? If you think about it and picture an invoice, there are more items required than might occur to you. Do you assess sales tax? If you do, that's an item. Do you accept prepayments or give discounts? Those are items. Do you subtotal sections of your invoices to apply discounts or taxes? That subtotal is an item.

In this chapter I'll go over the item types you can use in QuickBooks, with the exception of inventory items (which are covered in Chapter 7) and payroll items (covered in Chapter 17).

Understanding How Items Are Used

When you create a sales transaction, each line in the transaction is an item that you've created and configured. Every item is linked to an account, so that when you're creating a sales transaction you don't have to worry about the account to which any individual line item on an invoice or sales receipt is posted.

Most items are linked to an income account, because most of the items that appear on a sales transaction are things you're selling to the customer. You can link all of your items to one income account (called "Income" or "Sales"), or you can track different types of items by linking them to different income accounts. For example, you might want to link all product sales to an income account named "Product Sales" and link the services you sell to an income account named "Sales Of Services." The advantage of linking certain types of items to certain income accounts is that when you look at a standard Profit & Loss report, you can tell at a glance what your sales totals are for each group of item types. You can also create reports on your items themselves, which is the way to see what's hot and what's not.

Some items, however, are not linked to income accounts, because they're not income. Sales tax isn't income; it's money you collect for someone else (your state or local government) and have to turn over to the proper tax authority. Because you're holding someone else's money, sales tax items are linked to a liability account.

Discounts you give your customers are items, and you should link them to accounts specifically designed for that purpose so you can easily see what you've "spent" on discounts (or you may want to use the terminology "given away as incentives").

As you can see, items are a bit more complicated than you may have thought, but creating items and configuring them is a task that's easy to accomplish if you follow the directions in this chapter.

Understanding Item Types

It isn't always clear how and when some of the item types are used (or why you must define them). Here are some guidelines you can use as you plan to enter your items:

Service   A service you provide to a customer. You can create services that are charged by the job or by the hour.

Inventory Part   A product you buy for the purpose of reselling. Inventory parts are treated differently in accounting; you post their cost as you sell them (not when you write the check to purchase them). This item type isn't available if you haven't enabled inventory during the EasyStep Interview or activated inventory in the Items & Inventory section of the Preferences dialog. Chapter 7 covers inventory part setup.

Non-Inventory Part   A product you sell but don't track as inventory.

Other Charge   You'll need this item type for things like shipping charges or other line items that don't fit into a service or product item.

Subtotal   This item type automatically adds up the line items that come before it on a sales transaction. It provides a subtotal before you add other charges or subtract discounts.

Group   This item type is a clever device. You can use it to enter a group of items (all of which must exist in your Item list) all at once, instead of entering each individual item on the sales transaction.

   For example, if you always have a shipping charge accompanying the sale of a particular item, you can create a group item that includes those two items.

Discount   You can't give a customer a discount as a line item if this item type doesn't exist. You may have more than one item that falls within this item type—for example, a discount for wholesale customers and a discount for a volume purchase. When you create the item you can indicate a flat rate or percentage of the original price.

Payment   If you receive a prepayment (either a total payment or a partial payment as a deposit), you must indicate it as a line item, using this item type.

Sales Tax Item   Create one of these item types for each sales tax authority for which you collect (available only if sales tax is enabled).

Sales Tax Group   This is for multiple sales taxes (state and local) that apply to the customer.

> **T I P :** I've described all of the item types in terms of their use on your invoices, but some of them are also used on your purchase orders.

Creating Items

Setting up items requires some planning. Each of your items must have a unique identification (QuickBooks calls that the Item Name/Number), which you can think of as an item code. Try to create a system that has some logic to it so your codes are recognizable and meaningful when you see them in the drop-down list of a sales transaction window.

To create an item, open the Item List by choosing Lists | Item List. Then press CTRL-N to open the New Item window, which displays the list of item types.

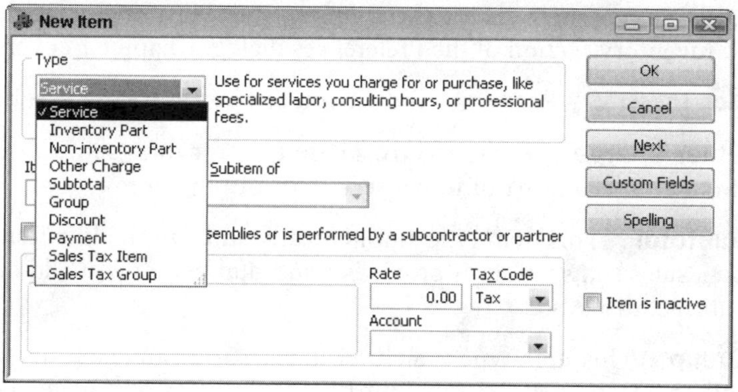

Select an item type to display the appropriate New Item window. The fields in the dialog vary, depending on the item type you chose, but by and large the data you have to enter follows a pattern. I'll go over a few item types so you can see the basic approach to configuring an item.

Creating Service Items

Figure 6-1 shows a New Item dialog for a service. The Item Name/Number field is the place to insert a unique identifying code for the item. When you are filling out sales transactions this is the listing you see in the drop-down list.

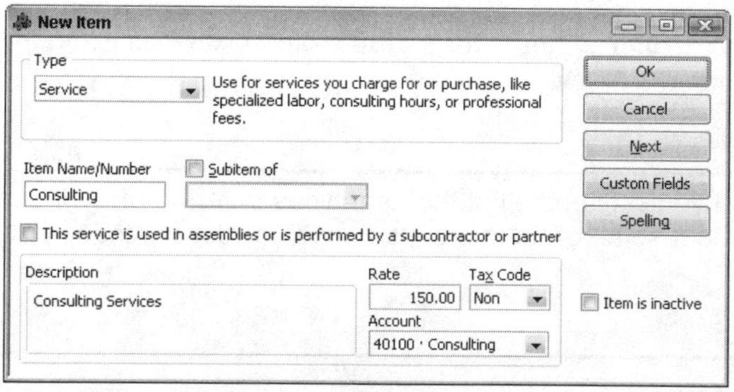

FIGURE 6-1 The fields in the New Item dialog hold the information you need to use the item, post it correctly to your general ledger, and produce accurate reports.

In the Rate field, you can enter a price for the item, or leave the rate at zero for the items you want to price when you are preparing the invoice. Don't worry—nothing is etched in stone. You can change any rate that appears automatically when you're filling out an invoice.

In the Account field, link the item to an income account in your chart of accounts and indicate whether the item is taxable (choose Tax) or not (choose Non). (The tax option is only available if you've configured your company to collect sales tax.)

When you finish filling out the fields, choose Next to move to the next blank New Item window. When you finish entering items, click OK.

Creating Subcontracted Service Items

If you sub out service work, eventually you create two separate types of transactions:

- You invoice the customer for the work.
- You pay the subcontractor for the work.

QuickBooks helps you manage this sometimes complicated paradigm by letting you set up a service item so that the income and expense amounts are preconfigured. To accomplish this, click the option This Service Is Used In Assemblies Or Is Performed By A Subcontractor Or Partner. The dialog changes to include fields necessary to track expenses as well as income (see Figure 6-2).

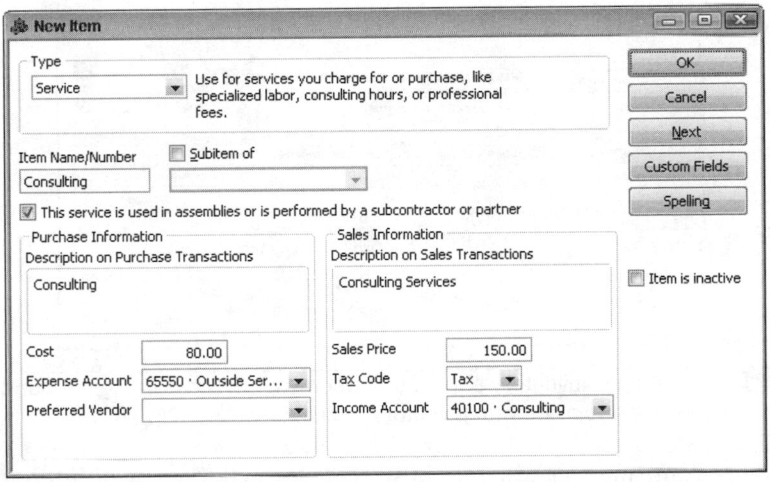

FIGURE 6-2   You can preset both the cost and the price of a service that is outsourced.

When you pay vendors for an item that is configured in this manner, use the Items tab of the Bill Or Write Checks window, instead of posting the expense to an expense account. Then, when you create a QuickReport on the item you can see the net profit/loss for the item.

> **NOTE:** The assemblies referred to in the configuration option are not available in QuickBooks Pro (which is the focus of this book). They are a QuickBooks Premier feature, and if you're running a QuickBooks Premier edition, or are considering upgrading to a Premier edition, you can learn about assemblies in *Running QuickBooks 2009 Premier Editions* from CPA911 Publishing, available at your favorite bookstore.

Creating Non-Inventory Part Items

If you use physical items (goods) as part of your services or sales, and you don't need to track quantities, values, cost of goods, and all the other complications involved in tracking inventory, you should use a non-inventory part.

The configuration dialog for a non-inventory part (seen in Figure 6-3) is straightforward and easy to fill out. Like the Services item, you can configure this item for sales and for purchasing (the Manufacturer's Part Number field is handy for purchasing).

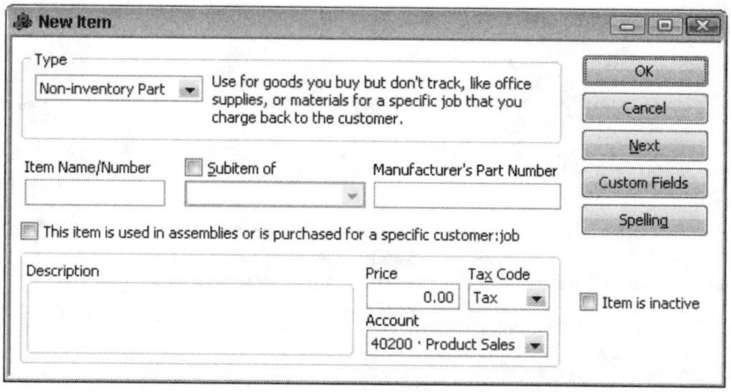

FIGURE 6-3 Create a non-inventory part to use when you sell physical items but don't need to complicate your life with inventory tracking.

Many companies that invoice customers for materials in addition to time and services don't need to spell out the specific items included in those materials, so it's common to have a non-inventory part named Materials (or Parts). You can indicate the specifics in the Description field at the time you create the invoice or sales receipt if your customer wants those details. You can also create a set of subitems for a parent item with a generic name if you want to categorize these items. (Subitems are discussed later in this chapter.)

Creating Other Charge Items

Use an Other Charge item type (see Figure 6-4) to include incidental items on a sales transaction. The definition of "incidental" is up to you. Some businesses use Other Charge items for materials (instead of using a non-inventory part), others use them for shipping, and some businesses use an Other Charge item type for handling charges (because you can set an Other Charge item as a percentage of another item or a subtotal).

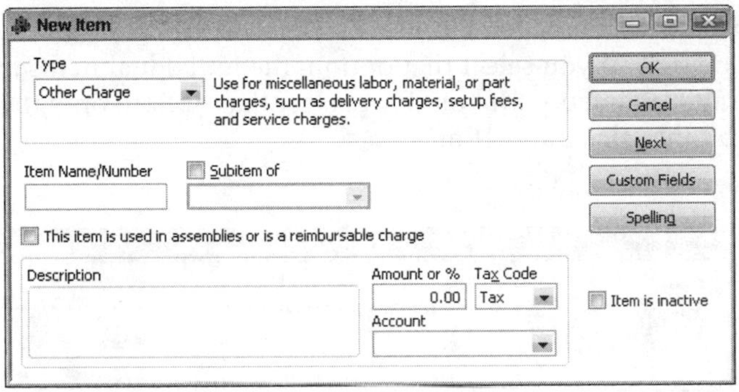

FIGURE 6-4   Other Charge item types can be used for any type of miscellaneous sales item.

The way you use this item type determines the account to which you post its use. If it's a generic item, you can post sales to your regular (generic) income account or create an income account for this item type. For example, if you use an Other Charge item type for shipping, you can post transactions to your shipping expense or you can create an income account for shipping charges. This is another item type that you may consider using with subitems in order to categorize your sales. Use a generic parent item and then subitems for specific categories. Then you can create a report on the earnings for each subitem. You can also configure an Other Charge item type for both sales and purchases.

Creating Group Items

If you have multiple items that are frequently (or always) sold together, you can create a group, which means you can enter a single line item on a sales transaction. For example, you may track inventory items that are occasionally combined to create a separate item you sell (a combo item you put together).

Or, you may have a product for which you always add a handling charge or a local delivery charge. Perhaps you have a product for which customers frequently buy an add-on. Instead of entering separate line items every time you fill out a sales transaction, create a group.

To create a group, the individual items in the group have to exist, so create your regular items first, then create the group item using the following steps:

1. With the Item List open, press CTRL-N to open the New Item dialog.
2. Select Group from the Type drop-down list.
3. Enter a name for this group in the Group Name/Number field.
4. Optionally enter a description.
5. Select each item that is part of this group, and enter the quantity for each item.
6. Click OK.

The New Item dialog for a group item includes a Print Items In Group check box (see Figure 6-5). If you select that option, the individual items are listed on the printed sales transaction. If you don't select that option, only the name of the group is listed on the sales transaction.

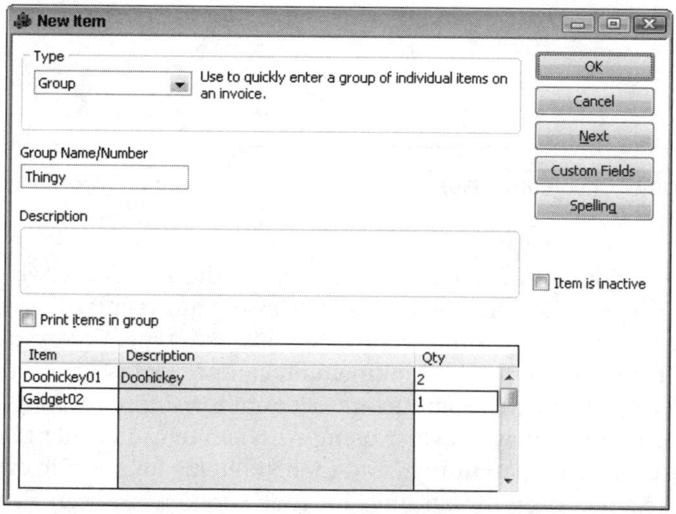

FIGURE 6-5   Creating a group is merely a matter of selecting existing items.

Creating Sales Transaction Helper Items

Some item types exist solely for the purpose of helping you create sales transactions that cover every possible financial circumstance.

Subtotal Items

Use a subtotal item to have QuickBooks automatically add the total price of everything that comes before the line in which you enter the subtotal. If you have a previous subtotal on the transaction, the calculation starts at the first item after the last subtotal.

You probably only need to create one subtotal item, because it's not necessary to plan all the reasons you'd need a subtotal and give each reason a discrete item name. If you want to indicate what the subtotal represents when you enter it in a sales transaction, type the appropriate text into the Description field.

Discount Items

Discount items provide a way to give a customer a discount as a line item. You may have more than one item that falls within this item type—for example, a discount for wholesale customers and a discount for a volume purchase. When you create the item, you can indicate a flat rate or percentage (or you can apply the rate or percentage when you create the sales transaction).

Payment Items

Use a Payment item to record a prepayment from a customer against an invoice you're preparing. QuickBooks treats the prepayment as a cash receipt and deposits it into the Undeposited Funds account or into the bank (depending on the way you configure the item).

Creating Subitems

Most of the item types offer the ability to create a subitem. This means you can create a generic parent item and then track the sales (and purchases) of categories of that item. When you use subitems, always post sales transactions to the subitems, not to the parent item.

Custom Fields for Items

You can add custom fields to your items (except subtotal items and sales tax items) and use those fields on transactions and in reports. This is a two-step process; first create the custom field, then populate the field with data on an item-by-item basis.

Creating Custom Fields for Items

Use the following steps to create a custom field for items:

1. Open the Item List and select any item.
2. Press CTRL-E to edit the item.
3. Click the Custom Fields button. (The first time you create a custom field, a message appears telling you that there are no custom fields yet defined; click OK.)

4. When the Custom Fields dialog appears, click Define Fields.
5. When the Define Custom Fields For Items dialog opens, enter a name for each field you want to add.

6. Click the Use check box to use the field. (You can deselect the box later if you don't want to use the field any more.)
7. Click OK.

You can add fields that fit services, inventory items, non-inventory items, and so on. Any custom field you create is available for all items, but not all custom fields are appropriate to use in every item type; use the appropriate field for the item type when you enter data in an item's record.

The first time you enter a custom field on an item, a dialog appears to tell you that you can use these fields on templates (forms such as Invoices, Purchase Orders, or Packing Slips). Select the option to stop displaying this message in the future, and click OK. See Chapter 28 to learn how to add custom fields to templates.

When you click Custom Fields on the New Item, or Edit Item dialog for any item, your existing custom fields appear. If you want to add more custom fields, click the Define Fields button to open the Define Custom Fields For Items dialog and add the additional custom field. You can create up to five custom fields for items.

Entering Data in Custom Fields

To enter data for the custom fields in an item, press CTRL-E to edit the item and click the Custom Fields button on the Edit Item window. Then enter the appropriate data.

Sales Tax Items

QuickBooks uses sales tax items to calculate the Tax field at the bottom of sales forms and to prepare reports for tax authorities. If the state in which you operate has a complicated sales tax structure, you may be able to use some workarounds to automate the process, even if the QuickBooks sales tax feature doesn't support the paradigm your state uses. There are some states in which the sales tax law is rather complicated and not supported by QuickBooks—in those cases you'll have to prepare sales tax returns outside of QuickBooks.

Enabling the Sales Tax Feature

To access any of the sales tax features (including the ability to create a sales tax item), you must enable the sales tax feature. Choose Edit | Preferences and click the Sales Tax icon in the left pane. Move to the Company Preferences tab (see Figure 6-6), and select Yes for the Do You Charge Sales Tax? option.

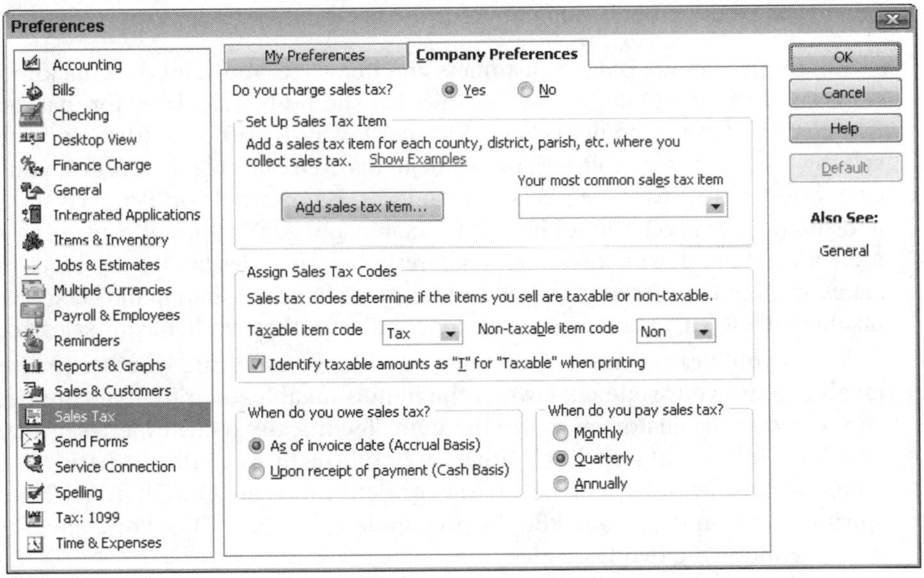

FIGURE 6-6 You must enable the sales tax feature before you can create sales tax items.

The steps needed to create a sales tax item are covered in "Creating Sales Tax Items," later in this section. After you create a sales tax item (or multiple sales tax items, if needed) you must assign a sales tax item to the Your Most Common Sales

Tax Item field. That item becomes the default sales tax item for sales transactions, but you can change the sales tax item when you're creating a transaction.

Sales Tax Codes

The Sales Tax Preferences dialog has a section named Assign Sales Tax Codes. Sales tax codes are not the same things as sales tax items.

QuickBooks has two discrete entities for configuring sales tax: Tax Codes and Tax Items. Lots of people get them confused, so I'll attempt to clarify their definitions and use. Let's start with definitions:

- A *tax code* indicates tax liability, which means the entity to which it's linked (a customer or an item) is deemed to be taxable or nontaxable, depending on the code. In addition, if you take the trouble to do so, you can have tax codes that explain *why* an entity is taxable or nontaxable. Tax codes contain no information about the tax rate or the taxing authority.
- *Tax items* contain information about the tax rate and the taxing authority to which you remit taxes and reports. Like any other item, they appear on sales forms, and the tax is calculated for the taxable line items.

Linking a sales tax *code* to customers and items lets you (and the QuickBooks sales transactions features) know whether sales tax should be calculated for that item for this customer. If a customer is liable for sales tax, it doesn't mean that every item you sell the customer is taxable because some items aren't taxable. I can't give you a list of categories because each state sets its own rules. For example, in Pennsylvania, food and some other necessities of life aren't taxable, but some types of consulting services are. Other states don't tax services at all, reserving the sales tax for products. Some states seem to tax everything—California comes to mind. If an item is taxable, it's taxable only to customers whose tax code indicates they are liable for sales tax.

When you create items in your company file, you indicate whether the item is taxable under your state tax laws. If the item is taxable, the rate that's applied is connected to the customer, not to the item. Technically, a customer's sales tax liability is like a light switch; it's either on or off (techies call this scenario "Boolean," which means the only possible answers or definitions are On/Off or Yes/No). In the spirit of Boolean logic, QuickBooks prepopulates the Sales Tax Preferences dialog with the following two tax codes:

- **Tax** Means liable for sales tax
- **Non** Means not liable for sales tax

For many of us, that's enough; we don't need any additional tax codes for customers or for items. We can move on to creating tax items so their rates are calculated on sales forms. However, for some companies, those two tax codes aren't enough. State rules governing sales tax reports and state reporting forms sometimes require more information.

For nontaxable customers, some states want to know why a nontaxable customer isn't charged sales tax. Is a customer nontaxable because it's out of state and the rules say you don't have to collect taxes for out-of-state sales? Is a customer nontaxable because it's a nonprofit organization? Is a customer nontaxable because it's a government agency? Is a customer nontaxable because it's a wholesale business and collects sales tax from its own customers? (The last definition may describe your business, and your suppliers may have you configured as nontaxable.) If your state requires this information, you must create tax codes to match your reporting needs.

For taxable customers, you may want to use tax codes to specify customers as taxable in another state (if you collect taxes from out-of-state customers and remit those taxes to that state's taxing authority).

States that have instituted multiple tax rates depending on a customer's location want to know which location within the state the customer occupies, because that location determines the tax rate. Your reports on sales taxes have to subtotal your collections by location. In fact, in some states, you have to send individual sales tax reports to individual local tax authorities. If your state operates in this manner, you should solve this with tax items, not tax codes, because part of your configuration task is the tax rate (which isn't part of a tax code, it's only part of a tax item) and the taxing authority (which also isn't part of a tax code).

If you want to create codes to track customer sales tax status in a manner more detailed than "taxable" and "nontaxable," follow these steps to add a new sales tax code:

1. Choose Lists | Sales Tax Code List.
2. Press CTRL-N to open the New Sales Tax Code dialog.
3. Enter the name of the new code, using up to three characters.
4. Enter a description to make it easier to interpret the code.
5. Select Taxable if you're entering a code to track taxable sales.
6. Select Non-Taxable if you're entering a code to trace nontaxable sales.
7. Click Next to set up another tax code, or click OK if you've finished adding tax codes.

This procedure works nicely for specifying different types of nontaxable customers. For example, you could create the following tax codes for nontaxable categories:

- NPO for nonprofit organizations
- GOV for government agencies
- WSL for wholesale businesses
- OOS for out-of-state customers (if you aren't required to collect taxes from out-of-state customers)

For taxable customers, the permutations and combinations are much broader, of course. If you're required to collect and remit sales tax for some additional states, just create codes for customers in those states, using the postal abbreviations for each state.

The problem is that tax codes don't work well for categorizing taxable customers if you do business in a state with complicated multiple tax rates. Those states issue codes that match the rules and rates (frequently location-based), and the codes are almost always more than three characters—but three characters is all QuickBooks permits for a sales tax code. The workaround for this is in the ability to assign a sales tax item to a customer, as long as the customer's configuration indicates "taxable" (using the built-in tax code or any taxable code you created). The sales tax item can be specific to the location, rate, and taxing authority.

Sales Tax Remittance Options

The bottom section of the Sales Tax Preferences dialog contains options for the way you report your sales and remit the collected taxes to the tax authorities. Check your sales tax license for the circumstances that rule your reporting and remittances.

QuickBooks does not provide an option for businesses that file sales tax reports on a semiannual basis. If your business is one of the many businesses that face this problem, select Quarterly and then just ignore any "quarterly tax reports are due" reminders you get from QuickBooks until it's time to remit your sales tax collections.

Creating Sales Tax Items

You can create a sales tax item in either of the following ways:

- In the Sales Tax Preferences dialog, click the Add Sales Tax Item button.
- Choose Lists | Item List from the menu bar to open the Item List. Then press CTRL-N.

Both actions open the New Item dialog, where you create the item using the following steps:

1. Select Sales Tax Item as the item type.
2. Enter a name for the item. If you're in a state that has codes for each county, ZIP code, or other regional tax area, use the state's code for the specific sales tax rate and taxing authority.
3. Optionally, enter a description.
4. Enter the tax rate. QuickBooks knows the rate is a percentage, so it automatically adds the percent sign to the numbers you type (for instance, enter **6.5** if the rate is 6.5 percent).

5. Select the tax agency (a vendor) to which you pay the tax from the drop-down list, or add a new vendor by choosing <Add New>.
6. Click OK.

Creating Tax Groups

In some states, the tax imposed is really two taxes, and the taxing authority collects a single check from you but insists on a breakdown in the reports you send. For example, in Pennsylvania, the state sales tax is 6 percent, but businesses in Philadelphia and Pittsburgh must charge an extra 1 percent. The customer pays 7 percent, and a check for 7 percent of taxable sales is remitted to the state's revenue department. However, the report that accompanies the check must break down the remittance into the individual taxes—the total of the 6 percent tax and the total of the 1 percent tax.

In other states, the basic state sales tax is remitted to the state, and the locally added tax is remitted to the local taxing authority.

The challenge is to display and calculate a single tax for the customer and report multiple taxes to the taxing authorities. Tax groups meet this challenge. A tax group is a single entity that appears on a sales transaction, but it is really multiple entities that have been totaled. QuickBooks creates the tax amount by calculating each of the multiple entries and displaying its total (the customer is being charged the "combo" rate). For example, in Pennsylvania a Philadelphia business uses a tax group (totaling 7 percent) that includes the 6 percent state sales tax and the 1 percent Philadelphia sales tax.

To create a tax group, you must first create the individual tax items and then use the following steps to create the group item.

1. Open the Item List by choosing Lists | Item List.
2. Press CTRL-N to open the New Item dialog.
3. Select Sales Tax Group as the type.

4. Enter a name for the group.

5. Optionally enter a description, which will appear on sales transactions.

6. In the Tax Item column, choose the individual sales tax items you need to create this group. As you move to the next item, QuickBooks fills in the rate, tax agency, and description (if one exists) of each sales tax item you select. The calculated total (the group rate) appears at the bottom of the dialog (see Figure 6-7).

7. Click OK.

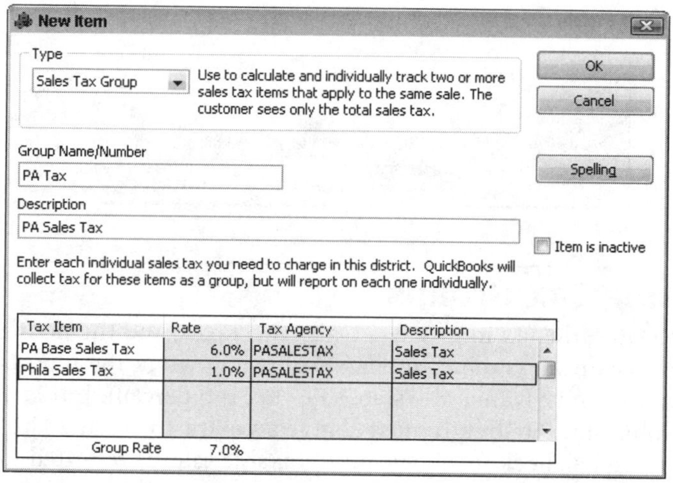

FIGURE 6-7   Create a Sales Tax Group to apply multiple taxes to transactions.

Select this item for the appropriate customers when you're creating sales transactions.

Assigning Tax Codes and Items to Customers

By default, QuickBooks assigns the Tax (taxable) tax code to all customers, as well as the tax item you specify as the default in the Sales Tax Preferences dialog. These fields are on the Additional Info tab of the customer's record, and you can edit each customer's record to make changes to either field.

Most of the time, it's the default tax item (not the tax code) for a customer that requires changing, especially if you're in a state that bases tax rates (and perhaps taxing authorities) on the delivery location for customers.

If you already created a great many customers, opening each record to make changes is onerous, so wait until you use a customer in a sales transaction. Then, in the transaction window, select a new tax code or tax item (or both) from the drop-down list in the appropriate field.

When you save the transaction, QuickBooks cooperates with this approach by asking you if you want to change the customer's tax information permanently. Click Yes to change the customer record, and hereafter the new tax information appears in any transaction window for this customer.

NOTE: Information about producing sales tax reports and remitting sales tax to taxing authorities is in Chapter 12.

Setting Up Inventory

n this chapter:

- Create inventory items
- Use purchase orders
- Deal with physical inventory counts
- Adjust inventory numbers
- Create builds
- Manage backorders

For many businesses, the warehouse is a source of frustration, bewilderment, rage, and erroneous information. I'm using the term "warehouse" generically to indicate the place where you store inventory (which may be your basement instead of a real warehouse). In this chapter, I'll discuss the ways to set up, configure, and track inventory to make the process less of a nightmare.

What Is an Inventory Item?

An inventory item is a product you manufacture, assemble, or purchase for the purpose of selling it to a customer.

Items that you store to use in the normal course of business that are resold to customers as part of other services being involved are not inventory. This means that if you're a plumber and you store valves, pipes, and other plumbing parts to use when you perform a job, you don't track those parts as inventory. If you're a consultant who uses consumables or supplies in the course of your consulting work, and you keep those products on hand to sell to customers, don't track those supplies as inventory.

 N O T E : QuickBooks provides an item type called a non-inventory part you can use to indicate products you used when you invoice customers. You can create reports on those items to track quantity and revenue amounts. These item types don't require you to attend to the kind of details and tax reports that inventory items do.

The hallmark of an item that is configured as an inventory part is that it is made or purchased solely for the purpose of resale; the trade your business engages in is the sale of products. Usually, the only types of businesses that track inventory are manufacturers (who may use inventory parts to create other inventory parts), wholesale distributors, and retailers.

Setting Up QuickBooks for Inventory Tracking

To track inventory, you must enable the inventory function in QuickBooks (which you might have done during the EasyStep Interview when you set up your company file). In addition, QuickBooks adds accounts to your chart of accounts that are earmarked for tracking inventory.

Enabling Inventory Tracking

To enable inventory tracking, choose Edit | Preferences and select the Items &
Inventory category in the left pane. Move to the Company Preferences tab
(see Figure 7-1) to see the inventory options.

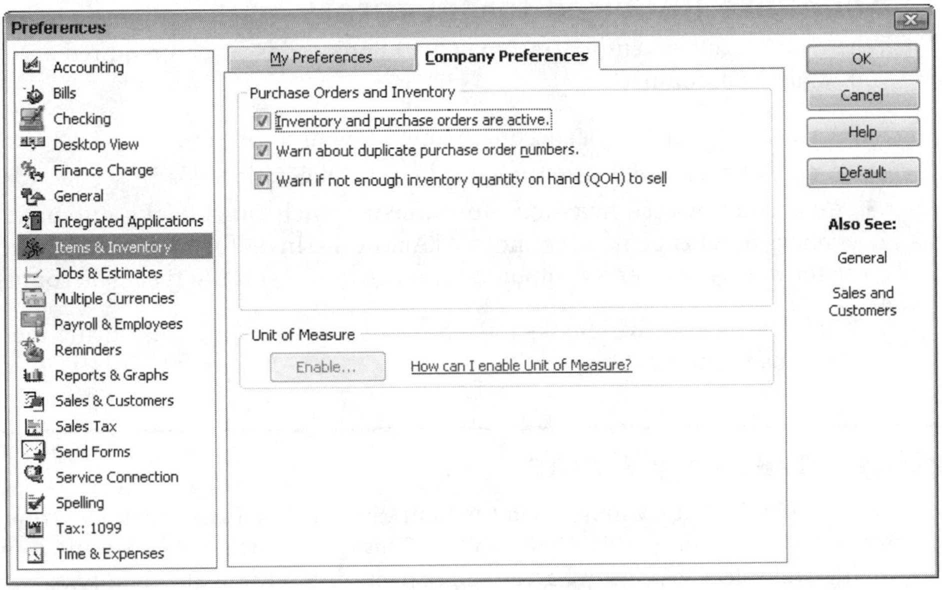

FIGURE 7-1 Enable inventory and set the protocols to use for inventory tracking.

When you turn on the inventory feature, you also turn on the purchase order
feature (although you don't have to use purchase orders to use the inventory
feature). In addition, the dialog offers two options that help you keep your
inventory records accurately:

- **Warn About Duplicate Purchase Order Numbers.**   When enabled, if you use
  a PO number that's already in use, QuickBooks will display a message warning
  you of that fact. (The system doesn't prevent you from using the duplicate
  number, but it's a good idea to heed the warning to avoid problems.)

- **Warn If Not Enough Inventory Quantity On Hand (QOH) To Sell.**   When
  enabled, QuickBooks flashes a warning if you fill out a sales transaction that
  has a quantity greater than the current available units of that product. You can
  continue the sale if you wish and track the unfilled quantity as a backorder
  (covered later in this chapter).

NOTE: The Company Preferences tab of the Items & Inventory Preferences dialog contains a reference to Units of Measure. This feature is only available in QuickBooks Premier editions.

Accounts Required for Inventory

When you enable inventory tracking QuickBooks adds several required accounts to your chart of accounts:

- An Other Current Asset account named Inventory Asset.
- A cost of goods sold account named Costs Of Goods Sold.
- An account named Inventory Adjustment, which QuickBooks automatically creates as an expense account (see "About the Inventory Adjustment Account" later in this chapter for important information about the type of account).

You'll learn how QuickBooks posts amounts to these accounts during the discussions in this chapter.

Creating Inventory Items

To create an inventory item, open the Item List (choose Lists | Item List from the menu bar) to open the Item List window. Then press CTRL-N to open the New Item dialog and select Inventory Part from the drop-down list as the item type.

Fill in the information using the guidelines that follow (Figure 7-2 is an example of an inventory item record).

- The Item Name/Number is your code for the item. This field must be unique in your Item List.
- The Manufacturer's Part Number (useful if you're a distributor or retailer) lets you include the part number on your purchase orders. If you purchase from a distributor instead of a manufacturer, enter the distributor's part number. This makes creating an accurate purchase order much easier.
- The text you enter in the Description On Purchase Transactions field automatically appears when you create a purchase order. The text you enter in the Description On Sales Transactions field automatically appears in sales transaction forms, such as invoices, estimates, and sales receipts.
- You can enter a cost, but it's really a convenience for creating purchase orders (the cost appears automatically in the PO, which is useful if the cost doesn't change often). QuickBooks does not use this figure for posting cost of goods sold; instead it uses the average cost of this item based on your item receipt and inventory adjustment transactions (all covered later in this chapter).

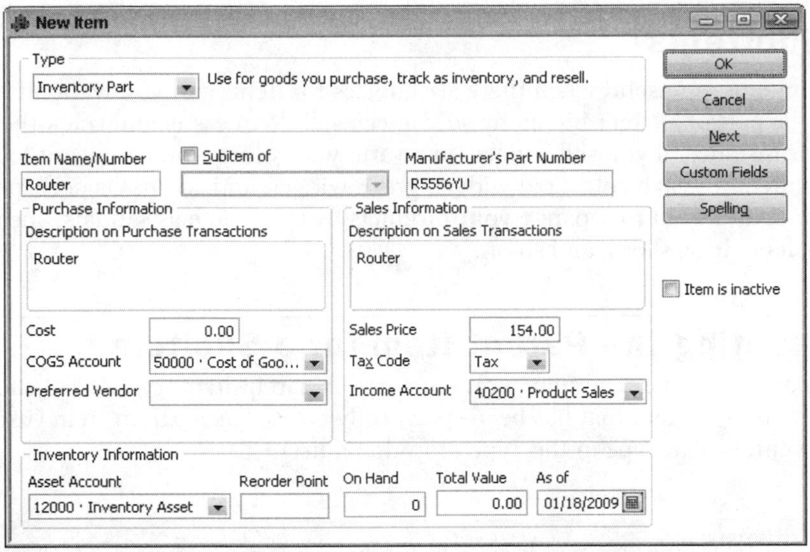

FIGURE 7-2 An inventory item record contains all the information you need to use it in transactions.

- If you enter a Sales Price, that amount is automatically entered when you create sales transactions (but you can change the price on an individual sales transaction).

- Choose the Tax Code for this item, which indicates whether the item is taxable to customers.

- Select the appropriate posting accounts for Cost of Goods and Income.

- Enter a number in the Reorder Point field that reflects the minimum quantity you want to have in stock. When this quantity is reached, QuickBooks will issue a reminder about reordering if you've enabled the Reminders feature. To turn on the Reminders feature, choose Edit | Preferences and click the Reminders category. On the My Preferences tab, check Show Reminders List When Opening A Company File check box. On the Company Preferences tab, choose either Show Summary or Show List for the Inventory To Reorder option.

- *Do not* enter anything in the On Hand or Total Value fields, because the data won't provide the accurate financial trail your accountant needs. Instead, let QuickBooks track these values as you receive items into inventory and/or use the inventory adjustment feature. Inventory adjustments are covered later in this chapter. Chapter 11 has information about receiving items into inventory from your vendors so that your costs of goods sold numbers are accurate.

Using Subitems

Subitems are useful when there are choices for items and you want all the choices to be part of a larger hierarchy so you can sell them easily and track them efficiently. For instance, if you sell widgets in a variety of colors, you may want to create a subitem for each color: red widget, green widget, and so on. Or perhaps you sell shoes and want to separate your products by type, such as sandals, sneakers, loafers, dress shoes, and so on.

Creating the Parent Item for a Subitem

In order to have a subitem, you must have a parent item. Figure 7-3 shows the record of an item that has been specifically created as a parent item (using the Inventory Part type in the Type drop-down list).

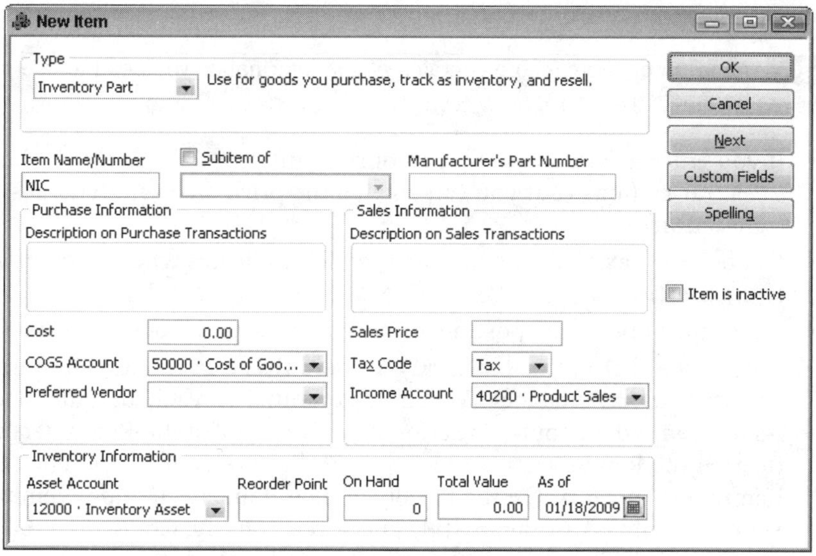

FIGURE 7-3 This item isn't sold to customers—it exists only as a parent item.

Here are some guidelines for creating an inventory item that's designed to be a parent:

- Use a generic name for the item; the details are in the subitem names.
- Don't enter a description, save that for the subitems.
- Don't enter the cost.
- Don't enter the price.

- Don't enter a reorder point.
- Don't enter the quantity on hand.
- Enter the Inventory Asset, COG, and Income accounts because they are required fields for all inventory items.

Creating Subitems

Having created the parent item, subitems are easy to create. Open a blank New Item window (press CTRL-N) and follow these steps:

1. In the Item Name/Number field, enter the code for this item. It can be a color, a size, a manufacturer name, or any other code that makes this subitem unique when compared to other subitems under the same parent item (see Figure 7-4).
2. Check the box named Subitem Of, and then select the parent item from the drop-down list that appears when you click the arrow to the right of the field.
3. Enter the Manufacturer's Part Number (for creating purchase orders).
4. Optionally, enter any descriptions you want to appear on purchase orders and sales transactions.
5. Optionally, enter the price.
6. Enter the general ledger account information (Inventory Asset, Cost of Goods, and Income accounts).
7. Enter the reorder point if you're using that feature.
8. Click Next to enter another inventory item, or click OK if you're finished.

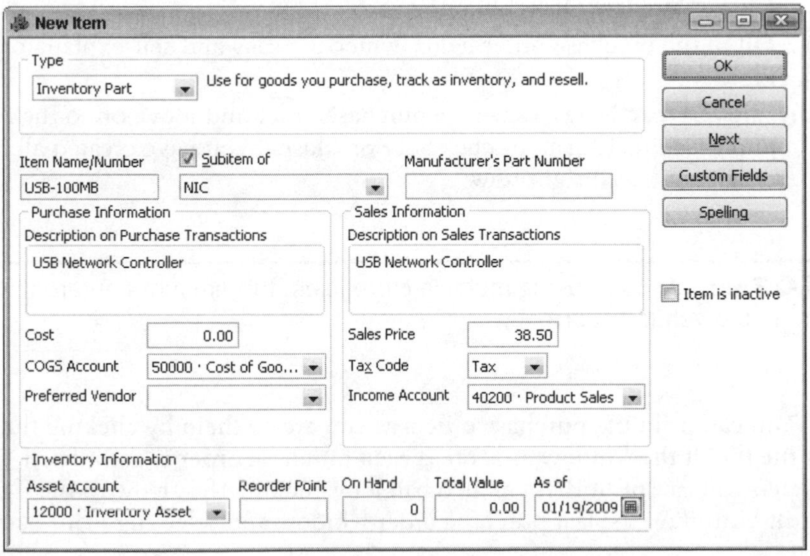

FIGURE 7-4   Creating inventory subitems is almost the same as creating inventory items.

Using Purchase Orders

You can use purchase orders to order inventory items or manufacturing parts from your suppliers. It's not a good idea to use purchase orders for goods that aren't in your inventory, such as office supplies or consulting services—that's not what purchase orders are intended for.

If you want to order services or other non-inventory items, and the vendor wants a purchase order, create a PO document in Microsoft Word, to avoid crowding your QuickBooks company file with POs that will never be used to receive inventory items.

Creating a purchase order has no effect on your financial records. No amounts are posted because purchase orders exist only to help you track what you've ordered against what you've received. You create the financial transactions when the items and the vendor's bill are received.

When you enable the Inventory and Purchase Order features, QuickBooks creates a nonposting account named Purchase Orders. You can double-click the account's listing to view and drill down into the purchase orders you've entered, but the data in the register has no effect on your finances and doesn't appear in financial reports.

Creating a Purchase Order

Use the following steps to create a purchase order:

1. Choose Vendors | Create Purchase Orders from the menu bar to open a blank Create Purchase Orders window.
2. Fill in the purchase order fields, which are easy and self-explanatory (see Figure 7-5).
3. Click Save & New to save the purchase order and move on to the next blank purchase order form, or click Save & Close if you have created all the purchase orders you need right now.

 N O T E : If you're using multiple currencies, the amounts entered in the PO are in the vendor's currency.

You can print the purchase orders as you create them by clicking the Print icon at the top of the window as soon as each purchase order is completed. If you'd prefer, you can print them all in a batch by clicking the arrow to the right of the Print button on the last purchase order window and selecting Print Batch. If you

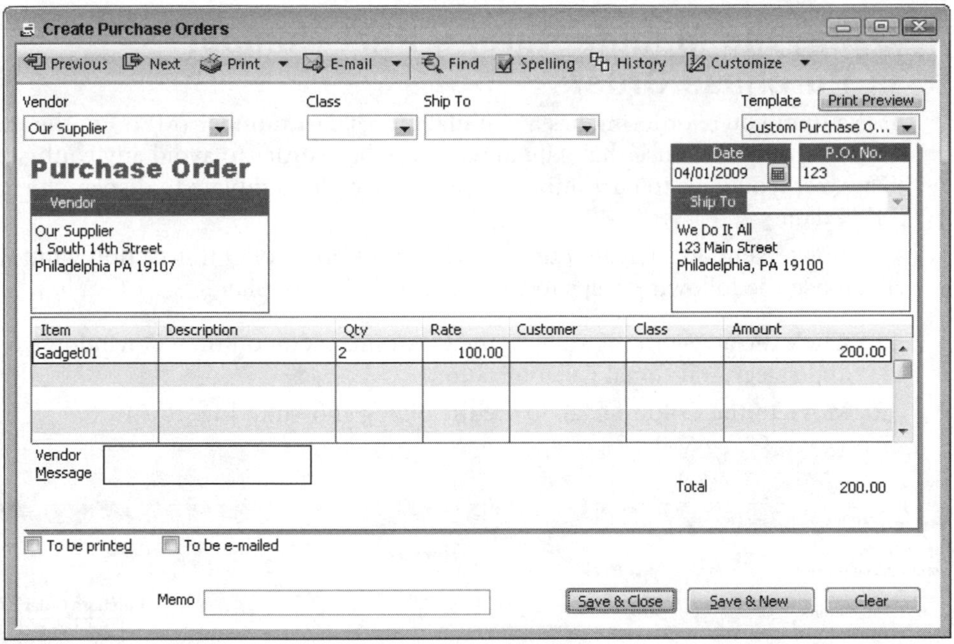

FIGURE 7-5 A purchase order looks like a vendor bill, but it doesn't post amounts to accounts payable.

want to print them later, be sure the option To Be Printed is selected on each PO. When you're ready to print, choose File | Print Forms | Purchase Orders.

You can also e-mail the purchase orders as you create them, or e-mail them as a batch by selecting Send Batch from the drop-down list next to the E-mail icon on the transaction window's toolbar.

TIP: Many companies don't send purchase orders; instead, they notify the vendor of the purchase order number when they place the order over the telephone, via e-mail, or by logging into the vendor's Internet-based order system.

When the inventory items and the bill for them are received, you can use the purchase order to automate the receiving of inventory into your warehouse as well as the entry of the vendor's bill (covered in Chapter 11).

Using the Manufacturer's Part Number in Purchase Orders

If the item you're ordering has a manufacturer's part number (MPN) in the item record, you should use that data in your purchase order to avoid any confusion. However, you have to customize the purchase order template to display the MPN data.

Choose Vendors | Create Purchase Orders to open a PO transaction window. Then use the following steps to customize the PO template.

1. Click the arrow to the right of the Customize icon on the PO window's toolbar and select Additional Customization.
2. Move to the Columns tab to see the dialog shown in Figure 7-6.

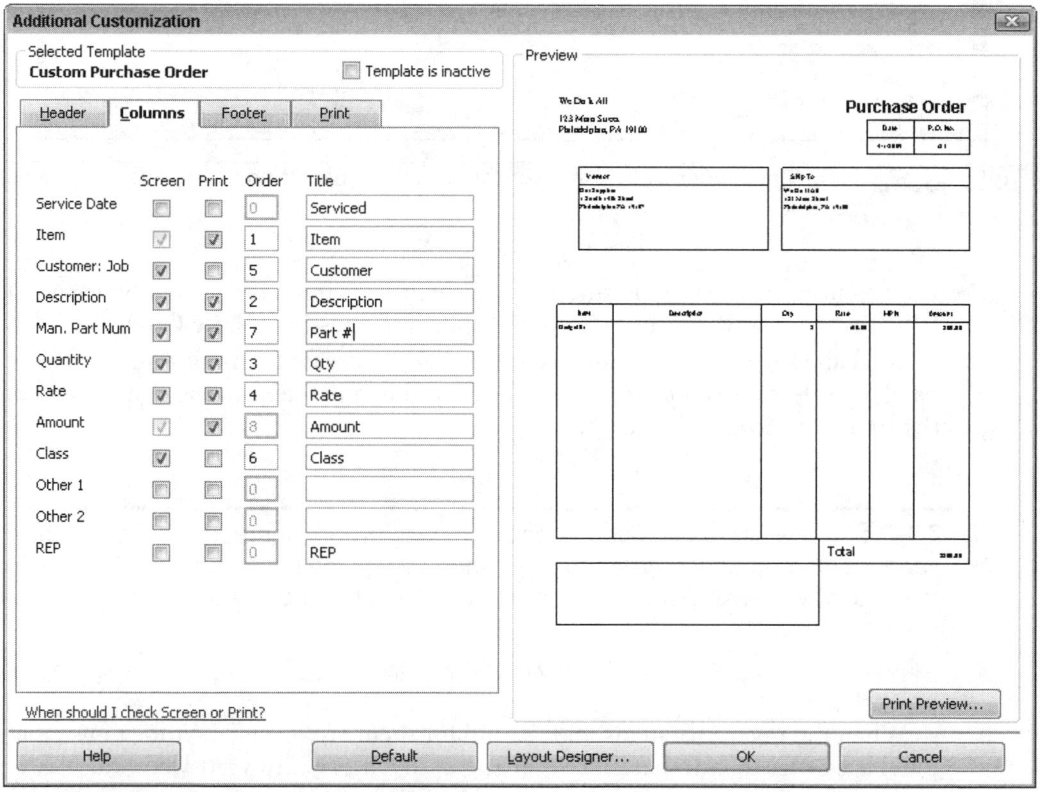

FIGURE 7-6 Add a column for the MPN to your PO template.

3. Add the Man. Part Num field to the screen, printed copy, or both by clicking in the appropriate boxes to add a check mark (adding the field to both the screen and print versions is best).

4. Enter the number for this column, working from left to right across the columns. For example, entering 3 puts the MPN in the third column. When you press TAB, QuickBooks automatically renumbers the column order to accommodate your selection.

5. Optionally, change the text that appears as the column title. By default, the title is MPN, but you might want to change it to something like Part # or Part No.

Check the Print Preview pane on the right side of the dialog to make sure the layout works. Adding this column doesn't overcrowd the template, but if you previously customized the template to add columns or fields, you may have to rework your changes (see Chapter 28 to learn everything about customizing templates). If the layout looks presentable, click OK to save your changes.

Hereafter, when you create a PO for an item that has the MPN stored in its record, the data appears automatically in the MPN column.

Running Inventory Reports

You'll probably find that you run reports on your inventory status quite often. For many inventory-based businesses, tracking the state of the inventory is the second most important set of reports (right behind reports about the current accounts receivable balances).

QuickBooks provides several useful, significant inventory reports, which you can access by choosing Reports | Inventory. The available reports are discussed in this section.

Inventory Valuation Summary Report

This report gives you a quick assessment of the value of your inventory. By default, the date range is the current month to date, but you can change that to suit your needs. Each item is listed with the following information displayed in columns:

Item Description   The description of the item, if you entered a description for purchase transactions.

On Hand   The current quantity on hand, which is the net number of received items and sold items. Because QuickBooks permits you to sell items you don't have in stock (a very bad step, which can wreak havoc with your financials), it's possible to have a negative number in this column.

Avg Cost   QuickBooks uses the totals from each transaction for receipt of inventory to calculate this figure.

Asset Value   The value posted to your Inventory account in the general ledger. The value is calculated by multiplying the number on hand by the average cost.

% Of Tot Asset   The percentage of your total inventory assets that this item represents.

Sales Price   The price you've set for this item. This figure is obtained by looking at the item's configuration window. If you entered a price when you set up the item, that price is displayed. If you didn't enter a price (because you chose to determine the price at the time of sale), $0.00 displays. QuickBooks does not check the sales records for this item to determine this number, so if you routinely change the price when you're filling out a customer invoice, those changes aren't reflected in this report.

Retail Value   The current retail value of the item, which is calculated by multiplying the number on hand by the retail price (if the retail price is set).

% Of Tot Retail   The percentage of the total retail value of your inventory that this item represents.

Inventory Valuation Detail Report

This report lists each transaction that involved each inventory item. The report shows no financial information about the price charged to customers because your inventory value is based on cost. You can double-click any sales transaction line to see the details of that transaction (including the amount you charged for the item).

Inventory Stock Status

There are two Stock Status reports: Inventory Stock Status By Item and Inventory Stock Status By Vendor. The information is the same in both reports, but the order in which information is arranged and subtotaled is different. You can use these Stock Status reports to get quick numbers about inventory items, including the following information:

- The preferred vendor
- The reorder point
- The number currently on hand
- A reminder (a check mark) for ordering items that are below the reorder point
- The number currently on order (a purchase order exists but the order has not yet been received)
- The next delivery date (according to the data in the purchase orders)
- The average number of units sold per week

Physical Inventory Worksheet

This is the report you print when it's time to take an inventory count. See the section "Counting Inventory," later in this chapter, for more information.

Pending Builds

This report details the current state of items you assemble from existing inventory items (called *builds*). Only QuickBooks Premier editions offer built-in features for creating builds (although in the Premier editions they're called *assemblies*).

QuickBooks personnel tell me that this report is listed in case you've opened a company file in your copy of QuickBooks Pro that was created (or worked on) in a QuickBooks Premier edition. Apparently, this report exists so you can view the details on builds that were created in a Premier edition, even though you can't access the QuickBooks build features in QuickBooks Pro.

To learn about a workaround for builds so you can create them in QuickBooks Pro, see the section "Creating Builds," later in this chapter. To learn how to create real builds (called *assemblies*) in QuickBooks Premier Edition, read *Running QuickBooks 2009 Premier Editions* from CPA911 Publishing (www.cpa911publishing.com). You can purchase the book at your favorite bookstore.

Inventory QuickReports

QuickBooks provides a reporting feature called QuickReports that provides sales and purchase information about an individual inventory item. QuickReports are available from the Item List window.

In the Item List window, select an item and press CTRL-Q to open a QuickReport that shows you the bills (purchases) and sales transactions. You can change the date range for the report, and you can double-click any transaction line to drill down to the transaction details.

Counting Inventory

I can hear the groans. I know—there's nothing worse than doing a physical inventory. However, no matter how careful you are with QuickBooks transactions, no matter how pristine your protocols are for making sure everything that comes and goes is accounted for, it's not uncommon to find that your physical inventory does not match your QuickBooks figures. Sorry about that, but it's an old story.

Printing the Physical Inventory Worksheet

The first thing you must do is print a Physical Inventory Worksheet (see Figure 7-7), which is one of the choices on the Inventory Reports submenu. This report lists your

Physical Inventory Worksheet					
Modify Report...	Memorize...	Print...	E-mail ▾	Export...	Hide Header	Refresh

We Do It All

Physical Inventory Worksheet

All Transactions

	◇ Item Description ◇	Pref Vendor ◇	On Hand	◇ Physical Count ◇
Inventory				
Cables ▸			10	_____ ◂
Doohickey01	Doohickey		5	_____
Gadget01			2	_____
Gadget02		Toro	7	_____
Monitor	Monitor		8	_____
NIC				
100MB			8	_____
1GB			2	_____
NIC - Other			0	_____
NIC - End				
Software			12	_____
Sound Card	Sound Card		7	_____
VideoCard	Video Controller		8	_____
Widgets	Widgets		41	_____

FIGURE 7-7   The most important column is the one with blank lines, which is where you enter the physical count.

inventory items and subitems in alphabetical order, along with the current quantity on hand, which is calculated from your QuickBooks transactions. In addition, there's a column that's set up to record the actual count as you walk around your warehouse with this printout (and a pen) in hand.

 CAUTION: The Physical Inventory Worksheet displays only the inventory items that are active. If you made any items inactive and you think (or know) there are units in stock, make the items active before creating this report.

If you have a large number of inventory items, you may have some problems with this worksheet:

- You cannot change the way the worksheet is sorted, so you cannot arrange the items to match the way you've laid out your warehouse.
- If you use bins, rows, or some other physical entity in your warehouse, QuickBooks has no feature to support it, so you cannot enter or sort on the location on this worksheet.
- The Pref Vendor column, which usually isn't needed (or even useful) for a physical count can't be removed. However, if you drag the diamond on the right side of the column all the way to the left, you can close the column so it won't print.

Click the Print button in the worksheet window to bring up the Print Reports window. In the Number Of Copies box, enter as many copies as you need.

> **TIP:** Don't hand every person a full report—cut the report apart to give each person the pages he or she needs, and keep one full copy to use as a master.

Planning the Physical Count

QuickBooks lacks an automatic "freeze" feature like the one found in many inventory-enabled accounting software applications. Freezing the inventory means that after you've printed the worksheet and begun counting, any transactions involving inventory are saved to a holding file in order to avoid changing the totals. When you've finished your physical count, you unfreeze the inventory count and print a report on the holding file. You make your adjustments to the count using the information in that file, and then you can fill your orders.

In QuickBooks, you can perform these actions manually. After you print the worksheet (which you don't do until you're ready to start counting), be sure that all sales transactions will be handled differently until after the inventory count is adjusted. There are a number of ways to do this:

- Print an extra copy of each invoice and save the copies in a folder. Don't pick and pack the inventory for the invoices until after the count.
- Prepare a form for salespeople to fill out the name and quantity of inventory items sold during the freeze, and delay picking and packing the inventory until after the count.
- Delay entering invoices until after the count is over. (This is not a good idea if counting takes a couple of days.)
- Don't receive inventory in QuickBooks (don't fill out a Receive Items or Enter Bill for Received Items form) until after the count.
- If inventory arrives in the warehouse during the count, don't unpack the boxes until after the count.

When you start counting the inventory, be sure there's a good system in place. The most important element of the system is *having somebody in charge*. One person, with a master inventory worksheet in hand, must know who is counting what. When each counter is finished, his or her sheet should be handed to the person in charge and the numbers should be copied onto the master inventory worksheet. (This is why you print multiple copies of the worksheet.) Note the date and time the count was reported.

After the count, bring in any inventory that's arrived during the count. Then start picking and packing your orders so you can generate income again.

Making Inventory Adjustments

After you've finished counting the inventory, you may find that the numbers on the worksheet don't match the physical count. In fact, it's almost a sure bet that the numbers won't match.

Most of the time the physical count is lower than the QuickBooks figures. This is called *shrinkage*. Shrinkage is jargon for "stuff went missing for an unexplained reason," but most of the time the reason is employee theft. Unfortunately, that's a well-documented fact. Another reason for shrinkage is breakage, but most of the time that's reported by employees, and you can adjust your inventory because you know about it. When you don't know about it, suspect the worst, because statistics prove that suspicion to be the most accurate.

Adjusting the Count

You have to tell QuickBooks about the results of the physical count, and you accomplish that by choosing Vendors | Inventory Activities | Adjust Quantity/Value On Hand. The Adjust Quantity/Value On Hand window opens, which is shown in Figure 7-8.

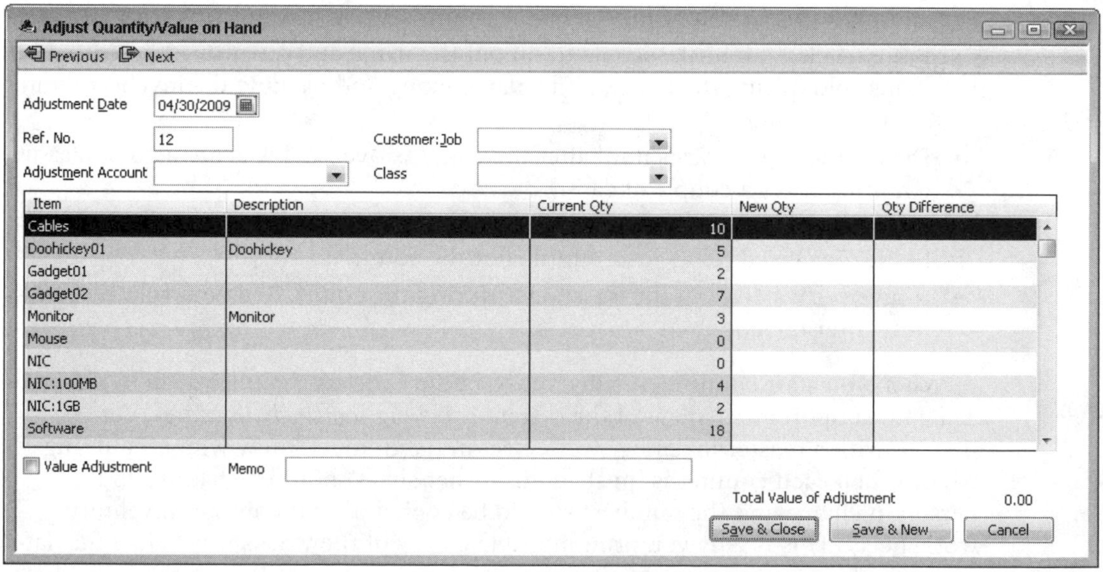

FIGURE 7-8 Correct the quantity to match the physical count.

NOTE: Inactive items appear on the Adjust Quantity/Value On Hand window.

Here are the guidelines for filling out this window:

- Enter the date (usually inventory adjustments are made at the end of the month, quarter, or year, but there's no rule about that).
- Use an optional reference number to track the adjustment.
- In the Adjustment Account field, enter the inventory adjustment account in your chart of accounts. (See the section "About the Inventory Adjustment Account" for important information about the type of account.)
- The Customer:Job field is there in case you're sending stuff to a customer but didn't include the items on any invoices for that customer or job. This is a way to effect a transfer of the inventory; the inventory count is changed and the cost is posted to the customer or job.
- If you've enabled the class tracking feature, a Class field appears.
- Use either the New Qty column or the Qty Difference column to enter the count (depending on how you filled out the worksheet and calculated it). Whichever column you use, QuickBooks fills in the other column automatically.
- Anything you enter in the Memo field appears on your Profit & Loss Detail report, which eliminates the question "what's this figure?" from your accountant.

When you complete the entries, the total value of the adjustment you made is displayed below the Qty Difference column. That value is calculated by using the average cost of your inventory. For example, if you received ten widgets into inventory at a cost of $10.00 each and later received ten more at a cost of $12.00 each, your average cost for widgets is $11.00 each. If your adjustment is for minus one widget, your inventory asset value is decreased by $11.00.

Adjusting the Value

You can be more precise about your inventory valuation; in fact, you can override the average cost calculation and enter a true value when you fill out this transaction window.

Click the Value Adjustment check box at the bottom of the window. Two new columns named Current Value and New Value appear in the window (see Figure 7-9).

The value of the total adjusted count is displayed for each item, and you can change the value to eliminate the effects of averaging costs up to this point (although as you continue to receive inventory items, QuickBooks continues to use average costing). You can change the current value of any item.

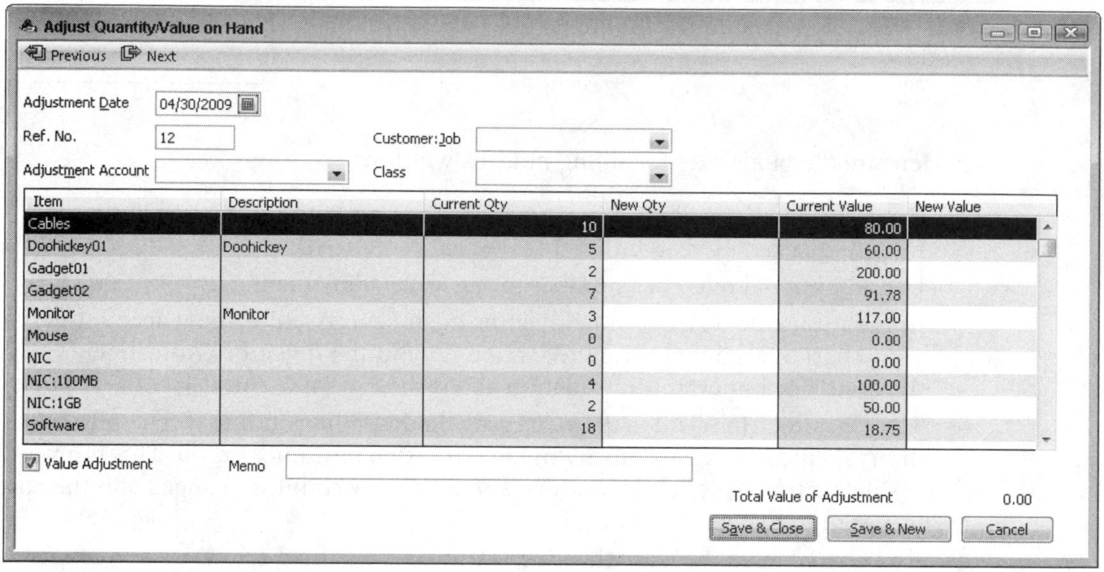

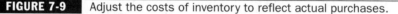

FIGURE 7-9 Adjust the costs of inventory to reflect actual purchases.

Of course, in order to enter the correct total value, you must have the information you need and then make the appropriate calculations. To obtain the information, choose Reports | Purchases | Purchases By Vendor Detail. This report presents a history of your purchases so you can make the necessary calculations.

Return to the Adjust Quantity window and enter the data. When you've finished making your changes, click Save & Close to save your new inventory numbers.

QuickBooks does not support FIFO or LIFO costing for inventory. Essentially, when you use current figures to update the cost, you're updating the current average cost, you are not creating FIFO/LIFO inventory costing.

About the Inventory Adjustment Account

QuickBooks automatically creates an expense account named Inventory Adjustment when you enable inventory tracking. However, most accountants prefer to have the Inventory Adjustment account configured as a cost of goods sold account, not as an expense account. Check with your accountant, and if you need to change the account type, follow these steps:

1. Open the chart of accounts.
2. Select the expense account named Inventory Adjustment and press CTRL-E to open the account record in Edit mode.

3. Click the arrow to the right of the Account Type field and select Cost Of Goods Sold from the drop-down list.

4. If you're using account numbers, change the number to reflect the numbers you're using for cost of goods sold.

5. Click Save & Close.

Unfortunately, if you use a COGS account when you use the Adjust Quantity/ Value On Hand window, QuickBooks issues a warning message when you enter your adjustment account in the Adjustment Account field.

Ask your accountant about the account type for your inventory adjustments, and if he or she wants you to use a cost of goods account, be sure to select the option to stop showing this message before you click OK to continue working in this window.

I've never met an accountant who agreed with the import of this message (and it's a question I ask frequently in my newsletter, seminars, and when I'm leading CPE classes), but obviously there must be quite a few who do, and Intuit has been in contact with them.

Most of the accountants who don't agree with this paradigm are especially emphatic about not posting an increase in inventory value to an income account. They explain that while an adjustment of inventory may increase or decrease profit, that is not the same thing as recorded income or expenses and shouldn't be posted as such (some call it "unrealized income" and "unrealized expense"). In addition (and terribly important), if your local government imposes a gross receipts tax, posting an inventory adjustment as if it were income will increase your taxable gross receipts without any real sales-based income being received.

Understanding the Postings

When you adjust the inventory count, you're also changing the value of your inventory asset. After you save the adjustment, the inventory asset account register reflects the differences for each item.

But this is double-entry bookkeeping, which means there has to be an equal and opposite entry somewhere else. For example, when you sell items via customer invoices, the balancing entry to the decrement of your inventory account is made to cost of goods sold. When you're adjusting inventory, however, there is no sale involved (nor is there a purchase involved). In this case, the balancing entry is made to the inventory adjustment account, which must exist in order to adjust your inventory.

If your inventory adjustment lowers the value of your inventory, the inventory asset account is credited and the adjustment account receives a debit in the same amount. If your adjustment raises the value of your inventory, the postings are opposite.

Making Other Adjustments to Inventory

You can use the Adjust Quantity/Value On Hand window to make adjustments to inventory at any time and for a variety of reasons unconnected to the periodic physical count:

- Breakage or other damage
- Customer demo/sample units
- Gifts or bonuses for customers or employees
- Removal of inventory parts in order to create built or preassembled inventory items (see the upcoming section on builds).

The important thing to remember is that tracking inventory isn't just to make sure that you have sufficient items on hand to sell to customers (although that's certainly an important point). Equally important is the fact that inventory is a significant asset, just like your cash, equipment, and other assets. It affects your company's worth in a substantial way.

Creating Builds

Builds are products that are assembled or partially assembled using existing inventory parts. Some manufacturers call them *kits* or *assembly items*. Only QuickBooks Premier and Enterprise editions offer the software features for assembly items. However, even though QuickBooks Pro doesn't have any capacity for building or tracking builds automatically, you can still create a system that works.

I'll start by examining the elements that go into a build. Accounting software that supports builds automates all the processes using the following rules:

- Asking which existing inventory parts (and how many of each) are used to build the product
- Asking how many builds you want to make (the number is limited by the available quantity of the individual parts)
- Receiving the built item into inventory (after you notify the software that you've built it) and automatically removing the individual parts that were used from inventory
- Automatically creating a cost for the new built item based on the cost of the individual parts

Each of these steps can be performed manually in QuickBooks and, although it's more time consuming, it means you can create builds if you need them.

$ **TIP:** If builds are a large part of your business, you should move up to QuickBooks Premier or QuickBooks Enterprise Solutions. You can learn how to use this feature in *Running QuickBooks 2009 Premier Editions* from CPA911 Publishing (www.cpa911publishing.com). The book is available at your favorite bookstore or online book seller.

Creating the Built Item

Start a build by putting the item into your Item List, as shown in Figure 7-10. The protocols I've used for entering the item are specially designed for builds, and you may find the guidelines I present here helpful as you make your own entries:

- The Item Name/Number is unique in its starting character to make it clear that this is a special line of products. Use a unique letter for the first character of your builds so they appear together in drop-down lists and announce themselves as a build (X or Z usually works well).
- The cost is the aggregate current average cost of the original inventory parts (which means you have to look them up and add them up before you create this item).

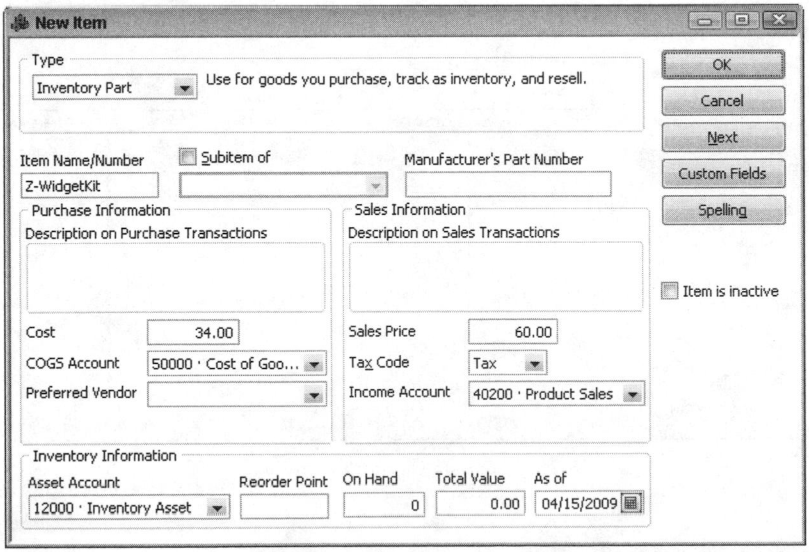

FIGURE 7-10 Create a build the same way you create a regular, purchased item.

- No startup quantity is entered (it's brought into inventory when you build it).
- If the item is built-to-order for individual customers, no reorder point is needed.

Putting Builds into Inventory

When you bring your built items into inventory, you don't receive them the way you receive the inventory items you purchase (there's no vendor and you don't write a check to purchase them).

Instead, you must take the items you used to build the new product out of inventory and put the new built product into inventory, using the following steps:

1. Choose Vendors | Inventory Activities | Adjust Quantity/Value On Hand to open the Adjust Quantity/Value On Hand window.
2. In the Qty Difference column, remove the appropriate quantities of items that are used to create this build (or multiple builds of this item if you're creating more than one) by using a minus sign before the quantity.
3. Enter a positive number to indicate the number of builds.

As you can see in Figure 7-11, the total value of the inventory adjustment is zero (the adjustment value is in the lower-right corner of the window) because you're replacing components that total a certain amount with a build that costs the same amount.

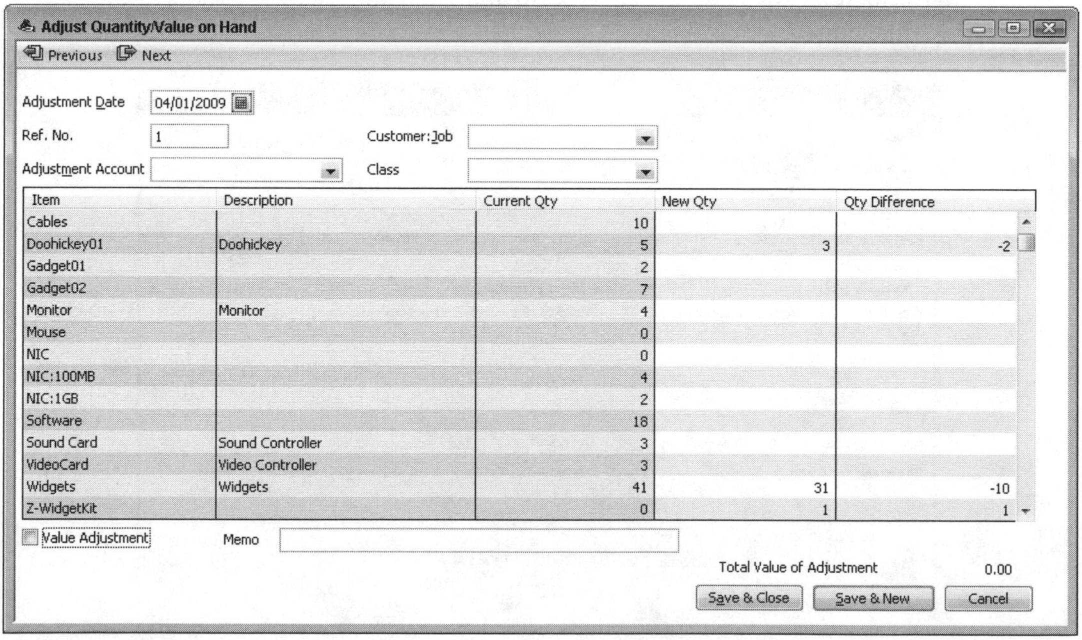

FIGURE 7-11 The cost of the build is equal to the cost of the parts removed to create it.

Workaround for Backorders

Backorders are nerve-wracking on both ends, whether you're waiting for items that your supplier didn't have (your supplier's backorder problem), or you need to ship items to customers and you're out of them (your backorder problem). Although QuickBooks Pro doesn't offer a backorder feature, you can use existing features to create your own backorder protocols.

 N O T E : QuickBooks Premier and Enterprise Solutions editions have backorder features built in. If backorders are common in your business, consider upgrading. You can learn how to create and track backorders in *Running QuickBooks 2009 Premier Editions* from CPA911 Publishing (www.cpa911publishing.com). The book is available at your favorite bookstore or online retailer.

Tracking Customer Backorder Preferences

Part of the trick of keeping your customers' business is keeping your customers' preferences straight. The issue of backorders is important because not all customers have the same attitude. Generally, there are three different approaches your customers take:

- "Okay, ship me whatever you have and send the backorders when you get them."
- "Just ship me what you have and take the other items off the order, and I'll order the other stuff when you get it." (This may really mean, "I'm going to look elsewhere, but if everyone else is out of it, I'll call you back.")
- "Hold the order until the backordered items are in, and then ship everything at once."

Nobody expects you to remember each customer's preference, but QuickBooks has some features that help you handle backorders to each customer's satisfaction.

Using the Notepad for Backorder Instructions

QuickBooks has this nifty item called "customer notes," which you can use for keeping backorder instructions. Use the following steps to add a note about backorder preferences to a customer's file:

1. Open the Customers & Jobs List, select the customer's listing, and click the Edit Notes button in the right pane of the Customer Center.
2. In the Notepad window, enter a notation about the customer's attitude regarding backorders.
3. Click OK to save the note.

When you're filling out an invoice for this customer, you can view the customer notepad. With the customer's invoice on the screen, choose Edit | Notepad from the QuickBooks menu bar, and the notepad for that customer appears.

Using a Backorder Handling Field

You can formalize your backorder handling by creating a Backorders field on the customer records. Then you can put the field on the invoice form so it's right in front of you when you're filling out an order. To do this, you have to perform the following three tasks (all of which are covered in this section):

- Create the custom field for backorder preferences.
- Add data to the field for each customer.
- Add the field to your invoice form.

Create a Custom Field for Customers

You can add a custom field to all the customer records in your system by creating the new field in any existing customer record (when you add a custom field to one customer record, you're adding the field to all customer records). Use the following steps to accomplish this task:

1. Open the Customers & Jobs List and double-click the listing for any existing customer.
2. Click the Additional Info tab, and then click Define Fields.
3. Enter a label for the backorder preferences field and select Customers:Jobs as the list for this custom field.

4. When you click OK, QuickBooks displays a message telling you that you can use this custom field in templates (which is exactly what you're going to do). Click OK to make the message go away (and notice that you can tell it never to come back).

5. When you return to the customer record, click OK to close the record.

Enter Backorder Preferences Data in the Customer Records

The customer list is still on your QuickBooks screen, which is handy because now you must enter information in the new field for each customer who orders inventory items from you and for whom you know the backorder preference. Enter the information using the following steps:

1. Double-click a customer listing to open an Edit Customer window.

2. Move to the Additional Info tab.

3. Enter this customer's backorder preference in the BO Pref field you created (see Figure 7-12).

4. Click OK to save the information.

5. Repeat the process for each customer.

FIGURE 7-12 Use the custom field to track each customer's backorder preference.

Unlike most of the fields that are built into the customer record, custom fields don't have their own list files; therefore, you don't have a drop-down list available when you want to enter data—data entry is manual.

You must create some rules about the way you use this field so everyone in the office uses the same phrases. Don't let people create abbreviations or "cute" entries; make sure the data makes the customer's backorder status absolutely clear. For example, for a backorder preference, consider creating easy-to-understand data entries such as ShipSeparately, HoldOrder, and NoBO.

Put the Field on Your Invoice Forms

The information about a customer's backorder preferences is important when you're filling an order and you're out of something the customer wants. So you might as well have the information in front of you, which means putting it right on the invoice form. Complete instructions for customizing invoices appear in Chapter 28, but I'll give you some guidelines for this particular change in order to complete the instructions for tracking backorders.

- In the Header tab of the Additional Customization dialog, you'll find the custom field you added to the customer records. Enter the text you want to use for this field on the invoice (see Figure 7-13).

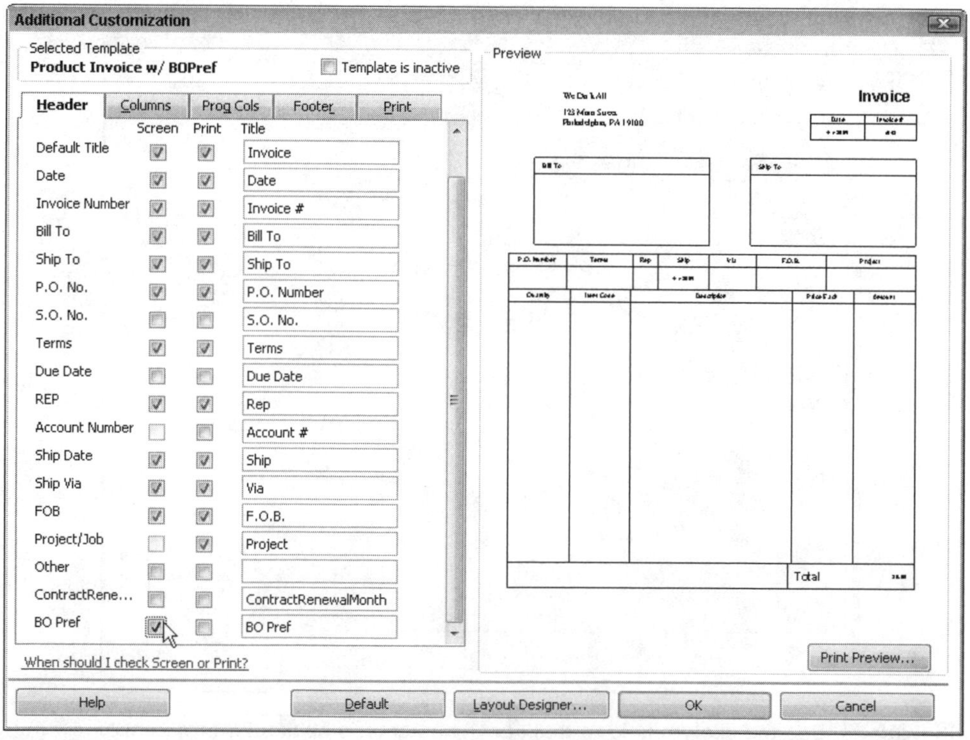

FIGURE 7-13   Put the custom field on the invoice template.

- Select Screen to make sure this field and its data are on the screen when you're filling out an invoice.
- If you want to print the field and its data when you print the invoice (so the customer is reminded of the preference), also select Print.

Now when you need to enter a product invoice, use this new template. As soon as you enter the customer name in the Create Invoices window, the backorder preference for that customer is displayed (see Figure 7-14).

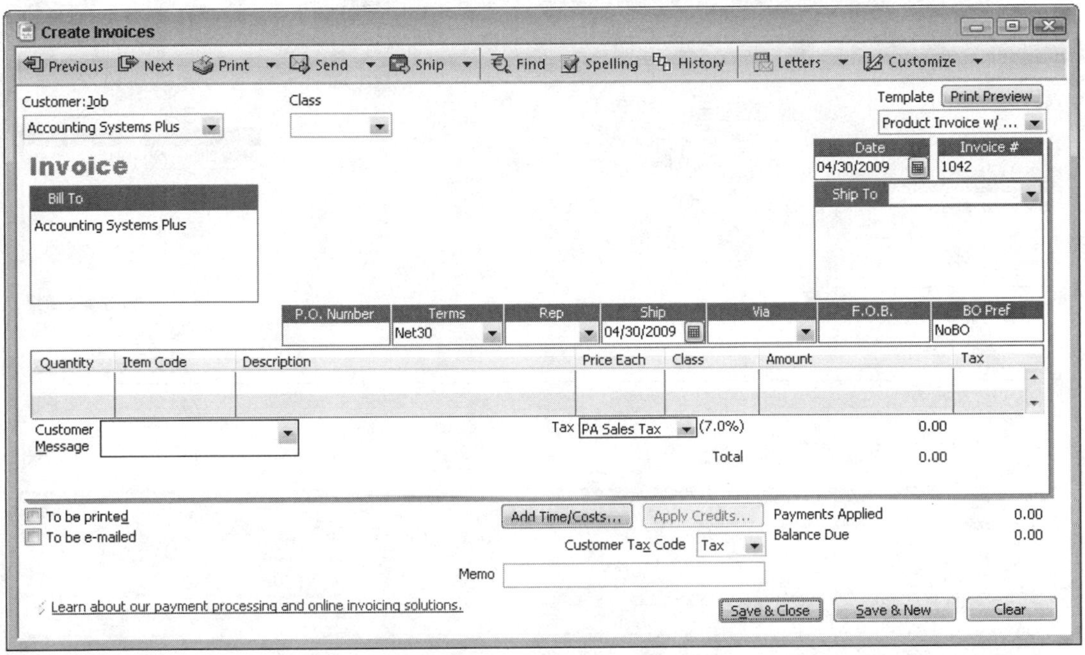

FIGURE 7-14 You can see what each customer's backorder preference is while you're filling the order.

Recording a Backorder Invoice

Now you're all set and can fill backorders the way your customers want them filled, using the following guidelines:

- If your customer wants you to ship the products on hand and then ship backordered products separately, complete the invoice for the products on hand. Then create a new Backorder Invoice.
- If your customer wants you to hold the shipment until the backordered products are available, create a Backorder Invoice for the entire order.
- If the customer doesn't accept backorders, just create the invoice for the quantity on hand.

To create a Backorder Invoice, fill out the invoice as usual, entering the appropriate quantities on the line items. QuickBooks displays a message telling you there's insufficient quantity to fill the order (which is not a problem now, so click OK).

When the invoice form is completely filled out, right-click in the header or footer area of the form and choose Mark Invoice As Pending from the shortcut menu. The word "Pending" appears on the invoice form (see Figure 7-15). Save the invoice by clicking Save & Close (or click Save & New if you have more invoices to create).

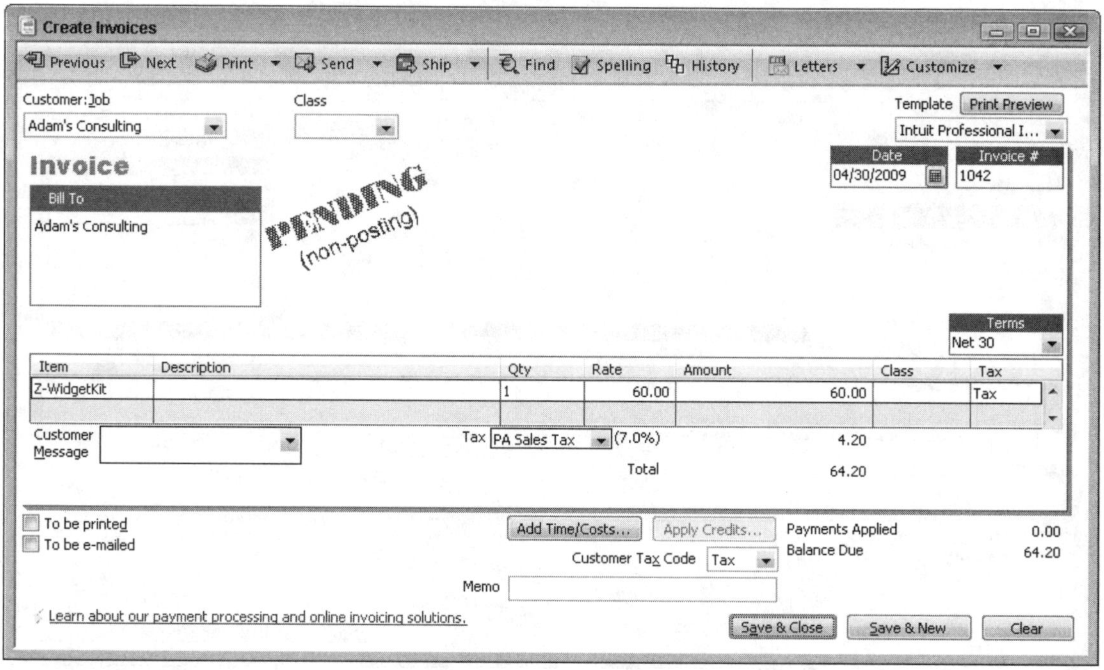

FIGURE 7-15 This order can't be filled until you receive the product, so it's not really a sale yet.

NOTE: A pending invoice does not post any amounts to the general ledger.

Later, when the backordered products arrive and have been entered into inventory, you can release the pending status using the following steps:

1. Choose Reports | Sales | Pending Sales.
2. When the list of pending sales appears, double-click the listing for the sale you want to finalize. The original invoice (still marked "Pending") opens.

3. Right-click in the header or footer section and choose Mark Invoice As Final.
4. Click Save & Close to save the invoice.
5. Pick it, pack it, and ship it.

The point of going through this work is to reinforce the notion that the better you satisfy your customers, the more money you'll make.

Another important lesson in this chapter is that even though your edition of QuickBooks doesn't inherently support a feature you want to use, once you understand the software, you can frequently manipulate it to do what you need.

Entering Historical Data

*I*n this chapter:

- Understand the opening trial balance

- Enter historical customer and vendor data

- Enter inventory

- Create the final trial balance for the previous year

Unless you started your business the first day of the current fiscal year and made your first bank deposit the same day and installed QuickBooks the same day, you have some historical data to put into your QuickBooks company file.

QuickBooks does not have a feature called the "Opening Balance," per se. However, every account register is sorted by date, so when you begin entering transactions in QuickBooks, you can follow these rules:

- Enter current transactions using dates on or after the first day of your current fiscal year.
- Enter historical transactions using any date prior to the first day of your current fiscal year.

Enter the customer, vendor, and inventory history using QuickBooks transactions windows, then use journal entries to record other totals (assets, liabilities, and equity). Confer with your accountant to develop your final opening balances, which usually requires adjusting the equity accounts (which are affected by the historical transactions you enter) to match your final retained earnings as of last year.

In this chapter, I'm assuming the following:

- You're setting up your QuickBooks company file to track transactions from the first day of your fiscal year, even if you started using QuickBooks later in the year. This gives you all the information you need to create final reports on your business year, making it much easier to file your tax returns.
- You've entered your lists—customers, vendors, items, and chart of accounts.

Opening Trial Balance

The goal you seek when you enter historical transactions is to build an opening trial balance for the first day of your fiscal year. A trial balance is a list of all your accounts and their current balances. However, the report called the *opening trial balance* is a bit different from the trial balance reports you create normally. The opening trial balance is the balance of the accounts on the first day of the fiscal year (usually the same as the calendar year for small businesses).

On the first day of a fiscal year, you do not have any income or expenses. The previous year's income and expenses have been calculated as a net number by subtracting the total expenses from the total income. Let's hope the result is a positive number so you have a net profit (a negative number means a loss).

That net number is posted to an equity account (called Retained Earnings), and the income and expense accounts all show zero balances, waiting for your first sales and expense transactions of the current year. Therefore, the opening trial balance only has balances for asset, liability, and equity accounts (generally referred to as *balance sheet accounts*).

To get to this point, you need to enter historical balances, and QuickBooks will automatically create the opening trial balance accurately for the first day of the current year.

 CAUTION: Before you start entering any transactions (historical or current), be sure your chart of accounts, items (including inventory if you track inventory), vendors, and customers are in the company file. Instructions for performing these tasks are found throughout this book—check the Index or the Table of Contents to find the chapters you need.

Entering Current Transactions While Entering Historical Transactions

Because QuickBooks is date sensitive, you can begin using the software for current transactions before you've entered all your historical transactions. To make it easier for your accountant to validate the opening trial balance for your fiscal year, don't enter any current transactions that are dated the first day of the year. Using a calendar year as an example (since most small businesses operate on a calendar year), that means that even if you had sales or wrote checks on January 1, 2007, enter those transactions with the date January 2, 2007. That leaves January 1 "pristine" and your opening trial balance on that date reflects only the totals of your historical transactions, and it is your ending balance for the previous year as well as the starting balance for the current year.

After you're sure your opening trial balance for January 1 is correct, you can edit the January 2 transactions that were really created on January 1 to correct the date (or you can leave the date as January 2).

Entering Open Customer Balances

You have to get all of your open customer balances as of the last day of the year into QuickBooks. If any of the invoices were paid this year (with any luck, all of them were paid, especially if you start using QuickBooks a couple of months into the current year), you enter those payments as current transactions. You also have to track any outstanding customer credits as of the end of last year, so you can use those credits against current or future transactions.

Creating an Item for Historical Transactions

Since all sales transactions require you to use an item, one efficient way to do this is to create an item specifically for these historical open invoices. You can call the item Historical Sales or something similar and link it to an existing income account.

Use a Service or Other Charge item type (see Chapter 6 for a full discussion of creating items).

If you remitted sales tax for the last reporting period of last year with a check dated before the end of the year (which means you don't have to track sales tax for historical transactions), make the item nontaxable.

If you haven't yet paid sales taxes for the last reporting period of last year, create two items: HistoricalSalesTaxable and HistoricalSalesNonTaxable, and mark their tax status appropriately. See the next section "Tracking Historical Sales Tax" for more information on this topic.

For each customer, you can enter the open invoices in either of two ways:

- Enter each individual invoice, using the real date of that invoice. This works well for customers who send payments earmarked for a specific invoice and also permits you to generate an accurate A/R aging report.

- Enter one invoice representing the total outstanding balance, dating it December 31. This is less data entry but only works well if your customers send payments to be applied against a running open balance, and you don't track aging by due dates of individual invoices.

Tracking Historical Sales Tax

If you filed and paid all of your previous year sales taxes by the last day of last year, you don't have to worry about sales tax when you enter the historical transactions. However, if you hadn't yet remitted sales taxes for the last period of last year (either the last quarter or the last month, depending on the frequency of your tax reporting), you have to build the tax liability as you enter the transactions.

If you're using actual invoice dates as you enter historical transactions, do not use the taxable item in any transaction that falls in a period for which you already remitted your sale tax payment. For example, if you're a quarterly filer, make all transactions in the first three quarters nontaxable, and create taxable transactions for the last quarter. Then, in the current year, use the QuickBooks Sales Tax feature to generate the appropriate report for the quarter and remit the taxes.

If you prefer to enter summarized total transactions, you must create one summary nontaxable transaction for the periods covered by sales tax reports you remitted to the tax authorities last year (use the nontaxable item for those transactions) and another summary taxable transaction for the period yet to be reported (using the taxable item).

Creating the Historical Invoices

Use the following guidelines to enter historical transactions:

- Use the original invoice date to make it easier to track aging.

- Use the original invoice number to make sure you and your customers can discuss open balances intelligently.

- In the Item column, select the historical transaction item you created.
- Move directly to the Amount column to enter the total for each invoice (skip the Qty and Description fields).
- Use the Memo field for any notes you think might be important if you have to discuss this invoice with your customer.
- Deselect any check marks in the To Be Printed or To Be E-mailed boxes at the bottom of the window.

TIP: I use the Intuit Service Invoice template for historical transactions because it has fewer fields and columns than other built-in templates.

Figure 8-1 shows an invoice for a customer who pays against a running balance, so the invoice is a summary of open invoices through the third quarter of the previous year and has no taxes (because those taxes were collected and remitted). A similar invoice is created for the last quarter, and that invoice has sales taxes applied because the sales tax hadn't been remitted as of the last day of the previous year.

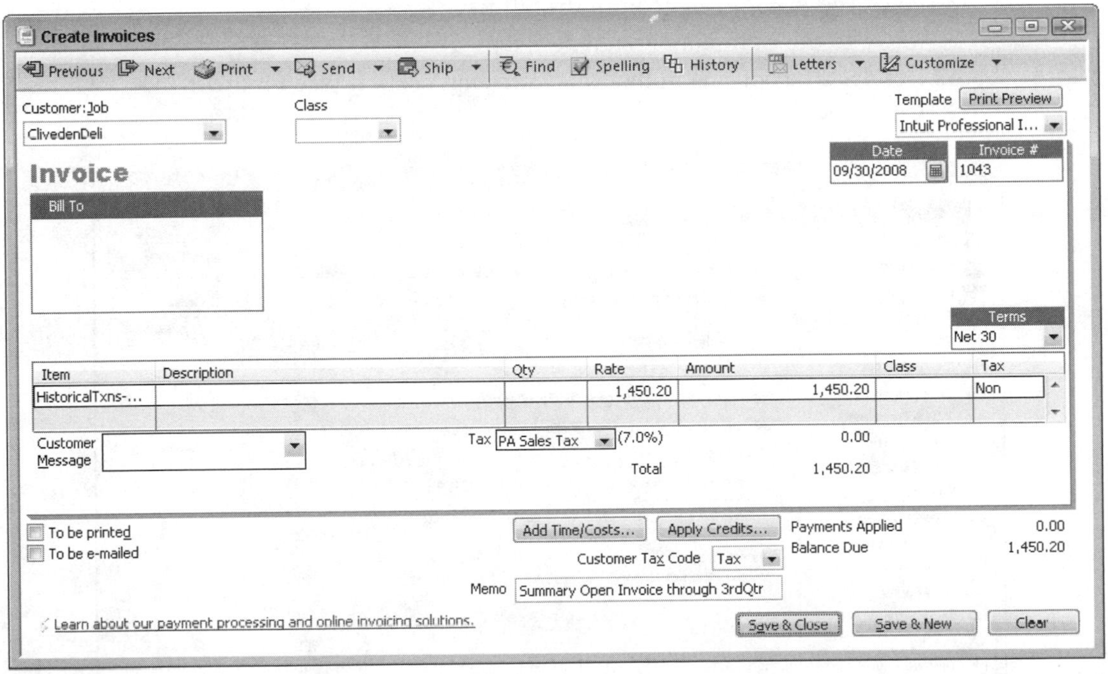

FIGURE 8-1 Enter historical invoices using the item you created for this purpose.

When you enter a transaction that is 90 days before the current date, or 30 days after the current date, QuickBooks issues a warning (which is wonderful because it avoids typos that can create some very strange financial reports).

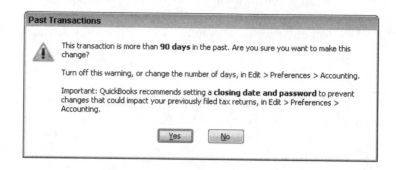

If you're entering individual historical transactions and you don't want to click Yes after saving each transaction, you can turn off this function, using the following steps:

1. Choose Edit | Preferences to open the Preferences dialog.
2. Click the Accounting icon in the left pane.
3. Move to the Company Preferences tab.
4. Deselect the options in the Date Warnings section (see Figure 8-2).
5. Click OK.

FIGURE 8-2   Turn off the Date Warnings function while you're entering old transactions.

Don't forget to turn the warnings on again after you've completed your historical transactions.

Creating Historical Credits

If any of your customers had outstanding credit balances at the end of the year, you must enter them. You can apply them against customer payments or invoices that are entered in the current year. Chapter 9 has detailed information on creating credit memos.

When you create the credit memo, use the real date from the previous year if you're tracking payments by invoices, or summarize multiple credit memos and use the last day of the previous year if you're using running balances.

Use the item you created for historical transactions. The same rules about sales tax apply as discussed in the previous section. When you save a credit memo, QuickBooks asks how to handle the transaction.

Since this is a prior year transaction that will be applied against a current year transaction, select the option Retain As An Available Credit. Chapter 10 has instructions for applying credits against customer invoices and payments.

Entering Open Payables

Enter all the vendor bills that were due as of the last day of the previous year (you'll record any payments you've made this year as a current transaction). If multiple bills existed for any vendors, you can enter individual bills, or enter one bill to cover the entire amount.

If you normally pay your bills to match invoice amounts, it's best to enter each bill individually. This makes recording payments more straightforward and also makes it easier to have conversations with the vendor in the event of a dispute.

Entering Inventory

If you track inventory, enter the quantity and value of each inventory item as of the last day of the year. Choose Vendors | Inventory Activities | Adjust Quantity/Value On Hand. When the transaction window opens, click the Value Adjustment check box at the bottom of the window to add the Current Value and New Value columns to the window (see Figure 8-3).

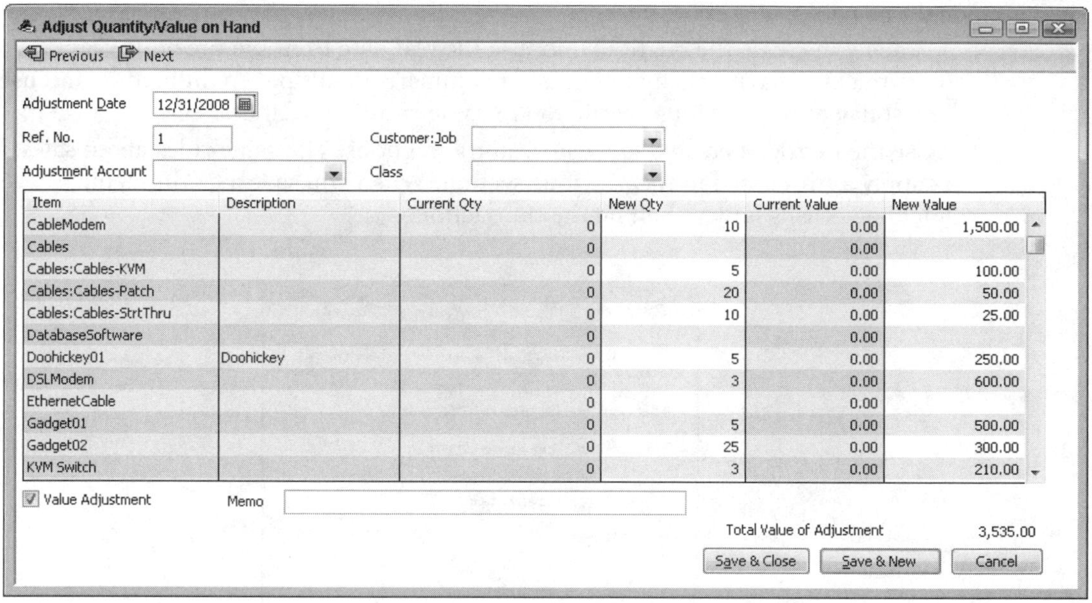

FIGURE 8-3 All your inventory items are displayed so you can enter the quantity and value of each.

For each inventory item, enter the appropriate numbers in the New Qty and New Value columns. When you complete this task, you end up with the following:

- The total value of your inventory is posted (as a debit) to your inventory asset account as of the last day of the year.
- The cost per unit of your inventory items has been calculated by QuickBooks. This number is used to post amounts to the cost of goods account when you enter sales transactions in the current year.
- The inventory adjustment account has been credited with the offsetting total.

The inventory adjustment account requires some discussion with your accountant. If you're adding inventory as an adjustment instead of receiving goods via a purchase order and vendor bill (as is the case in this opening entry), the inventory adjustment account is credited, essentially becoming a contra-expense (increasing your profit). By default, QuickBooks wants you to use an income account or an expense account, but most accountants prefer a cost of goods account type (see the discussion on this issue in Chapter 7).

Creating the Trial Balance for Last Year

When your historical transactions are posted, you can begin to create a trial balance report as of the last day of the previous year. Start by viewing the current trial balance, which shows the totals posted for all the historical transactions you entered. You probably have balances for the following accounts (depending on the types of historical transactions you entered):

- Accounts receivable
- Inventory
- Accounts payable
- Sales tax payable
- Income (the account you linked to the item you created for entering historical invoices)
- Expenses (postings from the open vendor bills you entered)

To generate the report, choose Reports | Accountant & Taxes | Trial Balance. When the report opens, set the date range to the previous fiscal year (see Figure 8-4).

		Debit	Credit
10600 · Checking Accnt		8,459.07	
10000 · Operating Account		25,339.22	
10100 · Money Market Accnt		19,000.00	
10200 · Payroll Account		1,000.00	
11000 · Accounts Receivable		950.20	
12000 · Inventory Asset		3,613.00	
22000 · Sales Tax Payable		0.00	
31310 · Owner Capital In			20,000.00
40100 · Consulting			18,540.36
40200 · Product Sales			6,876.86
40300 · Other Regular Income			950.20
50100 · Inventory Adjustments			3,535.00
67040 · Janitorial Exp		100.00	
63400 · Telephone		102.50	
70300 · Other Income			9,739.80
80100 · Other Expenses		1,078.23	
TOTAL		59,642.22	59,642.22

FIGURE 8-4 Your trial balance for last year now has the totals for the historical transactions you created.

Print this report; you need it as a reference when you create the journal entry to enter balances in all your accounts, because you don't want to enter these totals twice.

You also need to create a balance sheet report as of the end of the year, so you can see the effect of your entries on your balance sheet accounts, including equity accounts. To generate the report, choose Reports | Company & Financial | Balance Sheet Standard. When the report window opens, select a date range for the previous year to see a report that resembles the one seen in Figure 8-5.

Print the report, because you have to know what's already posted and calculated (net profit or loss in the equity account) when you enter the remaining account totals.

We Do It All
Balance Sheet
As of December 31, 2008

Accrual Basis

	Dec 31, 08
ASSETS	
Current Assets	
Checking/Savings	
10000 · Operating Account	25,339.22
10100 · Money Market Accnt	20,000.00
Total Checking/Savings	45,339.22
Other Current Assets	
12000 · Inventory Asset	5,653.74
Total Other Current Assets	5,653.74
Total Current Assets	50,992.96
TOTAL ASSETS	50,992.96
LIABILITIES & EQUITY	
Equity	
31300 · Owner's Capital	
31310 · Owner Capital In	21,200.00
Total 31300 · Owner's Capital	21,200.00
Net Income	29,792.96
Total Equity	50,992.96
TOTAL LIABILITIES & EQUITY	50,992.96

FIGURE 8-5 The balance sheet reflects the activity in your company file, in this case the historical transactions you entered.

Entering the Remaining Account Totals

The totals for the remaining accounts can be entered as a journal entry dated the last day of the previous year. Remember not to use the accounts that received postings as a result of your transaction entries (with the exception of the sales tax liability account, which is discussed in the section "Entering Sales Tax Liabilities Balances").

Remember that the goal is to create an opening trial balance for the first day of the current year, which has only balance sheet accounts. The best way to get there is to create a journal entry as of the last day of the previous year that uses all your accounts (including income and expense accounts). Then let QuickBooks perform the calculations that turn the numbers into an opening trial balance on the first day of the current year.

Enter all the totals you calculate from your manual or spreadsheet-based former bookkeeping system. This puts all the income and expense totals into your QuickBooks company file, which makes it easier to create budgets for the current year and also lets you create reports comparing sales and expenses between the current year and last year.

Some of the entries in your journal entry are easy to figure out, but others require some thought. For example, the totals for accounts of the type Other Current Assets (excluding inventory) and Other Assets are usually easy to calculate. Most Current Liabilities and Long Term Liabilities totals are equally straightforward. However, the totals you enter for your bank accounts, fixed assets, and payroll liabilities merit special attention, explained in the following sections.

Entering Bank Account Balances

To enter bank account balances, use the reconciled balance as of the last day of the last fiscal year in your journal entry (most banks generate statements as of the last day of each month for business accounts). Don't include any transactions that hadn't cleared as of the last day of the year.

After you save the journal entry, use individual transactions to enter the unreconciled transactions, which allows you to see those transactions when you reconcile the bank account in QuickBooks. Enter each deposit and withdrawal (including checks and any electronic payments), all of which should be dated earlier than the first day of the year. You can make the entries directly in the account register, which is faster than using transaction windows (Write Checks or Make Deposits). See Chapter 14 to learn how to reconcile bank accounts, including performing the first reconciliation in QuickBooks.

Entering Fixed Asset Balances

You can enter your current balances for fixed assets in either of the following ways:

- Enter the net amount (the purchase amount less accumulated depreciation).
- Enter the original purchase amount and also enter the historical depreciation.

I prefer the latter, because I like my accounting system to provide as much information as possible. (I present a rather lengthy discussion on the various methods for tracking depreciation in Chapter 19.) This task takes only a couple of minutes, and the accounts are there, waiting for you, when you enter the opening balances for fixed assets in your journal entry.

Entering Payroll Liabilities Balances

If you ended the year with payroll liabilities still unpaid, enter them in the opening balance journal entry. They'll wash when you enter the transaction that paid them during the current year. If you're using QuickBooks payroll, during setup the system asks about those liabilities and prompts you to enter payroll liability payments you have made in the current year. If you don't use QuickBooks payroll you can enter the transaction as of its real date. See Chapter 17 to learn how to set up and run QuickBooks payroll and Chapter 18 to learn how to remit payroll payments. Chapter 19 covers the steps needed to record payroll when you have an outside payroll service.

Entering Sales Tax Liabilities Balances

If you have taxable sales for the last reporting period, you have to enter the total sales tax liability for those transactions *not* included in the historical transactions you entered. Paid (not open as of the end of the year) transactions also contributed to your tax liability, and you have to add that total to the sales tax liability account in order to remit taxes accurately.

Entering Income and Expense Balances

If you're working with calculated totals from the previous year (that you calculated in your old bookkeeping system), you may have to "back out" the amounts you posted when you entered the open receivables and payables.

For example, if you know your calculated sales total from your old system includes the unpaid invoices you entered in QuickBooks, subtract the total of the entered unpaid invoices from your year-end total. Do the same for your expense balances.

Entering Equity Account Balances

When you enter equity account balances you have to build in the accumulated equity (retained earnings) for your business. The way you enter equity account balances depends on the way your business is organized. If your business is a proprietorship or partnership, and you track capital in and draws out, you need to enter those individual totals.

If your accountant has prepared an end-of-year trial balance, including final equity balances as of the last day of the year, you can use those figures as a starting point. However, you have to subtract the equity that resulted from the historical transactions you entered. Ask your accountant for help and advice on recalculating that equity.

Creating the Historical Journal Entry

To create the journal entry that populates the account balances as of the last day of the prior year, choose Company | Make General Journal Entries to open the Make General Journal Entries transaction window.

Select the last day of the prior year as the transaction date. Remember to omit the balance sheet accounts you used when you entered your open transactions (except for sales tax liabilities as described earlier). For income and expense accounts, subtract the totals of the individual transactions you entered from the totals you have from your previous system (if those previous totals included open transactions).

Checking the Results

You need to check your work against two standards:

- The closing reports for the previous year to make sure the numbers match your accountant's numbers, including the numbers used for your tax return.
- The opening trial balance for the current year, which should contain no accounts except balance sheet accounts, and the account balances should match your accountant's numbers.

Creating Reports on the Previous Year

To make sure your previous year numbers are correct (they're the basis of your tax return in addition to being the basis of your starting numbers for the current year), run the following standard financial reports and set the date range for each report to the previous year:

- Profit & Loss Standard
- Balance Sheet Standard
- Trial Balance

Check the numbers against your accountant's figures. If they don't match, you can drill down through the reports to find the entries that are causing the problem.

Generating the Trial Balance for the Current Year

Run a trial balance report for the first day of the current year. Only the balance sheet accounts should display on the report; if you see any income or expense accounts, drill down to the offending transaction (which has a date entered incorrectly).

Congratulations, you're starting off in QuickBooks with accurate numbers!

Bookkeeping with QuickBooks

Part Two contains chapters about the day-to-day bookkeeping chores you'll be performing in QuickBooks. The chapters are filled with instructions, tips, and explanations. There's information that you can pass along to your accountant, who wants to know just how you're performing tasks in QuickBooks.

The chapters in Part Two take you through everything you need to know about sending invoices to your customers and collecting the money they send back as a result. You'll learn how to track and pay the bills you receive from vendors. There's plenty of information about dealing with inventory—buying it, selling it, and counting it—and keeping QuickBooks up to date on those figures. There are chapters that cover payroll, discussing the ways to manage both in-house payroll systems and outside services.

You'll also learn how to manage your bank accounts, create transactions in a way that provides job costing data, and make adjustments to account balances by creating journal entries.

Invoicing Customers

n this chapter:

- Create invoices
- Use price levels
- Work with estimates
- Create and edit credit memos
- Use memorized invoices
- Invoice customers for reimbursable expenses

For many businesses, the only way to get money is to send an invoice to a customer (the exception is retail, of course). Creating an invoice in QuickBooks is easy once you understand what all the parts of the invoice do and why various functions exist.

In addition to invoices, you often have to create credits, packing slips, estimates, and other sales-related transactions. In this chapter, I'll go over all those transactions, and after I've explained how to create them, I'll move on to describe the choices you have for sending them to your customers.

> **N O T E :** If you've enabled multicurrency (see Appendix A), your invoices use the currency linked to the customer.

Creating Invoices

QuickBooks offers several ways to open the Create Invoices window. You can select Customers | Create Invoices from the menu bar, press CTRL-I, or click the Create Invoices icon in the Customers section of the Home page (there are additional methods, but three choices should be enough). Any of those actions opens the Create Invoices window, which is a blank invoice form (see Figure 9-1).

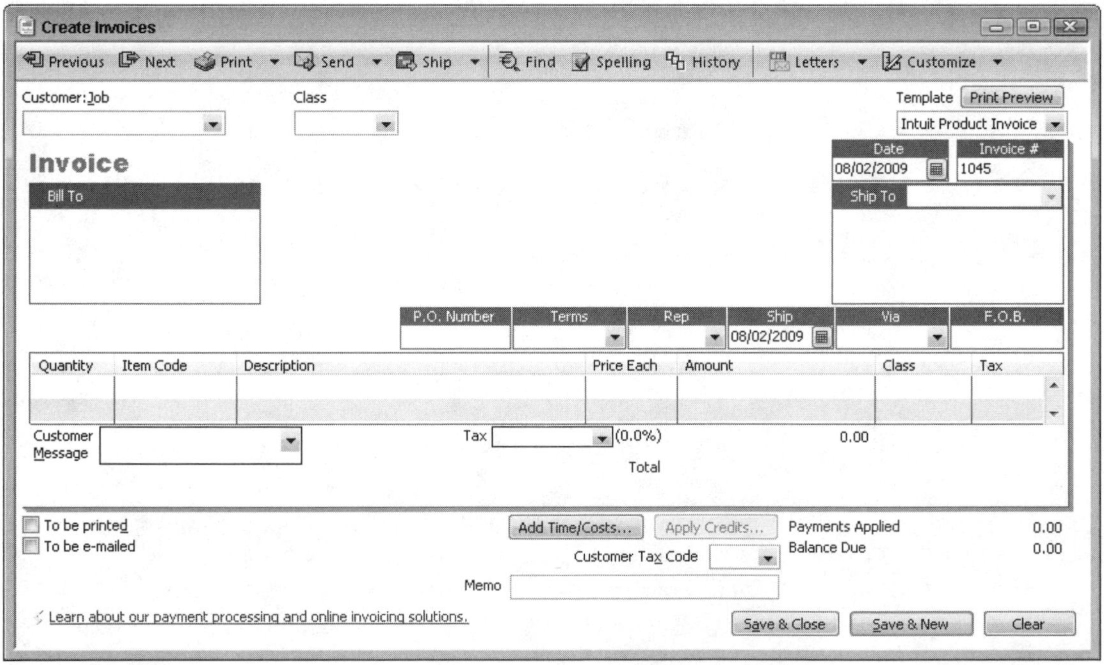

FIGURE 9-1 The Create Invoices window has all the fields you need to track your sales activity.

There are several invoice templates built into QuickBooks, and you can use any of them. The first thing to do is decide whether or not the displayed template suits you. You should probably look at the other templates before settling on the one you want to use. To do that, click the arrow below the Template field and select another invoice template from the drop-down list:

- The Professional and Service templates are almost identical. There's a difference in the order of the columns, and the Service template has a field for a purchase order number.
- The Product template has more fields and different columns because it's designed for product sales, including inventory items.
- The Progress template, which is covered later in this chapter in the "Creating Progress Billing Invoices" section, is designed specifically for progress billing against a job estimate. It doesn't appear in the Template list unless you have specified Progress Invoicing in the Company Preferences tab of the Jobs & Estimates category of the Preferences dialog.
- The Finance Charge template appears if you enable finance charges in the Finance Charge category of the Preferences dialog. Information about finance charges is in Chapter 10.
- The Packing Slip template is discussed in the section "Printing Packing Slips," later in this chapter.

For this discussion, I'll use the Product template, because it's the most complicated. If you're using any other template, you'll still be able to follow along, even though your invoice form lacks some of the fields related to products.

The top portion of the invoice is for the basic information and is called the *invoice header*. The middle section, where the billing items are placed, is called the *line item* section. The bottom section, called the *footer*, holds the totals and other details (such as customer messages). Each section of the invoice has fields into which you enter data.

Entering Header Information

To create an invoice, start with the customer or the job. Click the arrow to the right of the Customer:Job field to see a list of all your customers. If you've attached jobs to any customers, those jobs are listed under the customer name. Select the customer or job for this invoice.

If the customer isn't in the system, choose <Add New> to open a new customer window and enter all the data required for setting up a customer. Read Chapter 3 for information on creating customers and jobs.

If you've charged reimbursable expenses or time charges to this customer, QuickBooks displays a message reminding you to add those charges to this invoice. You learn how to charge customers for reimbursable expenses in Chapter 11.

NOTE: If you have more than one Accounts Receivable account, the top of the Invoice window has a field to select the A/R account you want to use to post this transaction. You must select the same A/R account when you receive payment for the invoice.

In the Date field, the current date is showing, but if you want to change the date you can either type in a new date, or click the calendar icon at the right side of the field to select a date. If you change the date, the new date appears automatically in each invoice you create during this session of QuickBooks (the current date returns after you close and then re-open the software). You can change that behavior by changing its configuration option in the My Preferences tab of the General category of the Preferences dialog (choose Edit | Preferences to open the dialog). Select the option Use Today's Date As Default instead of the default option Use The Last Entered Date As Default.

The first time you enter an invoice, fill in the invoice number you want to use as a starting point. Hereafter, QuickBooks will increment that number for each ensuing invoice.

The Bill To address is taken from the customer record, as is the Ship To address that's available on the Product Invoice template (using the Ship To address you configured to be the default Ship To address). You can select another Ship To address from the drop-down list, or add a new Ship To address by choosing <Add New> from the list.

If you have a purchase order from this customer, enter the PO number in the P.O. Number field (not available on the Professional template).

The Terms field is filled in automatically with the terms you entered for this customer when you created the customer. You can change the terms for this invoice if you wish. If terms don't automatically appear, it means you didn't enter that information in the customer record. If you enter it now, when you save the invoice QuickBooks offers to make the entry the new default for this customer by adding it to the customer record.

TIP: If you enter or change any information about the customer while you're creating an invoice, QuickBooks offers to add the information to the customer record when you save the invoice. If the change is permanent, click the Yes button in the dialog that displays the offer. This saves you the trouble of going back to the customer record to make the changes. If the change is only for this invoice, click the No button. If you never make permanent changes, you can tell QuickBooks to turn off this feature by changing the option in the Company Preferences tab in the General category of the Preferences dialog. Select the option Never Update Name Information When Saving Transactions.

The Rep field (only in the Product template) is for the salesperson attached to this customer. If you didn't link a salesperson when you filled out the customer record, you can click the arrow next to the field and choose a name from the drop-down list. If the Rep you want to use doesn't exist, see Chapter 5 to learn how to add reps to your system.

The Ship field (only in the Product and Packing Slip templates) is for the ship date, and the date defaults to the invoice date. You can change the date if you're not shipping until a later date.

The Via field (only in the Product and Packing Slip templates) is for the method of shipping. Click the arrow next to the field to see the available shipping choices. (See Chapter 5 for information about adding to this list.)

The F.O.B. field (only in the Product and Packing Slip templates) is used by some companies to indicate the point at which the shipping costs are transferred to the buyer and the assumption of a completed sale takes place. (That means, if it breaks or gets lost after that point, the customer owns it.) If you use FOB terms, you can enter the applicable data in the field; it has no impact on your QuickBooks financial records and is there for your convenience only.

NOTE: FOB stands for Free On Board, and I'm sure there's some meaningful reason for the term, but I suspect it's been lost in history.

Entering Line Items

Now you can begin to enter the items for which you are billing this customer. Click in the first column of the line item section.

If you're using the Product invoice template, that column is Quantity. (If you're using the Professional or Service invoice template, the first column is Item.) Enter the quantity of the first item you're invoicing.

In the Item Code column, an arrow appears on the right edge of the column—click it to see a list of the items you sell. (See Chapter 6 to learn how to enter items.) Select the item you need. The description and price are filled in automatically, using the information you provided when you created the item. If you didn't include description and/or price information when you created the item, you can enter it manually now.

QuickBooks does the math, and the Amount column displays the total of the quantity times the price. If the item and the customer are both liable for tax, the Tax column displays "Tax."

Repeat this process to add all the items that should be on this invoice. You can add as many rows of items as you need; if you run out of room, QuickBooks automatically adds pages to your invoice.

Applying Price Levels

If you've created entries in your Price Level List (explained in Chapter 5), you can change the amount of any line item by applying a price level. Most of the time, your price levels are a percentage by which to lower (discount) the price, but you may also have created price levels that increase the price.

If you have already assigned a price level to this customer, the appropriate price shows up automatically. If not, to assign a price level, click your mouse within the Price Each column to display an arrow. Click the arrow to see a drop-down list of price level items, and select the one you want to apply to this item. As you can see in Figure 9-2, QuickBooks has already performed the math, so you not only see the name of your price level, you also see the resulting item price for each price level. After you select a price level, QuickBooks changes the amount you're charging the customer for the item and adjusts the amount of the total for this item if the quantity is more than 1.

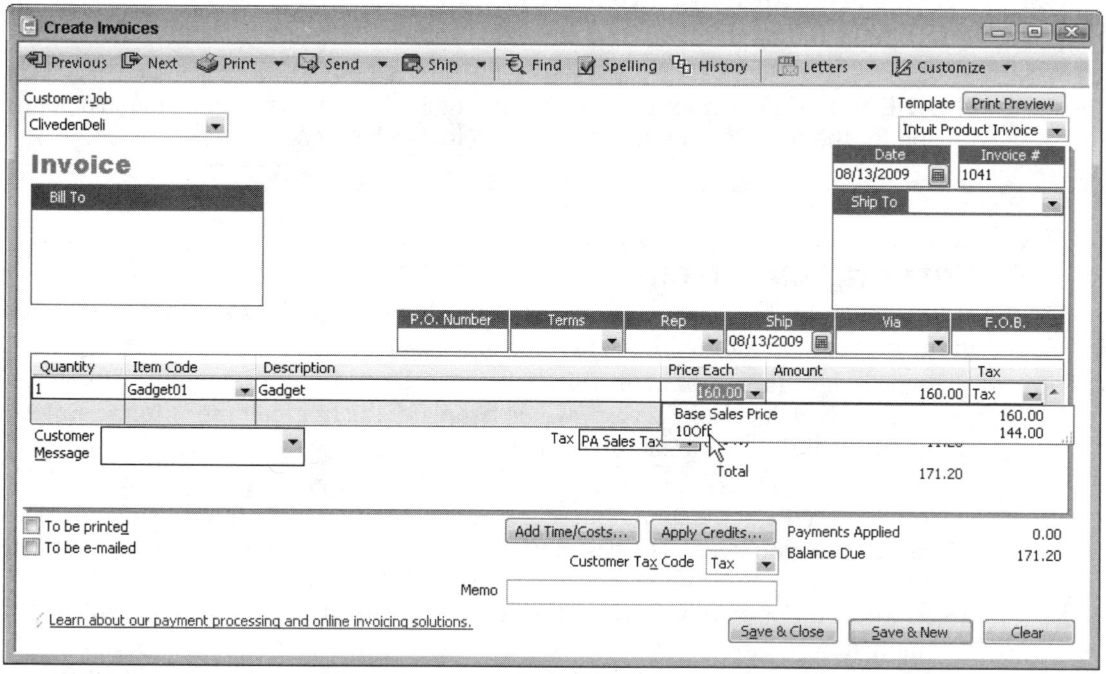

FIGURE 9-2 Assign a predefined price level to the price of any item.

The invoice displays no indication that you've adjusted the price. This is different from applying a discount to a price (covered in the next section), where a discrete line item exists to announce the discount.

Entering Discounts

You can also adjust the invoice by applying discounts. Discounts are entered as line items, so the discount item has to exist in your Item List.

When you enter a discount, its amount (usually a percentage) is applied based on the line item immediately above it. For example, let's suppose you have already entered the following line items:

- Qty of 1 for Some Item with a price of $100.00 for a total line item price of $100.00
- Qty of 2 for Some Other Item with a price of $40.00 for a total line item price of $80.00

Now you want to give the customer a 10 percent discount (you created a 10 percent discount item in your Item List). If you enter that item on the next line, QuickBooks will calculate its value as 10 percent of the last line you entered—an $8.00 discount.

Entering Subtotals

If you want to apply the discount against multiple (or all) line items, you must first enter a line item that subtotals those lines. To do this, use a subtotal item type that you've created in your Item List. Then enter the discount item as the next line item, and when the discount is applied to the previous amount, that previous amount is the amount of the subtotal. The discount is based on the subtotal.

Subtotals work by adding up all the line items that have been entered after the last subtotal item. (The first subtotal item adds up all line items starting at the first line item on the invoice.) This gives you the ability to discount some line items but not others and to apply a different discount rate to each group (subtotaled) of items.

Because discounts are displayed on the invoice, your discount policies are made clear to the customer.

Checking the Footer Section

When you're finished entering all the line items, you'll see that QuickBooks has kept a running total, including taxes, in the footer section of the invoice (see Figure 9-3).

Adding a Message

If you want to add a message, click the arrow in the Customer Message field to see the messages you created in the Customer Message list (as described in Chapter 5). You can create a new message if you don't want to use any of the existing text by choosing <Add New> from the message drop-down list and entering your text in the New Customer Message window. Click OK to enter the message in the invoice.

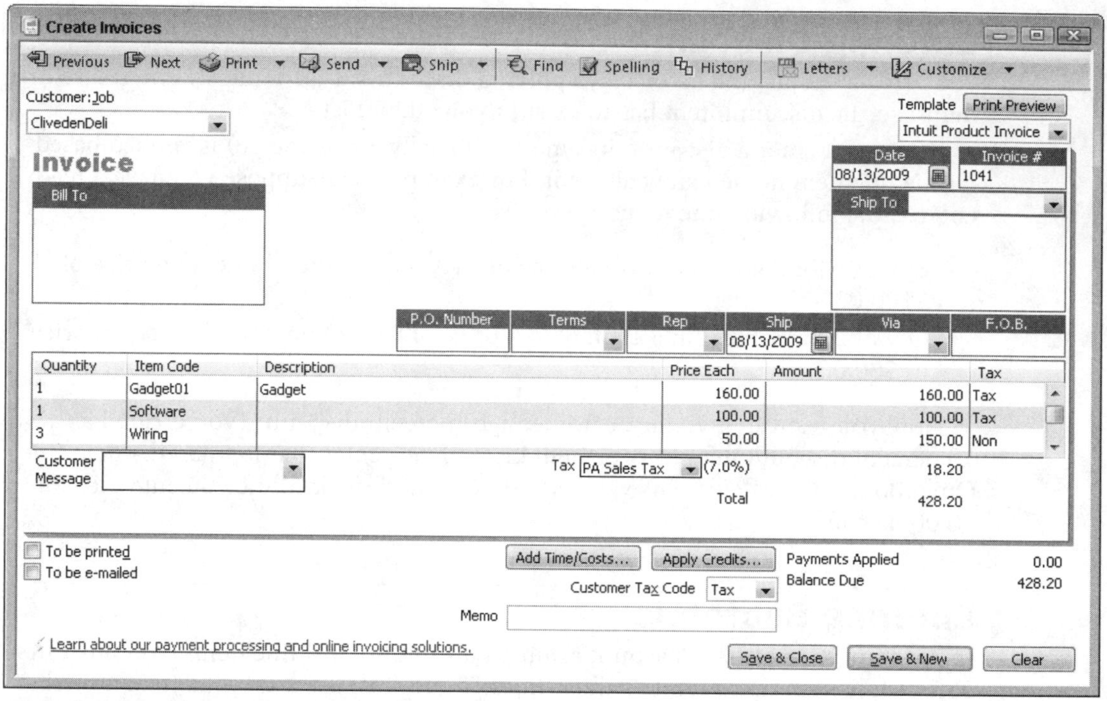

FIGURE 9-3 The invoice is complete, and there are no math errors because computers never make math errors.

QuickBooks automatically saves the message in the Customer Message list so you can use it again. You can also type the message directly in the Customer Message field, which opens a Customer Message Not Found dialog that offers you the chance to do a QuickAdd to put your new message in the Customer Message list.

Adding a Memo

You can add text to the Memo field at the bottom of the invoice. This text doesn't print on the invoice—it appears only on the screen (you'll see it if you re-open this invoice to view or edit it). However, the memo text *does* appear on statements, next to the listing for this invoice. Therefore, be careful about the text you use—don't enter anything you wouldn't want the customer to see (unless you never send statements).

Choosing the Method of Sending the Invoice

At the bottom of the invoice template are two options for sending the invoice: To Be Printed and To Be E-mailed. You can print or e-mail each invoice as you complete it, or just save the invoice and then batch-print or batch-mail all of your invoices.

▶ FYI

Printing Invoices without Saving Them

For many years, QuickBooks permitted users to print invoices (and packing slips) without saving those invoices. Because this is one of the most often used schemes to purloin products (employees would create an invoice and packing slip to have products shipped to friends or relatives), almost all accounting software prevents users from printing an invoice unless it has been saved.

In older versions of QuickBooks you could create and print an invoice (or even a check), and then close the transaction window without saving the transaction. In QuickBooks 2007, the paradigm changed to meet the standards of the accounting industry; if you printed a transaction, QuickBooks automatically saved it. If the user later deleted the transaction to hide it, the QuickBooks audit trail would show that action.

Unfortunately, quite a few users who liked to print invoices without saving them, for reasons they deemed valid, complained about the requirement to save before printing. As a result, Intuit has made it possible to turn off the option to save transactions before printing (in the General section of the Preferences dialog). Don't turn this default setting off; it's good business practice to save a transaction before you print it.

Your choices about printing and e-mailing invoices (and other transaction documents) are varied, and you can learn about sending transaction documents in Chapter 25.

Saving the Invoice

Choose Save & New to save this invoice and move on to the next blank invoice form. If this is the last invoice you're creating, click Save & Close to save this invoice and close the Create Invoices window.

Using Estimates

For certain customers or certain types of jobs, it may be advantageous to create estimates. An estimate isn't an invoice, but it can be the basis of an invoice (or multiple invoices if you choose to send invoices as the job progresses).

 NOTE: Estimates are only available if you enable them in the Jobs & Estimates section of the Preferences dialog (Edit | Preferences).

Creating an Estimate

The first (and most important) thing to understand is that creating an estimate doesn't impact your financial records. When you indicate that you use estimates in your QuickBooks preferences, a nonposting account named Estimates is added to your chart of accounts. The amount of the estimate is recorded in this account, but nothing shows up on your Profit & Loss statement because the estimate isn't a sale and doesn't affect your bottom line.

To create an estimate, choose Customers | Create Estimates from the menu bar. As you can see in Figure 9-4, the Create Estimates transaction window looks very much like an invoice. Fill out the fields in the same manner you use for invoices.

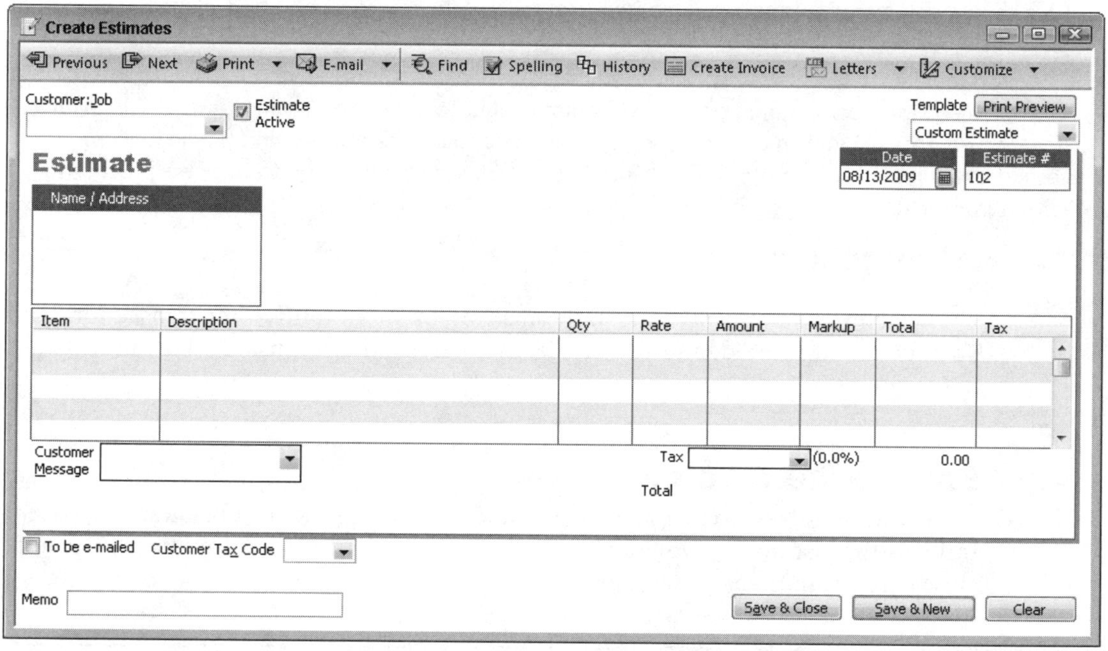

FIGURE 9-4 Estimates provide a way to bid for, and then track, a job.

Some estimate templates permit you to invoice customers with a markup over cost (such as the built-in Custom Estimate template). This is often the approach used for time and materials on bids. Just enter the cost and indicate the markup in dollars or percentage. Incidentally, if you decide to change the total of the item, QuickBooks will change the markup to make sure the math is correct.

If the item you use has been configured for both a cost and price, the estimate uses the cost. If the item you use is only configured for a price, the estimate uses the price as the cost.

The Cost and Markup fields are only displayed on the screen version of the estimate—those columns don't appear on the printed version.

Creating Multiple Estimates for a Job

You can create multiple estimates for a customer or a job, which is an extremely handy feature. You can create an estimate for each phase of the job or create multiple estimates with different prices. Of course, that means each estimate has different contents.

When you create multiple estimates for the same job, the Estimate Active option is checked by default. If a customer rejects any estimates, you can either delete them or deselect the Estimate Active option (effectively closing the estimate).

Duplicating Estimates

You can duplicate an estimate, which provides a quick way to create multiple estimates with slightly different contents. Choose Edit | Duplicate Estimate while the estimate is displayed in your QuickBooks window (or right-click in the estimate header or footer and choose Duplicate Estimate from the shortcut menu). The Estimate # field changes to the next number, while everything else remains the same. Make the required changes, and then click Save & Close.

Memorizing Estimates

If you frequently present the same estimated items to multiple customers, you can use the Memorize Estimate feature to create boilerplate estimates for future use. Memorized estimates do not contain the customer name (QuickBooks removes the name when memorizing the document).

Create an estimate, filling in the items that belong on this type of estimate. Don't fill in amounts that usually change (such as quantities, or even prices). Then press CTRL-M to memorize the estimate. Use the following guidelines to fill out the Memorize Transaction dialog:

- Give the estimate a name that reminds you of its contents.
- Select the option Don't Remind Me.
- Click OK.

To use this boilerplate estimate, press CTRL-T to open the Memorized Transaction list. Double-click the estimate, fill in the Customer:Job information and any pricing information that's not automatically included, and then save it. The memorized estimate isn't changed, only the new estimate is saved.

Creating Progress Billing Invoices

If you've enabled estimates and progress billing in the Jobs & Estimates category of the Preferences dialog (reached by choosing Edit | Preferences), you can use the Progress invoice template to invoice your customers as each invoicing plateau arrives.

Choosing the Estimated Job

Progress invoices are invoices that are connected to estimates. Open the Create Invoices window, select Progress Invoice from the Template drop-down list, and choose the customer or job for which you're creating the Progress invoice. Because you've enabled estimates in your QuickBooks preferences, the system always checks the customer record to see if you've recorded any estimates for this job, and if so, presents them.

Select the estimate you're invoicing against and click OK. QuickBooks then asks you to specify what to include on the invoice:

Fill out the dialog, using the following guidelines:

- You can bill for the whole job, 100 percent of the estimate. When the line items appear, you can edit individual items.
- You can create an invoice for a specific percentage of the estimate. The percentage usually depends upon the agreement you have with your customer. For example, you could have an agreement that you'll invoice the job in a certain number of equal installments, or you could invoice a percentage that's equal to the percentage of the work that's been finished.
- You can create an invoice that covers only certain items on the estimate, or you can create an invoice that has a different percentage for each item on the estimate. This is the approach to use if you're billing for completed work on a job that has a number of distinct tasks. Some of the work listed on the estimate may be finished, other work not started, and the various items listed on the estimate may be at different points of completion.

TIP: You can use a percentage figure larger than 100 to cover overruns (make sure your customer has agreed to permit that option).

After you've created the first progress billing invoice for an estimate, a new option is available for subsequent invoices. That option is to bill for all remaining amounts in the estimate (it replaces the (100%) option). This is generally reserved for your last invoice, and it saves you the trouble of figuring out which percentages of which items have been invoiced previously.

As far as QuickBooks is concerned, the items and prices in the estimate are not etched in stone; you can change any amounts or quantities you wish while you're creating the invoice. Your customer, however, may not be quite so lenient, and your ability to invoice for amounts that differ from the estimate depends on your agreement with the customer.

Entering Progress Invoice Line Items

After you choose your progress billing method and click OK, QuickBooks automatically fills in the line item section of the invoice based on the approach you selected. For example, in Figure 9-5, I opted to create a progress bill for 50 percent of the estimate (because half the work was done).

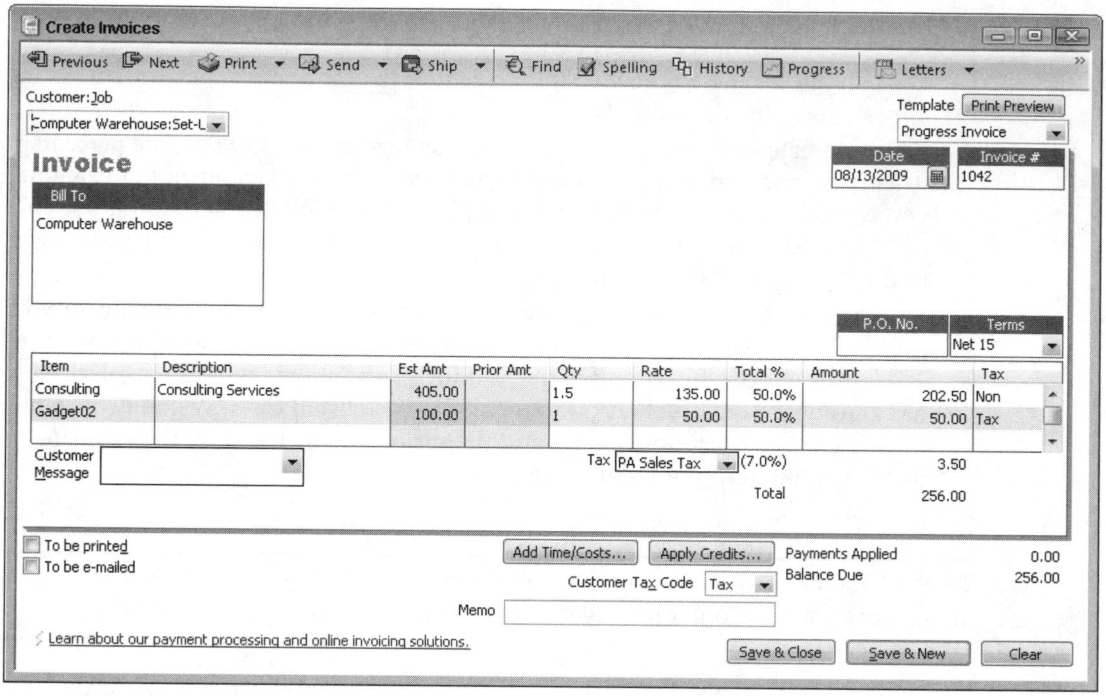

FIGURE 9-5 Progress invoices are automatically filled in, using the information in the estimate.

Changing Line Items

If you chose to invoice a percentage of the estimate's total, the amount of every line item on the estimate reflects that percentage. This doesn't work terribly well for those lines that have products (it's hard to sell a percentage of a physical product). You can leave the invoice as is, because the customer will probably understand that this is a progress invoice. Or, you can make changes to the invoice.

In addition to strange or inaccurate line items for products, the line items for services rendered may not be totally accurate. For example, some of the line items may contain service categories that aren't at the same percentage of completion as others.

To change the invoice and keep a history of the changes against the estimate, don't just make changes to the line items on the invoice. Instead, click the Progress icon on the toolbar of the Create Invoices window. This opens a dialog (see Figure 9-6) that allows reconfiguration of the line items. You can change the quantity, rate, or percentage of completion for any individual line item.

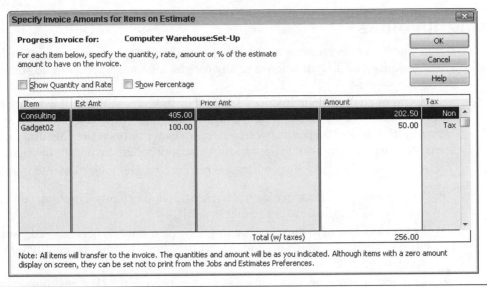

FIGURE 9-6 You can make changes to the data that QuickBooks automatically inserted in the invoice.

If you select Show Quantity And Rate, the columns in the dialog display the columns from the estimate, and you can make changes to any of them. Click the Qty column for any line item to highlight the number that's been used to calculate the invoice. Replace the number with the amount you want to use for the invoice. You can also change the rate, but generally that's not cricket unless there are some circumstances that warrant it (which you and the customer have agreed upon).

If you select Show Percentage, the dialog displays the Curr % column, which shows the percentage of completion for this and previous billings. The percentages compare the dollar amounts for invoices against the estimated total. You can change the percentage for any line item.

Select both options if you need to make changes to one type of progress on one line item and another type of progress on another line item. All the columns (and all the previous billings, if any exist) appear in the window.

Click OK when you have finished making your adjustments. You return to the invoice form, where the amounts on the line items have changed to match the adjustments you made. Click Save & New to save this invoice and move on to the next invoice, or click Save & Close to save this invoice and close the Create Invoices window.

Using this method to change a line item keeps the history of your estimate and invoices intact (as opposed to making changes in the amounts directly on the invoice form, which does not create a good audit trail).

Editing Invoices

If you want to correct an invoice (perhaps you charged the wrong amount or forgot you'd promised a different amount to a particular customer), you can do so quite easily.

You can open the Create Invoices window (or perhaps you're still working there) and click the Previous button to move back through all the invoices in your system. However, if you have a great many invoices, it's faster to open the Customer Center, select the customer or job, and double-click the appropriate invoice in the right pane.

Use the following guidelines when you're editing a previously entered invoice:

- If a previously entered invoice has been paid, don't change anything (unless you want to edit the text in the memo field).
- If a previously entered invoice has not been paid but has been mailed, you shouldn't edit anything, although it's probably safe to enter or modify text in the memo field if necessary.
- If the previously entered invoice has not yet been sent to the customer, you can make any changes you wish.

When you click Save & Close, QuickBooks displays a message dialog asking whether you want to save the changes you made. Click Yes.

Voiding and Deleting Invoices

There's an enormous difference between voiding and deleting an invoice. Voiding an invoice makes the invoice nonexistent to your accounting and customer balances. However, the invoice number continues to exist (it's marked "VOID") so you can account for it—missing invoice numbers are just as frustrating as missing check numbers. To void an invoice, open it and right-click a blank spot in the header or footer section. Choose Void Invoice from the right-click menu and close the Invoice window. When QuickBooks asks if you want to record your change, click Yes.

> **NOTE:** When you void an invoice, QuickBooks marks the status of the invoice as Paid. This means nothing more than the fact that the invoice isn't "open." If you're discussing the status of open and paid invoices with a customer, remember that an invoice marked Paid may not really be paid; it may be a voided transaction.

Deleting an invoice, on the other hand, removes all traces of it from your transaction registers and reports, which is dangerous and breaks all sorts of accounting rules of conduct. However, if you insist, open the invoice, right-click a blank spot in the header or footer section and choose Delete Invoice. QuickBooks asks you to confirm your action.

> **CAUTION:** Never remove an invoice to which a customer payment has been attached. Straightening out that mess is a nightmare.

Understanding the Postings for Invoices

It's important to understand what QuickBooks is doing behind the scenes, because everything you do has an impact on your financial reports. Let's look at the postings for an imaginary invoice that has these line items:

- $500.00 for services rendered
- $30.00 for sales tax

Because QuickBooks is a full, double-entry bookkeeping program, there is a balanced posting made to the general ledger. For this invoice, the following postings are made to the general ledger:

Account	Debit	Credit
Accounts Receivable	530.00	
Sales Tax		30.00
Income—Services		500.00

If the invoice includes inventory items, the postings are a bit more complicated. Let's post an invoice that sold ten widgets to a customer. The widgets have an average cost of $50.00 each and you sold them for $100.00 each. This customer was shipped ten widgets and was also charged tax and shipping.

Account	Debit	Credit
Accounts Receivable	1077.00	
Income—Sales of Items		1000.00
Sales Tax		70.00
Shipping		7.00
Cost of Sales	500.00	
Inventory		500.00

There are two theories on posting shipping:

- Separate your own shipping costs (an expense) from the shipping you collect from your customers (revenue).
- Post everything to the shipping expense.

To use the first method, create an income account for shipping and link that account to the shipping item you created.

If you use the latter method, don't be surprised at the end of the year if you find your shipping expense is reported as a negative number, meaning that you collected more than you spent for shipping. You won't have a shipping expense to deduct from your revenue at tax time, but who cares—you made money.

Issuing Credits and Refunds

Sometimes you have to give money to a customer. You can do this in the form of a credit against current or future balances, or you can write a check and refund money you received from the customer. Neither is a lot of fun, but it's a fact of business life.

Creating Credit Memos

A credit memo reduces a customer balance. This is necessary if a customer returns goods, has been billed for goods that were lost or damaged in shipment, or wins an argument about the price of a service you provided.

Creating a credit memo is similar to creating an invoice. The credit memo itself is usually printed and sent to the customer, to let the customer know the details about the credit that's being applied.

The totals are posted to your accounting records just as the invoice totals are posted, except there's an inherent minus sign next to the number. (Information about applying the credit memo against the customer's account when you're entering customer payments is in Chapter 10.)

To create a credit memo choose Customers | Create Credit Memos/Refunds from the menu bar to open a blank Create Credit Memos/Refunds window (see Figure 9-7).

Select the appropriate customer or job, and then fill out the rest of the heading. Move to the line item section and enter the item, the quantity, and the rate for the items in this credit memo. Do *not* use a minus sign—QuickBooks knows what a credit is.

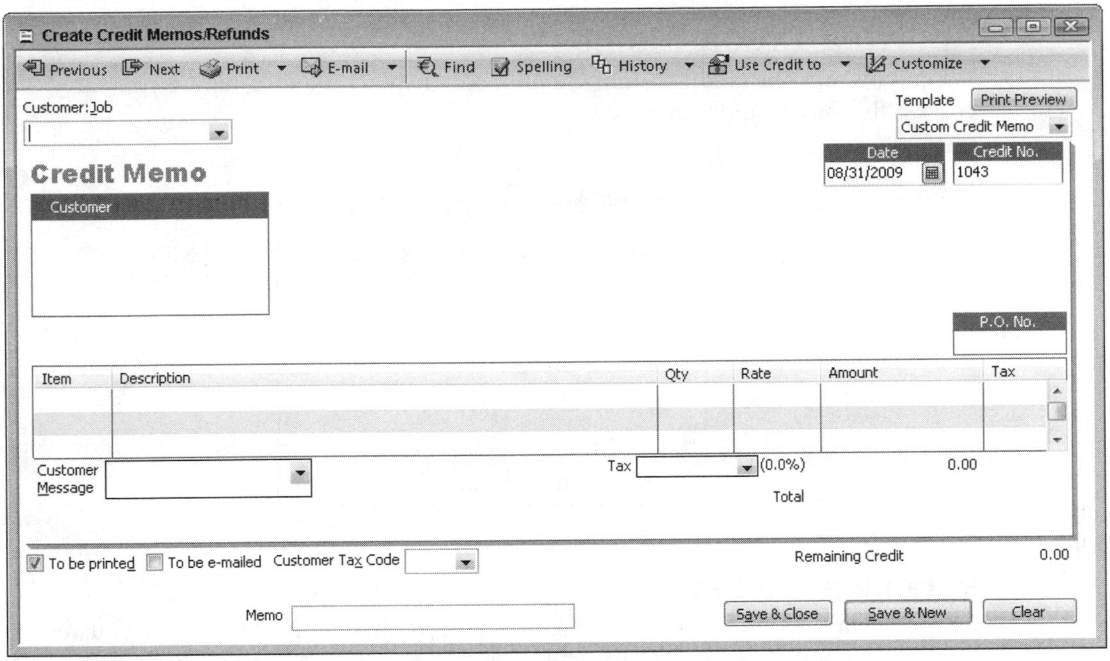

FIGURE 9-7 The Custom Credit Memo template has all the fields needed to provide information to the customer about the credit.

TIP: Remember to insert all the special items you need to give credit for, such as shipping or handling costs you previously invoiced.

Click Save & Close to save the credit memo (unless you have more credit memos to create—in which case, click Save & New). When you save the credit memo, QuickBooks asks you to specify the way you want to apply the credit amount. See the next section, "Applying Credit Memos."

NOTE: By default, the credit memo number is the next available invoice number. If you change the number because you want a different numbering system for credit memos, you'll have to keep track of numbers manually. QuickBooks will use the next number (the one after this credit memo) for your next invoice. Therefore, it's easier to use the default procedure of having one set of continuous numbers for invoices and credit memos.

Applying Credit Memos

When you save the credit memo, QuickBooks displays a dialog where you can choose the way to apply this credit.

Retaining the Credit

Choose Retain As An Available Credit to let the credit amount stay with the customer. You can apply the credit to a future invoice, or apply it to a current open invoice later if the customer sends a payment that deducts the credit. When you create new invoices, or apply customer payments to existing invoices, the credit is available.

 TIP: The jargon for a credit that is not yet applied to an invoice is *floating credit.*

If the credit is for a job, and the job doesn't have any outstanding invoices, you should retain the credit, because you can apply it against a different job for the same customer.

Giving a Refund for the Credit

Choose Give A Refund to give money back to the customer. When you click OK, the Issue A Refund window opens (see Figure 9-8). Use the following guidelines to configure the Issue A Refund window:

- In the Issue This Refund Via field, select the method for the refund from the drop-down list (cash, check, or credit card).
- If you choose Cash, QuickBooks assumes you're taking the money out of a cash register and deducts the amount from the bank account you set up for the cash register. (Be sure to select the appropriate bank account in the Account field.)

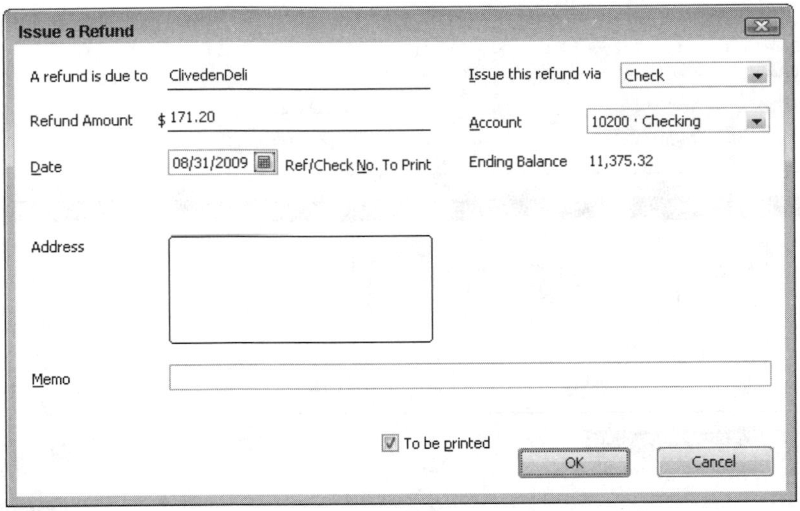

FIGURE 9-8 Tell QuickBooks how to manage the refund you want to send to the customer.

- If you choose Check, the dialog adds an option labeled To Be Printed, which is selected by default.
- If you print checks, leave the check mark in the check box, and click OK. The check is added to the list of checks to be printed when you choose File | Print Forms | Checks. (The check also appears in the bank account register with the notation "To Print.")
- If you write checks manually, deselect the check mark in the To Be Printed check box, and click OK. The check is added to your bank account register, using the next available check number. Don't forget to create and send the check.
- If you choose Credit Card, follow the usual procedure for creating a credit card transaction.

Applying the Credit to an Invoice

Choose Apply To An Invoice to apply the credit to a current invoice. When you click OK, QuickBooks displays a list of open invoices for this customer (or this job, if the credit is for a job) and automatically applies the credit against the oldest invoice (see Figure 9-9).

If the credit is larger than the oldest invoice, QuickBooks applies the remaining amount of the credit to the next oldest invoice. If there are no additional invoices, the remaining amount of the credit is held in the customer's record and is treated as a retained credit. Click Done to save the transaction.

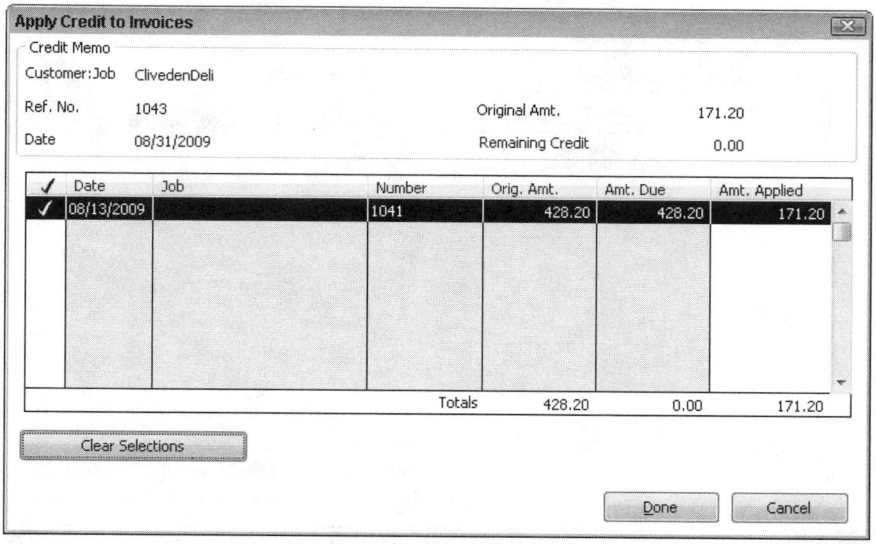

FIGURE 9-9 Select the invoice against which you want to apply the credit.

Printing Packing Slips

QuickBooks provides a template for a packing slip, which is basically an invoice that doesn't display prices. The theory behind packing slips is that for the warehouse personnel who manage and pack products, or unpack them at the customer's site, the cost of those products falls under the category "none of your business."

Printing the Default Packing Slip

To print the default packing slip, complete the invoice. Then click the arrow next to the Print icon at the top of the Create Invoices window, and select Print Packing Slip from the drop-down list. The Print Packing Slip dialog opens so you can select your printing options (see Figure 9-10).

Changing the Default Packing Slip

If you create your own, customized, packing slip template, you can select it each time you print a packing slip, or you can make that new form the default packing slip by choosing Edit | Preferences to open the Preferences dialog.

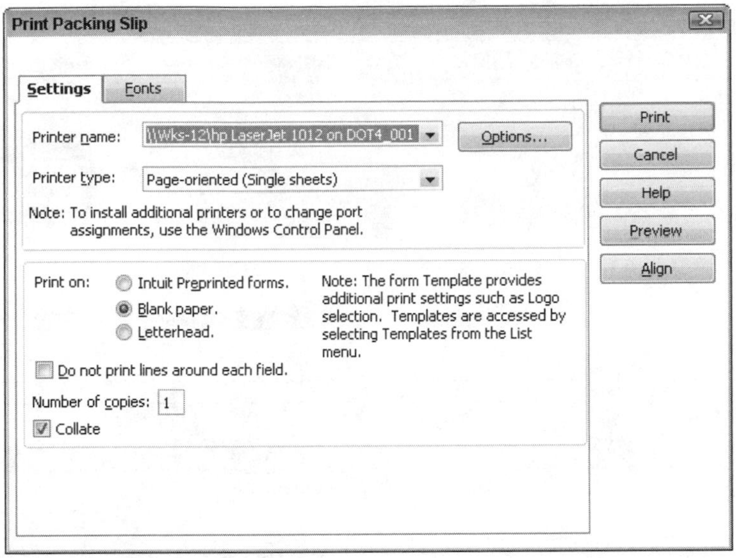

Print Packing Slip

| Settings | Fonts |

Printer name: \\Wks-12\hp LaserJet 1012 on DOT4_001 ▾   Options...

Printer type: Page-oriented (Single sheets) ▾

Note: To install additional printers or to change port assignments, use the Windows Control Panel.

Print on: ◯ Intuit Preprinted forms.
◉ Blank paper.
◯ Letterhead.

☐ Do not print lines around each field.

Number of copies: 1
☑ Collate

Note: The form Template provides additional print settings such as Logo selection. Templates are accessed by selecting Templates from the List menu.

Print | Cancel | Help | Preview | Align

FIGURE 9-10 Select the appropriate options for printing the packing slip.

Go to the Sales & Customers category and click the Company Preferences tab. In the Choose Template For Invoice Packing Slip field, select your new packing slip form from the drop-down list, and click OK.

If you have multiple packing slips, you can choose any of them for printing. With the completed invoice in the Create Invoices window, instead of selecting Print Packing Slip from the Print button's drop-down list, select a packing slip template from the drop-down list in the Template field. The Create Invoices window changes to display the packing slip, as shown in Figure 9-11.

I know I just told you that a packing slip doesn't display any amounts, and there they are! Well, no they're not. Confused? Don't be—the packing slip in Figure 9-11 is the Intuit Packing Slip, which has one set of configuration options for the screen and another set of configuration options for the printed version. This is true for any packing slip template you create as a customized template, and it's a handy feature, as you'll learn when you read the section on customizing templates in Chapter 28.

To see what the printed version of the packing slip looks like, click the arrow next to the Print icon on the Create Invoices window toolbar, and choose Preview. Satisfied? Close the Preview window and return to the Create Invoices window. Now you can print the packing slip.

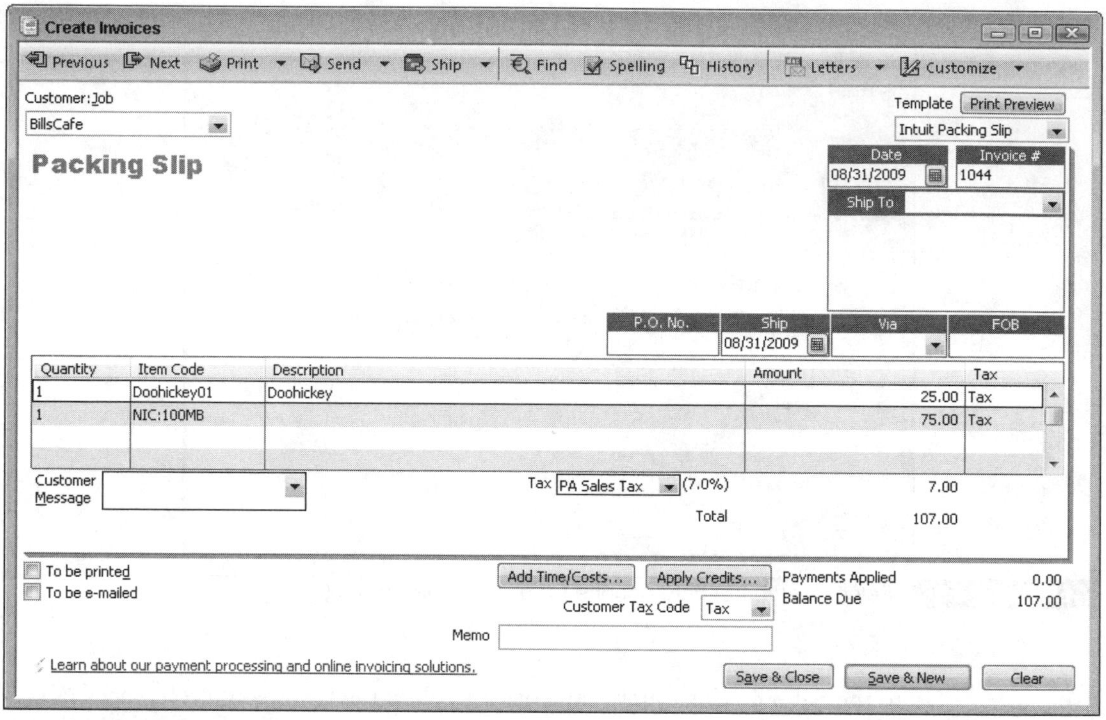

FIGURE 9-11 View a packing slip before you print it.

Using Memorized Invoices

If you have a recurring invoice (common if you have a retainer agreement with a customer or you collect rent from tenants), you can automate the process of creating it. Recurring invoices are those that are sent out at regular intervals, usually for the same amount.

Create the first invoice, filling out all the fields. If there are any fields that will change each time you send the invoice, leave those fields blank and fill them out each time you send the invoice. Then press CTRL-M to open the Memorize Transaction dialog.

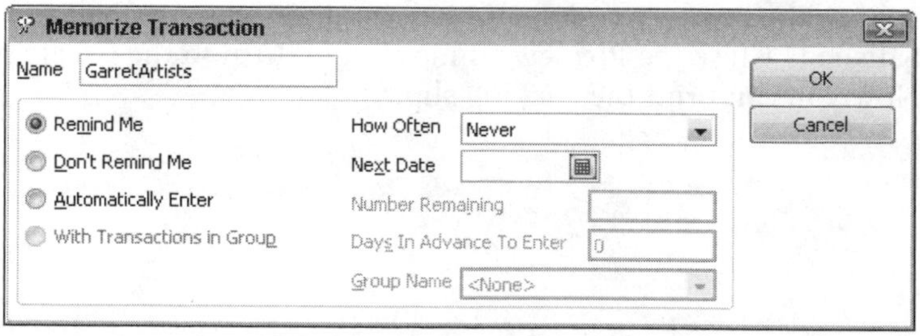

Fill in the fields using the following guidelines:

- Change the title in the Name box to reflect what you've done. It's easiest to add a word or phrase to the default title (which is the customer or job name), such as Retainer. You can use up to 31 characters, including spaces, in the Name box.
- Choose Remind Me and specify how and when you want to be reminded in the How Often and Next Date fields. The reminder will appear in the automatic QuickBooks Reminder window.
- Choose Don't Remind Me if you have a great memory, or if you only use this memorized invoice for special occasions.
- Choose Automatically Enter if you want QuickBooks to issue this invoice automatically. If you opt for automatic issuing of this invoice, you must fill in the fields so that QuickBooks performs the task accurately, as follows:
  - The How Often field is where you specify the interval for this invoice, such as monthly, weekly, or so on. Click the arrow to see the drop-down list and choose the option you need.
  - The Next Date field is the place to note the next instance of this invoice.
  - The Number Remaining field is a place to start a countdown for a specified number of invoices. This is useful if you're billing a customer for a finite number of months because you only have a one-year contract.
  - The Days In Advance To Enter field is for specifying the number of days in advance of the next date you want QuickBooks to create the invoice.

Click OK when you have finished filling out the dialog. Then click Save & Close in the Invoice window to save the transaction. Later, if you want to view, edit, or remove the transaction, you can select it from the Memorized Transaction List, which you open by pressing CTRL-T.

Invoicing Customers for Reimbursable Expenses

When you pay vendors, some purchases may be made on behalf of a customer or they may be purchases needed to complete a job. When you create a vendor bill, or write a check to a vendor, you can specify expenses as reimbursable and link those expenses to a specific customer or job (covered in Chapter 11).

NOTE: QuickBooks calls this feature "Reimbursed Expenses" when you configure it in the Time & Expenses Preferences dialog, and refers to it as "Billable Time and Costs" when you use the feature in a sales transaction. I use both phrases in this chapter; remember, they're interchangeable terms for the same feature.

You can automatically invoice customers for those expenses. In addition, you can link mileage costs and time costs (for employees or subcontractors) to customers and automatically invoice customers for those expenses. (Chapter 16 has information on tracking mileage and time.)

Any amounts you link to a customer are saved in the customer record, and you can collect the money by adding those amounts to the next invoice you create for that customer. In fact, you could create an invoice specifically for the purpose of collecting reimbursable expenses, with no other services or products included on the invoice.

Configuring Reimbursement Settings

In addition to enabling the option to track reimbursable costs when entering transactions for vendors (vendor bills are covered in Chapter 11 and writing checks to vendors is covered in Chapter 12), QuickBooks offers configuration options for the way you invoice customers when you want to recover your reimbursable expenses. To establish your own preference, choose Edit | Preferences and select the Sales & Customers category in the left pane. In the My Preferences tab, select one of the available options:

Prompt For Time/Costs To Add Choosing this option tells QuickBooks to open the Choose Billable Time And Costs dialog, which displays the current reimbursable expenses whenever you create an invoice or sales receipt for a customer with outstanding reimbursable costs. This is the option to select if you always (or almost always) collect reimbursable costs from customers.

Don't Add Any   Selecting this option prevents the automatic display of the Choose Billable Time And Costs dialog. Choose this option if collect reimbursable expenses periodically, on separate invoices. When you're ready to create an invoice for these expenses, click the Add Time/Costs button on the sales transaction form.

Ask What To Do   Select this option to tell QuickBooks to ask you what you want to do whenever you create a sales transaction for a customer with outstanding reimbursable costs. Depending on your selection in that dialog (discussed in the next section), you can add the costs to the sales transaction or omit them.

Creating a Transaction for Reimbursable Expenses

When you're creating a sales transaction (an invoice or a sales receipt) for a customer that has outstanding reimbursable costs, QuickBooks uses the preference you set (as described in the previous section) to determine how to manage those costs.

If you selected the preference Prompt For Time/Costs To Add, when you select the customer, QuickBooks automatically displays the current reimbursable expenses so you can select those you want to include in the current transaction.

If you selected the preference Don't Add Any, the invoice or sales receipt transaction window opens as usual. If you want to check for reimbursable costs for this customer, and then decide whether you want to recover any of them, click the Add Time/Costs button at the bottom of the transaction form (the button is grayed out if no billable expenses have been transferred to the customer or job record). When the Choose Billable Time And Costs dialog opens, you can see if there are any reimbursable expenses you want to collect. If so, follow the instructions presented in the next section, "Adding Reimbursable Costs to the Sales Transaction."

If you selected the preference Ask What To Do, when you select a customer that has unpaid reimbursable costs in the transaction window, QuickBooks displays a dialog asking how you want to handle those amounts. Your response determines whether the Choose Billable Time And Costs dialog opens automatically.

Adding Reimbursable Costs to the Sales Transaction

To collect reimbursable costs from a customer, select those costs from the Choose Billable Time And Costs dialog. Each type of expense is displayed in its own tab, and you must examine each tab to see if any amounts exist. Unfortunately, the amount displayed on each tab doesn't help you head for the appropriate tab—all the amounts are set at $0.00 because those numbers represent the amount you selected to add to the sales transaction, not the amount accumulated in reimbursable expenses. So, start clicking each tab to find reimbursable expenses to transfer to the transaction.

When you find a tab that has contents, click in the leftmost column to place a check mark next to the expense(s) you want to include (see Figure 9-12).

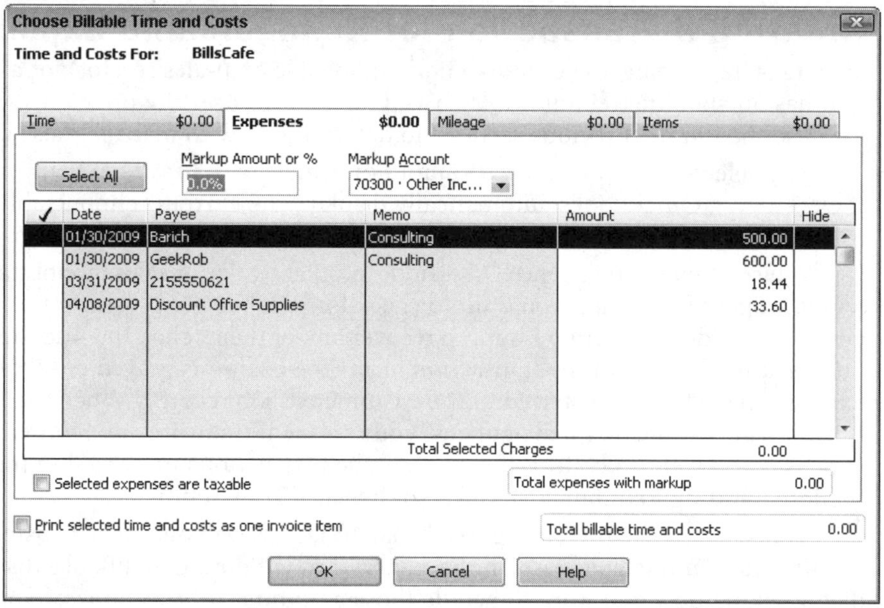

FIGURE 9-12   Select the reimbursable expenses you want to add to the transaction you're preparing.

Click OK to move the item(s) to the transaction window, to join any other items you're entering in that transaction. You may find reimbursable expenses on more than one tab; for example, you may have expenses on the Expenses tab and items on the Items tab. You have to check each tab.

QuickBooks automatically transfers the selected reimbursable costs to the Invoice. The description of reimbursable expenses on the invoice is taken from the text you entered in the Memo column when you entered the vendor's bill. If you didn't use that Memo column, you'll have to enter text manually in the Description column of the invoice (which is a real test of your memory). Otherwise, the customer sees only an amount and no explanation of what it's for. (The description of mileage or item costs is taken from the Description field of the item you configured.)

Adding Taxes to Reimbursable Expenses

If an expense is taxable and the customer is not tax exempt, choose the option Selected Expenses Are Taxable. When the expenses are passed to the invoice, the appropriate taxes are applied. If you select the taxable option and the customer is tax exempt, QuickBooks won't add the sales tax to the invoice.

If some expenses are taxable and others aren't, you have to separate the process of moving items to the invoice. First, deselect each nontaxable expense by clicking its check mark to remove it (it's a toggle). Click OK to put those expenses on the invoice. Then return to the Choose Billable Time And Costs window, put a check mark next to each nontaxable expense, deselect the Selected Expenses Are Taxable option, and click OK.

Omitting the Details on the Invoice

Each of the tabs has the option Print Selected Time And Costs As One Invoice Item. When you click OK and view the results in the invoice, you still see each individual item. Don't panic—you're not losing your mind. The screen version of the invoice continues to display the individual items. However, when you print the invoice, you'll see a single line item with the correct total in the Amount column.

TIP: You can preview the printed invoice by clicking the arrow next to the Print icon on the invoice window and choosing Preview.

QuickBooks changes the format of the printed invoice to eliminate the details but doesn't change the data in the onscreen version of the invoice. This means you can open the invoice later and see the detailed items, which is handy when the customer calls to ask, "What's this reimbursable expenses item on my bill?"

Excluding a Reimbursable Expense

If you have some reason to exclude one or more expenses from the current invoice, just avoid putting a check mark in the column. The item remains in the system and shows up on the Choose Billable Time And Costs window the next time you open it. You can add the item to the customer's invoice in the future.

Removing a Reimbursable Expense from the List

Suppose when it's time to invoice the customer, you decide that you don't want to ask the customer to pay an expense you marked as reimbursable; you've changed your mind. The Choose Billable Time And Costs window has no Delete button and no method of selecting an item and choosing a delete function. You could deselect the check mark that tells QuickBooks to move the item to the sales transaction, but afterwards, every time you open the window, the item is still there—it's like a haunting.

The solution lies in the Hide column. If you place a check mark in the Hide column, the item is effectively deleted from the list of reimbursable expenses that you see when you're preparing invoices (but the amount is still in your system). This means you won't accidentally invoice the customer for the item, but the link to this expense for this customer continues to appear in reports about this customer's activity (which is helpful for job costing). In effect, by selecting the Hide option, you've marked the expense as "nonbillable," and it's not available in the future.

Changing the Amount of a Reimbursable Expense

You're free to change the amount of a reimbursable expense. To accomplish this, select (highlight) the amount in the Amount column of the Billable Time And Costs window on the Expenses tab, and enter the new figure.

If you reduce the amount, QuickBooks does not keep the remaining amount on the Billable Time And Costs window. You won't see it again, because QuickBooks makes the assumption you're not planning to pass the remaining amount to your customer in the future.

You may want to increase the charge for some reason (perhaps to cover overhead), but if you're increasing all the charges, it's easier to apply a markup (covered next) than to change each individual item.

Marking Up Reimbursable Expenses

You can mark up any expenses you're invoicing, which many companies do to cover any additional costs incurred such as handling, time, or general aggravation. To apply a markup, select the items you want to mark up by placing a check mark in the Use column in the Expenses tab of the Choose Billable Time And Costs window. Then enter a markup in the Markup Amount Or % field in either of the following ways:

- Enter an amount.
- Enter a percentage (a number followed by the percent sign).

Specify the account to which you're posting markups. You can create an account specifically for markups (which is what I do because I'm slightly obsessive about analyzing the source of all income) or use an existing income account.

When you click OK to transfer the reimbursable expenses to the customer's invoice, you'll see the reimbursable expenses and the markup as separate items.

Although it would be unusual for you to be marking up items without having discussed this with your customer, if you don't want your customer to see the markup amounts, select the Print Selected Time And Costs As One Invoice Item option. You'll see the breakdown on the screen version of the invoice, but the printed invoice will contain only the grand total.

One big difference between using the markup function and just changing the amount of the reimbursable expense in the Amount column is the way the amounts are posted to your general ledger. If you use the markup function, the difference between the actual expense and the charge to your customer is posted to the markup account. If you change the amount of the expense, the entire amount is posted to the income account you linked to the reimbursable expense account.

C A U T I O N : If you void or delete a saved sales transaction that contains reimbursable expenses, the expenses are not put back into the "to be collected from customer" category. They're gone and cannot be used in future invoices for this customer.

Receiving and Tracking Customer Payments

I n this chapter:

- Apply customer payments

- Apply credits and discounts to invoices

- Handle cash sales

- Deposit customer payments into your bank account

- Track receivables

- Impose finance charges

- Send statements to customers

The best accounts receivable task is receiving the payments. However, you need to make sure you apply customer payments correctly so that you and your customers have the same information in your records.

Handling Invoice Payments

As you create invoices and send them to your customers, there's an expectation that money will eventually arrive to pay off those invoices. And, in fact, it almost always works that way. In accounting, there are two ways to apply the monies that pay off invoices:

Balance Forward   This is a system in which you consider the total of all the outstanding invoices as the amount due from the customer, and you apply payments against that total. It doesn't matter which particular invoice is being paid because it's a running total of payments against a running total of invoices.

Open Item   This is a system in which payments you receive are applied to specific invoices. Most of the time, the customer either sends a copy of the invoice along with the check or notes the invoice number that is being paid in the Memo field of the check, or on a check stub, to make sure your records agree with the customer's records.

Setting Default Options for Receiving Customer Payments

QuickBooks assumes you're using a balance forward system, but you can override that default easily. In fact, changing the system so you apply payments directly to specific invoices is just a matter of a mouse click or two, using the following steps:

1. Choose Edit | Preferences and click the Sales & Customers icon in the left pane.
2. Move to the Company Preferences tab.
3. In the Receive Payments section at the bottom of the dialog, select or deselect options to match your needs:
   - Automatically Apply Payments means that when you enter the amount you've received from the customer, QuickBooks will automatically pay off invoices, starting with the oldest.
   - Automatically Calculate Payments tells QuickBooks to let you omit the amount of the customer's payment in the transaction window, and select invoices to pay off. QuickBooks adds up the invoice amounts and applies the total as the customer's payment. (This assumes the customer has sent a payment that matches the total.)
   - Use Undeposited Funds As A Default Deposit To Account automatically posts the payments you receive to the Undeposited Funds account, and you deposit the funds into a bank account.

Recording Invoice Payments

When a check arrives from a customer, choose Customers | Receive Payments to open a blank Receive Payments window, as shown in Figure 10-1. If you have multiple A/R accounts, a field exists at the top of the window so you can select the A/R account to which this customer's invoices were posted.

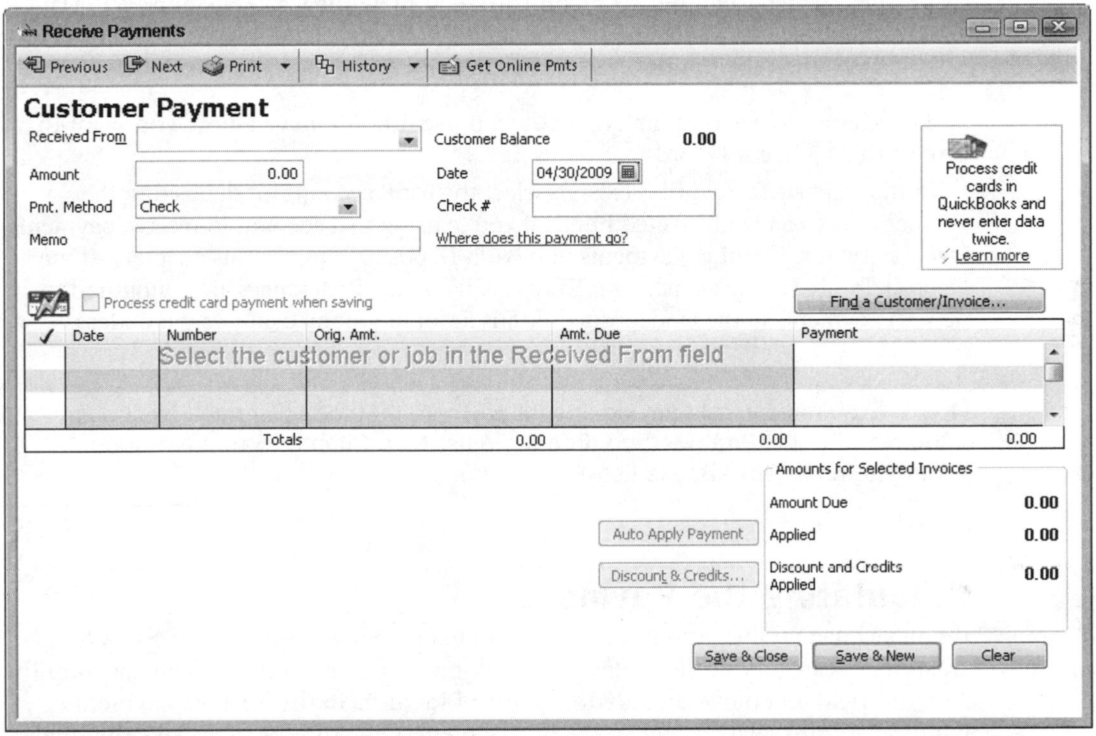

FIGURE 10-1   The Customer Payment form has all the fields needed to apply payments accurately.

Click the arrow to the right of the Received From field and select the customer or job from the drop-down list using the following guidelines:

• If the payment is from a customer for whom you're not tracking jobs (or for an invoice that wasn't related to a job), select the customer. The current balance for this customer automatically appears in the Customer Balance field.

• If the payment is for a job, select the job. The current balance for this job automatically appears in the Customer Balance field.

• If the payment covers multiple jobs, select the customer to see all invoices for all jobs. The current balance for this customer automatically appears in the Customer Balance field.

In the Amount field, enter the amount of this payment. (You can omit this step and let QuickBooks calculate the amount of the payment—see the section "Calculating the Payment").

Click the arrow to the right of the Pmt. Method field and select the payment method:

- If the payment method is a check, enter the check number in the Check # field that appears.
- If the payment method is a credit card, complete the Card No. and Exp. Date fields. (If you have a merchant account with the QuickBooks Merchant Account Service, click the option Process Credit Card Payment When Saving.)

The Memo field is optional, and you can use it if you have a note you want to link to this payment record.

In the Deposit To field (if it exists), select the bank account for depositing the payment, or select Undeposited Funds if you're using that account to receive payments (see the section "Turning Payments into Bank Deposits," later in this chapter). If the Deposit To field doesn't exist, your Sales & Customers Preferences are configured to deposit payments to the Undeposited Funds account automatically (a good idea).

NOTE: You can add any additional payment methods you need by choosing <Add New> in the Pmt. Method drop-down list (see Chapter 5 to learn about adding items to QuickBooks lists).

Calculating the Payment

If you've enabled the Automatically Calculate Payments option in the Sales & Customers category of the Preferences dialog (the default setting), you can skip the Amount field and move directly to the list of invoices in the Receive Payments window. As you select each invoice for payment, QuickBooks calculates the total and places it in the Amount field. (For some reason, if you selected the option to calculate payments, when you click the first invoice listing, QuickBooks opens a dialog asking you if want to continue to use this option.)

If you haven't enabled the option to calculate payments automatically, and you select an invoice listing without entering the amount of the payment first, QuickBooks issues an error message, telling you that the amount of the payment you're applying is higher than the amount you entered in the header section (the amount you received from the customer). In that case, enter the amount of the payment in the Amount field at the top of window.

Applying Payments to Invoices

By default, QuickBooks automatically applies the payment to the oldest invoice(s), as seen in Figure 10-2, unless the amount of the payment exactly matches the amount of another invoice.

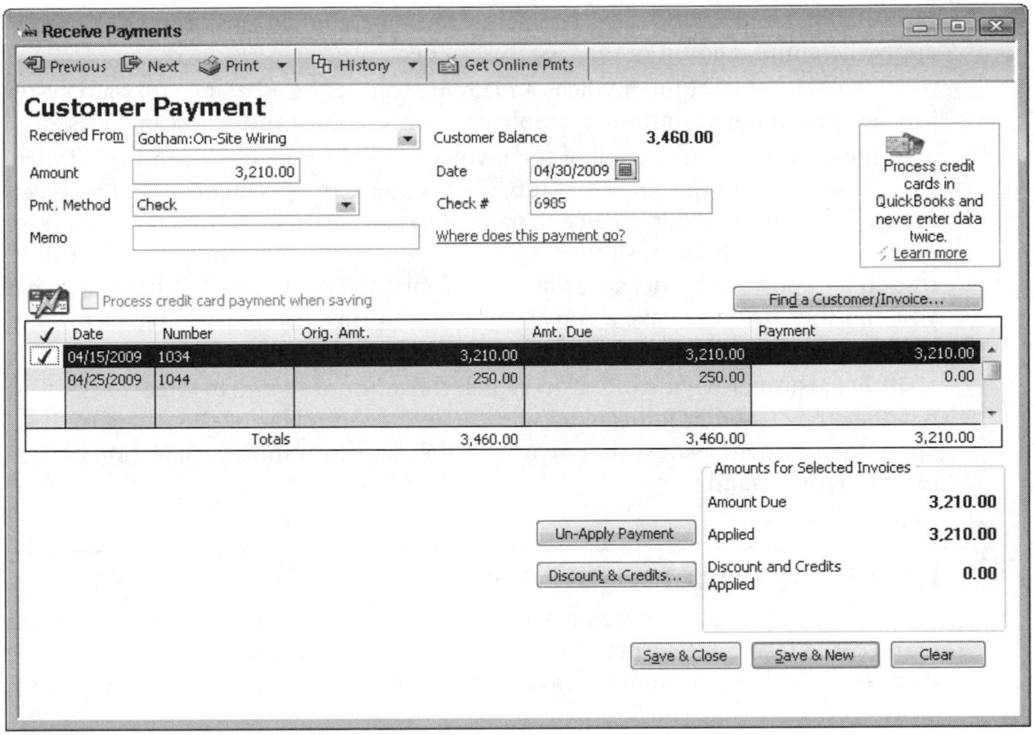

FIGURE 10-2 QuickBooks has applied the payment in a logical manner.

You could face any of several scenarios when receiving customer payments:

- The customer has one unpaid invoice, and the payment is for the same amount as that invoice.
- The customer has several unpaid invoices, and the payment is for the amount of one of those invoices.
- The customer has several unpaid invoices, and the payment equals the total of multiple invoices.
- The customer has one or more unpaid invoices, and the payment is for an amount lower than any single invoice.
- The customer has several unpaid invoices, and the payment is for an amount greater than any one invoice but not large enough to cover two invoices.
- The customer has one or more unpaid invoices, and the payment is for a lesser amount than the current balance. However, the customer has a credit equal to the difference between the payment and the customer balance.

You have a variety of choices for handling any of these scenarios, but for situations in which the customer's intention isn't clear, the smart thing to do is call the customer and ask how the payment should be applied. You must, of course, apply the entire amount of the customer's check.

If you are not tracking invoices and are instead using a balance forward system, just let QuickBooks continue to apply payments against the oldest invoices.

If the customer sent a copy of the invoice with the payment or indicated the invoice number on the check or stub, always apply the payment to that invoice, even if it means an older invoice remains unpaid. Customers sometimes do this deliberately, usually because there's a problem with the older invoice. The rule of thumb is "apply payments according to the customers' wishes." Otherwise, when you and the customer have a conversation about the current open balance, your bookkeeping records won't match.

If the customer payment doesn't match the amount of any invoice, check to see whether the customer indicated a specific invoice number for the payment. If so, apply the payment against that invoice; if not, let the automatic selection of the oldest invoice stand.

Handling Underpayments

After you apply the customer's payment, if it isn't sufficient to pay off an existing invoice, the lower left corner of the Receive Payments window displays a message that asks whether you want to leave the underpaid amount as an underpayment, or write it off.

If you want to ask the customer about the reason for the underpayment, click the button labeled View Customer Contact Information. The customer record opens, and you can call your contact at the customer's place of business (assuming you entered the name and telephone number of a contact when you created the customer).

If you opt to retain the underpayment, the invoice you selected for payment remains as a receivable, with a new balance (the original balance less the payment you applied). When you click Save & Close (or Save & New if you're entering more customer payments), QuickBooks makes the appropriate postings.

If you select the option to write off the underpayment, when you click Save & Close or Save & New, QuickBooks opens the Write Off Amount dialog so you can choose the posting account, and, if applicable, apply a class to the transaction.

Discuss the account to use for a write off with your accountant. You can create an Income or Expense account for this purpose, depending on the way your accountant wants to track receivables you've decided to forgive.

Do not use this feature as a "bad debt" solution, because writing off bad debts for tax purposes is a more complicated function than merely deciding, "Oh, what the heck, I'll let this slide."

Applying Credits to Invoices

You can apply any existing credits to an open invoice, in addition to applying the payment that arrived. If credits exist, customers usually let you know how they want credits applied, and it's not unusual to find a note written on the copy of the invoice that the customer sent along with the check (a check that probably represents the net due when the credit is applied).

When credits exist for the customer or job you select in the Receive Payments transaction window, QuickBooks displays a note to that effect in the window (see Figure 10-3).

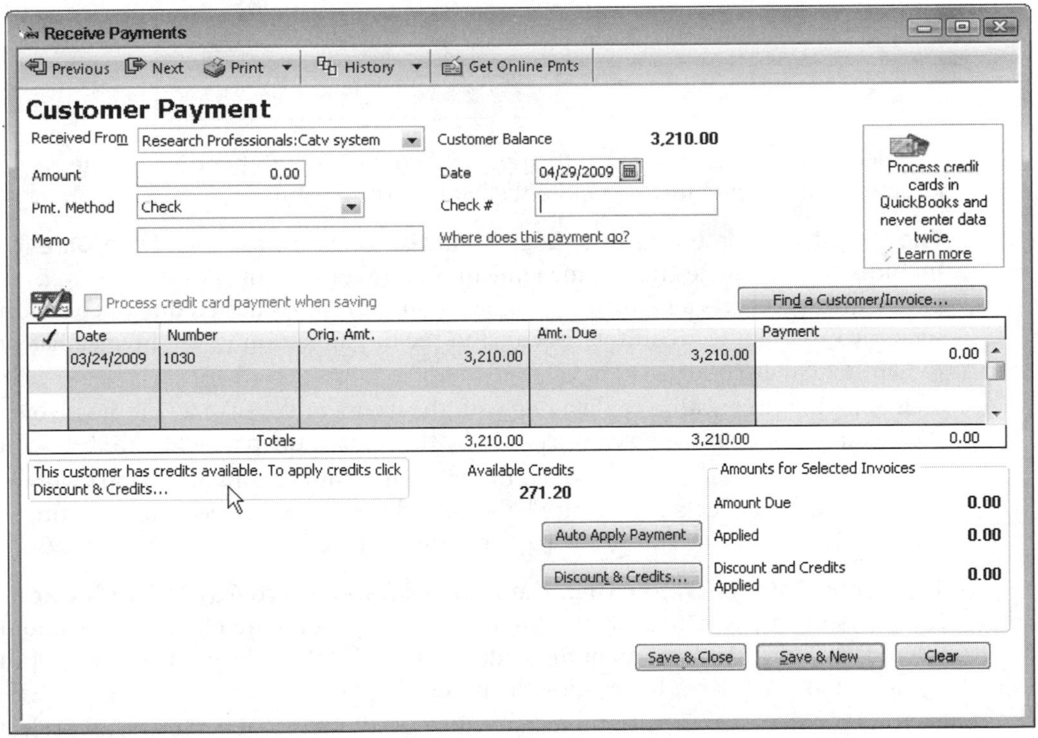

FIGURE 10-3 This customer has a credit balance that can be applied to the invoice along with the payment the customer sent.

To apply a credit balance to an invoice, click the Discounts & Credits button on the Receive Payments window, which opens the Discount And Credits dialog.

Select the credit(s) you want to apply and click Done. Depending on the circumstances, here's how QuickBooks handles the credits:

The Credit Total Is Equal to or Less Than the Unpaid Amount of the Oldest Invoice

This reduces the balance due on that invoice. If the customer sent a payment that reflects a deduction for the amount of his or her credits (a common scenario) so that the credit total is equal to the unpaid amount, the invoice has no remaining balance.

If applying the existing credit along with the payment doesn't pay off the invoice, the balance due on the invoice is reduced by the total of the payment and the credit.

The amount of the credit is added to the postings for the invoice. Don't worry—this change only affects the invoice balance and the accounts receivable posting; it doesn't change the amount of the payment that's posted to your bank account.

The Credit Total Is Larger Than the Amount Required to Pay Off an Invoice

If the customer payment is smaller than the amount of the invoice, but the amount of credit is larger than the amount needed to pay off the invoice, the balance of the credit remains available for posting to another invoice.

To apply the unapplied credit balance to another invoice, click Done and select the next invoice in the Receive Payments window. Then click the Discounts & Credits button and apply the credit balance (or as much of it as you need) against the invoice. Any unused credits remain for the future.

You should send a statement to the customer to reflect the current, new invoice balances as a result of applying the payments and the credits to make sure your records and your customer's records match.

Applying Credits to a Different Job

You may have a situation in which a customer has already paid the invoices for a job when the credit is created, or has paid for part of the job, exceeding the amount of the credit. If the customer tells you to apply the credit balance to another job or to float the credit and apply it against the next job, open the credit transaction and change the job. Then apply the credit to an invoice for the job you specified, or tell QuickBooks to retain it as an available credit that you'll apply when payment arrives.

Applying Discounts for Timely Payments

If you offer your customers terms that include a discount if they pay their bills promptly (for instance, 2%10 Net30), you must apply the discount to the payment if it's applicable.

Figure 10-4 shows the Receive Payments window for a customer who has an invoice that is eligible for a discount for timely payment. QuickBooks has displayed

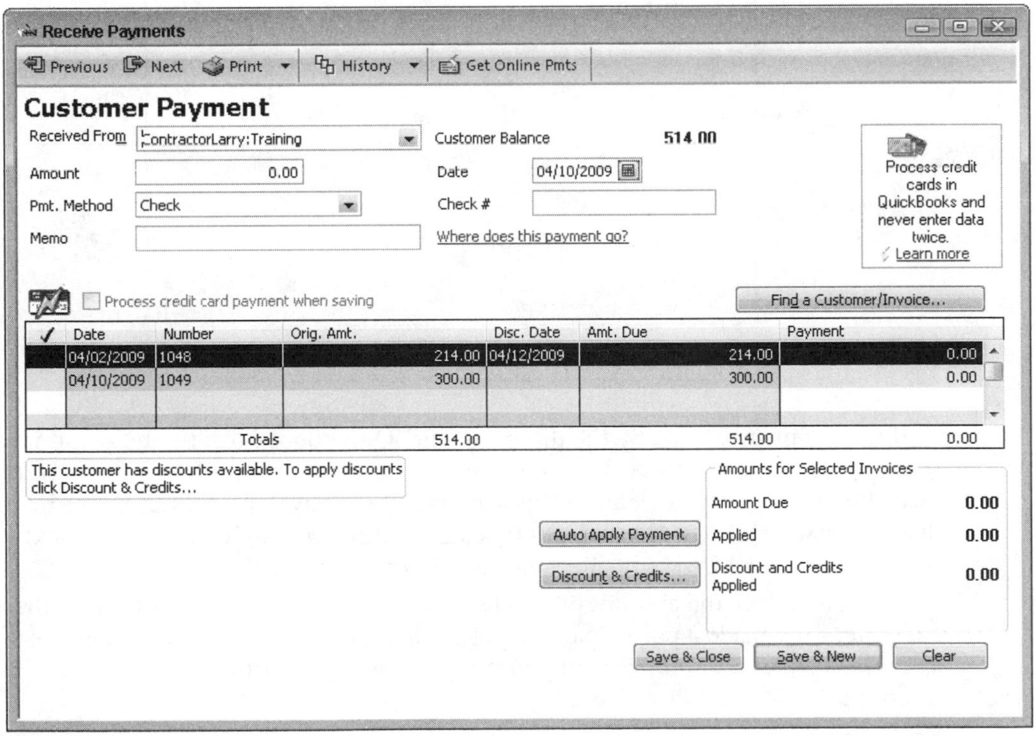

FIGURE 10-4 A discount date appears for invoices that have terms offering discounts.

a message that discounts are available. However, if there are multiple invoices listed in the transaction window, the only clue you have to recognize an invoice with such a discount is the fact that the Disc. Date column shows the date by which the invoice must be paid to receive the discount. For invoices without discount terms, that column is blank in the Receive Payments window.

QuickBooks doesn't apply the discount automatically, for instance by offering a column with the discount amount and selecting that amount as part of the payment. Instead, you must select the invoice (unless QuickBooks automatically selected it in order to apply the payment) and click the Discount & Credits button to see the Discount And Credits dialog connected to this invoice.

If the payment arrived by the discount date, QuickBooks inserts the amount of the discount to use. Accept the amount of discount and enter a Discount Account (see "Posting Discounts" later in this section). If the payment did not arrive by the discount date, QuickBooks displays 0.00 as the discount amount—see the next section, "Applying Discounts for Untimely Payments," for the solution.

You can change the amount of the discount, which you may want to do if the customer only made a partial payment (less than is required to pay off the invoice after the discount is applied) and you want to give a proportionately smaller discount.

Click Done to return to the Receive Payments window. You'll see that QuickBooks has added a discount column and displayed the discount amount in that column. If the net amount and the customer payment amount are the same, the invoice is now paid off.

Applying Discounts for Untimely Payments

Sometimes customers take the discount even if the payment arrives after the discount date. (It's probably more accurate to say that customers *always* take the discount even if the payment arrives later than the terms permit.) You can apply the payment to the invoice and leave a balance due for the discount amount that was deducted by the customer, if you wish. However, most companies give the customer the discount even if the payment is late, as part of "good will."

When you click the Discount & Credits button in that case, QuickBooks does not automatically fill in the discount amount—it's too late, and no accounting software is forgiving, generous, or aware of the need to humor customers to preserve good will. Simply enter the amount of the discount manually, select the posting account, and then click Done to apply the discount to the invoice.

Posting Discounts

To track the amount of money you've given away with discounts, you should create a specific account in your chart of accounts. You could post discounts to your standard income account(s), which will be reduced every time you apply a discount. The math is right, but the absence of an audit trail bothers me (and bothers many accountants). It's better to create an Income account (I call mine "Discounts Given").

 C A U T I O N : If there's an account named "Discounts" in the part of your chart of accounts that's devoted to expenses or cost of goods, don't use that account for your customer discounts, because it's there to track the discounts you take with your vendors.

Turning Payments into Bank Deposits

Use the Deposit To field in the Receive Payments window to select an account for depositing the payments. You can select a bank account or select the Undeposited Funds account.

If you don't see the Deposit To field, it means you set your configuration options to post cash automatically to the Undeposited Funds account. (The option is in the Preferences dialog in the Sales & Customers category.)

Using the Undeposited Funds account is almost always the best way to handle income you receive.

Depositing Cash Receipts into the Undeposited Funds Account

When you enable automatic use of the Undeposited Funds account (or manually select that account in the transaction window), each payment you receive is entered into the account named Undeposited Funds (QuickBooks establishes this account automatically). It's an account type of Other Current Asset.

When you finish applying customer payments in QuickBooks, and you're ready to make your bank deposit, you move the money from the Undeposited Funds account into a bank account by choosing Banking | Make Deposits from the menu bar. See the section "Making Bank Deposits" later in this chapter for the rest of the details.

While the Undeposited Funds account shows each individual payment you received, the bank account shows only the total amount of each bank deposit (the payments you selected for transfer to the bank in the Undeposited Funds account). This matches the bank statement that shows up each month, making it easier to reconcile the account.

Depositing Cash Receipts into a Bank Account

Depositing each payment directly to the bank means you don't have to take the extra step involved in moving cash receipts from the Undeposited Funds account into the bank account. However, each payment you receive appears as a separate entry when you reconcile your bank account.

If you receive six payments totaling $10,450.25 and take the checks to the bank that day, your bank statement shows that amount as the deposit. When you reconcile the bank statement, each deposit you made (for each individual payment you received) is listed in your bank register. You'll have to select each payment individually, mark it as cleared, and make sure it matches the day's deposits on the bank statement. (See Chapter 14 for detailed instructions on reconciling bank accounts.)

Printing a Receipt for an Invoice Payment

You can print a receipt for an invoice payment by clicking the Print icon on the transaction window. Most customers don't expect printed receipts for invoice payments, but you may have a customer who requests one.

Understanding Customer Payment Postings

When you receive money in payment for customer invoices, QuickBooks automatically posts all the amounts to your general ledger. Following are the postings if you select the Undeposited Funds account:

Account	Debit	Credit
Undeposited Funds	Total of cash receipts	
Accounts Receivable		Total of cash receipts

When you make the actual deposit, using the Make Deposits window, QuickBooks automatically posts the following transaction:

Account	Debit	Credit
Bank	Total of deposit	
Undeposited Funds or Bank Account		Total of deposit

Here are the postings for a sale to a customer who has terms that permit a 1% discount. Let's assume the sale was for $100.00. The original invoice posted the following amounts:

Account	Debit	Credit
Accounts Receivable	$100.00	
Income		$100.00

Notice that the postings are unconcerned with the discount amount. You don't have to account for the discount until it's used by the customer. In addition, the discount isn't posted against the receivable, so the customer's invoice is paid in full even though the check was not for the full amount.

When the customer's payment arrives, the 1% discount is deducted from the invoice total. When you enter the customer payment, which is in the amount of $99.00, the following postings occur:

Account	Debit	Credit
Undeposited Funds or Bank Account	$99.00	
Accounts Receivable		$100.00
Discounts Given	$1.00	

Handling Cash Sales

A *cash sale* is a sale for which you haven't created an invoice, because the exchange of product and payment occurred simultaneously. Cash sales are the same as invoiced sales insofar as an exchange of money for goods or services occurs. The difference is that there's no period of time during which you have money "on the street" (you have no receivable as a result of the transaction). You can have a cash sale for either a service or a product, although it's far more common to sell products for cash. Most service companies use invoices, and most retail companies deal with cash.

 NOTE: QuickBooks uses the term *sales receipt* instead of *cash sale*. However, the term *cash sale* is the common jargon (a sales receipt is a piece of paper a cash-paying customer receives).

I'm assuming that a cash sale is not your normal method of doing business (you're not running a candy store). If you *are* running a retail store, the cash sale feature in QuickBooks isn't an efficient way to handle your cash flow. You should either have specialized retail software (that even takes care of opening the cash register drawer automatically and also tracks inventory) or use QuickBooks to record your daily totals of bank deposits as a journal entry. You might want to look at the QuickBooks Point of Sale product, which is designed for retailers. More information is available on the QuickBooks website, www.quickbooks.com.

 NOTE: Don't take the word "cash" literally, because a cash sale can involve a check or a credit card.

There are two methods for handling cash sales in QuickBooks:

- Record each cash sale as a discrete record. This is useful for tracking sales of products or services to customers. It provides a way to maintain historical records about those customers in addition to tracking income and inventory.
- Record sales in batches (usually one batch for each business day). This method tracks income and inventory when you have no desire to maintain historical information about each customer that pays cash.

To record a cash sale, choose Customers | Enter Sales Receipts from the menu bar, which opens the Enter Sales Receipts window shown in Figure 10-5.

Entering Cash Sale Data

If you want to track customer information, enter a name in the Customer:Job field or select the name from the drop-down list. If the customer doesn't exist, you can add a new customer by choosing <Add New>.

| FIGURE 10-5 | A Sales Receipt form is like an invoice, a receive payment form, and a printable customer receipt, all rolled into one transaction window. |

TIP: If you track customers who always pay at the time of the sale, and you never send them invoices, you might want to consider creating a customer type for this group ("Cash" seems an appropriate name for the type). You can separate this group for reports or for marketing and advertising campaigns. See Chapter 5 to learn about creating customer types.

If you're not tracking customers, invent a customer for cash sales (I name the customer "Cash Sale," which seems appropriate, if not creative).

Even if you use a generic "cash sale" customer name, you can put the customer's name and address in the Sold To box. After you print and save the transaction, QuickBooks asks if you want to update the information in the customer record of your generic cash customer. Click No to avoid changing the record of the "cash sale" customer. In the future, when you view the transactions for the generic customer, or generate a report that includes the Name field, you can view the name and address of the specific customer for each cash sale.

Every field in the Enter Sales Receipts window works exactly the way it works for invoices and payments—just fill in the information. To save the record, click Save & New to bring up a new blank record, or click Save & Close if you're finished.

Printing a Receipt for a Cash Sale

Some cash customers want a receipt. Click the Print button in the Enter Sales Receipts window to open the Print One Sales Receipt dialog. If you're not printing to a dot-matrix printer with multipart paper and you want a copy of the receipt for your files, be sure to change the specification in the Number Of Copies box to 2.

Customizing the Cash Receipts Template

I think a lot is missing from the default QuickBooks cash receipts template (which is named Custom Sales Receipt). For example, there's no place for a sales rep, which is needed if you're paying commissions on cash sales, or you just want to track the person who made the sale. There's no Ship To address if the customer pays cash and wants delivery, nor is there a Ship Via field.

The solution is to customize the Custom Sales Receipts form. Specific instructions on customizing templates are in Chapter 28, and I won't go over all those steps here; instead, use the guidelines in the following sections to change the Custom Sales Receipt template.

Change the Options in the Header Tab

Depending on your needs, you should consider one or more of the following suggestions for making changes in the Header tab of the Additional Customization dialog box:

- If you wish, change the Default Title. You might prefer the term Cash Receipt, or just Receipt.
- If you ever ship products to cash customers, select the Ship To field for both the Screen and the Print forms.
- If you're tracking salespersons (either for commission or just to know who made the sale), add the Rep field. You can add the field to the screen version and omit it from the print version.
- If you ship products to cash customers, add the Ship Date and Ship Via fields to the screen and print versions.

Change the Options in the Columns Tab

Use the Columns tab to add or remove columns in the line item section of the form. You can also change the order in which the columns appear. (For instance, perhaps you'd rather have Qty in the first column instead of the Item number.)

Handling Batches of Cash Sales

If you sell products or services and receive instant payment on a more frequent basis, you might want to consider batching the transactions. This works only if you don't care about maintaining information about the customers and no customer expects a printed receipt (except for one that may be produced by your cash register).

This technique also works if you have a business in which sales and service personnel return to the office each day with customer payments in hand.

Create a customized template using the steps described in Chapter 28, with the following guidelines:

- Name the form appropriately (for example, "Batch Sales" or "Sales Batch").
- On the Header tab, keep only the Date and Sale Number fields in the header part of the template.
- On the Header tab, deselect all the optional fields.
- On the Footer tab, remove the Message field.

To batch-process cash sales, use the new template with the following procedures:

- Use a customer named "CashSale" or "RetailSale."
- In the line item section, use a new line for each sale, regardless of whether the same customer is purchasing each item, each item is purchased by a different customer, or there's a combination of both events.
- Use the Save & Close button at the end of the day. If you need to close the window during the day (perhaps you'd like to get some other work done in QuickBooks), open the Sales Receipt window and click the Previous button to find your previous record.

Understanding the Cash Sale Postings

Accounting standards treat cash sales in the simplest, most logical manner. If you've sold a service instead of an inventory item for cash (perhaps a service call for a one-time customer you don't want to invoice), the postings are very straightforward:

Account	Debit	Credit
Undeposited Funds or Bank Account	Total cash sales	
Revenue		Total cash sales

If the cash sale involved inventory items, here are the postings:

Account	Debit	Credit
Undeposited Funds or Bank Account	Total cash sales	
Income		Total cash sales
Cost of Sales	Total cost of items sold	
Inventory Asset		Total cost of items sold

Tracking the Till in QuickBooks

Now I'm going to suggest you make it a bit more complicated, but don't panic, because it's not difficult. In the long run, these suggestions will make your bookkeeping chores easier. There's also a chance you'll make your accountant happier.

If you haven't enabled the automatic posting of received funds to the Undeposited Funds account (in the Sales & Customers category of the Preferences dialog), you can choose any bank account you wish. If you use a regular bank account, your sales won't appear in the Payments To Deposit window when you tell QuickBooks you're taking your cash receipts to the bank. (See the section "Making Bank Deposits" later in this chapter.) In fact, your bank account will be incremented by the amount of cash you post to it from cash sales, even though the money isn't really there until you make the trip to the bank. There are two other ways to track receipts from cash sales separate from customer payments; pick the one that appeals to you:

- Opt to post the receipts to the Undeposited Funds account but deposit those funds separately when you work in the QuickBooks Payments To Deposit window.
- Opt to post the receipts to a new bank account called "Undeposited Till" (or something similar) and move the money into your bank account with a journal entry.

The advantage of having a "Till" account is that you can match the contents of the physical till of your cash register to the posting account. Create an account of the type Other Current Asset to represent the cash till, and select it as the account when you use the Enter Sales Receipts window.

If you deal in real cash and have a cash register, you need to fill the till to make change. Cash a check from your operating account and post the amount to the new account (which I call "Undeposited Till"). Then put the cash (small bills and change) into your physical till. This produces the following posting (assuming $100.00 was the amount of the check).

Account	Debit	Credit
Checking		$100.00
Undeposited Till	$100.00	

When it's time to go to the bank, leave the original startup money (in this example, $100.00) in the till, count the rest of the money, and deposit that money into your checking account. When you return from the bank, make the following journal entry:

Account	Debit	Credit
Checking	Amt. of deposit	
Undeposited Till		Amt. of deposit

In a perfect world, after you make the deposit and the journal entry, you can open the register for the Undeposited Till account and see a balance equal to your original startup cash. The world isn't perfect, however, and sometimes the actual amount you were able to deposit doesn't equal the amount collected in the Enter Sales Receipts transaction window. To resolve this, see the section "Handling the Over and Short Problem" later in this chapter.

Incidentally, if you want to raise or lower the amount you leave in the till for change, you don't have to do anything special. Just deposit less or more money, and the remainder (in the register for the Undeposited Till account and also in the physical till) just becomes the new base.

Making Bank Deposits

If you use the Undeposited Funds account, when it's time to go to the bank you have to tell QuickBooks about your bank deposit. Otherwise, when it's time to reconcile your bank account you'll have a nervous breakdown.

Choosing the Payments to Deposit

As you've been filling out the payment and cash sales forms, QuickBooks has been keeping a list in the Undeposited Funds account. That list remains designated as Undeposited Funds until you clear it by depositing them. (If you've been depositing every payment and cash receipt to a specific bank account, this section doesn't apply to you.)

To tell QuickBooks to make a bank deposit, choose Banking | Make Deposits from the menu bar, which brings up the Payments To Deposit window, shown in Figure 10-6.

 N O T E : You may have other deposits to make, perhaps refunds, loan proceeds, capital infusion, or some other type of deposit. Don't worry—you can tell QuickBooks about them in the next transaction window. This window is only displaying the payments you've entered into QuickBooks through customer-based transaction windows.

Notice the following about the Payments To Deposit window:

- The Type column displays information about the payment type for each transaction—PMT for payment of an invoice and RCPT for a cash sale.
- The Payment Method column displays the specific payment method for each transaction, such as cash, check, a specific credit card, and so on.

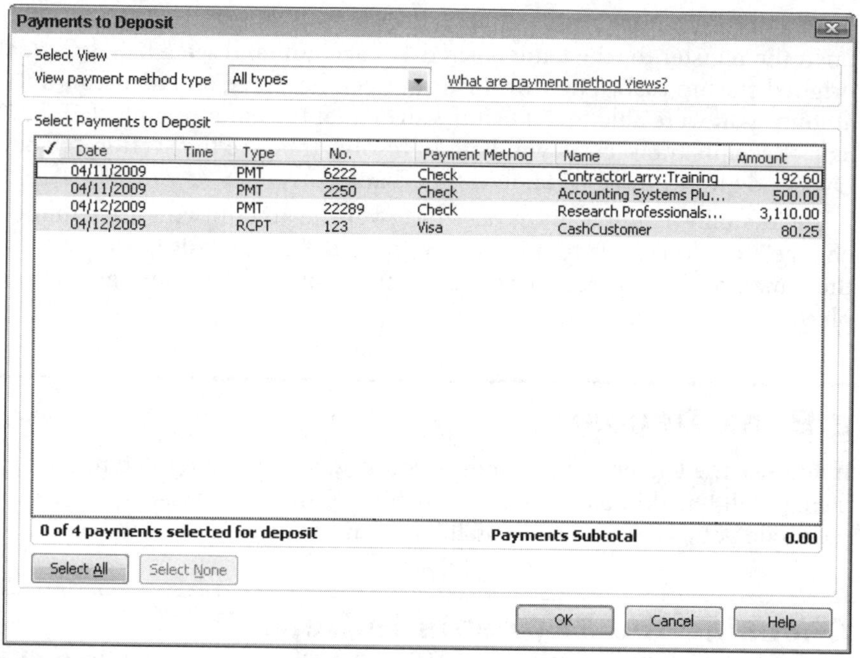
Payments to Deposit
Select View
View payment method type
All types
What are payment method views?
Select Payments to Deposit
✓ Date Time Type No. Payment Method Name Amount
04/11/2009 PMT 6222 Check ContractorLarry:Training 192.60
04/11/2009 PMT 2250 Check Accounting Systems Plu... 500.00
04/12/2009 PMT 22289 Check Research Professionals... 3,110.00
04/12/2009 RCPT 123 Visa CashCustomer 80.25
0 of 4 payments selected for deposit
Payments Subtotal
0.00
Select All
Select None
OK
Cancel
Help

FIGURE 10-6 All the income you've collected since the last bank deposit is waiting to be deposited.

This information is important because you should match it to the way your bank records deposits; otherwise, bank reconciliation becomes much more complicated.

For example, your bank probably lists credit card deposits separately from a deposit total for cash and checks, even if all the money was deposited the same day. That's because your credit card deposits are probably made directly to your bank account by your merchant account bank.

Select Deposit Items

If you only have a few transactions to deposit, select those you just deposited (when you went to the bank) by clicking their listings to place a check mark in the left column. Click Select All if you took all the payments to the bank for deposit.

Separate Deposit Items by Payment Method

If you have to separate deposits by type, select a payment method from the drop-down list at the top of the Payments To Deposit window. Choose Selected Types to open the Select Payment Types list and choose multiple payment types to include in the same deposit.

For example, you may use the Other category to signify a money order or a traveler's check, and you're listing those items on the same deposit slip in which you listed checks. The listings on the Payments To Deposit window change to include only the deposits that match the selected payment method.

Separate Cash From Checks

The drop-down list for payment method types doesn't provide separate payment methods for cash and checks. However, if you take a cash bag to the bank (sometimes deposited in a night deposit safe available after banking hours), select only the checks and deposit them. Then start the process over to select only the cash (or do it the other way around). You end up with two deposits of different payment types being transferred to the bank on the same day.

This is a common practice when depositing cash, because sometimes the bank notifies you that their automatic counting machine produced a different total from the total on your deposit slip (you probably don't own counting machines for coins and paper money). If that happens, you can edit the cash sales deposit item in your bank register, and the cause of the edit will be obvious.

Separate Deposits by Bank Account

If you're depositing money into multiple bank accounts, select only the transactions that go into the first account. After you complete the deposit, start this process again and deposit the remaining transactions into the other account(s).

Credit Card Deposits

You can't deposit credit card payments until your merchant bank notifies you that the funds have been placed in your account.

- If you have QuickBooks online banking, the deposit shows up in the downloaded report from your bank (see Chapter 15 to learn about managing online banking transactions).
- If you have online access to your merchant card account, the transfer will appear on the activities report on the website.
- If you don't have any form of online access, you'll have to wait for the monthly statement to arrive (or contact the bank periodically to see if anything showed up in your account).

If your merchant bank deducts fees before transferring funds, learn how to deposit the net amount in the section "Calculating Merchant Card Fees," later in this chapter.

Filling Out the Deposit Slip

After you select the appropriate payment method (or select all payments), click OK in the Payments To Deposit window to bring up the Make Deposits window shown in Figure 10-7.

Select the bank account you're using for this deposit. Then make sure the date matches the day you physically deposit the money.

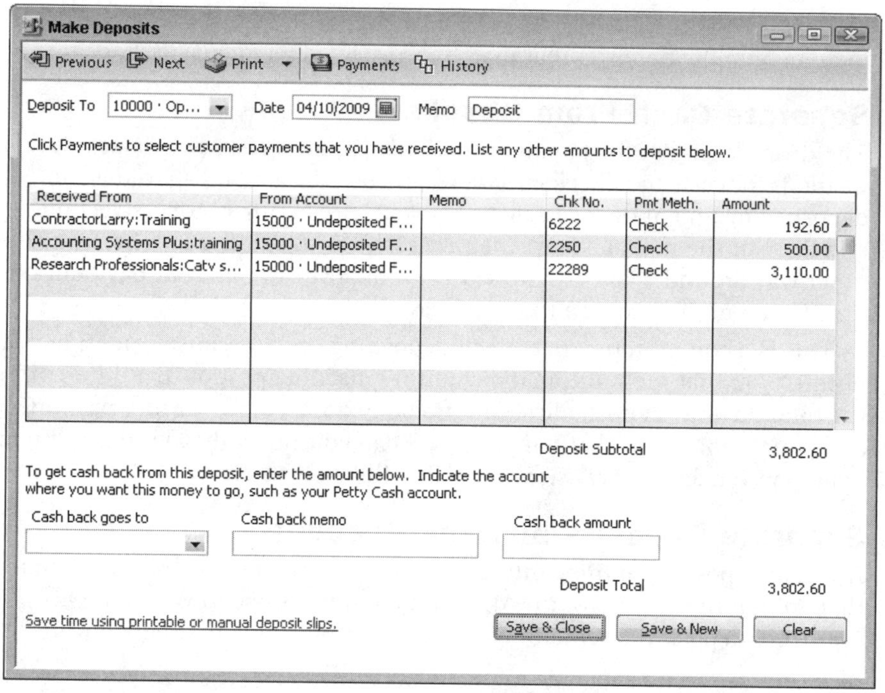

FIGURE 10-7 The Make Deposits form is a virtual bank deposit slip.

Adding Items to the Deposit

If you want to add deposit items that weren't in the Payments To Deposit window, click anywhere in the Received From column to make it accessible and select an existing name by clicking the arrow, or click <Add New> to enter a name that isn't in your system. If the source of the check is any entity that isn't a customer or vendor (perhaps you're depositing your own check to put additional capital into the company, or you have a check representing a bank loan), you can either skip the Received From column or add the name to the Other Names List. (If you don't need to track the entity as a customer or vendor, it's fine to skip the name.)

Press TAB to move to the From Account column and enter the account to which you're posting this transaction. Following are some common scenarios:

- If the check you're depositing represents a bank loan, use the liability account for that bank loan (you can create it here by choosing <Add New> if you didn't think to set up the account earlier). The bank should be in your Vendor List because you have to write checks to repay the loan.
- If the check you're depositing represents an infusion of capital from you, use the owner's capital account in the Equity section of your chart of accounts.

- If the check is a refund for an expense (perhaps you overpaid someone, and they're returning money to you), use the vendor's name, and post the deposit to the same expense account you used for the original transaction.
- If the check is a rebate from a manufacturer instead of the vendor, skip the Received From column and post the amount to the original expense account you used when you purchased the item.

Use the TAB key to move through the rest of the columns, which are self-explanatory.

Calculating Merchant Card Fees

If your merchant card bank deposits the gross amount of each transaction and charges your bank account for the total fees due at the end of the month, you don't have to do anything special to deposit credit card payments. You can deal with the fees when your bank statement arrives by entering the fee directly in the bank account register, posting the amount to the merchant card fee expense account.

If your merchant card bank deducts fees from transactions and deposits the net proceeds to your account, it takes a few extra steps to track credit card transactions and deposit the correct amount.

Select the credit card transactions in the Payments To Deposit window. These are gross amounts, representing the sales price you charged (and the customer paid). Then click OK to move the deposits to the Make Deposits window.

In the first empty line below the transactions that were transferred to the Make Deposits window, click the Account column and select the account to which you post merchant card fees.

Move to the Amount column and enter the fee as a negative number. Now, the net matches the amount that the merchant card company deposited in your bank account, and your merchant card expense has been posted to the general ledger.

Getting Cash Back from Deposits

If you're getting cash back from your deposit, you can tell QuickBooks about it right on the Make Deposits window, instead of making a journal entry to adjust the total of collected payments against the total of the bank deposit.

> **NOTE:** If you're keeping the money for yourself and your business isn't a corporation, use the Draw account to post the cash back. If your business is a corporation, you can't keep the money for yourself.

Enter the account to which you're posting the cash (usually a petty-cash account), and enter the amount of cash you want back from this deposit. Even though you can put the cash in your pocket, you must account for it, because these are business funds. As you spend the cash for business expenses, post the expense against the same petty-cash account with a journal entry, eventually washing out the amount you took back when you made this deposit.

> **($) CAUTION:** Many banks will not cash checks made out to a company, so your ability to get cash back may be limited to checks made out to you, personally.

Printing Deposit Slips

If you want to print a deposit slip or a deposit summary, click the Print button in the Make Deposits window. QuickBooks asks whether you want to print a deposit slip and summary, or just a deposit summary.

If you want to print a deposit slip that your bank will accept, you must order printable deposit slips from QuickBooks. The QuickBooks deposit slips are guaranteed to be acceptable to your bank. You must have a laser printer or inkjet printer to use them. When you print the deposit slip, there's a tear-off section at the bottom of the page that has a deposit summary. Keep that section for your own records and take the rest of the page to the bank along with your money.

If you don't have QuickBooks deposit slips, select Deposit Summary Only and fill out your bank deposit slip manually.

Handling the Over and Short Problem

If you literally take cash for cash sales, when you count the money in the till at the end of the day, you may find that the recorded income doesn't match the cash you expected to find in the till. Or you may find that the money you posted to deposit to the bank doesn't match the amount of money you put into the little brown bag you took to the bank.

This is a common problem with cash, and, in fact, it's an occasional problem in regular accrual bookkeeping. One of the ensuing problems you face is how to handle this in your bookkeeping system. QuickBooks is a double-entry bookkeeping system, which means the left side of the ledger has to be equal to the right side of the ledger. If you post $100.00 in cash sales but only have $99.50 to take to the bank, how do you handle the missing 50 cents? You can't just post $100.00 to your bank account (well, you could, but your bank reconciliation won't work and, just as important, you're not practicing good bookkeeping).

The solution to the over/short dilemma is to acknowledge it in your bookkeeping procedures. Track it. You'll be amazed by how much it balances itself out—short one day, over another. (Of course, if you're short every day, and the shortages are growing, you have an entirely different problem, and the first place to look is at the person who stands in front of the cash register.)

Creating Over and Short Accounts

To track over/short, you need to have some place to post the discrepancies, which means you have to create some new accounts in your chart of accounts, as follows:

- Create an account named Over, using the account type Income.
- Create an account named Short, using the account type Income.

If you're using numbered accounts, use sequential numbers on the next level from your regular Income accounts. For example, use 49000 if your regular Income accounts are 40000, 40100, 40300, and so on.

If you want to see a net number for over/short (a good idea), create three accounts. Create the parent account first and name it Over-Short (or Over&Short), and then make the Over and Short accounts subaccounts of the parent account. If you use account numbers, make the three numbers sequential; for instance:

- 49000 Over/Short (parent account)
- 49010 Over (subaccount)
- 49020 Short (subaccount)

Creating Over and Short Items

If you track cash sales by tracking batches of sales in a Sales Receipt transaction, you need items for your overages and shortages (in QuickBooks, you need items for everything that's connected with entering sales data in a transaction window). Create items for overages and shortages as follows:

- Create two Other Charge items, one named Overage, the other named Shortage.
- Don't assign a price.
- Make the item nontaxable.
- Link each item to the appropriate account (or subaccount) that you just created for Over/Short.

Now that you have the necessary accounts and items, use the Over and Short items right in the Enter Sales Receipts window to adjust the difference between the amount of money you've accumulated in the cash-sale transactions and the amount of money you're actually depositing to the bank. It's your last transaction of the day. Remember to use a minus sign before the figure when you use the Short item.

Tracking Accounts Receivable

Collecting the money owed to you is one of the largest headaches in running a business. You have to track what's owed and who owes it, and then expend time and effort to collect it. All of the effort you spend on the money your customers owe you is called *tracking accounts receivable* (or, more commonly, *tracking A/R*).

You can track overdue invoices and then remind your customers, in gentle, or not-so-gentle ways, to pay. In this chapter I go over the tools and features QuickBooks provides to help you track and collect the money your customers owe you.

Using Finance Charges

You can impose finance charges on overdue amounts as an incentive to get your customers to pay on time. Incidentally, this isn't "found money"; it probably doesn't cover its own cost. The amount of time spent tracking, analyzing, and chasing receivables is substantial, and in all businesses "time is money."

Configuring Finance Charges

To use finance charges, you have to establish the rate and circumstances under which they're assessed. Your company's finance charges are configured as part of your company preferences. Choose Edit | Preferences to open the Preferences dialog. Then click the Finance Charge icon in the left pane and select the Company Preferences tab (see Figure 10-8).

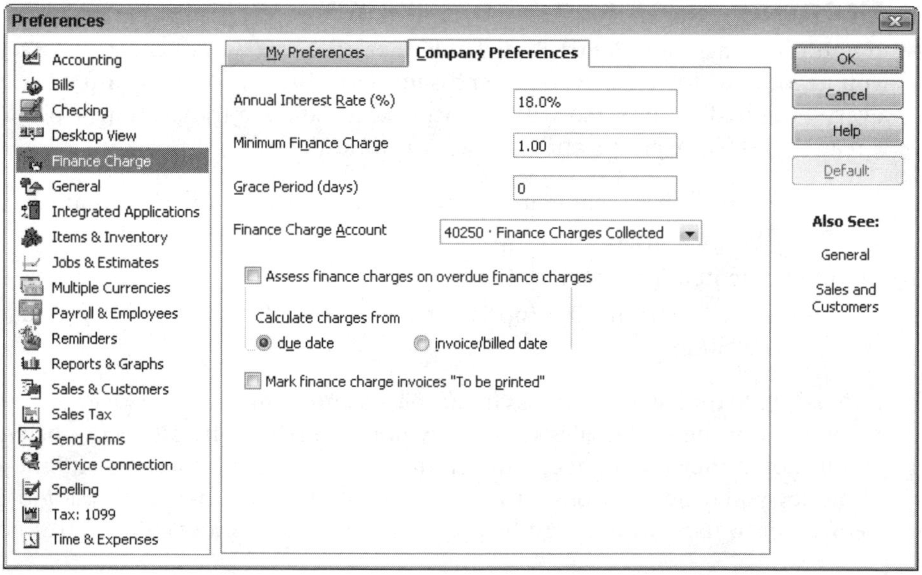

FIGURE 10-8 Configure the way in which you'll impose finance charges on overdue balances.

Here are some guidelines for filling out this dialog:

- In the Annual Interest Rate field, replacing the default data (0.00%) with any positive number automatically enables the Finance Charges feature (the dialog has no Yes/No check box to enable or disable finance charges).
- Notice that the interest rate is annual. If you want to charge 1.5 percent a month, enter **18%** in the Annual Interest Rate field.
- You can assess a minimum finance charge for overdue balances. QuickBooks will calculate the finance charge, and if it's less than the minimum, the amount will be rolled up to the minimum charge you specify here.
- Use the Grace Period field to enter the number of days of lateness you permit before finance charges are assessed.
- During setup, QuickBooks probably created an account for finance charges. If so, select it. If not, enter (or create) the account you want to use to post finance charges (it's an income account).
- The issue of assessing finance charges on overdue finance charges is a sticky one. The practice is illegal in many states. Selecting this option means that a customer who owed $100.00 last month and had a finance charge assessed of $2.00 now owes $102.00. As a result, the next finance charge is assessed on a balance of $102.00 (instead of on the original overdue balance of $100.00). Regardless of state law, the fact is that very few businesses opt to use this calculation method.
- Specify whether to calculate the finance charge from the due date or the invoice date (it's common to use the due date).
- QuickBooks creates an invoice automatically when finance charges are assessed in order to have a permanent record of the transaction. By default, these invoices aren't printed; they're just accumulated along with the overdue invoices so they'll print as a line item on a monthly statement. You can opt to have the finance charge invoices printed, which you should do only if you're planning to mail them to nudge your customers for payment.

Click OK to save your settings after you've filled out the window.

Assessing Finance Charges

You should assess finance charges just before you create customer statements, which is commonly a monthly chore. Choose Customers | Assess Finance Charges from the menu bar. The Assess Finance Charges window opens (see Figure 10-9) with a list of all the customers with overdue balances.

If you have any customers that have made payments that you haven't yet applied to an invoice, or if any customers have credits that you haven't yet applied to an invoice, an asterisk (*) appears to the left of the customer or job name. Close the Assess Finance Charges window and correct the situation, then return to this window.

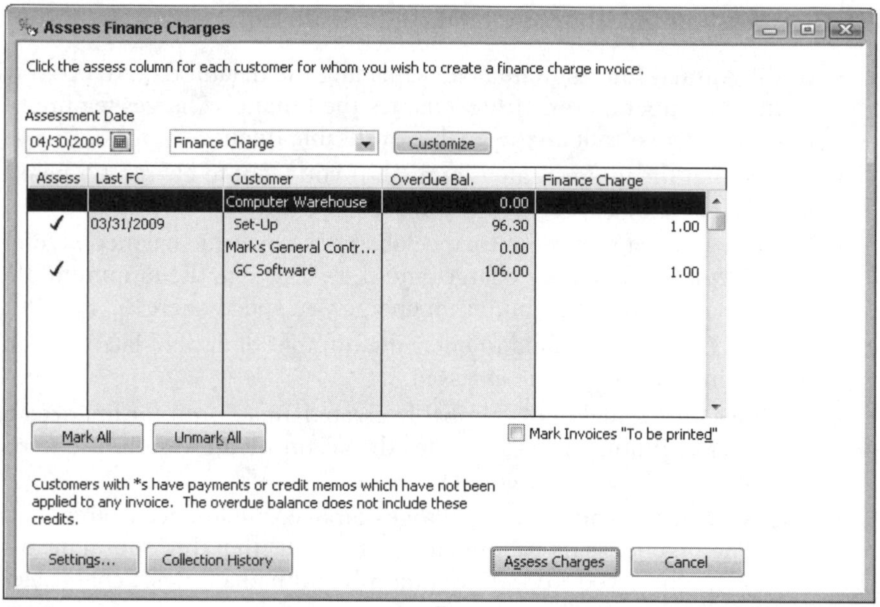

FIGURE 10-9 QuickBooks automatically assesses finance charges as of the assessment date you specify.

Choosing the Assessment Date

Change the Assessment Date field (which displays the current date) to the date on which you actually want to impose the charge—this date appears on customer statements. It's common to assess finance charges on the last day of the month. When you press TAB to move out of the date field, the finance charges are recalculated to reflect the new date.

Selecting the Customers

You can eliminate a customer from the process by clicking in the Assess column to remove the check mark. Unfortunately, QuickBooks does not have a finance charge assessment option on each customer record. Therefore, all customers with overdue balances are included when you assess finance charges. This means you have to know off the top of your head which customers are liable for finances charges and which aren't—or you have to keep a list near your desk.

It can be time consuming to deselect each customer, so if you have only a few customers for whom you reserve this process, choose Unmark All, then reselect the customers you want to include.

Changing the Amounts

You can change the calculated total if you wish (a good idea if there are credit memos floating around that you're not ready to apply against any invoices). Just click the amount displayed in the Finance Charge column to activate that column for that customer. Then enter a new finance charge amount. If you need to calculate the new figure (perhaps you're giving credit for a floating credit memo), press the equal sign (=) on your keyboard to use the QuickBooks built-in calculator.

Checking the History

To make sure you don't assess a charge that isn't really due (or fair), you can double-check by viewing a customer's history from the Assess Finance Charges window. Highlight a customer listing and click the Collection History button to see a Collections Report for the selected customer (see Figure 10-10). Your mouse pointer turns into a magnifying glass with the letter "z" (for "zoom") in it when you position it over a line item. Double-click any line item to display the original transaction window if you need to examine the details.

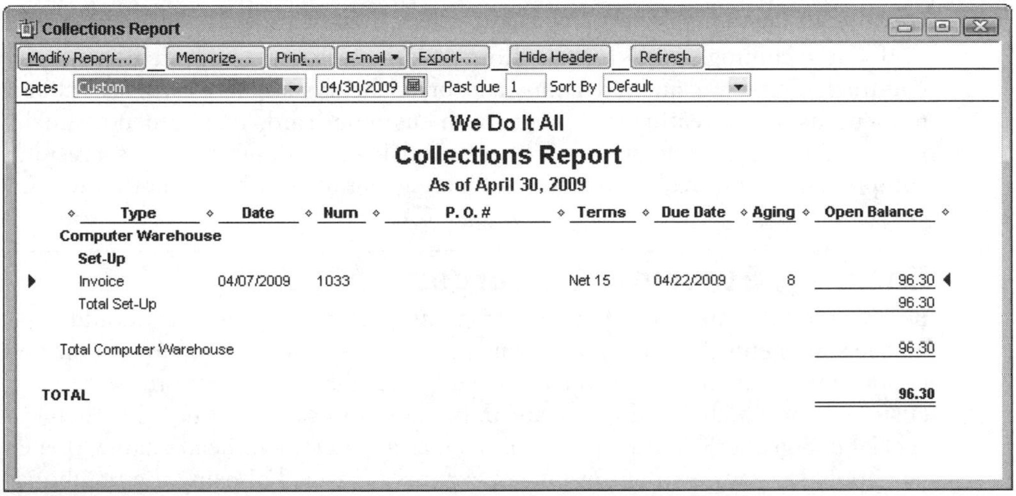

FIGURE 10-10 You can check a customer's history to make sure the finance charges are legitimate.

Saving the Finance Charge Invoices

If you're sure all the calculations and figures are correct, click Assess Charges in the Assess Finance Charges window. When you create your customer statements, the finance charges will appear. If you've opted to skip printing the finance charge assessments as invoices, there's nothing more to do. If you're printing the finance charges, see the next paragraph.

Selecting Printing Options

If you want to print the finance charge invoices (they really are invoices because they add charges to the customer balance), be sure to select the Mark Invoices

"To Be Printed" check box on the Assess Finance Charges window. You can send the printed copies to your customers as a nagging reminder. If you only care about having the finance charge on the monthly statement (the common method for most businesses), deselect the printing option.

To print the finance charge invoices, choose File | Print Forms | Invoices. The list of unprinted invoices appears, and unless you have regular invoices you didn't print yet, the list includes only the finance charge invoices. If the list is correct, click OK to continue on to the printing process.

Sending Statements

On a periodic basis, you should send statements to your customers. (Most businesses send statements monthly.) They serve a couple of purposes: they remind customers of outstanding balances, and they provide detailed documentation of your records, which your customers can match against their own records.

If you're coming to QuickBooks from a manual system or a system in which you tracked invoices and payments in a spreadsheet, statements will seem like a miraculous tool. Creating statements from customer cards maintained manually, in a word processing document or in a spreadsheet, is a nightmare. As a result, companies without real accounting software generally don't even bother to try.

Entering Statement Charges

Before creating statements, you should create any transactions that should appear on the statements. Invoices and payments appear automatically, but you may want to add statement charges. A *statement charge* is a charge you want to pass to a customer for which you don't create an invoice. You can use statement charges for special charges for certain customers, such as a general overhead charge, or a charge you apply for your own out-of-pocket expenses (instead of using the reimbursable expenses feature for expenses incurred on behalf of the customer). Some companies use statement charges instead of invoices for invoicing regular retainer payments.

You must add statement charges before you create the statements (or else the charges won't show up on the statements). Statement charges use items from your Item List, but you cannot use any of the following types of items:

- Items that are taxable, because the statement charge can't apply the tax
- Items that have percentage discounts (instead of discounts with specific amounts), because the statement charge can't look up the discount percentage (and therefore can't apply it)
- Items that represent a payment transaction, because those are negative charges, which a statement charge doesn't understand

Statement charges are recorded directly in a customer's register or in the register for a specific job. To create a statement charge choose Customers | Enter Statement Charges from the menu bar to open the customer register, which looks like Figure 10-11. By default, QuickBooks opens the register for the first customer in your Customers & Jobs List; you can use the drop-down list at the top of the window to select a different customer. Then use the following steps to add statement charges (use the TAB key to move through the register's fields):

Date	Number	Item	Qty	Rate	Amt Chrg	Amt Paid	Balance
	Type		Description		Billed Date	Due Date	
04/11/2009	2250					500.00	725.00
	PMT						
04/15/2009	445896					428.00	297.00
	PMT						
04/15/2009	445896					197.00	100.00
	PMT						
04/13/2009	Number	Mileage	20	0.45	9.00		
	STMTCHG						

Accounting Systems Plus - Accounts Receivable

Print...   Edit Transaction   Time/Costs...   QuickReport

Customer:Job Accounting Systems Plus

1-Line   Show open balance   Ending balance   100.00

Sort by Date, Type, Number/...

Record   Restore

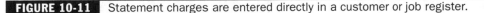

FIGURE 10-11   Statement charges are entered directly in a customer or job register.

1. Select the appropriate customer or job from the drop-down list in the Customer:Job field at the top of the register.
2. Enter the date on which the statement charge is being assessed.
3. In the Item field, select the item for the statement charge from the drop-down list.
4. Enter a quantity in the Qty field if the item is invoiced by quantity.
5. Enter a rate (or accept the default rate if one exists) if you're using the Qty field.
6. Enter the amount charged if the Qty and Rate fields aren't used (if they are, the total amount is entered automatically).
7. Optionally, edit the item description.
8. Optionally enter the billed date, which does not have to match the transaction date in the first column of the register. Postdating or predating this field determines which statement it appears on.

9. Optionally enter the due date, which affects your aging reports and your finance charge calculations.

10. When all the fields you want to use are filled in, click Record to save the transaction.

Continue to select customers and/or jobs to enter additional statement charges.

Creating Statements

Before you start creating your statements, be sure that all the transactions that should be included on the statements have been entered into the system. Did you forget anything? Applying credit memos? Applying payments? Assessing finance charges? Entering statement charges?

When all customer accounts are up to date, choose Customers | Create Statements to open the Create Statements dialog, shown in Figure 10-12.

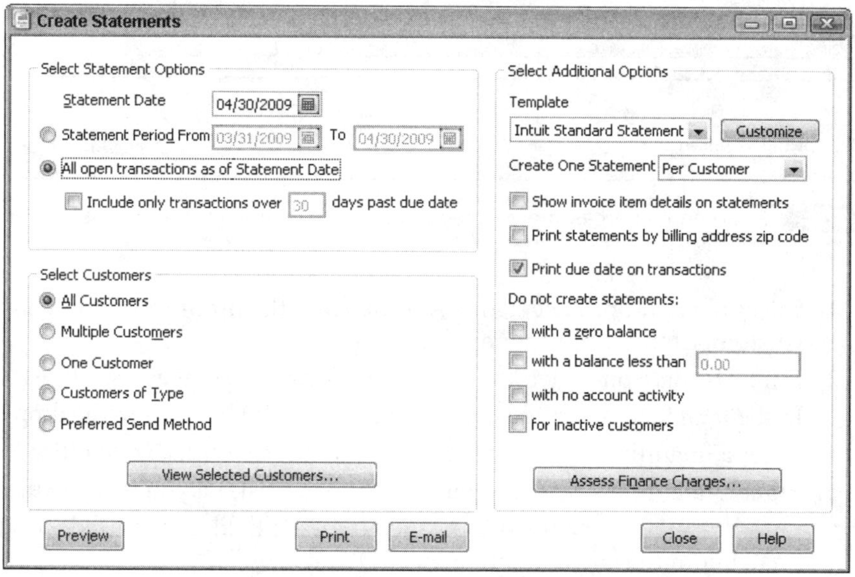

FIGURE 10-12 Configure the specifications for selecting customers who receive statements.

Selecting the Date Range

The statement date range determines which transactions appear on the statement. The printed statement displays the previous balance (the total due before the

"From" date) and includes all transactions that were created within the date range. The starting date should be the day after the last date of your last statement run. If you do monthly statements, choose the first and last days of the current month; if you send statements quarterly, enter the first and last dates of the current quarter—and so on.

If you choose All Open Transactions As Of Statement Date, the printed statement just shows unpaid invoices and charges and unapplied credits. You can narrow the criteria by selecting the option to include only transactions overdue by a certain number of days (which you specify). However, this makes the printed statement more like a list than a standard statement.

Selecting the Customers

It's normal procedure to send statements to all customers, but if that's not the plan, you can change the default selection.

If you want to send statements to a group of customers, click the Multiple Customers option to display a Choose button next to the option. Click the Choose button to bring up a list of customers and select each customer you want to include. You can manually select each customer, or select Automatic and then enter text to tell QuickBooks to match that text against all customer names and select the matching customers. (The automatic match option isn't efficient for multiple customers because it only matches exact text, not partial text, and therefore only matches one customer at a time.) Click OK when all the appropriate customers are selected.

If you're sending a statement to one customer only, select One Customer, and then click the arrow next to the text box to scroll through the list of your customers and select the one you want.

To send statements to customers who are designated with a specific customer type, select the Customers Of Type option, and then select the customer type you want to include from the drop-down list. This works, of course, only if you created customer types as part of your QuickBooks setup.

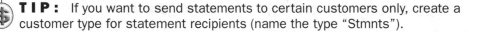

TIP: If you want to send statements to certain customers only, create a customer type for statement recipients (name the type "Stmnts").

Filtering for Send Methods

If your customers vary in the way you send them statements (the option selected in the Preferred Send Method field of the customer record), you can opt to handle your statement delivery in batches, using one delivery method per batch. To do this, select the Preferred Send Method option, and then select the send method for this batch from the drop-down list that appears:

- **E-mail**   Sends the statements by e-mail, using the QuickBooks e-mail services feature.
- **Mail**   Sends the statements to QuickBooks Billing Solutions, where the invoice is created with a tear-off slip that the customer can use to pay the invoice. QuickBooks mails the invoice. (This is a fee-based service.)
- **None**   Means no special handling. You print the statements, put them in envelopes, and mail them.

Specifying the Printing Options

You can specify the way you want the statements to print using the following criteria and options in the Select Additional Options section:

- You can print one statement for each customer, which lists all transactions for all that customer's jobs, or you can print a separate statement for each job.
- You can opt to show invoice item details instead of just listing the invoice on the statement. If your invoices have a lot of line items, this could make your statements very long (possibly too many pages to get away with a single postage stamp). I don't see any particular reason to select this option, because most customers have copies of the original invoices—if they don't, they'll call you with questions and you can look up the invoice number and provide details (or reprint the invoice and send it).
- Printing statements in order by ZIP code is handy if you're printing labels that are sorted by ZIP code. This option is also important if you have a bulk mail permit, because the post office requires bulk mail to be sorted by ZIP code.
- By default, the original due date for each transaction listed on the statement is displayed on the statement. If you have some reason to hide this information from your customers (I can't think of a good reason), QuickBooks offers the opportunity to deselect the option.

Specifying the Statements to Skip

You may want to skip statement creation for customers who meet the criteria you set in the Do Not Create Statements section of the dialog. If statements are the only documents you send to customers (you don't send the individual invoices and credits you create), selecting any of these options makes sense.

If, however, you use statements to make sure you and your customers have matching accounting records, you should create statements for all customers except inactive customers.

Last Call for Finance Charges

If you haven't assessed finance charges and you want them to appear on the statements, click the Assess Finance Charges button. The Assess Finance Charges window opens, showing customers who have been selected for finance charges.

If you've already assessed finance charges, QuickBooks will warn you (when you click the Assess Charges button) that finance charges have already been assessed as of the selected date. If you ignore the message, another round of finance charges is imposed (and you'll have a lot of angry and distrustful customers). Therefore, this window is useful only if you don't assess finance charges as described earlier in this chapter.

Previewing the Statements

Before you commit the statements to paper, you can click the Preview button to get an advance look. This is not just to see what the printed output will look like; it's also a way to look at the customer records and to make sure that all the customers you selected are included.

Use the Zoom In button to see the statement and its contents close up. Click the Next Page button to move through all the statements. Click Close to return to the Create Statements window.

Printing the Statements

When everything is just the way it should be, print the statements by clicking the Print button in either the Print Preview window or the Create Statements window. If you click Close in the Preview window, you return to the Create Statements window—click Print to open the Print Statement(s) window. Then change the printing options as needed.

CAUTION: If you click Print in the Preview window, all the statements are immediately sent to the default printer with no opportunity to change printers or set other print options.

Customizing Statements

You don't have to use the standard statement form—you can design your own. The instructions for creating a template with customized fields and columns are in Chapter 28. If you want to create a customized template for statements, think about adding the Terms field to the statement (which is not selected by default). It doesn't seem fair to tell a customer of amounts past due without reminding the customer of the terms.

Running A/R Aging Reports

A/R aging reports are lists of the money owed you by your customers, and they're available in quite a few formats. They're for you, not for your customers. You run them whenever you need to know the extent of your receivables. Many companies run an aging report every morning, just to keep an eye on the amount of money on the street ("on the street" is business jargon for uncollected receivables).

➡ **FYI**

A/R Totals

The total amount of A/R is the value of your A/R asset. It can be an important asset and, in fact, banks give lines of credit and loans using the A/R balance as part of the collateral.

When your accountant visits, you can bet one of the things he or she will ask to see is this report. When your accountant asks for an aging report, another safe bet is that you'll receive a request to see the amount posted to A/R in your general ledger. The general ledger A/R balance and the total on the aging report must be the same (for the same date)—not close, not almost, but *exactly* the same. If the figures are not identical, your general ledger isn't "proved" (jargon for, "I'm sorry, we can't trust your general ledger figures because they don't audit properly").

If your A/R account balance doesn't prove to your A/R report for the same date, you've messed up some transactions. Most of the time, this means you used the A/R account in a journal entry, and that's a no-no. You or your accountant, or both of you, must find the bad entry and correct it, because your A/R report total must match the A/R account balance for the same date.

A couple of aging reports are available in QuickBooks, and you can also customize any built-in reports so they report data exactly the way you want it. To see an aging report, choose Reports | Customers & Receivables, and then choose either A/R Aging Summary or A/R Aging Detail (these reports are explained next).

A/R Aging Summary Reports

The quickest way to see how much money is owed to you is to select A/R Aging Summary, which produces a listing of customer balances (see Figure 10-13).

	Current	1 - 30	31 - 60	61 - 90	> 90	TOTAL
Accounting Systems Plus						
training	0.00	100.00	0.00	0.00	0.00	100.00
Accounting Systems Plus - Other	9.00	0.00	0.00	0.00	0.00	9.00
Total Accounting Systems Plus	9.00	100.00	0.00	0.00	0.00	109.00
Adam's Consulting	1,000.00	0.00	0.00	0.00	0.00	1,000.00
Computer Warehouse						
Set-Up	0.00	0.00	96.30	9.22	0.00	105.52
Total Computer Warehouse	0.00	0.00	96.30	9.22	0.00	105.52
ContractorLarry						
Training	0.00	300.00	0.00	0.00	0.00	300.00
Total ContractorLarry	0.00	300.00	0.00	0.00	0.00	300.00
Gotham						
Audio	3,210.00	0.00	0.00	0.00	0.00	3,210.00
On-Site Wiring	0.00	3,460.00	0.00	0.00	0.00	3,460.00
Total Gotham	3,210.00	3,460.00	0.00	0.00	0.00	6,670.00
Mark's General Contracting						
GC Software	0.00	0.00	106.00	0.00	0.00	106.00
Total Mark's General Contracting	0.00	0.00	106.00	0.00	0.00	106.00
Research Professionals						
Staff training	0.00	428.80	0.00	0.00	0.00	428.80
Total Research Professionals	0.00	428.80	0.00	0.00	0.00	428.80
TOTAL	**4,219.00**	**4,288.80**	**202.30**	**9.22**	**0.00**	**8,719.32**

FIGURE 10-13 A summary report provides totals for each customer, broken down by aging periods.

A/R Aging Detail Reports

If you choose Aging Detail from the Accounts Receivable reports menu, you see a much more comprehensive report, such as the one seen in Figure 10-14. The report is sorted by aging interval, showing individual transactions, including finance charges, for each aging period.

Customizing Aging Reports

If you don't use (or care about) all of the columns in the A/R Aging Detail report, or you'd prefer to see the information displayed in a different manner, you can customize the report. Start by clicking the Modify Report button on the report to see the Modify Report window shown in Figure 10-15.

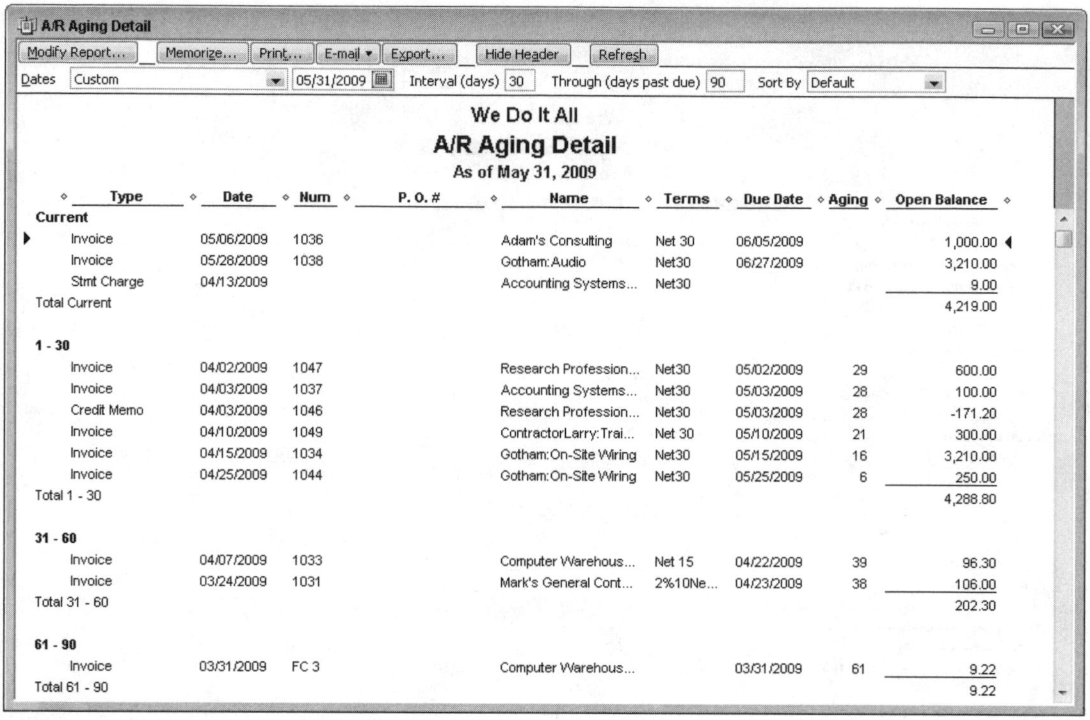

We Do It All
A/R Aging Detail
As of May 31, 2009

Type	Date	Num	P. O. #	Name	Terms	Due Date	Aging	Open Balance
Current								
Invoice	05/06/2009	1036		Adam's Consulting	Net 30	06/05/2009		1,000.00
Invoice	05/28/2009	1038		Gotham:Audio	Net30	06/27/2009		3,210.00
Stmt Charge	04/13/2009			Accounting Systems...	Net30			9.00
Total Current								4,219.00
1 - 30								
Invoice	04/02/2009	1047		Research Profession...	Net30	05/02/2009	29	600.00
Invoice	04/03/2009	1037		Accounting Systems...	Net30	05/03/2009	28	100.00
Credit Memo	04/03/2009	1046		Research Profession...	Net30	05/03/2009	28	-171.20
Invoice	04/10/2009	1049		ContractorLarry:Trai...	Net 30	05/10/2009	21	300.00
Invoice	04/15/2009	1034		Gotham:On-Site Wiring	Net30	05/15/2009	16	3,210.00
Invoice	04/25/2009	1044		Gotham:On-Site Wiring	Net30	05/25/2009	6	250.00
Total 1 - 30								4,288.80
31 - 60								
Invoice	04/07/2009	1033		Computer Warehous...	Net 15	04/22/2009	39	96.30
Invoice	03/24/2009	1031		Mark's General Cont...	2%10Ne...	04/23/2009	38	106.00
Total 31 - 60								202.30
61 - 90								
Invoice	03/31/2009	FC 3		Computer Warehous...		03/31/2009	61	9.22
Total 61 - 90								9.22

FIGURE 10-14 Detail reports display information about every transaction that's involved in each customer's A/R balance.

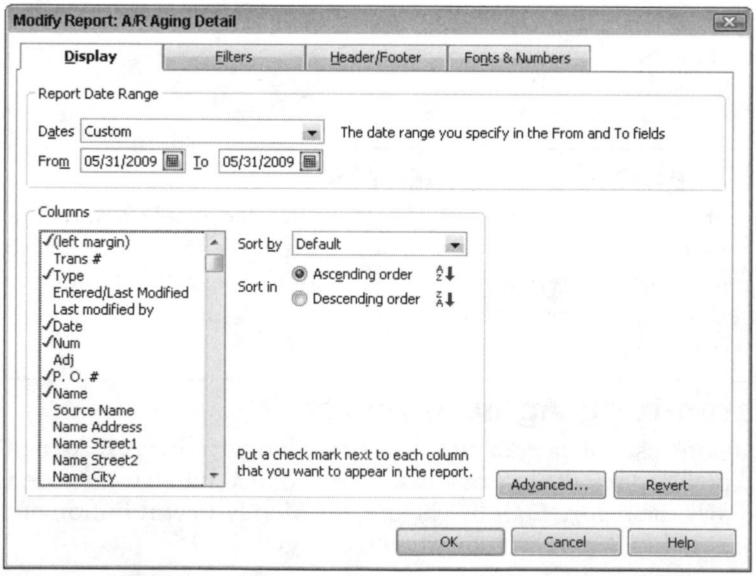

FIGURE 10-15 Customize the A/R Aging Detail report to get exactly the information you need.

Customizing the Columns

The most common customization is to get rid of any column you don't care about. For example, if you use the Classes feature but don't care about that information in your aging report, get rid of the column. Or you might want to get rid of the Terms column since it doesn't impact the totals. To remove a column, scroll through the Columns list and click to remove the check mark. The column disappears from the report.

While you're looking at the list of column names, you may find a column heading that's not currently selected but that contains information you'd like to include in your report. If so, click that column listing to place a check mark next to it. The column appears on the report and the data linked to it is displayed.

Filtering Information

If you want to produce an aging report for a special purpose, you can easily filter the information so it meets criteria important to you. To filter your aging report, click the Filters tab (see Figure 10-16).

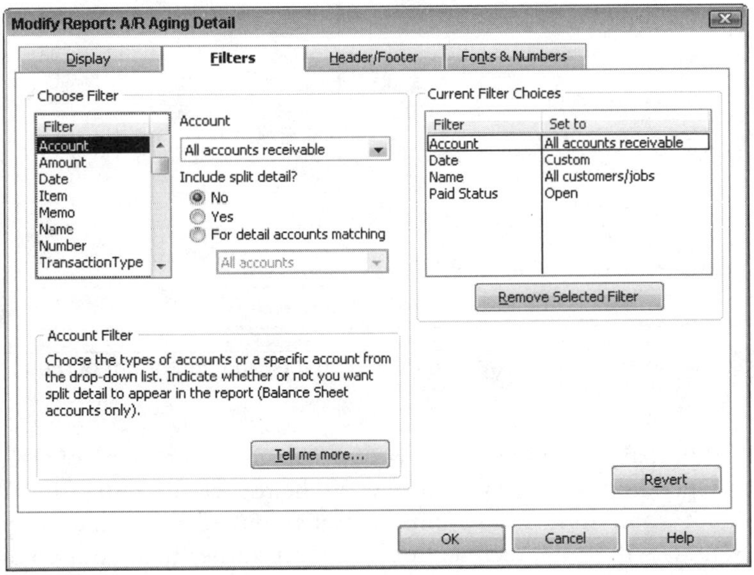

FIGURE 10-16 Filters let you specify criteria for displaying data.

Select a filter and then set the conditions for it. (Each filter has its own specific type of criteria.) For example, you can use this feature if you want to see only those customers with receivables higher than a certain figure or older than a certain aging period.

C A U T I O N : If you filter the report in a way that affects the amounts, your report total will not match your A/R account balance. Use this type of filter only to get certain types of information for yourself, not for an "official" aging report.

Configuring Header/Footer Data

You can customize the text that appears in the header and footer of the report by making changes in the Header/Footer tab shown in Figure 10-17.

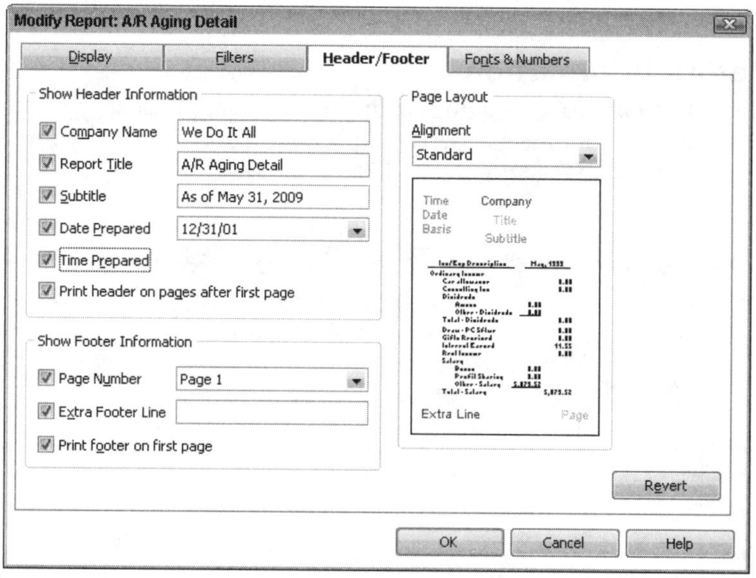

FIGURE 10-17 Specify the text you want to display on the top and bottom of the report.

You'll probably find that your decisions about the contents of the header and footer depend on whether you're viewing the report or printing it. And, if you're printing it, some stuff is more important if an outsider (a banker or your accountant) will be the recipient of the report, rather than your credit manager.

For example, the date and time of preparation is more important for outsiders than for you. Incidentally, on the Header/Footer tab, the Date Prepared field has a meaningless date—don't panic, your computer hasn't lost track of the date. That date is a format, not today's date. Click the arrow to the right of the field to see the other formats for inserting the date. The Page Number field also has a variety of formats to choose from.

You can eliminate a Header/Footer field by removing the check mark from the field's check box. For fields you want to print, you can change the text. You can also change the layout by choosing a different Alignment option from the drop-down list.

Customizing the Appearance

Click the Fonts & Numbers tab to change the format of the report. You can change the way negative numbers are displayed, and you can change the fonts for any or all the individual elements in the report.

When you close the report window, QuickBooks may ask if you want to memorize the report with the changes you made (if you told QuickBooks to stop asking, you won't see the message). Click Yes so you don't have to go through all the modifications again. If QuickBooks doesn't ask, memorize the report using the instructions in the next section.

Memorizing Aging Reports

If you've customized a report and have the columns, data, and formatting you need, there's no reason to reinvent the wheel the next time you need the same information. Instead of going through the customization process again next month, memorize the report as you designed it. Then you can fetch it whenever you need it.

Click the Memorize button in the report window. When the Memorize Report dialog appears, enter a new name for the report, optionally save it within a report group, and click OK.

From now on, this report name will be on the list of memorized reports you can select from when you choose Reports | Memorized Reports from the menu bar.

> **NOTE:** When you use a memorized report, only the criteria and formatting is memorized. Each time you open the report, the data is generated from the QuickBooks transaction records, so you get current, accurate information.

Printing Reports

Whether you're using the standard format or one you've customized, you'll probably want to print the report. When you're in a report window, click the Print button at the top of the window to bring up the Print Reports dialog. If the report is wide, use the Margins tab to set new margins, and use the options on the Settings tab to customize other printing options.

Running Customer and Job Reports

Customer and job reports are like aging reports, but they're designed to give you information about the selected customers/jobs instead of providing information on the totals for your business. There are plenty of customer reports available from the menu that appears when you choose Reports | Customers & Receivables:

- **Customer Balance Summary Report**   Lists current total balance owed for each customer.
- **Customer Balance Detail Report**   Lists every transaction for each customer with a net subtotal for each customer and job.
- **Open Invoices Report**   Lists all unpaid invoices, sorted and subtotaled by customer and job.
- **Collections Report**   A nifty report for nagging customers. Includes the contact name and telephone number, along with details about invoices with balances due. You're all set to call the customer and have a conversation, and you can answer any questions about invoice details.
- **Accounts Receivable Graph**   Shows a graphic representation of the accounts receivable. For a quick overview, there's nothing like a graph.
- **Unbilled Costs By Job**   Tracks job expenses that were linked to customers or jobs that you haven't yet invoiced.
- **Transaction List By Customer**   Displays individual transactions of all types for each customer.
- **Online Received Payments**   Shows payments received from customers who pay you online (only appears on the menu if you've signed up with QuickBooks to accept online payments).
- **Customer Phone List**   Displays an alphabetical list of customers along with the telephone number for each (if you entered the telephone number in the customer record).
- **Customer Contact List**   Displays an alphabetical list of customers along with the contact, telephone numbers, billing address, and current open balance for each. Give this list to the person in charge of collections.
- **Item Price List**   Lists all your items with their prices and preferred vendors.

Managing Vendor Bills

In this chapter:

- Enter vendor bills

- Track reimbursable expenses

- Receive inventory purchases

- Enter vendor credit memos

- Enter recurring bills

You have two ways to send money to vendors: You can enter the bill you received into QuickBooks, and then pay it later, or you can simply write a check without entering a bill. This chapter covers the process of entering bills, and also shows you how to link expenses on those bills to customers, so you can later send an invoice to the customer in order to be reimbursed for the vendor expense.

Chapter 12 covers paying vendors, either by paying the bills you entered into QuickBooks, or writing a check without entering a bill first.

Entering your bills into QuickBooks and then paying them in a separate transaction is accrual accounting. That means an expense is posted to your Profit & Loss statement when you enter the bill, not when you actually pay the bill. Your Accounts Payable account should always equal the total of unpaid bills in your company file.

However, if your taxes are filed on a cash basis (which means an expense isn't posted until you actually pay the bill), be assured (and assure your accountant) that QuickBooks understands how to report your financial figures on a cash basis. (See Chapter 21 for information on preparing financial reports.)

Recording Vendor Bills

When the mail arrives, after you open all the envelopes that contain checks from customers (I always do that first), you should tell QuickBooks about the bills that arrived.

To enter your bills, choose Vendors | Enter Bills from the menu bar. When the Enter Bills window opens (see Figure 11-1), you can fill out the information from the bill you received.

 NOTE: If you're using multicurrency (see Appendix A), the Amount Due field uses the currency of the vendor you select, along with the appropriate amount in your currency.

The window has two sections: the heading section, which contains information about the vendor and the bill, and the details section, in which you record the data related to your general ledger accounts.

The details section has two tabs: Expenses and Items. In this section, I'll cover bills that are posted to Expenses; entering Items is covered later in this chapter when I discuss the purchase of inventory items.

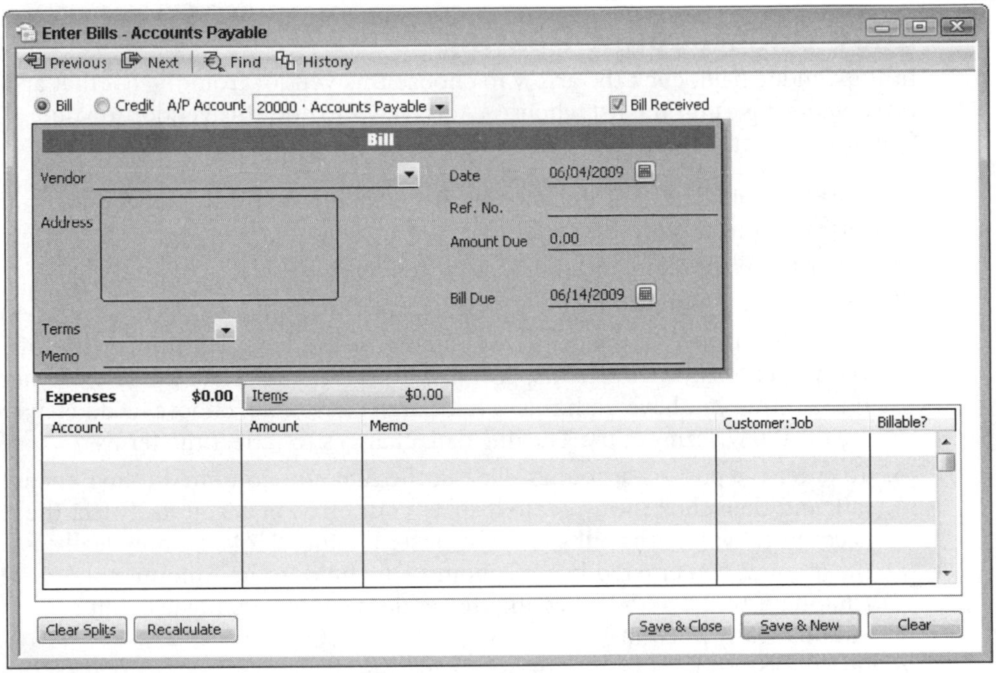

FIGURE 11-1 The Enter Bills window has a heading section and a details section.

NOTE: The A/P Account field (and accompanying drop-down list) appears at the top of the Enter Bills window only if you have multiple Accounts Payable accounts. For example, some manufacturers and distributors separate payables for overhead expenses from payables to suppliers of inventory parts (usually called Accounts Payable—Trade).

Depending on the bill, you may be able to assign the entire bill to one expense account (the easiest task), or you may have to split the bill among multiple expense accounts. For example, your utility bills are usually posted to the appropriate utility account (electric, heat, and so on). However, credit card bills may be split among numerous expenses, and loan payments are split between interest (an expense account) and principal (a liability account).

Easy One-Account Posting

In the Vendor field, click the arrow to choose this vendor from the list that appears. If the vendor isn't on the list, choose <Add New> to add this vendor to your QuickBooks vendor list. Then fill out the rest of the bill window as follows:

1. Enter the bill date. The due date then fills in automatically, depending on the terms you have with this vendor.
2. Enter the vendor's invoice number in the Ref. No. field.
3. Enter the amount of the bill in the Amount Due field.
4. In the Terms field, if the displayed data doesn't reflect your terms with this vendor, click the arrow to display a list of terms, and select the one you need. If the terms you have with this vendor aren't available, choose <Add New> to create a new Terms entry. The due date changes to reflect the terms.
5. To enter the posting accounts, click in the Account column on the Expenses tab, and then click the arrow to display your chart of accounts. Select the account to which this bill should be posted. QuickBooks automatically assigns the amount you entered in the Amount Due field to the Amount column. (See Chapter 4 to learn how to configure vendors so the posting account is automatically filled in.)
6. If you wish, enter a note in the Memo column.
7. In the Customer:Job column, enter a customer or job if you're paying a bill that you want to track for job costing, or if this bill is a reimbursable expense. See the discussions on tracking and charging customers for reimbursable expenses later in this chapter.
8. If you're tracking classes, a Class column appears; enter the appropriate class.
9. When you're finished, click Save & New to save this bill and bring up another blank Enter Bills window. When you've entered all your bills, click Save & Close.

NOTE: If you don't set up terms for a vendor, the due date is automatically filled out using the default number of days for paying bills. QuickBooks sets this default at 10 days, but you can change the default by choosing Edit | Preferences and going to the Company Preferences tab of the Bills category.

Splitting Expenses Among Multiple Accounts

Some bills aren't neatly assigned to one account in your general ledger; instead, they're split among multiple accounts. The most common examples are a loan repayment where you post the interest to your Interest expense account and the principal to the liability account for the loan, or a credit card bill that covers multiple categories of expenses (if you're treating those bills as vendor bills and not managing your credit card as a liability, as discussed in Chapter 13).

Entering a vendor bill with split expenses is the same as entering a vendor bill that's assigned to one expense (as described in the previous section), until you begin assigning the expense accounts and amounts in the details section of the Enter Bills window.

When you enter the first account in the Account column, QuickBooks automatically applies the entire amount of the bill in the Amount column. Replace that data with the amount you want to assign to the account you selected.

Then, on the next row, select the next account. As you add each additional account to the column, QuickBooks assumes that the unallocated amount is assigned to that account (see Figure 11-2). Repeat the process of changing the amount and adding another account until the total amount assigned to accounts equals the amount of the vendor bill.

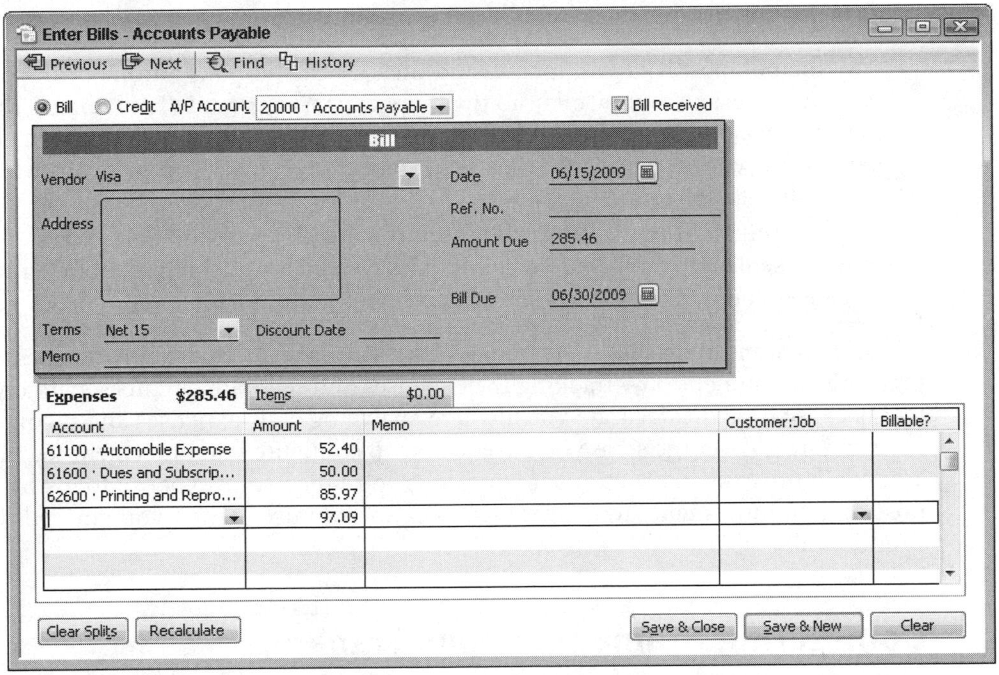

FIGURE 11-2 QuickBooks keeps recalculating, so the last account posting entry automatically has the correct amount.

TIP: If you don't fill in an amount for the bill in the header section, or you make a typo and the amounts in the line items don't match the total, click Recalculate to have QuickBooks add the line items and insert the total in the Amount Due field.

Reimbursable Expenses

A reimbursable expense is one that you incurred on behalf of a customer. Even though you pay the vendor bill, there's an agreement with your customer that you'll send an invoice to recover your costs. There are two common types of reimbursable expenses:

- General expenses, such as long-distance telephone charges, parking and tolls, and other incidental expenses, might be incurred on behalf of a client. Those portions of the vendor bill that apply to customer agreements for reimbursement are split out when you enter the bill.
- Specific goods or services are purchased on behalf of the customer.

Options for Managing Reimbursable Expenses

You have two ways to manage reimbursable expenses:

- Pay the bill, post it to an expense, and then let QuickBooks automatically post the customer's reimbursement to the same expense account. This cancels the original expense and reduces the expense total in your Profit & Loss statements, so that the expense amount reflects the net between what you paid and what you collected for reimbursement.
- Pay the bill and then let QuickBooks automatically post the customer's reimbursement to an income account that's created for tracking reimbursements. This lets you track totals for both expenses and reimbursements.

You may want to discuss these choices with your accountant. Many businesses prefer the second option—tracking the expenses and reimbursements separately—just because it's more accurate when you're analyzing your expenses and income. I'll therefore go over the steps you have to take to configure reimbursement tracking. You can ignore the instructions if you prefer to reduce your expense totals by posting reimbursements to the expense account you used when you entered the vendor's bill.

Configuring Reimbursement Tracking

To track reimbursed costs from customers, you need to enable reimbursement tracking in QuickBooks, and you must also create income accounts that are used for collecting reimbursements.

Enabling Reimbursement Tracking

To tell QuickBooks that you want to track reimbursable costs, you must enable the feature in the Preferences dialog box, using the following steps:

1. Choose Edit | Preferences to open the Preferences dialog.
2. Select the Time & Expenses icon in the left pane.
3. Click the Company Preferences tab.
4. In the Invoicing Options section of the dialog, click the check box next to the option labeled Track Reimbursed Expenses As Income to put a check mark in the box.
5. Click OK.

Applying Automatic Markups

The Time & Expenses Preferences dialog has an option for setting a default markup percentage. You can use this feature to have QuickBooks automatically mark up expenses you're linking to a customer for reimbursement.

This field is unrelated to the option to track reimbursed expenses as income. You can apply this markup whether you're tracking reimbursed expenses as income, or posting the reimbursements to the original expense account.

NOTE: It's not uncommon to mark up reimbursed expenses; in fact, if you look at the P&L of many companies you see that the shipping expense is a negative number (meaning it's really a credit, like income, instead of a debit). That's because the markups applied when charging customers for shipping exceeded the cost of shipping for the company.

The markup percentage is *not* just a markup for reimbursed expenses, it's a system-wide markup. If you enter a default markup percentage here, when you enter an amount in the Cost field when you're creating or editing an item, QuickBooks will automatically fill in the item's Price field by marking up the cost with this percentage.

You can override any automatic markup that QuickBooks applies, so filling in a percentage in this field doesn't prevent you from setting up your own pricing formula for any individual item.

Setting up Income Accounts for Reimbursement

As a result of enabling this option, QuickBooks adds a new field to the dialog you use when you create or edit an expense account. As you can see in Figure 11-3, you can configure an expense account so that reimbursements for the expense are posted to an income account. Whenever you post a vendor expense to this account and also indicate that the expense is reimbursable, the amount you charge to the customer when you create an invoice for that customer is automatically posted to the income account that's linked to this expense account.

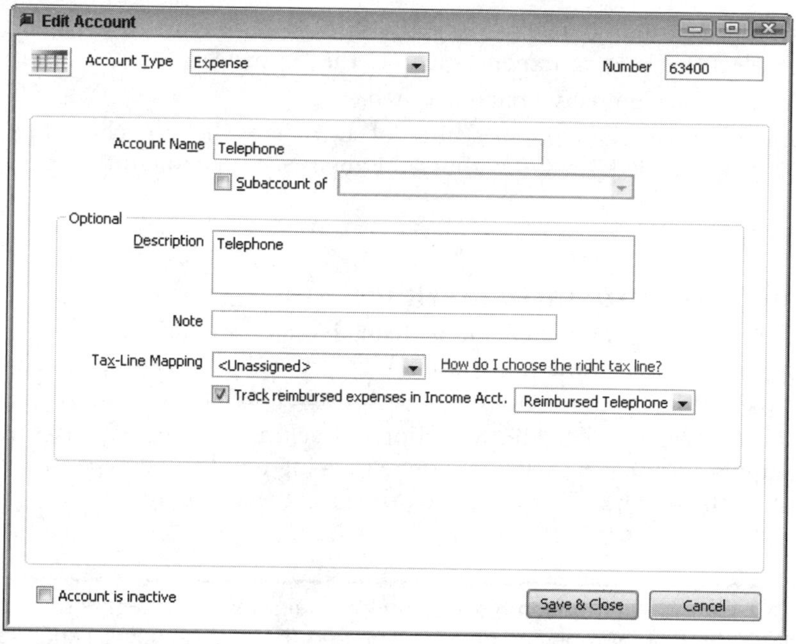

FIGURE 11-3 Configure expense accounts to post reimbursements to an income account.

You may have numerous expense accounts that you want to use for reimbursable expenses; in fact, that's the common scenario. Portions of telephone bills, travel expenses, subcontractor expenses, and so on are frequently passed on to customers for reimbursement.

The easiest way to manage all of this is to enable those expense accounts to track reimbursements and post the income from customers to one account named Reimbursed Expenses. However, QuickBooks insists on a one-to-one relationship between a reimbursable expense and the reimbursement income from that expense. As a result, if you have multiple expense accounts for which you may receive reimbursement (a highly likely scenario), you must also create multiple income accounts for accepting reimbursed expenses.

This is a one-time chore, however, so when you've finished setting up the accounts, you can just enter transactions, knowing QuickBooks will automatically post reimbursed expenses to your new income accounts.

The best way to set up the income accounts you'll need for reimbursement is to use subaccounts. That way, your reports will show the total amount of income due to reimbursed expenses, and you have individual account totals if you have some reason to audit a total.

Depending on the company type you selected during the EasyStep Interview, QuickBooks may have already created a Reimbursed Expenses account in the Income section of your chart of accounts. If so, you already have a parent account, and you only have to set up subaccounts.

Start by creating the parent account, if you don't already have an Income account named Reimbursed Expenses, using the following steps:

1. Open the chart of accounts by pressing CTRL-A.
2. Press CTRL-N to open the Add New Account: Choose Account Type dialog.
3. Select Income as the account type and click Continue.
4. In the Add New Account dialog, enter an account number (if you use numbers) and name the account Reimbursed Expenses (or something similar).
5. Click Save & New.

Now that you've created the parent account you can create all the subaccounts you need, using the same steps you used to create the parent account, with the following changes:

- If you're using numbered accounts, use the next sequential number after the number you used for the parent account.
- Name the account for the type of expense you're tracking, such as Telephone Reimbursements.
- Select the Subaccount Of check box and link it to the parent account you created.

Repeat this process as many times as necessary. Your reports show the individual account postings as well as a total for all postings for the parent account.

Don't forget to edit any of your existing expense accounts that you'll use to invoice customers for reimbursements. Select the account and press CTRL-E to open the account record in Edit mode. Then select the check box to track reimbursed expenses and enter the appropriate income account.

Recording Reimbursable Expenses

If you want to be reimbursed by customers for expenses you incurred on their behalf, you must enter the appropriate data while you're filling out the vendor's bill (or writing a direct disbursement check to a vendor for which you don't enter bills). After you enter the account and the amount, click the arrow in the Customer:Job column and select the appropriate customer or job from the drop-down list.

Entering data in the Customer:Job column automatically places a check box with a check mark inserted in the column named Billable?. The expense is charged to the customer and you can pass the charge along to the customer when you create an invoice (covered in Chapter 9).

NOTE: You can click the check box to remove the check mark if you don't want to bill the customer for the expense but you still want to track what you're spending for the customer or the job. This disables the reimbursement feature, but the expense is still associated with the customer/job so that you can track job costs.

Sometimes, a vendor's bill is for an amount that's not entirely chargeable to a customer. Some of the amount may be your own responsibility, and it may also be that multiple customers owe you reimbursement for the amount. (This is often the case with telephone expenses when your customers reimburse you for long-distance charges.)

Use the following steps to create a vendor bill (or a direct disbursement check if you're not entering vendor bills) that splits expenses between you and a customer or multiple customers:

1. Select the vendor and enter the amount and other data needed in the header section.
2. Select the expense account, and then enter the portion of the bill that is your own responsibility.
3. In the next line, select the same account, and then enter the portion of the bill you are charging back to a customer.
4. Enter an explanation of the charge in the Memo column. (When you create the invoice, the text in the Memo column is the only description the customer sees.)
5. In the Customer:Job column, choose the appropriate customer or job.
6. Repeat steps 3 through 5 to include any additional customers for this expense account.

When you're finished, the total amount entered should match the amount on the vendor's bill (see Figure 11-4).

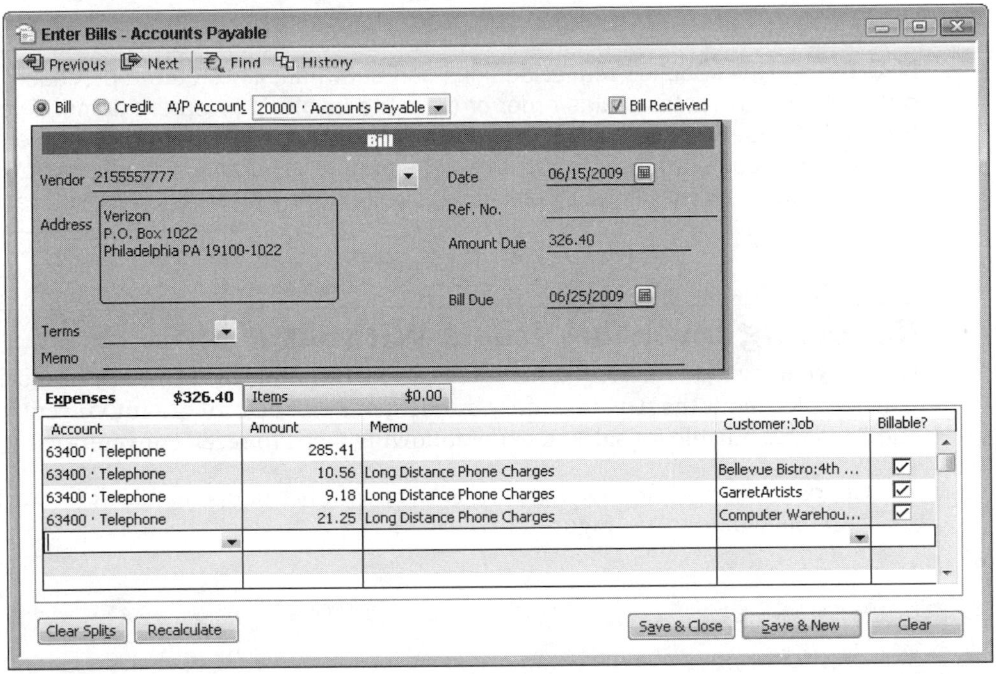

FIGURE 11-4 Charge portions of an expense to one or more customers by splitting the total expense among customers when you enter the vendor bill.

Managing Inventory Item Purchases

If the vendor bill you're recording is for inventory items, you need to take a different approach, because the accounting issues (the way you post amounts) are different. Frequently, two transactions are involved when you buy items for inventory:

- You receive the inventory products.
- You receive the bill for the inventory products.

Sometimes the bill comes before the products, sometimes the products arrive first, and sometimes both events occur at the same time (the bill is in an envelope pasted to the carton or included inside the carton). In this section, I'll go over all the available scenarios, including how to receive inventory through purchase orders.

If you create a purchase order, you can use it to automate the receiving and vendor bill entry processes when the inventory items and the bill for them arrive. (See Chapter 7 to learn how to create purchase orders.)

N O T E : QuickBooks Premier editions can automatically create a purchase order when you create a sales order or estimate involving inventory items. If you think this is useful for your company, consider upgrading to one of the Premier editions. You can learn how to use this nifty feature in *Running QuickBooks 2009 Premier Editions* from CPA911 Publishing, available at your favorite bookstore.

Receiving Inventory Items Without a Bill

If the inventory items arrive before you receive a bill from the vendor, you must tell QuickBooks about the new inventory, so the items can be brought into inventory and become available for sales. Use the following steps to receive inventory:

1. Choose Vendors | Receive Items from the menu bar to open a blank Create Item Receipts window (see Figure 11-5).

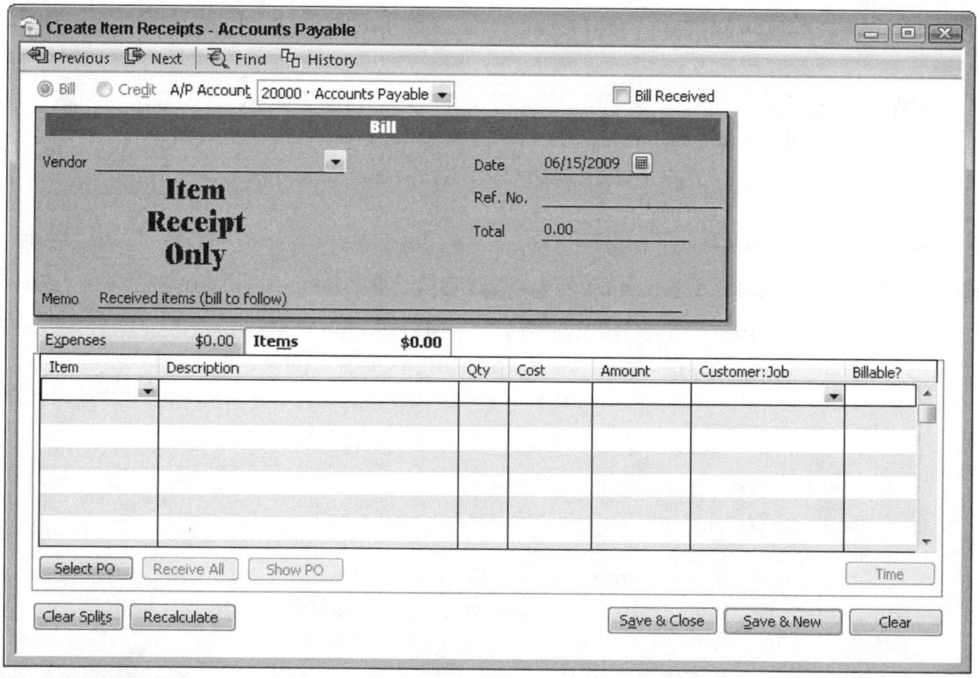

FIGURE 11-5 Receive items into inventory so you can sell them.

2. Select the vendor name, and if open purchase orders exist for this vendor, QuickBooks notifies you:

Open POs Exist

⚠ Open purchase orders exist for this vendor. Do you want to receive against one or more of these orders?

[Yes]   [No]

---

3. If you know there isn't a purchase order for this particular shipment, click No, and just fill out the Create Item Receipts window manually.

4. If you know a purchase order exists for this shipment, or if you're not sure, click Yes. QuickBooks displays all the open purchase orders for this vendor so you can put a check mark next to the appropriate PO (or multiple POs if the shipment that arrived covers more than one PO). If no PO matching this shipment is listed on the Open Purchase Orders list for this vendor, click Cancel on the Open Purchase Orders window to return to the receipts window and fill in the data manually.

5. If a PO exists, QuickBooks fills out the Create Item Receipts window using the information in the PO. Check the shipment against the PO and change any quantities that don't match.

6. Click Save & New to receive the next shipment into inventory, or click Save & Close if this takes care of all the receipts of goods.

QuickBooks posts the amounts in the purchase order to your Accounts Payable account. This is not the standard, Generally Accepted Accounting Procedure (GAAP) method for handling receipt of goods (because only a vendor bill should be posted to A/P), and if your accountant asks about the transaction, you can explain how QuickBooks handles this. (See the sidebar "How QuickBooks Posts Inventory Receipts and Bills")

In order to avoid double-posting the A/P liability when the bill does arrive, you must use a special QuickBooks transaction window (discussed next). Because warehouse personnel frequently handle the receipt of goods, and receipt of bills is handled by a bookkeeper, a lack of communication may interfere with using the correct transaction methods. QuickBooks prevents this problem by alerting the data-entry person of a possible error. If the bookkeeper uses the standard Enter Bills transaction window, as soon as the vendor is entered in the window QuickBooks displays a message stating that goods have been received from this vendor and the bill should not be recorded with the standard Enter Bills window, if the bill is connected to the receipt of goods.

▶▶ FYI

How QuickBooks Posts Inventory Receipts and Bills

Technically, an accounts payable liability should only be connected to a bill. When a bill comes, you owe the money. While it's safe to assume that if the goods showed up the bill will follow, technically you don't incur the A/P liability until you have a bill.

Even if you used a PO, the costs on the PO may not be the current costs for the items, and the vendor bill that shows up may have different amounts. Maybe the PO amounts you filled in were taken from your inventory records or by your own manual entry (perhaps using an out-of-date price list from the vendor). It's not uncommon for purchasing agents to fill out a PO without calling the vendor and checking the latest cost. The bill that arrives will have the correct costs, and those costs are the amounts that are supposed to be posted to the A/P account.

If this situation occurs, QuickBooks changes (totally replaces) the posting it made to A/P when you received the items, so that the new amounts match the bill. This means that on one date your A/P total and inventory valuation may have one amount, and a few days later, the amount may magically change even though no additional transactions are displayed in reports. If the interval between those days crosses the month, or even worse, the year, your accountant might have a problem trying to figure out what happened. But now that you understand what happens, you can explain it.

Recording Bills for Items Already Received

After you receive the items, eventually the bill comes from the vendor. To enter the bill, do *not* use the regular Enter Bills icon in the Vendors Navigator window, which would cause another posting to Accounts Payable. Instead, do the following:

1. Choose Vendors | Enter Bill For Received Items to open the Select Item Receipt dialog.
2. Select the vendor, and you see the current items receipt information for that vendor.

3. Select the appropriate listing and click OK to open an Enter Bills window. The information from the items receipt is used to fill in the bill information.

4. Change anything in the Items tab that needs to be changed, such as a different cost per unit.

5. To add any shipping or handling charges, move to the Expenses tab and enter the appropriate accounts and amounts.

6. If you made any changes, you must click the Recalculate button so QuickBooks can match the total in the Amount Due field to the changed line item data.

7. Click Save & Close.

Even if you didn't make any changes, and the bill matches the Receipts transaction, QuickBooks displays a message asking if you're sure you want to save the changes. Say Yes. The message appears because you've changed the transaction from a receipt of goods transaction to a vendor bill transaction and QuickBooks overwrites the original postings that were made when you received the items. If you look at the Accounts Payable register (or the Inventory Assets register) after you receive the items, the transaction type is ITEM RCPT. When you save this transaction, QuickBooks overwrites the entire transaction, changing the transaction type to BILL (and also uses the new amounts if you made changes).

Receiving Items and Bills Simultaneously

If the items and the bill arrive at the same time (sometimes the bill is in the shipping carton), you must tell QuickBooks about those events simultaneously. To do this, choose Vendors | Receive Items And Enter Bill. The standard Enter Bills window opens, and when you enter the vendor's name you may see a message telling you an open PO exists for the vendor. The message dialog asks if you want to receive these goods (and the bill) against an open PO.

Click Yes to see the open POs for this vendor and select the appropriate PO. The line items on the bill are filled in automatically, and you can correct any quantity or price difference between your original PO and the actuals. When you save the transaction, QuickBooks receives the items into inventory in addition to posting the bill to A/P.

If no PO exists, enter the item quantities and amounts. When you save the transaction, QuickBooks receives the items into inventory in addition to posting the bill to A/P.

Recording Vendor Credits

If you receive a credit from a vendor, you must record it in QuickBooks. Then you can apply it against an open vendor bill or let it float until your next order from the vendor. (See Chapter 12 for information about paying bills, which includes applying vendor credits to bills.)

QuickBooks doesn't provide a discrete credit form for accounts payable; instead, you can change a vendor bill form to a credit form with a click of the mouse. Follow these steps to create a vendor credit:

1. Choose Vendors | Enter Bills to open the Enter Bills window.
2. Select the Credit option at the top of the window, which automatically deselects Bill and changes the fields on the form (see Figure 11-6).

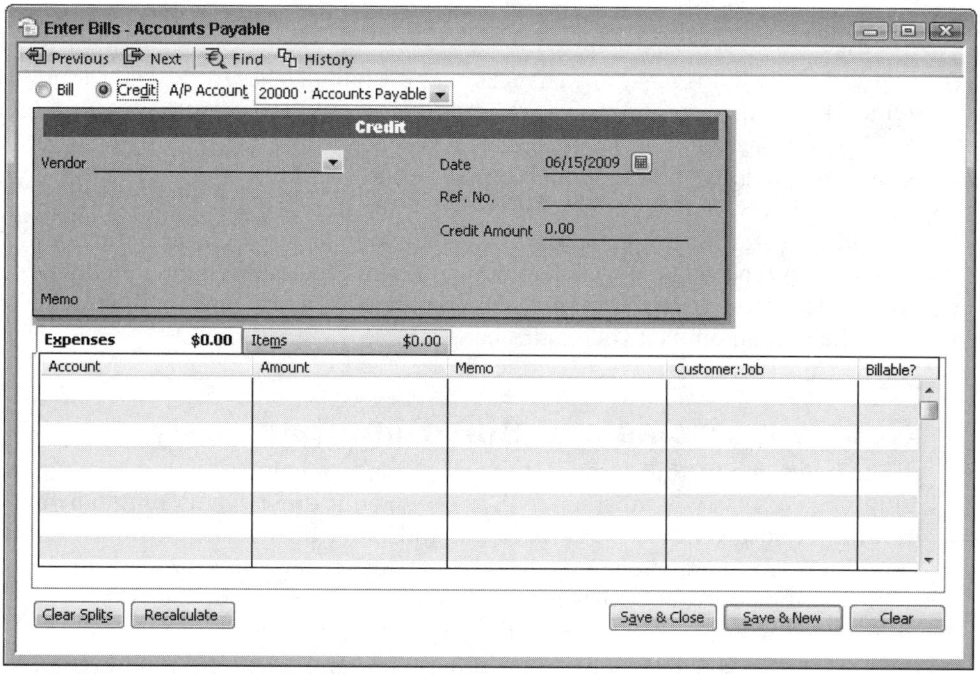

FIGURE 11-6 When you select the Credit option, the Enter Bills transaction window changes—the fields for terms and due date disappear.

3. Choose the vendor from the drop-down list that appears when you click the arrow in the Vendor field.
4. Enter the date of the credit memo.
5. In the Ref. No. field, enter the vendor's credit memo number.
6. Enter the amount of the credit memo.
7. If the credit is not for inventory items, use the Expenses tab to assign an account and amount to this credit.
8. If the credit is for inventory items, use the Items tab to enter the items, along with the quantity and cost, for which you are receiving this credit.
9. Click Save & Close to save the credit (unless you have more credits to enter—in which case, click Save & New).

NOTE: If you've agreed that the vendor pays the shipping costs to return items, don't forget to enter that amount in the Expenses tab.

Here are the postings to your general ledger when you save a vendor credit:

Account	Debit	Credit
Inventory Asset		Amount of returned items
Applicable expense account(s)		Amounts of expenses in the credit
Accounts Payable	Total credit amount	

TIP: Don't use an RA (Return Authorization) number you received on the telephone as the basis for your credit. Wait for the credit memo to arrive so your records and the vendor's records match. This makes it much easier to settle disputed amounts.

Entering Recurring Bills

You probably have quite a few bills that you must pay every month. Commonly, the list includes your rent or mortgage payment, loan payments, or a retainer fee (for an attorney, accountant, or subcontractor).

You can make it easy to pay those bills every month without entering a bill each time. QuickBooks provides a feature called *memorized transactions,* and you can put it to work to make sure your recurring bills are covered.

Creating a Memorized Bill

To create a memorized transaction for a recurring bill, first open the Enter Bills window and fill out the information as you normally would.

TIP: If the amount of a recurring bill isn't always exactly the same it's okay to leave the Amount Due field blank. You can fill in the amount each time you use the memorized bill.

Before you save the transaction, memorize it. To accomplish this, press CTRL-M to open the Memorize Transaction dialog.

Use these guidelines to fill out the Memorize Transaction dialog:

- Use the Name field to enter a name for the transaction. QuickBooks automatically enters the vendor name, but you can change it. Use a name that describes the transaction so you don't have to rely on your memory.
- Select Remind Me (the default) to tell QuickBooks to issue a reminder that this bill must be put into the system to be paid.
- Select Don't Remind Me if you want to forego getting a reminder and enter the bill yourself.
- Select Automatically Enter to have QuickBooks enter this bill as a payable automatically, without reminders. Specify the number of Days In Advance To Enter this bill into the system. At the appropriate time, the bill appears in the Select Bills To Pay List you use to pay your bills (covered in Chapter 12).
- Select the interval for this bill from the drop-down list in the How Often field.
- Enter the Next Date this bill is due.
- If this payment is finite, such as a loan that has a specific number of payments, use the Number Remaining field to specify how many times this bill must be paid.

TIP: If you created the bill only for the purpose of creating a memorized transaction and you don't want to enter the bill into the system for payment at this time, after you save the memorized transaction, close the Enter Bills window and respond No when QuickBooks asks if you want to save the transaction. The memorized transaction is saved even if you don't save this bill.

Click OK in the Memorize Transaction window to save it, and then click Save & Close in the Enter Bills window to save the bill.

CAUTION: When you select the reminder options for the memorized bill, the reminders only appear if you're using reminders in QuickBooks. Choose Edit | Preferences and click the Reminders category icon to view or change reminders options.

Using a Memorized Bill

If you've opted to enter the memorized bill yourself instead of having it automatically added to the Select Bills To Pay List, you must open it to make it a current payable. To open a memorized bill, use the following steps:

1. Press CTRL-T to open the Memorized Transaction List window.
2. Double-click the appropriate listing to open the bill in the usual Enter Bills window with the next due date showing.
3. If the Amount Due field is blank, fill it in.
4. Click Save & Close to save this bill so it becomes a current payable and is listed as a bill that must be paid when you write checks to pay your bills. (See Chapter 12 for information about paying bills.)

Creating Memorized Bill Groups

If you have a whole bunch of memorized transactions to cover all the bills that are due the first of the month (rent, mortgage, utilities, car payments, whatever), you don't have to select them for payment one at a time. You can create a group and then invoke actions on the group (automatically performing the action on every bill in the group). To accomplish this, use the following steps:

1. Press CTRL-T to display the Memorized Transaction List.
2. Right-click any blank spot in the Memorized Transaction window and choose New Group from the shortcut menu.
3. In the New Memorized Transaction Group window, give this group a name (such as 1st Of Month or 15th Of Month).
4. Fill out the fields to specify the way you want the bills in this group to be handled.
5. Click OK to save this group.

Adding Memorized Bills to Groups

After you create the group, you can add memorized transactions to it as follows:

1. In the Memorized Transaction List window, select the first memorized transaction you want to add to the group.
2. Right-click and choose Edit Memorized Transaction from the shortcut menu.
3. When the Schedule Memorized Transaction window opens with this transaction displayed, select the option named With Transactions In Group.
4. Select the group from the list that appears when you click the arrow next to the Group Name field and click OK.

Repeat this process for each bill you want to add to the group. As you create future memorized bills, just select the With Transactions In Group option to add the bills to the appropriate group straightaway.

If you have other recurring bills with different criteria (perhaps they're due on a different day of the month, or they're due annually), create groups for them and add the individual transactions to the group.

Paying Vendors

In this chapter:

- Choose bills to pay
- Apply discounts and credits
- Make direct disbursements
- Remit sales tax

Periodically you have to pay your vendors, and in QuickBooks you have some choices about the way you perform that task:

- You can enter vendor bills into QuickBooks when they arrive (covered in Chapter 11) and then pay them.
- You can save the bills in a large envelope or box and write checks (called direct disbursements), skipping the step of recording the bills in QuickBooks.

Some companies do both. They enter vendor bills into QuickBooks and write direct disbursements for vendors that don't send bills (such as the landlord, the mortgage company, the bank loan, and so on).

> **NOTE:** If you're using the Multicurrency feature (see Appendix A), amounts are displayed in the vendor's currency as well as your own currency.

Choosing What to Pay

You don't have to pay every bill that's entered, nor do you have to pay the entire amount due for each bill. Your current bank balance and your relationships with your vendors have a large influence on the decisions you make.

There are all sorts of rules that business consultants recite about how to decide what to pay when money is short, and the term "essential vendors" is prominent. I've never figured out how to define "essential," since having electricity can be just as important as buying inventory items. Having worked with hundreds of clients, however, I can give you two rules to follow that are based on those clients' experiences:

- The government (taxes) comes first. Never, never, never use payroll withholding money to pay bills.
- It's better to send lots of vendors small checks than to send gobs of money to a couple of vendors who have been applying pressure. Vendors hate being ignored much more than they dislike small payments on account.

Viewing Your Unpaid Bills

Start by examining the bills you entered in QuickBooks that are due. The best way to see that list is in detailed form instead of a summary total for each vendor. To accomplish this, choose Reports | Vendors & Payables | Unpaid Bills Detail to see a list of your outstanding vendor bills (see Figure 12-1).

Type	Date	Num	Due Date	Aging	Open Balance
2155557777					
Bill	06/15/2009		06/25/2009	5	326.40
Total 2155557777					326.40
Discount Office Supplies					
Bill	04/08/2009	1258...	05/08/2009	53	129.65
Total Discount Office Supplies					129.65
GeekRob					
Bill	05/12/2009	36987	05/22/2009	39	1,005.00
Total GeekRob					1,005.00
ISP					
Bill	05/27/2009	1548...	06/06/2009	24	139.90
Total ISP					139.90
Our Supplier					
Bill	06/15/2009		06/25/2009	5	210.00
Total Our Supplier					210.00
Visa					
Bill	06/15/2009		06/30/2009		285.46
Total Visa					285.46

FIGURE 12-1 Check the details for your current unpaid bills.

By default, the report is sorted by vendor name, and you may find that choosing Date from the drop-down list in the Sort By field is helpful in deciding which bills need urgent attention.

Double-click any entry if you want to see the original bill you entered, including all line items and notes you made in the Memo column.

You can filter the report to display only certain bills. To accomplish this, click Modify Report and go to the Filters tab in the Modify Report dialog. Use the filters to change the display, perhaps filtering for bills that are more or less than a certain amount, or for bills that are more than a certain number of days overdue.

Print the report, and if you're short on cash, work out a formula that will maintain good relationships with your vendors.

Choosing the Bills to Pay

When you're ready to tell QuickBooks which bills you want to pay, choose Vendors | Pay Bills. The Pay Bills window appears (see Figure 12-2), and you can make your selections using the following guidelines.

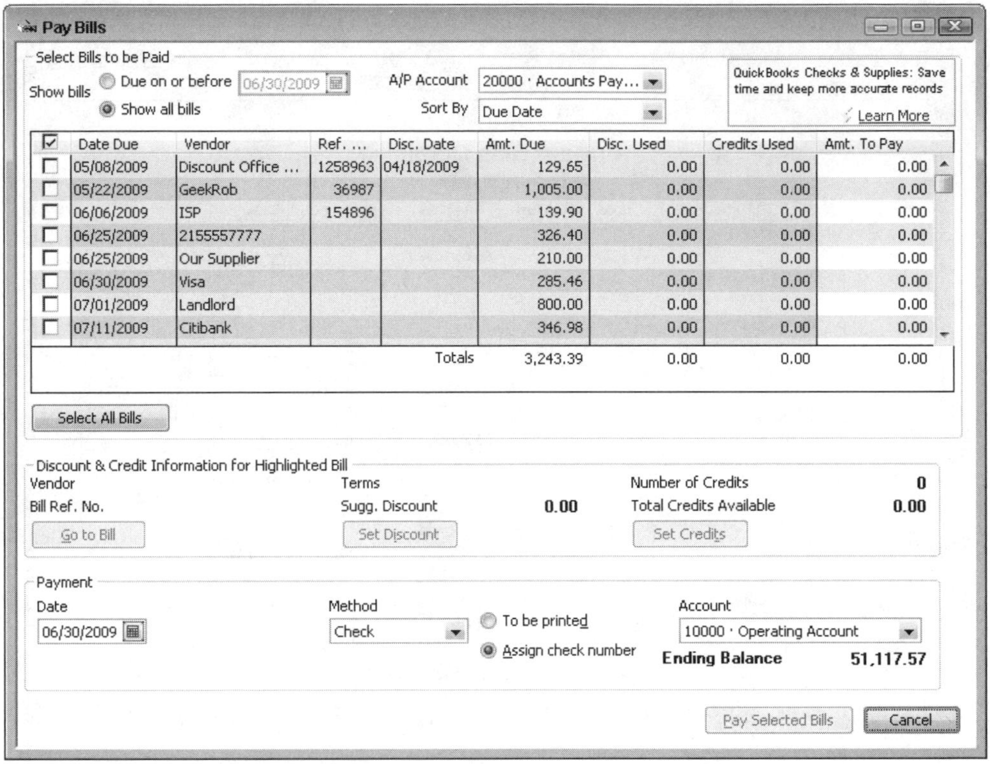

FIGURE 12-2 Paying bills starts in the Pay Bills window.

Due On Or Before Selecting this option displays all the bills due within ten days of the last bill you entered (the date that's automatically inserted), but you can change the date to display more or fewer bills. If you have discounts for timely payments with any vendors, this selection is more important than it seems. The due date isn't the same as the discount date. Therefore, if you have terms of 2%10Net30, a bill that arrived on April 2 is due on May 2 and won't appear on the list if the due date filter you select is April 30. Unfortunately, the discount date is April 12, but you won't know because the bill won't appear. If you want to use a due date filter, go out at least 30 days. (See the section "Applying Discounts" later in this chapter.)

Show All Bills Shows all the bills in your system, regardless of when they're due. This is the safest option (and it's selected by default), because you won't accidentally miss a discount date. On the other hand, the list can be rather long.

A/P Account If you have multiple A/P accounts, select the account to which the bills you want to pay were originally posted. If you don't have multiple A/P accounts, this field doesn't appear in the window. If you do have multiple A/P accounts, you have to repeat this process for each of them.

Sort Bills By   Determines the manner in which your bills are displayed in the Pay Bills window. The choices are

- Due Date (the default)
- Discount Date
- Vendor
- Amount Due

Payment Method   The Method drop-down list displays the available methods of payment: Check and Credit Card are listed by default, but if you've signed up for QuickBooks online bill payment services, that payment method also appears in the list (see Chapter 15 to learn about using QuickBooks for online banking, including online bill payments).

If you are paying by check and QuickBooks prints your checks, be sure the To Be Printed option is selected. When you finish selecting payments click the Pay Selected Bills button, and QuickBooks opens the Payment Summary dialog where you can choose to print the checks now, or wait until later. (See Chapter 25 to learn how to set up and configure check printing.)

If you prepare checks manually, select Assign Check Number, and when you click the Pay Selected Bills button, QuickBooks opens the Assign Check Numbers dialog so you can specify the starting check number for this bill paying session.

Payment Account   The checking or credit card account you want to use for these payments.

Payment Date   This is the date that appears on your checks. By default, the current date appears in the field, but if you want to predate or postdate your checks, you can change that date. If you merely select the bills today and wait until tomorrow (or later) to print the checks, the payment date set here still appears on the checks.

TIP: You can tell QuickBooks to date checks on the day of printing by changing the Checking Preferences.

If you made changes to the selection fields (perhaps you changed the due date filter), your list of bills to be paid may change. If all the bills displayed are to be paid either in full or in part, you're ready to move to the next step. If there are still some bills on the list that you're not going to pay, you can just select the ones you do want to pay. Selecting a bill is simple—just click the leftmost column to place a check mark in it. You can also click Select All Bills to select all of them (and click the leftmost column to toggle off the check mark of any bills you don't want to pay in this bill-paying session).

Paying Bills in Full

The easiest bills to pay (if you have enough cash in the bank) are those you want to pay in full, when none of them have credits or discounts to worry about. Select the bills, and then click Pay Selected Bills.

Making Partial Payments

If you don't want to pay a bill in full, you can easily adjust the amount by clicking the check mark column on the bill's listing to select the bill for payment. Then move to the Amt. To Pay column and replace the amount that's displayed with the amount you want to pay. When you press TAB, the total at the bottom of the column is recalculated (and QuickBooks reserves the unpaid balance for your next bill payment session).

Using Discounts and Credits

QuickBooks has a configuration option you can set to determine whether you make the decision about applying discounts and credits at the time you select the bill for payment, or let QuickBooks apply the amounts automatically to bills that you select for payment.

To set your default options, choose Edit | Preferences and select the Bills category in the left pane. In the Company Preferences tab, select the option Automatically Use Discounts And Credits, and enter the account to which you post the discounts.

➡ FYI

Applying Discounts for Timely Payments

It's probable that the only vendors who offer discounts are those from whom you buy inventory items, so you should put the discount account in the section of your chart of accounts that holds the Cost Of Goods Sold accounts. In fact, the most efficient way to do this is to have a parent account called Cost Of Goods Sold and then create two subaccounts:

- Cost Of Goods Purchased
- Discounts Taken

Only post to the subaccounts (make sure your inventory items are linked to the Cost of Goods Purchased subaccount). You'll be able to see the individual amounts on your financial reports, and the parent account will report the net COGS.

QuickBooks may have created a Cost Of Goods Sold account automatically during your company setup. If not, create one and then create the subaccounts.

The account for the discounts you take (sometimes called *earned discounts*) can be either an income or expense account. There's no right and wrong here, although I've seen accountants get into heated debates defending a point of view on this subject. If you think of the discount as income (money you've brought into your system by paying your bills promptly), make the account an income account. If you think of the discount as a reverse expense (money you've saved by paying your bills promptly), make the account an expense account (it posts as a minus amount, which means it reduces total expenses).

Applying Discounts

Bills that have terms for discounts for timely payment display the Discount Date (in the Disc. Date column). Bills that have no data in that column do not have discount terms.

If you enabled automatic application of discounts and credits, when you select the bill by clicking the check mark column, the discount is automatically applied. You can see the amount in the Disc. Used column, and the Amt. To Pay column adjusts accordingly.

If the discount isn't applied automatically, it's probably because today's date is later than the discount cutoff date. Don't worry, you can take the discount anyway—see the next section "Taking Discounts After the Discount Date."

If you're making a partial payment and want to adjust the discount, click the Set Discount button to open the Discount And Credits window and enter the amount of the discount you want to take. Click Done, and when you return to the Pay Bills window, the discount is applied and the Amt. To Pay column has the correct amount.

Taking Discounts After the Discount Date

Many businesses deduct the discount amount even if the discount period has expired. The resulting payment, with the discount applied, is frequently accepted by the vendor. Businesses that practice this protocol learn which vendors will accept a discounted payment and which won't (most will). Seeing that the discount you took has been added back in the next statement you receive is a pretty good hint that you're not going to get away with it.

To take a discount after the discount date, select the bill for payment and then click the Set Discount button to open the Discount And Credits window. The amount showing for the discount is zero. Enter the discount you would have been entitled to if you'd paid the bill in a timely fashion and click Done.

How QuickBooks Posts Your Bill Payments

When you pay bills, QuickBooks posts the financial data to your general ledger. I've had users ask why they don't see the expense accounts when they look at the postings for bill paying. The answer is that the expenses were posted when they entered the bills.

If you just write checks (without entering the bills), you enter the accounts to which you're assigning those expenses. For that system (the cash-based system) of paying bills, the postings debit the expense and credit the bank account. See the section "Using Direct Disbursements" later in this chapter for more information.

Understanding the Postings for Bill Payments Without Discounts

Here's what happens in your general ledger when you pay bills that don't have discounts or credits:

Account	Debit	Credit
Accounts Payable	Total bill payments	
Bank		Total bill payments

Understanding the Postings for Discounts

Here's what posts to your general ledger when you take a discount. For example, suppose the original amount of the bill was $484.00 and the discount was $9.68; therefore, the check amount was $474.32. (Remember that the original postings when you entered the bill were for the total amount without the discount.)

Account	Debit	Credit
Accounts Payable	$484.00	
Bank		$474.32
Discounts Taken		$9.68

Applying Credits

If you configured QuickBooks to take credits automatically, when you select a bill for payment, if credits exist for the vendor, the amount of the credit appears in the Credits Used column, and the Amt. To Pay column is adjusted.

If you didn't enable automatic credit application, when you select the bill, the amount of existing credits appears below the list of bills. Click Set Credits to open the Discounts And Credits window. Make the appropriate selections of credit amounts, and click Done to change the Amt. To Pay column to reflect your adjustments.

If credits are applied automatically and you don't want to take the credit against this bill (perhaps you want to save it for another bill), click Set Credits to open the Discounts And Credits window. Deselect the credit and click Done.

If your total credits with the vendor are equal to or exceed the bill you select, QuickBooks does not create a check, because the bill is paid in its entirety with credits (the Payment Summary window that displays indicates an Amount Paid of $0.00).

Sending the Payments

When you finish selecting the bills to pay, click Pay Selected Bills. QuickBooks transfers all the information to the general ledger and fills out your checkbook account register with the payments.

If you chose the option to print checks, QuickBooks displays a Payment Summary dialog (see Figure 12-3) that offers several choices for your next step:

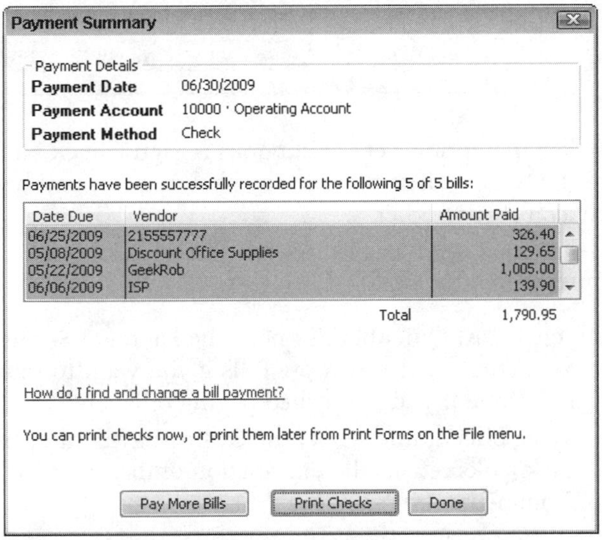

FIGURE 12-3 You can print checks now, or wait until later.

- Choose Pay More Bills to return to the Pay Bills window and select other bills to pay (you'll print these checks later). Use this choice to pay bills without printing checks, such as sending payments to vendors you've configured for online payments.
- Choose Print Checks to print your checks now.
- Click Done to close the Payment Summary dialog and close the Pay Bills window, and print your checks later.

When you defer printing, the checks are posted to the bank account register with the notation To Print. Choose File | Print Forms | Checks to print your checks.

If you selected the Assign Check Number option because you manually write checks, QuickBooks displays the Assign Check Numbers dialog.

- If you select the option Let QuickBooks Assign Check Numbers, QuickBooks looks at the last check number in the bank register and begins numbering with the next available number.
- If you select the option Let Me Assign The Check Numbers Below, enter the check numbers in the dialog.

When you click OK, QuickBooks opens the Payment Summary dialog that displays the payments. Click Pay More Bills if you want to return to the Pay Bills window, or click Done if you're finished paying bills.

If you're paying bills online, select the Online Payment option when you select those bills. QuickBooks retains the information until you go online. (See Chapter 15 to learn about online banking.)

Using Direct Disbursements

A *direct disbursement* is a disbursement of funds (usually by check) that is performed without matching the check to an existing bill. This is check writing without entering bills.

If you're not entering vendor bills, this is how you'll always pay your vendors. However, even if you are entering vendor bills, you sometimes need to write a quick check without going through the process of entering the vendor bill, selecting it, paying it, and printing the check—for example, when a delivery person is standing in front of you waiting for a COD check and doesn't have time for you to go through all those steps.

Manual Direct Disbursement Checks

If you use manual checks, you can write your checks and then tell QuickBooks about it later, or you can bring your checkbook to your computer and enter the checks in QuickBooks as you write them. You have two ways to enter your checks in QuickBooks: in the bank register or in the Write Checks window.

Writing Checks in the Bank Register

To use the bank register, open the bank account register and enter the check directly in a transaction line, as follows:

1. Enter the date.
2. Press the TAB key to move to the Number field. QuickBooks automatically fills in the next available check number.
3. Press TAB to move through the rest of the fields, filling in the name of the payee, the amount of the payment, and the expense account you're assigning to the transaction.
4. Click the Record button to save the transaction.
5. Repeat the steps for the next check and continue until all the manual checks you've written are entered into the register.

Using the Write Checks Window

If you prefer a graphical approach, you can use the Write Checks window to tell QuickBooks about a check you manually prepared. To get there, press CTRL-W. When the Write Checks transaction window opens (see Figure 12-4), select the bank account you're using to write the checks.

The next available check number is already filled in unless the To Be Printed option box is checked (if it is, click it to toggle the check mark off and put the check number in the window). QuickBooks warns you if you enter a check number that's already been used (unfortunately, the warning doesn't appear until you fill in all the data and attempt to save the check).

Fill out the check, posting amounts to the appropriate accounts. If the check is for inventory items, use the Items tab to make sure the items are placed into inventory. When you finish, click Save & New to open a new blank check. When you're through writing checks, click Save & Close to close the Write Checks transaction window. All the checks you wrote are recorded in the bank account register.

 CAUTION: You can't use the check register to purchase items—you must use the Write Checks transaction window.

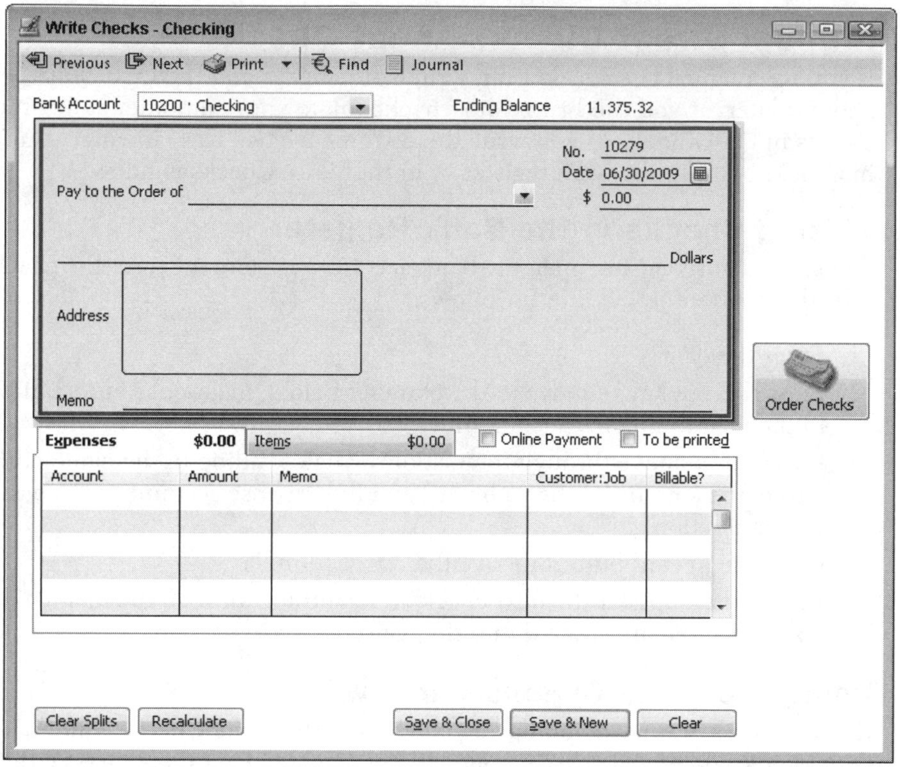

FIGURE 12-4 Fill out the onscreen check the same way you'd fill out a paper check—they look the same.

Printing Direct Disbursement Checks

If you pay your bills as direct disbursements by printing checks from the Write Checks window, by default QuickBooks saves the checks you prepare and then prints them in a batch instead of one at a time.

Open the Write Checks window and make sure the To Be Printed option is selected. Fill out all the fields for the first check and click Save & New to move to the next blank Write Checks window. Continue to fill out checks, until every check you need to print is ready. Then print the checks using one of the following methods:

- Click Save & Close when you are finished filling out all the checks, and then choose File | Print Forms | Checks from the menu bar.
- In the last Write Checks window, click the arrow to the right of the Print button at the top of the Write Checks window, and choose Print Batch.

Postings for Direct Disbursements

The postings for direct disbursements are quite simple:

Account	Debit	Credit
Bank account		Total of all checks written
An account	Total of all checks assigned to this account	
Another account	Total of all checks assigned to this account	
Another account	Total of all checks assigned to this account	

Remitting Sales Tax

If you collect sales tax from your customers, you have an inherent accounts payable bill because you have to turn that money over to the state taxing authorities.

In order to print reports on sales tax (so you can fill out those complicated government sales tax forms), you have to configure your sales tax collections in QuickBooks. If you collect multiple sales taxes, that configuration effort can be more complicated than the government forms.

While I will sometimes use the term "state" in the following sections, your tracking and reporting needs may not be limited to state-based activities. In recent years many states have created multiple sales tax authorities within the state (usually a specific location such as a county, a city, or a group of ZIP codes, each having its own tax rate). Businesses in those states may have to remit the sales tax they collect to both the state and the local sales tax authority (or to multiple local sales tax authorities). As a result, tracking sales tax properly (which means in a manner that makes it possible to fill out all the forms for all the authorities and send each authority the correct remittance) has become a very complicated process.

This discussion assumes you've created the sales tax items you need (covered in Chapter 6), and each item is linked to the right tax authority as a vendor.

QuickBooks' Manage Sales Tax Feature

QuickBooks provides a feature called Manage Sales Tax that acts as a "home page" for information and help, as well as links to reports and payment forms covered in this section. You can open the Manage Sales Tax window (see Figure 12-5) by choosing Vendors | Sales Tax | Manage Sales Tax.

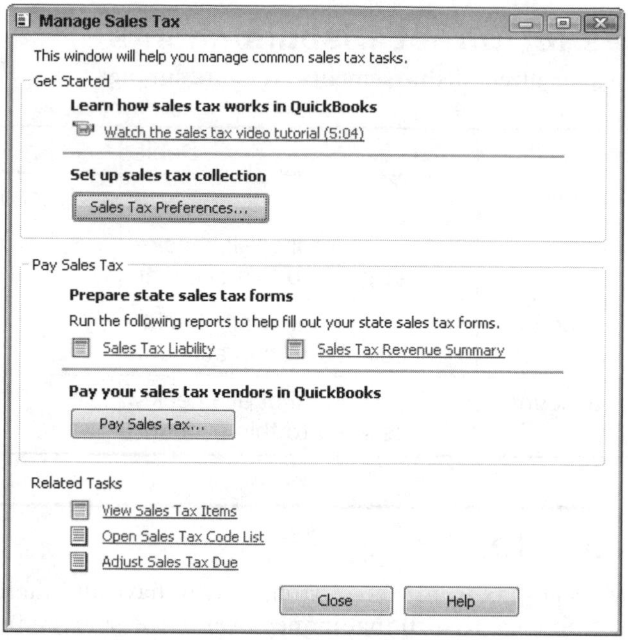

FIGURE 12-5 The Manage Sales Tax window has links to sales tax functions.

In the following discussions, I'll provide the menu commands to access features in functions, but you can also use the links on the Manage Sales Tax window for some of those chores.

Running Sales Tax Reports

At some interval determined by your taxing authority, you need to report your total sales, your nontaxable sales, and your taxable sales, along with any other required breakdowns. Oh, yes, you also have to write a check (or multiple checks) to remit the taxes.

Sales Tax Liability Report

QuickBooks has reports to help you fill out your sales tax forms. Choose Vendors | Sales Tax | Sales Tax Liability. Use the Dates drop-down list to select an interval that matches the way you report to the taxing authorities. By default, QuickBooks chooses the interval you configured in the Preferences dialog, but that interval may only apply to your primary sales tax. If you collect multiple taxes, due at different intervals, you must create a separate report with the appropriate interval to display those figures. Figure 12-6 shows a Sales Tax Liability report for a monthly filer.

	Total Sales	Non-Taxable Sales	Taxable Sales	Tax Rate	Tax Collected	Sales Tax Payable As of May 31, 09
PASALESTAX						
PA Base Sales Tax	9,600.00	1,000.00	8,600.00	6.0%	516.00	1,750.74
Phila Sales Tax	9,600.00	1,000.00	8,600.00	1.0%	86.00	260.79
Multiple taxes for PASALESTAX	-9,600.00	-1,000.00	-8,600.00		▶ 0.00	◀ 0.00
Total PASALESTAX	9,600.00	1,000.00	8,600.00		602.00	2,011.53
TOTAL	**9,600.00**	**1,000.00**	**8,600.00**		**602.00**	**2,011.53**

FIGURE 12-6 The Sales Tax Liability report displays taxable and nontaxable sales for each tax code.

Tax Code Reports

If you have to report specific types of taxable or nontaxable sales, you can obtain that information by creating a report on the tax code you created to track that information. Choose Lists | Sales Tax Code List and select (highlight) the tax code for which you need a report. Press CTRL-Q to see a report on the sales activity with this tax code. Change the date range to match your reporting interval with the sales tax authority (this isn't a sales tax report, so QuickBooks doesn't automatically match the settings in the Sales Tax Preferences dialog).

You don't have to create these reports one code at a time; you can modify the report so it reports all of your tax codes or just those you need for a specific tax authority's report. In fact, you can modify the report so it reports totals instead of every sales transaction.

Click the Modify Report button on the report window. In the Display tab, use the Columns list to deselect any items you don't require for the report (for example, the Type, Date, and Number of an invoice/sales receipt, and the contents of the Memo field).

In the Filters tab, choose Sales Tax Code from the Filter list. Click the arrow to the right of the Sales Tax Code field and select the appropriate option from the drop-down list, choosing one of the following options:

- All Sales Tax Codes, which displays total activity for the period for every code
- Multiple Sales Tax Codes, which opens the Select Sales Tax Code window, listing all codes, so you can select the specific codes you want to report on
- All Taxable Codes, which displays total activity for the period for each taxable code
- All Non-Taxable Codes, which displays total activity for the period for each nontaxable code

Click OK to return to the report window, where your selections are reflected. Unless you want to take all these steps again when you need this report, click the Memorize button to memorize the report.

Remitting the Sales Tax

After you check the figures (or calculate them, if you have multiple reports with different standards of calculation), it's time to pay the tax, using the following steps:

1. Choose Vendors | Sales Tax | Pay Sales Tax, to open the Pay Sales Tax dialog.

2. Select the bank account to use.
3. Check the date that's displayed in the field named Show Sales Tax Due Through. It must match the end date of your current reporting period (for instance, monthly or quarterly).
4. Click in the Pay column to insert a check mark next to those you're paying now. If you're lucky enough to have the same reporting interval for all taxing authorities just click the Pay All Tax button (the label changes to Clear Selections).
5. If you're going to print the check, be sure to select the To Be Printed check box at the bottom of the dialog. If you write the check manually, or if you remit sales tax online using an electronic transfer from your bank, deselect the To Be Printed check box. Then, if you're writing a manual check, insert the check number, and if you're remitting online either remove the check number entirely, or enter EFT (for electronic payment) in the No. field.
6. Click OK when you've completed filling out the information.

The next time you print or write checks, the sales tax check is in the group waiting to be completed.

> ($) **NOTE:** QuickBooks doesn't ask for a start date because it uses the period duration defined in your Sales Tax Preferences.

Adjusting Sales Tax Amounts

If you need to adjust the amount of sales tax due (most states offer a discount for timely payment), select the appropriate sales tax item in the Pay Sales Tax window and click the Adjust button to open the Sales Tax Adjustment dialog.

Specify the amount by which to reduce the tax amount for timely payment or to increase the amount, if you're late and paying a penalty. Specify an Adjustment Account (you should create a specific account for this adjustment to make it easier to track and audit your work), and click OK to return to the Pay Sales Tax window, where the amount has been changed to reflect your adjustment.

Managing Complicated Sales Tax Structures

States and local governments are getting extremely creative about imposing sales taxes. At the time of this writing there are more than 7,000 sales taxes imposed within the 50 states!

As if that isn't complicated enough, the rules governing what's taxable and what's not vary from state to state, and some states only tax a percentage of certain types of items.

QuickBooks is not yet able to manage some of the complicated sales tax schemes automatically, and you'll have to change the way you fill out sales transactions or do some of your calculations outside of QuickBooks (or both). Go to www.cpa911.com for some workarounds that let you track nonstandard tax schemes within QuickBooks (click the Navigation Button for the QuickBooks Tips section of the website).

Managing Bank and Credit Card Accounts

In *this chapter:*

- Make deposits that aren't customer payments

- Transfer funds between accounts

- Deal with bounced checks

- Void disbursements

- Manage cash

- Manage credit card purchases

Every penny that goes through your bank accounts has to be entered in QuickBooks. Most deposits and withdrawals are easy to enter in bank accounts because the transaction windows you use take care of adding or removing funds automatically.

But there are times when money is deposited or withdrawn outside of the usual transaction windows, and this chapter covers the methods you need to apply to take care of these situations.

Depositing Money That Isn't from Customers

Even though QuickBooks takes care of depositing money into your bank account when you receive money from customers (covered in Chapter 10), there are times when you receive money that's unconnected to a customer payment. Some of the common reasons for such deposits are

- Rebate checks from manufacturers or stores
- Checks from vendors with whom you have a credit balance and requested a check
- Infusion of capital from an owner or partner
- Loan from an owner, partner, officer, or bank

Entering a noncustomer deposit into a bank account is easy, and you can work directly in the account register or use the Make Deposit window.

- If the deposit is the only deposit you're making and it will appear on your statement as an individual deposit, you can work directly in the account register.
- If you're going to deposit the check along with other checks, use the Make Deposits window.

Using the Account Register for Deposits

To work directly in the bank account register, open the register by choosing Banking | Use Register, and then select the appropriate bank account. When the account register window opens, the next available transaction line is highlighted and the current date is displayed. Use the following steps to record the deposit directly into the bank account register:

1. Change the date if necessary, and then press TAB to move to the Number field.
2. Delete the check number if one automatically appears (or wait until you enter the amount in the Deposit column, at which point QuickBooks deletes the check number).
3. Press TAB to move past the next three columns to get to the Deposit column, or click in the Deposit column to move there immediately. (See "Assigning a Payee to a Noncustomer Deposit" later in this section to learn about your options in tracking a payee for this type of deposit.)

4. Enter the amount of the deposit.

5. Move to the next field (Account) and assign the deposit to the appropriate account. (See "Assigning Accounts to Noncustomer Deposits" later in this section for guidelines.)

6. Use the Memo field to enter an explanation in case your accountant asks you about the deposit.

7. Click the Record button.

Using the Make Deposits Window

Sometimes it's better to use the Make Deposits window for an unusual deposit, because you're planning to deposit the check along with other checks, and you want your deposit records to match the bank statement. Use the following steps to accomplish this:

1. Choose Banking | Make Deposits to open the Payments To Deposit window.

2. In the Payments To Deposit window, select the deposits you're taking to the bank (the check you want to deposit at the same time is not listed, because the window only shows the money you've received through customer transactions).

3. Click OK to move to the Make Deposits window.

4. Click in the From Account column of the blank line under the last entry (or in the Received From column if you need to track the payee).

5. Select the appropriate account for this deposit.

6. Optionally, enter data in the Memo, Chk No., and Pmt Meth. fields (and don't forget the Class field if you're tracking classes).

7. Enter the amount.

Your check is added to the total of the deposit you're making (see Figure 13-1).

Assigning a Payee to a Noncustomer Deposit

You can, if it's necessary, enter a payee name in the Received From column, but QuickBooks doesn't require that. Most of the time, a payee isn't needed. For example, if you're depositing a rebate on a purchase you made, there's a good chance the company that wrote the check doesn't exist in your QuickBooks system, and there's no point in adding a name you don't need to produce reports about. Most rebates are issued by manufacturers, and you probably bought the product from a vendor who is a retailer. In fact, even if the vendor is sending you the rebate, if you paid for the original purchase with a credit card the vendor doesn't exist in your system (the credit card company is the vendor).

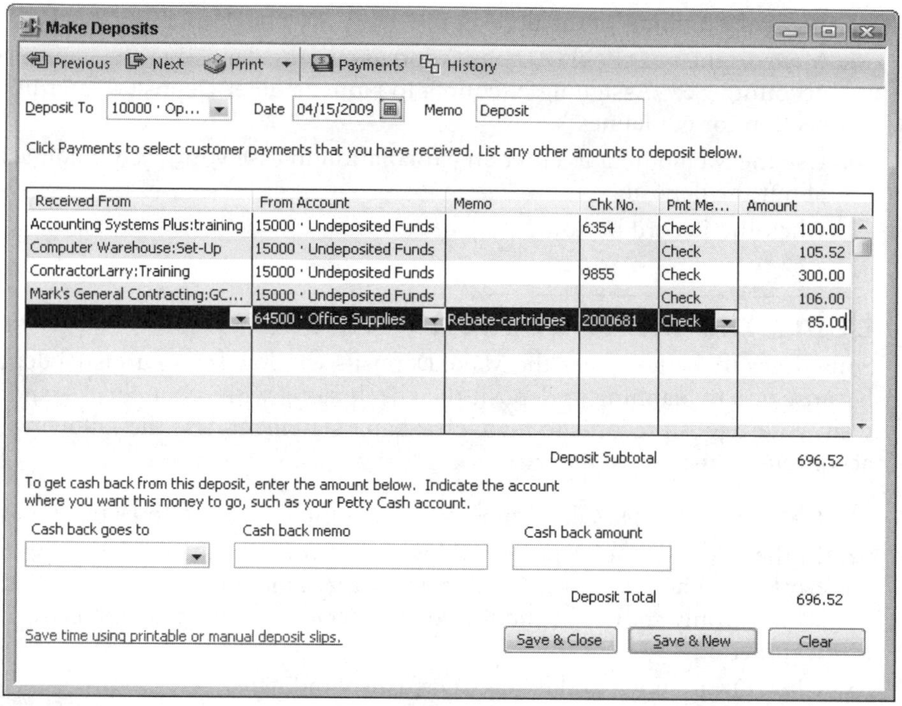

FIGURE 13-1 I'm taking the rebate check to the bank, along with a customer payment.

If the money is from an owner or partner, the name should exist in your system in the Other Names list. If the money is from a corporate officer, that officer probably exists as an employee, but you cannot use the employee name for this transaction. Instead, create the name in the Other Names list to track this deposit. Use a different name because you can't have duplicate names; so if the employee name is Casper Cashbucks, use something like CasperCash for the Other Names list.

If you're depositing the proceeds of a bank loan, you need a vendor because you'll be writing checks to pay back the principal and interest.

If you type a payee name that doesn't exist in any of your name lists, QuickBooks displays a Name Not Found message offering you the following selections:

- **Quick Add**   Lets you enter a name without any additional information
- **Set Up**   Lets you create a new name using the regular New Name window
- **Cancel**   Returns you to the original window you were working in so you can either choose another name or delete the name of the nonexistent payee

N O T E : If you've enabled multiple currencies, the Name Not Found dialog includes a currency selection drop down list.

If you select Quick Add or Set Up, you're asked which type of name you're adding: Vendor, Customer, Employee, or Other. Unless this payee will become a vendor or customer (I think we can eliminate employee from this procedure), choose Other.

Assigning Accounts to Noncustomer Deposits

If you're depositing your own money into the business, and the business is a proprietorship or partnership, that's capital and you should post the deposit to a capital account (it's an equity account). If you're depositing the proceeds of a loan (from yourself as a corporate office, or from a bank), post the deposit to the liability account for the loan (you may have to create the liability account). If you're making a deposit that's a refund from a vendor, you can post the amount to the expense account that was used for the original expense.

When in doubt, post the amount to the most logical place and ask your accountant (or post the amount to the Ask My Accountant account if you have one). You can always edit the transaction later or make a journal entry to post the amount to the right account.

Transferring Funds Between Accounts

Moving money between bank accounts is a common procedure in business. If you have a bank account for payroll, you have to move money out of your operating account into your payroll account every payday. Some people deposit all the customer payments into a money market account (which pays interest) and then transfer the necessary funds to an operating account when it's time to pay bills. Others do it the other way around, moving money not immediately needed from the business operating account to a money market account. Lawyers, agents, real estate brokers, and other professionals have to maintain escrow accounts and move money between them and the operating account. You can use either of two methods to transfer funds between bank accounts:

- Use the QuickBooks Transfer Funds transaction window.
- Post a check from the sending bank to a transfer account and then bring the funds into the receiving account from the funds transfer account.

Both methods are quite easy, and I'll go over them in this section.

Using the Transfer Funds Transaction Window

QuickBooks offers a Transfer Funds feature, which is the best solution if both checking accounts are in the same bank and you don't write a check to transfer funds (you call the bank or use their online website to move the funds).

The Transfer Funds feature also works if you write a check (either because the bank accounts are in separate banks or because you prefer to have a check as a record of the transfer), but adding the check number to the transaction involves an extra step, and QuickBooks insists on inserting the same check number in both bank accounts (which can mess up your check number system in the receiving bank account). If you don't mind the fact that a check number from one bank account appears in the other bank account, then the Transfer Funds feature remains an easy method for transferring funds.

(If you want to write a check from one bank and take it to the other bank, and you don't want to see the same check number in both accounts, see the next section, "Using a Transfer Account.")

To transfer money between accounts using the Transfer Funds transaction window, follow these steps:

1. Choose Banking | Transfer Funds from the menu bar to open the Transfer Funds Between Accounts dialog.
2. Fill out the fields.

3. Click Save & Close (or Save & New if you have another transfer to make).

QuickBooks posts the transaction (you'll see it marked as TRANSFR in both bank accounts if you open their registers) without affecting any totals in your financial reports. All the work is done on the balance sheet, but the bottom line of your balance sheet doesn't change because money was neither added nor removed from your company.

If you wrote a check from one account and took it to the bank to effect the transfer, open the register of the sending bank, select the transaction line, enter the check number in the Number field, and click Record. QuickBooks displays a dialog asking you to confirm the fact that you're changing the transaction (click Yes). That number is also recorded on the transaction line in the receiving bank register, and you cannot remove it.

Using a Transfer Account

If the bank accounts you want to use for transferring funds are not at the same bank, and you use a check to move the money, you might find it easier to use a transfer account. In fact, you might find a transfer account easier even if both accounts are in the same bank. This way, check numbers are correct in both bank accounts, and online banking downloads match (the fake check number in the receiving account can interfere with automatic matching of transactions in the receiving account).

Create a new account in your chart of accounts named Funds Transfer. You can use either a Bank account or an Other Current Asset account as the account type.

Creating a Check to Transfer Funds

In the sending bank, create the check to transfer the funds with the following steps:

1. Enter the date, check number (if you're using a check), and the amount. If you're not using a check (you use the telephone or your bank's online website), leave the check number blank or enter a code such as EFT (for Electronic Funds Transfer).
2. Post the account to the Funds Transfer account you created.
3. Save the transaction.

Receiving the Funds Transfer Check

In the receiving bank, this bank deposit is not connected to a customer, so you don't use the normal customer payment windows. Instead, to make sure you can reconcile your bank statement easily, use one of the following methods:

- If this check is the only check you are going to deposit when you go to the bank, open the account register and record the deposit. Use the Funds Transfer account as the posting account.
- If this check is part of a deposit that includes other checks, use the Make Deposits window. After you've selected the other items in the Payments To Deposit window and clicked OK, add this check to the next line of the Make Deposits window (you only need to enter the posting account and the amount). Be sure you select the appropriate bank account at the top of the window.

Handling Bounced Checks

Customer checks sometimes bounce. When that happens, you face the following tasks:

1. Configure items to manage bounced checks and service charges.
2. Deduct the amount of the bounced check from your checking account.
3. Recover the money from the customer, including any service charge you incurred from your bank.
4. Record any bank service charges you incurred as a result of the bounced check.

Following are the instructions to accomplish these tasks in a manner that is rather easy and logical (especially when compared to some of the complicated instructions found in some books and articles).

Configuring Items to Manage Bounced Checks

You need items to use in the transactions you create to notify the customer and attempt to collect the money still owed to you. You use these items to invoice the customer to recover your loss.

Creating an Item for a Bounced Check

For the amount of the check, create an Other Charge item named NSF Check (NSF stands for NonSufficient Funds, the bank's term for a bounced check). The item is nontaxable and is linked to the bank account into which you deposit customer checks (instead of using an income account). Don't enter an amount; when you create a transaction you use the amount of the bounced check.

Creating an Item for Bank Service Charges

You also have to have an item to use when you charge the customer for the service charge from your bank. Use an Other Charge item named NSF BankServChg, with the description "Service Charge for Returned Check." Use the bank service charges expense account as the linked account.

> $ **NOTE:** Some of the complicated instructions for managing bounced checks insist that creating a vendor for bounced checks, special expense accounts for bounced checks, and so on, are needed in order to track and report on the bounced checks you encounter. None of that is necessary—if you want to see a history of bounced checks and the customers that bounced them, just select this item in the Item List and press CTRL-Q to see a quick report on the transactions attached to this item.

Create an Invoice to Recover the Amounts Owed

Create an invoice (service or professional works best) that includes the items you created to handle bounced checks (see Figure 13-2). When (or if) the payment arrives, you use Receive Payments to record the amounts.

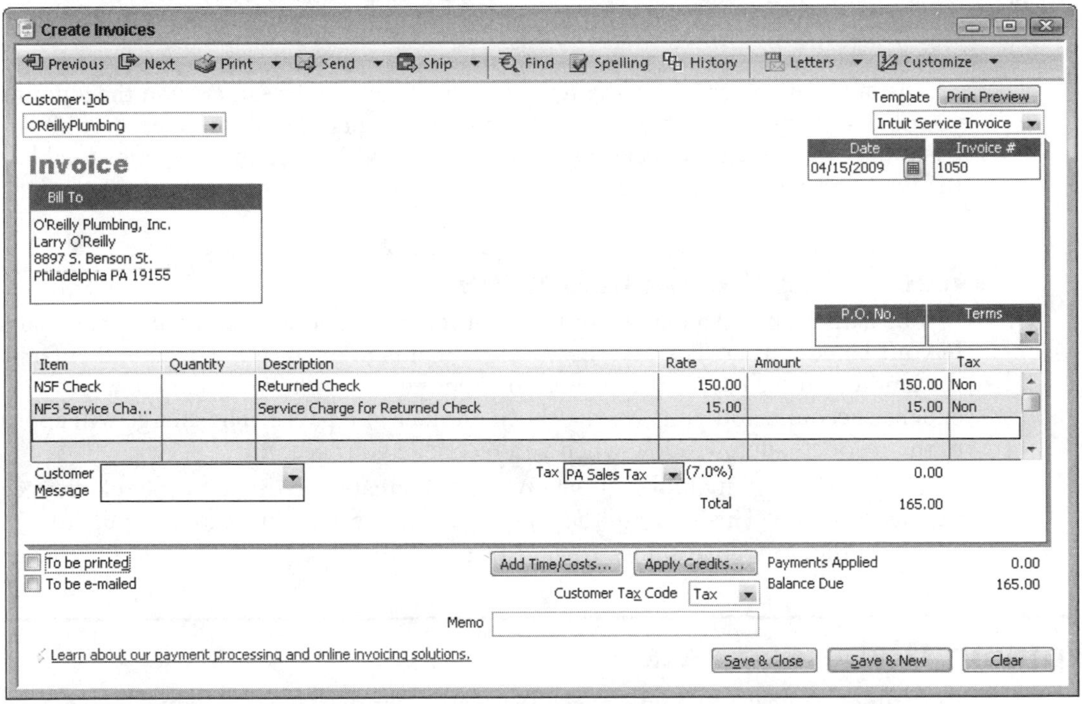

FIGURE 13-2 An invoice for a bounced check takes care of all the postings you need to adjust your accounting totals.

When you enter the NSF item on the invoice, it credits the bank account, which washes the amount of the original deposit of the check. It also provides both transactions in the Reconcile window when your statement arrives, so you can

➡ FYI

Redepositing Bounced Checks

As part of your design for managing bounced checks you also must decide whether you're going to redeposit the check. Most banks permit you to redeposit a bounced check, but only once—you cannot keep depositing against the hope that the customer's bank balance will grow large enough to cover the check.

Many business owners don't redeposit bounced checks; instead, they insist on receiving a new check, a certified check, or an envelope filled with cash. If your bank charges a service fee for bounced checks, it's probably not a good idea to redeposit the check and risk incurring another charge you may not be able to collect from your customer.

select the original deposit (if that's all that shows up on your statement) or both transactions (if all of these transactions occurred in time to appear on the statement).

The amount you enter for the service charge item can be larger than the amount your bank charged (check your state's laws on this matter). If you have a lot of customers who bounce checks, you could end up with a negative expense total for the bank service charge account.

Recording the Bank Charge

If your bank imposed a charge for the returned check, you have to enter that charge in your bank register. The easiest way to do that is to open the register and enter the amount in the Payment column. Post the transaction to your bank charges expense account. You don't need a check number or a payee. The charge will appear in the reconciliation window when you reconcile your account.

The bank charge included in the invoice you created credited your bank charges expense account. This entry in the register debits the account, and also puts the charge in the reconciliation window.

Voiding Disbursements

Sometimes you have to void a check that you've written. Perhaps you decided not to send it for some reason, or perhaps it was lost in the mail. Whatever the reason, if a check isn't going to clear your bank, you should void it.

The process of voiding a check is quite easy, and the only trouble you can cause yourself is *deleting* the check instead of *voiding* it. Deleting a check removes all history of the transaction, and the check number disappears into la-la land. This is not a good way to keep financial records. Voiding a check keeps the check number but sets the amount to zero.

To void a check, open the bank account register and click anywhere on the check's transaction line to select the transaction. Right-click to open the shortcut menu and choose Void Check. The corresponding entry in the expense account (or multiple expense accounts) to which the check was written is automatically adjusted. Click Record to save the transaction (QuickBooks asks you to confirm your action).

Tracking Cash

Many businesses maintain a petty cash box to dispense cash to employees (or owners) who need cash to recover money they've spent for the company, or as an advance against future expenditures. This box functions like a cash register till and requires similar accounting processes to make sure QuickBooks has the correct balance for the till.

Some businesses have debit cards for the business account, which they use to withdraw money from an ATM machine or use at the cash register to pay for a business purchase.

When you use cash, whether it's cash from the petty cash box or a withdrawal via an ATM machine, you have to account for it. In this section, I'll cover the accounting procedures involved with these cash transactions.

Tracking the Petty Cash Till

If you keep a cash box for business expenses, your chart of accounts should have a petty cash account. This account functions like a cash register till: you put money in it, then you account for the money that's spent, leaving the rest in the till until it too is spent. Then you put more money into the till. The petty cash account doesn't represent a real bank account; it just represents that portion of the money in the real bank account that moved into the till. If you don't have a petty cash account in your chart of accounts, create one using the following guidelines:

- The account type is Bank.
- If you number your accounts, use a number that places your new petty cash account near the other (real) bank accounts in your chart of accounts.
- Leave the opening balance at zero.

Putting Money into the Petty Cash Till

You have to put money into your petty cash till, both literally (get cash) and figuratively (record a withdrawal from your bank account to your petty cash account). Most of the time you write a check for petty cash using the following setup guidelines:

- Create a name in the Other Names list for the payee (usually the name is "Cash").
- Write the check from your bank account and post it to the petty cash account.

You can use the Write Checks window to accomplish the task, or enter the transaction directly in the bank account register. Don't use the Transfer Funds feature for this because you actually wrote a check and stood in line at the bank to cash it, and you have to account for the check number.

You don't post a petty cash check to an expense, nor to a class. Those postings are recorded when you account for the spent funds, not for the moment at which you withdraw the cash.

Recording Petty Cash Disbursements

As you take cash out of the petty cash box in the office (which was put into the box after you cashed a check), you must record those expenditures in the petty cash register.

> **TIP:** Don't let anyone take money out of the petty cash till without a receipt. If the money is an advance against a purchase instead of payment for a receipt, use an IOU. Later, replace the IOU with the purchase receipt.

I find it easiest to use the Write Checks window to record petty cash expenses, because I can record the customer or job when necessary (either for reimbursement or for job costing) and also assign a class.

Open the Write Checks window and select the petty cash bank account. You can delete the check number QuickBooks automatically inserts in the Number field, or you can leave the number there (you'll never get a statement that you have to reconcile, so it doesn't matter). You can either skip the Payee field or use a payee named Cash or PettyCash (in the Other Names list).

You can create the check when the first expense occurs, and then open the same check and continue to add to it until the next time you put cash into the till; you can wait until you're running out of cash and need to replenish the till; or you can create a weekly or monthly transaction.

The disbursements you enter track what was spent, not what was taken out of the till. If you spent less than the amount of cash you withdrew from the till, the balance goes back into the till. You'll probably spend it later, and at that point you'll repeat this task to account for that spending.

➡ FYI

Don't Track Vendors for Petty Cash Disbursements

I constantly encounter bookkeepers who enter a real payee for each petty cash transaction ("Joe's Hardware Store," "Mary's Office Supplies," and so on). As a result, their QuickBooks files grow larger than they need to because the system is carrying the weight of all these vendors. The vendors they enter appear in all their vendor reports, crowding those reports with extraneous names that nobody has any interest in tracking.

Reserve vendors for those payees from whom you receive bills or to whom you disburse checks and for whom you want to track activity. If it's so important to know that you spent a buck eighty for a screwdriver at Joe's Hardware Store, enter that information in the Memo field of the transaction.

TIP: When the receipts have been entered into QuickBooks, mark them with a "Paid" notation so you know which receipts are entered and which aren't.

Replacing the Cash Spent

As you dispense cash from the till, you need to replace it. The usual method is to bring the cash till back to its original balance (the amount of the first check you wrote to petty cash). Use the same steps you used to write the first check to petty cash, and use the total amount of funds disbursed as the amount of the check.

Tracking Cash Bank Withdrawals

If your business bank account comes with a debit card, the amount you withdraw using that card is a direct reduction of your bank balance and has to be recorded in order to keep an accurate balance in QuickBooks.

Creating a set of rules that ensure your ATM withdrawals are accounted for is *your* problem—QuickBooks cannot help you remember to enter these transactions when you return to the office. (Well, you could set up a QuickBooks reminder that appears frequently with the message "Did you ATM today????")

TIP: If your bank account is set up for online services, you don't have to enter your ATM withdrawals as you make them. You can see your ATM withdrawals when you download transactions, and you can enter the transaction at that time. (Learn about online banking in Chapter 15.)

Posting Cash Withdrawals

Because this money is removed directly from your bank account (a credit to the bank account), you have to post it to an account, using a debit. If you already know what the money was used for, you can debit the appropriate expense account when you enter the transaction in QuickBooks.

However, it's unusual for the ATM withdrawal amount to match the money spent on business expenses. Either there is money left over, or there is money still owed to the person who withdrew the funds and made purchases.

- The money that's left belongs to the business, not to the person who withdrew it. It's easiest to have that person put the money into your petty cash till (and post that portion of the transaction covering the withdrawal to the petty cash account).
- The money that the person spent over and above the withdrawal has to be reimbursed to that person. You can take the money out of your petty cash till and post it to the appropriate expense when you record your petty cash transactions.

Sometimes a business owner or an employee uses a debit card just to have "walking around money," and you need to track that when you create the transaction for the withdrawal from your bank account.

Create an account of the type Other Current Asset and name it "Petty Cash Owed to Company," or "Walking Around Money" (whatever name is easy for you to recognize). Post the withdrawal to that account. Then, as the person spends the money for business-related expenses (handing in receipts, of course), you can create a JE to credit the Other Current Asset account and debit the appropriate expense.

When you withdraw money from your bank account with a debit card and use the cash for business expenses, it's easiest to record the transaction with a check, using the same principles and steps explained earlier for tracking the money that moves through your petty cash till.

Managing Your Credit Cards

When you use a credit card, you have choices about the way you track and pay the credit card bill. You can either pay the entire bill every month, or pay part of the bill and keep a running credit card balance. For either approach, you can choose between two methods of handling credit card purchases in QuickBooks:

- Treat the credit card bill as an ordinary vendor and enter the bill when it arrives. This is an easy, almost effortless way to pay your credit card if you always pay the entire balance.
- Treat the credit card bill as a liability and enter each transaction as it's made. If you usually make partial payments, this method makes it easier to track the running balance.

Treating Credit Cards as Vendors

You can set up your credit card as an ordinary vendor (instead of a liability account) and enter the bill into QuickBooks when it arrives, or use the Write Checks function to create a direct disbursement. Most of the time, the expenses are posted to multiple accounts, so the credit card bill transaction is a split transaction (see Figure 13-3).

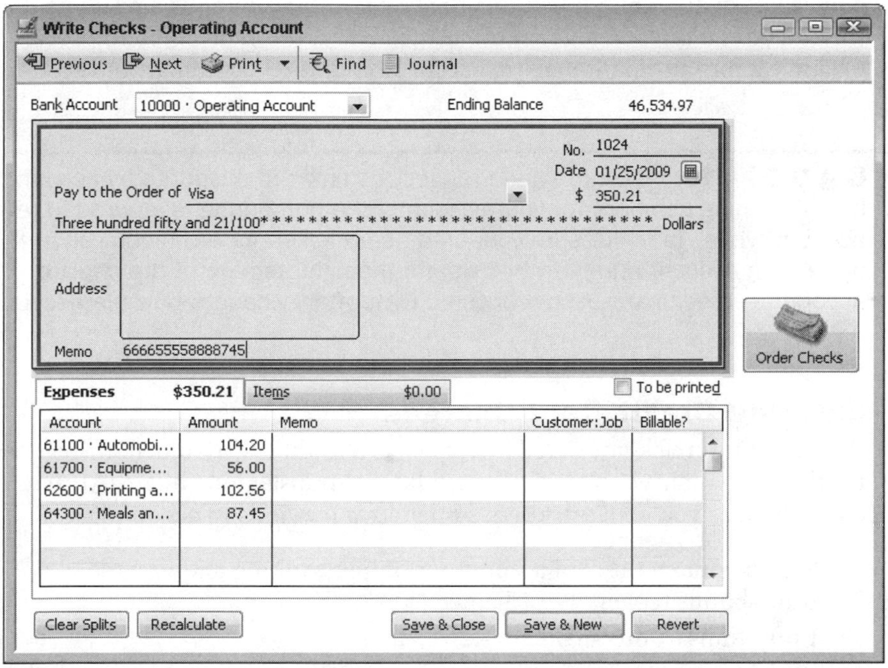

FIGURE 13-3 Credit card bills are usually posted to multiple accounts.

If you don't pay off the card balance, each month you'll have a new bill to enter that has interest charges in addition to your new purchases. (Post the interest charges to an interest expense account.)

If you enter the bill in the Enter Bills window, and then use the Pay Bills window to write the checks, enter the amount you want to pay against each bill in the system. Always start with the oldest bill, making a partial payment or paying it in full. Then move to the next oldest bill, making a partial payment or paying it in full.

Treating Credit Cards as Liability Accounts

You can treat credit cards as liability accounts, tracking each transaction against the account as it occurs. Then when the bill arrives, you match the transactions against the bill and decide how much to pay. Your running balance is tracked specifically against the credit card, instead of being part of your Accounts Payable balance.

Creating a Credit Card Account

To use credit cards in this manner, you must have an account for each credit card in your chart of accounts. If you don't have such an account as a result of the EasyStep Interview, you can create one now, using an account type of Credit Card. Check out Chapter 2 for information about adding accounts to your chart of accounts.

 CAUTION: QuickBooks arranges the chart of accounts by account types. If you're using numbers for your accounts, the numbering is ignored in favor of account types. To make sure your credit card accounts are displayed in the right order, use account numbers that fit into the right section of the chart of accounts—credit card accounts come right after accounts payable accounts.

Entering Credit Card Charges

If you want to track your credit card charges as they're assumed, instead of waiting for the bill, you have to treat your credit card transactions like ATM transactions—enter them as you go. QuickBooks offers two methods to accomplish this:

- Set up your credit card account for online banking and download the transactions (covered in Chapter 15).
- Enter transactions manually.

If your credit card account is enabled for online banking, these are not mutually exclusive methods. You can use either of the following methods:

- Enter the transactions manually and download data from your credit card server to match those transactions.
- Download the transactions and then add each transaction to the credit card register.

To enter credit card charges manually, choose Banking | Enter Credit Card Charges to open the Enter Credit Card Charges window seen in Figure 13-4.

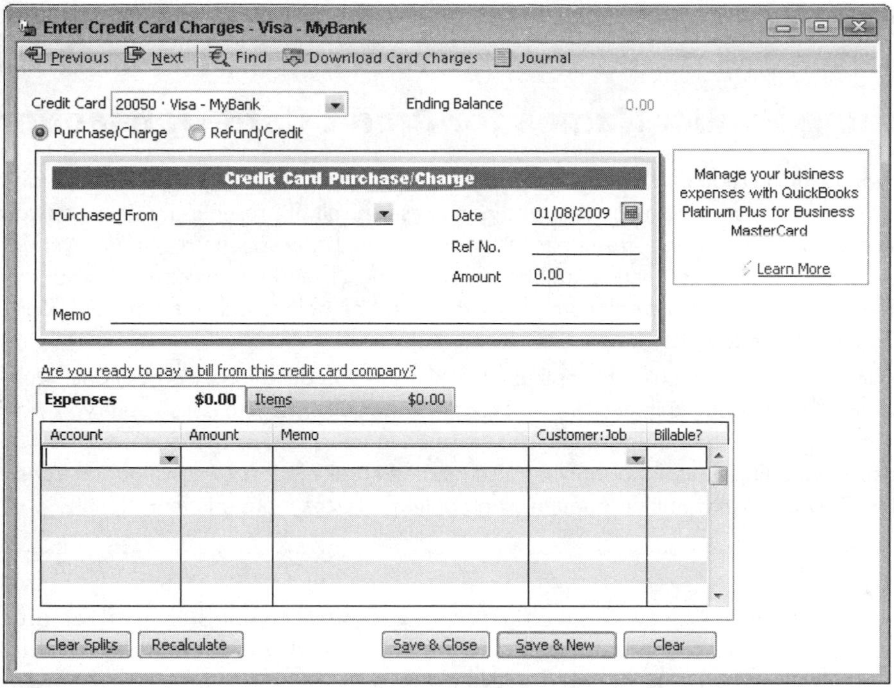

FIGURE 13-4 To track credit card charges as liabilities, enter each transaction.

Select the appropriate credit card account and then use the store receipt as a reference document to fill in the transaction. Here are some guidelines for making this transaction easy and quick to complete:

- You can skip the Purchased From field because if you type a vendor name in the Purchased From field, QuickBooks will force you to add the vendor to your vendor list. If the name is important to you for some reason, use the Memo field for each transaction to note the name of the vendor. (See the sidebar, "Tracking Vendor Names for Credit Card Transactions," for more information on this issue.)
- If the transaction is a return, be sure to select the Refund/Credit option at the top of the window.
- Enter the date of the purchase.
- Optionally, enter the receipt number in the Ref No. field.
- Use the Expenses tab for general expenses; use the Items tab if you used the credit card to buy inventory items for resale.
- If you used the credit card for an expense or an item for a customer, enter the customer information so you can bill the customer for reimbursement, or just track the expense for job costing.
- If you track classes, select the appropriate class for this transaction.

➡ FYI

Tracking Vendor Names for Credit Card Transactions

When you incur a credit card charge or pay your credit card bill, the vendor is the credit card, not the merchants from whom you received goods as a result of presenting your credit card. If you enter a vendor name in a credit card transaction you'll end up with a gazillion vendors with whom you don't have a real vendor relationship (they don't send you bills, at least not for purchases you made with a credit card), and you won't be able to delete them from your QuickBooks file because they have transactions.

If your credit card is enabled for online access, when you download transactions, QuickBooks not only lists the vendors as if they are real vendors, the software also asks you if you want to set up a renaming rule if the vendor name isn't matched in your Vendor List. See Chapter 15 to learn more about renaming rules, ignoring vendors that aren't real vendors in downloaded transactions, and other important information about making online services more efficient.

Click Save & New to save the record and move to another blank credit card entry window to enter another credit card transaction, or click Save & Close if you're finished entering credit card charges.

Reconciling the Credit Card Bill

Eventually, the credit card bill arrives, and you have to perform the following chores:

- Reconcile the bill against the entries you recorded.
- Decide whether to pay the entire bill or just a portion of it.
- Write a check (or create an electronic transfer).

Choose Banking | Reconcile from the QuickBooks menu bar to open the Begin Reconciliation window seen in Figure 13-5. In the Account field, select the credit card from the drop-down list.

In the Begin Reconciliation dialog box enter the following data:

- The ending balance from the credit card bill
- Any finance charges on the bill in the Finance Charge box, along with the date on which the charges were assessed
- The account you use to post finance charges (create one if you don't have one—it's an expense)

Click Continue to open the Reconcile Credit Card window, which displays the purchases you entered into QuickBooks (either manually or by downloading transactions), as well as any payments you made. Click the check mark column for

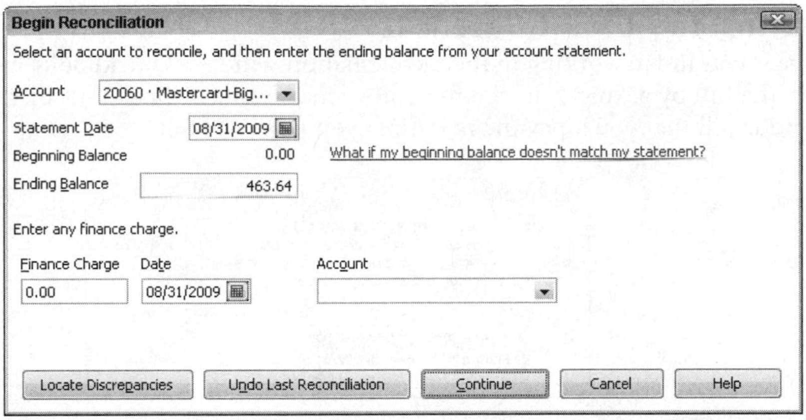

FIGURE 13-5 The first time you reconcile a credit card, the opening balance is $0.00.

each transaction on your window that has a matching transaction on the credit card bill (make sure the amounts match, too). That includes payments, credits, and charges.

> **TIP:** If the list of transactions is very long, select the option Hide Transactions After The Statement's End Date. This removes transaction listings past that date, none of which would have cleared yet.

Add any transactions you forgot to enter by opening the credit card register and entering the transactions. (To find the receipts, search your pockets, desk, pocketbook, the floor of your car, and the kitchen junk drawer.) When you return to the Reconcile Credit Card window, the new transactions are automatically added and you can check them off.

> **TIP:** Finance charges for businesses are tax deductible; the finance charges you incur for your personal credit cards, or for personal expenses, aren't.

Now look at the box at the bottom of the window where the totals are displayed. If the difference is $0.00, congratulations! Everything's fine. Click Reconcile Now.

If the difference is not $0.00, you have to figure out the problem and make corrections. Read Chapter 14, which is dedicated to the subject of reconciling bank accounts, to learn how to troubleshoot reconciliations (the problems and solutions are the same for credit card accounts as for bank accounts).

Paying the Credit Card Bill

When you finish working in the reconciliation window, QuickBooks moves on to pay the bill by asking you whether you want to write a check now or create a vendor bill that you'll pay the next time you pay your bills.

Select the appropriate response and click OK. QuickBooks offers congratulations and also offers to print a reconciliation report. Select the report type you want, or click Close to skip the report.

If you opted to pay the bill, a transaction window that matches your response to paying the bill opens (either the Write Checks window or the Enter Bills window), so you can enter the appropriate transaction.

Reconciling Bank Accounts

In *this chapter:*

- Get ready to reconcile

- Use the QuickBooks reconciliation windows

- Adjust the beginning balance for your first reconciliation

- Troubleshoot differences in the beginning balance

Reconciling bank accounts is fancy terminology for "I have to balance my checkbook," which is one of the most important tasks connected with financial record keeping.

Getting Ready to Reconcile

After your bank statement arrives, you must find some uninterrupted moments to compare it to the information in the QuickBooks account register.

If your bank sends your canceled checks in the envelope along with the statement (many banks don't include the physical checks), you can arrange the checks in numerical order before you start this task.

However, instead of sorting and collating the physical checks, it's much easier to use the list of check numbers that appears on your statement. An asterisk or some other mark usually indicates a missing number. The missing number is usually a check that hasn't cleared yet (which includes any checks you voided) or a check that cleared previously.

Checking the Register

Open the register for the bank account you're about to reconcile by pressing CTRL-R to open the Use Register dialog and selecting the account. Then compare the bank register to the statement.

If the bank statement shows deposits or checks (or both) that are absent from your bank register, add them to the register. If you miss any, don't worry; you can add transactions to the register while you're working in the Reconcile window, but it's usually quicker to get this task out of the way before you start the reconciliation process.

Interest payments and bank charges don't count as missing transactions because the bank reconciliation process treats those transactions separately. You'll have a chance to enter those amounts in the bank reconciliation windows.

Adding Missing Disbursements to the Register

The way you add missing disbursements to the register depends on whether the checks were payments of vendor bills you entered into your QuickBooks file or direct disbursements.

- To enter a payment, use the Pay Bills command on the Vendors menu.
- To enter a direct disbursement, use the Write Checks window (press CTRL-W) or enter the check directly into the register.

Adding Missing Deposits to the Register

Check for payments that were deposited to the Undeposited Funds account, which you neglected to move to the bank account. Choose Banking | Make Deposits from the menu bar and select any deposits that appear on your statement. If you have multiple transactions listed, deposit the funds in amounts (batches of transactions) that match the statement.

For example, your bank statement may show a deposit of $145.78 on one date and another deposit for $3,233.99 on another date. Both deposits appear in the Make Deposits window. Select one of the deposits, process it, and then repeat the procedure for the other deposit. When you reconcile the account, your transactions reflect the transactions in your bank statement.

If a missing deposit isn't in the Undeposited Funds account, you have to create the deposit, which may have been a customer payment of an invoice, a cash sale, a transfer of funds between banks, a payment of a loan, or a deposit of capital.

For customer invoice payments or cash sales, fill out the appropriate transaction window. If you deposit the proceeds to the Undeposited Funds account, don't forget to take the additional step to deposit the funds in the bank so the transaction appears in the reconciliation window. If you deposit the proceeds directly to the bank, the transaction appears in the reconciliation window automatically.

If you made deposits unconnected to customers and earned income, such as putting additional capital into your business or depositing the proceeds of a loan, the fastest way to enter the transaction is to work directly in the bank account's register. Enter the deposit amount and post the transaction to the appropriate account.

Reconciling in QuickBooks

Most of the time, performing a bank reconciliation in QuickBooks is easy and straightforward. You don't have a lot of data entry because most of the data you need is already in your bank register. The following sections explain the steps.

The Begin Reconciliation Window

Reconciling your bank account starts with the Begin Reconciliation window, which you open by choosing Banking | Reconcile (see Figure 14-1). If you have more than one bank account, or you have credit card accounts you reconcile in addition to bank accounts, select the account you want to reconcile from the drop-down list in the Account field.

Check the Beginning Balance field in the window against the beginning balance on the bank statement. (Your bank may call it the *starting balance*.) If your beginning balances match, enter the ending balance from your statement in the Ending Balance field and enter the statement date.

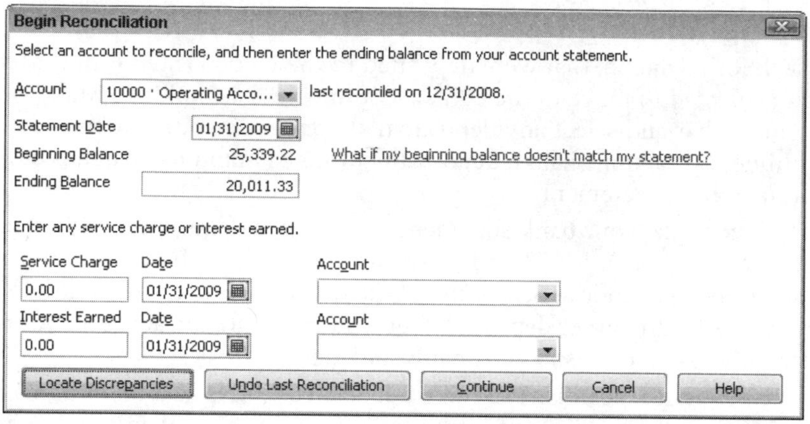

FIGURE 14-1 The first window summarizes bank activity.

If the beginning balances don't match because this is the first time you're reconciling the bank account in QuickBooks, read the section, "Adjusting the Beginning Balance for the First Reconciliation" and then return to this section of the chapter to finish reconciling.

If the beginning balances don't match and this is not the first time you're reconciling the bank account in QuickBooks, read the section "Troubleshooting Differences in the Beginning Balance" later in this chapter, and then return to this section of the chapter to perform the reconciliation.

Enter Interest Income and Service Charges

Your bank statement lists interest and bank service charges if either or both are applicable to your account. Enter those numbers in the Begin Reconciliation window and choose the appropriate account for posting.

If you have online banking and the interest payments and bank charges have already been entered into your register as a result of downloading transactions, do *not* enter them again in the Begin Reconciliation window—they'll be in the register list you see in the next window and you can clear them the way you clear checks and deposits.

By "bank charges," I mean the standard charges banks assess, such as monthly charges that may be assessed for failure to maintain a minimum balance. Bank charges do not include special charges for bounced checks, fees for electronic bank transfers, or any purchases you made that are charged to your account (such as the purchase of checks or deposit slips). Those should be entered in your bank register as discrete transactions (using the Memo field to explain the transaction), which makes them easier to find in case you have to talk to the bank about your account.

Clearing Transactions

After you've filled out the information in the Begin Reconciliation dialog, click Continue to open the Reconcile window, shown in Figure 14-2.

| FIGURE 14-2 | Uncleared transactions appear in the Reconcile window. |

Configuring the Reconcile Window

You can configure the way transactions are displayed to make it easier to work in the window by changing the way the data is displayed.

Sorting the Data

By default, QuickBooks sorts transactions by date, with a subsort by transaction number. For example, in the Checks And Payments pane, if multiple checks have the same date, those checks are sorted in numerical order.

Reconciling is easier if you sort the data to match the way your bank arranges the statement. For instance, if you have a lot of electronic payments in addition to checks, and your bank lists the electronic payments separately from checks, click the Chk # column to list withdrawals without check numbers separately from checks.

Eliminating Future Transactions

If the list is long, you can shorten it by selecting the option Hide Transactions After The Statement's End Date. Theoretically, transactions that weren't created before the ending date couldn't have cleared the bank. Removing them from the window leaves only those transactions likely to have cleared. If you select this option and your reconciliation doesn't balance, deselect the option so you can clear the transactions in case one of the following scenarios applies:

- You issued a postdated check and the recipient cashed it early. Since it's rare for a bank to enforce the date, this is a real possibility.
- You made a mistake when you entered the date of the original transaction. You may have entered a wrong month or even a wrong year, which resulted in moving the transaction date into the future.

Clearing Transactions

Now you must tell QuickBooks which transactions have cleared. All the transactions that are on your bank statement are cleared transactions. If the transactions are not listed on the statement, they have not cleared.

In the Reconcile window, click each transaction that cleared. A check mark appears in the leftmost (Cleared) column to indicate that the transaction has cleared the bank. If you clear a transaction in error, click again to remove the check mark—it's a toggle.

Use the following shortcuts to speed your work:

- If all, or almost all, of the transactions have cleared, click Mark All. Then deselect the transactions that didn't clear.
- Mark multiple, contiguous transactions by dragging down the Cleared column.
- If the account you're reconciling is enabled for online access, click Matched to automatically clear all transactions that were matched in the QuickStatements you've downloaded over the month. QuickBooks asks for the ending date on the statement and clears each previously matched transaction up to that date.

As you check each cleared transaction, the Difference amount in the lower-right corner of the Reconcile window changes. The goal is to get that figure to 0.00.

Adding Transactions During Reconciliation

While you're working in the Reconcile window, if you find a transaction on the statement that you haven't entered into your QuickBooks software (probably one of those ATM transactions you forgot to enter), you don't have to shut down the reconciliation process to remedy the situation. You can just enter the transaction into your register.

To open the bank account register, right-click anywhere in the Reconcile window and choose Use Register from the shortcut menu. When the account register opens, record the transaction. Return to the Reconcile window, where that transaction is now listed. Pretty nifty! Check it off as cleared, of course, because it was on the statement.

You can switch between the Reconcile window and the register for the account you're reconciling all through this process. Use the Window menu on the QuickBooks Menu bar to move between them.

Adding Undeposited Funds During Reconciliation

If the statement shows a deposit that doesn't appear in your reconcile window, don't add the deposit to your register until you check the Payments To Deposit window (choose Banking | Make Deposits). Most of the time you'll find the payments listed there, still awaiting deposit, even though you obviously went to the bank and deposited those checks. Select the payments that match the total shown on the bank statement and go through the Make Deposits function. When you're finished, the deposit appears in the Reconcile window. If the deposit isn't in the Payments To Deposit window, then you forgot to enter a transaction. Enter the transaction now, using the appropriate transaction window. Make sure you deposit it into the bank account to have it appear in the Reconcile window.

Deleting Transactions During Reconciliation

Sometimes you find that a transaction that was transferred from your account register to this Reconcile window shouldn't be there. This commonly occurs if you entered an ATM withdrawal twice. Or perhaps you forgot that you'd entered a deposit, and a couple of days later you entered it again. Whatever the reason, occasionally there are transactions that should be deleted.

To delete a transaction, double-click its listing in the window, which opens the original transaction. Then, right-click and select Delete (QuickBooks asks you to confirm the deletion). The transaction disappears from the Reconcile window and the bank register.

Editing Transactions During Reconciliation

Sometimes you'll want to change some of the information in a transaction. For example, when you see the real check, you realize the amount you entered in QuickBooks is wrong. You might even have the wrong date on a check. (These things only happen, of course, if you write checks manually; they don't happen to QuickBooks users who let QuickBooks take care of printing checks.)

Whatever the problem, you can correct it by editing the transaction. Double-click the transaction's listing in the Reconcile window to open the original transaction window. Enter the necessary changes and close the window. Answer Yes when QuickBooks asks if you want to record the changes, and you're returned to the Reconcile window where the changes are reflected.

Resolving Missing Check Numbers

Most bank statements list your checks in order and indicate a missing number with an asterisk. For instance, you may see check number 1234 followed by check number *1236 or 1236*. When a check number is missing, it means one of three things:

- The check cleared in a previous reconciliation.
- The check is still outstanding.
- The check number is unused and is probably literally missing.

If a missing check number on your bank statement is puzzling, you can check its status. To see if the check cleared in the last reconciliation, open the Previous Reconciliation report (discussed later in this chapter) by choosing Reports | Banking | Previous Reconciliation.

To investigate further, right-click anywhere in the Reconcile window and choose Missing Checks Report from the shortcut menu. When the Missing Checks dialog opens, select the appropriate account (if you have multiple bank accounts). You'll see asterisks indicating missing check numbers, as seen in Figure 14-3.

We Do It All

Missing Checks

All Transactions

Type	Date	Num	Name	Memo	Account	Split	Amount
Check	01/30/2009	1012	2155550621	2155550621...	10000 · Operating...	-SPLIT-	-104.22
Check	01/30/2009	1013	Alberts	123456789	10000 · Operating...	-SPLIT-	-2,000.00
Check	02/27/2009	1014	2155550621	2155550621...	10000 · Operating...	-SPLIT-	-84.22
Check	01/30/2009	1015	Barich		10000 · Operating...	-SPLIT-	-1,000.00
Check	01/30/2009	1016	GeekRob		10000 · Operating...	-SPLIT-	-2,500.00
Check	01/30/2009	1017	USPS		10000 · Operating...	-SPLIT-	-150.00
Check	01/30/2009	1018	Our Supplier		10000 · Operating...	12000 · Inven...	-24.00
Check	12/30/2008	1019	Our Supplier		10000 · Operating...	12000 · Inven...	-78.00
Check	01/02/2009	1020	Our Supplier		10000 · Operating...	-SPLIT-	-214.00
Bill Pmt -Check	01/19/2009	1021	Alberts	123456789	10000 · Operating...	20000 · Acco...	-1,190.00
Bill Pmt -Check	01/19/2009	1022	Barich		10000 · Operating...	20000 · Acco...	-1,000.00
Bill Pmt -Check	01/19/2009	1023	Visa		10000 · Operating...	20000 · Acco...	-450.26
Check	01/25/2009	1024	Visa	6666555588...	10000 · Operating...	-SPLIT-	-350.21
*** Missing numbers here ***							
Bill Pmt -Check	02/06/2009	1026	DelValSupplies	IV0006	10000 · Operating...	20000 · Acco...	-654.20
Bill Pmt -Check	02/06/2009	1027	Our Supplier		10000 · Operating...	20000 · Acco...	-610.00

FIGURE 14-3 Quite a few checks are missing.

If the check number is listed in your Missing Checks Report, it's truly missing; it doesn't exist in the register. Investigate the following possible causes:

- You deleted the check that was assigned that number.
- The check is physically missing (usually because somebody grabbed one or more checks to carry around).
- Checks jammed while printing, and you restarted the print run with the number of the first available check (QuickBooks doesn't mark checks as void in that case, it just omits the numbers in the register so they show up in the Missing Checks Report).

Finishing the Reconciliation

If this isn't the first reconciliation you're performing, there's a good chance that the Difference figure at the bottom of the Reconcile window displays 0.00. If this is the first reconciliation and you changed the opening balance in the account register (as explained earlier in this chapter), you probably also see 0.00 as the difference.

Click Reconcile Now and read the section, "Printing the Reconciliation Report," later in this chapter. If the Difference amount is an amount other than 0.00, read the following sections.

Pausing the Reconciliation Process

If the account doesn't reconcile (the Difference figure isn't 0.00), and you don't have the time, energy, or emotional fortitude to track down the problem at the moment, you can stop the reconciliation process without losing all the transactions you cleared.

Click the Leave button in the Reconcile window and do something else for a while. Have dinner, play with the cat, go to the movies, whatever. When you restart the reconciliation process, all the entries you made are still there.

Finding and Correcting Problems

When you're ready to investigate the cause of a difference between the ending balance and the cleared balance, follow the guidelines presented here to find the problem.

Count the number of transactions on the bank statement. Then look in the lower-left corner of the Reconcile window, where the number of items you have marked cleared is displayed. Mentally add another item to that number for each of the following:

- A service charge you entered in the Begin Reconciliation box
- An interest amount you entered in the Begin Reconciliation box

If the numbers differ, the problem is in your QuickBooks records; there's a transaction you should have cleared but didn't or a transaction you cleared that you shouldn't have.

If you're sure you didn't make any mistakes clearing transactions, do the following:

- Check the amount of each transaction against the amount in the bank statement.
- Check your transactions and make sure a deposit wasn't inadvertently entered as a payment (or vice versa). A clue for this is a transaction that's half the difference. If the difference is $220.00, find a transaction that has an amount of $110.00 and make sure it's a deduction if it's supposed to be a deduction (or the other way around).
- Check for transposed figures. Perhaps you entered a figure incorrectly in the register, such as $549.00 when the bank clears the transaction as $594.00. A clue that a transposed number is the problem is that the reconciliation difference can be divided by nine.

If you find the problem, correct it. When the Difference figure is 0.00, click Reconcile Now.

TIP: You might want to let somebody else check over the statement and the register, because sometimes you can't see your own mistakes.

Permitting an Adjusting Entry

If you cannot find the problem, you can tell QuickBooks to make an adjusting entry to force the reconciliation to balance. The adjusting entry is placed in the bank account register and is offset in an expense account named Reconciliation Discrepancies (the account is created automatically the first time you encounter this problem). If you ever figure out what the problem is, you can make the proper adjustment transaction and delete the adjusting entry.

To force a reconciliation, click Reconcile Now, even though there's a difference. A message appears to offer the opportunity to make an adjusting entry. Click Enter Adjustment.

Printing the Reconciliation Report

When you have a balanced reconciliation (even if it results from an adjusting entry), QuickBooks offers congratulations and also offers to print a reconciliation report.

(The dialog has a Close button to skip the report, but you should keep a copy of all your reconciliation reports.)

Select Reconciliation Report

Congratulations! Your account is balanced. All marked items have been cleared in the account register.

Select the type of reconciliation report you'd like to see.

○ Summary
○ Detail
● Both

To view this report at a later time, select the Report menu, display Banking and then Previous Reconciliation.

[Display] [Print...] [Close]

QuickBooks saves the report whether you print it, view it, or cancel it. You can view it in the future by choosing Reports | Banking | Previous Reconciliation.

Deciding on the Type of Report

QuickBooks offers two reconciliation report types: Detail and Summary. Here are the differences between them:

- The Detail Report shows all the transactions that are cleared and all the transactions that haven't cleared (called *in transit* transactions) as of the statement closing date. Any transactions dated after the statement closing date are listed as *new transactions*.
- The Summary Report breaks down your transactions in the same way, but it doesn't list the individual transactions; it shows only the totals for each category: Cleared, Uncleared (in transit), and New.

Selecting the Detail Report makes it easier to resolve problems in the future. You have a list of every check and deposit and when it cleared.

Print vs. Display

You also have to decide whether to print or to display the report. Make your decision according to how you think you might use the report.

Printing a Reconciliation Report

If you opt to print both reports, the Print Reports dialog opens so you can select the printer. If you select either the Summary or Detail Report, the Print Reports dialog offers options, as follows:

- Print the report to the selected printer. You can file the printout in case you ever need to refer to it.

- Print the report to a file. The file option offers several formats in a drop-down list, so you can load the resulting file into the software of your choice. This gives you the opportunity to store multiple reports in one application (or even one file) and sort the data as you wish. The following file options are available:
  - **ASCII text**   Is straight, unformatted text.
  - **Comma delimited**   Automatically puts a comma between each field (column). Select this option if you want to use the file in a spreadsheet or database program capable of importing comma-delimited files. Most spreadsheet software can handle comma-delimited files.
  - **Tab delimited**   Is the same as comma delimited, but the field delimiter is a tab marker instead of a comma. All spreadsheet and database software can handle tab-delimited files.

When you print a report to a disk file, QuickBooks opens a Create Disk File window with the folder that holds your QuickBooks software as the target folder. The file extension matches the file type you selected.

You can change the container to any other folder in the system—you might want to create a subfolder in your My Documents folder to hold these files. Hereafter, that folder becomes the default container for your reconciliation reports. Be sure to save each month's reconciliation report file with a unique name—the date and the account name (if you reconcile more than one bank account) are good selections for filenames.

Displaying the Reconciliation Report

If you choose to display a report (or both reports), you see the usual QuickBooks report format. You can modify the report to change the font, the columns, and so on. In addition, you can click the Export icon at the top of the report window and send the report to Excel, where you can manipulate the data to match your needs.

Adjusting the Beginning Balance for the First Reconciliation

The beginning balance in the Begin Reconciliation window probably doesn't match the opening balance on your bank statement the first time you reconcile the account. The beginning balance should be 0.00.

The bank, of course, is using the last ending balance as the current beginning balance. The last ending balance represents a running total that began way back when, starting when you first opened that bank account. The only QuickBooks users who have it easy are those who opened their bank accounts the same day they started to use QuickBooks. (A minuscule number of people, if any, fit that description.)

To get your QuickBooks bank reconciliation in sync with your bank balance, you have to create a "fake previous reconciliation."

Follow these steps to create a previous reconciliation:

1. Set the Statement Date field in the Begin Reconciliation dialog to the day before the date of the bank statement.

2. In the Ending Balance field (see Figure 14-4), enter the amount of the closing balance on the bank statement.

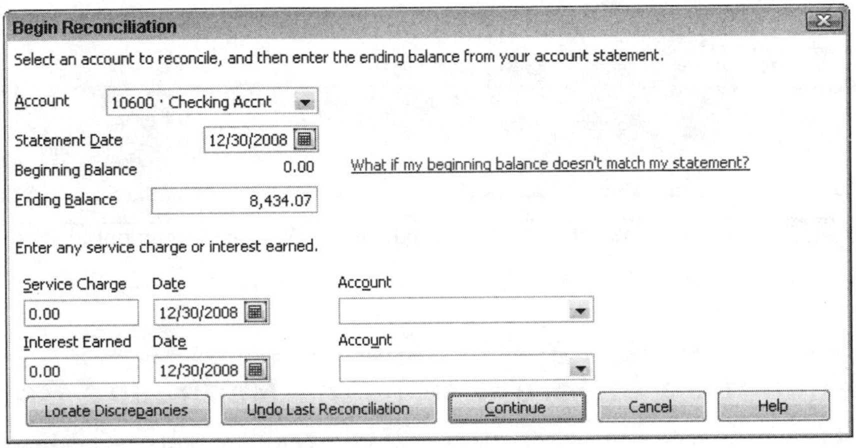

Begin Reconciliation

Select an account to reconcile, and then enter the ending balance from your account statement.

Account	10600 · Checking Accnt ▾
Statement Date	12/30/2008 📅
Beginning Balance	0.00 What if my beginning balance doesn't match my statement?
Ending Balance	8,434.07

Enter any service charge or interest earned.

Service Charge	Date	Account
0.00	12/30/2008 📅	▾
Interest Earned	Date	Account
0.00	12/30/2008 📅	▾

[Locate Discrepancies] [Undo Last Reconciliation] [Continue] [Cancel] [Help]

FIGURE 14-4   Use an earlier statement date to catch up to your real bank statements.

3. Click Continue to move to the Reconcile dialog.

4. Select all the transactions dated on or before the date of the statement.

5. The Difference figure (in the lower-right corner of the Reconcile dialog) should now be zero (see Figure 14-5).

6. Click Reconcile Now.

QuickBooks announces a successful, balanced reconciliation, and you can print a report if you wish. Now you can return to the bank reconciliation feature and use the real statement date to reconcile your bank account. This time, you have the same amounts for the opening and closing balances, and you don't have to select any transactions to set the Difference figure to 0.00. Finish the reconciliation to set the previous date and opening balance for future months.

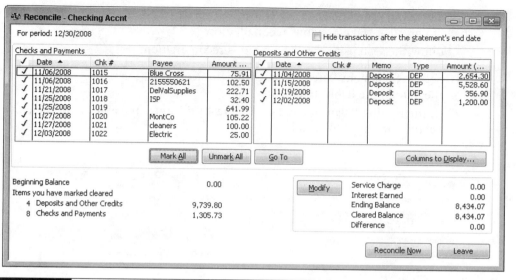

FIGURE 14-5 Clear all the earlier transactions to match the current statement to QuickBooks.

Troubleshooting Differences in the Beginning Balance

If this isn't the first time you've reconciled the bank account, the beginning balance that's displayed on the Begin Reconciliation window should match the beginning balance on the bank statement. That beginning balance is the ending balance from the last reconciliation, and nothing should change its amount.

If the beginning balance doesn't match the statement, you have to find out why. Search your memory, because you probably performed one of the following actions (these are all things you should *never* do, and you need to undo the damage):

- You changed the amount on a transaction that had previously cleared.
- You voided a transaction that had previously cleared.
- You deleted a transaction that had previously cleared.
- You removed the cleared check mark from a transaction that had previously cleared.
- You manually entered a cleared check mark on a transaction that had not cleared.

You have to figure out which one of those actions you took after you last reconciled the account, and luckily, QuickBooks has a tool to help you. Click the Locate Discrepancies button on the Begin Reconciliation window to open the Locate Discrepancies dialog seen in Figure 14-6.

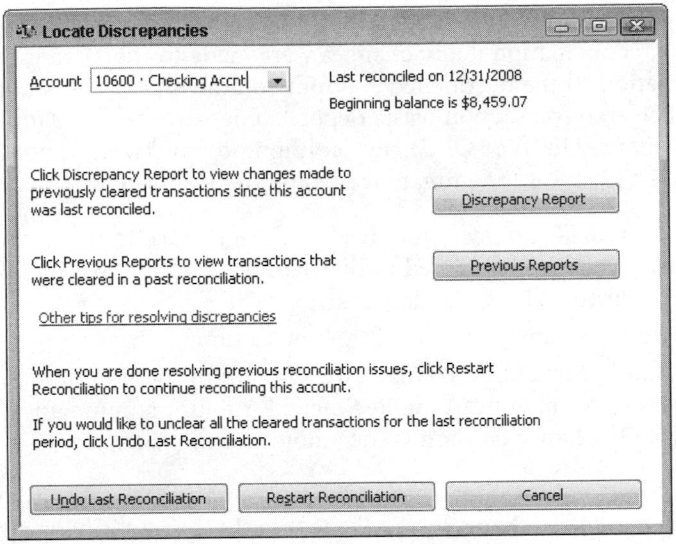

FIGURE 14-6 You have tools to help you track down the reason for an incorrect starting balance.

Viewing the Discrepancy Report

Click Discrepancy Report to see if any transactions that were cleared during a past reconciliation were later changed or deleted (see Figure 14-7).

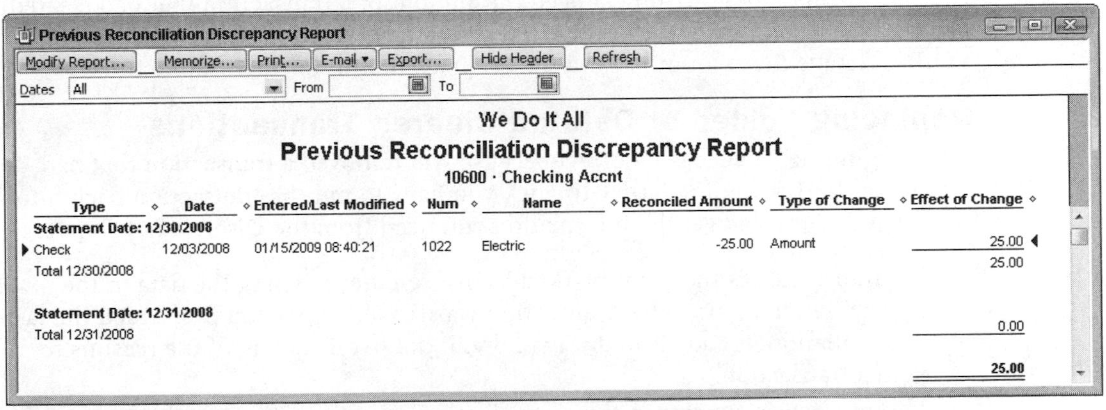

FIGURE 14-7 Someone voided a transaction that was cleared during a previous reconciliation.

This report shows you the details of the transactions that cleared during a previous reconciliation if any changes were made to those transactions since that reconciliation. If the Reconciled Amount column shows a positive number, the original cleared transaction was a deposit; a negative number indicates a disbursement. The Type Of Change column provides a clue about the action you must take to correct the unmatched beginning balances.

- **Uncleared** Means you removed the check mark in the Cleared column of the register (and you persisted in this action even though QuickBooks issued a stern warning about the dangers).
- **Deleted** Means you deleted the transaction.
- **Amount** Means you changed the amount of the transaction. The difference between the amount in the Reconciled Amount column and the amount in the Effect Of Change column is the amount of the change.

This report doesn't offer a Type Of Change named "Void," so a voided transaction is merely marked as changed, and the text in the Type Of Change column is Amount. A transaction with a changed amount equal to and opposite of the original amount was almost certainly a transaction you voided after it cleared.

Correcting Opening Balance Differences

Use the information in the Discrepancy Report to correct the problems you created by changing previously cleared transactions.

Correcting Changed Transactions

If you cleared or uncleared a transaction manually, open the bank register and undo your erroneous action. If you changed the amount of a transaction that had cleared, and the transaction still exists in the register with an amount (it's not marked VOID), change the amount back to the original amount for that transaction.

Replacing Voided or Deleted Cleared Transactions

If the beginning balance is incorrect because you removed a transaction that had cleared (either by voiding or deleting it), you have to put the transaction back into your register. You can get the information you need from the Discrepancy Report.

- If a transaction is there but marked VOID, re-enter it, using the data in the reconciliation report. That transaction wasn't void when you performed the last reconciliation, it had cleared. Therefore, it doesn't meet any of the reasons to void a transaction.
- If a transaction appears in the reconciliation report but is not in the register, it was deleted. If it cleared, it can't be deleted. Re-enter it, using the data in the reconciliation report.
- Check the amounts on the printed check reconciliation report against the data in the register to see if any amount was changed after the account was reconciled. If so, restore the original amount.

Making these changes is safe because you're undoing your own mistake. You can't justify changing a cleared transaction—*a transaction that cleared cannot have the amount changed, be voided, be deleted, or be uncleared.*

If you re-enter a transaction that was voided or deleted after it cleared, and you put a check mark into the Cleared Column (the column with a check mark as the column title), QuickBooks adds it to your reconcile window with a check mark already in place. This is a nifty feature, probably born from need as the QuickBooks programmers realized how often people improperly void or delete previously cleared transactions. This action doesn't adjust your opening balance on the Begin Reconciliation window, but it does re-adjust the math so the current reconciliation works and next month's opening balance will be correct.

> **TIP:** You don't have to be in the Begin Reconciliation window to see a Discrepancy Report. You can view the contents at any time by choosing Reports | Banking | Reconciliation Discrepancy.

Viewing the Last Reconciliation Report

Even if you don't display or print a reconciliation report after you reconcile an account, QuickBooks saves the report. If you're trying to track down a discrepancy in the beginning balance, viewing the last reconciliation report may be helpful.

Click Previous Reports to open the Select Previous Reconciliation Report dialog, and select the options for the type and format of the report you want to see.

> **TIP:** You can view the Previous Reconciliation Report at any time by choosing Reports | Banking | Previous Reconciliation.

Undoing the Last Reconciliation

QuickBooks lets you undo the last reconciliation, which means that all transactions cleared during the reconciliation are uncleared. This is a good way to start over if you're mired in difficulties and confusion during the current reconciliation, and the problems seem to stem from the previous reconciliation (especially if you forced reconciliation by having QuickBooks make an adjusting entry).

Click the Undo Last Reconciliation button on the Begin Reconciliation dialog. QuickBooks suggests you click Cancel and back up your company file before continuing, which is an excellent idea (just in case this process doesn't work properly, so you can restore the data in its reconciled state). Then, begin reconciling, click Undo Last Reconciliation, and click Continue.

QuickBooks performs the following actions:

- Removes the cleared status of all transactions you cleared during the last reconciliation.
- Leaves the amounts you entered for interest and bank charges (so don't re-enter them).

When the process completes, QuickBooks displays a message to describe those actions and tell you they were performed. Click OK to clear the message and return to the Begin Reconciliation dialog.

If QuickBooks made an adjustment entry during the last reconciliation (which almost certainly is the case; otherwise, you wouldn't have to undo and redo the reconciliation), click Cancel to close the Begin Reconciliation dialog. Open the account's register and delete the adjustment entry—it's the entry posted to the Reconciliation Adjustment account. Hopefully, this time the reconciliation will work and you won't need another adjusting entry.

Start the reconciliation process again for the same month you just "undid." When the Begin Reconciliation window opens, the data that appears is the same data that appeared when you started the last reconciliation—the last reconciliation date, the statement date, and the beginning balance are back.

Enter the ending balance from the bank statement. Do *not* enter the interest and bank charges again; they were *not* removed when QuickBooks undid the last reconciliation. Instead, find them in the Reconcile window and clear them (they're not labeled, so you have to look for the appropriate date and amount).

Good luck!

Giving Up the Search for a Reason

You may not be able to find a reason for the difference in the beginning balances. There's a point at which it isn't worth your time to keep looking, so just give up and perform the reconciliation. If your bank account doesn't balance, QuickBooks will make an adjusting transaction at the end of the reconciliation process, and if you ever learn the reason, you can remove that transaction with a journal entry that transfers the amount to the appropriate account (with the help of your accountant).

Using Online Banking Services

You can use your Internet connection to access a wide range of online services that QuickBooks offers to financial institutions, including the following:

- Transaction download, which means you can view the status of your bank accounts, see which transactions have cleared, and generally keep an eye on your accounts via your Internet connection.
- Online payments, which means you send vendor checks through your bank, directly from QuickBooks, instead of writing checks.

Another online service is access to your credit card accounts, so you can download credit card transactions and enter them in your credit card account register. To take advantage of online credit card tracking, you must set up your credit cards as credit card accounts in your chart of accounts (all of which is discussed in Chapter 13). Some financial institutions offer online banking for liability accounts you've established in QuickBooks, such as lines of credit.

Understanding Online Banking

Online banking is nothing more than using the Internet to move funds and access information about your accounts from your financial institution. The financial institution's computer is a server, configured for secure exchange of data, that provides information and services related to your accounts. QuickBooks supports two methods for online banking services, and your financial institution selects the method it wants to use:

- **Web Connect**   This is the method you use when your financial institution doesn't provide a way to connect your QuickBooks data directly to the data on their own server. Actually, this means your financial institution chose not to install the software required to work interactively with QuickBooks. Instead, there's a page on its website that lets you view and download your transactions and import the downloaded file into QuickBooks.
- **Direct Connect**   Your financial institution exchanges data interactively with QuickBooks. This allows you to take advantage of all types of additional online banking services, such as transaction data downloads directly into your QuickBooks bank register, transfers between bank accounts, electronic messages between you and the financial institution, and online bill payments (optional at some financial institutions). Some financial institutions charge a fee for some or all of the services available through Direct Connect.

NOTE: Some financial institutions offer both Web Connect and Direct Connect and you can choose the method you prefer. Usually, banks that offer both methods charge a fee for Direct Connect.

Setting Up Online Banking

To use online banking, your bank must support at least one QuickBooks online access feature. There are three online banking services available:

- Transaction download
- Online bill paying
- Online credit card services

You can sign up for any or all of these services. If your bank supports only online account access and doesn't support online bill paying or online credit card services, you can work directly with the QuickBooks online banking services. See "Using the QuickBooks Bill Pay Service" later in this chapter.

The process of enabling online banking has three steps (all of which are covered in this section):

1. Apply for online services with your bank.
2. Receive a personal identification number (PIN) or password from your bank to make sure your online account is secure.
3. Enable a QuickBooks account (or multiple accounts) for online services.

Once a QuickBooks bank account is enabled for online banking, you can download transaction information from your bank and match it to your bank register.

To get started, choose Banking | Online Banking from the menu bar. The submenu has four commands related to online banking services:

- Set Up Account For Online Services
- Participating Financial Institutions
- Import Web Connect File
- Learn About Online Bill Payment

Finding Your Bank Online

If you haven't signed up for (or discussed) online services with your bank, and you're not sure if your bank has online services, choose Participating Financial Institutions to see if your bank participates. QuickBooks may display a dialog telling you it has to open a browser to travel to the Internet. Click OK, and when you're connected to the Internet, you see the Financial Institutions Directory website (see Figure 15-1).

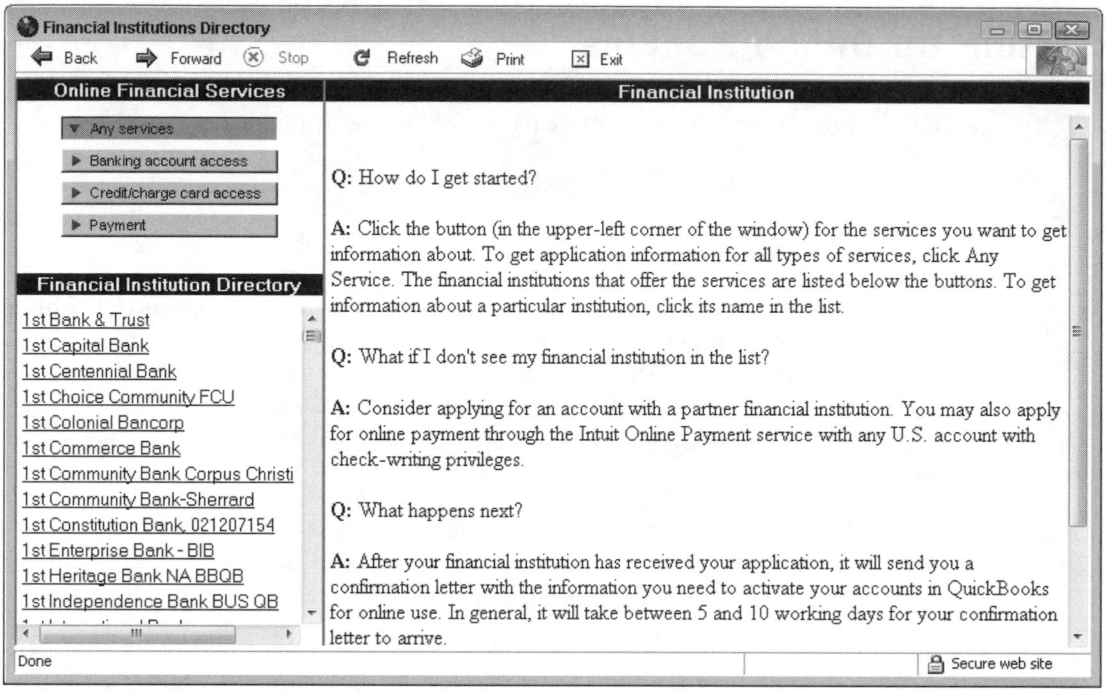

FIGURE 15-1 Select the type of online service you want, and then scroll through the list to see if your bank is included.

The four choices at the top of the left pane determine the contents of the Financial Institutions Directory list that QuickBooks displays. The window opens with the choice labeled Any Services preselected, and all the banks listed provide some type of online service.

If you're interested in a particular online service (for example, you only care about bank account access to download transactions), select that option, and the list of banks changes to those banks that offer the selected service.

Scroll through the list to find your bank and click its listing. The right pane of the Financial Institutions Directory window displays information about your bank's online services (see Figure 15-2). If your bank isn't listed, you cannot set up any QuickBooks online banking services.

Click the Apply Now button if you want to start the application process here and now. If no Apply Now button exists, follow the instructions for setting up online services at the bank—usually the bank displays a phone number. If online applications are available, fill out the form and submit the information. Your bank will send

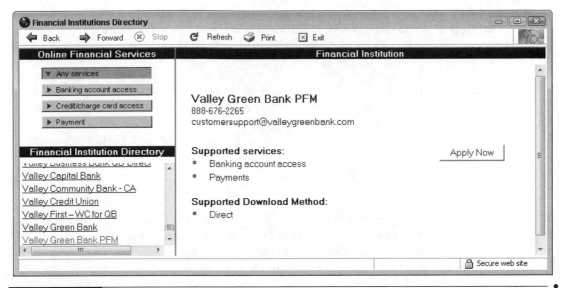

FIGURE 15-2 This bank has Direct Connect.

you information about using its online service, a login name (sometimes called a company ID), and a PIN or a password. This is the information you need to enable the bank account for online access.

> **NOTE:** Most banks that support Direct Connect provide a PIN (a four-digit number), and most banks that support Web Connect use a password.

After you've completed the paperwork at your bank and received your login ID and a PIN or a password, QuickBooks walks you through the process of enabling your bank account for online banking in QuickBooks.

Those steps differ depending on whether your bank uses Direct Connect or Web Connect. The following sections cover both scenarios.

> **NOTE:** Banks that are enabled for online access have a symbol that looks like a lightning bolt in the Online Access column of your chart of accounts—the column heading doesn't say "Online Access," it just has the lightning bolt symbol.

Enabling Online Access for Direct Connect

After you receive your ID and PIN, you can enable a bank account for online access with Direct Connect in any of the following ways:

- Choose Banking | Online Banking | Setup Account For Online Services and select the bank account you want to configure for online services in the Set Up Account For Online Services dialog.
- Open an existing bank account (select the account in the Chart of Accounts List and press CTRL-E) and click Set Up Online Services.
- Click Yes in the Set Up Online Services dialog that appears when you create a new bank account.

QuickBooks opens the Set Up Account For Online Services For *<Name you used for your bank account in the chart of accounts>* dialog seen in Figure 15-3. Select your bank from the drop-down list of participating financial institutions and click Next. (You don't have to scroll through the list; instead, as you type the characters for the name of your bank, QuickBooks moves to the appropriate listing.)

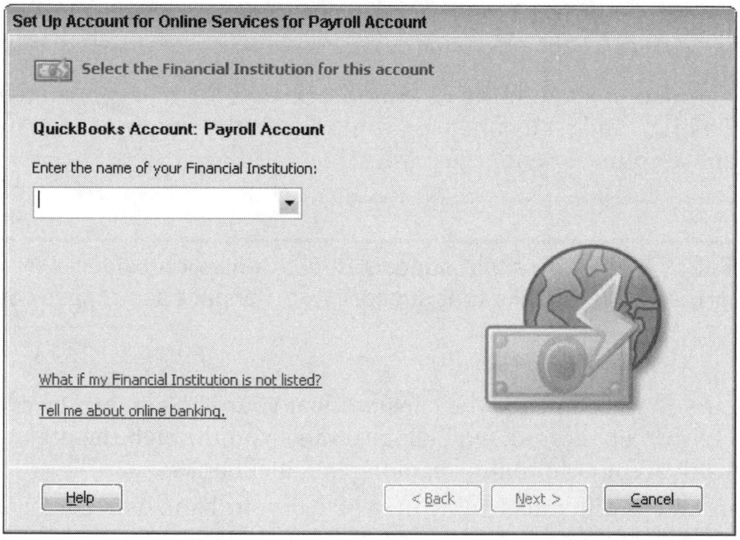

Set Up Account for Online Services for Payroll Account

Select the Financial Institution for this account

QuickBooks Account: Payroll Account

Enter the name of your Financial Institution:

What if my Financial Institution is not listed?

Tell me about online banking.

Help   < Back   Next >   Cancel

FIGURE 15-3   The first step is to select your bank.

NOTE: If your bank has a nationwide presence with regional headquarters, after you select the bank you may see a second dialog asking you to select the appropriate bank region. For example, if your bank is BigAsTheNation, you may have to select BigAsTheNation-Pennsylvania-NJ if the bank you use is part of that division.

QuickBooks contacts the bank over the Internet (to determine the information your bank requires to configure your bank account for online access), and then displays information about the bank's online access. As you can see in Figure 15-4, this bank requires a PIN (it offers Direct Connect). QuickBooks reminds you that if you signed up for your bank's own website-based online banking features, the User ID and password required to enter that website may be different from the User ID and PIN/password required for access via QuickBooks (your financial institution sets these rules).

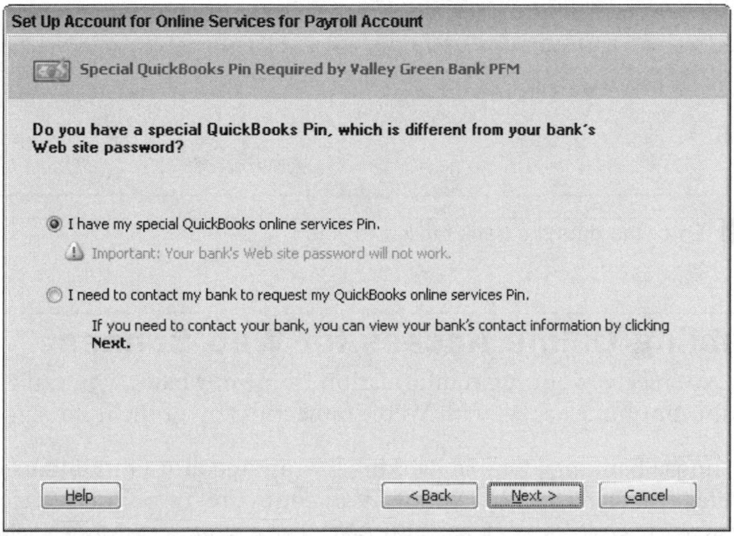

FIGURE 15-4 This bank requires a PIN for Direct Connect.

Click Next and use the information the bank sent you to fill in the fields for your Customer ID and PIN/password (see Figure 15-5). Depending on the way your bank maintains account information to configure online services, you may be asked to enter a routing number for the bank and the account number for your bank account instead of only the Customer ID and PIN.

Click Sign In to access your bank account online. QuickBooks contacts the bank over the Internet and downloads the transactions for your bank account, displaying a dialog that tells you how many transactions were downloaded. Click Finish to open the Online Banking Center automatically, where you can view the downloaded transactions (using the Online Banking Center and matching transactions is covered later in this chapter).

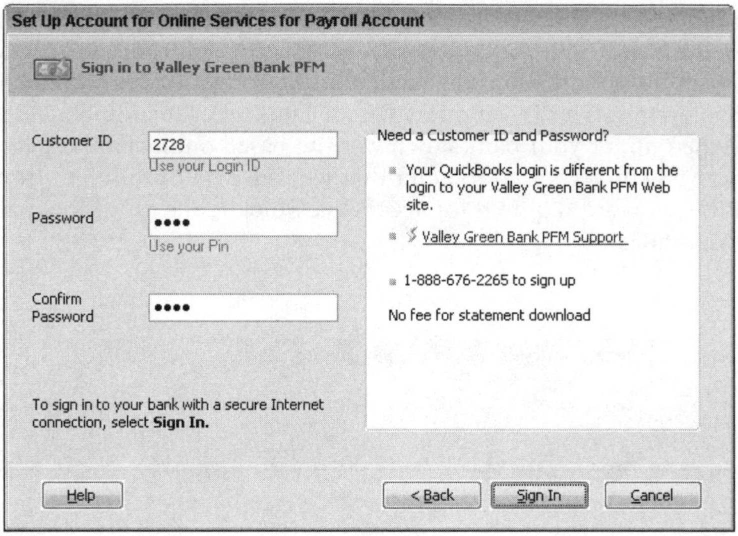

FIGURE 15-5 Enter the data the bank mailed to you.

Enabling Online Access for Web Connect

After you receive your login information from your bank, you can enable a bank account for online access with Web Connect in any of the following ways:

- Choose Banking | Online Banking | Setup Account For Online Services and select the bank account you want to configure for online services.
- Open an existing bank account (select the account in the Chart of Accounts List and press CTRL-E) and click Set Up Online Services.
- Click Yes in the Setup Online Services dialog that asks you whether you want to enable this new account for online services.

QuickBooks opens the Set Up Account For Online Services For <*Name you used for your bank account in the chart of accounts*> dialog. Select your bank from the drop-down list. You don't have to scroll through the list; instead, as you type the characters for the name of your bank, QuickBooks moves to the appropriate listing.

Click Next to have QuickBooks travel to your bank's website to check the bank's type of online services (which will be Web Connect). QuickBooks displays the dialog seen in Figure 15-6.

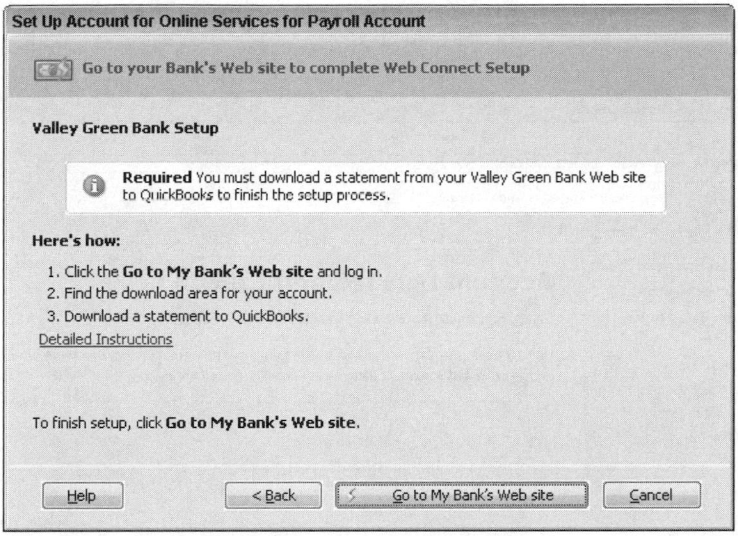

Set Up Account for Online Services for Payroll Account

Go to your Bank's Web site to complete Web Connect Setup

Valley Green Bank Setup

ⓘ **Required** You must download a statement from your Valley Green Bank Web site to QuickBooks to finish the setup process.

Here's how:

1. Click the **Go to My Bank's Web site** and log in.
2. Find the download area for your account.
3. Download a statement to QuickBooks.

Detailed Instructions

To finish setup, click **Go to My Bank's Web site**.

| Help | < Back | Go to My Bank's Web site | Cancel |

FIGURE 15-6 To enable a bank account for Web Connect online services, you must download a transactions file from the bank's website.

Click the button labeled Go To My Bank's Web Site. QuickBooks opens its Help files with instructions, information, and explanations about connecting to banks that offer Web Connect.

If you see a message telling you that QuickBooks must launch a browser and travel to the Internet, click OK (no, wait, click the option labeled Do Not Display This Message In the Future, *then* click OK).

When QuickBooks connects to your bank's website, use the login information the bank gave you when you signed up for online services. Depending on the type of software the bank uses, you may be asked for a company ID and a User ID (or both), as well as a password. Some bank software doesn't present the password field on the same web page as the sign-in ID; instead, you must click Continue or Next to move to the web page that asks for your password.

Click the button or link that connects you to your account transactions. The label might be Reports, Reporting, Download Statements, Download Transactions, Exports, or any other terminology that indicates, "Get a report on the transactions that have passed through your bank account."

In the options or criteria page, select QuickBooks File as the report type. Your bank may have several choices for QuickBooks files, for instance, according to the version (year). Some banks use a file named "QBO file" instead of "QuickBooks File."

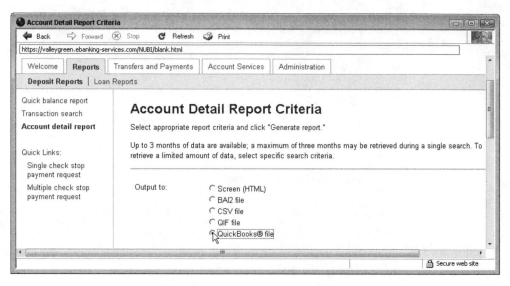

Your bank probably displays criteria selections for a date range (yesterday, today, or a From Date–To Date range of dates) and may also offer an option labeled Since Last Download (which you can select after this initial download).

After you make your selections and click the appropriate button (Generate, Download, or some other similar label), your bank generates the file and displays a File Download dialog asking whether you want to open the file or save it to your computer.

- If you click Save, QuickBooks downloads the file to your computer and saves it in a folder you select. When you're ready to import the file and view it in the Online Banking Center, choose File | Utilities | Import | Web Connect Files and select the file you saved.
- If you click Open, QuickBooks asks if you want to import the file into your bank account now, or save it and import it later.

The first time you import your Web Connect file into QuickBooks, you must link the file to a QuickBooks bank account.

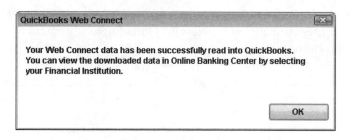

- If you've already created this bank account in QuickBooks, select the option Use An Existing QuickBooks Account, and select the account from the drop-down list. Click Continue and QuickBooks enables the account for online access.

- If you haven't created this bank account in QuickBooks, select the option Create A New QuickBooks Account, and then click Continue. QuickBooks creates a new bank account automatically, naming it Checking At *<Name of Bank>* and enables the account for online access.

QuickBooks displays a message telling you the data has been imported.

Click OK to open the Online Banking Center (covered next) so you can view the downloaded data and match it to your bank register. Hereafter, you use the Online Banking Center to download your transaction data.

Using the Online Banking Center

To connect to your financial institution, choose Banking | Online Banking | Online Banking Center to open the Online Banking Center window.

As discussed in the previous section, if you've just enabled an account for online banking and downloaded transactions for the first time, the Online Banking Center opens automatically and you can skip the beginning of this section that tells you how to effect a transaction download—go right to the section on viewing the downloaded transactions. Hereafter, you'll both download and view transactions from the Online Banking Center.

If you have online banking at more than one financial institution, select the appropriate one from the drop-down list in the Financial Institution field at the top of the window. For example, you may have online bank account access at one financial institution and online credit card access at another.

NOTE: If your financial institution supports Web Connect, you can only download transactions; all the other functions covered in this section (such as exchanging electronic messages, making online payments within QuickBooks, and so on) are available only for Direct Connect.

Downloading Transactions

To download transactions from your bank, open the Online Banking Center and click Send/Receive Transactions.

- For Direct Connect, QuickBooks opens the Access To *<Name of Bank>* dialog. Enter your PIN and click OK. QuickBooks automatically downloads new transactions.
- For Web Connect, QuickBooks travels to the bank's website, where you must log in and then select a QuickBooks download (as described earlier in this chapter).

Viewing the Downloaded Transactions

When your data has been downloaded, the Online Banking Center dialog displays a summary of the items received from your bank in the Items Received section.

(For Direct Connect, you can select the electronic messages listing, read the messages, and delete those you don't care to save. It would be unusual to want to save any, since most of the time the messages contain information about upcoming bank holiday closings or announcements about new mortgage or CD rates.)

> **NOTE:** After the first time you download transactions, QuickBooks checks your company file to see which transactions were already downloaded and only downloads transactions not downloaded previously. This means you don't have to worry about duplicate transactions.

Matching Transactions

To match downloaded transactions to your QuickBooks bank register, click the button labeled Add Transactions To QuickBooks and select the account. QuickBooks displays the downloaded transactions (see Figure 15-7).

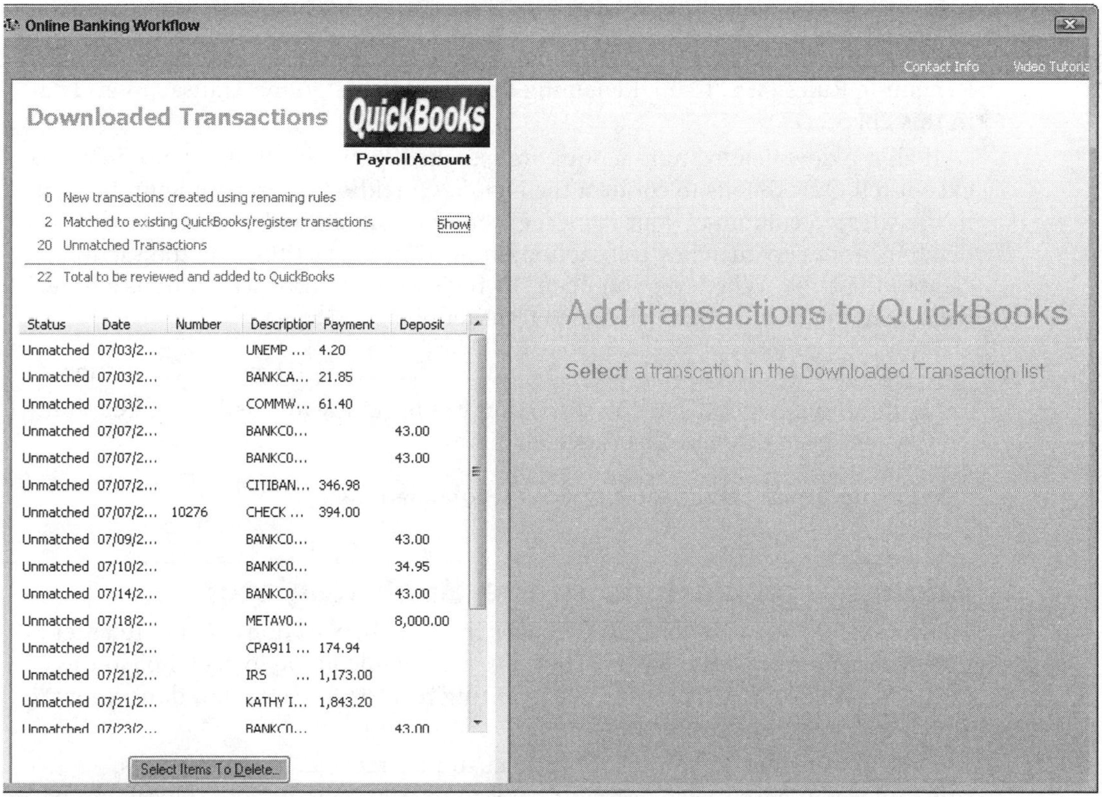

Status	Date	Number	Description	Payment	Deposit
Unmatched	07/03/2...		UNEMP ...	4.20	
Unmatched	07/03/2...		BANKCA...	21.85	
Unmatched	07/03/2...		COMMW...	61.40	
Unmatched	07/07/2...		BANKCO...		43.00
Unmatched	07/07/2...		BANKCO...		43.00
Unmatched	07/07/2...		CITIBAN...	346.98	
Unmatched	07/07/2...	10276	CHECK ...	394.00	
Unmatched	07/09/2...		BANKCO...		43.00
Unmatched	07/10/2...		BANKCO...		34.95
Unmatched	07/14/2...		BANKCO...		43.00
Unmatched	07/18/2...		METAVO...		8,000.00
Unmatched	07/21/2...		CPA911 ...	174.94	
Unmatched	07/21/2...		IRS ...	1,173.00	
Unmatched	07/21/2...		KATHY I...	1,843.20	
Unmatched	07/23/2...		BANKCO...		43.00

FIGURE 15-7 All the downloaded transactions are available in the Online Banking Center.

QuickBooks automatically tries to match the transactions in the file to the transactions in your register and marks the status of each transaction with one of the following conditions:

- **Matched** Means the downloaded transaction matches a transaction in the register.
- **Unmatched** Means no match was found in your register for the downloaded transaction.

By default, only the unmatched transactions are listed in the left pane of the window. The top of the left pane displays the number of matched transactions, but doesn't display the details. To see the details, click the link labeled Show and QuickBooks displays the matched transactions. To hide the matched transactions listings, click the Hide link at the top of the window. (Since you don't need to do anything with matched transactions, it's easier to work with the list when those transactions are removed.)

The top of the left pane also displays the number of transactions matched via Renaming Rules (see "Using Renaming Rules to Match Online Transactions" later in this chapter).

If all the downloaded transactions are matched, you have nothing else to do except tell QuickBooks to confirm the match. QuickBooks inserts a lightning bolt in the Cleared column of your bank register (the column with a check mark heading) for every matched transaction, indicating the fact that the transaction has cleared the bank. Whenever you open the register, you know which transactions have been matched with downloaded transactions:

- A check mark indicates a transaction has been through bank reconciliation.
- A lightning bolt indicates a transaction has been downloaded as cleared, but has not been through a bank reconciliation.

(Chapter 14 covers the topic of bank reconciliations.)

Adding Transactions to the Bank Register

Many users (those who don't print checks in QuickBooks) don't bother to enter all transactions in the bank register. They use the download file to accomplish the task. This isn't a good way to keep accounting records, because you don't know which transactions are outstanding.

Even if you enter all your checks and customer receipts in QuickBooks, sometimes you have to wait for your bank to tell you whether the transaction has cleared to learn the amount of the transaction (such as merchant card receipts or payments taken out of your bank automatically by a vendor).

To add an unmatched transaction to the bank register, select its listing in the Add Transactions To QuickBooks window. Depending on the type of transaction (payment or deposit), the right pane displays options for adding the transaction to the bank register.

Adding a Downloaded Payment to the Register

When you select an unmatched payment, QuickBooks opens the Record An Expense window in the right pane (see Figure 15-8).

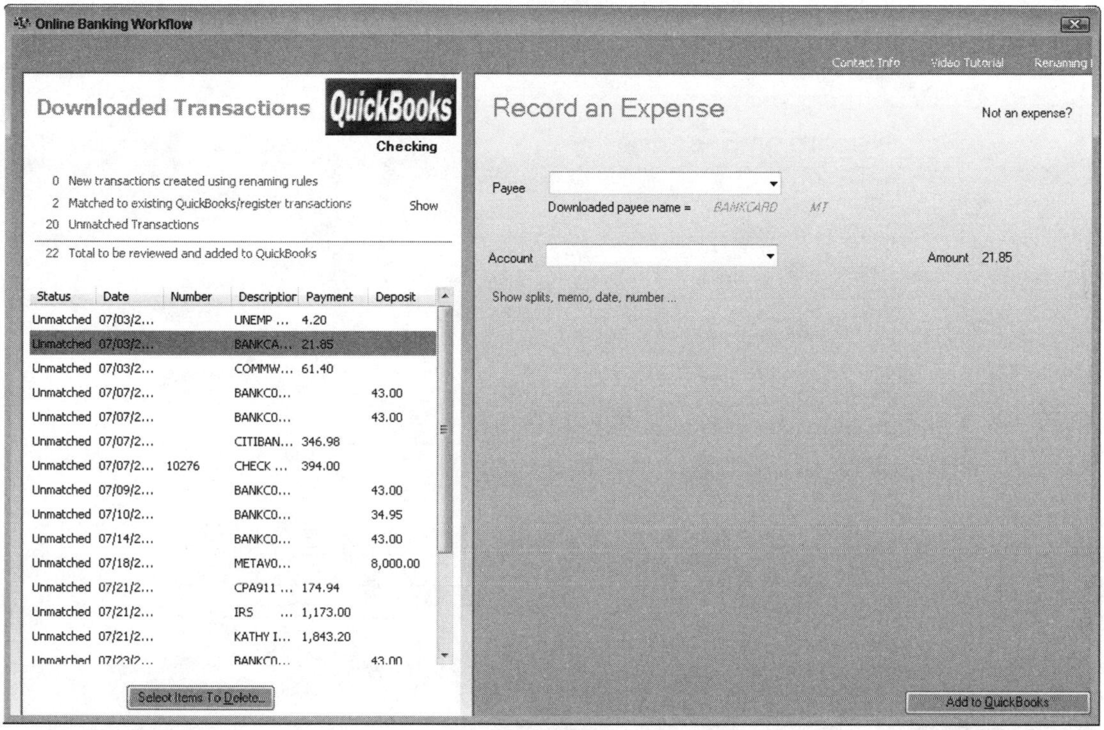

FIGURE 15-8 A downloaded payment is assumed to be an expense.

If the vendor exists in your company file, select the vendor from the drop-down list in the Payee field (there is no <Add New> listing, so you cannot add vendors in the Online Banking window).

If the vendor name on the downloaded transactions doesn't exist in your company file you have several options:

- Enter the transaction without a vendor name (which is appropriate only for those payments to vendors you don't care about tracking, such as monthly payments for merchant account charges or your bank's monthly service charges).

- Enter the transaction without a vendor name, and create the vendor after you're finished with the Online Banking window. Then edit the transaction to add the vendor name.
- Link the vendor name on the downloaded transaction to a vendor name in your company file via a renaming rule.

If the payment is posted to multiple accounts, or should be linked to a customer (or both), click the link "Show splits, memo, date, number" to open an entry window that looks like Figure 15-9.

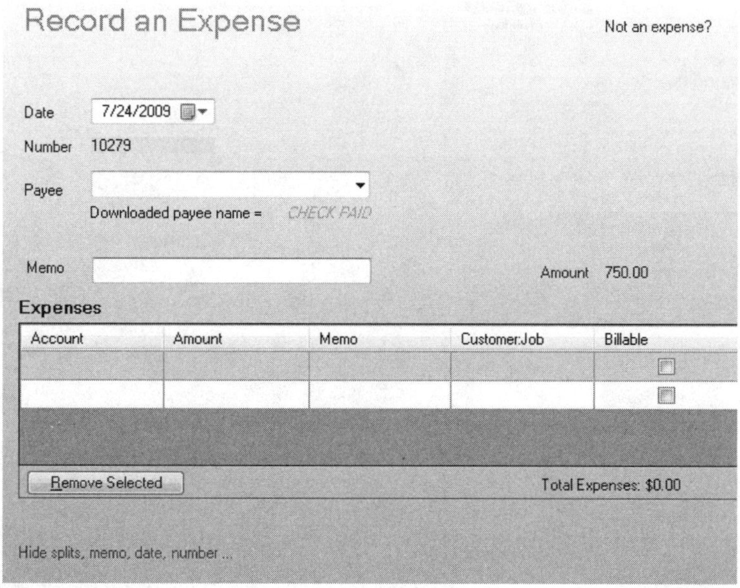

FIGURE 15-9 Enter the payment with the details you need.

If the downloaded payment represents a check or online payment you created to pay a vendor bill that is entered in your system, click the link "Not an expense?" and select the option Select Open Bills In QuickBooks To Pay.

In the Vendor field, select the vendor with an open A/P bill that this downloaded payment is linked to. QuickBooks displays the open bills for the vendor (see Figure 15-10).

Select the bill to pay with this transaction, and change the paid amount if the transaction represented a partial payment. You can also select multiple bills for this vendor, if you paid more than one bill with this payment. QuickBooks does some quick arithmetic to make sure that all the bills you select total up to match the downloaded amount.

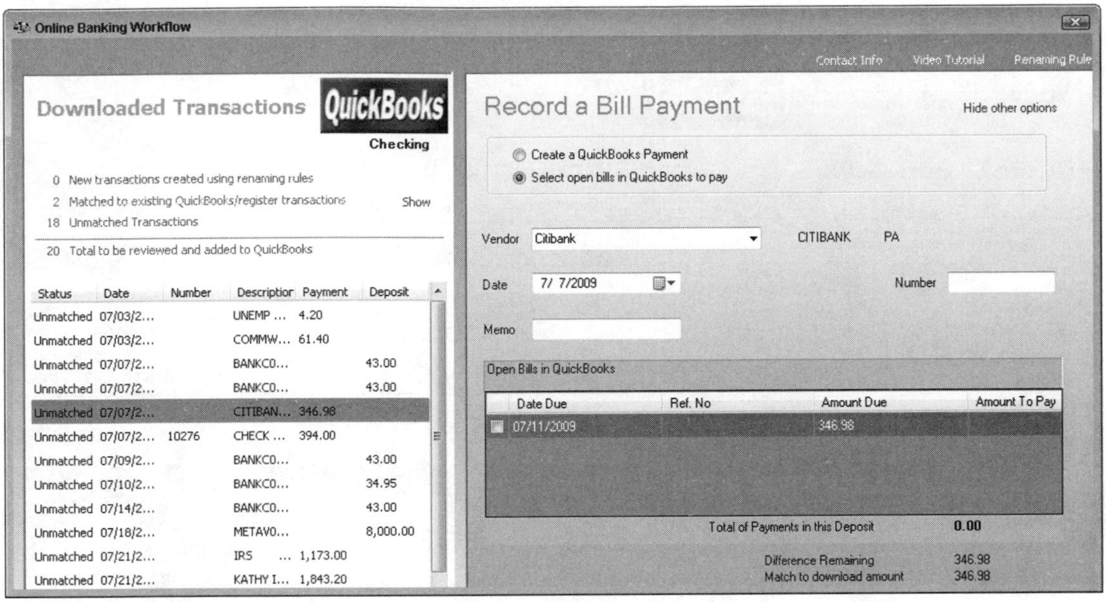

FIGURE 15-10 This downloaded transaction was a bill payment.

Adding a Downloaded Deposit to the Register

When you select a downloaded deposit, the right pane of the Online Banking Center displays the Record A QuickBooks Deposit window, which could have either or both of the following tabs:

- Undeposited Funds, which contains all the current transactions waiting for deposit (the transactions you see when you open the Make Deposits window). If no entries exist in Undeposited Funds, the tab isn't displayed.

- Open Invoices, which lists all the current open invoices in your company file. If no open invoices exist, the tab isn't displayed.

Choose the appropriate tab, and then choose the matching transaction (or multiple transactions that total up to the amount of the downloaded transaction). As you can see in Figure 15-11, the selected downloaded transaction matches a credit card sale transaction that was waiting for the merchant bank to deposit the funds.

If the merchant card company deducts fees before depositing the sale, the downloaded transaction amount is lower than the amount received for the sale. To match the amount, enter those fees in this window, in the next blank row. Click the From Account column and select the merchant account fees expense account. Then, in the Amount column, enter the difference between the original transaction and the downloaded deposit (it's a minus amount). The net amount matches the

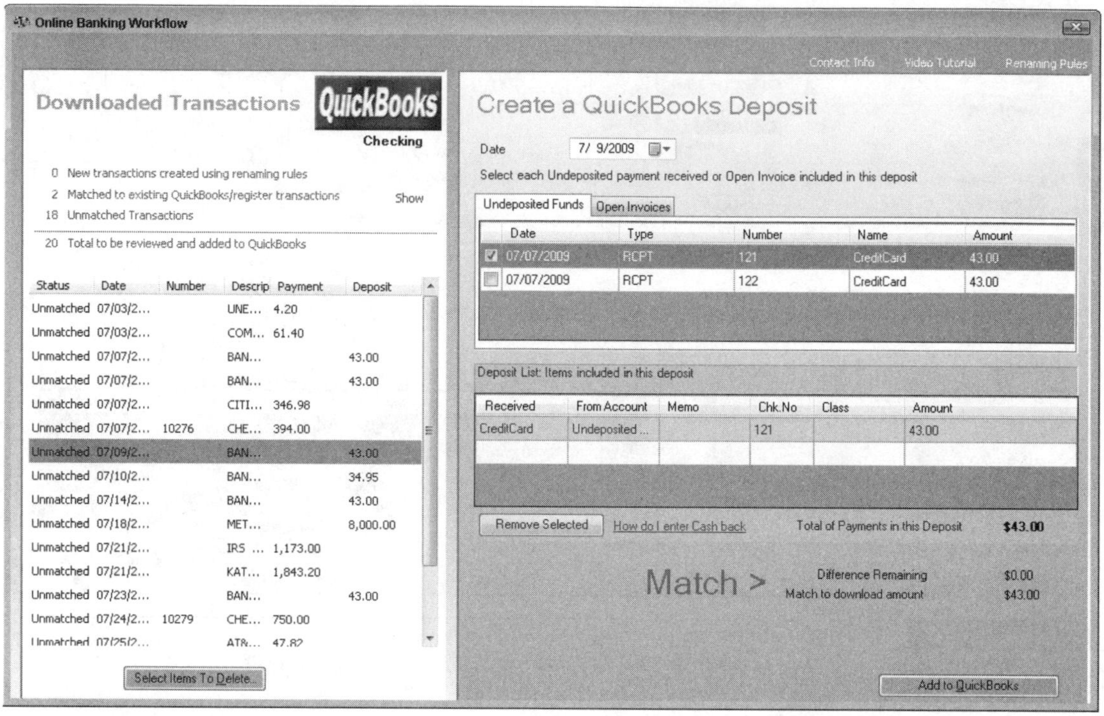

FIGURE 15-11 The merchant bank has deposited the proceeds of this sale.

downloaded transaction and you can deposit it into your account by clicking the
Add To QuickBooks button at the bottom of the window.

Using Renaming Rules to Match Online Transactions

You can use a renaming rule to match the payee name on a downloaded electronic
payment to a vendor name in your QuickBooks company file when the names
don't match. (In previous versions of QuickBooks, this feature was called Creating
An Alias.)

When you download transactions, QuickBooks checks the payee name only for
electronic payments. For regular checks, the payee name isn't compared because
the payee name isn't recorded when checks clear your bank. Instead, you see the
word "Check" in the Payee section of the downloaded transaction file, and QuickBooks
uses the check number and amount to match the downloaded transaction against
your check register.

Use renaming rules to let QuickBooks know how to match a downloaded
transaction when you did not enter the transaction in your bank register or your
credit card account register, and the payee name doesn't match an existing vendor
name when you select the option to add the transaction to QuickBooks.

Understanding How and When Payee Names Differ

It's not uncommon for the payee name on a downloaded electronic payment to differ from the vendor name you're using in your company file. For example, you may have a vendor named BigBank that automatically deducts payments from your account, but the bank uses BB4445 (representing your loan account number) when creating online payments. In that case, you have two options for matching (or adding) the transaction in the Online Banking Center dialog:

- Use a renaming rule to create an alias to match BB4445 to BigBank when a payment appears in a downloaded file. You can create additional renaming rules for any other loans or other types of payments made to this vendor.
- Close the Online Banking Center and change the name of the vendor to BB4445 in your QuickBooks file. This works if the only payments to this bank are for this loan. If you have multiple loans from the bank (or other types of payments to the bank), and you're tracking them in different accounts, using a loan number as the vendor name doesn't work, so you must create a renaming rule.

The first option is easier and quicker.

The same problem occurs when the difference in the payee name is inadvertent. For example, you may have a vendor named Backstroke, with a company name Arthur Backstroke, but when you create the vendor on your bank's online payment website, you may fill in the payee name as Art Backstroke, or Artie Backstroke. If you aren't consistent about the way you fill in payee names when you create online vendor accounts, creating a renaming rule for the payee means that transactions are matched (although a better solution is to be careful about the way you enter data).

In the future, when you download transactions with this payee name, QuickBooks recognizes the renaming rule and matches the transaction if it exists in the register. If the transaction doesn't exist in the register, select the downloaded transaction and click Add To QuickBooks. QuickBooks automatically adds it to the register, using the renaming rule to link the transaction to the right vendor name.

Creating a Renaming Rule

You cannot create a renaming rule in QuickBooks the way you can create other components in your company file (by adding it to a list). The QuickBooks Online Banking Center lets you create the renaming rule when you run into a problem matching or adding an online transaction that's been downloaded. Even if you know that your vendor named BigBank is automatically taking money out of your checking account every month, and you also know the loan number the bank uses as Payee, you can't set this up ahead of time. You have to wait for the first unmatched transaction to create the rule.

One commonly encountered need for a renaming rule is the downloaded transaction you see when you remit taxes (especially payroll or sales tax) on the tax authority's website, using an ACH transfer from your bank account. For example, in

Figure 15-12, a payroll liability transaction doesn't match the vendor name in the company file.

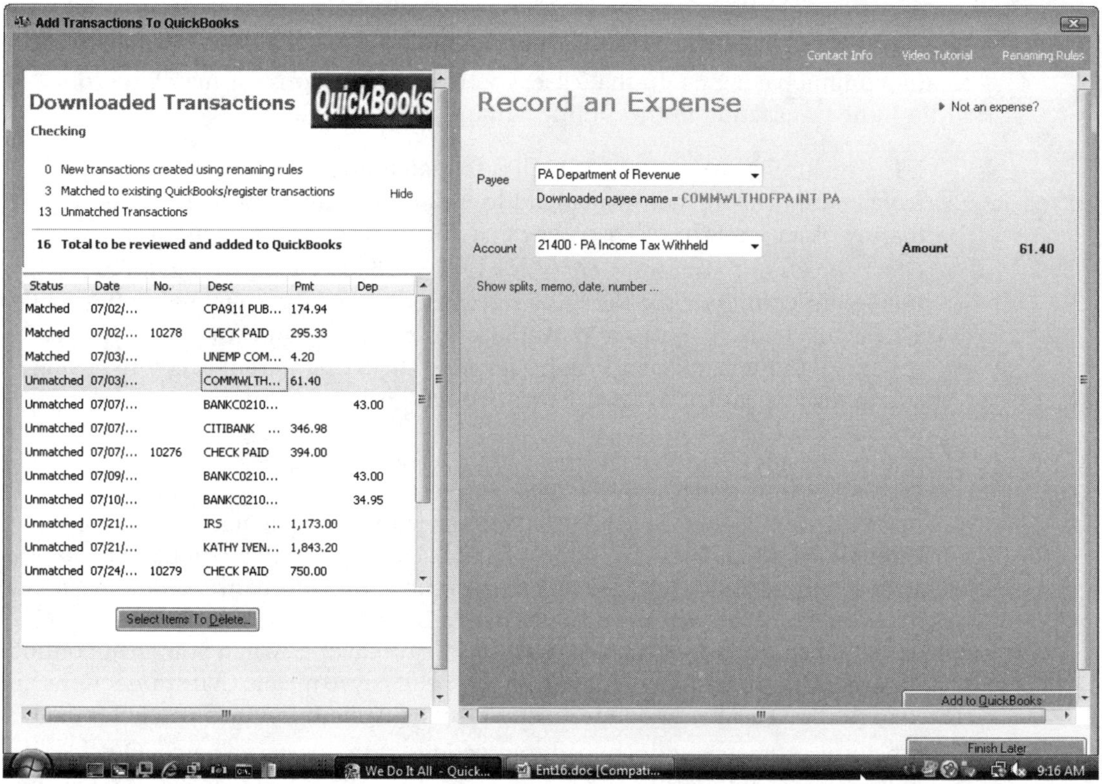

FIGURE 15-12 Create a naming rule by selecting the transaction in the left pane and selecting the QuickBooks vendor name in the right pane.

Select the vendor to whom this transaction should be linked. QuickBooks automatically fills in the account, based on your configuration settings for that vendor, but you can change the account if necessary. When you click Add To QuickBooks, the renaming rule is automatically saved.

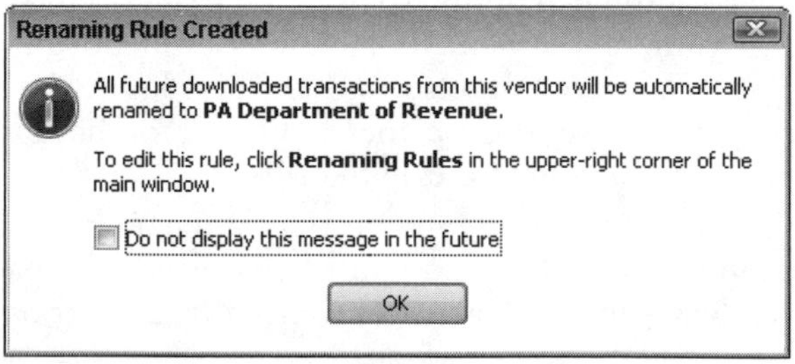

Managing Renaming Rules

You can view, edit, and delete renaming rules by clicking the Renaming Rules link at the top right of the Online Banking Center or the Add Transactions To QuickBooks window.

If downloaded transactions from a vendor have differing payee names for individual transactions, you can create a special renaming rule instead of creating multiple renaming rules for that vendor. For example, suppose you have monthly auto-payments from a vendor who includes a unique internal reference as part of the payee name on each transaction. (Some companies include the invoice number of the invoice being paid by electronic transfer in the payee name.)

In the Renaming Rules window, specify the way you want QuickBooks to examine the name, and enter the appropriate text in the name field. Then click Save.

The following choices for creating a wild-card are available, and for each vendor you should select the choice that's appropriate to the way the vendor names the payee:

- Begins With
- Ends With
- Contains (this is the default matching specification)
- Exactly Matches

Skipping Renaming Rules

You don't have to create or use a renaming rule for an unmatched transaction. Ignoring this feature can be helpful if your unmatched downloaded payments always fall into one of three categories:

- The payee is your bank (service charge) or your credit card merchant bank (the monthly sweep of your account to collect the fees). You don't really need to track these payees as vendors, you don't create vendor reports for them, and you don't care if the vendor doesn't appear on the vendor list in the Vendor Center. The only thing you care about is the account to which the transaction is posted (which is where you can get a report on the totals posted).

- The payee is one that changes the payee name with every payment. It's silly to create a renaming rule for every downloaded name because the payee name won't ever appear again. Some debit card transactions include the name of the store and the date in the Payee name, some delivery/courier services add the Invoice Number to the Payee name, and so on and so on. These payee names, because they're based on a unique transaction, will never appear in the future; therefore, there's no point in collecting a slew of renaming rules that will never be used again.

To post a downloaded transaction without creating a renaming rule, merely fill in the posting account in the Record An Expense dialog in the right pane of the Add Transactions To QuickBooks window and click Add To QuickBooks. Later, you can edit the transaction in the register to add a payee name, or you can leave the

▶ FYI

Vendors and Renaming Rules for Credit Card Downloads: Are They Necessary?

The QuickBooks support documentation (Help files or website articles) often explains the advantage of creating renaming rules by using downloaded credit card transactions as examples. For instance, suppose you use your credit card at your local famous gourmet coffee shop? The downloaded transaction has a payee name similar to "CoffeePlace 098," where 098 is the store number. The vendor CoffeePlace doesn't exist in your system (unless you've opened a charge account at the store and they send you monthly bills). QuickBooks wants you to add the vendor when you match the transactions to your credit card register.

A couple of days later you use your credit card at the same coffee chain, but a different store (Store #876), and the downloaded transaction has a payee name like "CoffeePlace 876," so you create an alias for the vendor you created.

Given the fact that this chain may have six or seven stores between your house, your office, and the local football stadium where you have season tickets, you can add a renaming rule for each store as it appears in the credit card download file and eventually every downloaded transaction will be matched with one of the rules.

Here's a question to ask yourself: "Why are you entering the coffee place as a vendor and creating renaming rules?" The credit card company is the vendor; you do not have a customer-vendor relationship with the store that accepts your credit card. Adding the stores where you use your credit card as vendors unnecessarily takes up a vendor slot (remember, except for the Enterprise editions, QuickBooks permits a finite number of "names" in the Names lists). Unless you have some reason to track these transactions by linking them to a vendor, enter the vendor's name in the Memo field, don't create the vendor or renaming rule.

transaction "payee-less" if it's your bank, merchant card account, or another expense you don't track by vendor.

Although you'll have transactions in your bank register that have no Payee name, that omission doesn't interfere with keeping accurate books and getting the reports you need. The reason this all works so efficiently is that QuickBooks only requires two things to create a direct transaction (a direct transaction is one that isn't posting to A/R or A/P):

- An amount
- An account

This makes perfect sense in terms of business bookkeeping because sometimes the only thing you care about for certain transactions is the posting account.

Deleting Unmatched Transactions

Sometimes the download file contains transactions that can't be matched. This usually occurs when you don't download transactions frequently, and some of the transactions you download have already been cleared during a reconciliation (After the first time you download transactions, QuickBooks omits cleared transactions).

You should delete these transactions; otherwise they'll be there waiting for you every time you download new transactions. Click the button labeled Select Items To Delete at the bottom of the left pane. QuickBooks opens the Select Items To Delete dialog, where you can get rid of the transactions you don't want to see again.

The top of the dialog offers two options:

- Select Individual Transactions, which leaves the selection check boxes unchecked until you manually click each box to delete its transaction.
- Select All Download Transactions Older Than <Date>, which automatically adds check marks to the check boxes of transactions that are older than the specified date.

CAUTION: The Select Items To Delete dialog includes matched transactions, so pay attention to the Status column to avoid deleting transactions you've matched.

Paying Bills Online

Online bill payments are a wonderful invention. You save the costs of checks, envelopes, and stamps, and, if you don't print checks in QuickBooks, you save the time and energy required to write a check.

Today, most banks offer online bill payments either on their website or by supporting online bill payments directly through QuickBooks:

- If your bank supports Direct Connect for QuickBooks and offers online bill payment as part of its Direct Connect feature, you can enter checks in QuickBooks and send them to your bank electronically via the Online Banking Center.
- If your bank supports Web Connect for QuickBooks (offering a download file instead of interacting directly with your QuickBooks bank account register), you can use your bank's website online bill payment feature (if one exists).
- If your bank doesn't support online payments of checks created in QuickBooks, and you want to enter checks in QuickBooks and have them automatically transfer to an electronic bill payment service, you can sign up for the QuickBooks Bill Pay service (covered later in this chapter).

Some vendors (almost always large companies) accept payments via electronic transfers. These vendors are registered in a database, and that database is checked when an online payment is being processed. If the vendor is in the database, with e-pay information, the online payment service electronically transfers the funds directly into the vendor's bank account instead of writing and mailing a check.

QuickBooks Bill Pay vs. Bank Website Bill Pay

If your bank supports bill payment through Direct Connect, you can enter checks in QuickBooks (in the Pay Bills window or the Write Checks window) and mark them as online bill payments so they are automatically uploaded to your bank. Detailed instructions for performing this task appear later in this chapter in the section, "Paying Bills Online in QuickBooks."

Banks that support QuickBooks Direct Connect almost always also provide website features for paying bills online (after all, regardless of the immense popularity of QuickBooks, some businesses choose other accounting software). You can go to the bank's website and create online vendors and initiate online checks to those vendors from the website.

If your bank offers both methods of paying bills online, you have to determine whether you want to create your online payments in QuickBooks and upload them, or go to the bank's website, enter the payments, and then add them to your QuickBooks file (either manually or by adding them during a direct connect download). You should weigh the pros and cons by deciding on your own priorities.

Setup Processes Are the Same for QuickBooks and Bank Website Payments

For both methods, you have to set up the vendor for online payments. This means the vendor information has to include the vendor name (the Payee), address, telephone number, and your account number with that vendor (in QuickBooks, your account number is entered in the Additional Info tab of the vendor record).

For both methods, if the payee is registered in the database of e-pay recipients, the online payment is automatically sent electronically instead of mailing a check.

The reason you have to provide your customer account number with the vendor is that the payment the vendor receives doesn't come from you or your bank account. It comes from the bank's bank account. The payment includes your customer account number so the vendor knows which account to credit with the payment. (See the section, "Following the Money Trail: How Online Payments Work" later in this chapter for a complete explanation.)

Now that you know what's the same, let's look at what's different. You can decide which of the differences are pros and which are cons as you decide how you want to manage online payments.

Data Entry Considerations

Using QuickBooks means you only have to enter check data once. Using the bank's website means you enter the amount while you're connected to the bank, and then you have to enter the check in QuickBooks (not as an online payment). If you fail to enter the check in QuickBooks you won't have an accurate running balance until you download transactions and see the payment, and then you'll have to enter it in the bank register anyway, using the Add To QuickBooks function described in the previous section of this chapter. If you don't add the transaction when it's downloaded, you'll have to add it when your statement arrives or your reconciliation fails. This is double work, but once the vendor exists in your QuickBooks file, you only have to enter the date and amount when you duplicate the online transaction.

Elapsed Time Considerations

Using the bank's website means the bank begins processing the payment almost immediately (unless you configure the payment for a future date).

Using QuickBooks means a delay in processing because QuickBooks gives the bank several days to process the payment and additional days to create and mail the check. For example, if you enter a check dated July 27, as soon as you select the Online Payment option, QuickBooks changes the processing date to July 31 (which means the bank won't even look at the uploaded check until that date) and changes the check date to August 3 (which is the date the bank will use to send the payment).

Paying Vendors Electronically

Many banks let you convert any payee you've created on the bank's website to an e-pay vendor, so you can transfer funds electronically for every transaction when you use the bank's website to create the online payment. To do this, you must provide the bank with the vendor's bank information (routing number, bank account number, and bank account name). Most banks have a form for this.

QuickBooks only sends e-payments to vendors registered in the "official" e-pay database.

In addition, many banks are equipped to handle ACH files for the transfer of funds directly from your bank account to the bank accounts of all the payees in the ACH file (this is the technology QuickBooks uses for payroll direct deposits).

NOTE: *ACH* stands for *Automated Clearing House,* which is a payment transfer system that connects all financial institutions in the United States. The ACH network is the central clearing facility for all *Electronic Fund Transfer (EFT)* transactions. ACH transfer files are text files that contain all the information required to move money from an account in one financial institution to an account in another financial institution. The data in an ACH file must follow strict rules about layout and formatting to ensure accuracy.

If your bank doesn't accept ACH file transfers, it probably will add that service soon, because this is a very popular service and banks are marketing electronic services to lure customers—electronic banking is a hot issue! QuickBooks does not offer ACH file creation (at least not yet). If you don't know how to build an ACH file from scratch, there is software available that will read your QuickBooks file and create an ACH file from the checks you prepare. You upload that ACH file to your bank by going to the bank's website and using the ACH transfer functions available on that site; you cannot send the file through QuickBooks.

Following the Money Trail: How Online Payments Work

When you send your own checks to vendors, the money isn't removed from your bank account until the check is presented to your bank for payment by the payee's bank. This means the payee has received, endorsed, and deposited the check.

When you create an online payment (either in QuickBooks or on your bank's website), the money is immediately removed from your checking account and placed into the bank's checking account.

The bank sends the check to the payee, and after the vendor deposits it in its own bank account, the check is sent to the bank's checking account for payment and clearance. No notification is sent to you when the check is presented for payment.

It's important to know that very few banks manage online payments directly; instead they outsource this process (as well as most other software-based processes including setting up online bank accounts for customers, statement preparations, etc.) to large, high-tech software companies that specialize in bank "back-end" processes.

These companies are "bank processors" and are usually referred to as "processors" by bank personnel. This means when you contact your bank about a problem with an online payment, the bank has to contact the processor to get you the information you need (which may delay the response). In this section, when you see the word "bank" you should think "processor." For example, when the discussion in this chapter says that money is removed from your bank account and placed in the bank's bank account, it's almost certainly placed in a bank account that belongs to the processor, not into a bank account that belongs to your bank.

When you download bank transactions, you see the deduction for the online payment. However, unlike deductions you see for the checks you create and send, this doesn't mean that the vendor has received and deposited your payment; instead it means the bank has moved the money from your account to its account.

 NOTE: If you create an online payment that is an e-payment, the same process applies; that is, the money is removed from your account before the e-payment is transmitted.

When you get your statement from the bank, you don't see physical checks or pictures of checks (depending on the way your bank sends you checks with the statement) that were online payments. Those checks are sent to, and retained by, the bank (because it's the bank's checking account that processed the check).

What to Do When Vendors Don't Receive Online Payment Checks

If you create and mail your own checks, when a vendor calls to say that the check wasn't received, you can check with your bank to see if the check cleared. If it didn't clear, you can stop payment and issue a new check. If it cleared, you can request a copy of the back of the check in order to see the endorsement. When you send the endorsement information to the vendor (a copy of the back of the check), the vendor can correct its records to apply your payment. If the vendor claims the endorsement is bogus, your bank has procedures for recovering the funds and you can send another check to the vendor.

It's not quite as straightforward when the check is an online payment, but your bank has procedures that cover this situation. However, when you talk to your bank's personnel about problems with online services, the banker you speak to almost certainly has to convey your query or complaint to the processor, which means you may not get an answer immediately (although the delay should never exceed a business day).

NOTE: You can determine the current status of an online payment you uploaded from QuickBooks by choosing Banking | Online Banking | Inquire About Online Banking Payment. The message you see tells you whether the payment is in process (which means the bank has it but has not yet created the check) or has been processed (the check has been created and mailed). This information does not tell you whether the check has been deposited by the payee or whether it has cleared the bank's bank account.

If an online payment check is not presented for payment to the bank's bank account within 90 days, a flag goes up in the bank's software (some processors may use a different number of elapsed days, but 90 days is the common interval). The money is automatically returned to your bank account, and a "stop payment" order is issued within the bank's bank account (not your bank account).

Ninety days is a long time, and well before this automatic stop payment is issued, you're being dunned by the payee. You have to remit payment immediately. Go to your bank and explain the problem. Your bank should offer you the following options:

- The bank will reissue the check and send it to the payee using the funds that were removed for the original payment. The money doesn't have to be withdrawn from your account again because the bank still has it since the check wasn't presented for payment by the payee's bank. (Most banks call you or the vendor to check the vendor's address in case a bad address is the problem; if so, the check is reissued to the corrected address.)
- The bank will return the money to your account so you can issue your own check (or cash) to the vendor.

If the bank discovers that the check it sent was presented for payment, the procedures are the same as if this happened with your own check. The bank will provide a picture of the endorsement that you can send to the vendor. The vendor will either discover its mistake in entering your payment, or will claim the endorsement is bogus (and the same remedies are available as for your own checks that have forged endorsements).

Paying Bills Online in QuickBooks

You can pay your bills in QuickBooks, then use the Online Banking Center to send the payments to the payees. You can either use your own bank (if it provides Direct Connect and also offers QuickBooks online payments), or use the QuickBooks Bill Pay service. In this section, when you see the word "bank," you can mentally substitute the QuickBooks Bill Pay service instead of your own bank, if that's what you're using. (See the section, "Using the QuickBooks Bill Pay Service," later in this chapter.)

If the vendor is set up to receive electronic payments (the company appears in the national e-pay database), the money is transferred directly from your bank account to the vendor's bank account. If the vendor's account is not accessible for online payments, your bank writes a check and mails it.

There are three methods for creating the transaction in QuickBooks, explained in detail in this section.

Using the Write Checks Transaction Form for Online Payments

If there's no bill in the system for this vendor and you're preparing a direct disbursement in the Write Checks window, complete the check as usual, and then select the option labeled Online Payment.

> **NOTE:** If you have multiple bank accounts, you must select the bank account that's enabled for online bill payments from the drop-down list in the Bank Account field at the top of the Write Checks window. If the selected bank account is not enabled for online bill payments, the Online Payment option doesn't appear on the check form.

If you usually print checks, the To Be Printed option is preselected, and you must deselect it by clicking the check box to remove the check mark in order to make the Online Payment check box available. As soon as you deselect the To Be Printed option, QuickBooks inserts the next available check number in the No. field.

When you select the Online Payment option, QuickBooks displays a message about the date of your check. Remember, the processing date (when the bank is notified of the transaction) is delayed, and the check date (when the check is actually mailed) is delayed until after the processing date.

(If the vendor is in the national e-pay vendor database, the date is changed to three days from the current date.)

When you click OK, QuickBooks makes the following changes to the Write Checks window:

- Displays a lightning bolt symbol in the top-left corner of the check.
- Replaces the check number with the word SEND (later, when the payment is sent to the bank from the Online Banking Center, the word SEND is replaced with a check number that QuickBooks chooses).
- Replaces the label on the Date field from Date to Delivery Date.
- Replaces the label on the Memo from Memo to Transmit Memo, and puts a check box next to the field.
- Places your account number with this vendor at the bottom of the check (where the signature line would be for a regular check).

If you want to add a memo to the transaction, select the Transmit Memo check box and enter the text you want to include on this check. If you use this option, your payment can only be delivered as a voucher or stub attached to a physical check. This means that your payment will not be made electronically if the vendor is able to accept electronic payments. Instead, a check is sent, which delays the payment.

Click Save & Close or Save & New (if you have another check to write) to save the payment. QuickBooks displays a message telling you that you've created an online payment that will appear in the Online Banking Center. (See the section "Uploading Online Payments" to learn how to transfer the payment to your bank.)

Using the Pay Bills Window for Online Payments

If this vendor has a bill in your system, you must use the Pay Bills function to create the payment, not the Write Checks transaction. Select the appropriate bill and then choose Online Bank Pmt from the drop-down list in the Payment Method field.

> **NOTE:** If you have multiple bank accounts, you must select the bank account that's enabled for online bill payments from the Payment Account field at the bottom of the Pay Bills window. If the selected bank account is not enabled for online bill payments, the Online Bank Pmt option doesn't appear in the Payment Method drop-down list.

When you choose the online payment option, QuickBooks automatically changes the date in the Payment Date field at the bottom of the window as described earlier for the Write Checks window.

When you click Pay Selected Bills, QuickBooks displays the usual Payment Summary dialog message, where your payment is noted as an online bank payment. (See the section "Uploading Online Payments" to learn how to transfer the payment to your bank.)

Using the Bank Register for Online Payments

You can use the register for the bank account you use for online payments instead of the Write Checks transaction form to create an online payment, using the following steps:

1. Open the register and go to the next blank line to create the payment.
2. The Date field has the current date, which you should accept.
3. Press TAB to move to the Number field and enter the text **SEND**.
4. QuickBooks displays a message telling you it has to change the check date; click OK.
5. Finish filling out the check information and click Record.

QuickBooks displays a message telling you that you've created an online payment.

Uploading Online Payments

To send your online payments to your bank, open the Online Banking Center (choose Banking | Online Banking | Online Banking Center). In the Online Banking Center window, you can see your payments in the Items Ready To Send section, along with the request to download bank transactions.

You can perform any of the following actions on the online payments that are listed:

- Deselect the check mark to prevent the payment from being uploaded (you can select it for upload another time).
- Select the payment and click Edit to view or change the transaction.
- Select the payment and click Delete to remove the payment from your system (clicking Delete doesn't just delete the payment from the upload; it deletes the transaction from your company file). QuickBooks asks you to confirm your action.
- Click Send/Receive Transactions to begin uploading your payments along with the request for a download transaction file.

Sending Electronic Messages to the Bank

If your bank supports Direct Connect, you can send a message to your bank by choosing Banking | Online Banking | Create Online Banking Message. QuickBooks opens the Online Banking Message transaction window where you can enter your message.

The message appears in the Online Banking Center in the list of items to be uploaded.

Using the QuickBooks Bill Pay Service

If your bank doesn't participate in online bill payment services directly from QuickBooks, and you want to pay your bills online using QuickBooks, you can sign up for online payments directly with QuickBooks. This is a fee-based service.

From the Online Banking submenu, choose Participating Financial Institutions. When the Financial Institutions list is displayed in your browser window, scroll through the list to find QuickBooks Bill Pay Service in the left pane.

You'll see two listings:

- QuickBooks Bill Pay—New!, which is the listing you should select
- QuickBooks Bill Pay-TM, which is the listing for existing customers of this older service (for users of older versions of QuickBooks) and doesn't provide online signup anymore

When you select QuickBooks Bill Pay—New!, the right pane displays information about this service (see Figure 15-13).

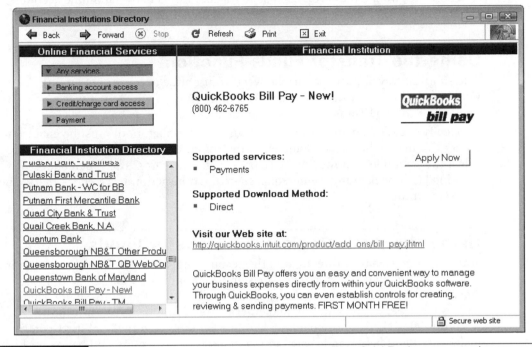

FIGURE 15-13   If your bank doesn't offer online bill paying within QuickBooks, you can sign up with QuickBooks Bill Pay.

To sign up, click Apply Now. After you answer a couple of questions about your business, click the Continue button. An application form appears on your screen. Follow the prompts and instructions to complete the enrollment process. QuickBooks will send you the information you need to begin using the service for online bill payments.

Transferring Money Between Accounts Online

If you have multiple accounts at your financial institution, and the financial institution uses Direct Connect, you can transfer money between those accounts within QuickBooks. For example, you may have a money market account for your business in addition to your checking account.

To transfer money online, you must have applied at your financial institution for online banking for both accounts. You'll probably have a unique PIN for each account. (To make your life less complicated, you should make changes while you're online to ensure both accounts have the same PIN, so you don't inadvertently enter the wrong PIN). In addition, you must have enabled both accounts for online access within QuickBooks.

There are two methods you can use to transfer funds between online accounts: the transfer funds function or direct data entry in the register for either account.

Using the Transfer Funds Function

The simplest way to move money between your online accounts is to use the QuickBooks Transfer Funds Between Accounts window, which you reach by choosing Banking | Transfer Funds from the menu bar.

Specify the sending and receiving accounts (remember, both must be enabled for Direct Connect online access) and enter the amount you want to transfer. Be sure to select the option for Online Funds Transfer. Click Save & Close. Then choose Banking | Online Banking Center, make sure the transaction has a check mark, and click Go Online.

Using the Bank Register to Transfer Funds

You can enter a transfer directly into the account register of the bank account from which you are sending the money. The significant data entry is the one in the Check Number column; instead of a check number, type the word **SEND**. Don't enter a payee; enter the amount, and enter the receiving bank account in the Account field. Then choose Banking | Online Banking | Online Banking Center, make sure the transaction is listed in the Items To Send section and has a check mark, and click Send/Receive Transactions.

Receiving Customer Payments Online

Besides the online activities that permit you to track your own bank account activity, transfer money, and pay your own bills, QuickBooks offers a way for your customers to pay you online. This is a fee-based service provided by the QuickBooks Billing Solutions service.

If you sign up for this service, you can notify your customers about this feature by e-mailing the invoice with the online service URL in the cover note, or by snail-mailing the invoice and sending an e-mail message with the online service URL. The customer clicks the link to the URL to travel to the QuickBooks website and arrange for payment (usually by filling out a form with a credit card number—the site is secure).

QuickBooks notifies you when the payment is made, and you can download the payment into your bank register using the standard online banking procedures.

To learn more about this service or to sign up, go to the QuickBooks Billing Solutions page at http://quickbooks.intuit.com/product/add_ons/getting_paid_faster.jhtml.

Tracking Time and Mileage

In *this chapter:*

- Enable the time tracking feature
- Use QuickBooks timesheets
- Learn about the online timesheets feature
- Track mileage

You can track time and mileage and use the information to recover reimbursable costs from customers, develop an accurate job costing system, prepare tax returns, analyze expenses, and pay employees. All the tools you need to perform these functions are available in QuickBooks, and in this chapter, I'll go over the time and mileage tracking features.

Setting Up Time Tracking

When you create a company in QuickBooks, one of the EasyStep Interview windows queries you about your desire to track time. If you respond affirmatively, QuickBooks turns on the time-tracking features.

If you're not sure whether you turned on time tracking when you installed your company, choose Edit | Preferences from the QuickBooks menu bar. Select the Time & Expenses category in the left pane, and click the Company Preferences tab. Make sure the Yes option is selected.

By default, QuickBooks assumes your workweek starts on Monday. However, some businesses use a different workweek, such as a Sunday-to-Saturday pattern for tracking time.

If you're tracking time for employees and you plan to use the timesheets for payroll, it's a good idea to match the workweek to the week your pay period covers. Of course, since timesheets are weekly, this works best if your pay periods are weekly.

Configuring Workers

By "workers" I mean anyone who spends time performing work for your company. Workers can be employees, outside contractors, owners, or partners. To track time, every worker must exist in the company file.

Tracking Employee Time

If you're running the QuickBooks payroll feature, you already have employees in your QuickBooks system. You can track the time of any employee who fills out a timesheet (timesheets are covered later in this chapter).

You can also use the timesheet data to create a paycheck automatically, using the number of hours reported in the time-tracking system to determine the number of hours for which the employee is paid. For this to work, however, the employee must be linked to his or her timesheet. As a result, you must modify the employee record as follows:

1. Open the Employee Center.
2. Click the Employees tab to display the list of employees
3. Double-click the listing of the employee you want to link to time tracking.
4. In the Change Tabs field at the top of the window, select Payroll And Compensation Info from the drop-down list.
5. Select the Use Time Data To Create Paychecks check box (see Figure 16-1).
6. Click OK.

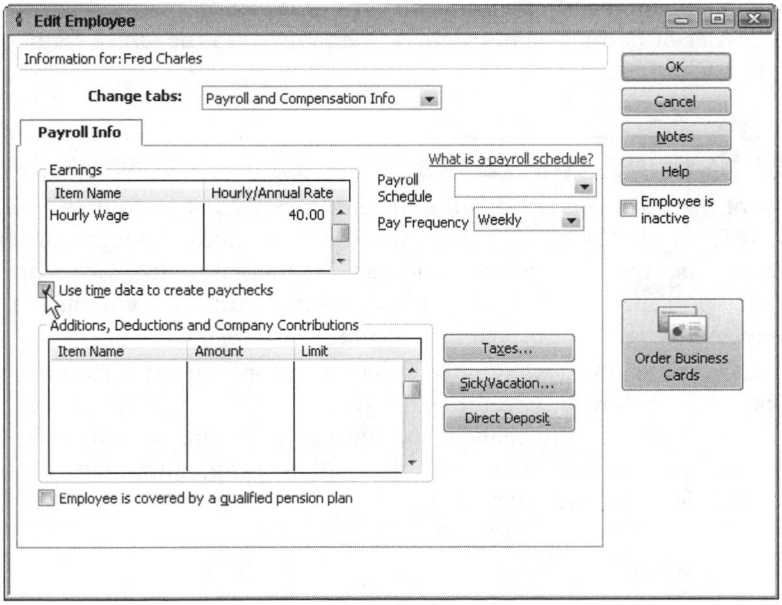

FIGURE 16-1 Link employees to time tracking if you want to use timesheets to prepare paychecks automatically.

You don't have to link employees to time tracking in order for them to use timesheets to record their time—your employees can track time unconnected to the preparation of paychecks in order to make it possible to create job costing reports, or to invoice customers for their time.

Even if you're not doing your own payroll in QuickBooks, you can create employees (in the Employee Center) for the purpose of tracking time (and you can use the timesheets data for your payroll service).

Tracking Vendor Time

Any vendor in your system who is paid for his or her time can have that time tracked for the purpose of billing customers. Most of the time, these vendors are outside contractors or subcontractors. You don't have to do anything to the vendor record to effect time tracking; you merely need to record the time used as the vendor sends bills.

Tracking Other Worker Time

You may need to track the time of people who are neither employees nor vendors. QuickBooks provides a system list called Other Names, and you can use this list to collect names that don't fit in the other QuickBooks lists. Following are some situations in which you'll need to use the Other Names list:

- You have employees and use QuickBooks payroll, but you are not an employee because you take a draw instead of a paycheck. In this case, you must add your name to the Other Names list if you want to track your own time.
- You have no employees and your business is a proprietorship or a partnership. Owner or partner names should be entered into the Other Names list in order to track time.

Configuring the Tasks

Most of the tasks you track in timesheets already exist in your system as service items. These are the items you use when you invoice customers for services. However, because you can use time tracking to analyze the way people in your organization spend their time, you may want to add service items that aren't connected to tasks performed for customers.

For example, if you want to track the time people spend performing administrative tasks for the business, you can add a service item called Administrative to your items list. If you want to be more specific, you can name the particular administrative tasks you want to track (for example, bookkeeping, equipment repair, new sales calls, public relations, and so on).

To enter new items, choose Lists | Item List from the menu bar. When the Item List window opens, press CTRL-N to open the New Item dialog. Select Service as the item type (only service items are tracked in timesheets) and name the new item. Here are some guidelines for administrative items:

- If you're specifying administrative tasks, create a service named Administration and then make each specific administrative task a subitem of Administration.
- Don't put an amount in the Rate box unless every employee and outside contractor performing this service has the same hourly pay rate (highly unlikely). You can enter the amount when you make the payment (via payroll or vendor checks).
- Because QuickBooks insists that you assign an account to a service, choose or create an innocuous revenue account (such as Other Revenue or Time Tracking Revenue). Don't worry, no money is ever posted to the account because you don't ever sell these services directly to customers.

Because time tracking is linked to customers, in order to track administrative work in reports you must also create a customer for the occasions when no real customer is being tracked (those in-house administrative tasks). The easiest way to do that is to create a new customer to represent your company, such as a customer named House or InHouse.

Using Timesheets

In this section I'll go over the way you use timesheets within QuickBooks. Later in this chapter (in the section "Using Online Timesheets"), I'll go over the way you can use the online timesheets feature, Time Tracker, to let employees and subcontractors enter timesheets when they're working in remote locations.

QuickBooks timesheets offer two methods for recording the time you spend on tasks: Single Activity and Weekly Timesheet.

- Single Activity is a form you use to enter what you did when you performed a single task at a specific time on a specific date. For example, a Single Activity form may record the fact that you made a telephone call on behalf of a customer, you repaired some piece of equipment for a customer, or you performed some administrative task for the company.
- Weekly Timesheet is a form in which you indicate how much time and on which date you performed work. Each Weekly Timesheet entry can also include the name of the customer for whom the work was performed.

Your decision about which method to use depends on the type of work you do and on the efficiency of your workers' memories. People tend to put off filling in

Weekly Timesheets and then attempt to reconstruct their activities in order to complete the timesheets. This frequently ends up being a less-than-accurate approach. The method works properly only if everyone remembers to open the timesheets and fill them in as soon as they complete each task. Many workers say they do this. Uh huh, sure.

TIP: When you fill out a Single Activity form, its data is automatically inserted into a Weekly Timesheet form.

Setting the Format for Displaying Time

When you enter time in the various timesheet forms, you can use either the hh:mm format, or a decimal format such as 6.5. To establish a default, choose Edit | Preferences and click the General category. Then select the Company Preferences tab and use the options in the Time Format section of the dialog to select the format you prefer.

If you set the preference to decimal, and then enter time as 1:30, when you press TAB to move to the next field, QuickBooks changes the entry to 1.50 (or the other way around).

Tracking a Single Activity

To track one event or task with a Single Activity form (see Figure 16-2), choose Employees | Enter Time | Time/Enter Single Activity. Use the following guidelines to use this form.

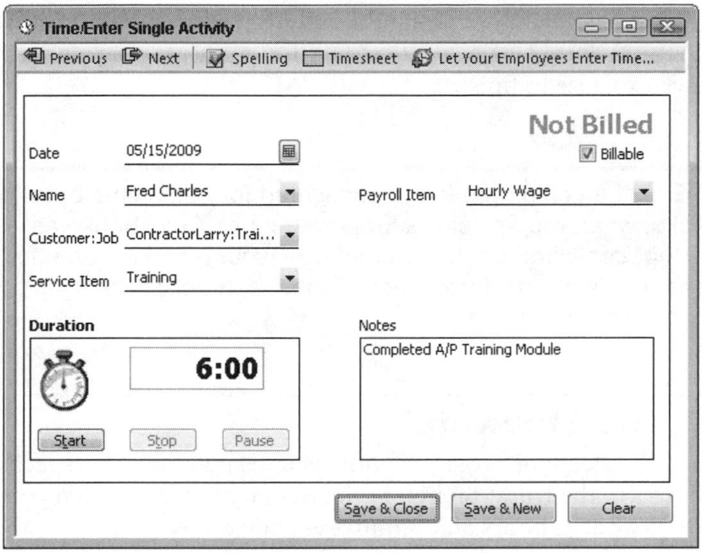

FIGURE 16-2 Fill out the details to indicate how you spent your time.

- The Date field is automatically filled in with the current date. If this activity took place previously, you can change the date (but you cannot change the date if you're using the stopwatch).
- Click the arrow to the right of the Name field and select the name of the person who performed the work from the drop-down list. The list contains vendors, employees, and names from the Other Names list. Most of the time, the worker who performed the work is filling out the form.
- Select the customer or job in the Customer:Job field. Do this whether or not the customer is going to be billed for the time.
- In the Service Item field, select the task, and in the Duration box, enter the amount of time you're reporting, using the format hh:mm.
- If this time is billable to the customer, the Billable check box should be marked (it is by default). If the time is not going to be billed to the customer (it's going to be tracked for job costing), click the box to remove the check mark.

- If the Payroll Item field appears, select the payroll item that applies to this time (for example, salary or hourly wages). This field appears only if the selected name is an employee and the employee record has been linked to the time-tracking system (explained earlier in this chapter).
- Use the Notes box to enter any comments or additional information you want to record about this activity.

When you've finished creating the activity, click Save & New to fill out another Single Activity form (many workers perform multiple single activities each day) or click Save & Close to finish.

N O T E : If an employee is not configured for using time data to create paychecks, when you select the Employee name QuickBooks asks if you'd like to change that configuration. If the employee is just tracking time for job-costing purposes and is not paid from these timesheets, click No.

Using the Stopwatch

You can let QuickBooks track the time you're spending on a specific task. Click the Start button in the Duration box of the Activity window when you begin the task. QuickBooks tracks hours and minutes as they elapse.

- To pause the counting when you're interrupted, click Pause. Then click Start to pick up where you left off.
- To stop timing, click Stop. The elapsed time is displayed.

The stopwatch always displays time in the hh:mm:ss format. If you set your format preference to decimal, QuickBooks converts the time when the stopwatch is stopped.

Using Weekly Timesheets

A Weekly Timesheet records the same information as the Single Activity form, except that the information is recorded in day-at-a-time and week-at-a-time blocks. To use this form (shown in Figure 16-3), choose Employees | Enter Time | Use Weekly Timesheet. Use the instructions that follow to fill out the timesheet.

1. Select the name of the worker from the drop-down list in the Name field.
2. The current week appears by default; use the calendar if you need to select a different week.

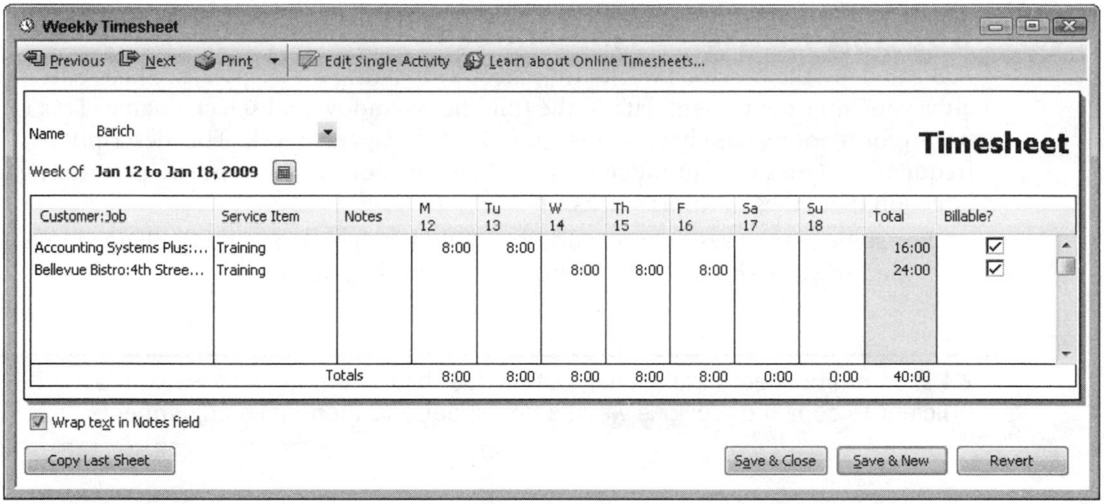

FIGURE 16-3 Some people find it easier to enter information on a weekly basis.

3. In the Customer:Job column select the customer or job connected to the activity (or select the in-house listing to enter administrative work unconnected to a customer).

4. In the Service Item column, select the appropriate service item.

5. For an employee whose paycheck is linked to timesheets, use the Payroll Item column to select the Payroll Item that fits the activity. (If the name selected in the Name field is not an employee whose paycheck is linked to timesheets, the Payroll Item column disappears.)

6. In the Notes column, enter any necessary notes or comments.

7. Click the column that represents the day in which an activity occurred and enter the number of hours worked on this task. Repeat across the week for each day that the same activity was performed for the same customer or job.

8. Move to the beginning of the next row to enter a different activity, or the same activity for a different customer, repeating this action until the timesheet is filled in for the week.

9. For each row, indicate whether the time is billable in the Billable column. By default, all time entries linked to a customer are marked as billable. Click the check box to remove the checkmark in the Billable column if the time on this row is not billable.

10. Click Save & New to use a timesheet for a different week. Click Save & Close when you are finished entering time.

Copying Previous Timesheets

You can copy the previous week's timesheet by clicking the Copy Last Sheet button after you enter the current date in the timesheet window and select a name. This is useful for workers who have similar timesheet data every week. This description frequently applies to your office staff or to outside contractors who are performing a large job that takes multiple weeks.

For some employees, whose work is usually for the office and not charged to a customer, the timesheet may be identical from week to week.

TIP: If timesheets are similar, but not identical, from week to week, it's efficient to copy the previous week's timesheet and then make adjustments.

Reporting Timesheet Information

Before you use the information on the timesheets to bill customers or pay workers, you should go over the data on the timesheet reports. You can view and customize reports, edit information, and print the original timesheets.

Running Timesheet Reports

To run reports on timesheets, choose Reports | Jobs, Time & Mileage. You'll see a long list of available reports, but the following reports provide information on time tracking:

- **Time By Job Summary**   Reports the amount of time spent for each service on your customers and jobs.
- **Time By Job Detail**   Reports the details of the time spent for each customer and job, including dates and whether or not the time was marked as billable. A billing status of Unbilled indicates the time is billable but hasn't yet been used on a customer invoice.
- **Time By Name**   Reports the amount of time each user tracked.
- **Time By Item**   Provides an analysis of the amount of time spent on each service your company provides, including the customers for whom the services were performed.

Editing Entries in a Report

While you're browsing the report, you can double-click an activity listing to see the original entry. You can make changes in the original entry, such as selecting or deselecting the billable option, or changing the Notes field by adding a note or editing the content of the existing note.

Editing the Original Timesheets

Before you use the timesheets for customer billing or payroll, make sure you examine them and make any needed corrections. In fact, you may want to take this step before you view any of the Jobs & Time reports.

The most common revision is the billable status. If you have outside contractors or employees filling out timesheets, it's not unusual to have some confusion about which customers receive direct time billings. In fact, you may have customers to whom you send direct time bills only for certain activities and provide the remaining activities as part of your basic services.

To check timesheets, just open a new weekly timesheet and enter the name of the person connected to the timesheet you want to view. Use the Previous or Next arrows at the top of the timesheet window or use the calendar to move to the timesheet you want to inspect. Then edit the information as necessary:

- If needed, change the number of hours for any activity item.
- Change the billable status.
- View (and edit if necessary) any notes.

CAUTION: If you've already used the timesheet data to create an invoice for the customer or to pay the employee, the changes you make are useless. It's too late. Customer invoices and payroll records are not updated with your edits.

Printing the Weekly Timesheets

It's a common practice to have employees print their weekly timesheets and deliver them to the appropriate management people. Usually that means your payroll person (or the person who phones in the payroll if you use a payroll service) or a personnel manager. However, instead of having each user be responsible for handing in the timesheet, it's a good idea to designate someone (such as your payroll manager) to print all the timesheets to make sure they're available when needed.

To print timesheets, choose File | Print Forms | Timesheets from the QuickBooks menu bar to open the Select Timesheets To Print window shown in Figure 16-4.

- Change the date range to match the timesheets you want to print.
- By default, all timesheets are selected. To remove a timesheet, select its listing and click the column with the check mark to deselect that listing. You can click Select None to deselect all listings, then select one or more specific users.
- To see any notes in their entirety, select the Print Full Activity Notes option. Otherwise, the default selection to print only the first line of any note is empowered.

FIGURE 16-4 Print the timesheets for every person who tracks time.

The Select Timesheets To Print dialog has a Preview button, and clicking it displays a print preview of the selected timesheets. If you click the Print button in the Preview window, the timesheets are sent to the printer immediately, giving you no opportunity to change the printer or any printing options. Clicking the Close button in the Preview window returns you to the Select Timesheets To Print dialog. Click OK to open the Print Timesheets window, where you can change the printer or printing options. You should change the number of copies to print to match the number of people to whom you're distributing the timesheets.

One thing you should notice about printed (or previewed) timesheets is the last column, which indicates the billing status. The entries are codes, as follows:

- **B**   Billable but not yet invoiced to the customer
- **N**   Not billable
- **D**   Billable and already invoiced to the customer

Using Online Timesheets

You can use the fee-based QuickBooks Time Tracker service to let timekeepers fill out their timesheets online (a real boon for offsite workers). QuickBooks Time Tracker is easy to use and administer for both the company bookkeeper and the workers.

To fill out timesheets, workers only need access to a computer that can reach the Internet. The computer they use does not need QuickBooks or any other software. This means workers who are performing tasks at customer sites or working at home can easily track and report their time.

To learn more about this service, and to sign up for a free 60-day trial, choose Employees | Enter Time | Let Your Employees Enter Time.

Tracking Mileage

QuickBooks provides a way to track the mileage of your vehicles. You can use the mileage information to track the expenses connected to vehicle use, to use mileage as part of your job-costing efforts, to bill customers for mileage expenses, or to maintain records for your vehicle-use tax deduction.

To track a vehicle, you must add that vehicle to your Vehicle list (covered in Chapter 5). Once the vehicle is in your QuickBooks system, you can begin tracking its mileage. Of course, you also need to make sure that everyone who uses the vehicle is tracking mileage properly. Create, print, and distribute a form for this purpose, with the following categories to fill in:

- Trip Start Date
- Trip End Date
- Starting Odometer
- Ending Odometer
- Customer:Job

Entering Mileage Rates

To track the cost of mileage, you must make sure you have accurate mileage rates in your system. These change frequently, so you'll have to keep up with the latest IRS figures. QuickBooks calculates the cost of mileage based on the information you enter. To get the current rate, check with the IRS (www.irs.gov) or ask your accountant. To enter mileage rates for your own use, use the following steps:

1. Choose Company | Enter Vehicle Mileage to open the Enter Vehicle Mileage dialog.
2. Click the Mileage Rates button on the toolbar to open the Mileage Rates dialog.
3. Select a date from the calendar as the Effective Date.
4. Enter the IRS rate for that date.
5. Click Close.
6. Close the Enter Vehicle Mileage dialog (unless you're using it to enter mileage).

The Mileage Rates dialog accepts multiple dates and rates. When you track mileage, QuickBooks uses the appropriate rate, based on the date of your mileage entry, to calculate costs.

Creating a Mileage Item

If you plan to invoice customers for mileage expenses you must create an item (call it mileage, travel, or something similar). The item you create can be either a Service or Other Charge type.

- If you want to charge your customers for mileage as a reimbursable expense and post your reimbursements as income (as explained in Chapter 11), select the option This Item Is Used In Assemblies Or Is A Reimbursable Charge. Then enter the appropriate expense and income accounts.
- If you want to charge your customers for mileage and reduce your mileage expenses with reimbursed amounts, select the expense account to which you post your mileage expenses.

It's important to understand that the mileage rate you entered in the Mileage Rates window (described in the previous section) is *not* automatically transferred to the item you create for mileage. Therefore, you must manually fill in the rate for the item and update it when the IRS rate changes. You can use the same rate you used in the Mileage Rates window or enter a different rate to create a markup (or a markdown, if you wish to take that approach).

Entering Mileage

After you've configured your company file for mileage charges, you can track the mileage in the Enter Vehicle Mileage dialog as follows:

1. Choose Company | Enter Vehicle Mileage
2. Select the appropriate vehicle from the drop-down list in the Vehicle field.
3. Enter the following data:
   - The dates of the trip.
   - The odometer readings (QuickBooks calculates the total miles for you). You can skip the odometer readings and enter the total mileage manually, but entering the odometer numbers creates a report entry that's closer to what an IRS auditor wants to see (the IRS likes "logs" that include odometer readings).
   - If you want to bill the customer for mileage, place a check mark in the Billable check box and select the Customer:Job, the item you created for mileage, and the Class (if you're tracking classes).
   - If you don't want to bill a customer but you want to track job costs, select the Customer:Job, but don't place a check mark in the Billable check box.

To learn how to add mileage charges to customer invoices, read Chapter 9.

> **TIP:** To track mileage for administrative use, use the in-house customer named House or InHouse.

Creating Mileage Reports

QuickBooks includes four vehicle mileage reports, which you can access by choosing Reports | Jobs, Time & Mileage and selecting the appropriate mileage report from the submenu. If you're working in the Enter Vehicle Mileage dialog box, the reports are available in the drop-down list you see if you click the arrow next to the Mileage Reports button.

Mileage By Vehicle Summary

Use the Mileage By Vehicle Summary report to see the total miles and the mileage expense for each vehicle you're tracking. You can run this report for any date range that you want to check, which is a way to determine whether vehicles need servicing. For example, you may need to change the oil and filter every 6,000 miles, or schedule a 50,000-mile checkup. If you deduct mileage expenses on your income tax form, use the entire year as the date range.

Mileage By Vehicle Detail

Use the Mileage By Vehicle Detail report to view details about each mileage slip you created. For each vehicle, the report displays the following information:

- Trip End Date
- Total Miles
- Mileage Rate
- Mileage Expense

No customer information appears in the report, but you can double-click any listing to open the original mileage slip, which shows you whether the trip is linked to a job and whether it's marked billable.

Mileage By Job Summary

Use the Mileage By Job Summary report to view the total number of miles linked to customers or jobs. The report displays total miles for all customers or jobs for which you entered an item and displays billable amounts for any mileage entries you marked billable.

Mileage By Job Detail

Use the Mileage By Job Detail report to see the following information about each trip for each customer or job:

- Trip End Date
- Billing Status
- Item
- Total Miles
- Sales Price
- Amount

To gain more knowledge, you can modify the report by clicking the Modify Report button on the report window to open the Modify Report dialog. In the Display tab, select additional columns to reflect what you want to see in this report. For example, you may want to add the Mileage Rate or Mileage Expense (or both). Memorize the report so you don't have to repeat the modifications next time.

Running Payroll

In this chapter:

- Choose a payroll service
- Set up payroll
- Set up employee information
- Enter historical data
- Issue payroll checks
- Use the Employee Center

Chapter 17

If you plan to do your own payroll rather than employ a payroll service, the information you need to set up and run payroll is in this chapter.

QuickBooks Do-It-Yourself Payroll Services

QuickBooks offers a variety of do-it-yourself payroll services, and if you want to do your payroll in-house, here's a brief overview of the offerings:

- Basic Payroll, which provides tax tables and automatic calculations of paycheck deductions and employer expenses for up to three employees. No tax forms are included, so you either need to work with your accountant on tax filings or prepare your tax forms manually. QuickBooks makes it easy to prepare tax forms manually by providing detailed reports in Excel (covered in Chapter 18).
- Enhanced Payroll, which adds tax forms and e-filing for both federal and state reporting.
- Assisted Payroll, which lets you run payroll and then turns the job of depositing withholdings, paying employer contributions, and printing and filing government forms over to QuickBooks.

Additional plans are available based on these payroll offerings, such as Enhanced Payroll for Accountants, which lets you prepare payroll for up to 50 companies.

Updating with an Existing Payroll Subscription

If you're updating to QuickBooks 2009, and currently subscribe to Standard Payroll (no longer offered for new subscribers), which provides tax tables, automatic calculations of paycheck deductions, and automatic creation of federal forms (941, W-2, and so on), you can continue your Standard Payroll subscription.

Direct Deposit

With any of the payroll services, you can purchase direct deposit services for your employees. Employees must sign a form giving permission for direct deposit, and you can print those forms directly from your QuickBooks software (QuickBooks provides a link to display and print the forms during the sign-up process). Employees can opt to deposit their entire paychecks into one bank account or split the amount between two bank accounts.

N O T E : Unless you've signed up for QuickBooks payroll services, no calculations occur against the gross amount of any paycheck you create. No withholding appears, no amounts are posted to employee and employer liability accounts, and there is no net amount. You can, if you wish, use your own printed tax table (Employer's Circular E from the IRS), calculate the deductions manually, and then issue a paycheck for the net amount to each employee. If you don't want to face that, you must sign up for payroll services.

Signing Up for Payroll Services

To learn about the QuickBooks payroll offerings, choose Employees | Payroll and then, from the submenu, choose either Learn About Payroll Options or Order Payroll Service (both menu choices produce the same result).

After you've used the links on the Payroll Services website to learn about all the payroll offerings, follow the prompts to sign up.

When the sign-up process is completed, you download the files you need to run payroll. The new files are automatically added to your QuickBooks system; you don't have to do anything to install them. In addition to the payroll software, the current tax table is added to your system. After payroll is installed, your Employees menu has all the commands you need to run payroll.

Configuring Payroll Elements

To produce accurate paychecks, you need to complete setup tasks, including adding accounts to your chart of accounts, creating payroll items (salary, wages, and so on), identifying the payroll taxes you have to withhold, the payroll taxes you have to pay as an employer, and the deductions or company contributions for benefits. And you also need to set up tax information for each employee, such as dependents and deductions.

You can set up payroll in either of two ways:

- Manually
- Using the Payroll Setup Wizard

The following sections cover all the elements and components involved in setting up payroll manually, and later in this chapter there's a "walk-through" of the Payroll Setup Wizard. You can read both to decide the way you want to approach setup.

Accounts

You may need to create new accounts in your chart of accounts for payroll. If you want to use a bank account specifically for payroll instead of using your main bank account (generally a good idea), you must open the account at your bank and also add the new bank account to your chart of accounts. In addition, you'll need at least the following accounts:

- Payroll Liabilities, which tracks the deductions from paychecks
- Payroll Expenses, which tracks company payroll expenses (company social security, Medicare, pension, medical, and so on)

QuickBooks automatically adds the Payroll Liabilities and Payroll Expenses accounts when you enable payroll. You can use each account for all payroll transactions or create subaccounts to track individual payroll liabilities and expenses.

You should use subaccounts for payroll liabilities and payroll expenses, because it's much easier to determine the current status of individual liabilities and expenses (see Figure 17-1). Link your payroll items to the subaccounts and never post to the parent account. (When you create reports, any balances in the subaccount are totaled in the parent account.)

Chart of Accounts			
Name	§	Type	Balance Total
◆21000 · Payroll Liabilities		Other Current Liability	0.00
◆21100 · FWT		Other Current Liability	0.00
◆21200 · FICA Withheld		Other Current Liability	0.00
◆21300 · Medicare Withheld		Other Current Liability	0.00
◆21400 · PA Income Tax Withheld		Other Current Liability	0.00
◆21500 · Phila Wage Tax		Other Current Liability	0.00
◆21600 · Blue Cross		Other Current Liability	0.00
◆22000 · Sales Tax Payable		Other Current Liability	2,003.48
◆30000 · Opening Bal Equity		Equity	0.00

Account ▾   Activities ▾   Reports ▾   ☐ Include inactive

FIGURE 17-1   It's easy to track payroll financial data if you use subaccounts.

Vendors

Running payroll creates liabilities for payroll taxes, other deductions that your company must remit, and possibly employer benefits that must be paid. To be able to send the money you owe to the appropriate vendors, set up those vendors before you set up payroll items so that you can assign the payroll items to the proper vendors. (Payroll items are discussed in the next section.)

For withholding of federal income taxes, Medicare, FICA, and the matching employer Medicare and FICA payments, the vendor you use depends on the way you transmit the funds. If you use electronic transfer of funds, the vendor is the United States Treasury Department. If you use a physical check (along with coupons provided by the IRS), the vendor is the bank that has the checking account for your payroll checks.

For local and state income tax, unemployment, disability, workers comp, and deductions for benefits such as health insurance, set up a vendor for each agency you need to pay. Most states now offer electronic payments for payroll remittances on their websites, but if you use checks you probably have forms or coupons for the required payment interval (usually monthly or quarterly).

Payroll Items

A QuickBooks *payroll item* is any element that is part of a payroll check. The number of individual elements that go into a paycheck may be more than you thought. Consider this list, which is typical of many businesses:

- Salaries
- Wages (hourly)
- Overtime (time and a half)
- Double-time
- Federal tax withholdings (including FIT, FICA, and Medicare)
- State tax withholdings
- State unemployment and disability withholdings
- Local tax withholdings
- Pension plan deductions
- Medical insurance deductions
- Life insurance deductions
- Garnishes
- Union dues
- Reimbursement for auto expenses
- Bonuses
- Commissions
- Vacation pay
- Sick pay
- Advanced Earned Income Credit

Whew! And don't forget that you also have to track company-paid payroll items, such as matching FICA and Medicare, employer contributions to unemployment (both state and federal), state disability funds, pension and medical benefit plans, and more!

You can view your payroll items and create new payroll items by choosing Lists | Payroll Item List to open the Payroll Item List seen in Figure 17-2. QuickBooks adds some items to the list automatically when you enable payroll services. Usually, local taxes, medical benefits deductions, and other payroll items are missing (and the items that *do* exist may be missing information about the vendor, so you'll have to edit them to add that information).

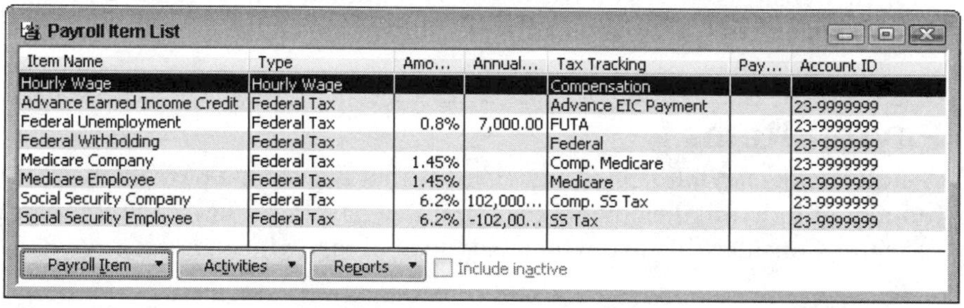

FIGURE 17-2 The payroll items created automatically don't include everything you need.

To add a new payroll item, press CTRL-N to open the Add New Payroll Item Wizard shown in Figure 17-3.

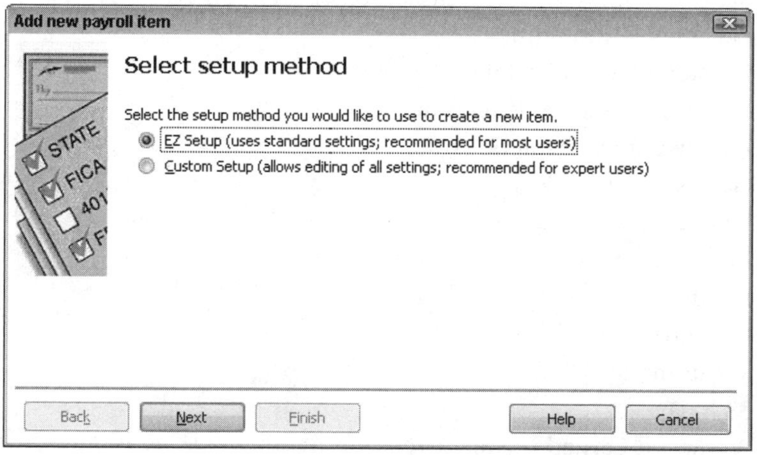

FIGURE 17-3 This wizard helps you create a payroll item.

The two options presented on the first wizard window don't offer full explanations of their differences, so I'll explain what happens with each option.

EZ Setup of Payroll Items

If you select the EZ Setup option, when you click Next you see a list of payroll item types. The descriptions are brief, but essentially you can create any type of pay, deduction, or company benefit, including payroll items that are paid in full by the company, deducted in full from employees, or paid by both the company and the employee. The only types of payroll items you cannot create in the EZ Setup are state and local payroll taxes, including state unemployment and/or disability taxes.

When you use the EZ Setup option, after you select the type of item, QuickBooks loads the Payroll Setup Wizard and then displays the Add New dialog from that feature. (The Payroll Setup Wizard is an alternate method of setting up all the elements in your payroll system—see "Using the QuickBooks Payroll Setup Wizard" later in this chapter).

The questions and explanations you see in the Payroll Setup Wizard are more basic than the questions you're asked if you select the Custom option for setting up a payroll item. You need less knowledge of accounting jargon to complete the setup, but you'll spend more time moving through more wizard windows, because most of the data you provide is entered one wizard window at a time. Most of the wizard windows ask one question or require a single answer.

This does not mean you can set up a payroll item accurately if you know nothing about deductions, benefits, or about the accounting and legal issues involved with payroll benefits and deductions; it merely means the explanations you see when you're asked to provide information are somewhat user-friendly.

For example, if you're setting up a benefit such as health insurance, pension benefit, or any form of a benefit in a cafeteria plan, the wizard asks you if the benefit cost is borne entirely by the company, entirely by the employee, or shared between both parties. Depending on your answer, the wizard moves through the ensuing windows to set up the necessary payroll item (or multiple items if you require the employee deduction and the employer contribution). If the employee contributes some or all of the cost, you have to know whether it's a pre-tax or after-tax deduction, and you have to know how the deduction affects the employee's W-2 form. This means that even if you choose the EZ Setup option you can't do this properly if you have no information about payroll issues; it is imperative that you discuss the payroll items required for your company with your accountant.

Custom Setup of Payroll Items

If you select the Custom Setup option, the list you see when you click Next is all inclusive, because you can set up all the payroll item types offered in the EZ Setup list of payroll types, and you can also set up state and local payroll items.

When you select a payroll item type, the wizard moves through information windows without asking the kind of easy-to-understand questions the EZ Setup presents; on the other hand, each window contains all the fields for the required information instead of walking you through multiple windows to answer questions and fill out a single field.

For example, if you have a health benefit with costs shared between the company and the employee, the wizard isn't going to remind you that you have to set up two items, one for the company payment and another for the employee deduction. You just have to know that both tasks must be completed (they are separate items). In the second wizard window, you select Deduction and establish the employee contribution (and you have to know which types of deductions are pre-tax and which are after-tax, and whether the deduction affects the W-2 form). Then you have to start the wizard again to select Company Contribution in the second wizard window to set up the company side of the health benefits item. If you have detailed instructions from your accountant, the Custom option is a quicker way to set up all your payroll items.

Use the wizard to create all the payroll items you need.

Setting Up Employees

The information about your employees must be perfectly, pristinely accurate, or you may hear about it in a very unfriendly manner. Your employees won't be happy if the deductions are incorrect, and the IRS won't be happy if your payroll records don't accurately reflect employee tax status categories and withholding data.

Create an Employee Template

There is a great deal of information to fill out for each employee, and some of it is probably the same for all or most of your employees. For example, you may have many employees who share the same type of pay (salary or hourly wage) or the same deductions for medical insurance.

To avoid entering the same information over and over, you can create a template and then apply the information to all the employees who match that data. You'll save yourself lots of time, even if you have to edit one or two entries for some employees because their data differs from the template.

To get to the template, you have to open the Employee Center by choosing Employees | Employee Center from the menu bar.

Click the button labeled Manage Employee Information at the top of the window, and choose Change New Employee Default Settings from the submenu that appears. This opens the Employee Defaults window, where you can enter the data that applies to most or all of your employees.

The information you put into the template is automatically added to the Payroll Info tab for each employee you create hereafter (discussed in the next section, "Creating Employees"). You can skip any field for which there isn't a common payroll item.

- Click in the Item Name column of the Earnings box, and then click the arrow to see a list of earnings types that you've defined as payroll items. Select the one that is common enough to be suitable for a template.

- In the Hourly/Annual Rate column, enter a wage or salary figure if there's one that applies to most of your employees. If there's not, just skip it and enter each employee's rate in the individual employee record later.

- Use the arrow to the right of the Payroll Schedule field and select a schedule (if you've established payroll schedules). See the section "Payroll Schedules" later in this chapter for more information.

- Select a pay frequency (if you created schedules and selected one, QuickBooks automatically uses that schedule to fill in the Pay Frequency field).

- Use the Class field if you've enabled classes to track data.

- If you're using QuickBooks' time tracking features to pay employees, you also see a check box labeled Use Time Data To Create Paychecks. Put a check mark in the check box to enable the feature.

- If all or most of your employees have the same additional adjustments (such as insurance deductions, 401(k) deductions, or reimbursement for car expenses), click in the Item Name column in the Additions, Deductions, And Company Contributions box, and then click the arrow to select the appropriate adjustments.

- Click the Taxes button to open the Taxes Defaults dialog, and select those taxes that are common and therefore suited for the template. The State tab and the Other tab (usually local payroll taxes) contain tax data that probably applies to all or most of your employees.
- Click the Sick/Vacation button to set the terms for accruing sick time and vacation time if your policy is similar enough among employees to include it in the template.

When you are finished filling out the template, click OK to save it.

Creating Employees

Now you're ready to tell QuickBooks about your list of employees. Open the Employee Center and click New Employee to open a New Employee form.

The New Employee form opens with the Personal Info tab selected in the Change Tabs drop-down list at the top of the form. This selection displays three tabs: Personal, Address And Contact, and Additional Info.

Additional tab sets exist, and you use the drop-down list in the Change Tabs field at the top of the window to access them. The following tab categories are available in the drop-down list:

- **Personal Info**   A three-tab dialog where you enter personal information about the employee.
- **Payroll And Compensation Info**   Where you enter information about earnings, taxes, deductions, and other financial data.
- **Employment Info**   Where you enter information about the employee's hiring date and other employment history.
- **Workers Compensation**   Only available if you signed up for Enhanced Payroll. If so, workers comp is automatically enabled (you can disable it in the Payroll & Employees category of the Preferences dialog).

All of these tabs are covered in the following sections.

Personal Info Tab Set

The Personal Info tab set (see Figure 17-4) is the place to record personal information about this employee. It has three tabs because the information is divided into three categories.

Personal Tab   Enter the employee's name, social security number, and the way the name should be printed on paychecks. Enter the gender and/or date of birth if you have a company policy of recording this information, or if any tax or benefits agency requires it. For example, your state unemployment form may require you to note the gender of all employees; your medical or life insurance carrier may require the date of birth.

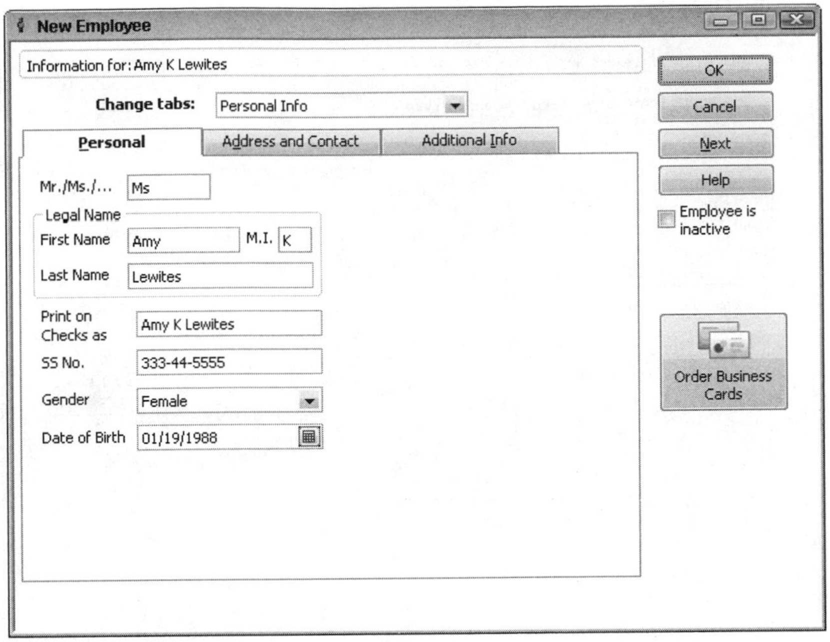

FIGURE 17-4 Start by entering personal information about the employee.

Address And Contact Tab   Use this tab to record the employee's address, as well as information about contacting the employee (phone number, e-mail, fax, and so on). The address is required for W-2 forms.

Additional Info Tab   Use this tab to enter the employee number (if your company uses employee numbers). This tab also contains a Define Fields button, so you can create custom fields for employee records.

Payroll And Compensation Info Tab Set

This tab set has only one tab, and it contains the information QuickBooks needs to pay employees (see Figure 17-5). Where the employee's payroll items and amounts match information already filled in from the default template, just accept the items. Otherwise, make additions and changes as necessary for this employee.

If the amount of the earnings or the deduction is the same every week, enter an amount. If it differs from week to week, don't enter an amount on the employee card. Instead, you'll enter that information when you create the payroll check.

Employee Tax Information   Click the Taxes button to open the Taxes dialog, which starts with Federal tax information, as seen in Figure 17-6. Fill in any data that wasn't automatically filled in from the Employee Template, and modify data that is different for this employee.

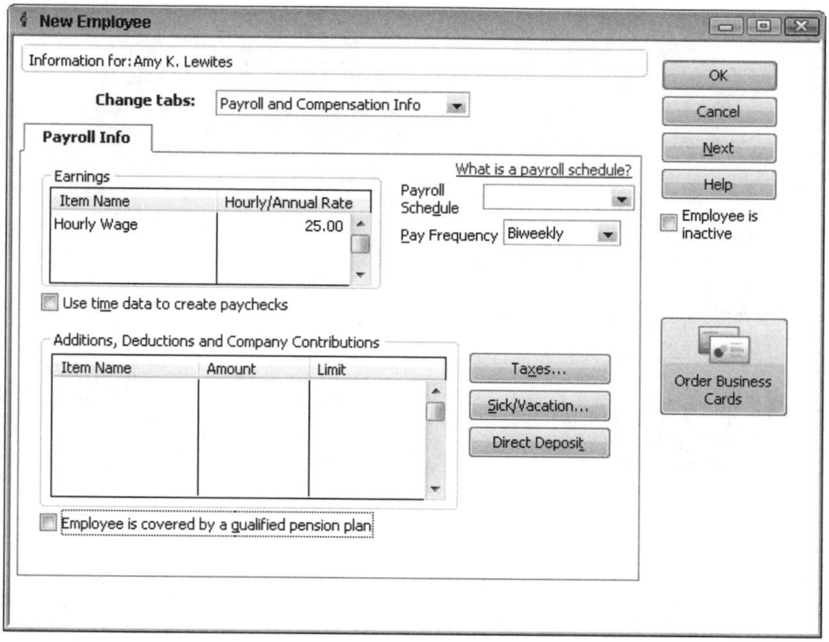

FIGURE 17-5 Enter information about this employee's compensation and deductions (excluding tax deduction).

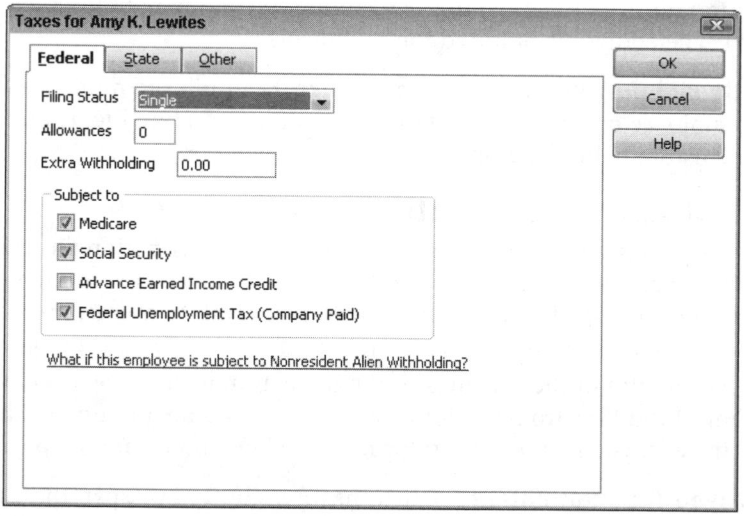

FIGURE 17-6 Configure the employee's tax information.

Move to the State tab and configure the employee's status for the state. This varies from state to state, of course, and you should check with your accountant if you aren't sure of something you find there.

NOTE: QuickBooks has built in a great deal of state information. Depending on the state, you should see the appropriate withholdings and company-paid items. For example, states that don't deduct SUI from employees have a check box for SUI (Company Paid); while states that collect disability funds from employees will display the appropriate check box.

In the Other tab, apply any local payroll tax that applies to this employee. If you haven't already configured that tax in the Payroll Item List, you can click <Add New> in the Item Name column to enter it now.

Click OK to save the tax status information and return to the Payroll Info tab.

Sick and Vacation Pay Information   Click the Sick/Vacation button and enter the configuration for this employee (which may include data from the Employee Template). When you are finished, click OK to return to the employee card.

Direct Deposit   The Payroll Info tab has a Direct Deposit button, which you can use to establish direct deposit of the employee's paycheck to his or her bank account. If you haven't signed up for direct deposit, the window that opens offers the chance to enroll.

Employment Info Tab Set

Select Employment Info in the Change Tabs drop-down list to see the Employment tab, which lets you track the following information about the employee:

- Hire Date
- Release Date (fill this in when an employee leaves your company)
- Employee Type

For more information on employee types, see the section "Understanding Employee Types."

Workers Compensation Tab Set

For Enhanced Payroll subscribers, if you haven't disabled workers-comp tracking in the Payroll & Employees category of the Preferences dialog, choose Workers Compensation from the Change Tabs drop-down list. Assign the workers-comp code that applies to the employee, or select Exempt if this employee is exempt from workers comp.

Understanding Employee Types

The Type field on the Employment Info tab offers four choices, which are explained in this section. The selection you make has an impact on the way your tax returns are prepared. You must check with your accountant if you have any questions about the type you should assign to any employee.

Regular Employee

A Regular employee is exactly what it seems to be: a person you hired for whom you deduct withholdings, issue a W-2, and so on. It's important to have every employee fill out a W-4 form every year (don't accept "I did that last year, nothing has changed").

 TIP: If you need extra W-4 forms, you can download them from the IRS at www.irs.ustreas.gov. Go to the forms section, select W-4, and print or download the form and print as many copies as you need.

Officer Employee

An *officer* is someone who is an officer of a corporation. If your business isn't incorporated, you have no officers. On federal corporate tax returns, you are required to report payroll for officers of the corporation separately from the regular payroll amounts. Selecting Officer as the type has no impact on running your payroll (calculations, check printing, and so on); it only affects reports.

Statutory Employee

A *statutory employee* is someone who works for you that the IRS has decided qualifies as an employee instead of as an independent contractor. The list of the job types that the rules cover and the definition of *independent contractor* is the subject of much debate (especially in IRS audit hearings). The IRS has a list of criteria that must be met in order to qualify as an independent contractor (which means you don't have to put that person on your payroll, you don't have to withhold taxes, and you don't have to pay employer taxes). The rules that govern this change frequently, so it's important to check the rules in Circular E or with your accountant.

Owner Employee

Owner and Employee are mutually exclusive terms to the IRS. If you own a company, that means the company is a proprietorship; it's not a corporation (a corporation doesn't have owners; it has officers and directors). The same thing is true of a partnership, which has multiple owners. You cannot put yourself on the payroll; when you draw checks they cannot be paychecks. Post the checks against a Draw account in the Equity section of your chart of accounts.

QuickBooks puts this type in the list in case it's too late and you've already listed the proprietor or partners in the Employee List. The QuickBooks payroll program won't perform payroll tasks for any employee of this type. If you did add a proprietor or partner name to the Employee List, delete it rather than assign this type.

Entering Historical Data

If you're not starting your use of QuickBooks at the very beginning of the year, you must enter all the historical information about paychecks. This is the only way to perform all those tasks required at the end of the year. You cannot give your employees two W-2 forms, one from your manual system and another from QuickBooks, nor can you file your annual tax reports on a piecemeal basis.

No matter what your fiscal year is, your payroll year is the calendar year. Even though you can start using payroll for the current period before you enter the historical data, remember that the absence of historical data may affect some tax calculations. If there are withholding amounts that cease after a certain maximum (perhaps your state only requires SUTA/SUI for the first $8,000.00 in gross payroll), you'll have to adjust the deductions on the current paychecks manually. If the historical data is entered, QuickBooks can calculate the maximum deduction properly and stop deducting these amounts.

TIP: To make historical data entry easier, go live with payroll at the beginning of a calendar quarter.

Understanding Historical Data

The historical data is the payroll you issued before the date on which you let QuickBooks take over your payroll chores (which is called the *go live date*). Starting with the go live date, you'll be entering payroll checks in QuickBooks; those checks are not part of the historical data. It's important to understand how the go live date affects the task of entering historical data, so here are some guidelines:

- Payroll records are summarized quarterly, because your 941 reports are due quarterly.
- You can't enter summarized data for the quarter that's current (the quarter that the go live date falls in). Instead, for the current quarter, you must enter data for each individual pay period (weekly, biweekly, semimonthly, or monthly). For previous quarters, you can enter quarterly totals.

- If your go live date is any date in the first quarter, you have to enter historical data for each pay period because you don't have a full quarter to summarize.
- If your go live date is in the second quarter, enter a quarterly total for the first quarter and then enter the individual pay period numbers for the second quarter, up to the go live date.
- If your go live date is in the third quarter, enter quarterly totals for the first two quarters and then enter each pay period up to the go live date.
- If your go live date is in the fourth quarter, you can follow the same pattern, but it might be just as easy to wait until next year to begin using QuickBooks payroll.

Entering the History Manually

The truth is, payroll is so easy to do if everything is set up properly that entering each historical payroll run individually isn't difficult, and it's great training for creating payroll checks. For the first couple of pay periods, stop to look at the details (the postings to general ledger accounts) after you enter historical totals, and compare them to your manual records. This gives you an opportunity to understand what QuickBooks is doing, in addition to checking accuracy.

However, if it's close to the end of the year, this is a lot of work. You can enter the history in batches, using the "secret" Payroll History feature ("secret" because it's not documented in QuickBooks but a lot of accountants know about it), or use the QuickBooks Payroll Setup Wizard (covered in the section, "Using the QuickBooks Payroll Setup Wizard"), which walks you through all payroll setup processes, including payroll history, using easy-to-understand wizard windows.

Manually Entering Payroll History in Batches

Here's an undocumented shortcut for entering year-to-date payroll information (you must have created all your employees to use it).

Choose Help—About QuickBooks to display the Product Information window. Then press the keyboard combination CTRL-SHIFT-Y. The Set Up YTD Amounts Wizard opens to walk you through the steps of entering year-to-date summary information for each employee (see Figure 17-7).

Click Next to begin. The wizard replicates the historical balance entry information that the QuickBooks Payroll Setup Wizard offers, but most people find this easier to use, especially if they've chosen to enter basic components manually.

The wizard asks you to specify three dates:

- The date your payroll liability and expense accounts are affected. That means, "When should the data you're entering be posted to liability and expense accounts that are associated with payroll items?"

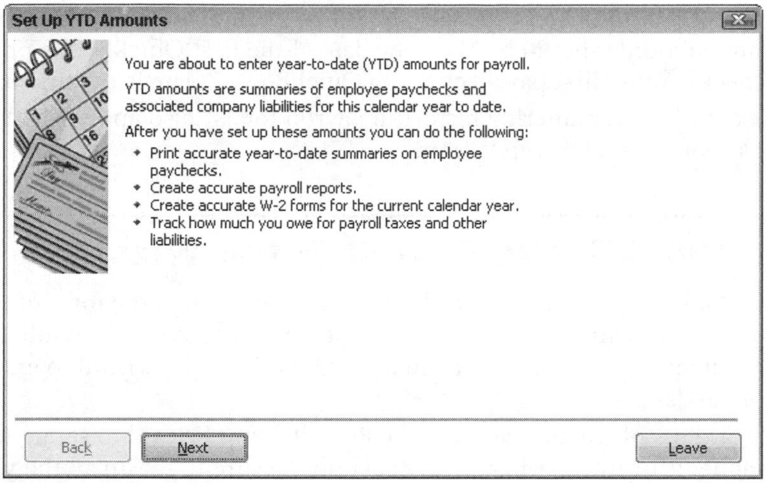

FIGURE 17-7   This is a quick way to use your manual payroll records to summarize year-to-date payroll information.

- The date your payroll bank accounts are affected. That means, "When should the net paycheck amounts be posted to your payroll bank account?"
- The check date of the first paycheck you'll create using QuickBooks payroll. This paycheck posts to all relevant accounts; there are no historical balances.

The correct dates might not be the same for all three categories. Following are some examples of possible scenarios that should help you understand how to enter the dates in these categories. For the purpose of these explanations, let's assume you're entering historical information as of the end of April; your first QuickBooks-produced paychecks will be the first payday in May.

If you've been doing payroll manually or through an outside service, and you've remitted your liabilities and expenses, those amounts should have been posted when you set up your opening QuickBooks balances. You don't want QuickBooks to post the liabilities, expenses, and net check amounts again; instead, you're entering historical data for the purpose of producing accurate reports and W-2 forms. Tell QuickBooks that the first date of your liability, expense, and bank accounts is the day of your first May paychecks. Enter the first quarter payroll totals for each employee, and then enter the individual payroll data for April (so you have running totals for your quarterly reports). Your "first paycheck using QuickBooks" date is the first payday in May.

If you've been using an outside payroll service, you've certainly posted the payroll totals to the bank account you use for payroll, but you might not have been posting liabilities and expenses to date, because the payroll service was taking care of it and you wait for the quarterly reports to post amounts. Your last journal entry for liabilities and expenses was at the end of the quarter (March 31). Your first posting of liabilities and expenses should be April 1, and your first posting of bank account amounts should be May (the date of the first QuickBooks-produced paycheck). Your "first paycheck using QuickBooks" date is the first payday in May.

These "rules for entering historical payroll totals" also apply when you use the QuickBooks Payroll Setup Wizard.

Using the QuickBooks Payroll Setup Wizard

QuickBooks provides assistance for setting up payroll in the form of a wizard. You can use the wizard to set up all the components required for payroll, or set up your payroll items and employees manually and then use the wizard to enter your historical data.

Regardless of whether you use the Payroll Setup Wizard to set up all your components or to enter historical data only, be sure to set up all the vendors and accounts you need to remit payroll withholding and employer payroll expenses before using the wizard.

To use the wizard, choose Employees | Payroll Setup from the QuickBooks menu bar. The wizard window opens with all the tasks listed in the left pane (see Figure 17-8).

QuickBooks Payroll Setup

QuickBooks
Payroll Setup

1 **Introduction**
2 **Company Setup**
3 **Employee Setup**
4 **Taxes**
5 **Payroll History**
6 **Data Review**
7 **Finishing Up**

Welcome to QuickBooks Payroll Setup

We'll walk you through setting up the basics of payroll by asking you questions and giving you guidance along the way. When you're done with setup, you'll be ready to start using QuickBooks Payroll-- customized just for you!

Before you begin:

1. Review the payroll setup checklist.
2. Gather all the documents and information ahead of time that you'll need to answer the interview questions.

[Finish Later]   UPS1.1020   [Continue >]

FIGURE 17-8   The QuickBooks Payroll Setup Wizard is divided into logical sets of tasks.

If you're using the wizard to set up your payroll from scratch (you didn't preconfigure any of the components as described in the previous sections of this chapter), the setup process can take more time than it takes to perform those tasks manually, but the wizard is rather user-friendly, demanding no knowledge of accounting jargon, so you may prefer to use it. The wizard has a Finish Later button, which you can click if you have to do other work, get tired, or get bored. When you open the wizard again, you pick up where you left off.

The first few wizard screens are informational, indicating the data you need to complete the wizard (the same information about employees, payroll items, deductions, etc., discussed earlier in this chapter). The real work starts with Section 2, where the wizard starts configuring payroll for your company.

Company Setup for Payroll

In the Company Setup section, the wizard starts with compensation, which means payroll items that are compensation—salary, hourly wages, and so on. When you've finished with that section, the wizard moves on to other payroll item types.

If you've configured payroll items manually, they appear in the wizard window, and you can click Edit to view or change the settings.

If you haven't yet set up payroll items, click Add New to open a mini-wizard that walks you through the process (the same process initiated if you choose EZ Setup of Payroll Items, which is covered earlier in this chapter).

The types of payroll items the wizard offers to set up include the following:

- Types of compensation, such as salary, hourly wages, overtime, bonuses, commissions, tips, and so on.
- Benefits, such as insurance, pension, and so on. For each benefit you select, you configure the employee/employer contribution rates.
- Paid time off, such as sick leave and vacations. You can configure your formulas for calculating vacation time and sick time (if you let employees accrue time according to time worked).
- Other additions and deductions, such as workers comp, auto expense reimbursement, garnishments, union dues, and so on.

Setting Up Employees in the Wizard

In Section 3, the wizard moves on to the task of setting up employees. If you didn't set up your employees manually, you can add each employee in the wizard, moving through a series of windows in which you enter information about the employee's personal information, pay structure, and tax status. For each employee, you designate the taxes and benefits that affect the employee.

When you finish entering your employee information, the wizard displays the list of employees. If any employee is missing information, the wizard indicates the problem (if you entered your employees manually, the wizard automatically finds the employee records and displays the same list if problems exist).

Some missing information isn't critical to issuing paychecks (for example, the hire date), but QuickBooks requires the information in the employee record. If any employee in the list has the notation Fix This Error Now, it means critical information is missing, and the system either won't be able to issue a paycheck or won't be able to issue a W-2 form at the end of the year. Regardless of whether the missing information is critical or not, select the employee and click Edit to move through the wizard and fix the problem.

Incidentally, if you use the wizard to set up employees, when you fail to fill in required information the wizard displays a reminder, something that doesn't happen when you set up employees manually.

Setting Up Payroll Taxes in the Wizard

In Section 4, you tell the wizard about the federal, state, and local taxes you're responsible for. These are payroll items, so if you haven't set up all these items beforehand, you can use the wizard.

If you're setting up your taxes in the wizard, as you finish each section, the wizard displays a list of all the taxes for that section. If you set up your taxes as payroll items manually, the wizard finds those entries and uses them to populate the list.

If the wizard finds anything amiss in your setup of any tax, the problem is displayed in the Description column. Choose Edit to make the needed changes.

Entering Payroll History in the Wizard

In Section 5, you enter your historical payroll data. The wizard presents a set of windows, starting with a window that asks if you've issued paychecks this year (meaning outside of QuickBooks, of course). If you answer Yes, the wizard walks you through each appropriate quarter, asking about the following for the quarter:

- Did you create paychecks?
- Did you remit your payroll tax liabilities?
- Did you remit your nontax payroll liabilities (company contributions to benefits, and so on)?

Depending on the date you perform this setup, you may be asked for weekly totals instead of quarterly totals.

The wizard walks you through multiple windows to ascertain the details for those categories. It starts with the paychecks, where the wizard presents each employee and walks you through the steps required to enter the payroll history.

In the ensuing windows, you'll enter the batch totals for employer contributions and other employer payments (which depend on the benefits you offer and the state or local municipality in which your business operates).

When you finish entering the batch totals for completed quarters, the wizard asks for the financial information about the paychecks in the current quarter. If you are performing this task in the second month of the current quarter, the wizard asks for batch information for the first month of the quarter and then individual paycheck information for the current month.

After the paycheck data is entered, the wizard walks you through the process of entering employer payments (withholding remittances, employer taxes, payments to pension and benefit plans, and so on).

Payroll Checkup

Step 6 is the Data Review, which you can run if you choose. QuickBooks asks if you'd like to go over your payroll settings, and if you select Yes, the wizard runs a payroll checkup. You can also run a Payroll Checkup whenever you make changes to your payroll components (employees, taxes, etc.) by choosing Employees | My Payroll Service | Run Payroll Checkup.

The QuickBooks Payroll Checkup is a wizard that walks through all the elements required for running payroll (a task list). Each section of the wizard's task list is checked for errors. The errors the checkup may find include missing information, invalid information (the format of an EIN number or state reporting number may be incorrect), or any other data that doesn't match the standards built into the QuickBooks payroll feature.

The program displays a report on the integrity of the data for prior quarters (unless you're working in the first quarter, of course), and then, separately, the integrity of the data for the current quarter.

Then, the program asks you about the federal and state forms you've filed to remit withholdings and pay employer taxes. After you've filled in the information, the program reconciles the totals against the payroll totals you entered previously. If there are errors, the specifics are displayed, and you can correct the problem and re-run the checkup.

Payroll Schedules

A payroll schedule is a way to separate different payroll intervals. For example, if your company pays salaried employees and officers on a weekly basis and pays hourly workers on a biweekly basis, you can run payroll by selecting the appropriate schedule in order to make sure you pay the right employees on the right dates.

When you create a payroll schedule you define how often you pay your employees (weekly, biweekly, semimonthly, and so on), the pay period (the workdays covered by the paycheck), the date on the paycheck, and the date you prepare the payroll.

> **NOTE:** The date you prepare the payroll differs from the paycheck date if you're using direct deposit, which requires you to transfer payroll information two days before the paycheck date.

The number of payroll schedules you have to create depends on the manner in which you issue paychecks; following are some common scenarios:

- If all your employees are paid on the same frequency, and all of them receive physical paychecks, you don't need payroll schedules.
- If all your employees are paid on the same frequency, and all of them have signed up for direct deposit, you don't need payroll schedules.
- If all your employees are paid on the same frequency, but some are signed up for direct deposit and others receive physical paychecks, you may want to set up two payroll schedules (because preparation for direct deposit is two days earlier than the date on which you'd normally print paychecks). On the other hand, you can omit payroll schedules, print the paychecks early while you're preparing the direct deposit checks, and put the paychecks away until payday.
- If your employees are paid on different frequency sets (for example, some weekly, some monthly), you can eliminate the need to select/deselect the appropriate employees for a given pay date by creating payroll schedules.

Creating a Payroll Schedule

To create a payroll schedule, choose Employees | Add Or Edit Payroll Schedules. When the Payroll Schedule List window opens, press CTRL-N to create a new payroll schedule. In the New Payroll Schedule dialog, fill out the required information as follows:

- A name for this schedule. Use descriptive text if you're setting up multiple payroll schedules, such as "weekly-checks," "weekly-DirDep," "CommissionsOnly," and so on.
- The pay period frequency for this schedule.
- The next pay period end date. This is the time period covered by the paycheck, which often is not the same as the paycheck date. For example, you may issue paychecks on Thursday for the period ending the previous Friday.
- The next paycheck date.

➡ **FYI**

The Paycheck Date Is All That Really Counts

All the information in the payroll schedule except the paycheck date is for your convenience in running payroll and has no impact on your finances or tax liabilities. For direct deposit employees, the deposit date is the paycheck date.

Your QuickBooks reports are based only on the paycheck dates, and your 941/W-2 forms use only the paycheck dates. For example, if you issue a paycheck dated October 5, 2009, for the period ending September 29, 2009, that paycheck is not included in your third-quarter reports, nor in your September reports for any tax reports that are due monthly.

If your payroll is monthly or semimonthly, the dialog includes additional fields. For example, if you issue paychecks semimonthly, you can select specific dates, such as the 10th and the 25th, or you can select one midmonth date and then select Last Day Of Month for the second check in that month.

After you create the schedule, QuickBooks offers to assign the schedule automatically to any employees who are configured for the same pay frequency as the new schedule.

Assigning Payroll Schedules to Employees

Each employee record has a field for the applicable payroll schedule in the Payroll And Compensation Info tab. When you link the payroll schedule to the appropriate employees, those employees appear when you select the schedule on the day you're preparing paychecks.

Special Payroll Runs

QuickBooks offers a way to issue a paycheck, or multiple paychecks, outside of the schedules you create. When you choose Employees | Pay Employees, in addition to the subcommand Scheduled Payroll, you see two commands you can use for special payroll runs:

- Unscheduled Payroll
- Termination Check

Unscheduled Payroll Select this special payroll category if you need to create bonus checks, commission checks, or any other type of paycheck that differs from a regularly scheduled payroll run. You also have the option of adding the additional compensation to a "regular" paycheck instead of running an unscheduled payroll.

Termination Checks   Selecting this special payroll type, the use of which is rather obvious from its name, opens the Enter Payroll Information dialog. Select the terminated employee (put a check mark in the column to the left of the employee name), the pay period ending date, the check date, the termination date, and the hours (or amount if the employee is salaried). Click Continue, approve or change the paycheck details; then print the check, assign a check number for a manual check, or issue a direct deposit check. You must enter a Release Date in the Employment Info tab of the employee's record, or QuickBooks will not create a termination check.

Running Payroll

It's payday. All the historical data is entered. It's time to run the payroll. Begin creating payroll checks as follows:

- If you don't use payroll schedules, choose Employees | Pay Employees to open the Enter Payroll Information dialog seen in Figure 17-9.

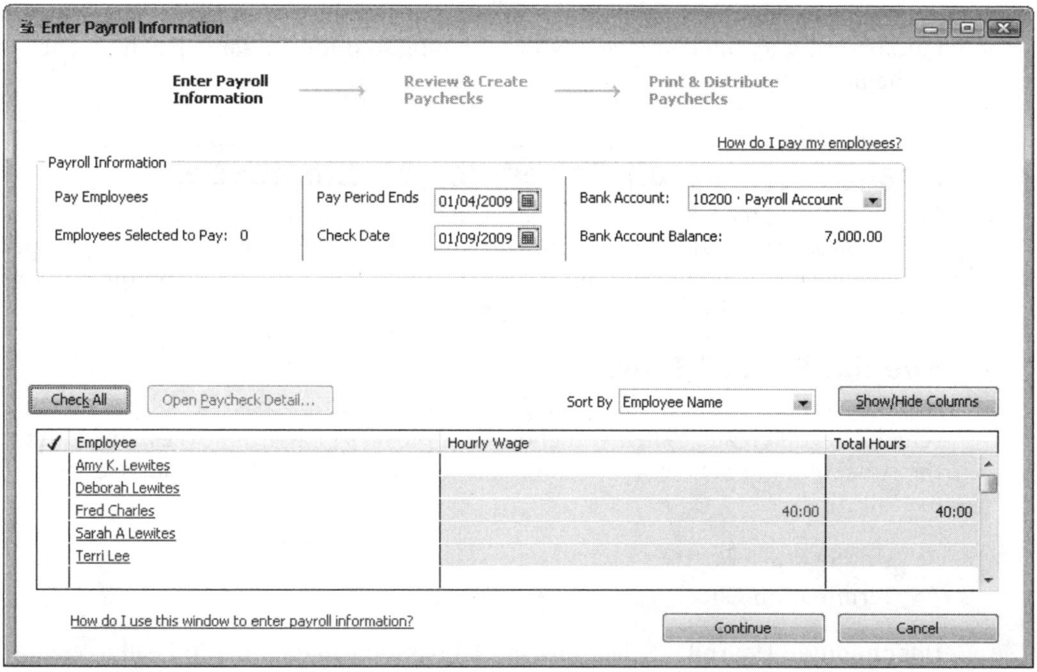

FIGURE 17-9   Begin configuring paychecks in the Enter Payroll Information dialog.

- If you have payroll schedules, choose Employees | Pay Employees | Scheduled Payroll to open the Employee Center with the Payroll tab selected (the Pay Employees function appears in the right pane). Select the appropriate schedule and click Start Scheduled Payroll to open the Enter Payroll Information dialog, which looks the same as Figure 17-9, but only lists the employees linked to this payroll schedule.

Select the employees to pay. If all the employees are receiving paychecks (the usual scenario), click Check All.

- For hourly employees who are configured for automatic payroll amounts using timesheets, the number of hours is prefilled.
- For hourly employees who are not paid from timesheets, you must fill in the number of hours for this paycheck.

> **N O T E :** The column names are deceiving; you'd expect to see the wage rate in a column named Hourly Wage, but that column is for the number of hours worked by employees configured for hourly wages.

Changing Paycheck Data

If you want to make changes to the paycheck, click the employee's name to open the Preview Paycheck dialog. You can add a payroll item such as a bonus, assign the paycheck to a customer or job, or add a deduction such as a repayment of a loan or garnishment. Click Save & Next to move to the next employee or click Save & Close to return to the Enter Payroll Information dialog. (There's also a Save & Previous button in case you think you should go back to a previous check.)

Reviewing the Payroll Run

Click Continue in the Enter Payroll Information dialog to display the Review And Create Paychecks window (see Figure 17-10), which displays all the financial information for this payroll run. If anything is amiss, click Back to reconfigure the paychecks or make other needed corrections.

Fill out the options for producing the paychecks (print the checks or automatically assign check numbers in the bank account register for manual

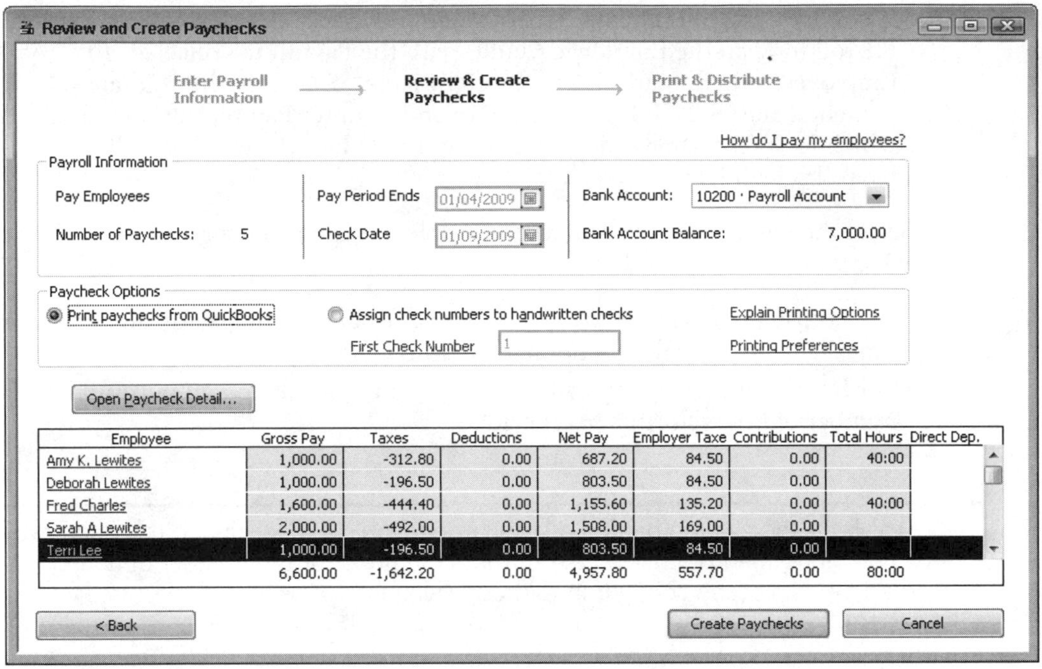

FIGURE 17-10 The details for each paycheck have been entered.

checks), and then click Create Paychecks. QuickBooks creates the checks and displays the Confirmation And Next Steps dialog.

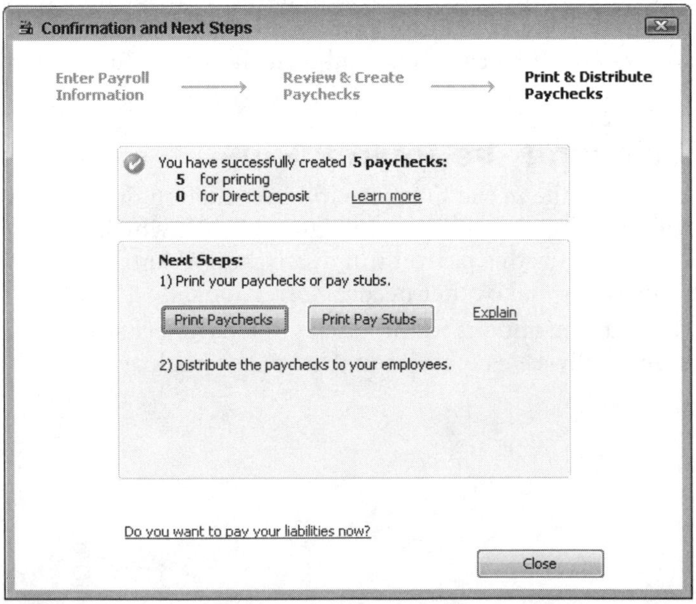

➡ **FYI**

Net to Gross Calculations
for Enhanced Payroll Subscribers

If you subscribe to Enhanced Payroll you can enter the net amount of a check and let QuickBooks calculate the gross amount. This is useful for bonus checks or another special payroll check for which you need to make sure the employee receives a net check of a certain amount.

During the payroll run (either a regular payroll or a special payroll for this individual paycheck), select the employee for this payroll run. In the Preview Paycheck window, select the option Enter Net/Calculate Gross, and then enter the net amount for this paycheck. QuickBooks automatically calculates the gross amount and the deductions to arrive at the net amount you entered.

If you're printing paychecks you can click Print Paychecks, or you can wait and print them from the Print Forms command in the File menu (in case you have another payroll schedule to process today, and you want to load the payroll checks and process them in one fell swoop).

If you have direct deposit employees, click Print Pay Stubs. When the pay stubs are printed, click the Send Payroll Data button on the Confirmation And Next Steps dialog. This opens the Send Center window and you can upload the direct deposit data to Intuit for processing. You can e-mail the pay stubs using the security standards built into the process (see the Help files for details).

If you have another payroll schedule to run today (perhaps both weekly and biweekly employees are paid today), repeat all the processes enumerated here.

The Employee Center

The Employee Center, seen in Figure 17-11, contains all the information about your payroll components and also provides links to all the functions in the payroll system. It's a central location for everything you need to do or need to know. To open this window, choose Employees | Employee Center.

($) **N O T E :** Users who do not have QuickBooks permissions to see payroll or other sensitive information do not see payroll financial information when they open the Employee Center.

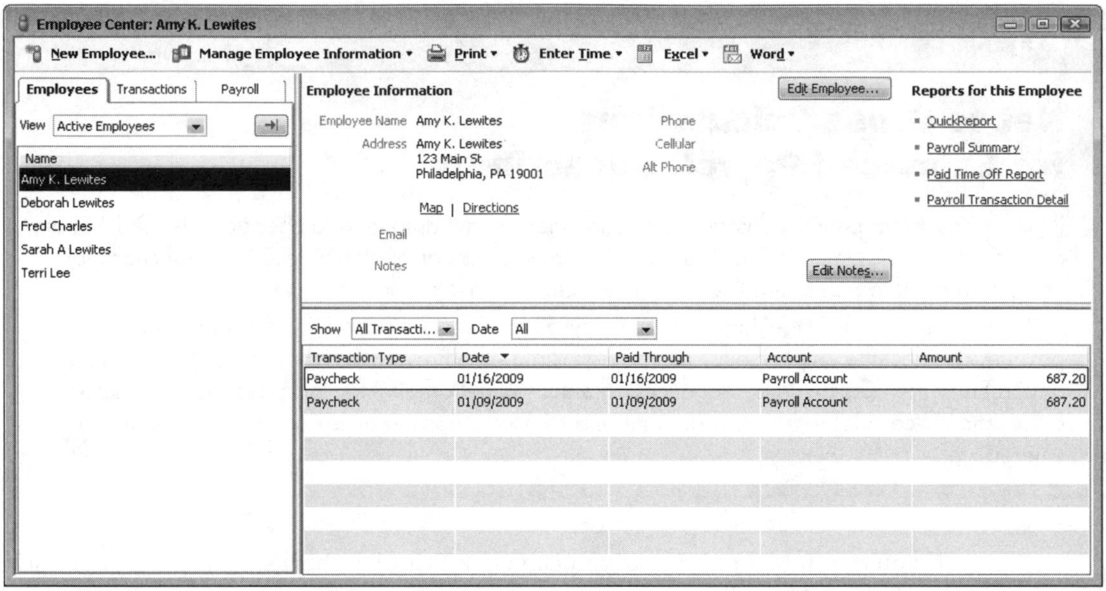

FIGURE 17-11 The Employee Center is the repository of all payroll information and functions.

If you subscribe to a QuickBooks payroll service, the left pane of the Employee Center contains three tabs: Employees, Transactions, and Payroll. If you don't have a payroll plan subscription, the pane lacks a Payroll tab.

Employee Tab

When you select an employee on the Employees tab, QuickBooks displays information from the employee's record on the top part of the right pane and displays transaction information for that employee on the bottom part of the right pane. You can change the choices in the Show and Date fields to filter the transactions information.

You can open any listed transaction by double-clicking its listing. For example, if you open a paycheck you can see the original check along with a summary of the financial information. If you need to check any of the details, click Paycheck Detail to see all the calculated amounts.

Transactions Tab

The Transactions tab (see Figure 17-12) lists all payroll-related transaction types. Select a type to display the transactions you've created. You can use the Date field to narrow the breadth of information.

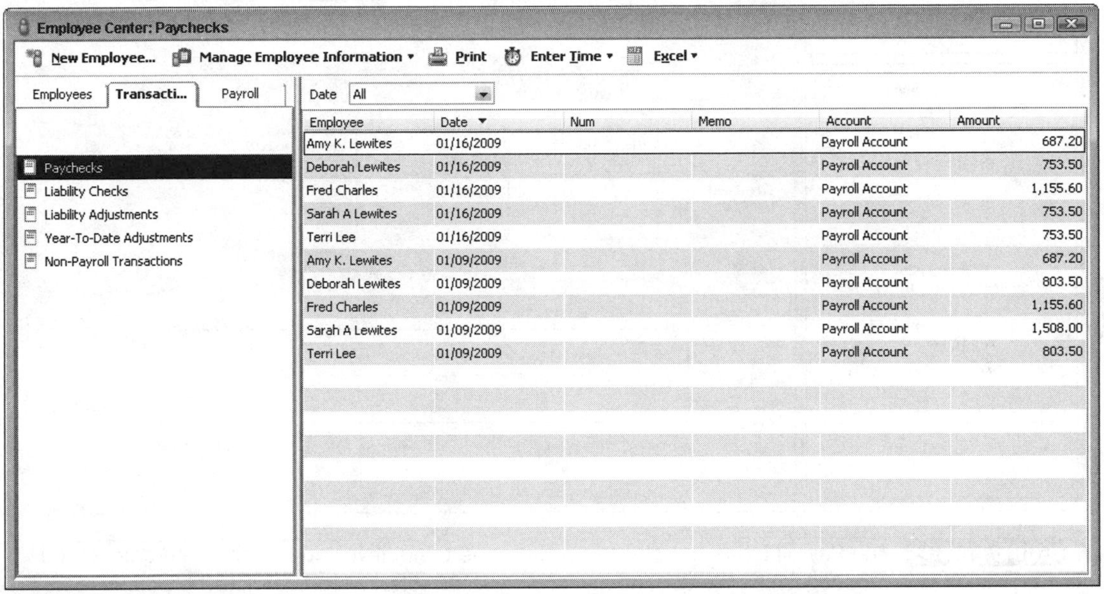

Employee Center: Paychecks
New Employee...
Manage Employee Information
Print
Enter Time
Excel
Employees
Transacti...
Payroll
Date
All
Paychecks
Liability Checks
Liability Adjustments
Year-To-Date Adjustments
Non-Payroll Transactions
Employee
Date
Num
Memo
Account
Amount
Amy K. Lewites 01/16/2009 Payroll Account 687.20
Deborah Lewites 01/16/2009 Payroll Account 753.50
Fred Charles 01/16/2009 Payroll Account 1,155.60
Sarah A Lewites 01/16/2009 Payroll Account 753.50
Terri Lee 01/16/2009 Payroll Account 753.50
Amy K. Lewites 01/09/2009 Payroll Account 687.20
Deborah Lewites 01/09/2009 Payroll Account 803.50
Fred Charles 01/09/2009 Payroll Account 1,155.60
Sarah A Lewites 01/09/2009 Payroll Account 1,508.00
Terri Lee 01/09/2009 Payroll Account 803.50

FIGURE 17-12 Use the Transactions tab to view transactions of the selected type.

Payroll Tab

The Payroll tab provides a one-stop center for all your payroll tasks (see Figure 17-13). You can view transactions, create transactions, and generate the payroll forms you need. Visit this tab periodically to make sure you don't miss any deadlines.

Customizing the Employee Center

You can tailor the way the Employee Center displays information. Resize the panes by moving your mouse pointer over the edge of any pane; when the pointer changes to a vertical bar with right and left arrows, drag the pane in either direction.

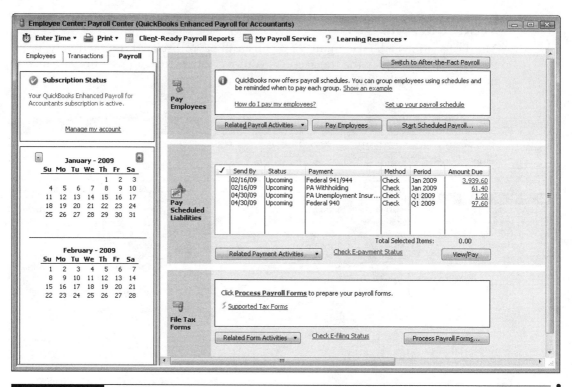

FIGURE 17-13 The Payroll tab is the place to access the tasks involved in payroll—the links and messages change depending on the QuickBooks payroll service you purchased.

You can customize the columns that QuickBooks displays in the left pane of the Employees tab by right-clicking anywhere on the list and choosing Customize Columns.

You can also customize the information displayed in the right pane when you select an employee's name in the Employees tab. Right-click anywhere in the right (Transaction) pane and select Customize Columns.

Of course, after you create and deliver paychecks to employees, you have to send the government agencies, insurance companies, and other vendors the money you're holding for them. Instructions for those tasks are in Chapter 18.

Payroll Reports and Remittances

In *this chapter:*

- Confirm payroll liability payment schedules

- Remit liabilities

- Prepare quarterly and annual returns

- Print W-2 forms

Doing payroll in-house means having a lot of reports to print, forms to fill out, and checks to write. There's a logical order to these tasks, although the logic differs depending on the state and municipality you're in. In this chapter, I'll go over the procedures in the order in which most businesses have to perform the tasks.

Confirming Payroll Remittance Schedules

QuickBooks provides a method of tracking due dates for all the payroll liabilities and employer expenses that accumulate during payroll runs. You can use this payment schedule to make sure you remit your payroll obligations on time. Most of the information required for scheduling payments is probably already in your system as a result of the information you provided when you set up payroll items. To view the schedule, and correct any problems, choose Employees | Payroll Taxes And Liabilities | Edit Payment Due Dates/Methods.

This action opens the Payroll Setup Wizard's Schedule Payments window, and if any data is missing or does not match the content or format the payroll system expects, the wizard highlights the listing with a problem (see Figure 18-1).

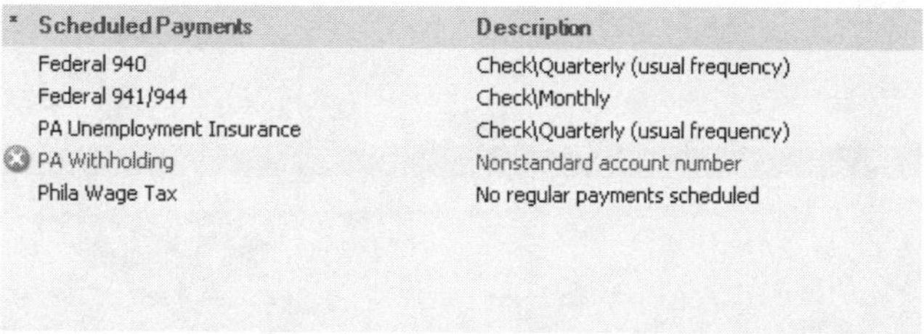

Scheduled Payments	Description
Federal 940	Check\Quarterly (usual frequency)
Federal 941/944	Check\Monthly
PA Unemployment Insurance	Check\Quarterly (usual frequency)
⊗ PA Withholding	Nonstandard account number
Phila Wage Tax	No regular payments scheduled

FIGURE 18-1   If a listing has an icon, there's a problem with the configuration of that listing.

Double-click the errant listing so you can edit its configuration to correct the problem. QuickBooks usually provides a hint about the problem in the window that opens for editing. For example, in Figure 18-1 the problem with the highlighted listing is the format of the account number for state payroll withholding in Pennsylvania. QuickBooks knows that the account number has to follow a specific format, and this data was originally entered in the wrong format.

Using the Scheduled vs. Using the Unscheduled Liabilities Window

In the following sections covering payroll remittances, you have a choice of methods for performing the each task:

- For liabilities that have a scheduled configured, choose Employees | Payroll Taxes And Liabilities | Pay Scheduled Liabilities. Select the payments to remit from the schedule that displays.

- For liabilities that don't have a schedule configured, choose Employees | Payroll Taxes And Liabilities | Create Custom Liability Payments. Select the paycheck date range you need, and then select the payments to remit. All your liabilities (both scheduled and unscheduled) are included in the list.

- If you set up a schedule for most liabilities, but one or more of your payments didn't match the options available in the schedule, it's easier to use the Create Custom Liability Payments command than to use the scheduled liabilities command and then use the unscheduled liabilities command.

Remitting Liabilities

When you create payroll checks, QuickBooks tracks the liabilities you accrue as a result of those checks. To see your scheduled liabilities, choose the appropriate command (as described in the preceding section). QuickBooks displays the currently owed liabilities (see Figure 18-2).

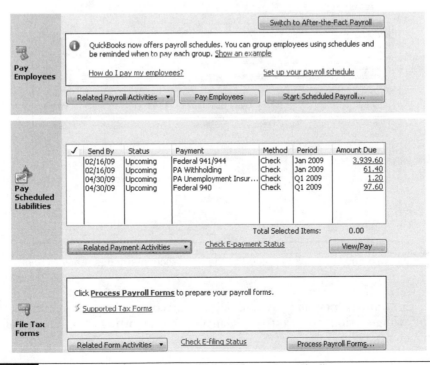

FIGURE 18-2 QuickBooks tracks your payroll liabilities automatically.

Select the liability you want to pay and click View/Pay. The first time you pay liabilities, QuickBooks asks you to select the right bank account (if you have more than one bank account).

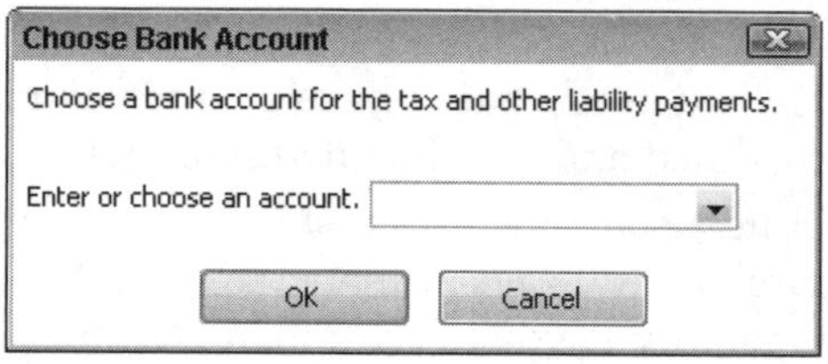

The payment transaction window opens, as seen in Figure 18-3.

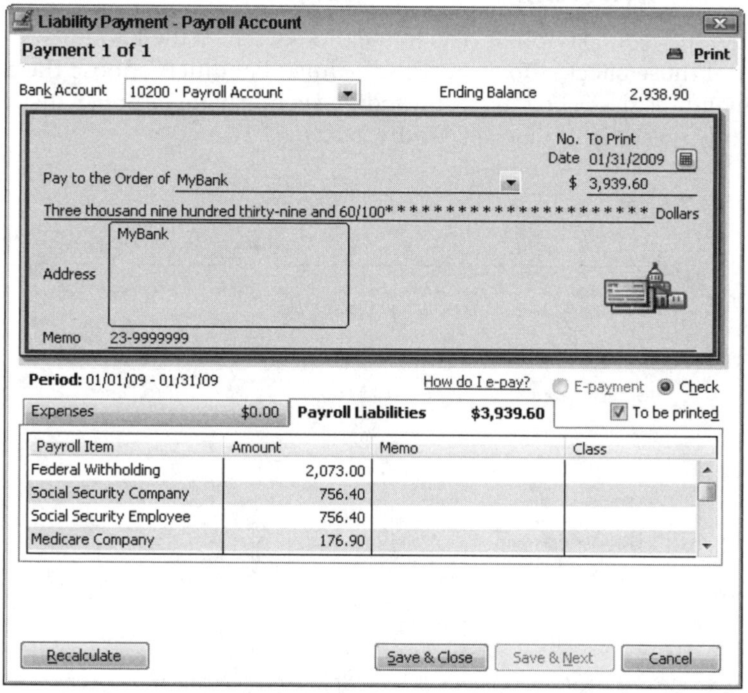

FIGURE 18-3 This liability check is posted to the right accounts and is ready to print.

Continue to view and pay until all the current liabilities are remitted. The following sections cover the details involved in remitting common payroll liability payments.

Sending Federal Tax Payments

Payments to the federal government involve two payroll taxes:

- 941/944/943 taxes, which cover withholding, social security, and Medicare
- 940 taxes, which are the federal unemployment taxes

NOTE: This section is specific to liabilities payments made by companies that file Form 941/943 on a quarterly basis. If you use Form 944, you file annually.

941/943 Payments

The federal government requires you to deposit the withheld amounts, along with the matching employer contributions, at a specified time. That time period is dependent upon the size of the total withholding amount you've accumulated. You may be required to deposit monthly, semimonthly, weekly, or within three days of the payroll. Check the current limits with the IRS or your accountant.

There's a formula for determining the size of the 941/943 payment—it's the sum of the following amounts for the period:

- Federal withholding
- FICA withholding
- Medicare withholding
- FICA matching contribution from employer
- Medicare matching contribution from employer

You don't have to do the math—QuickBooks does it for you. But it's a good idea to know what the formula is so you can check the numbers yourself (and make sure you have sufficient funds in your bank account to cover the next payment).

Creating a Check for 941/943 Payments

If you write or print the 941/943 payment check and deposit it at the bank in which you have your payroll account, use the coupons the federal government sent you (Form 8109). Fill out a coupon and take it, along with your check, to the bank in which you have your payroll account. Make the check payable to the bank. Don't forget to fill in the little bullets on the coupon: one to indicate the type of deposit (941 or 943), the other to indicate the quarter for which this payment is remitted.

E-Paying 941/943 Payments

If you remit your payments electronically (either through QuickBooks Enhanced Payroll or by using the Electronic Federal Tax Payment System (EFTPS) operated by the IRS), the payee is the IRS. The payment appears in your bank register as an e-payment, either automatically (if you're using QuickBooks e-pay), or manually (if you use EFTPS).

Employers who e-pay directly through EFTPS usually enter text in the check number field such as "ACH," which is the method the IRS uses to take the payment out of your bank account. ACH stands for *Automated Clearing House*, which is a network operated by the Federal Reserve and the Electronic Payments Network that provides a way for financial institutions to exchange funds electronically. You can also leave the check number field blank.

940 Payments

The Federal Unemployment Tax Act (FUTA) provides unemployment compensation to workers who have lost their jobs, usually after the workers' state benefits have been exhausted. The FUTA tax is paid by employers; no deductions are taken from employee wages. Companies must make FUTA payments if either of the following scenarios exist:

- During this year or last year you paid wages of at least $1,500 in any calendar quarter.
- During this year or last year you had one or more employees for at least part of a day for a period of 20 weeks (the weeks do not have to be contiguous).

If you print the check, use Form 8109 (the same coupon you use to deposit federal withholding and employer matching contributions for Form 941/943) and mark the coupon for 940 Tax and the quarter in which you are making your deposit. You don't have to make the deposit until you owe the entire amount, but you can make deposits until you reach that amount if you wish.

 CAUTION: Always use a separate coupon and check for FUTA; don't mix the payment with your other federal liabilities payment.

Technically, FUTA tax is 6.2 percent of gross wages up to $7,000.00 per employee, but the federal government gives employers a 5.4 percent credit for paying their state unemployment taxes. Therefore, unless you deliberately ignore your state unemployment payments, you can calculate FUTA at the rate of .8 percent of gross wages (.008 × $7,000.00), which is $56.00 per employee who reaches the $7,000.00 goal. QuickBooks assumes you're paying your state unemployment taxes and calculates your FUTA liability accordingly.

Remitting State and Local Liabilities

Your state and local payroll liabilities vary depending upon where your business is located and where your employees live (and pay taxes). Besides income taxes, you may be liable for unemployment insurance and disability insurance.

Remitting State and Local Income Taxes

Most states have some form of an income tax, which might be calculated in any one of a variety of ways:

- A flat percentage of gross income
- A sliding percentage of gross income
- A percentage based on the federal tax for the employee

Local (municipal or county) taxes are also widely varied in their approach:

- Some cities have different rates for employees of companies that operate in the city. There may be one rate for employees who live in the same city and a different rate for nonresidents.
- Your business might operate in a city or town that has a *payroll head tax* (a once-a-year payment that is a flat amount per employee).
- You may have a head tax for the town in which your business operates and still be required to withhold local taxes for employees who live in another city.

State and local taxing authorities provide coupons or forms or an online service for remitting income tax withholding. The frequency with which you must remit might depend on the size of your payroll, or it might be quarterly, semiannual, or annual, regardless of the amount. Some municipal authorities have e-pay available.

Remitting Other State Liabilities

If your state has SUI or SDI or both, you have to pay those liabilities when they're due. Commonly, these are quarterly payments.

> **TIP:** It's a good idea to create different vendor names for SUI, SDI, and state income tax withholding to make sure you don't accidentally send checks for the wrong component and to prevent QuickBooks from issuing a single check for the grand total. The vendor record for each vendor name may have the same payee (State Department of Revenue), but the vendor names are different.

Not all states have SUI or SDI, and some have one but not the other. Some states collect SUI and SDI from the employee and the company; some collect only from the company. Check the rules for your state.

Remitting Other Payroll Liabilities

The rules for remitting the paycheck deductions and employer contributions for other reasons—such as health benefits, pension, and workers compensation—are specific to your arrangements with those vendors.

There are a great many ways to handle the way these payments are posted, and you have to decide what makes sense to you (or to your accountant). For example, if you pay a monthly amount to a medical insurer, you may want to post the employee deductions back to the same expense account you use to pay the bill. That way, only the net amount is reported as an expense on your taxes.

Workers Comp

QuickBooks Enhanced Payroll offerings include workers comp, and the setup options are available in the Payroll & Employees category of the Preferences dialog. Click Workers Compensation on the Company Preferences tab to open the Workers Comp Preferences dialog. Select Track Workers Comp to enable the feature.

When workers comp is enabled, you can also opt to see reminder messages to assign workers comp codes when you create paychecks or timesheets. In addition, you can select the option to exclude an overtime premium from your workers comp calculations (check your workers comp insurance policy to see if you can calculate overtime amounts as regular pay).

Preparing Your 941/943 Form

Unless you've been notified that you're a Form 944 filer, you must file a 941 or 943 form every quarter to report the total amount you owe the federal government for withheld taxes, FICA, and Medicare. If you have been paying the deposits regularly, no check is remitted with the 941/943. Instead, it's a report of amounts due and amounts paid, and they should match so that Line 12 is $0.00.

- If you underpaid, use the payment voucher to send your check for the underpaid amount. The vendor for the check is United States Treasury (you do not take this check to the bank; only deposits accompanied by Form 8109 are deposited at your bank). Use the address provided on the form instructions (QuickBooks prints the instruction page).
- If you overpaid, you can select the option to take a credit toward the next 941/943 or you can select the option for a refund.

The 941/943 is concerned with the following data:

- Gross wages paid
- Federal income tax withholding
- FICA (social security) withholding and matching employer contributions
- Medicare withholding and matching employer contributions

Creating a 941/943 Form

QuickBooks will prepare your 941/943 report using the information in your QuickBooks registers.

If QuickBooks isn't preparing your federal forms (either because you're doing payroll manually or you subscribed to the QuickBooks Basic Payroll service), you can prepare your forms manually with the use of Excel worksheets that QuickBooks provides. See the section "Tax Form Worksheets in Excel" at the end of this chapter. Creating the form is quite easy.

Follow these steps to create a 941/943 form:

1. Choose Employees | Payroll Tax Forms & W-2s | Process Payroll Forms.
2. In the Select Form Type dialog, select Federal Form and click OK.
3. In the Select Payroll Form dialog select (highlight) Quarterly Form 941 or Annual Form 943.
4. Select the filing period and click OK.

The Payroll Tax Form window opens with Form 941 or 943 selected. This process is a wizard, so you fill out information and click Next to move through all the steps in the process. The first window is an interview; enter the appropriate data (see Figure 18-4) and click Next to continue.

N O T E : Schedule B is the Employer's Record of Federal Tax Liability. If you are a semiweekly depositor or your payroll tax liability on any day in the quarter exceeds the standard amount for a monthly depositor, you must file Schedule B with Form 941/943.

Move through the wizard, following the prompts, using the guidelines presented in the following sections.

Filling in Blank Fields

To enter information in a blank field, click your cursor in the field to activate it, then type the data. The typed text appears blue, but that's just a signal to you that the data was entered manually; QuickBooks doesn't print the form in color.

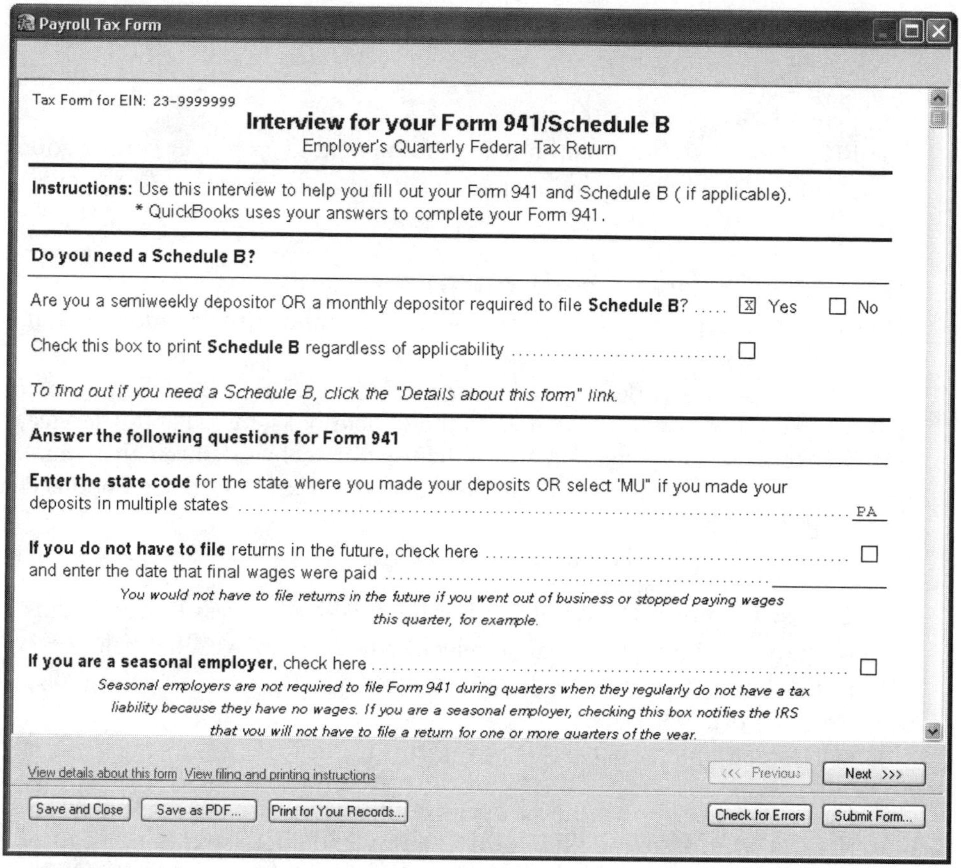

FIGURE 18-4 Start by answering questions; the answers are transferred to the form in the appropriate places.

Editing Prefilled Data

Follow these steps to edit data:

1. Right-click the field and choose Override from the menu that appears.
2. Enter the replacement data in the Override box and press the TAB key.
3. The new data replaces the original data in the field, and it's green (to remind you that you manually replaced the data that was exported from QuickBooks).

If you change your mind and decide that the data automatically supplied by QuickBooks should remain in the form, right-click in the field and choose Cancel Override.

Data You Cannot Change

Do *not* edit the following types of data on the 941 form (or on any payroll tax form for that matter):

- Federal Employer Identification Number (EIN)
- Filing period (if you're trying to change the filing period, start the process again and select the appropriate date range)
- Totals (these are calculated by QuickBooks; if a total is wrong, edit the erroneous number and QuickBooks will recalculate the total)

Checking for Errors

Before you finalize the contents of Form 941/943, click the Check For Errors button. QuickBooks examines the content and displays any errors in the Errors box that opens at the top of the form. If there aren't any problems, the Errors box reports this.

Click the error to move automatically to the field that's causing the problem, and correct the information:

- If the problem is in a field you filled out, correct the data and press TAB.
- If the problem is in a field that was prefilled, but you changed the content by overriding the data, right-click the field and select Cancel Override.

When you press TAB to replace the data in the field, the error listing should disappear from the Errors box. If it doesn't, you have to do some homework to figure out what's wrong with the data in the affected field and then correct it.

Close the Errors box by clicking the Close Errors button.

Saving and Re-opening an Unfinished Form

If you get interrupted or confused while you're preparing your 941, 943, or 940 form, you can save the form with the data you already filled in, so you don't have to start from scratch when you resume your work. Click Save and Close to save the form with its current contents. To return to work on the saved form, go through the steps enumerated earlier in this section to select the form and its date range. QuickBooks asks if you want to use the saved draft.

If you open a saved draft, QuickBooks does not examine your files and refresh the data, so if you made changes to payroll data, you have to start a new form instead of opening a saved draft. Changes could include an additional paycheck being issued within the date range for some reason, or a payment you made to the bank or IRS as a remittance deposit for this report period.

Printing Form 941/943

You can print the form from QuickBooks and send it to the IRS if you use these printing criteria:

- The form must be printed with black ink on white or cream paper.
- The paper must be 8"x11" or 8.5"x11".
- The paper must be 18-lb. weight or heavier.

The printed report doesn't look exactly like the blank form you received, but it's close. More importantly, it's perfectly acceptable to the government. Print two copies: one to mail and one for your files.

 NOTE: You could also use the information in the printed report to fill in the blank 941/943 form you receive if you don't want to send the QuickBooks printout. Save the printed report as your file copy.

If you're signed up for e-payments you can e-file your 941/943. Save the printed report as your file copy.

NOTE: If you subscribe to an Enhanced Payroll service, you can archive a copy of the form as a PDF file by clicking the Save As PDF button on the form. This is handy for people who believe that using computers creates a paperless environment and therefore use the hard drive as a file cabinet. This works if those people are religious about backing up every day to an external drive.

Preparing Annual Returns

All taxing authorities want annual returns. The feds, state, and local folks need reports in the form of coupons or longer forms. Some of them want money; some just want reports because the remittances were made earlier in the year. You can get all the information you need from QuickBooks; all the standard QuickBooks payroll reports work just fine, as long as you remember to set the Dates field to the entire year.

Preparing State and Local Annual Returns

The state and local taxing authorities usually send you a form that asks for a reconciliation for the year. You may have to present quarterly totals as you fill out the form, which you can accomplish by changing the date range in the QuickBooks payroll reports. For example, if your state returns require totals for each quarter, run payroll reports for Jan 1 through March 31, followed by April 1 through June 30, and so on.

Finish your State Unemployment annual report or 4th Quarter report as soon as possible, because the payments you make to the state are relevant to the Federal Unemployment report (Form 940). In many states, the year-end or 4th Quarter report doesn't require a check because there's a limit to the wages that are eligible for applying the unemployment contribution rate, and it's common to meet that limit fairly early in the year.

Preparing the 940 Form

The 940 form (FUTA) is filed annually; there are no quarterly forms to file. To create your Form 940, choose Employees | Payroll Tax Forms & W-2s | Process Payroll Forms from the QuickBooks menu bar. Select Federal Form, then select 940 and fill in the year.

The Payroll Tax Form window (it's the first window of a wizard) opens with the Form 940 Interview. The top section of the interview window asks about your state and federal unemployment payments. Your answers determine whether you can use Form 940EZ.

Below that section are a series of questions aimed at determining whether any of your payroll expenses covered exempt payment types. Exempt payments are wages you paid that are exempt from FUTA taxes. QuickBooks checks your payroll items to track several categories of exempt payments, and if you've used these payroll items QuickBooks fills in the amounts. If you had any exempt payments that are not in the payroll items that QuickBooks automatically checks, select them from the drop-down lists, and fill in the amount. The drop-down list is long and can be complicated. Check the IRS rules for preparing Form 940, or check with your accountant.

Click Next to see the form itself. Fill out any fields that aren't automatically prefilled by QuickBooks from your payroll records. Continue to click Next and follow the instructions that appear on the screen.

Preparing the 944 Form

If you were notified by the IRS that you should file Form 944 instead of Form 941, follow the instructions in the previous sections to open the federal form list and select Form 944. You can remit your liabilities when you send the form, or, if you wish, you can make deposits against your 944 liability by using the deposit coupon (8109), filling in the circle for Form 944, and taking the check to the bank.

You cannot use Form 944, even if you qualify financially, unless you've been notified by the IRS that you are a Form 944 filer. This form is shorter than Form 941, has no additional schedules, and has an annual filing frequency, all of which combine to make this a desirable filing method. If you think you qualify financially, but you didn't receive a notification to use Form 944, you can contact the IRS to request a notification at 800-829-0115.

 C A U T I O N : If the IRS notified you to file Form 944, use it even if your payroll liabilities exceed the Form 944 threshold. The IRS will notice and will switch you back to Form 941/943. You cannot make the decision on your own.

Printing W-2 Forms

You must print W-2 forms for your employees, the government agencies, and your own files. You start by selecting the form and the employees, and then move to the process of creating and printing the forms.

Follow these steps to produce W-2 forms:

1. Choose Employees | Payroll Tax Forms & W-2s | Process Payroll Forms to open the Select Form Type dialog.
2. Select Federal Form and click OK (if you subscribe to an Enhanced Payroll service, state forms are also listed).
3. In the next dialog, make sure the filing period year is correct, select Annual Form W-2/W-3, and then click OK.

Select Payroll Form

Choose a form
Choose the form you want to use: Auto-Fill Contact Info...

Form   Annual Form 940/Sch. A - Employer's Annual Federal Unemployment (FUTA) Tax Ret...
       Quarterly Form 941/Sch. B - Employer's Quarterly Federal Tax Return
       Annual Form 943/943A - Employer's Annual Federal Tax Return for Agricultural Empl...
       Annual Form 944/945A - Employer's Annual Federal Tax Return
       Annual Form W-2/W-3 - Wage and Tax Statement/Transmittal

Process W-2s for: ⦿ All Employees (5 Employees)   Which option should I choose?
                  ◯ Employee's Last Name - From: [▼] To: [▼]

Select Filing Period
       Year [2009]

[OK]   [Cancel]   [Help]

The Select Employees For Form W-2/W-3 window opens, listing all your employees (see Figure 18-5). By default all employees are selected, and the current status of the W-2 printing process is noted.

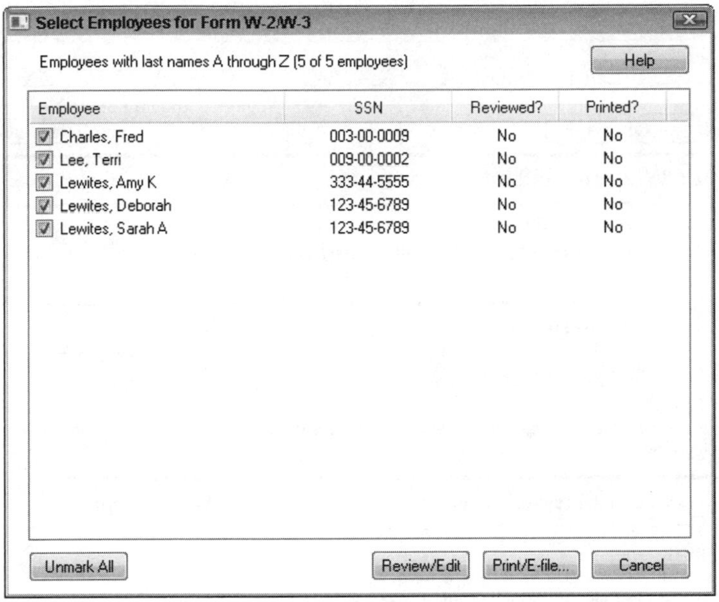

FIGURE 18-5 When you begin, none of the W-2s have been reviewed or printed.

Click Review/Edit to display the Payroll Tax Form window, which explains the steps you'll go through as you step through the wizard (see Figure 18-6). Click Next to move through the wizard.

Each employee's W-2 form is presented on the screen. If there is nonfinancial data missing (such as an address or ZIP code), you must fill it in. If prefilled information is incorrect, right-click the appropriate field and select Override. Enter the correct information, and press TAB to put that information into the field.

NOTE: Changes you make to nonfinancial information are not written back to the employee record. You must make the same changes there.

Because the financial information is prefilled from your payroll records, there should be no reason to make changes to those fields.

Click Check For Errors to see if anything is amiss on any employee's form. If errors appear in the Errors box at the top of the form, click the error's listing and QuickBooks automatically takes you to the appropriate field to correct the information.

When everything is correct, load your W-2 forms in the printer and click Submit Form to open the Print Form dialog. The Print W-2s window opens so you can choose a printer and print the forms. Click OK and click Print.

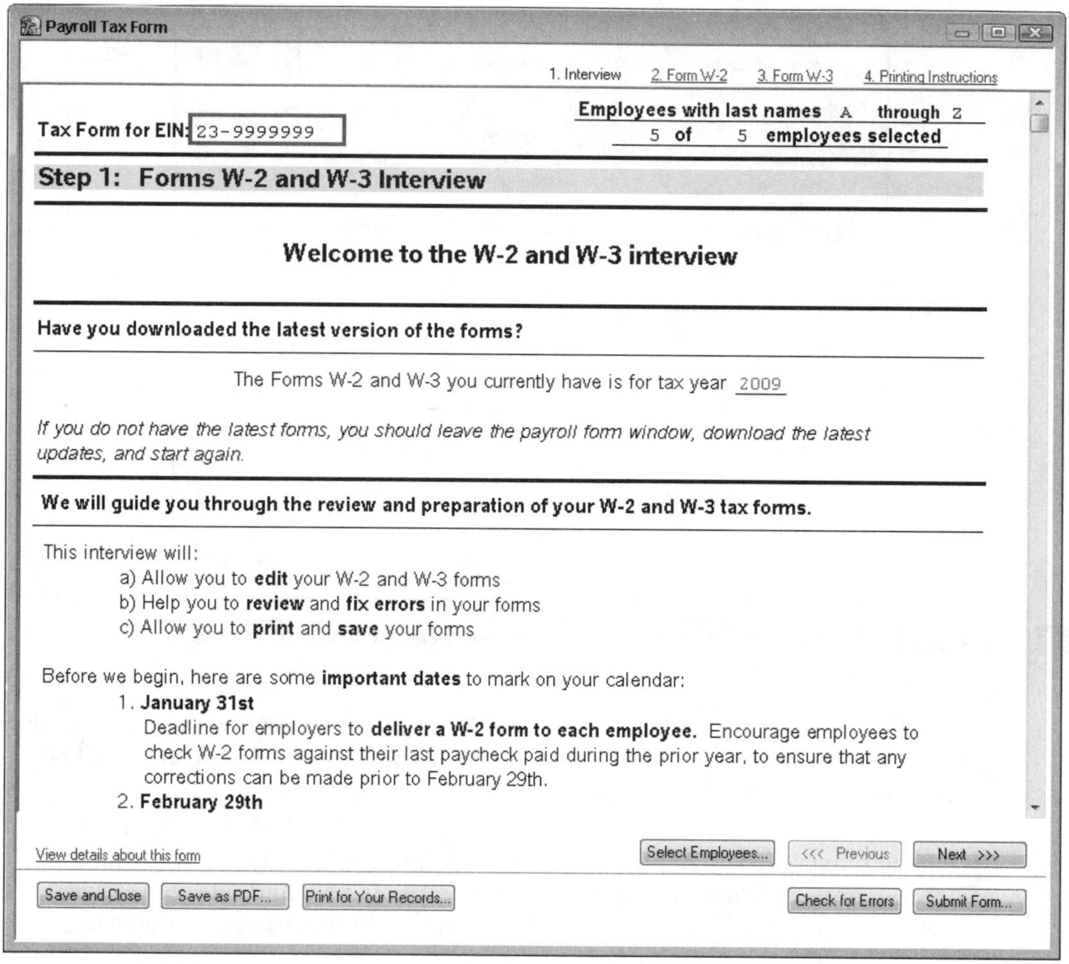

FIGURE 18-6 The wizard takes you through an interview to produce your W-2/W-3 forms.

You must also print the W-3 form, which is a summary of your W-2 forms. It must be in the package you send to the IRS when you transmit the W-2 forms.

NOTE: The IRS requires e-filing of W-2/W-3 forms if you have 250 or more employees, which is not common in small businesses. However, some states are now requiring e-filing for a much smaller number of employees. Check with your state's revenue department to determine the number of employees that kick off the e-filing requirement.

All these payroll reports are time consuming, but you have no choice: these tasks are legally necessary. At least it's easier because QuickBooks keeps the records and does the math.

Tax Form Worksheets in Excel

If QuickBooks isn't preparing your payroll forms (either because you're doing payroll manually or you subscribed to the QuickBooks Basic Payroll service) you can prepare your forms manually with the use of Excel worksheets that are available from QuickBooks.

To access the worksheets, choose Reports | Employees & Payroll | Tax Form Worksheets In Excel. Because this Excel file has macros (programming code to accomplish the required tasks), you might have to tell Excel to let the macros run (depending on how you've configured Excel's security options):

- In Excel 2003 and earlier, if you see a dialog warning you that the file contains macros, click Enable Macros to open the file with macros enabled. Depending on your version of Excel, you may have to choose Always Trust Macros From This Source before the Enable Macros button becomes available.
- In Excel 2007, the file opens without a warning dialog. However, if you haven't changed the default Excel setting which disables all macros, a Security Warning message bar appears under the toolbar to tell you that macros have been disabled. Click Options and enable macros for this worksheet.

When the QuickBooks Tax Worksheets dialog appears, select the form and date range you need.

Setting Report Options

Click Options/Settings on the QuickBooks Tax Worksheets dialog to configure the report using the guidelines discussed in the following sections.

Configuring Worksheet Headers

By default, the option to update headers is selected. This means that the header of a printout of the worksheet contains the company name and address information, as well as the date range of the report (the date range you selected in the previous dialog). If you are planning to print the report, it's important to know the date range, so make sure this option is selected.

Configuring the Level of Detail

By default, the option Hide Detailed Data Returned From QuickBooks is selected, which means that the workbook displays only the information connected to the report you selected. For example, Figure 18-7 displays a workbook with a single worksheet (the 941 report).

If you deselect the option to hide the detail, you must choose the detail level you want to see, as explained next.

Return Full Transaction Detail From QuickBooks— For Trouble-Shooting

If you select this option, QuickBooks adds a second worksheet named Data to the workbook. This worksheet contains all detailed information about the employees (every field on the employee record), the payroll items, and the job costing links (if you use timesheets to do job costing for payroll).

This is an enormous amount of information and should be used only if you need to troubleshoot the numbers you saw when you produced a report without detailed data. In fact, most of the information is available through other QuickBooks reports, such as the detail reports available in the Employees & Payroll section of

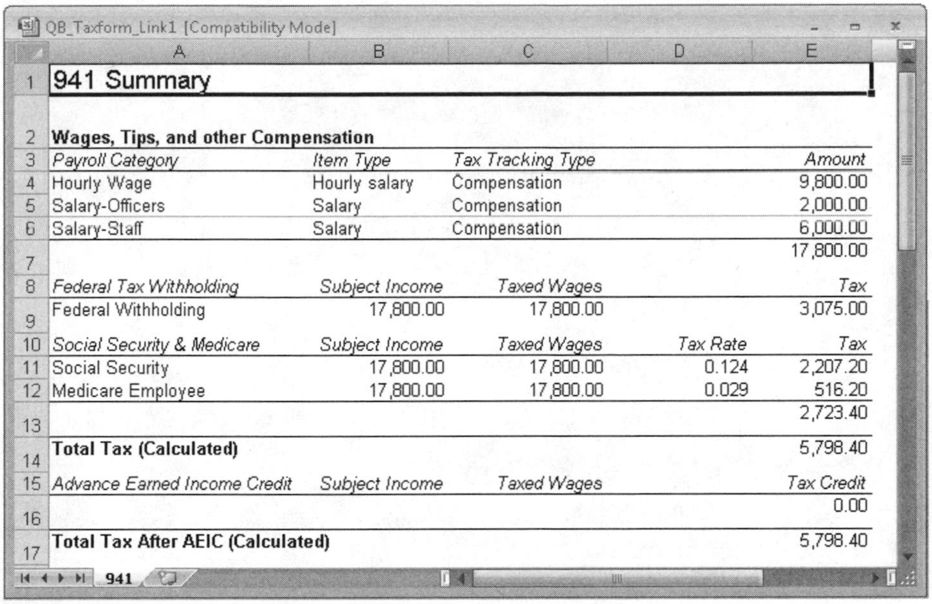

	A	B	C	D	E
1	941 Summary				
2	**Wages, Tips, and other Compensation**				
3	*Payroll Category*	*Item Type*	*Tax Tracking Type*		*Amount*
4	Hourly Wage	Hourly salary	Compensation		9,800.00
5	Salary-Officers	Salary	Compensation		2,000.00
6	Salary-Staff	Salary	Compensation		6,000.00
7					17,800.00
8	*Federal Tax Withholding*	*Subject Income*	*Taxed Wages*		*Tax*
9	Federal Withholding	17,800.00	17,800.00		3,075.00
10	*Social Security & Medicare*	*Subject Income*	*Taxed Wages*	*Tax Rate*	*Tax*
11	Social Security	17,800.00	17,800.00	0.124	2,207.20
12	Medicare Employee	17,800.00	17,800.00	0.029	516.20
13					2,723.40
14	**Total Tax (Calculated)**				5,798.40
15	*Advance Earned Income Credit*	*Subject Income*	*Taxed Wages*		*Tax Credit*
16					0.00
17	**Total Tax After AEIC (Calculated)**				5,798.40

FIGURE 18-7 Hide detailed data to produce only the report.

the Reports menu. Details on the employee records are available by customizing the Employee Contact List report available in the List section of the Reports menu (add additional columns to the report to display detailed information).

Minimize Detail From QuickBooks—For Speed In Excel And Large QB Files

If you select this option, QuickBooks adds a second worksheet named Data to the workbook. This worksheet contains detailed information about the paychecks involved in the date range you selected.

The detail data includes the details of payroll items and the amount of each payroll item in each individual paycheck.

Journal Entries

In *this chapter:*

- The QuickBooks journal entry window

- Make adjustments to the general ledger

- Depreciate fixed assets

- Journalize outside payroll services

- Allocate overhead to classes

As you work in QuickBooks, the amounts involved in the financial transactions you complete are transferred to your general ledger. In addition to transaction data, numbers can be placed into the general ledger directly. This action is called a *journal entry*.

Journal entries should be used with a specific purpose, and usually that purpose is to enter financial data that cannot be added to an account via a standard transaction.

> **NOTE:** The standard jargon for this transaction type is *journal entry*, usually abbreviated JE. However, QuickBooks refers to the transaction as *general journal entry* and uses GJE as the abbreviation. I use JE out of many years of habit.

The QuickBooks Journal Entry Window

For journal entries, QuickBooks provides the Make General Journal Entries window, seen in Figure 19-1. The format of the transaction window matches the standard approach to viewing the general ledger: columns for account numbers, debit amounts, and credit amounts (the accounting jargon for this format is *T-Account* format). In addition, QuickBooks provides columns you can use to link the data you enter to customers and classes and also enter a memo.

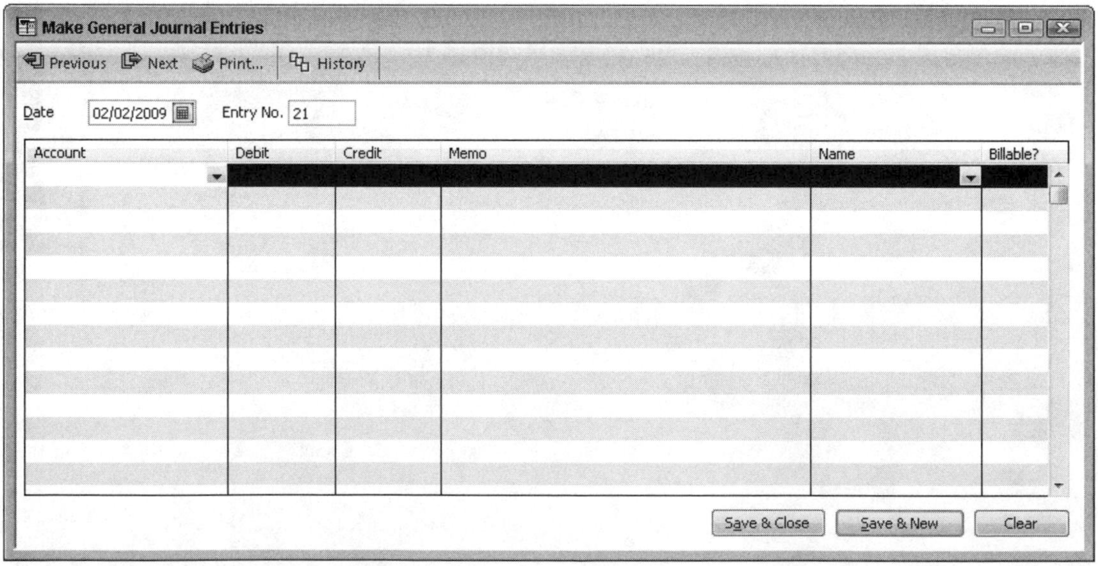

FIGURE 19-1 The QuickBooks GJE window has more columns than the standard T-Account format, so you can track additional information.

To create a journal entry, follow these steps:

1. Choose Company | Make General Journal Entries. QuickBooks displays a message telling you that automatic numbers are now assigned to journal entries. (You can select the option Do Not Display This Message In The Future before you click OK.) You can enable or disable the automatic numbering feature in the Accounting category of the Preferences dialog.
2. In the Account column, select the account you need.
3. Move to the Debit or Credit column (depending on the data you're entering) and enter the amount for this account.
4. Optionally, enter the appropriate data in the other columns.
5. Repeat for all the accounts in the journal entry.

As you enter each amount, QuickBooks presents the offsetting total in the next line. For example, if the line items you've entered so far have a higher total for the credit side than the debit side, the next entry presents the balancing offset (see Figure 19-2).

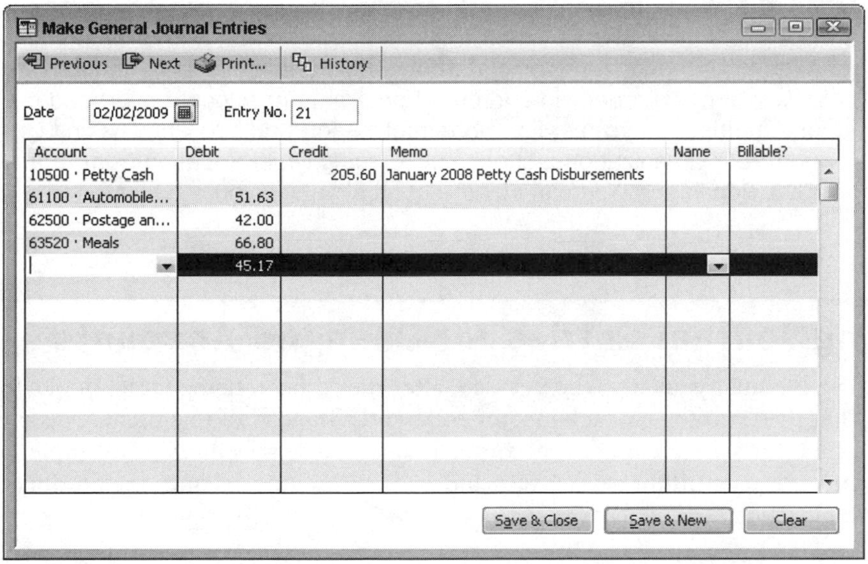

FIGURE 19-2 QuickBooks keeps the running offset figure available so you don't have to enter an amount for the last entry.

Here are the guidelines for using the columns QuickBooks adds to a traditional journal entry window:

- Use the Memo column to write a comment about the reason for the journal entry. The memo text appears in the entry of the account's register and on reports, so you should enter the text on every line of the entry in order to see the explanation no matter which account register you're viewing.
- Use the Name column to assign a customer, vendor, employee, or other name to the amount on this line of the entry, if you're linking the entry to a name. If the account you're posting to is an A/R or A/P account, an entry in the Name column is required.
- The Billable column indicates whether the amount is billable to the name in the Name column, if you are using an expense account and you enter a customer name in the Name column.
- If you are using the Classes feature, a Class column is present, and you can link the entry to a class. (See Chapter 5 for information about setting up classes.)

NOTE: If you're running QuickBooks in a nonprofit organization, your journal entries are almost always linked to classes (programs) and often also linked to jobs (grants). In fact, assigning journal entry transaction lines to classes is the best way to move money in and out of programs or allocate overhead expenses among multiple programs. For more information and tips about using QuickBooks for nonprofit organizations, check out *Running QuickBooks in Nonprofits* from CPA911 Publishing. You can buy the book at your favorite bookstore.

Creating Journal Entries for Changed Accounts

I've had many clients who decided, after they'd been using QuickBooks for a while, that they wanted to track income differently. Instead of one income account, they opted for separate income accounts that are more specific. For example, having an income account for service fees and another income account for products sold makes business analysis easier.

This transaction is quite simple. Create the new account and then take the appropriate amount of funds out of the original account and put it into the new account. Revenue is a credit-side item, so that means

- Debit the original account for the amount that belongs in the new account.
- Credit the new account for that same amount.

Then, of course, you'll have to go to the Item List and change the necessary items to reflect the new income account so you don't have to keep making journal entries.

The same decision is frequently made about expenses, as business owners decide to split heretofore comprehensive accounts. Perhaps you feel your insurance accounts should be separated for car insurance, equipment insurance, building insurance, malpractice insurance, and so on.

For expense accounts, the journal entry goes to the opposite side of the ledger because expenses are a debit-side item, so do the following:

- Credit the original expense account for the amount you're taking out of it and putting into the new account(s).
- Debit the new account(s) for the appropriate amount(s).

This logic also applies to fixed asset accounts. For example, you may have a fixed asset account named Vehicles that you want to divide to track the truck separately from the car (especially if they were purchased in different years). This means you can also separate out any accumulated depreciation so it's assigned to the correct asset. (See the following section to learn about JEs for depreciation.)

Creating Journal Entries for Depreciation

Depreciation is a way to track the current value of a fixed asset that loses value as it ages. The basis of an asset's depreciation from an accounting point of view is determined by a complicated set of rules, including IRS rules, and the rules change frequently.

Depreciation is a journal entry activity. Most small businesses enter the depreciation of their assets at the end of the year, but some companies perform depreciation tasks monthly or quarterly.

Depreciation is a special journal entry because the accounts involved are very restricted—this is not a free choice where you can use whichever account strikes your fancy. The account that is being depreciated must be a fixed asset. The offset entry is to an account named Depreciation Expense (or Depreciation), and it is in the expense section of your chart of accounts.

Creating Accounts for Tracking Depreciation

I'm assuming that you've created your fixed-asset account and that the assets you've purchased have been posted there. You might have multiple fixed-asset accounts if you want to track different types of fixed assets separately. (For instance, my chart of accounts has three fixed-asset account sections: Equipment, Furn & Fixtures, and Vehicles.)

When it comes to accounting procedures that have a direct bearing on my taxes and for which I might need information at a glance (especially if I'm called on to explain to the IRS or my bank's lending officer what I did and why I did it that way), I like to be very explicit in the way I work. Therefore, for every fixed-asset account in my chart of accounts, I have families of accounts for depreciation. I create a parent (account) and children (subaccounts) for each type of fixed asset. For example, the fixed-asset section of a chart of accounts I create would look like this:

Parent Accounts	Subaccounts
Equipment Assets	
	Equipment Purchases
	AccumDepr-Equipment
Furn & Fixtures Assets	
	Furn & Fixtures Purchases
	AccumDepr-Furn & Fixtures
Vehicle Assets	
	Vehicle Purchases
	AccumDepr-Vehicles

If you use numbers for your chart of accounts, create a numbering system that makes sense for this setup. For example, if Equipment is 16000, the subaccounts start with 16010; Furn & Fixtures starts with 16100, and the subaccounts start with 16110; Vehicle starts with 16200, and so on.

I post asset purchases to the subaccount I create for purchases, and I make my journal entry for depreciation in the AccumDepr subaccount. I never use the parent accounts. There are several reasons for this:

- Both the asset subaccount and the AccumDepr subaccount are "pure." I can look at either one to see a running total instead of a calculated net total.
- Tracing the year-to-year depreciation is easy. I just open the AccumDepr subaccount register—each line represents a year.
- It's easier and quicker to open the AccumDepr subaccount if I'm asked about the depreciation total (handy if you sell the asset and have to add back the depreciation).
- The net value of my fixed assets is correct. A Balance Sheet report shows me the details in the subaccounts and automatically displays the total of the subaccounts in the parent account.

You can further refine this paradigm by creating subaccounts for specific fixed assets. For instance, you may want to create a subaccount for each vehicle asset (or one that covers all cars and another that manages all trucks) and its accompanying accumulated depreciation. If your equipment falls under a variety of depreciation rules (for example, manufacturing equipment versus computer equipment), you may want to have a set of subaccounts for each type.

If you're really obsessive, you can create a different subaccount for each year of depreciation; for instance, under your AccumDepr-Vehicle subaccount, you could have Vehicle-Depr 2006, Vehicle-Depr 2007, Vehicle-Depr 2008, and so on. Then your balance sheet shows a complete year-by-year depreciation schedule instead of accumulated depreciation—and the math still works properly. However, after a number of years, you'll have destroyed an entire forest with all the paper it takes to print your balance sheet.

Creating a Depreciation Entry

To depreciate fixed assets, you must have a depreciation offset account in the Expense section of your chart of accounts. Once that account exists, open the Make General Journal Entries window and choose the first asset depreciation subaccount (for example, the AccumDepr account under the fixed asset "Equipment"). Enter the depreciation amount in the Credit column.

Choose the next asset depreciation subaccount and enter its depreciation amount in the Credit column. (QuickBooks automatically puts the offsetting amount in the Debit column, but just keep moving to the Credit column as you work.) Continue until all your depreciation figures are entered in the Credit column.

Choose the Depreciation Expense account. The total amount of the credits you've entered is automatically placed in the Debit column. Click Save & Close.

For example, here's a typical journal entry for depreciation. Notice the colon in the account names for the asset accounts—that's the QuickBooks indication of a subaccount.

Account	Debit	Credit
Equipment:AccumDepr-Equip		5,000.00
Furn & Fix:AccumDepr-Furn & Fix		700.00
LeaseholdImprov:AccumDepr-LeasImprov		1000.00
Depreciation Expense	6,700.00	

Journalizing Outside Payroll Services

If you have an outside payroll service, you have to tell QuickBooks about the payroll transactions that took place. You get a report from the service, so all the numbers are available. It's just a matter of entering them.

It's common for businesses to perform this task via a journal entry. Like all other journal entries, this one is just a matter of entering debits and credits. There are three parts to recording payroll:

- Transferring money to the payroll account
- Entering the payroll figures
- Entering the employer expense figures

Transferring Money to the Payroll Account

You should have a separate bank account for payroll if you have an outside payroll service—actually, a separate payroll account is a good idea even if you do your own payroll. Outside payroll services reach into your checking account; in fact, they have checks, and you shouldn't give away checks for your regular operating account.

Another reason for a separate payroll account even if you do your own payroll is the discipline involved in holding on to your employee withholdings until you pass them along to insurance companies, other vendors, and the government—*especially* the government. The money you withhold and leave in your bank account until you're ready to transmit it to the government is not your money. You cannot spend it. It doesn't matter if you need the money to save your business from total bankruptcy—you cannot spend the money. People have done that and gotten into serious trouble, including going to jail. Keeping all the money associated with payroll in a separate bank account makes it more difficult to "inadvertently" use that money to run your business.

To transfer the money you need for this payroll, choose Banking | Transfer Funds. Then, transfer the money from your regular operating account to your payroll account. Be sure to transfer enough money for the gross payroll plus the employer payroll expenses, which include the following:

- Employer-matching contributions to FICA and Medicare
- Employer-matching contributions to pension plans
- Employer-matching contributions to benefits
- Employer state unemployment assessments
- Employer FUTA
- Any other government or benefit payments paid by the employer

Even though some of these aren't transmitted every payday, you should transfer the amounts at that time anyway. Then, when it's time to pay them, the correct amount of money will have accumulated in the payroll account.

Recording the Payroll

The *payroll run* (jargon for "printing the paychecks") produces a fairly complicated set of debits and credits. Many businesses record a journal entry for the run, then a separate journal entry for the employer expenses when they're transmitted.

- If your payroll service takes care of remitting payroll liabilities, you can journalize those payments.
- If your payroll service doesn't remit your liabilities, when you create those checks your check-writing activity will record the payments, so you don't need a journal entry.

Table 19-1 shows a typical template for recording the payroll run as a journal entry. It's possible that you don't have all the expenses shown in this table (for instance, not all states have employee unemployment assessments). And you may have additional withholding categories such as union dues, garnishments against wages, and so on. Be sure you've created a liability account in your chart of accounts for each withholding category you need, and a vendor for each transmittal check.

Account	Debit	Credit
Salaries and Wages (expense)	Gross Payroll	
FWT (liability)		Total Federal Withheld
FICA (liability)		Total FICA Withheld
Medicare (liability)		Total Medicare Withheld
State Income Tax (liability)		Total State Tax Withheld
Local Income Tax (liability)		Total Local Tax Withheld
State SDI (liability)		Total State SDI Withheld
State SUI (liability)		Total State SUI Withheld
Benefits Contrib. (liability)		Total Benefits Withheld
401(k) Contrib. (liability)		Total 401(k) Withheld
Other Deductions (liability)		Total Other Deductions Withheld
Payroll Bank Account (asset)		Total of Net Payroll

TABLE 19-1 Typical Journal Entry to Record Payroll by an Outside Service

Recording Liabilities

You need to journalize the employer remittances of payroll liabilities if your payroll service is taking care of them for you (if you do it yourself, just write the checks from the payroll account and each item will post to the general ledger). Table 19-2 is a sample journal entry for recording payroll remittances.

Account	Debit	Credit
Federal Payroll Expenses (expense)	Employer FICA and Medicare	
Federal Withholdings (liability)	All federal withholding	
State and Local Withholdings (liability)	All local withholding	
SUTA (expense)	Employer SUTA	
FUTA (expense)	Employer FUTA	
Employer Contributions (expense)	All employer benefit, pension, etc.	
Payroll Bank Account (asset)		Total of checks written

TABLE 19-2   Typical Journal Entry for Employer-side Transactions

The entry involving the transmittal of withholdings is posted to the same account you used when you withheld the amounts. In effect, you "wash" the liability accounts; you're not really spending money, you're remitting money you've withheld from employees.

You can have as many individual employer expense accounts as you think you need, or you can post all the employer expenses to one account named "payroll expenses."

NOTE: Don't have your payroll service take their fee from the payroll account. Instead, write them a check from your operating account. The fee for the service is not a payroll expense; it's an operating expense. If the service insists on taking the money from the payroll account, include the amount in your JE and post it to the appropriate operating expense.

Creating a Boilerplate Payroll JE

You can save a lot of time and effort by creating a template for the payroll journal entries. Open a Make General Journal Entries window and fill out the Account column only. Enter the first account, then press the down arrow and enter the next account, and keep going until all accounts are listed.

Press CTRL-M to open the Memorize Transaction dialog. Name the memorized transaction Payroll (or something similar), and select the option Don't Remind Me (the reports from the payroll company are your reminder).

Close the Make General Journal Entries window. QuickBooks displays a message asking if you want to save the transaction you just created. Click No (you don't have to save a GJE to memorize it, isn't that handy?). Do the same thing for the boilerplate journal entry you create to record employer remittances.

Using the Boilerplate JE to Enter Payroll Data

When you're ready to record payroll, open the memorized transaction by pressing CTRL-T to open the Memorized Transaction List. Double-click your payroll boilerplate JE, enter the appropriate date, and then enter the data.

Click Save & New if you have to create another JE for the employer expenses; otherwise click Save & Close.

Reconciling the Payroll Account

The problem with journal entries for payroll is that when the bank statement comes for the payroll account, reconciling it is a bit different. You don't have a record of the check numbers and payees. When you open the payroll account in the Reconcile window, you see the journal entry totals instead of the individual checks.

Reconciling Outside QuickBooks

You have the report from the payroll service, and it lists each check number. You can therefore reconcile the account outside of the QuickBooks Reconcile window, using a manual system or using your spreadsheet software.

 TIP: See if your payroll service can send you a file containing check#/payee/ amount information that can be opened in a spreadsheet. A tab-delimited file is the best file type.

Entering Fake Payroll Checks in QuickBooks

If you want to perform the reconciliation in QuickBooks, you can enter the checks and post them back to the payroll account. (The journal entry took care of all the real postings.) You have a little bit of setup to do, and then you can perform this task every payday.

Create a name in the Other Names list, and name the new entity Payroll. You can use this name for every check (and put the employee's name in the memo field).

Alternatively, you can create a name for each employee in the Other Names list, using initials, last name only, or some other name that isn't the same as the original employee name as it exists in your Employee List.

Get the report from the payroll service and open the Payroll account register. Then enter the payroll checks using these guidelines:

- The date is the date of the payroll check.
- The number is the first check number on the payroll service report.
- The payee is Payroll (unless you've entered all your employee names as Other Names, in which case enter the appropriate name, but then you have to match the right check number, which is something I'm too lazy to do).
- The amount is the net paycheck (not the gross payroll amount).
- The account is the same bank account you're currently working in.

When you enter the account data, QuickBooks flashes a message warning you that you're posting the payment to the source account. Click OK (because that's exactly what you want to do) and click the check box that tells QuickBooks to omit this warning in the future.

You can also enter the checks the payroll service wrote to transmit your withholdings or pay your taxes. As long as each entry you make was entered into the journal entry, you can post everything back to the payroll account. You're "washing" every transaction, not changing the balance of the account. Then, when you want to reconcile the payroll account, the individual checks are in the Reconcile window. The fact is, this procedure is quite easy and fast, and you have to do it only on payday (or once a month if you want to wait until the bank statement comes in).

Allocating Overhead to Classes

If you're tracking locations, departments, or divisions by class, many of the transactions you create aren't directly connected to a particular class. This is particularly true of general operating expenses that are difficult to divide at the time you create the transaction. Those transactions are usually linked to a class you created for this situation, such as a class named Admin or Overhead. Or, as often happens, the Class column may have been omitted altogether when you created the transaction.

At the end of a given period (month, quarter, or year), you should allocate overhead expenses to make your class P&L more accurate. There isn't any hard and fast rule to determine amount you apply to each class; that figure is based on your own knowledge of the way your divisions share these expenses.

Some businesses split overhead expenses equally among the classes, other businesses use a formula based on the percentage of income the class supplied to the company (the theory being that a class that contributed 70 percent of the income probably used 70 percent of the expenses).

To allocate expenses to classes, you remove the total expense from the account and then put the total expense back into the account in multiple JE lines, each of which is linked to a class. For example, Figure 19-3 shows how you'd allocate an expense that was originally posted to the class named Admin (the class used to track general expenses and overhead).

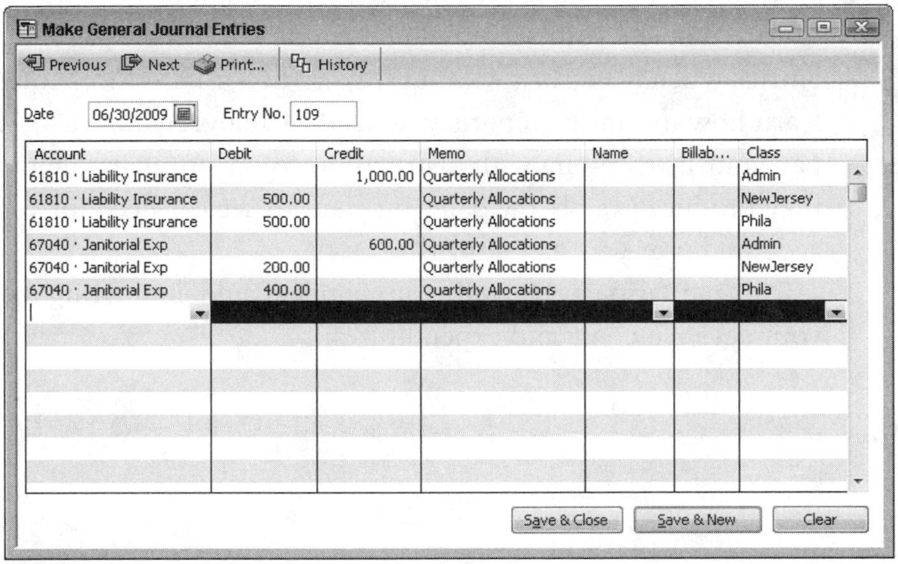

FIGURE 19-3 Divide overhead among classes to produce more accurate P&L by Class reports.

If the original transaction was not posted to a class, leave the Class column blank in the JE line that credits the expense.

Financial Planning and Reporting

Part Three of this book covers all the steps you need to take to track your finances. You'll learn about the Accountant's Copy, which is a feature that lets your accountant examine your books, and adjust entries when necessary, without leaving his or her office. You'll also learn how to run the reports you need to analyze your business and pay your taxes, along with instructions for customizing reports so they produce exactly the data you want to see (or need for your accountant or your tax return).

This part also covers setting up budgets, and comparing them to your actual income and expenditures.

Accountant's Copy

In *this chapter:*

- Understand the accountant's copy

- Create an accountant's copy

- Merge the accountant's changes into your file

Chapter 20

Many accountants support QuickBooks directly, which means they understand the software and know how to use it. In fact, they have a copy of QuickBooks on their own computer systems.

At various times during the year, your accountant might want to look at your books. There might be quarterly reports and adjustments, a physical inventory that resulted in serious changes in your Balance Sheet, expenses that should be posted to different accounts, or any of a hundred other reasons to examine your transactions. Almost definitely this will occur at the end-of-year process you have to go through in order to close your books for the year.

This could result in your accountant showing up and sitting in front of your computer, making the necessary changes (frequently journal entries), moving this, reversing that, and generally making sense out of your daily transaction postings. By "making sense," I mean putting transaction postings into categories that fit your tax reporting needs.

While your accountant is using the software, you can't get much accomplished. You could say, "Excuse me, could you move? I have to enter an invoice." But remember, you're paying for the accountant's time.

If your accountant doesn't want to visit, he or she may request printouts of various reports, then write notes on those printouts: "Move this, split that, credit this number here, debit that number there." Or you might receive a spreadsheet-like printout with a complicated journal entry, which means you have to stop entering your day-to-day transactions to make all those changes.

Some accountants ask for a copy of the company file, a backup of your company file (which they restore), or a portable company file. While the accountant has the file and is tweaking transactions or making journal entries, you can't do any work. If you continue to work, the transactions you enter won't be in the company file you restore when your accountant returns it to you, because it overwrites the company file you'd continued to use.

Understanding the Accountant's Copy

QuickBooks has a better solution. Give your accountant a specially designed copy of your company file. Let your accountant do the work back at his or her office, while you continue to work in your copy. When the file comes back to you, with the accountant's changes, QuickBooks can merge the changes in the accountant's copy into your copy of the company file, which means the work you do while the accountant is working isn't replaced by the work your accountant does.

When you create the accountant's copy, QuickBooks imposes restrictions on the type or extent of transactions you and your accountant can perform (to make sure you don't work at cross purposes). All of this is discussed in this chapter.

Creating an Accountant's Copy

QuickBooks provides two methods for delivering an accountant's copy to your accountant:

Send the File to Your Accountant You can save an accountant's copy on removable media (CD, DVD, or flash drive) and send or deliver it to your accountant. Most people can't e-mail the file because of the limits imposed by their ISP and/or their accountant's ISP.

Upload the File to a QuickBooks Secure Server You can upload an accountant's copy to a secure server provided by QuickBooks and have your accountant download the file (this is a free service). QuickBooks notifies the accountant of the existence of the file by e-mail and provides a link to the file in the e-mail message.

NOTE: Only the Admin user can create an accountant's copy, and the company file must be operating in Single-User mode to accomplish this task.

Saving the Accountant's Copy on Removable Media

To create an accountant's copy and save it on removable media, choose File | Accountant's Copy | Save File. In the Save Accountant's Copy dialog be sure the option labeled Accountant's Copy is selected.

Click Next to move to the window in which you set the dividing date for this accountant's copy (see the section "Choosing the Dividing Date" for more information about the significance of the dividing date).

Click Next to save the file. QuickBooks opens the Save Accountant's Copy dialog and creates a filename that incorporates your company filename as well as the date and time of the file's creation. That's an excellent filename and there's no reason to change it. By default QuickBooks saves the accountant's copy to your desktop, but you can change the location if you wish.

If you're sending the file on a flash drive, change the location by choosing the flash drive in the Save In field at the top of the dialog. If you're planning to send the file on a CD or DVD, save the file to your hard drive and then transfer the file to the CD/DVD. After you save the file, QuickBooks displays a message reminding you of the dividing date and also reminding you to send the file to your accountant.

If you've password-protected your QuickBooks data file, you must give your accountant the Admin password so your accountant can open the file.

Sending an Accountant's Copy to the QuickBooks Server

To create an accountant's copy that is uploaded to a secure server maintained by QuickBooks, from which your accountant can download the file, choose File | Accountant's Copy | Send To Accountant, which opens the Send Accountant's Copy dialog that explains the process.

Click Next to select the dividing date (covered in the next section, "Choosing the Dividing Date"). In the next window, enter your accountant's e-mail address (twice, to confirm the data), your name, and your e-mail address. If an e-mail address exists in the e-mail field of the Company Info dialog (in the Company menu) window, that address is automatically entered as your e-mail address, but you can change it.

In the next window (see Figure 20-1), enter a password for the upload/download of this file. This is not the Admin password your accountant needs to open the company file; it's a password required to download the file from the server. It must be a *strong password*, which means it contains at least seven characters, mixes letters and numbers, and at least one letter must be in a different case from the other letters (usually this means one letter is uppercase).

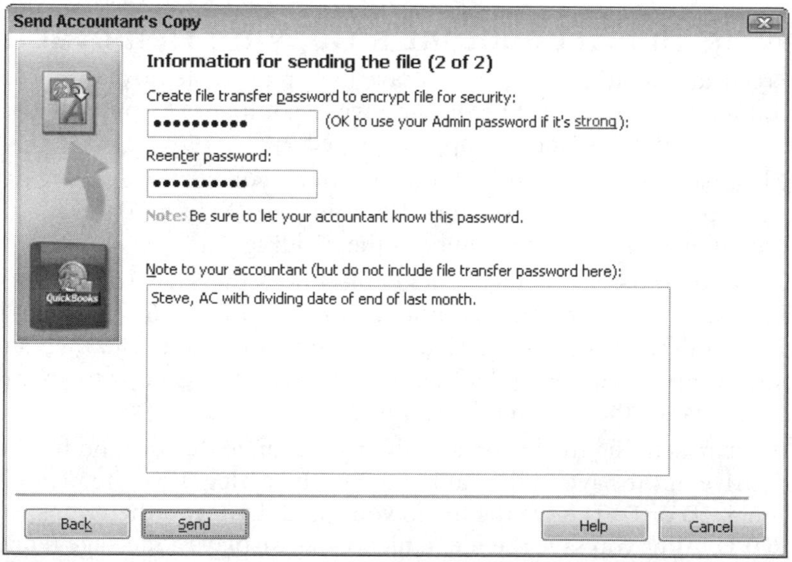

FIGURE 20-1 Secure the file's transfer over the Internet with a strong password.

If your Admin password is a strong password (because you enabled credit card security as explained in Chapter 3), then you can use the Admin password for the upload/download server access.

You can also enter a message for your accountant that will appear in the body of the e-mail message notifying your accountant that you've uploaded the file. E-mail text is not encrypted as it travels around the Internet, so don't use this message to give your accountant the password.

Click Send to upload the file to the server. QuickBooks displays a message telling you it must close all windows to create an accountant's copy; click OK to continue. When the accountant's copy has been created and uploaded, QuickBooks displays a success message.

QuickBooks sends e-mail to your accountant (see Figure 20-2) and to you (see Figure 20-3). (The text in both of the messages displayed in these figures has been edited to protect secure information.)

Accountant's Copy File Available

An Accountant's Copy Transfer File has been sent to you via the Intuit Accountant's Copy File Transfer secure server. To download this file, click here. (Just click "Save" in the box that comes up, not "Open". Go into QuickBooks to open the file.)

About this Accountant's Copy Transfer File:

File Name: WDIA (Acct Transfer Feb01,2009 05 46 PM).QBX

Sent by: Kathy.

Note:

Here's the file

Uploaded: 02-01-2009 05:48 PM

Expires: **02-15-2009**

What Next?

No automatic notification is sent to your client when you download the file. Please contact your client to confirm receipt of this file.

To start using this file, go into QuickBooks Accountant Edition. In the **File** menu, click on **Accountant's Copy** and then **Open and Convert Accountant's Copy Transfer File**. You will be asked for a file transfer password to decrypt this file. You will need to get that password from your client.

FIGURE 20-2 QuickBooks notifies your accountant that the file is available and explains what to do next.

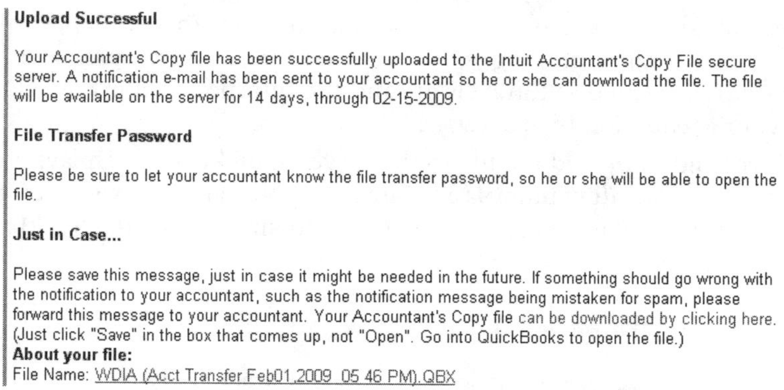

Upload Successful

Your Accountant's Copy file has been successfully uploaded to the Intuit Accountant's Copy File secure server. A notification e-mail has been sent to your accountant so he or she can download the file. The file will be available on the server for 14 days, through 02-15-2009.

File Transfer Password

Please be sure to let your accountant know the file transfer password, so he or she will be able to open the file.

Just in Case...

Please save this message, just in case it might be needed in the future. If something should go wrong with the notification to your accountant, such as the notification message being mistaken for spam, please forward this message to your accountant. Your Accountant's Copy file can be downloaded by clicking here. (Just click "Save" in the box that comes up, not "Open". Go into QuickBooks to open the file.)
About your file:
File Name: WDIA (Acct Transfer Feb01,2009_05 46 PM).QBX

FIGURE 20-3   QuickBooks sends you information about the file transfer.

Choosing the Dividing Date

The text in the Set The Dividing Date window (see Figure 20-4), explains that your accountant works on transactions on or before the dividing date, and you work on transactions that are dated after the dividing date. You and your accountant should discuss the date you select.

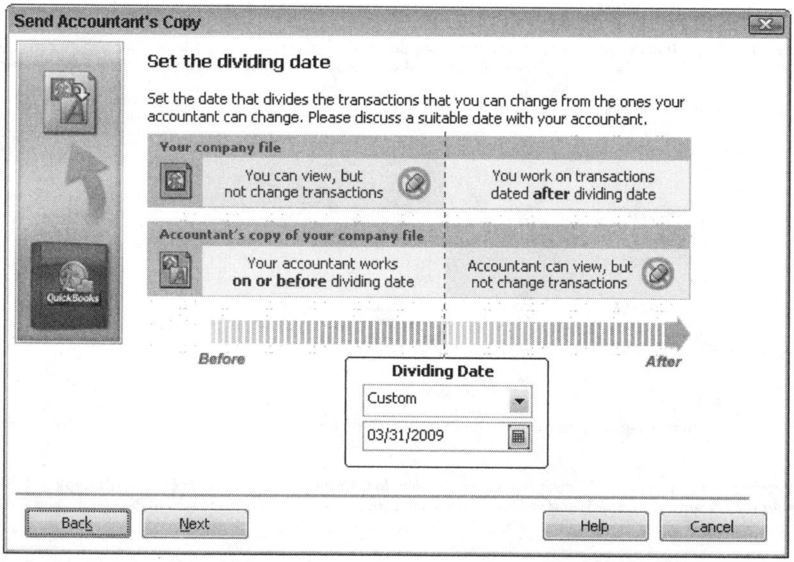

FIGURE 20-4   The dividing date establishes boundaries and limits for the type of work you and your accountant can perform.

The explanation on the wizard window is an overview—an oversimplified description of the dividing date and its impact on the work you can perform. To see (and download) a task-by-task table that explains what you can do and what your accountant can do while the accountant's copy exists, you can view or download a PDF file from the QuickBooks Tips section of www.cpa911.com.

The dividing date you select should be the period for which you need your accountant to examine your books and make needed changes, which may not be a year-end date.

Some people send an accountant's copy with a dividing date matching the date of a report they need for a special reason—such as an income statement and/or balance sheet the bank wants to see because of an existing or potential line of credit. Other users may need an "accountant-approved" detailed report of transactions for the company's partners or a nonprofit association's board (usually a month, quarter, or year-end date).

To give your accountant a period in which to insert changes such as adjusting journal entries or reversing journal entries, set the dividing date about two weeks after the end date you need. For example, if the report you need is as of the end of the last quarter, set the dividing date for two or three weeks after the last quarter end date.

Merging the Accountant's Changes into Your File

The file your accountant sends back is not a complete QuickBooks company file; it contains only the changes made by your accountant. The file is encrypted so it can only be imported into the company file you used to create it.

NOTE: The file is quite small and can easily be sent as an e-mail attachment. Because it's encrypted, transferring the file by e-mail is perfectly safe.

Use the following steps to open the file and import it into the original company file.

1. Be sure the company file from which you created the accountant's copy is open.
2. Choose File | Accountant's Copy | Import Accountant's Changes.
3. Navigate to the location where you saved the file your accountant sent and double-click the file listing; the file has the naming format *<CompanyName>* (Acct Changes).QBY.

4. The Incorporate Accountant's Changes window opens so you can preview the changes that will be merged into your company data file and read any notes your accountant wrote. (Before you import the changes you can save the report as a PDF file or print it).

5. Click Incorporate Accountant's Changes. QuickBooks walks you through the process of backing up your current file before importing the changes and then merges the changes into your company data file.

> **NOTE:** The printed report includes the accountant's notes, but the PDF file doesn't.

After the changes have been incorporated into your file, QuickBooks displays a window (that looks like the window displayed before you selected the option to incorporate the file, except the window indicates that the transactions are "incorporated" instead of "pending"). If any transactions failed to merge with your company file, a message appears to inform you of the failure.

The window has buttons you can click to save (as PDF) or print the information. It's a good idea to print this data so you know where to look in your file to see the changes.

Click Close (if you didn't save or print the import data, QuickBooks urges you to rectify your mistake). QuickBooks displays a message asking if you'd like to set a closing date and password-protect the closed period, as of the dividing date you set.

If the dividing date on this accountant's copy was the last day of the previous fiscal year, this is a good idea, so click Yes; but if not, it depends on your own judgment. (You can learn about setting a closing date to protect data in the previous fiscal year in Chapter 24.)

QuickBooks opens your company file, the text on the title bar changes back to its normal contents (instead of displaying a notice that an accountant's copy is outstanding), and you can work in the file with no restrictions.

> **TIP:** After you're up and running again normally, you can delete the file your accountant sent you, and you can also delete the accountant's copy file you created (if you saved it instead of uploading it).

Canceling the Accountant's Copy

If you're not going to get a file back from your accountant, you can cancel the accountant's copy in order to work normally in your company file.

Sometimes accountants report that they have no changes to make, sometimes accountants send you e-mail to notify you of a small change and ask you to enter the transaction manually, and sometimes you decide you made the accountant's copy in error and don't want to wait for a file to come back (don't forget to tell the accountant about your decision).

TIP: Another reason to cancel the accountant's copy is because you don't want to import the changes you saw in the Incorporate Accountant's Changes window. Call your accountant and discuss the problem. If the end result is that you prefer not to import the changes, close the Incorporate Accountant's Changes window without importing the changes and cancel the accountant's copy.

To return everything to normal, choose File | Accountant's Copy | Remove Restrictions. QuickBooks asks you to confirm your decision. Select the option labeled Yes, I Want To Remove The Accountant's Copy Restrictions, and click OK.

NOTE: Because this book is about QuickBooks 2009 Pro Edition, I covered only the client-side activities for the accountant's copy feature (you can only perform the accountant's tasks in QuickBooks 2009 Premier Accountant Edition). For information about using the accountant's copy, read *Running QuickBooks 2009 Premier Editions* (CPA911 Publishing), which is available at your favorite bookstore.

Creating Reports

In *this chapter:*

- The QuickBooks Report Center
- Standard financial reports
- Financial activity reports
- Reports on classes
- Job costing reports
- Company Snapshot
- Client Data Review tool

If QuickBooks is your first accounting software program and you've been using manual bookkeeping procedures, you've already discovered how much easier it is to accomplish bookkeeping tasks. However, it's the reports you get out of the software that are worth more than the price of buying and learning QuickBooks. These are reports you'd have to spend hours on using a manual bookkeeping system, and in fact a good deal of the data you obtain from QuickBooks reports couldn't be gained from a manual system. In addition, you can change, customize, and manipulate these reports to get all sorts of information about your business (see Chapter 22 to learn about customizing reports).

Using the Report Center

To get a preview of the built-in reports that are available you can explore the QuickBooks Report Center. Choose Reports | Report Center or click the Report Center icon on the toolbar to get there.

As you can see in Figure 21-1, you can select a report category in the left column, and QuickBooks displays all the reports available for that category in the main window.

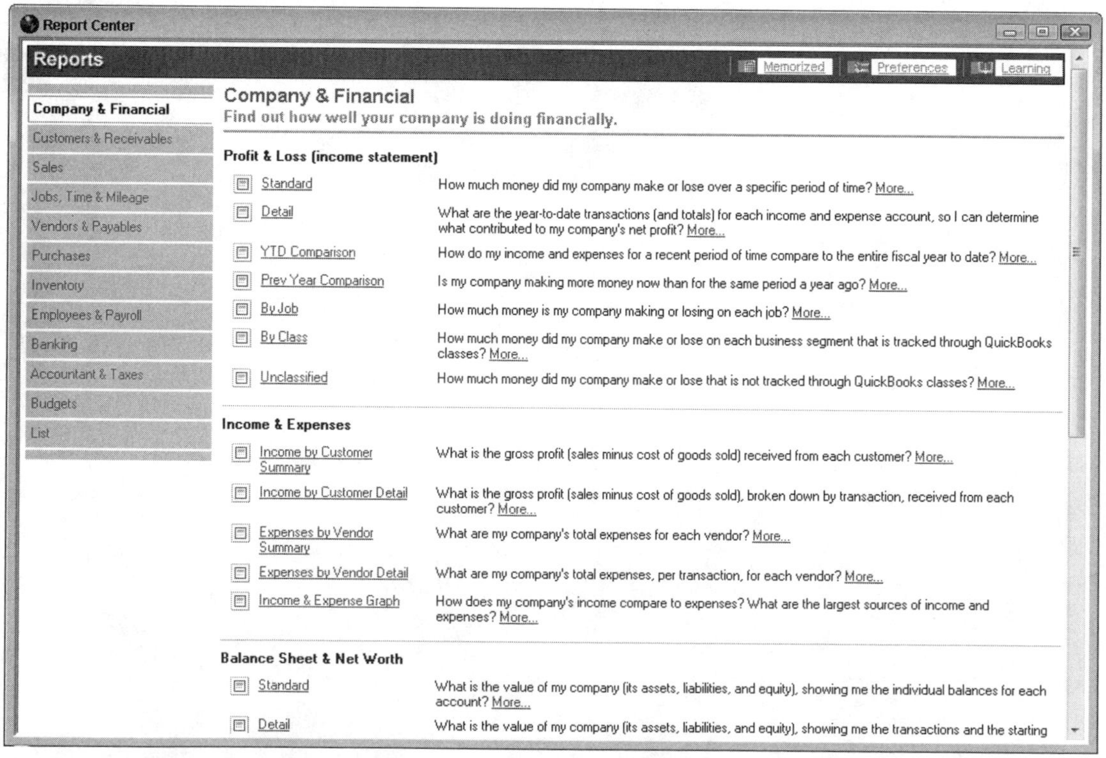

FIGURE 21-1   All the built-in reports are explained, by category, in the Report Center.

If you click a report's link, the report opens (see Figure 21-2); it's not a sample report, it's a report on your company.

	Jan - Jun 09
Ordinary Income/Expense	
Income	
40100 · Consulting	14,670.00
40200 · Product Sales	22,734.75
40250 · Finance Charges Collected	45.51
40300 · Other Regular Income	7,355.00
40400 · Reimbursed Expenses	
40402 · Reimbursed Telephone Expenses	35.71
Total 40400 · Reimbursed Expenses	35.71
Total Income	44,840.97
Cost of Goods Sold	
50000 · Cost of Goods Sold	234.09
50100 · Inventory Adjustments	13.00
51200 · Freight Costs	8.00
Total COGS	255.09
Gross Profit	44,585.88
Expense	
59000 · Discounts Given	104.70
61100 · Automobile Expense	403.07
61200 · Bank Service Charges	12.00
61700 · Equipment Rental	256.00
62500 · Postage and Delivery	302.60
62600 · Printing and Reproduction	247.03
62900 · Rent	2,400.00
63000 · Repairs & Maintenance	

FIGURE 21-2 Point and click to open a report.

Drilling Down for Details

When you create a report, the information that's presented can be investigated by drilling down to the details behind the displayed totals.

Position your mouse over a total, and your mouse pointer turns into a magnifying glass with the letter "z" (for zoom). Double-click to see the details behind the number.

- If the report is a Summary report, the detail report that opens is a list of transactions that made up the total on the original report. You can drill down into each listing to see the original transaction.
- If the report is a Detail report, the list of individual transactions is displayed. You can drill down into each listing to see the original transaction.

Standard Financial Reports

Accountants, bookkeepers, and business owners can keep an eye on the company's health and financial status with a group of reports that are generally deemed to be the *standard financial reports*.

These are also the reports your banker will ask to see for loans and lines of credit, and if you're selling your business, these are the initial reports the potential buyer wants to see. In this section, I'll go over some of these standard financial reports.

Trial Balance

A *trial balance* is a list of all your general ledger accounts and their current balances. It's a quick way to see what's what on an account-by-account basis. In fact, you can use the individual totals and subtotal them to create a Balance Sheet and a Profit & Loss (P&L) statement. However, you don't have to do that because both of those important reports are also available in QuickBooks. Most accountants ask to see a trial balance when they're preparing your taxes or analyzing the health of your business.

To see a trial balance, choose Reports | Accountant & Taxes | Trial Balance. Your company's trial balance is displayed on your screen and you can scroll through it to see all the account balances. The bottom of the report has a total for debits and a total for credits, and they're equal.

By default, the trial balance displays every account (including inactive accounts), even if an account has a zero balance. That's because most accountants want to see the entire list of accounts, and sometimes the fact that an account has a zero balance is meaningful.

Balance Sheet

A Balance Sheet report is specifically designed to show only the totals of the Balance Sheet accounts (assets, liabilities, and equity) from your chart of accounts. It's really a report on your financial health. The reason a Balance Sheet balances is that it's based on a formula:

```
Total Assets = Total Liabilities + Total Equity
```

QuickBooks offers several Balance Sheet reports, and each of them is explained in this section. Select the one you want to see from the Report Center, or by choosing Reports | Company & Financial and then one of these reports.

Balance Sheet Standard Report

The Balance Sheet Standard reports the balance in every Balance Sheet account (unless the account has a zero balance) and subtotals each type of asset, liability, and equity in addition to reporting the totals of those three categories. By default, the report displays totals as of the fiscal year-to-date figures, but you can change the As Of date.

Balance Sheet Detail Report

This report displays every transaction in every Balance Sheet account. By default, the report covers a date range of the current month to date. Even if it's early in the month, this report is lengthy. If you change the date range to encompass a longer period (the quarter or year), the report goes on forever.

If you want to see a Balance Sheet only to get an idea of your company's financial health, this is probably more than you wanted to know.

Balance Sheet Summary Report

This report is a quick way to see totals, and it's also the easiest way to answer the question, "How am I doing?" All the Balance Sheet accounts are subtotaled by type, as shown in Figure 21-3.

Balance Sheet Prev Year Comparison Report

The comparison Balance Sheet is designed to show you what your financial situation is compared to a year ago, and displays the following four columns:

- The year-to-date balance for each Balance Sheet account
- The year-to-date balance for each Balance Sheet account for last year
- The amount of change in dollars between last year and this year
- The percentage of change between last year and this year

If you've just started using QuickBooks this year, there's little reason to run this report. Next year, however, it'll be interesting to see how you're doing compared to this year.

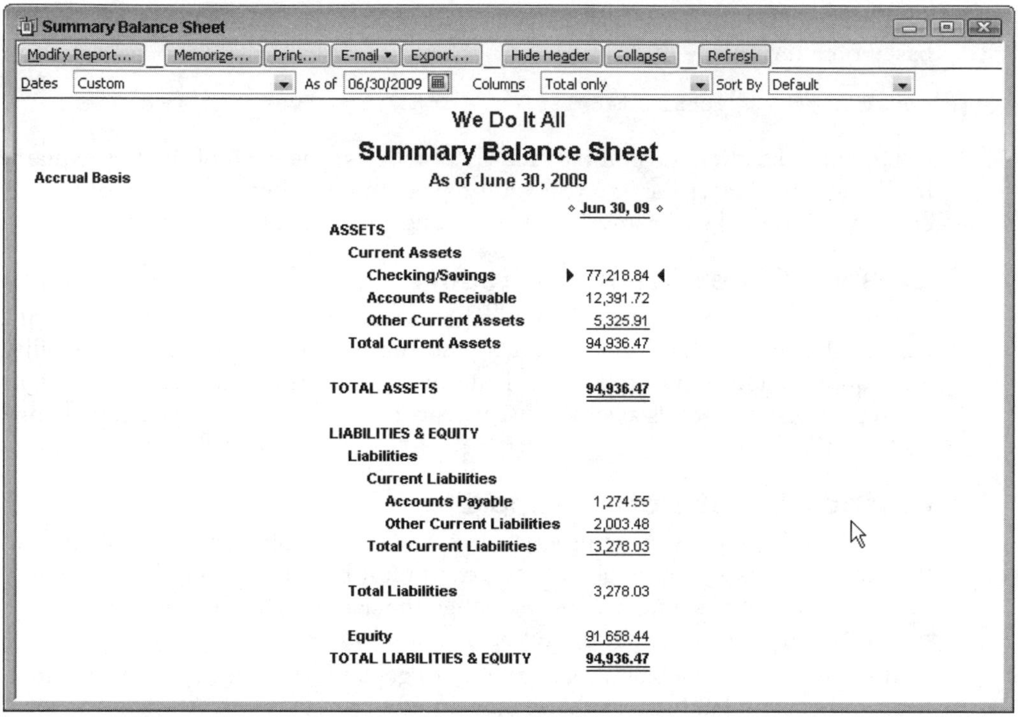

We Do It All

Summary Balance Sheet

Accrual Basis — As of June 30, 2009

	Jun 30, 09
ASSETS	
Current Assets	
Checking/Savings	77,218.84
Accounts Receivable	12,391.72
Other Current Assets	5,325.91
Total Current Assets	94,936.47
TOTAL ASSETS	94,936.47
LIABILITIES & EQUITY	
Liabilities	
Current Liabilities	
Accounts Payable	1,274.55
Other Current Liabilities	2,003.48
Total Current Liabilities	3,278.03
Total Liabilities	3,278.03
Equity	91,658.44
TOTAL LIABILITIES & EQUITY	94,936.47

FIGURE 21-3 Check your financial health with the Summary Balance Sheet.

Profit & Loss Report

Your P&L report is probably the one you'll run most often. It's natural to want to know if you're making any money. A P&L report is sometimes called an *income report*. It shows all your income accounts (and displays the total), all your expense accounts (displaying the total), and then puts the difference between the two totals on the last line. If you have more income than expenses, the last line is a profit; if not, that last line is a loss.

All of the P&L reports are available by choosing Reports | Company & Financial and are explained in this section.

Profit & Loss Standard Report

The standard P&L report is a straightforward document, following the normal format for an income statement:

- The income is listed and totaled.
- The Cost of Goods Sold accounts are listed (if any exist), and the total is deducted from the income total in order to show the gross profit.

- The expenses are listed and totaled.
- The difference between the gross profit and the total expenses is displayed as your Net Ordinary Income (or Loss).

NOTE: If you don't sell inventory items, you may not have a Cost of Goods Sold section in your P&L.

While the format is that of a normal income statement, the date isn't. The default date range for the QuickBooks Standard P&L is the current month to date. This is not a year-to-date figure; it uses only the transactions from the current month, and it's almost certainly not what you want to see. Click the arrow to the right of the Dates field and change the date range to This Fiscal Year-To-Date. The resulting display is what you want to see—an income statement for your business so far this year.

Profit & Loss Detail Report

The Profit & Loss Detail report is for terminally curious people. It lists every transaction for every account in the P&L format. It goes on and on.

This report is almost like an audit trail, and it's good to have if you notice some numbers that seem "not quite right" in the standard P&L. I don't recommend it as the report to run when you just need to know if you're making money.

Profit & Loss YTD Comparison Report

The YTD (year-to-date) comparison report compares the current month's income and expense totals with the year-to-date totals. Each income and expense account is listed.

Profit & Loss Prev Year Comparison Report

If you've been using QuickBooks for more than a year, this is a great report! If you recently started with QuickBooks, next year you'll say, "This is a great report!"

This is an income statement for the current year to date, with a column that shows last year's figures for the same period. This gives you an instant appraisal of your business growth (or ebb). So that you don't have to tax your brain doing the math, there are two additional columns: the difference between the years in dollars and in percentage.

Cash Flow Reports

The list of reports in the Company & Financial submenu includes two cash flow reports: Statement of Cash Flows and Cash Flow Forecast. The difference between them is that the Statement of Cash Flows reports history based on the data in your company file, and the Cash Flow Forecast looks ahead and forecasts cash flow (based on the history in your company file).

Statement of Cash Flows

As seen in Figure 21-4, the Statement of Cash Flows report displays the history of your cash position over a period of time (by default, the date range is Current Year To Date, but you can change the interval). This is one of the reports you'll probably be asked for by a banker or a potential buyer; it's not a report that provides quick analysis about whether you're making a profit.

	Statement of Cash Flows								— □ ✕
Modify Report...	Memorize...	Print...	E-mail ▾	Export...		Hide Header		Refresh	Classify Cash...

Dates Custom ▾ From 01/01/2009 ▦ To 06/30/2009 ▦

We Do It All

Statement of Cash Flows

January through June 2009

	◇ Jan - Jun 09 ◇
OPERATING ACTIVITIES	
Net Income	▸ 33,296.95 ◂
Adjustments to reconcile Net Income	
to net cash provided by operations:	
11000 · Accounts Receivable	-11,441.52
12000 · Inventory Asset	-1,712.91
20000 · Accounts Payable	1,274.55
22000 · Sales Tax Payable	2,003.48
Net cash provided by Operating Activities	23,420.55
Net cash increase for period	23,420.55
Cash at beginning of period	53,798.29
Cash at end of period	77,218.84

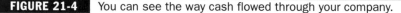

FIGURE 21-4 You can see the way cash flowed through your company.

This is an accrual report that self-modifies to report on a cash basis, and the lines on the report show you the adjustments that were made behind the scenes to provide cash-based totals. If you have no asset accounts that involve money owed to you (such as A/R or loans you made to others), and no liability accounts that involve money you owe (such as A/P or loans you're indebted for), then no adjustments have to be made (because you're essentially operating your business on a cash basis).

A cash flow report has several categories, and, depending on the general ledger postings, QuickBooks provides category totals as follows:

1. **Operating Activities**   The postings involved with general business activities
2. **Investing Activities**   The postings involved with the acquisition and sale of fixed assets
3. **Financing Activities**   The postings involved with long-term liabilities and, if the business is not a C-Corp, postings of owner/partner investments in the business and draws from the business

QuickBooks uses specific accounts for this report, and you can view and modify those accounts as follows:

1. Choose Edit | Preferences and select the Reports & Graphs category in the left pane.
2. Move to the Company Preferences tab, and click the button labeled Classify Cash.
3. In the Classify Cash dialog, you can add or remove accounts, or move an account to a different category.

C A U T I O N : Don't change anything in the Classify Cash dialog without discussing it with your accountant.

Cash Flow Forecast

The Cash Flow Forecast report (see Figure 21-5) predicts your cash flow as of a specific date range (by default, the next four weeks, but you can change the date range). The forecast predicts cash in and cash out and then displays the cash balances that result from those cash flows.

This report is based on income predicted from current receivables and outgo predicted by current payables. If your business operates mostly on a cash basis (you usually collect payment from customers at the time of the sale, and you usually write direct disbursement checks instead of entering vendor bills), there's not much future cash flow for QuickBooks to predict.

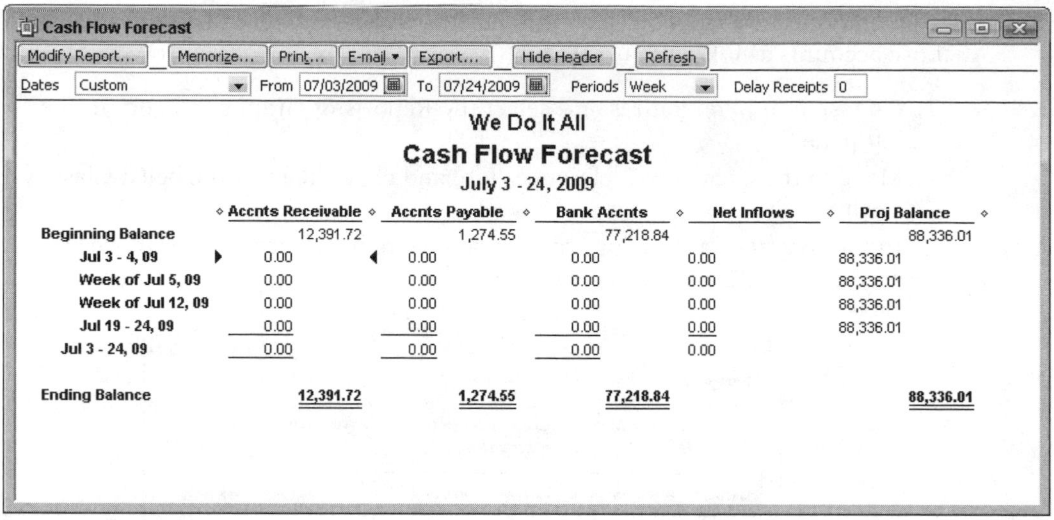

Cash Flow Forecast					
Modify Report...	Memorize...	Print...	E-mail ▾	Export...	Hide Header	Refresh

Dates Custom ▾ From 07/03/2009 ▦ To 07/24/2009 ▦ Periods Week ▾ Delay Receipts 0

We Do It All
Cash Flow Forecast
July 3 - 24, 2009

	Accnts Receivable	Accnts Payable	Bank Accnts	Net Inflows	Proj Balance
Beginning Balance	12,391.72	1,274.55	77,218.84		88,336.01
Jul 3 - 4, 09 ▶	0.00 ◀	0.00	0.00	0.00	88,336.01
Week of Jul 5, 09	0.00	0.00	0.00	0.00	88,336.01
Week of Jul 12, 09	0.00	0.00	0.00	0.00	88,336.01
Jul 19 - 24, 09	0.00	0.00	0.00	0.00	88,336.01
Jul 3 - 24, 09	0.00	0.00	0.00	0.00	
Ending Balance	**12,391.72**	**1,274.55**	**77,218.84**		**88,336.01**

FIGURE 21-5   Use the Cash Flow Forecast to predict the cash you'll end up with by the date you selected.

This report assumes that both you and your customers pay bills based on the terms of those bills. If your customers run late, you can tell QuickBooks to "re-predict" the flow of cash and the dates you can expect that cash by using the Delay Receipts field at the top of the report window. Enter the number of days after the due date you expect to receive money from your customers. For example, if your terms to customers are 30DaysNet, and you know from experience that most of your customers pay you in 60 days, enter **30** in the Delay Receipts field. (QuickBooks has no field on the report window for you to enter the number of days you take beyond the terms your vendors offer; this report always assumes you pay on time.)

Activity Reports

QuickBooks offers a great many financial reports on your transactions, categorized by the type of activity for those transactions. In the following sections I'll provide an overview of those reports.

Sales Reports

If you choose Reports | Sales you see a list of built-in reports you can open to see sales reports summarized by a variety of categories. Table 21-1 explains the contents of each report. All of these reports can be customized to include additional data, sort totals by a scheme you require, and subtotal by report components. See Chapter 22 to learn how to customize reports.

Report	Contents
Sales by Customer Summary	Total sales for each customer and job; does not include reimbursed expenses or sales tax.
Sales by Customer Detail	Each transaction that's included in the Sales by Customer Summary report.
Sales by Item Summary	Summary of sales, subtotaled by Item type.
Sales by Item Detail	Each transaction that's included in the Sales by Item Summary report.
Sales by Rep Summary	Summary of sales totaled by sales rep; does not include reimbursed expenses or sales tax.
Sales by Rep Detail	Each transaction that's included in the Sales by Rep summary report.
Sales Graph	Bar and pie graphs of sales totals (you can display data by customers, items, and reps).
Pending Sales	All sales transactions currently marked "Pending."

TABLE 21-1 Built-in Sales Reports

Vendor Reports

Choose Reports | Vendors & Payables to track financial data related to vendor payments. The list of reports in the submenu includes A/P aging, Form 1099 data, and other useful information.

A/P Aging Summary
A/P Aging Detail
Vendor Balance Summary
Vendor Balance Detail
Unpaid Bills Detail
Accounts Payable Graph
Transaction List by Vendor

1099 Summary
1099 Detail

Sales Tax Liability
Sales Tax Revenue Summary

Vendor Phone List
Vendor Contact List

Inventory Reports

If you've enabled inventory tracking, QuickBooks provides the following useful reports:

Purchases Reports   Purchases sorted and totaled by vendor or item, open POs.

Inventory Reports   Inventory reports on inventory value and stock status.

Employees & Payroll Reports

The Employees & Payroll submenu provides a number of reports that range from important to useful, depending on how you and your accountant want to analyze your financials.

```
Summarize Payroll Data in Excel
Tax Form Worksheets in Excel

Payroll Summary
Payroll Item Detail
Payroll Detail Review
Employee Earnings Summary
Employee State Taxes Detail
Payroll Transactions by Payee
Payroll Transaction Detail
Payroll Liability Balances

Employee Contact List
Employee Withholding
Payroll Item Listing
Paid Time Off List
```

Banking Reports

To track your banking/cash activities, you can display reports on banking activities, including check and deposit detail data, missing check numbers, and reconciliations. (See Chapter 14 to learn about reconciliation processes and troubleshooting reconciliation problems with the reconciliation reports in this Reports submenu.)

Accountant & Taxes Reports

Select the reports you need from the submenu under this Reports menu item to peruse the details of your financial transactions. You can also investigate user actions by opening one of the audit reports. And, of course, you can generate the reports you need to begin tax preparation. Chapter 24 covers the year-end procedures you must follow to prepare for filing your taxes.

Reports on Classes

If you've enabled class tracking (and you've been consistent about entering data in the Class column of transaction windows), you can create reports that show you the financial condition of each class.

Profit & Loss Unclassified Report

The first report you should run is the Profit & Loss Unclassified report, which tells you which transactions lack class information. Some of the transactions may not be linked to a class on purpose, but I find that most of the time this report displays many transactions that should have class information but don't.

Choose Reports | Company & Financial | Profit & Loss Unclassified. QuickBooks displays a P&L generated solely from transactions that had no class assignment.

Examine the report and drill down (double-click the listing) to view the individual transactions. If any transaction should have been assigned a class, you can add the class and click Yes when QuickBooks asks if you want to save the changes you made to the transaction. When you've fixed all the errors, you can be sure that the *real* P&L reports for classes contain all the information they should.

Profit & Loss By Class Report

Choose Reports | Company & Financial | Profit & Loss By Class to generate a report that displays a P&L report for each class (each class P&L is displayed in its own column).

Balance Sheet Class Report

QuickBooks does not offer a report on a class-by-class basis for Balance Sheet accounts (Assets, Liabilities, and Equity). However, I receive a lot of requests from readers who want to know how to do this, and I've advised a slightly kludgy trick to create a report that displays totals by class.

You can only generate a report for a single class, so you have to generate multiple reports to include all your classes. However, you can export each report to the same Excel workbook (each class gets its own worksheet).

To create a Balance Sheet report for a class, use the following steps:

1. Choose Reports | Company & Financial | Balance Sheet Standard.
2. Click the Modify Report button at the top of the report window.
3. Move to the Filters tab and select Class from the Filter list, and then select the class you want to report on.
4. Move to the Header/Footer tab and change the text in the Report Title field to add the name of the class to the title (so you're not confused about which report you're viewing).
5. Click OK to display the report, which now reflects data that has been filtered by class.

It's important to remember that the postings to many Balance Sheet accounts don't involve transactions that have a Class column, so this report isn't a valid Balance Sheet, it's just a vehicle for tracking activities on a class basis for Balance Sheet accounts.

Job Costing Reports

Many businesses track financial transactions in a manner that permits job costing, and QuickBooks provides plenty of reports to help. Choose Reports | Jobs, Time & Mileage to see a submenu of report titles that provide useful information about the expenses that are linked to customers and jobs.

Voided and Deleted Transactions Reports

QuickBooks offers two reports you can use to track voided and deleted transactions. Both reports are available by choosing Reports | Accountant & Taxes and then selecting either of these reports: Voided/Deleted Transactions Summary or Voided/Deleted Transactions Detail.

Voided/Deleted Transactions Summary Report

This report displays a summary of all voided and deleted transactions in the selected period. The report shows the current state (void or deleted) and the original state (including the amount) of each affected transaction.

Voided/Deleted Transactions Detail History Report

This report provides more information about both the original transaction and the change. In addition to the information provided by the Voided/Deleted Transactions Summary report, this report displays the credit and debit postings and the posting accounts. If items (including payroll items) were involved in the transaction, they're also displayed.

Company Snapshot

You can get a quick answer to the question, "How's business?" in the Company Snapshot window (see Figure 21-6). Choose Company | Company Snapshot to open this window.

In addition to displaying an easy-to-understand summary of the money that's moved in and out, this window provides information on tasks you should perform, account balances, and A/R and A/P data by customer/vendor.

Need details? Double-click an element in this window to see the particulars. For example, to see details about a customer's A/R balance, click the listing to display an Open Balance report for that customer, sorted and totaled by job (see Figure 21-7).

The data displayed in the Company Snapshot window is always appropriate for the permissions granted to the current user. If the user does not have permission to

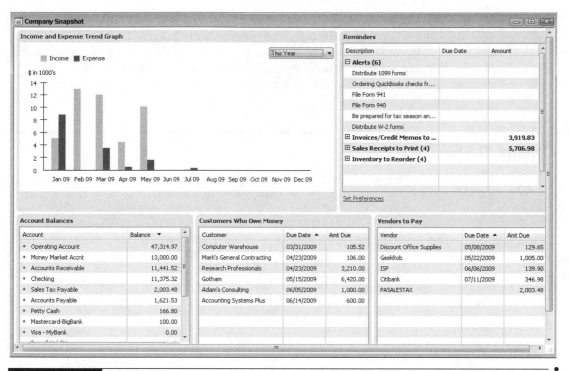

FIGURE 21-6 View a summary of your financial status.

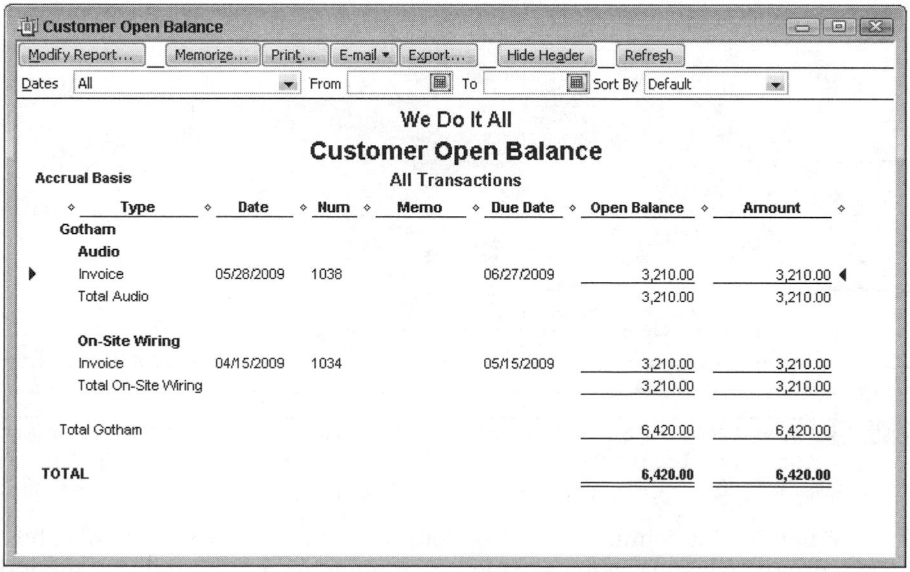

FIGURE 21-7 It's easy to see the details behind the figures in the Company Snapshot, and you can continue to drill down for more details.

see sensitive financial data, no bank balances appear in the Account Balances section of the window. Additionally, the Income And Expense Trend Graph section has no data; instead, the user sees a message explaining that she needs permission to view the area. Various elements of the window are displayed or hidden depending on the current user's permissions. (Learn about configuring users and permissions in Chapter 26.)

Client Data Review

Client Data Review (see Figure 21-8) provides a central place for investigating problems, or potential problems, in a company file.

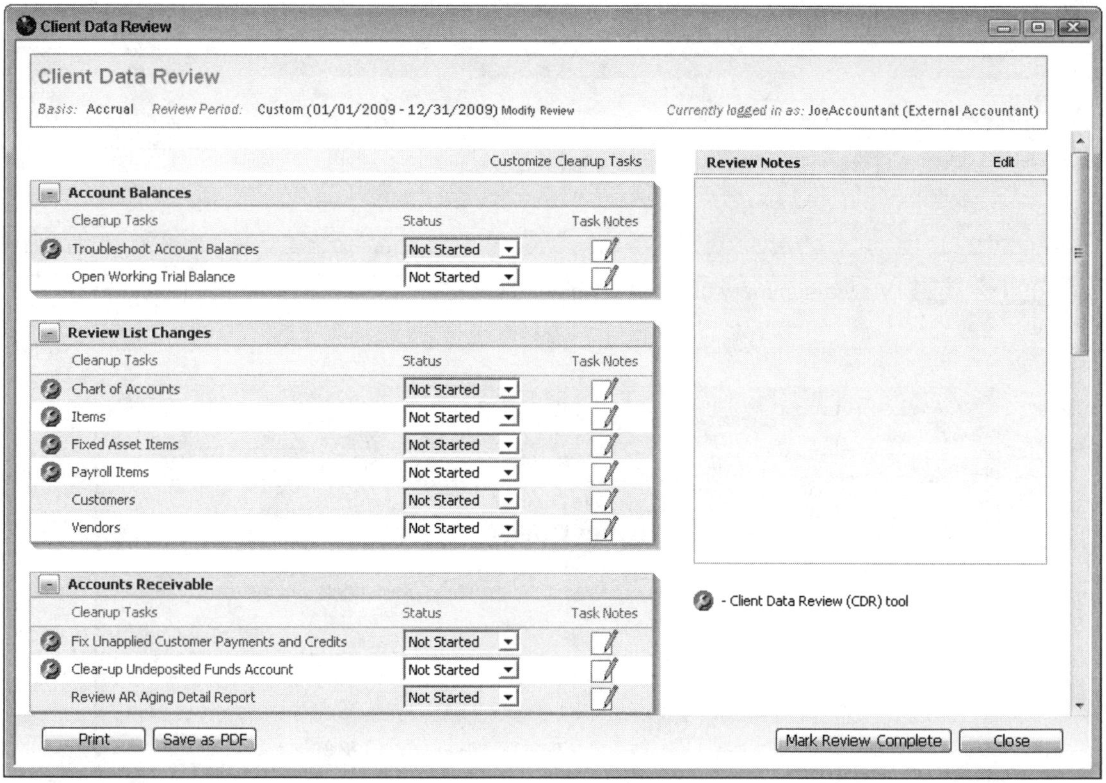

FIGURE 21-8 Your accountant can review your data to make sure your financial information is correct.

When your accountant comes to your office to work on your books, he or she can use the Client Data Review tool to examine the data and troubleshoot data entry problems (or potential problems).

The Client Data Review is only available for a user who has logged in as an "External Accountant" (discussed next). An External Accountant is a specific type of user who has the same rights as the QuickBooks Admin with the following exceptions:

- The External Accountant cannot create, edit, or remove users.
- The External Accountant cannot view customer credit card numbers if the QuickBooks Credit Card Protection feature is enabled (covered in Chapter 3).

External Accountant

You should create an External Accountant user so that when your accountant (or a bookkeeper from your accountant's office) comes to your office, the Client Data Review tools are available.

Creating an External Accountant

To create a user who is an External Accountant, you must be logged into QuickBooks as the Admin (only the QuickBooks Admin can create users).

1. Choose Company | Set Up Users And Passwords | Set Up Users.
2. In the User List dialog, select Add User.
3. Enter the User Name and Password and click Next.
4. Select External Accountant and click Next.
5. QuickBooks asks you to confirm this action—click Yes.
6. Click Finish to create the External Accountant.

Converting an Existing User to an External Accountant

Many companies have already set up a user name for the accountant. Even if the accountant's login provides full permissions, the Client Data Review tool isn't available on the Company menu unless an external accountant is logged in (except in Premier Accountant Edition). You can edit the accountant's user account to convert it to an External Accountant.

Select the accountant's user account and click Edit User. Don't change the user name and password data. Click Next, and in the next window, select External Accountant and follow the prompts to save this user name as an External Accountant.

 NOTE: A full discussion of the Client Data Review tool is available in *Running QuickBooks 2009 Premier Editions*, from CPA911 Publishing, available at your favorite bookstore.

Customizing Reports

*I*n *this chapter:*

- Understand report customization features
- Memorize customized reports

QuickBooks offers report customization features that provide an enormous amount of power. When you learn how to use the customization tools, you can select and sort almost any piece of information stored in your QuickBooks company file, from the teeniest details to the broadest overview. In this chapter, I'll go over the customization features and also provide some specific examples.

 NOTE: Usually, reports with the word "Summary" in the report name have fewer (and less powerful) customization opportunities than reports with the word "Detail" in the report name.

Customization Starts with a Built-in Report

All report customization efforts start with opening the report you want to customize. For this discussion, I opened the Sales By Customer Detail Report and set the date range for the first half of the year. Figure 22-1 shows you what it looks like before customization.

Type	**Date**	**Num**	**Memo**	**Name**	**Item**	**Qty**	**Sales Price**	**Amount**	**Balance**
Accounting Systems Plus									
software									
Invoice	03/06/2009	1027		Accounting System...	Software	4	100.00	400.00	400.00
Total software								400.00	400.00
training									
Sales Receipt	02/02/2009	103	Finished wo...	Accounting System...	Training	4	60.00	240.00	240.00
Sales Receipt	02/02/2009	103		Accounting System...	Training	4	60.00	240.00	480.00
Sales Receipt	02/02/2009	103		Accounting System...	Training	8	60.00	480.00	960.00
Sales Receipt	02/02/2009	103		Accounting System...	Training	8	60.00	480.00	1,440.00
Invoice	02/02/2009	1020	Staff Training	Accounting System...	Training	10	60.00	600.00	2,040.00
Invoice	03/30/2009	1032		Accounting System...	Gadget02	2	50.00	100.00	2,140.00
Invoice	03/30/2009	1032	Widgets	Accounting System...	Widgets	15	6.00	90.00	2,230.00
Invoice	05/15/2009	1037	Staff Training	Accounting System...	Training	10	60.00	600.00	2,830.00
Total training								2,830.00	2,830.00
Total Accounting Systems Plus								3,230.00	3,230.00
Adam's Consulting									
Invoice	01/02/2009	1011	Consulting S...	Adam's Consulting	Consulting	3	135.00	405.00	405.00
Invoice	01/02/2009	1011	Discount	Adam's Consulting	10%Dis...		-10.0%	-40.50	364.50
Invoice	01/02/2009	1011		Adam's Consulting	Gadget01	1	160.00	160.00	524.50
Invoice	01/02/2009	1011	Widgets	Adam's Consulting	Widgets	5	6.00	30.00	554.50
Credit Memo	01/15/2009	1013	Returned Ite...	Adam's Consulting	Widgets	-1	6.00	-6.00	548.50
Invoice	02/02/2009	1021	Consulting S...	Adam's Consulting	Consulting	4	135.00	540.00	1,088.50
Invoice	03/31/2009	FC 1	Finance Cha...	Adam's Consulting	*Fin Chg	1	24.36	24.36	1,112.86
Stmt Charge	03/31/2009			Adam's Consulting	Labor	1	200.00	200.00	1,312.86
Invoice	05/06/2009	1036	Administrativ...	Adam's Consulting	Admin	1	1,000.00	1,000.00	2,312.86
Total Adam's Consulting								2,312.86	2,312.86

FIGURE 22-1 This report has a lot of data, but I don't always need all this data and sometimes I need different data.

Click Modify Report to open the Modify Report dialog, where you can customize the format and content of the report. I cover each part of the Modify Report dialog in the following sections.

Customizing Report Display Settings

The Display tab (see Figure 22-2) is in the foreground when you open the Modify Report dialog, and it's filled with customization options. Some of the options are also on the report window, such as the Dates and Sort By fields.

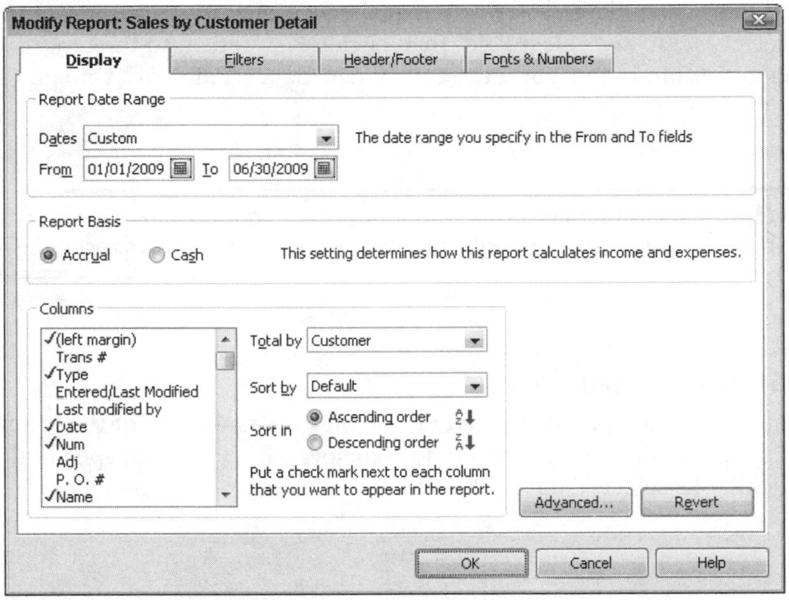

FIGURE 22-2 Use the Display tab to determine what type of data appears on the report and how it's sorted.

Selecting the Report Basis

You can select Accrual or Cash basis for most QuickBooks reports.

- When you create a cash basis report, the data is calculated by considering actual cash transactions. This means that revenue doesn't exist in the report until a customer pays you and expenses don't exist until you pay the vendor.
- When you create an accrual basis report, the data is calculated to reflect all the transactions you've entered. This means that revenue exists when you send an invoice to a customer and expenses exist when you enter a vendor bill.

By default, QuickBooks displays financial reports as accrual-based reports because accrual-based reports are more useful for getting an overview of the state of your business. However, if you file taxes on a cash basis, a cash-based report is easier to use for tax preparation.

Selecting Columns

The real power in the Display tab is in the Columns list (which only exists in Detail reports, not in Summary reports). You can select and deselect columns so the report displays only the information you need.

For example, in this report you may not care about the contents of the Memo field, but you'd like to know whether the invoice is paid. In the Columns list, deselect Memo and select Paid, then click OK to return to the report where the Memo column is gone, and the appropriate data ("Paid" or "Unpaid") appears in the Paid column.

> **TIP:** Any custom fields you created appear in the Columns list, which adds even more power to your ability to customize reports in a meaningful way.

Advanced Options

Some reports have an Advanced button on the Display tab of the Modify Report dialog to open the Advanced Options dialog, which lets you specify the way QuickBooks selects data for the report.

This dialog varies depending on the report, and the following discussion covers the various options you might encounter.

Include Option

These options determine which accounts appear in transaction detail reports.

- All includes all accounts, whether or not the account had postings in the date range selected for the report.
- In Use includes only those accounts that had postings in the date range selected for the report.

Open Balance/Aging Options

These options specify the way QuickBooks calculates an open balance in an aging report.

- Current (Faster) displays the open balance as of today, including all payments received through today's date.
- Report Date displays the open balance as of the ending date of the report, and payments received after the ending date of the report are not included in the calculation.

Display Rows Options

These options specify the rows to include or exclude, as follows:

- **Active** Only rows in which some financial activity occurred, which includes amounts of $0.00 if that total resulted from financial transactions.
- **All** All rows regardless of activity or balance.
- **Non-Zero** Only rows in which activity occurred and where the amounts are other than zero.

Display Columns Options

These options specify whether to include or exclude columns based on whether financial activity occurred in the time frame specified for the report, as follows:

- **Active** Only columns in which some financial activity occurred, which includes amounts of $0.00 if that total resulted from financial transactions.
- **All** All columns regardless of activity or balance.
- **Non-Zero** Only columns in which activity occurred and where the amounts are other than zero.

Reporting Calendar Options

These options specify the calendar basis of the report, as follows:

- **Fiscal Year** Uses the fiscal year as specified in the Company Info window, starting with the first month of the fiscal year. For example, if your fiscal year begins in October, configuring the report's date range to First Fiscal Quarter displays transactions from October through December.
- **Calendar Year** Uses the calendar year (starts in January).
- **Tax Year** Uses a year that starts in the first month of your company's tax year, as specified in the Company Info window.

 N O T E : Some reports have an option labeled Show Only Rows And Columns With Budgets, which you can use to customize a report so it displays only accounts that are used in your budgets.

Filtering Report Data

The Filters tab (see Figure 22-3) is a powerhouse of tools to help customize a report in very exact, granular ways. I'll go over some examples here, but when you have time you should play around with the options in this tab to get a feel for its capabilities and power.

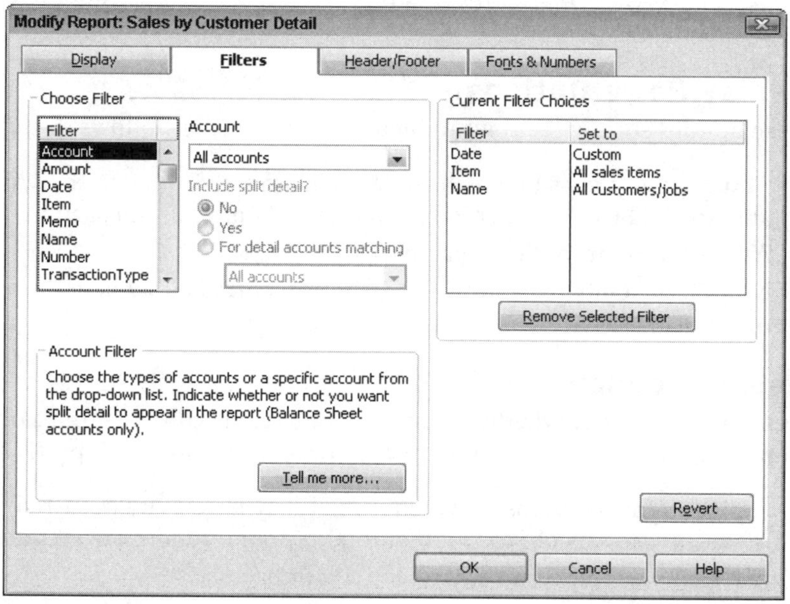

FIGURE 22-3   Change what's reported by filtering the data to meet your own criteria.

For the sales report currently under discussion, suppose you want to see only those transactions that are higher than a certain amount?

1. Select Amount in the Filter list. The filter changes to reflect the options available for the Amount item (see Figure 22-4).
2. In the filter, select the Equal To Or Greater Than (> =)option.
3. Enter the amount on which to filter the transaction.
4. Press TAB to add the filter to the Current Filter Choices list.
5. Click OK to return to the report, where the contents of the report have changed to match your filter.

If you want to see only certain types of transactions on the report, use the Transaction Type filter to select the type you want to see; for example, in this report on sales and customers, you might want to see only credit memos. At that point you've created a "Credit Memos by Customer Detail" report—the kind of report

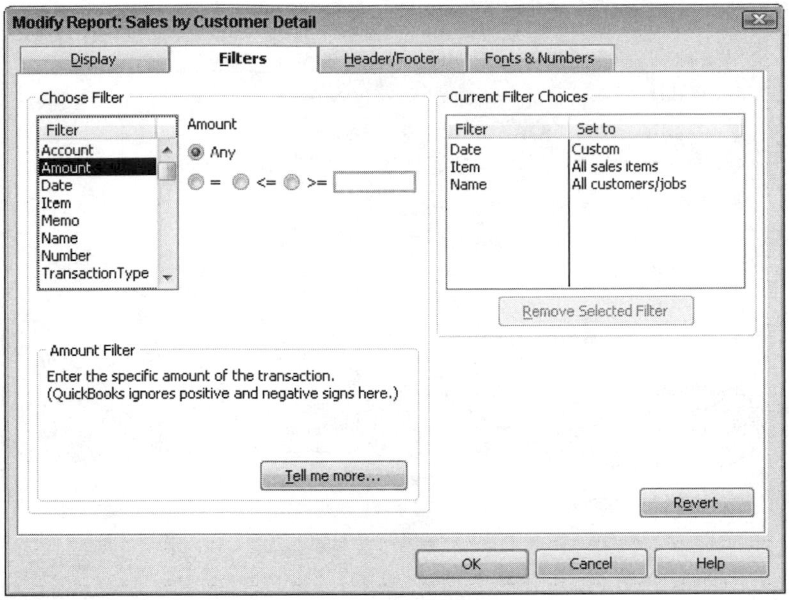

FIGURE 22-4 You can create precise filters to customize the criteria for displaying data.

you memorize so you can use it frequently (memorizing customized reports is covered later in this chapter).

If you select multiple filters, make sure they don't interfere with each other. In this discussion I mentioned filtering for amounts and also for transaction type. If you were following along, creating the same filters I created, at this point you're only seeing credit memos that exceed the amount you entered in the amount filter. If you want to see all credit memos, select the Amount filter in the Current Filter Choices list and click Remove Selected Filter.

TIP : Each filter has its own format of filter options. As you add and configure filters and notice the effect on your reports, you'll learn to use filters effectively.

Customizing Report Headers and Footers

You can customize what appears on the header and footer of your report by changing the options on the Header/Footer tab, shown in Figure 22-5.

The options you set here have no bearing on the figures in the report; this is just informational stuff. Most of the fields are self-explanatory, but the Date Prepared field bears mentioning. The date you see in this tab has nothing to do with the

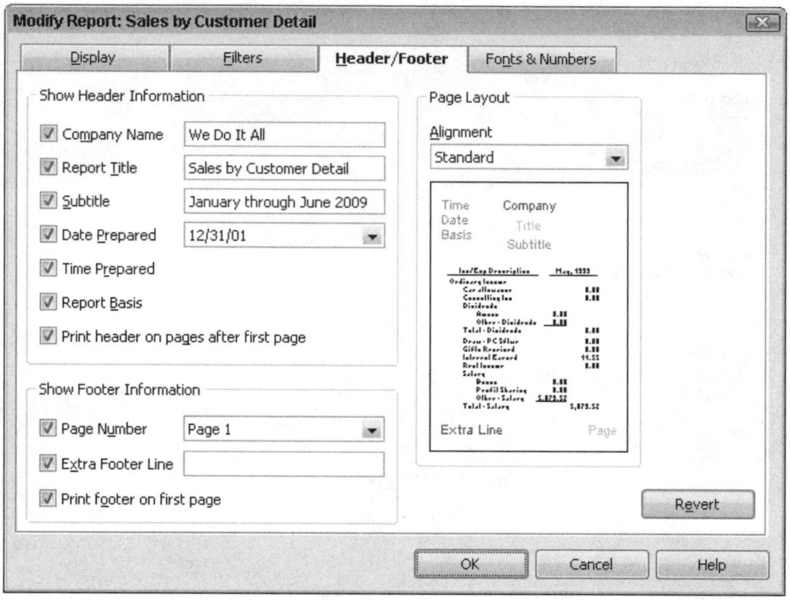

FIGURE 22-5 Customize the information on the top and bottom of the report page using the Header/Footer tab.

current date or the dates on the report; it's just a sample format. Click the arrow to the right of the field to see other formats for displaying the date.

Customizing Report Fonts & Numbers

The Fonts & Numbers tab, shown in Figure 22-6, lets you spiff up your report by changing fonts and also provides options for the way numbers display on the report.

The Change Font For list lets you select elements of the report and change their fonts. Select an element and click Change Font, then select a typeface, a style (bold, italic, etc.), a size, and a special effect such as underline.

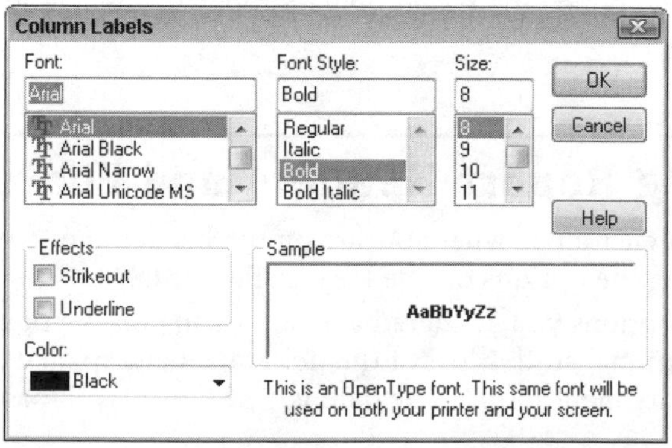

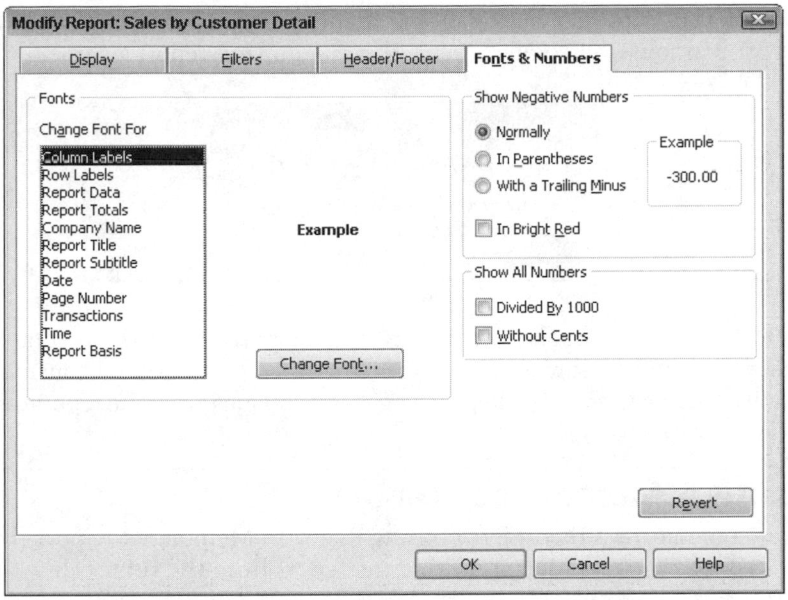

FIGURE 22-6 Change the appearance of the data in the report.

On the right side of the Fonts & Numbers dialog you can configure the way numbers display and print on your report. Select a method for showing negative numbers. If you wish, you can also select a method for displaying all the numbers on the report:

- Divided By 1000 reduces the size of the numbers by showing them as multiples of 1000. This is useful for companies that report seven- and eight-digit numbers.
- Without Cents eliminates the decimal point and the two digits to the right of the decimal point from every amount. Only the dollars show, not the cents. QuickBooks rounds the cents to the nearest dollar. (Accountants frequently enter numbers in this manner.)

Memorizing Customized Reports

After you've customized a report to display the information you want in the manner in which you want it, you can avoid the need to go through all this work again by memorizing the report.

TIP: Before you memorize a report, change its name in the Header/Footer tab so when you use it in the future you know exactly what you're looking at.

Click the Memorize button on the report's button bar to open the Memorize Report window where you can give this customized report a name.

By default, QuickBooks uses the report name in the Header/Footer tab. If you didn't change that title, be sure to use a reference to the report type in the memorized name. If you use a name such as My Report, you'll have no idea what the report displays.

Using a Memorized Report

Open a memorized report by choosing Reports | Memorized Reports from the QuickBooks menu bar and selecting the report from the submenu.

When you open the report, all your customized settings are the way you configured them, but the data changes to reflect up-to-date information. Incidentally, it's not uncommon for experienced QuickBooks users to open a memorized report, look at the data, and think, "Hmm, this makes me think that I'd like to know more about X than Y when I do my quarterly analysis." When that happens, use your memorized report as the basis of another customized report, and memorize that one, too.

Using Memorized Report Groups

After you discover the power available in creating and memorizing customized reports, you'll be creating special-data reports like crazy. After a while, it becomes difficult to select the report you need in the list of memorized reports. To save time and confusion, you have to get more organized in the way you store these reports. QuickBooks provides a nifty device called Memorized Reports Groups to help. These report groups let you store reports by category, which makes it easier to locate exactly the report you need.

Creating a Memorized Report Group

Memorized report groups are displayed in the Memorized Report List window, as well as on the submenu you see when you select Memorized Reports on the Reports menu. However, in order to create or manipulate groups you have to work in the Memorized Report List window. Choose Reports | Memorized Reports | Memorized Report List to open the Memorized Report List window.

Click the button labeled Memorized Report at the bottom of the window to display the window's menu, and choose New Group. Enter a name for this group in the New Memorized Report Group dialog and click OK. The group you created appears in the window list, and its listing is bold. Continue to add groups to reflect the types of memorized reports you've already created or expect to create in the future.

 TIP: Choose a name that fits the category for the group you're creating. Common names for these groups are Year-End, Monthly, and so on. The more straightforward the name, the easier it is to place reports in the group and find those reports when you need them.

Moving Existing Memorized Reports into Groups

Start by moving your existing memorized reports into the appropriate groups, and then you can save reports you memorize directly in the right group (covered next). You can use either of the following methods to move a report into a group:

- Edit each report to add the name of the group. Select the report's listing and press CTRL-E. Select the option labeled Save In Memorized Report Group and then select the appropriate group from the drop-down list.
- Drag each report to a group by indenting the report name under the group name. First, drag each report listing so it's under the group listing, and then drag to the right, indenting the report name under the group name.

Any report listing indented under a group listing is automatically a member of that group (you can check my veracity by pressing CTRL-E to see the group association in the Edit Memorized Report dialog).

NOTE: You can only drag listings to groups if the Report Name column heading bar at the top of the window is the only column heading. If you see a column to the left that has a diamond as the heading, click the diamond to hide that column (to reverse the process, click the Report Name heading to reveal the diamond).

Saving a Memorized Report in a Group

After you've created groups, you can save memorized reports directly to a group. When you've perfected the customizations you need, click Memorize on the report window. In the Memorize Report dialog, enter the report name, select the option labeled Save In Memorized Report Group, and then select the appropriate group from the drop-down list.

Processing Report Groups

One of the nifty things about creating groups for your memorized reports is that QuickBooks makes it easy to process all the reports in a group at once. You can print all the reports in one fell swoop or display all the reports (and then export them to Excel for your accountant).

For example, if you've created reports that are important at the end of each month or each quarter and placed them in a group named End of Month or End of Quarter, you can display or print all the reports with a single mouse click.

To process a group of reports, double-click the group's listing in the Memorized Report List window to open the Process Multiple Reports dialog seen in Figure 22-7. You can deselect any report you don't need at the moment.

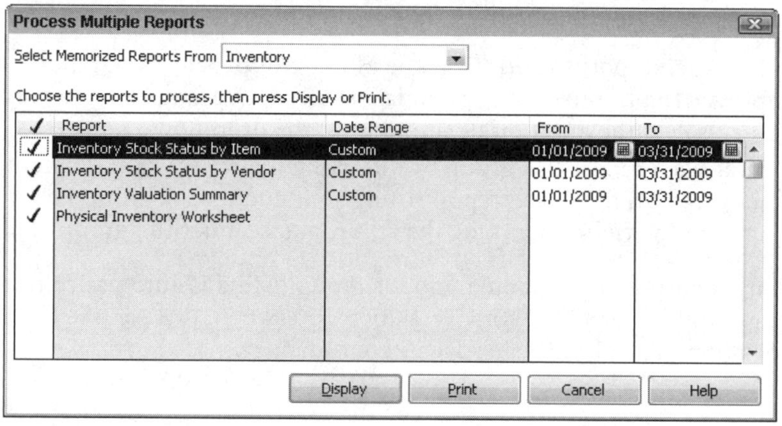

FIGURE 22-7 When it's time to evaluate and count inventory, print everything you need.

Adding Standard Reports to Memorized Reports Groups

Often, the report you want to include in a group is a standard, built-in report, available on the Reports menu. To add the report to a group, open the report and click the Memorize button. In the Memorize Report dialog, put the report into the appropriate group.

Budgets and Planning Tools

In this chapter:

- Configure a budget

- Report on budget versus actual figures

- Export budgets

- Project cash flow

A budget is a tool for tracking your progress against your plans. A well-prepared budget can also help you draw money out of your business wisely, because knowing what you plan to spend on staff, overhead, or other expenses in the future prevents you from carelessly withdrawing profits and living high on the hog whenever you have a good month.

For general planning, the ability to project cash flow by using actual data and then applying "what if" scenarios helps you decide whether you can increase or decrease expenses and prices.

I'll go over these tools in this chapter.

How QuickBooks Handles Budgets

Before you begin creating a budget, you need to know how QuickBooks manages budgets and the processes connected to budgets. In this section, I'll present an overview of the QuickBooks budget features, so you can understand them and bear them in mind when you create your budgets.

Types of Budgets

QuickBooks offers several types of budgets:

- Budgets based on your Balance Sheet accounts
- P&L budgets based on your income and expense accounts
- P&L budgets based on income and expense accounts and a customer or job
- P&L budgets based on income and expense accounts and a class

P&L budgets can be created from scratch or by using the actual figures from the previous year. The latter option, of course, only works if you've upgraded to QuickBooks 2009 from an earlier version.

Budgets Aren't Really Documents

In QuickBooks, a budget is the data you enter in a budget window. Once you begin creating a budget, the data you record is more or less permanently ensconced in the budget window and reappears whenever you open that budget window. You create a budget by choosing Company | Planning & Budgeting | Set Up Budgets.

You can only create one of each type of budget. For example, if you create a P&L budget, enter and record some figures, and then decide to start all over by launching the Create New Budget Wizard, you can't create a new P&L budget. Instead of creating a new budget, the wizard displays the data you already configured. You have no way of telling QuickBooks, "Okay, save that one, I'm going to do another one with different figures." You can change the figures, but the changes replace the original figures. You're editing a budget; you're not creating a new budget document.

Creating Multiple Budgets

Once you've created your first budget, regardless of type, the next time you select Company | Planning & Budgeting | Set Up Budgets, the budget window opens with the last budget you created.

If the budget is a P&L or Balance Sheet budget, you cannot create a second budget of the same type. However, you can create a budget of a different type (P&L with Customer:Job, or P&L with Class). To do so, click the Create New Budget button in the budget window and go through the wizard to select different criteria (Customer:Job or Class).

After you've created a Customer:Job budget or a Class budget, you can create another budget using a different customer or job or a different class (or using different accounts for the same customer, job, or class). See the sections "Customer:Job Budgets" and "Class Budgets" for instructions on creating multiple budgets of those types.

Deleting a Budget

QuickBooks lets you delete a budget. This means if you want to create multiple budgets of the same type (perhaps you feel better if you have a "Plan B" budget), you have a workaround to the "no two budgets of the same type" rule. Export the original budget to Excel, and then delete the original budget and start the process again. See the section "Exporting Budgets" later in this chapter.

To delete a budget, choose Edit | Delete Budget from the QuickBooks menu bar while the budget window is open.

Understanding the Budget Window

Before you start entering figures, you need to learn how to manage your work using the buttons on the budget window.

- **Clear** Deletes all figures in the budget window—you cannot use this button to clear a row or column.
- **Save** Records the current figures and leaves the window open so you can continue to work.
- **OK** Records the current figures and closes the window.
- **Cancel** Closes the window without any offer to record the figures.
- **Create New Budget** Starts the budget process anew, opening the Create New Budget Wizard. If you've entered any data, QuickBooks asks if you want to record your budget before closing the window. If you record your data (or have previously recorded your data with the Save button), when you start anew, the budget window opens with the same recorded data, and you can change the figures.

The other buttons in the budget window are used when you're entering data, and I go over them later in this chapter. See the section "Enter Budget Amounts."

Tasks to Perform Before You Start Your Budget

Before you create a budget, you need to check the following details:

- Make sure the accounts you need exist; adding accounts while you're working in a budget doesn't work properly because you won't see the accounts unless you close and re-open the budget.
- The first month of the budget must be the same as the first month of your fiscal year.
- All the accounts you want to include on the budget must be active; inactive accounts aren't available in the budget window.

A Word About Balance Sheet Budgets

It's highly unusual to need to create a Balance Sheet budget because you can't predict the amounts for most Balance Sheet accounts. Even if you want to keep an eye on the few accounts over which you have control (fixed assets and loans), there's little reason to use a budget to do so. The transactions for fixed assets and loans are usually planned and therefore don't need budget-to-reality comparisons to allow you to keep an eye on them.

As a result, I'm not going to spend time discussing Balance Sheet budgets. If you feel you need to create one, choose Company | Planning & Budgeting | Set Up Budgets. If this is your first budget, the Create New Budget Wizard opens. Otherwise, when an existing budget appears, click the Create New Budget button. When the Create New Budget Wizard opens, select the year for which you want to create the budget and select the Balance Sheet option. Then click Next, and because the next window has no options, there's nothing for you to do except click Finish. The budget window opens, listing all your Balance Sheet accounts, and you can enter the budget figures. See the following sections on creating P&L budgets to learn the procedures for entering budget figures.

P&L Budgets

The most common (and useful) budget is based on your income and expenses. After you've set up a good chart of accounts, creating a budget is quite easy.

Create the Budget and Its Criteria

To create a P&L budget, choose Company | Planning & Budgeting | Set Up Budgets. If this is the first budget you're creating, the Create New Budget Wizard opens to walk you through the process. (If you've already created a budget, the Set Up Budgets window appears with your existing budget loaded—click Create New Budget to launch the Create New Budget Wizard.) Enter the year for which you're creating the budget and select the P&L budget option.

Create New Budget

Create a New Budget

Begin by specifying the year and type for the new budget.

2009

Choose the budget type

● Profit and Loss (reflects all activity for the year)
○ Balance Sheet (reflects ending balance)

Back   Next   Finish   Cancel

NOTE: If you're not operating on a calendar year, the budget year field spans two calendar years, for instance 2009–10, to accommodate your fiscal year.

Click Next to select any additional criteria for this budget. You can include customers (and jobs) or classes in your budget.

Create New Budget

Additional Profit and Loss Budget Criteria

● No additional criteria
○ Customer:Job
○ Class

Back   Next   Finish   Cancel

For this discussion, I'll go over regular P&L budgets (unconnected to customers or classes), and I'll explain later in this chapter how to budget for customers and jobs and for classes. Click Next to choose between creating a budget from scratch or from the figures from last year's activities. I'll start by selecting the option to create a budget from scratch. Click Finish to open the budget window, where all your income and expense accounts are displayed (see Figure 23-1).

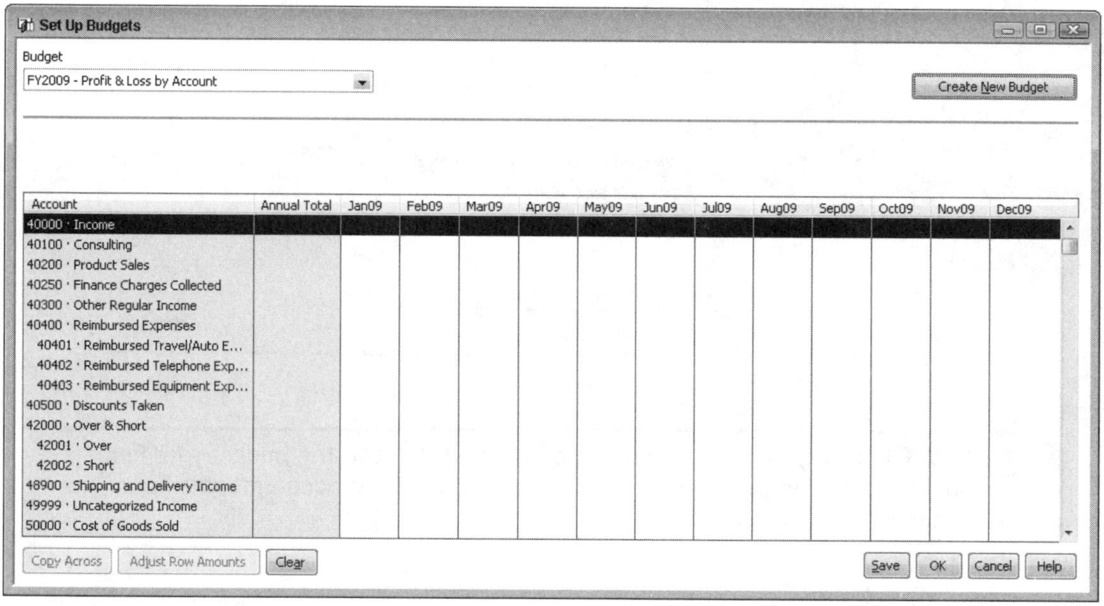

FIGURE 23-1   All active income and expense accounts are available for your budget.

Enter Budget Amounts

To create budget figures for an account, select the account and then click in the column of the first month you want to budget. Enter the budget figure, press TAB to move to the next month, and enter the appropriate amount. Repeat until all the months for this account have your budget figures. As you enter each monthly amount and press TAB, QuickBooks automatically calculates and displays the annual total for the account (see Figure 23-2).

Using Budget Entry Shortcuts

To save yourself from contracting a case of terminal ennui, QuickBooks provides some shortcuts for entering budget figures.

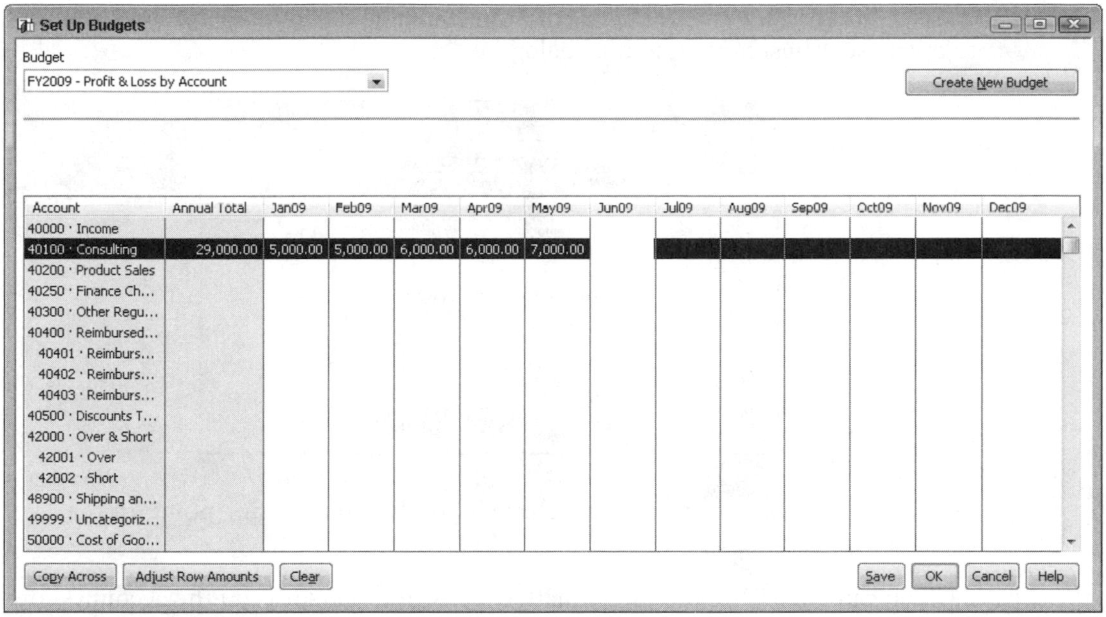

FIGURE 23-2 QuickBooks takes care of tracking the running totals.

Copy Numbers Across the Months

To copy a monthly figure from the current month (the month where your cursor is) to all the following months, enter the figure and click Copy Across. The numbers are copied to all the rest of the months of the year.

You can perform this shortcut as soon as you enter an amount (but before you press TAB), or you can return to the month you want to designate the first month by clicking its column (useful if you've entered figures for several months and then remember this shortcut).

This is handier than it seems at first glance. It's obvious that if you enter your rent in the first month and choose Copy Across, you've saved a lot of manual data entry. However, suppose your landlord sends you a notice that your rent is increasing beginning in July? To adjust the July–December budget figures, just move your cursor to July, enter the new rate, and click Copy Across.

The Copy Across button is also the only way to clear a row. Delete the figure in the first month (or enter a zero) and click Copy Across. The entire row is now blank (or filled with zeros).

Automatically Increase or Decrease Monthly Figures

After you've entered figures into all the months on an account's row, you can raise or lower monthly figures automatically. For example, you may want to raise an income account by an amount or a percentage starting in a certain month because you expect to sign a new customer or a new contract.

Select the first month that needs the adjustment and click Adjust Row Amounts to open the Adjust Row Amounts dialog.

Choose 1st Month or Currently Selected Month as the starting point for the calculations.

- You can choose 1st Month no matter where your cursor is on the account's row.
- You must click in the column for the appropriate month if you want to choose Currently Selected Month (you can click the first month to make that the currently selected month).
- To increase or decrease the amount in the selected month and all the months following by a specific amount, enter the amount.
- To increase or decrease the amount in the selected month and all columns to the right by a percentage, enter the percentage rate and the percentage sign.

Compound the Changes

If you select Currently Selected Month, the Adjust Row Amounts dialog adds an additional option named Enable Compounding.

> **TIP:** Although the Enable Compounding option appears only when you select Currently Selected Month, if your cursor is in the first month and you select the Currently Selected Month option, you can use compounding for the entire year.

When you enable compounding, the calculations for each month are increased or decreased based on a formula starting with the currently selected month and taking into consideration the resulting change in the previous month.

For example, if you entered $1,000.00 in the current month and indicated a $100.00 increase, the results differ from amounts that are not being compounded.

Compounding Enabled?	Current Month Original Figure	Current Month New Figure	Next Month	Next Month	Next Month	Next Month
Yes	1,000.00	1,000.00	1,100.00	1,200.00	1,300.00	1,400.00
No	1,000.00	1,100.00	1,100.00	1,100.00	1,100.00	1,100.00

Creating a Budget from Last Year's Data

If you used QuickBooks last year, you can create a budget based on last year's figures. To use last year's real data as the basis of your budget, open the Create New Budget Wizard by choosing Company | Planning & Budgeting | Set Up Budgets. When the Create New Budget Wizard opens, enter the year for which you're creating the budget, and select the P&L budget option. In the next window, select any additional criteria, such as a customer, job, or class. (I'm skipping additional criteria for this example.) In the next window, select the option to create the budget from the previous year's actual figures, and click Finish.

The budget window opens with last year's actual data used for the budget figures (see Figure 23-3). For each account that had activity, the ending monthly balances are entered in the appropriate month.

You can change any figures you wish using the procedures and shortcuts described earlier in this chapter.

Customer:Job Budgets

If you have a customer or a job that warrants it, you can create a P&L budget to track the financials for that customer or job against a budget. Usually, you only do this for a project that involves a substantial amount of money and/or covers a long period of time.

Account	Annual ...	Jan09	Feb09	Mar09	Apr09	May09	Jun09	Jul09	Aug09	Sep09	Oct09	Nov09	Dec09
4000 · Sales	180,084...	14,71...	7,340...	61,15...	5,568...	8,774...	7,408...	13,31...	10,49...	13,69...	7,388...	23,63...	6,587.40
4001 · Discounts Given	-39.48										-28.73		-10.75
4470 · Sales Tax Disc...	0.84		0.00						0.84				
4480 · OTHER REVEN...													
4490 · INTEREST INC...	113.44										8.88	54.59	37.74	12.23
4600 · Cost of Goods...	39,862.63	4,385...	2,035...	14,46...	1,126...	1,193...	1,672...	2,801...	2,448...	3,135...	1,607...	5,104...	-108.51
4610 · Discounts Taken													
4620 · Inventory Adj...	385.79	-122.69	-1,44...		1,451...	334.45	334.75	-65.00			-25.00	-75.00	
66900 · Reconciliatio...													
5010 · ADVERTISING	1,715.38	92.76		17.20					245.00				1,360.42
5120 · VEHICLE FUEL	1,141.13	120.30	96.00	102.40	111.31	98.54	88.71	106.22	96.55	85.58	55.47	90.06	89.99
5130 · BANK SERVIC...													
5150 · CONTRIBUTI...													
5160 · COMMISSIONS	5,762.00	1,450...	156.00	620.00	285.00	512.00	421.00	215.00	542.00	456.00	215.00	630.00	260.00
5170 · DEPRECIATIO...													
5180 · DUES & SUBS...													

FIGURE 23-3 Start your budget by looking at last year's figures.

Creating the First Customer:Job Budget

To create your first budget for a customer or a job, choose Company | Planning & Budgeting | Set Up Budgets. I'm assuming you're creating the budget from scratch, not from last year's P&L figures.

- If you already created another budget of a different type (P&L or Class), the budget window opens with the last budget you created. Click the Create New Budget button in the budget window to launch the Create New Budget Wizard.
- If this is your first-ever budget, the Create New Budget Wizard appears automatically.

Follow these steps to create a Customer:Job budget:

1. Select the year for your budget and choose Profit And Loss as the type.
2. In the next wizard window, select the option Customer:Job.
3. In the next window, specify whether you want to create the budget from scratch or from last year's data. Then click Finish.

In the Set Up Budgets window, select the Customer:Job for this budget from the drop-down list. Enter budget figures using the guidelines that follow.

- It's common to budget only expense accounts for a customer or job because the anticipated income is usually known.
- The expenses you track depend on the scope of the job. For example, you may only want to budget the cost of outside contractors or supplies, so if prices rise you can have a conversation with the customer about overruns.
- Enter a monthly budget figure for each account or for each month the project exists, or enter a total budget figure in the first month. The last option lets you compare accumulated data for expenses against the total budgeted figure by creating modified reports (where you change the report date to reflect the elapsed time for the project and filter the report for this job only).
- If the project is lengthy, you may budget some accounts for some months and other accounts for other months. For example, if you have a project that involves purchases of goods, followed by installation of those goods, or training for the customer's employees, you might choose to budget the purchases for the first few months and then the cost of the installation or training (either by tracking payroll or outside contractors) for the months in which those activities occur.
- If you want to track payroll costs against a job, use the QuickBooks Time and Billing features that are discussed in Chapter 16.

CAUTION: Customer:Job budget reports aren't accurate unless you're faithful about assigning every appropriate transaction to the customer or job.

Creating Additional Customer:Job Budgets

After you've created one budget based on a customer or job, creating a budget for a different customer or job requires different steps.

To create a budget for another customer immediately while the Customer:Job budget you just created is still in the budget window, select another customer from the drop-down list. When QuickBooks asks if you want to record (save) the budget you just finished, click Yes. Then begin entering data for the new budget.

To create a budget for another customer later, choose Company | Planning & Budgeting | Set Up Budgets. The budget window opens immediately with the last budget you worked on.

- If the budget that appears is a Customer:Job budget, select a different customer or job from the Current Customer:Job drop-down list and begin entering data.
- If the budget that appears is a different type of budget, click the arrow to the right of the Budget field and select Profit And Loss By Account And Customer:Job as the budget type. Then select a customer from the Current Customer:Job drop-down list and begin entering data.

Class Budgets

You can link your budget to any class you've created (if you're using class tracking). I've learned that this works well for certain types of classes and not for others. If you're using classes to track branch offices, company divisions, or company departments, you can create useful budgets. If, on the other hand, you're using classes to divide your transactions in some esoteric way, budgeting may not work well.

Look at your class-based reports, and if you find yourself asking, "Aren't those expenses higher than they should be?" or "Why is one class less profitable than the other classes?" you might want to budget each month to get a handle on where and when expenses got out of hand. Also, if you ask, "Is this department contributing the income I expected?" include income accounts in your budget. You can use income accounts in class budgets to provide incentives to your employees— perhaps a bonus to a manager if the reality is better than the budget.

To create a class-based budget, use the steps described earlier to create a budget and choose Class in the Additional Profit And Loss Budget Criteria Wizard window. When the budget window opens, a Current Class field appears. Select the class for which you're creating a budget from the drop-down list. Then begin entering data.

To create additional class budgets (for other classes, of course), use the same approach discussed in the previous section on creating additional customer or job budgets.

Budget Reports

QuickBooks provides a number of budget reports you can use to see how you're doing. I'll discuss each of them in this section. To get to the reports, choose Reports | Budgets from the menu bar and then select one of the following reports:

- Budget Overview
- Budget vs. Actual
- Profit & Loss Budget Performance
- Budget vs. Actual Graph

Budget Overview

This report shows the accounts you budgeted and the amounts you budgeted for each month. Accounts that you didn't include in the budget aren't displayed.

Profit & Loss Budget Overview

If you created multiple budgets, select the budget you want to view from the drop-down list and click Next. In the next window, select a report layout (the options differ depending on the type of budget). Click Next, and then click Finish. Essentially, the Overview report type produces the display you'd see if the window you use to create a budget had a button labeled Print The Budget.

This report includes inactive accounts, even though inactive accounts are not displayed when you create a budget. This may be confusing if you print this report as the "official" budget for your company.

If you use subaccounts in your budget, you can click the Collapse button at the top of the report window to see only the parent account totals. The button name changes to Expand, and clicking it puts the subaccount lines back into the display.

To condense the numbers, use the Columns drop-down list to select a different interval. The default is Month, but you can choose another interval and QuickBooks will calculate the figures to fit. For example, you might want to select Quarter to see four columns of three-month subtotals (and a Total column).

If you want to tweak the budget, or play "what if" games by experimenting with different numbers, click the Export button to send the report to Microsoft Excel.

Balance Sheet Budget Overview

If you created a Balance Sheet budget, select Balance Sheet By Account in the first window and then click Next. QuickBooks displays a graphical representation of the report's layout (it's a monthly layout similar to the layout for the P&L budget). Click Finish to see the report.

Customer:Job Budget Overview

If you created budgets for customers or jobs, select Profit & Loss By Account And Customer:Job in the first window and click Next. Select a report layout from the drop-down list (as you select each option from the list, QuickBooks displays a diagram of the layout). The following choices are available:

- **Account By Month**   Lists each account you used in the budget and displays the total budget amounts (for all customer budgets you created) for each month that has data. No budget information for individual customers appears.
- **Account By Customer:Job**   Lists each account you used in the budget and displays the fiscal year total for that account for each customer (each customer has its own column).
- **Customer:Job By Month**   Displays a row for each customer that has a budget and a column for each month. The budget totals (for all accounts—individual accounts are not displayed) appear under each month. Under each customer's row is a row for each job that has a budget.

TIP: The name of each layout choice is a hint about the way it displays in the report. The first word represents the rows, and the word after the word "by" represents the columns.

Class Budget Overview

If you created a Class budget, select Profit & Loss By Account And Class in the first window and click Next. Select a report layout from the drop-down list. You have the following choices:

- **Account By Month**   Lists each account you used in the budget and displays the total budget amounts (for all Class budgets you created) for each month that has data. No budget information for individual classes appears.
- **Account By Class**   Lists each account you used in the budget and displays the yearly total for that account for each class (each class has its own column).
- **Class By Month**   Displays a row for each class that has a budget and a column for each month. The total budget (not broken down by account) appears for each month.

Budget vs. Actual

This report's name says it all—you can see how your real numbers compare to your budget figures. For a straight P&L budget, the report displays the following data for each month of your budget, for each account:

- Amount posted
- Amount budgeted
- Difference in dollars
- Difference in percentage

The choices for the budget type are the same as the Budget Overview, so you can see account totals, customer totals, or class totals to match the budgets you've created.

The first thing you'll notice in the report is that all the accounts in your general ledger are listed, regardless of whether or not you included them in your budget. However, only the accounts you used in your budget show budget figures. You can change that by customizing the report to include only your budgeted accounts, using the following steps:

1. Click the Modify Report button at the top of the budget report window.
2. In the Modify Report window, click the Advanced button to open the Advanced Options dialog.
3. Click the option labeled Show Only Rows And Columns With Budgets.
4. Click OK to return to the Modify Report window.
5. Click OK again to return to the Budget vs. Actual Report window.

Now, the data that's displayed is only that data connected to your budgeted accounts.

You can also use the options in the Modify Report window to make the following changes:

- Change the report dates.
- Change the calculations from Accrual to Cash (which means that unpaid invoices and bills are removed from the calculations, and only actual income and expenses are reported).

You should memorize the report so you don't have to make these modifications the next time you want to view a comparison report. Click the Memorize button at the top of the report window and then give the report a meaningful name. Only the formatting changes you make are memorized, not the data. Every time you open the report, it displays current data. To view the report after you memorize it, choose Reports | Memorized Reports from the QuickBooks menu bar.

Profit & Loss Budget Performance

This report is similar to the Budget vs. Actual report, but it's based on the current month and the year to date. For that time period, the report displays your actual income and expenses compared to what you budgeted.

By default, the date range is the current month, but you can change that to see last month's figures or the figures for any previous month. This report is also available for all types, as described in "Budget Overview," earlier in this section, and can also be modified to customize the display.

Budget vs. Actual Graph

This report just opens; you have no choices to select first. All the choices are in the graph that displays, in the form of buttons across the top of the report window. Merely click the type of report you want to see.

Exporting Budgets

If you need to manipulate your budgets, export them to other software applications. One common task is to change the budget dates to the following year, so you can import your budgets back into QuickBooks and use them as the basis of next year's budgets.

You have two methods for exporting your budgets:

- Export all your budgets to a delimited text file that can be opened in Excel, Access (or another database program), or even Word (where you can convert the text to a table).
- Export a Budget Overview report to Excel.

Exporting Budgets to Delimited Text Files

When you export budgets to a delimited text file (the delimiter is a Tab) you can't select specific budgets to export—it's all or nothing. Use the following steps to export your budgets:

1. Choose File | Utilities | Export | Lists To IIF Files from the QuickBooks menu bar.
2. When the Export dialog opens, it displays all the QuickBooks lists. Select the item named Budgets and click OK.
3. Another Export dialog opens (this one looks like the Save dialog you're used to seeing in Windows software). Select a folder in which to save this exported file, or leave it in your QuickBooks folder (the default location). I usually change the folder to the location where I keep files for the program I'm going to use for the exported file.
4. Give the exported list a filename (for example, 2009 Budgets). QuickBooks will automatically add the extension .IIF to the filename.
5. Click Save. QuickBooks displays a message telling you that your data has been exported successfully.
6. Click OK.

Exporting a Budget Report to Excel

You can export any budget report to Excel, although it's common to use the Budget Overview report. Click the Export button at the top of the report window to open the Export Report dialog and select a new workbook if this is the first budget you're exporting; if you're exporting multiple budgets in this manner, you can select an existing workbook and create separate worksheets for each budget.

Importing Budgets Back into QuickBooks

The only circumstances under which you'd import budgets back into QuickBooks is to copy a budget to another year. If you wanted to edit figures, you'd work in the QuickBooks budget window. To play "what if" games or to sort the budget differently, you'd work in the appropriate software (such as Excel) because QuickBooks doesn't provide those features.

Before you can import the file you must save it as a delimited text file, choosing Tab as the delimiter. You must also change the filename extension to .IIF. Then follow these steps to bring the budget into QuickBooks:

1. Choose File | Utilities | Import | IIF Files from the menu bar to open the Import dialog.
2. Locate and double-click the file you saved.
3. When QuickBooks displays a message telling you the import was successful, click OK.

You can view the imported budgets in any budget report or in the budget window. QuickBooks checks the dates and changes the budget's name to reflect the dates. Budget names start with FY*xxxx*, where *xxxx* is the fiscal year.

When you select a budget report or choose a budget to edit in the budget window, the available budgets include both the budgets you created in QuickBooks (FY2009) and the budgets you imported after changing the date (FY2010). Next year, you can delete the FY2009 budgets.

Projecting Cash Flow

The Cash Flow Projector is a tool you can use to build a report that projects your cash flows using your own criteria. This tool uses data in your company file and then lets you remove and add accounts and even adjust figures. These features make it easier to achieve the projection parameters and results you need.

The Cash Flow Projector is rather powerful if you understand the accounting terminology and principles of determining cash flows. You can design very specific cash flow scenarios, which might be useful in planning for expansion or other major business events.

It's beyond the scope of this book to provide a detailed explanation of the best ways to use this tool, but in this section I'll give you an overview.

NOTE: Unless you have quite a bit of expertise in accounting, it's best to work with your accountant when you use the Cash Flow Projector.

To ensure accuracy, make sure you've entered all transactions, including memorized transactions, into your QuickBooks company file. Then launch the Cash Flow Projector by choosing Company | Planning & Budgeting | Cash Flow Projector. The program operates like a wizard, and the opening window (see Figure 23-4) welcomes you and offers links to information you should read before you begin.

TIP: Each ensuing wizard window has a button labeled Preview Projection. Click it to see your results so far.

Click Next to display the Beginning Balance window (see Figure 23-5), and select the cash accounts you want to include in your projection.

The software calculates a beginning balance by adding together the balances of all the accounts you select. You can make an adjustment to that calculated balance to change the beginning balance of the cash flows projection. This is useful if you

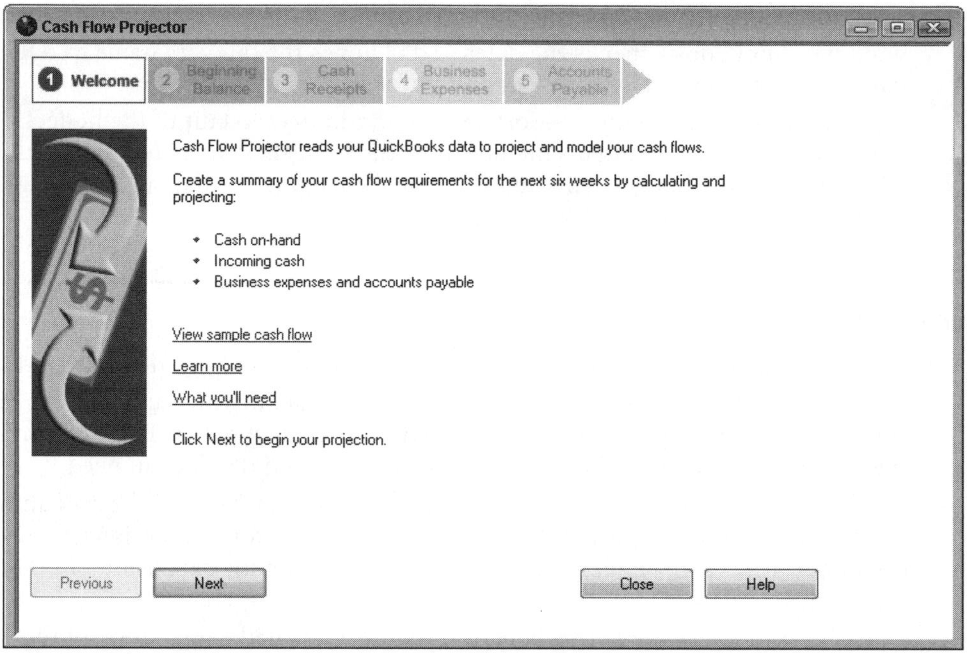

FIGURE 23-4 Use the links to familiarize yourself with the information the wizard needs.

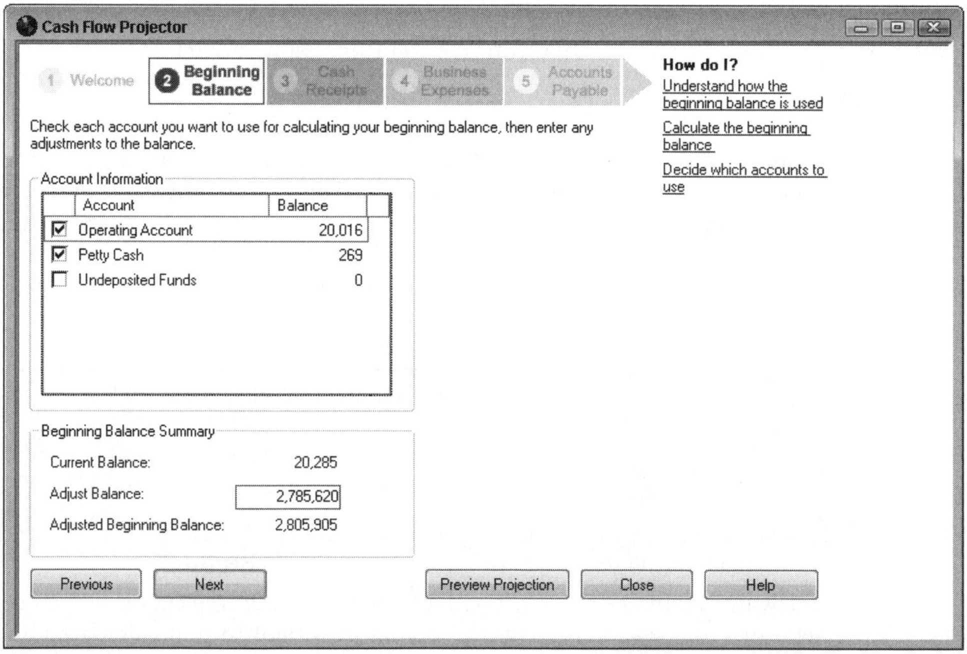

FIGURE 23-5 Select the accounts to use to project your cash flow.

know the current balance of any account contains an amount that you don't want included in the projection, such as an income item that is earmarked for spending today or tomorrow and therefore shouldn't be counted.

Click Next to move to the Cash Receipts window (see Figure 23-6). You must select a projection method from the drop-down list. If you don't understand the terminology in the list, discuss it with your accountant. One of the choices is manual entry, which is useful if your accountant has some particular paradigm in mind or if you don't have A/R totals to guide you because you run a retail business.

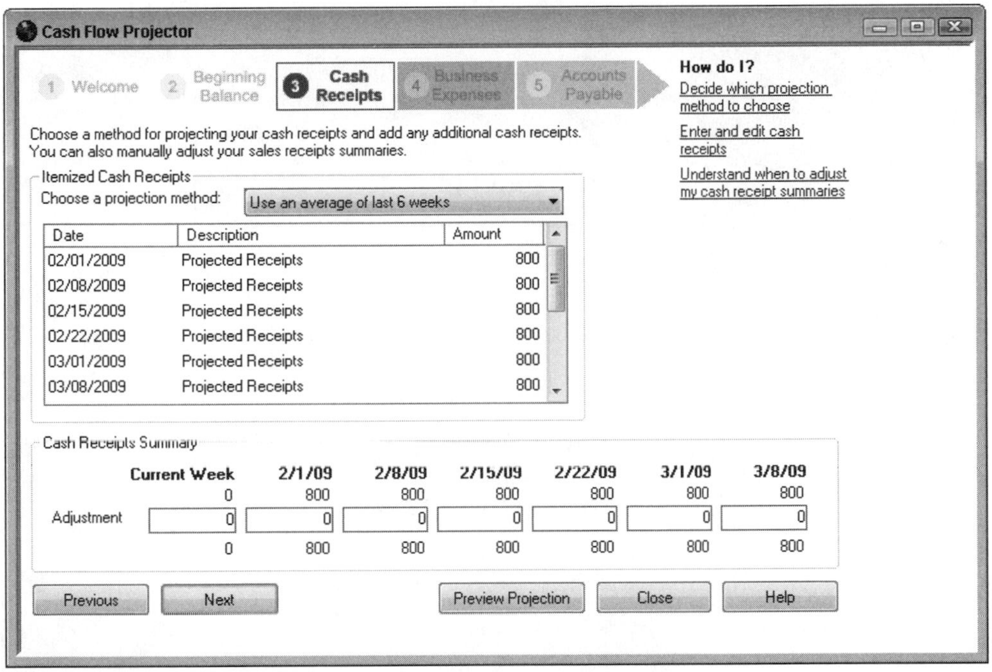

FIGURE 23-6 Summarize your projected cash receipts on a weekly basis.

The next two wizard windows look similar to Figure 23-6, but they deal with expenses, starting with expenses that are not accounts-payable expenses (expenses for which you write direct checks instead of entering bills, and any unique expenses that qualify as "one-time-only") and moving on to accounts-payable expenses (including recurring bills you've entered into your system). In both windows you can enter specific expenses or enter adjusted total expenses.

This brief discussion should help you examine the explanations and instructions and understand the possibilities in this tool. If you have a need for a variety of cash flow scenarios, you should go over this tool and the way it can be applied to your business needs with your accountant.

Year-End Procedures

In *this chapter:*

- The year-end To Do list

- Run financial reports

- Print 1099 forms

- Make year-end journal entries

- Get ready for taxes

- Close the books

- Create a year-end backup

The end of the year is a madhouse for bookkeepers, and that's true for major corporations as well as for small businesses. There is so much to do: so many reports to examine, corrections to make, entries to create, adjustments to apply— whew!

You can relax a bit. You don't have to show up at the office on January 1 (or the first day of your new fiscal year if you're not on a calendar year). Everything doesn't have to be accomplished immediately. QuickBooks is date sensitive so you can continue to work in the new year without impacting the totals of the previous year. As long as the dates of new transactions are after the last day of your fiscal year, the transactions won't work their way into your year-end calculations.

The Year-End To Do List

Most of the topics in this chapter are instructions for printing reports and creating transactions to make sure your company file is accurate at the end of the year (so your tax return is accurate). In addition to the specific year-end tasks covered in this chapter, you should create a year-end To Do list so you don't miss anything important. In this section I discuss some commonly needed year-end processes.

Bank Reconciliation

In January, when your December statement arrives from your bank, print an extra copy of the bank reconciliation report. Your cash position at year's end is important for planning, applying for credit, tax returns, and other purposes.

 N O T E : If your fiscal year is not a calendar year, substitute the appropriate months for January and December.

Inventory Stock Status

Perform a physical inventory immediately after the end of the year. Adjust the physical count to remove stock changes (sales and receipt of goods) that occurred after the last day of the year, and then create an inventory adjustment dated the last day of the previous year (see Chapter 7 to learn about using the QuickBooks inventory count processes and inventory adjustments).

Fixed Assets

Create a report on your fixed asset accounts to see purchases for the year, as well as accumulated depreciation totals for fixed assets that were purchased in prior years.

The easy way to create this report is to select any fixed asset account in your chart of accounts and press CTRL-Q to open a QuickReport on that account. Click Modify Report, move to the Filters tab, and select Account in the Filter list. Then select All Fixed Assets from the drop-down list in the Account field. The resulting report displays information about all your fixed assets, including purchases and accumulated depreciation.

Payroll

Payroll reports are always due as of the end of the calendar year, regardless of your company's fiscal year setup. See Chapter 18 to learn about year-end payroll processes, including W-2 forms.

If you run your payroll in-house, QuickBooks insists on using the check date as the basis for payroll, not the payroll time period covered by the check. For example, if you pay employees on Friday for the pay period ending the previous Saturday, all payroll reports are based on the Friday paycheck date. That means, for 2009, the last payroll figures are reported as of the last Friday in December. Paychecks issued in January 2010 for the period covering the end of December 2009 are not part of your payroll totals.

Some businesses (and accountants) prefer to track salaries and wages as a liability based on the work period and pay off that liability with the paycheck. Because QuickBooks won't manage payroll in this way, they create journal entries to track accrued salaries and wages. In 2009, that accrued entry covers December 21 through December 27 (and will be paid with the paycheck issued January 2, 2009).

If you're accruing payroll entries, and you file taxes on a cash basis, you need to make a journal entry for the accrued amounts that won't be paid by the end of the year. A reversing journal entry (dated December 31, 2009, and reversed on January 1, 2010) takes care of maintaining the figures you need.

Running Year-End Financial Reports

The standard financial reports you run at year-end provide a couple of services for you:

- You can see the economic health of your business.
- You can examine the report to make sure everything is posted correctly before you organize information for paying taxes.

Don't forget that reports have date ranges like "current year" and "last fiscal year." If you perform these tasks before the end of your fiscal year, you're still in the current year. However, if you're working after the last date of your fiscal year (which is quite common), the current year isn't the year of interest. Instead, choose Last Fiscal Year.

Profit & Loss Reports

Start with a Profit & Loss Standard report (also called an *income statement*) by choosing Reports | Company & Financial | Profit & Loss Standard. When the report opens, be sure the date range is the entire fiscal year—either the current fiscal year or the last fiscal year, depending on when you're generating the report (by default, the date range is the current month to date).

The report displays the year-end balances for all the income and expense accounts in your general ledger that had any activity this year. Examine the report, and if anything seems out of whack, double-click the line to see a list of the postings to that account. If the data you see doesn't reassure you, double-click any of the individual posting lines to see the original transaction.

If there's a transaction that seems to be in error, you can take corrective action. You cannot delete or void a bill you paid or a customer invoice for which you received payment, of course. However, you might be able to talk to a customer or vendor for whom you've found a problem and work out a satisfactory arrangement for credits. Or you may find that you posted an expense or income transaction to the wrong general ledger account. If so, either change the posting account in the transaction, or create a journal entry to correct it (see Chapter 19 for information on creating journal entries). Then run the year-end P&L report again and print it.

> **N O T E :** If you followed the advice in Chapter 2 about using numbered accounts and arranging your numbering scheme so that income and expenses are designed to match the totals and subtotals you need to file taxes (instead of being arranged alphabetically), you can export this report to Excel and insert subtotals to match the subtotals you need on your tax return. This makes tax preparation much easier.

Year-End Balance Sheet

Your financial health is demonstrated in your Balance Sheet, and you should look at this report toward the end of your fiscal year. To run a year-end balance sheet, choose Reports | Company & Financial | Balance Sheet Standard. The Balance Sheet figures are more than a list of numbers; they're a list of chores. Check with your accountant first, but often you'll find that the following advice is offered:

- Try to pay your payroll withholding liabilities in the current year (the year in which they were accumulated) in order to clear them from the Balance Sheet. Also pay employer contributions.
- If you have an A/P balance, pay as many bills as you can afford in the current year. Even if this means you pay vendor bills earlier than their due dates (if those dates fall in the next year), you can gain the expense deduction for this year.

Issuing 1099 Forms

If any vendors are eligible for 1099 forms, you need to print and mail the forms to them by the end of January. Most of the work involved in issuing 1099 forms is done during company setup, where you set up the conditions for 1099 tracking. Then, during the year, you must make sure the transactions you enter are posted to the proper accounts so that your configuration settings are met.

Checking the 1099 Setup

First, make sure your 1099 setup is correct by choosing Edit | Preferences, selecting the Tax: 1099 icon, and moving to the Company Preferences tab to see your settings (see Figure 24-1).

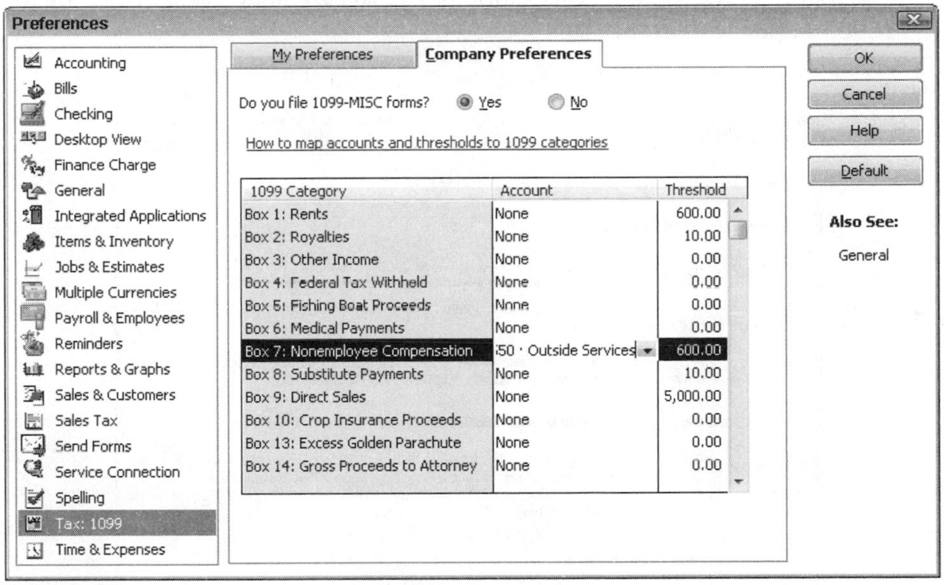

FIGURE 24-1 QuickBooks supports Form 1099-MISC, and you must configure the categories (boxes) for which you issue that form.

Be sure you assigned at least one account to the category for which you'll be issuing Form 1099 to vendors. You can assign multiple accounts to a 1099 category, but you cannot assign any accounts to more than one 1099 category.

For example, if you have an expense account "subcontractors" and an expense account "outside consultants," both of the accounts can be linked to the same 1099 category (Box 7—Nonemployee Compensation). However, once you link those accounts to that category, you cannot use those same accounts in any other 1099 category.

To assign a single account to a category, click the category to select it. Click the text in the account column (it probably says "None") and then click the arrow to select the account for this category.

To assign multiple accounts to a category, instead of selecting an account after you click the arrow, choose the Multiple Accounts option (at the top of the list). In the Select Account dialog, click each appropriate account to put a check mark next to its listing. Click OK to assign all the accounts you checked. Then click OK to close the Preferences dialog.

Using the 1099 Wizard

Before you print the forms, you need to run a checkup—it's essential to make sure everything is correct before you send forms to vendors and the government.

QuickBooks provides a wizard that walks you through the process to make sure every step is covered and every amount is correct. Choose Vendors | Print 1099s/ 1096 to open the wizard (see Figure 24-2).

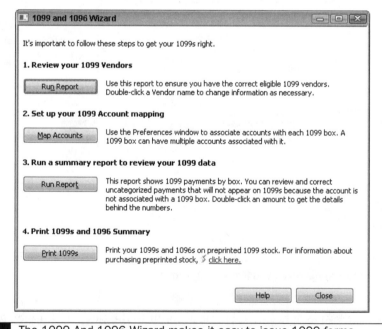

FIGURE 24-2   The 1099 And 1096 Wizard makes it easy to issue 1099 forms.

This isn't a standard wizard, because you don't walk through a series of windows. Instead, as you check each item in the window, QuickBooks opens the appropriate QuickBooks report window or print dialog so you can check, and if necessary, change the data. When you close each window, you're returned to the wizard window.

In the following sections I'll go over the wizard's functions in the order in which they appear, except for the function labeled Map Accounts, which opens the Preferences dialog for the Tax 1099 category, which I discussed in the previous section.

Vendor 1099 Review Report

Click Run Report in the 1099 Review section of the wizard window to display the report, which shows you all the vendors in your system. The important column is the one labeled Eligible For 1099 (see Figure 24-3).

Vendor	Tax ID	Eligible for 1099	Address	City	State
2155550621		No	Verizon P.O. Box 9999 Philadelphia PA 19100-9999	Philadelphia	PA
2155557777		No	Verizon		
2155559999		No	Verizon P.O. Box 1011 Philadelphia PA 19101-1011	Philadelphia	PA
Alberts	100-10-1000	Yes	12 Smith Rd Glenside PA 19038	Glenside	PA
Barich	123-45-6798	Yes	Tom Barich		
Bell		No	Bell Atlantic P.O. Box 1234 Philadelphia PA 19000	Philadelphia	PA
Blue Cross		No	Blue Cross		
cash		No	cash		
cleaners		No	cleaning		
DelValSupplies		No			
Discount Office Supplies		No	Discount Office Supplies		
Electric		No	Electric		
GeekRob	001-02-0001	Yes	3 Main Avenue Philadelphia PA 19919	Philadelphia	PA

FIGURE 24-3 Make sure your vendor information is correct for 1099 forms.

This report includes vendors you've marked as inactive, so you won't miss any vendor who must receive a 1099. Check the following data in the report:

- Be sure that every vendor who should be receiving a 1099 is marked Yes.
- Be sure that for every vendor marked Yes, you have a Tax ID and a complete mailing address.

TIP: If a Tax ID or an address is missing, or if a vendor who should be a 1099 recipient is marked as No (or the other way around), you can fix it immediately. Double-click the listing in this report to open the vendor's record. Make the appropriate changes, and when you click OK, the report data is updated.

1099 Summary Report

The wizard button labeled Run Report, in the 1099 Summary section, opens the 1099 Summary report (which you can view at any time by choosing Reports | Vendors & Payables | 1099 Summary). The report displays each vendor eligible for a 1099, along with the total amount paid to that vendor. The report is sorted by Box Number, but many small businesses only use Box 7:Nonemployee Compensation, so that may be the only Box Number you see on the report.

If the numbers don't seem right, you can double-click any vendor's total to see the transactions that made up the total, and you can double-click any transaction listing to see the original transaction.

Make sure you posted transactions to an account configured for 1099s when appropriate. If not, you can safely change the posting account on a transaction (the "unsafe" changes are those that change the amount of a paid bill or cleared check).

Click the Print button to create a hard copy of this report so you can use it to double-check your 1099 data (covered next).

Checking for 1099 Errors

After you print the 1099 Summary report, choose Reports | Vendors & Payables | 1099 Details to display the 1099 Details report. Make sure the date range is correct, and then perform the actions described in the following sections.

Checking Vendor Payments Posted to Accounts Configured for Form 1099

In the 1099 options fields (under the Dates field) change the default selection Only 1099 Vendors to All Vendors, and make sure the second field is configured for Only 1099 Accounts.

If another vendor name appears on the report, it means you posted at least one payment for that vendor to an account that you're tracking for 1099 payments.

- Is that vendor supposed to receive a 1099? If so, open the vendor's record and move to the Additional Info tab to enable Form 1099. Make sure you have a Tax ID number for this vendor.

- Is that vendor not supposed to receive a 1099? If that's the case, it's perfectly okay to post transactions to the account configured for 1099 tracking without sending the vendor a 1099 at the end of the year.

 NOTE: Vendors that are corporations do not receive Form 1099. Vendors that are organized as LLCs may be filing taxes as a corporation, a partnership, or a proprietorship (the IRS doesn't recognize an LLC as a tax entity). Ask your LLC vendors if they file corporate tax returns; if so, they won't need Form 1099.

Checking 1099 Vendor Payments Posted to Accounts Not Configured for Form 1099

To make sure all payments to your 1099 vendors appear in the total remittance amount on Form 1099, change the default selections on the 1099 Detail report to Only 1099 Vendors and All Allowed Accounts.

Compare the report to the totals on the 1099 Summary report. As you can see in Figure 24-4, you may find an additional amount, posted to an account that is not configured for 1099 tracking, which affects the total payments to this vendor.

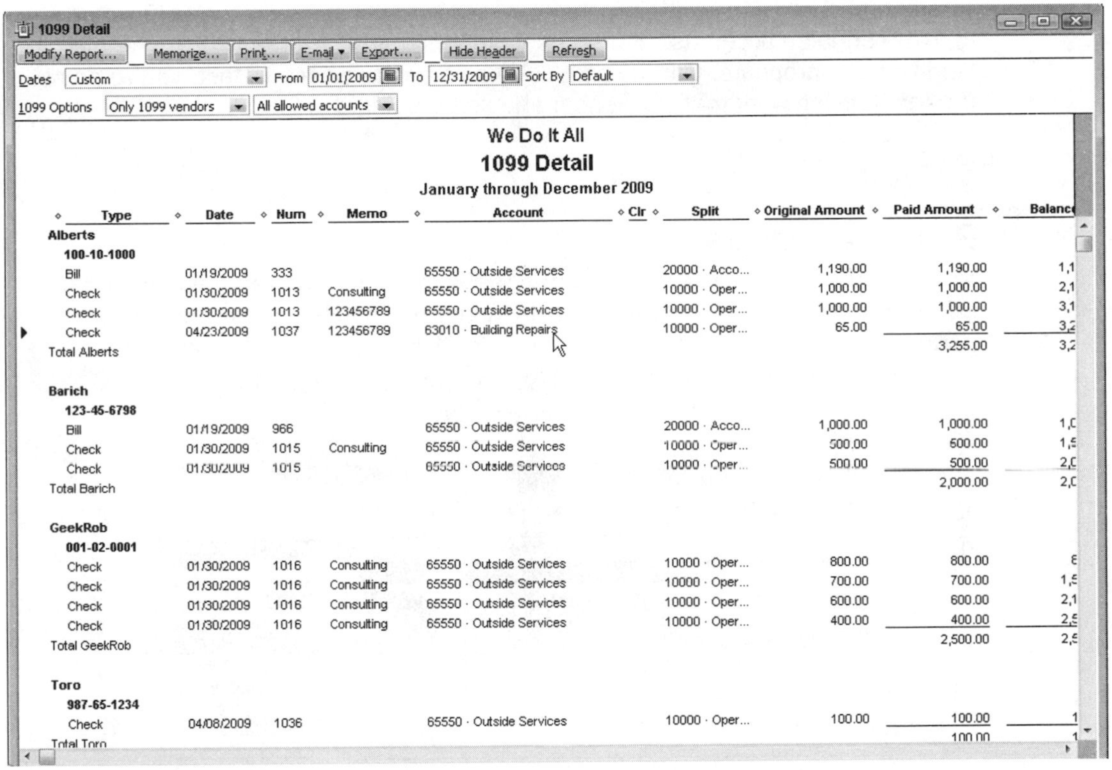

Type	Date	Num	Memo	Account	Clr	Split	Original Amount	Paid Amount	Balanc
Alberts									
100-10-1000									
Bill	01/19/2009	333		65550 · Outside Services		20000 · Acco...	1,190.00	1,190.00	1,1
Check	01/30/2009	1013	Consulting	65550 · Outside Services		10000 · Oper...	1,000.00	1,000.00	2,1
Check	01/30/2009	1013	123456789	65550 · Outside Services		10000 · Oper...	1,000.00	1,000.00	3,1
Check	04/23/2009	1037	123456789	63010 · Building Repairs		10000 · Oper...	65.00	65.00	3,2
Total Alberts								3,255.00	3,2
Barich									
123-45-6798									
Bill	01/19/2009	966		65550 · Outside Services		20000 · Acco...	1,000.00	1,000.00	1,0
Check	01/30/2009	1015	Consulting	65550 · Outside Services		10000 · Oper...	500.00	500.00	1,5
Check	01/30/2009	1015		65550 · Outside Services		10000 · Oper...	500.00	500.00	2,0
Total Barich								2,000.00	2,0
GeekRob									
001-02-0001									
Check	01/30/2009	1016	Consulting	65550 · Outside Services		10000 · Oper...	800.00	800.00	8
Check	01/30/2009	1016	Consulting	65550 · Outside Services		10000 · Oper...	700.00	700.00	1,5
Check	01/30/2009	1016	Consulting	65550 · Outside Services		10000 · Oper...	600.00	600.00	2,1
Check	01/30/2009	1016	Consulting	65550 · Outside Services		10000 · Oper...	400.00	400.00	2,5
Total GeekRob								2,500.00	2,5
Toro									
987-65-1234									
Check	04/08/2009	1036		65550 · Outside Services		10000 · Oper...	100.00	100.00	1
Total Toro								100.00	1

FIGURE 24-4 A check to this 1099 vendor was not posted to a 1099-enabled account.

If the posting account for the additional transaction(s) was an obvious error, double-click the listing to drill down to the original transaction window and change the account to the appropriate 1099-enabled account. Then create another 1099 Summary report to make sure the changes appear.

If the posting account was for reimbursement for an expense the 1099 vendor accrued on your behalf, talk to your accountant about the way to handle reimbursements for 1099 vendors. Some accountants prefer that you post all payments to 1099-enabled accounts (such as Outside Services or Consulting Services), and let the 1099 vendor take care of costs and reimbursements in his or her own tax return. Other accountants don't care if you separate reimbursements from payments for services and then only report the payments for services on the 1099.

CAUTION: IRS publications for Form 1099 specifically state that reimbursements for automobile expenses should be included in Form 1099 MISC. For other types of reimbursements to 1099 vendors, check with your accountant. The truth is, it's much easier to post all payments to 1099 vendors to 1099-enabled accounts, and enter "reimbursement" on the check's Memo field when appropriate. Otherwise, you're doing extra work—in fact, you're doing the tax tracking work that the vendor should be doing.

Printing 1099s

When all the data is correct, click Print 1099s in the wizard window. The wizard asks you to confirm the year for which you're printing (I'm assuming you're performing this task in January of next year, so choose Last Calendar Year).

Click OK to move to the Select 1099s To Print dialog. QuickBooks displays the vendors for whom you should be printing 1099s.

✓	Vendor	Valid ID	Valid Address	Total
✓	Alberts	Yes	Yes	3,190.00
✓	Barich	Yes	No	2,000.00
✓	GeekRob	Yes	Yes	2,500.00

Select 1099s to Print

Select vendors to print 1099-MISC / 1096 forms:

Buttons: Preview 1099, Print 1099, Print 1096, Cancel, Help, Select All, Select None

1096 Summary Information
Number of vendors selected: 3
Total for vendors selected: 7,690.00

Click Preview 1099 to see what the form will look like when it prints. Zoom in to make sure your company name, address, and EIN number are correct, and also check the vendor's information to make sure it's up to date.

Click Close on the Print Preview window to return to the Select 1099s To Print window. Then load the 1099 forms into your printer and click Print 1099. If you're using a laser or inkjet printer, set the number of copies at three. Dot-matrix printers use three-part forms.

When the forms are printed, click Print 1096 in the Select 1099s To Print dialog. Enter the name of the contact person in your company that can answer questions about these forms (the name is printed on the 1096 form).

Print two copies of the 1096, so you have one for your files. Send each vendor a copy of the 1099 form by January 31. Send the government a copy of each 1099, along with a 1096 Transmittal Form.

Repeat these procedures for each Box Number of the 1099-MISC form you are required to print (most small businesses only need Box 7).

Making Year-End Journal Entries

Your accountant may want you to make some journal entries before you close your books for the year, such as the following:

- Enter depreciation
- Move retained earnings to an account created to hold prior retained earnings, or move retained earnings to owner or partner equity retained earnings accounts
- Create adjustments needed for cash versus accrual reporting (these are usually reversed on the first day of the next fiscal year)
- Adjust prepaid expenses from asset accounts to expense accounts

N O T E : See Chapter 19 for detailed instructions for creating journal entries.

You can send the P&L and Balance Sheet reports to your accountant by exporting the reports to Excel.

You can also send your accountant an accountant's copy of your company data and let your accountant make the journal entries. You import the changes when the file is returned. (See Chapter 20 to learn how to use the Accountant's Copy feature.)

Getting Ready for Taxes

Most small businesses turn over the tax preparation chores to their accountants, but some business owners prepare their own taxes manually or by using a tax software program like TurboTax.

No matter which method you choose for tax preparation, you should run the reports that tell you whether your QuickBooks data files are ready for tax preparation. Is all the necessary data entered? Do the bottom-line numbers call for some special tax planning or special tax considerations? Even if your taxes are prepared by your accountant, the more organized your records are, the less time the accountant spends on your return (which makes your bill from the accountant smaller).

Check Tax Line Information

If you're going to do your own taxes, every account in your chart of accounts that is tax related must have the right tax form in the account's tax line assignment. To see if any tax line assignments are missing, choose Reports | Accountant & Taxes | Income Tax Preparation. When the report appears, all your accounts are listed, along with the tax form assigned to each account. If you created your own chart of accounts, instead of accepting a chart of accounts during company setup, the number of accounts that lack a tax form assignment is likely to be quite large.

Before you can prepare your own taxes, you should edit each account to add the tax information. To do so, open the chart of accounts and select an account. Press CTRL-E to edit the account and select a tax form from the Tax-Line Mapping drop-down list.

Your selections vary depending upon the organizational type of your company (proprietorship, partnership, S-Corp, C-Corp, and so on).

NOTE: Be sure the Income Tax Form Used field is filled out properly on the Company Information dialog (on the Company menu). If it's blank, you won't see the tax information fields on any accounts.

If you don't know which form and category to assign to an account, here's an easy trick for getting that information. Choose File | New Company to open the EasyStep Interview Wizard, and click Skip Interview to open the Creating New Company dialog.

Enter a name in the Company Name field (it doesn't matter what name you use; you're not really creating a company file). Click Next and select the correct organizational type and Income Tax Form. Next, enter the first month of your fiscal year, and in the next window select the type of company that best describes your business (if nothing comes close to matching your business, select General Business). Click Next, and save the new company file.

When the new company file is loaded into the QuickBooks window, open the chart of accounts list and press CTRL-P to print the list. The printed list has the tax form information you need. Open your real company, open the chart of accounts, and use the information on the printed document to enter tax form information.

Calculate Other Important Tax Information

There are some taxable numbers that aren't available through the normal QuickBooks reports. One of the most common is the report on company officer compensation if your business is incorporated.

If your business is a C-Corporation, you file tax Form 1120, while a Subchapter S-corporation files tax Form 1120S. Both of these forms require you to separate compensation for corporate officers from the other employee compensation. You will have to add those totals from payroll reports (either QuickBooks payroll or an outside payroll service).

You can avoid the need to calculate this by creating a separate Payroll item called Officer Compensation and assigning it to its own account (named something like Salaries & Wages—Officers, which you'll also have to create). Then open the Employee card for each officer and change the Earnings item to the new item. Do this for next year; it's probably too late for this year's end-of-year process.

Using TurboTax

If you purchase TurboTax to do your taxes, you don't have to do anything special in QuickBooks to transfer the information. Open TurboTax and tell it to import your QuickBooks company file.

Almost everything you need is transferred to TurboTax. There are some details you'll have to enter directly into TurboTax (for example, home-office expenses for a Schedule C form). You can learn more about TurboTax at www.turbotax.com.

Closing Your Books

After all the year-end reports have been run, any necessary journal entries have been entered, and your taxes have been filed, it's customary to go through the exercise of closing the books. Typically, closing the books occurs some time after the end of the fiscal year, usually within the first couple of months of the next fiscal year, as soon as your business tax forms have been filed.

The exercise of closing the books is performed to lock the books, so no user can add, remove, or change any transactions. After taxes have been filed based on the information in the system, nothing should ever be changed.

Understanding Closing in QuickBooks

QuickBooks doesn't use the traditional accounting software closing procedures. In most other business accounting software, closing the year means you cannot post transactions to any date in that year, nor can you manipulate any transactions in the closed year. Closing the books in QuickBooks does not set the information in cement; it can be changed and/or deleted by users with the appropriate permissions.

QuickBooks does not require you to close the books in order to keep working in the software. You can work forever, year after year, without performing a closing process. However, many QuickBooks users prefer to lock the transactions for the previous year as a way to prevent any changes to the data except by users with the appropriate permissions who know the password (you create the password when you close the books).

When transactions are locked, existing transactions can't be changed and new transactions cannot contain a date that is on or before the closing date. Users who know the password can overcome these restrictions, so make sure anyone given the password understands the bookkeeping ramifications of changing a transaction in a way that might change the totals you used for tax preparation.

Closing the Year

In QuickBooks, you close the year by entering a closing date. This inherently does nothing more than lock users out of the previous year's transactions. At the same time, you can configure user rights to enable or disable a user's ability to see, or even manipulate, closed transactions.

To enter a closing date and lock the books, follow these steps:

1. Choose Company | Set Closing Date.
2. In the Closing Date section of the dialog, click Set Date/Password.
3. In the Set Closing Date And Password dialog, enter the closing date (the last date of your fiscal year) and a password.

CAUTION: If you've set up users and passwords for access to your QuickBooks data file, only the QuickBooks user named Admin can set the closing date and password.

NOTE: If your fiscal year is different from a calendar year, don't worry about payroll. The payroll files and features, as well as 1099 records, are locked into a calendar year configuration, and closing your books doesn't have any effect on your ability to manage these transactions.

Creating a Year-End Backup

After all the numbers are checked, all the journal entries are made, and the books have been closed by entering a closing date as described in the previous section, do a separate backup in addition to your normal daily backup. Don't put this backup on the same media you use for your normal backups—the best option is a CD or DVD, which you label "Year-End Backup 2009" and store off-site. See Chapter 27 to learn about backing up your QuickBooks files.

Part Four

Managing QuickBooks

All software needs TLC, and accounting software needs regular maintenance to ensure its accuracy and usefulness.

In Part Four of this book, you'll learn how to set up and customize QuickBooks so it works efficiently. Of course, I'm going to cover backing up your data, which is the most important maintenance task in the world.

Printing and E-mailing in QuickBooks

I n this chapter:

- Set up printers for QuickBooks

- Print transaction forms and checks

- E-mail transaction forms

Most of the transactions you create are transmitted to customers, vendors, and employees in the form of printed copies. You can print and mail those forms, or e-mail them (except checks, of course, but the direct deposit feature in payroll and the ability to create online payments for vendors are almost the same as e-mailing).

In this chapter, I discuss setting up printers, printing, and e-mailing forms.

Setting Up Printing

You have to set up your QuickBooks printing processes by linking each type of document you print to a specific printer and configuring the way the printer processes each document type.

To begin setting up forms, choose File | Printer Setup. The Printer Setup dialog opens with the drop-down list of the Form Name field displayed, as seen in Figure 25-1.

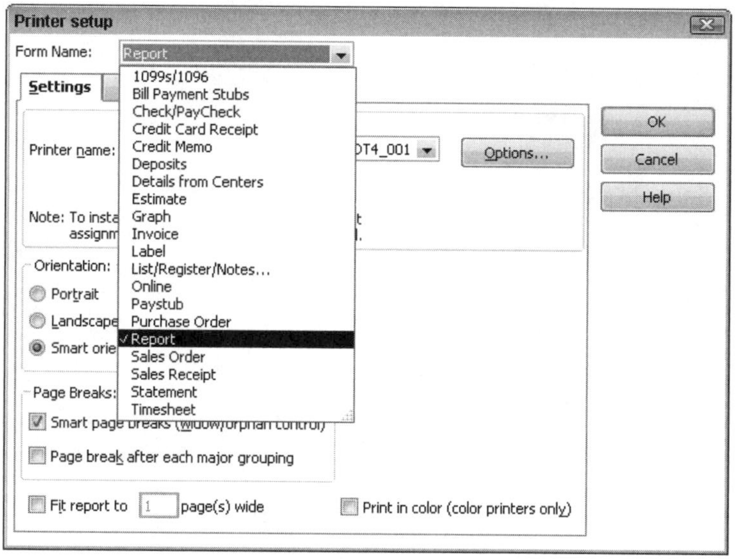

FIGURE 25-1 Start by selecting the form you want to configure.

NOTE: The form types you see may differ from the listing in Figure 25-1 because the available forms depend on the features you've enabled (for instance, if you haven't enabled Timekeeping, the Timesheet form won't appear).

The form type you select determines the contents of the Printer Setup dialog; where the tabs, fields, and options vary depending on the form. Many of the forms you print come out of the printer perfectly without any (or much) customization; however, some forms (such as checks) should be tweaked to make sure the output is what you want it to be. If you have multiple printers you can assign specific printers to specific types of forms, and QuickBooks will always select that printer when you print those forms.

Configuring Form Printing

In this section I cover setting up forms, with the exception of checks. See the section, "Configuring Check Printing" to learn how to set up check printing.

You must assign a printer and configure settings for the forms you print. Start by selecting the appropriate form in the Form Name field at the top of the Printer Setup dialog; the fields in the dialog change to match the needs of the form you selected. For example, Figure 25-2 shows the setup options for invoices; other forms have different (and sometimes fewer) options available.

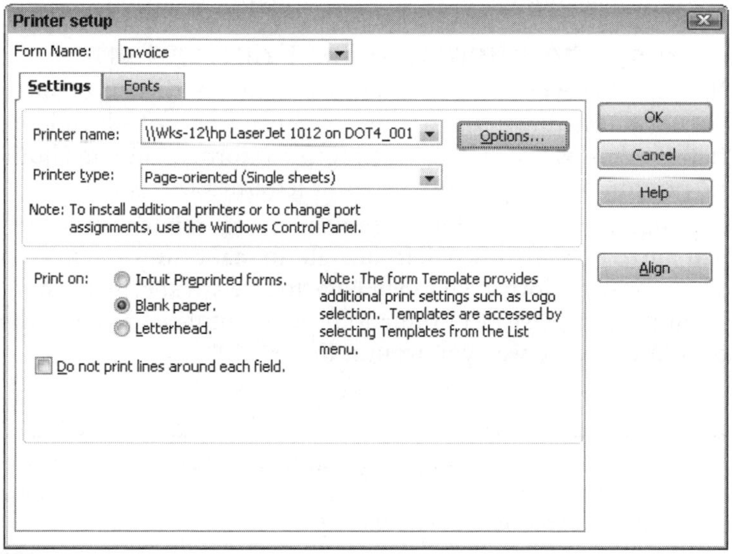

FIGURE 25-2   Configure the settings for printing a transaction form.

Choosing a Printer for a Form

The drop-down list in the Printer Name field displays the printers installed on your computer. (The printer selected in Figure 25-2 is a remote printer on a network, which is why the printer name might seem strange to you.) Select the appropriate printer for this form.

Selecting the Paper for Printing a Form

For transaction forms, the setup offers three types of paper:

Intuit Preprinted Forms These are forms you order from Intuit or your favorite form supplier (who carries forms specifically designed for QuickBooks). All the fields are preprinted and aligned to match the way QuickBooks prints the form. When you print, only the field data prints, not the field names.

Blank Paper If you use blank paper to print transaction forms, QuickBooks prints your company name and address at the top of the paper and prints the field names in addition to the data. Lines to separate fields and columns are also printed. You can deselect the option to print the lines, but without the column and field lines the invoice may be hard to read or understand.

Letterhead This setting is the same as the Blank Paper setting, except QuickBooks does not print the company name and address information at the top, and the top of the form begins printing two inches below the top of the paper to make sure the data doesn't print over your preprinted letterhead text.

Fine-tuning the Alignment for Printing Forms

To make sure that everything prints in the right place (or to change the placement if you're not satisfied with the output), you can fine-tune the alignment of text. It's important to do this if you're using preprinted forms, but you should also check the way the printout looks on blank paper or letterhead.

Click Align to open the Fine Alignment dialog in which you can print a sample, and then move text up, down, left, or right to make adjustments to the sample printout. (For some forms, you may have to select a specific form before the Alignment dialog opens.) Continue to print a sample and make adjustments until the printout looks the way you want it to.

 NOTE: If you're configuring a dot matrix printer, when you click Align, QuickBooks first presents a Coarse Alignment dialog, then you can fine-tune the alignment with the Fine Alignment dialog.

Adjustments affect all the text, as a block. You cannot adjust individual fields, rows, or other elements in the printed form. If you adjust the alignment by moving up 10/100ths of an inch, everything that prints on the form moves up 10/100ths of an inch.

▶▶ FYI

Printing Forms as PDF Files

QuickBooks automatically installs a PDF printer driver when you install the software (you can see it in your Windows Printers folder; it's named QuickBooks PDF Converter). This printer is not displayed in the drop-down list of printers you see when you are setting up form printing. It's also missing from the drop-down list of printers you see when you actually print forms. The printer driver is used by QuickBooks when you click Send in order to e-mail transaction forms to customers or vendors (covered in this chapter in the section, "E-mailing Forms and Reports").

If you want to print your forms as PDF documents, you must install a PDF printer driver from another company (search the Internet for PDF converters—you'll find a wide variety of them, some of which are free). After you install a PDF converter, it appears on the drop-down list of printers when you're setting up printing and when you print transaction forms and reports.

TIP: Don't waste preprinted forms to check the alignment. Print your samples to blank paper and then put the paper in front of the preprinted form (or the other way around) and hold it up against a window or a lamp so you can see where the printed text falls.

Configuring Check Printing

If you want to print your checks from within QuickBooks instead of creating manual checks, you must use checks that are designed specifically for QuickBooks.

Purchasing Checks that Work with QuickBooks

Many vendors sell computer checks, and you can shop for the price and style you prefer. If you purchase checks from any supplier except Intuit, you have to tell them you use QuickBooks. All check makers know about QuickBooks and offer a line of checks that are designed to work perfectly with the software.

Computer checks can be purchased for dot matrix printers (the check forms have sprocket holes and are available as multipart documents if you like to keep a copy of your checks) or for page printers (laser and inkjet). Investigate the prices and options at the following sources:

- Intuit, the company that makes QuickBooks, sells checks through its Internet marketplace, which you can reach at www.intuitmarket.com.
- Business form companies (there are several well-known national companies, such as Safeguard).

- Office supply stores.
- Some banks have a computer-check purchasing arrangement with suppliers who have QuickBooks checks available; check with your bank.

Computer checks come in several varieties (and in a wide range of colors and designs). For QuickBooks, you can order any of the following check types:

- Plain checks
- Checks with stubs (QuickBooks prints information on the stub)
- Checks with special stubs for payroll information (current check and year-to-date information about wages and withholding)
- Wallet-sized checks

Setting Up Your Printer for Checks

To configure your printer to manage check printing, choose File | Printer Setup from the menu bar. Select Check/PayCheck as the form, and then select the printer you're using for checks. Your Printer Setup window should look similar to Figure 25-3.

FIGURE 25-3 Set up your printer for check printing.

Choosing a Check Style

You have to select a check style, and it has to match the check style you purchased, of course. Three styles are available for QuickBooks checks, and a sample of each style appears in the window to show you what the style looks like.

- **Voucher checks** These have a detachable section on the check form. QuickBooks prints voucher information if you have voucher checks, including the name of the payee, the date, and the individual amounts of the bills being paid by this check. The voucher is attached to the bottom of the check. The check is the width of a regular business envelope.
- **Standard checks** These are just checks. They're the width of a regular business envelope (usually called a *#10 envelope*). If you have a laser or inkjet printer, there are three checks to a page. A dot matrix pin-feed printer just keeps rolling, since the checks are printed on a continuous sheet with perforations separating the checks.
- **Wallet checks** These are narrower than the other two check styles (so they fit in your wallet). The paper size is the same as the other checks (otherwise, you'd have a problem with your printer), but there's a perforation on the left edge of the check, so you can tear off the check. Most banks require the Check 21 format, so make sure you select that option when you select wallet checks, assuming your checks are printed for Check 21 requirements.

Adding a Logo

If your checks have no preprinted logo and you have a file of your company logo, select Use Logo or click the Logo button to open the Logo dialog. Click the File button to locate the graphics file.

There's also a selection box for printing your company name and address, but when you buy checks, you should have that information preprinted.

CAUTION: Dot matrix printers can't handle graphics printing, so don't bother choosing a logo if you're using a dot matrix printer for your checks.

Changing Fonts

Click the Fonts tab in the Printer Setup window to choose different fonts for the check information, such as the spelled-out amounts or the payee's address block. Click the appropriate button and then choose a font, a font style, and a size from the dialog that opens.

CAUTION: Before you change fonts, make a note of the current settings. No Reset or Default button exists in the Fonts tab. If you make changes and they don't work properly, without knowing the original settings you'll have to mess around with fonts for a long time to get back to where you started.

Handling Partial Check Pages on Laser and Inkjet Printers

If you're printing to a laser or inkjet printer, you don't have the advantage that a pin-feed dot matrix printer provides—printing a check and stopping, leaving the next check waiting in the printer for the next time you print checks. QuickBooks has a nifty solution for this problem, found on the Partial Page tab (see Figure 25-4). The solution that matches your printer's capabilities is preselected.

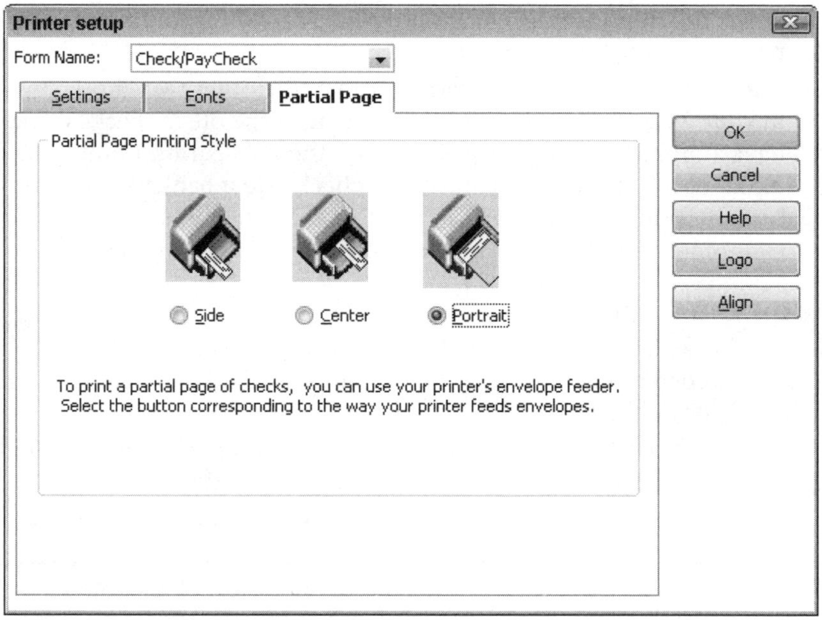

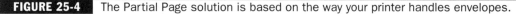

FIGURE 25-4   The Partial Page solution is based on the way your printer handles envelopes.

Aligning the Printout

Click the Align button to print a sample check and see where the printing lines up on the physical check. You can move the starting points for printing up/down or left/right to make sure everything prints where it's supposed to. When you're finished, click OK in the Printer Setup window to save the configuration data.

Printer Settings vs. Printer Options

When you configure a printer by assigning it a form (or multiple forms) and customize the printing setup for that form, QuickBooks memorizes the selection. If you change printers when you're ready to print, the next time you print the same form QuickBooks returns to the original printer and printer settings linked to that form type (unless you reconfigure the setup to change printers).

Every printer has its own set of options to control the way printing occurs. When you're ready to print a document, such as an invoice, you can set the printing options when you print. The Print dialog has an Options button that opens an additional dialog for selecting options for the selected printer. You can change the tray (or select manual feed), change the resolution of the printing, and perform other tweaks.

QuickBooks does not memorize these options; it uses the printer's defaults the next time you print the form type. If you want to make printer options permanent, you must change the printer configuration in the Windows Printers folder.

➡ FYI

Print Settings May Not Work for Multiple Companies

One of the most frustrating things about QuickBooks is the way it uses printer settings; the configuration options you set are applied to the software, not to the company file that's open when you set up printers. If you have multiple companies, and they require different print settings, you must go through the exercise of setting up printers and printing options every time you change the company file (all the steps enumerated in this chapter for setting up, configuring, and aligning print settings for different forms).

For example, if one company has payroll and buys voucher checks for all check printing, but the other company doesn't, you must go through a complete printer setup every time you switch company files and want to print checks. This is in addition to the frustration that's caused by the fact that even with one company file, QuickBooks doesn't let you perform separate setups for payroll checks (with vouchers) and vendor checks (without vouchers). You can solve that problem for a single company by buying voucher checks for both types of check printing.

If one company has preprinted invoice paper for a page printer, but the other company uses plain paper to print invoices (common in manufacturing and distribution companies that print multipart documents on plain paper on dot-matrix printers), you must go through a complete printer setup every time you print invoices...and so on and so on for every form you print that differs between companies.

If you've repositioned printing with the Align feature, you must write down your saved settings so you can enter them again each time you switch between companies.

The only way to avoid the aggravation of going through all the steps involved with printer setup whenever you change company files is to get another computer for each company that has different printer settings and install a copy of QuickBooks on each computer to manage each company.

Printing Transaction Forms

Most of the transactions you create are sent to the customer or vendor involved in the transaction. In this section I discuss the process of printing transactions (see the section, "E-mailing Forms and Reports," if you prefer electronic delivery).

You can print each transaction as you create it, or wait and print all your transactions in a batch.

Printing Transactions As You Create Them

If you want to print the current transaction as soon as you finish filling in the data (before you click Save & Close or Save & New), click the Print button on the top of the transaction window. QuickBooks opens the Print One *<NameOfTransactionType>* dialog (Figure 25-5 displays the dialog for Print One Invoice). Click Print to send the transaction form to the selected printer.

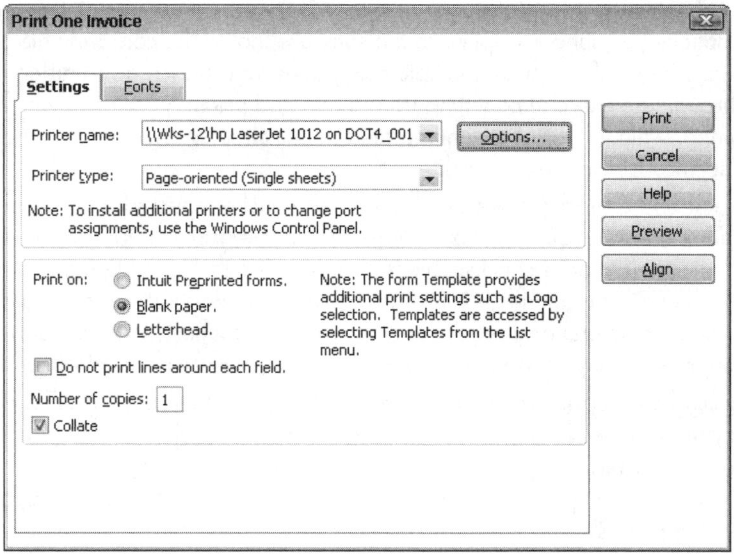

FIGURE 25-5   Printing a single transaction is quick and easy.

> **NOTE:** QuickBooks saves the transaction before opening the Print dialog. This is a security measure that almost all accounting software applications use to avoid employee theft. You can change this behavior in the General category of the Preferences dialog, but you shouldn't. See Chapter 9 for details about this security device.

Previewing Form Printouts

If you want to see what the printed document looks like, click the arrow to the right of the Print icon and select Preview.

Often, the printed form differs from the onscreen form. For example, if you're creating a packing slip, the onscreen form shows prices, but the printed form doesn't. If you create custom fields for lists or items, the custom field data may appear only in the onscreen form to help you prepare the transaction (such as backorder preferences for customers, advance payment requirements for vendors, and so on).

To learn how to customize transaction forms and decide which fields are seen only onscreen, only in the printed form, or on both, read Chapter 28.

Printing Transaction Forms in Batches

To print the transactions in batches, make sure the To Be Printed check box is selected on each transaction you create. Then follow these steps to batch print the documents:

1. Choose File | Print Forms | *<Transaction Type>* (substitute the transaction type for *<Transaction Type>*).
2. In the Select *<Transaction Type>* To Print window, all your unprinted transaction forms are selected with a check mark. If there are any you don't want to print at this time, click the check marks to remove them (it's a toggle).

✓	Date	Type	No.	Customer	Template	Amount
✓	01/02/2009	INV	1014	Bellevue Bistro:4...	Product Invoice ...	675.00
✓	01/05/2009	INV	1017	Jordan's Staffing...	Product Invoice ...	107.00
✓	01/07/2009	INV	1015	Gotham:On-Site ...	Product Invoice ...	3,317.00

3. Click OK to print. A Print dialog appears where you can change or select printing options. Click Print to begin printing. After sending the documents to the printer, QuickBooks asks you to confirm that all the documents printed properly.

Print Invoices - Confirmation

If your invoices printed correctly, click OK.

What if my invoices printed in reverse order?

If you need to reprint any invoices, select them and click OK. Then return to the Select Invoices to Print window to reprint them.

Reprint	Doc No.	Name	Amount
	1014	4th Street Restaurant	675.00
	1017	Software	107.00
	1015	On-Site Wiring	3,317.00

Select All

What if my invoices printed incorrectly?   Cancel   OK

4. If everything printed properly, click OK. If you have to reprint one or more forms, select the appropriate listing(s) and go through the steps to print batch forms again; the forms you selected for reprinting are listed in the Select *<Transaction Type>* To Print dialog, and you can finish printing your batch. (Of course, before taking this step, you need to unjam the printer, put in a new cartridge, or correct any other problem that caused the original failure.)

Printing Checks

If you print checks in QuickBooks, you can print each check as you create it in the Write Checks window, or wait until you've finished creating all your checks and then print them in a batch. When you use the Pay Bills window to create checks, check printing is treated as a batch process (even if only one check is created). I cover both individual check printing and batch check printing in this section.

Printing Each Check As You Create It

If you use the Write Checks window to create a check, when you've finished entering all the data, you can click the Print icon at the top of the window. The Print Check dialog opens, and the next printed check number is entered as the default.

Print Check

Printed Check Number 1044

OK   Cancel

➡ **FYI**

How QuickBooks Numbers Checks

QuickBooks tracks two sets of check numbers for each checking account:

- Numbers for checks that are entered manually. The next available number is automatically inserted when you enter checks in the check register, or deselect the To Be Printed option in the Write Checks or Pay Bill window.
- Numbers for checks that are printed in QuickBooks. The next available number is used automatically when you print checks.

This is a useful feature if you have preprinted checks in the office for printing checks and a checkbook you carry around so you can write checks when you're not in the office.

Peek at the checks in your printer to make sure this is the next check number; if not, change the number in the dialog. Then click OK to open the Print Checks dialog and click Print. After sending the check to the printer, QuickBooks displays the Print Checks-Confirmation dialog.

If the check printed properly, click OK. If not, you need to fix the problem and print the check again; see "Reprinting Checks After a Problem," later in this section.

If you have additional checks to create in the Write Checks window, you can repeat these steps. However, if you're creating multiple checks, it's faster to create all the checks and then print them in a batch.

Printing Checks in Batches

You can print all your checks in a batch after you've completed the task of creating the checks. If you've been working the Write Checks window, use the Save & New button to continue to create checks. When you're finished, use one of the following actions to print all the checks you've prepared:

- On the last check, click the arrow to the right of the Print icon on the check window and select Print Batch.
- Click Save & Close when you create the last check, and then choose File | Print Forms | Checks to print the batch.

Either action opens the Select Checks To Print dialog.

By default, all the unprinted checks are selected for printing, which is almost always what you want to do, but you can deselect checks if there's a reason to do so (they remain in the batch and will be waiting for you the next time you print checks). Click OK to open the Print Checks window.

NOTE: The first time you print checks, the First Check Number is 1; just replace that number with the first check number in the printer and QuickBooks will track printed check numbers thereafter.

If your checks were written on different bank accounts (perhaps you pay bills from your operating account and you use the Write Checks window to send checks to vendors for special purchases, using a different bank accounts), the Select Checks To Print window displays only the checks ready for printing from a specific bank account. After you print those checks, use the same steps to get to the Select Checks To Print window and change the bank account to see those checks. Don't forget to put the right checks in your printer.

If you use the Pay Bills window to create checks for vendors, when you finish selecting the bills and amounts to pay, click Pay Selected Bills. QuickBooks displays a Payment Summary window with a Print Checks button. (If you don't print checks, before you see the summary you must assign check numbers in the Assign Check Numbers dialog.)

Payment Summary

Payment Details
Payment Date   04/10/2009
Payment Account   10000 · Operating Account
Payment Method   Check

Payments have been successfully recorded for the following 4 of 4 bills:

Date Due	Vendor	Amount Paid
05/08/2009	Discount Office Supplies	129.65
05/22/2009	GeekRob	1,005.00
06/06/2009	ISP	139.90
05/03/2009	JM Securities	150.00
	Total	1,424.55

How do I find and change a bill payment?

You can print checks now, or print them later from Print Forms on the File menu.

[Pay More Bills] [Print Checks] [Done]

- If these are the only checks you're creating at the moment, click Print Checks.
- If you have additional checks to print (checks you have to create in the Write Checks window for vendors that do not have bills entered in your file), you can click Done and print all your checks at once from the File menu, as described earlier in this section.

In the Print Checks dialog, click Print to begin printing your checks. When all the checks have been sent to the printer, QuickBooks displays the Print Checks-Confirmation window. If all the checks printed correctly, click OK.

Reprinting Checks After a Problem

Sometimes things go awry when you're printing. The paper jams, you run out of toner, the ribbon has no ink left, the dog chews the paper as it emerges, the paper falls off the back tray and lands in the shredder—all sorts of bad things can occur.

If anything untoward happens, select the check(s) that didn't print properly in the Print Checks-Confirmation window and click OK. Put more checks into the printer (unless you're using a dot matrix printer, in which case the next check is waiting). Then click OK and choose File | Print Forms | Checks. Your unprinted checks are listed in the Select Checks To Print dialog, and the first check number is the next available check number (well, it should be, if not, change it).

E-mailing Forms and Reports

You can e-mail transaction forms and reports directly from QuickBooks as PDF attachments to e-mail messages. E-mailing works exactly the same as printing forms and reports, as described earlier in this chapter. That is, you can e-mail each individual transaction as you create it, or save the transactions and e-mail them in a batch.

If you're using Outlook Express, Windows Mail, or Outlook, QuickBooks sends e-mail to your customers directly through your e-mail software. If you use e-mail software other than the supported software, you can use QuickBooks Billing Solutions, which provides a server-based e-mail service. This is a free service, but you have to sign up for it.

You can e-mail any report (either as a QuickBooks report or as an Excel file), and you can also e-mail all of the following QuickBooks transaction forms:

- Invoices
- Estimates
- Sales Receipts
- Credit Memos
- Statements
- Purchase Orders
- Pay Stubs (if you use QuickBooks payroll and have signed up for direct deposit)

Setting Up E-mail

If QuickBooks finds a copy of one the supported e-mail software applications on your computer with an active profile installed, your QuickBooks e-mail is automatically sent using that software. (An *active profile* is an e-mail account established in the software, and the software is the default e-mail software on your computer.) In that case, the Send Forms category of the Preferences dialog shows the default e-mail method, as seen in Figure 25-6. If these options aren't displayed, you must use the QuickBooks e-mail service to send transaction forms and reports.

If the Send E-mail options don't appear on this dialog, it means QuickBooks didn't find supported e-mail software configured as the default e-mail software on your computer.

The dialog also contains an option to instruct QuickBooks to select To Be E-Mailed automatically on every transaction linked to a customer that is configured for E-mail as the preferred method for sending transactions forms. (The Preferred Send Method field is on the Additional Info tab of the customer record.) If you configure a customer for e-mail, make sure you enter the e-mail address in the customer's record.

On the Company Preferences tab (see Figure 25-7), you see the preset text for the e-mail message that's used for sending transaction forms and reports (the text

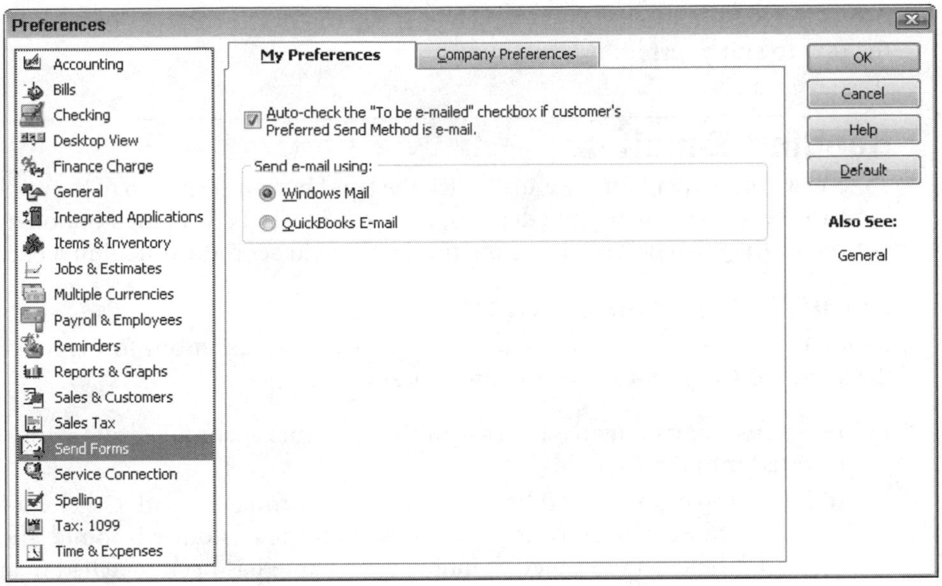

FIGURE 25-6 QuickBooks selects your e-mail software by default.

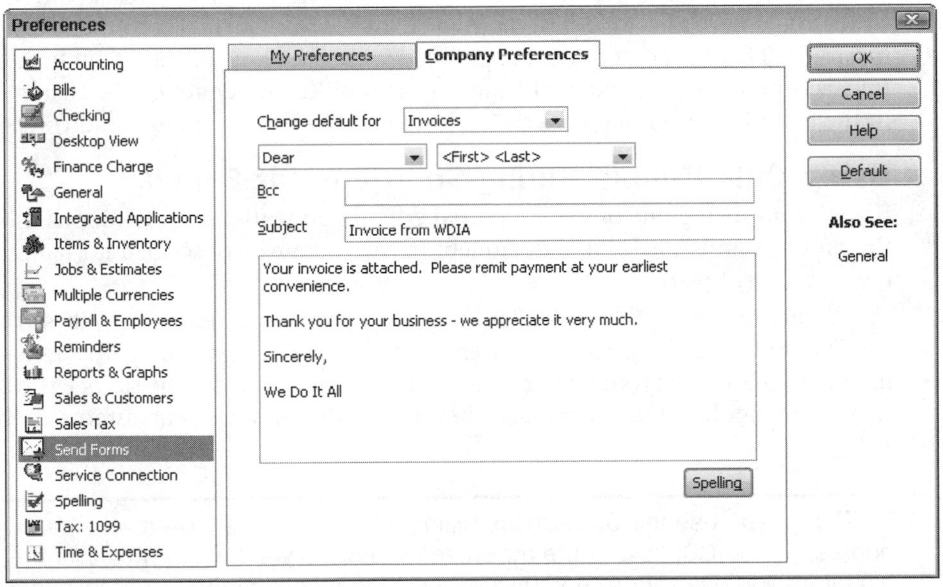

FIGURE 25-7 The text for the message body is the same whether you use your own e-mail software or the QuickBooks Billing Solutions.

differs depending on the form you select at the top of the dialog). You can change the text to suit yourself.

Sending E-mail

To send a transaction form by e-mail, click the Send button at the top of the transaction form (to send the e-mail immediately), or select the To Be E-mailed option at the bottom of the form before saving the transaction (to send the e-mail in a batch).

Using Your E-mail Software

If QuickBooks is using your e-mail software to send transactions forms (or reports), the standard Create Message window appears.

- If the customer's e-mail address is in the customer record, it's automatically inserted into the To: field.
- If the customer's e-mail address is not in the customer record, QuickBooks searches your e-mail software address book. If the customer is found, the entry in the To: field is underlined to indicate the name has been matched to an existing address book entry.
- If the customer's e-mail address is not available in either place, you have to add the customer's e-mail address to your e-mail software.

The Subject field is prefilled with the text "Invoice from <*YourCompanyName*>" (if the file you're attaching isn't an invoice, the correct form is automatically inserted). The Attachment field is prefilled with the name of the PDF file of the transaction form. The text of the message is prefilled by QuickBooks (using the text in the Send Forms Preferences dialog, discussed in the previous section).

Using QuickBooks Billing Solutions for E-mail

If you're not using one of the supported e-mail applications, QuickBooks fills out the message and attaches the document in the same way described for using your own e-mail software.

When you click Send, QuickBooks opens a browser window and takes you to the QuickBooks Billing Solutions website. If this is the first time you're e-mailing invoices, follow the prompts to complete the sign-up process (the service is free), and then QuickBooks sends the e-mail. Thereafter, your e-mail is sent automatically.

T I P : If you use the QuickBooks Billing Solutions, enter your own e-mail address in the CC: field of the message window so you have a record of the e-mail. (If you use your own software, you have a copy in the Sent Messages folder.)

Managing Users and Permissions

In this chapter:

- Learn about the QuickBooks administrator

- Create QuickBooks users

- Set permissions for users

Many businesses have multiple users accessing their QuickBooks company files. You can have multiple users who access QuickBooks on the same computer (taking turns using QuickBooks), or multiple users who access your company file from remote computers on a network. These businesses need to create user names and passwords.

Even companies that have only one user running QuickBooks on one computer should make sure at least one user exists, with a password, to ensure the security of the company file.

Why User Logins Are Important

If you run QuickBooks on a network, with multiple users accessing a company file from remote computers, QuickBooks requires user logins (you can't open a file in multi-user mode to permit simultaneous access by other users until you set up users).

If you're the only QuickBooks user, it's tempting to avoid the extra step of logging in and remembering a password. Don't yield to that temptation, because if anyone else wanders into the room that has your computer, it's possible for him or her to open QuickBooks and view your financial information. Worse, it's possible for him or her to create transactions that you might not notice for a very long time.

If you have only one computer running QuickBooks but more than one user shares the use of that computer to work in QuickBooks, you may need to know who did what. Without enforcing logins, that information won't be available. The QuickBooks Audit Trail feature (which tracks activities) displays the name of the logged in user for every transaction it tracks.

User names are linked to permission levels, which means you can limit the parts of QuickBooks that certain users can access to create or view transactions and reports. For example, you can keep users from seeing payroll information or sensitive reports that contain information about your profits, indebtedness, and so on.

Understanding Passwords

Passwords are the secret doors to entering computers or software. The word "secret" is important because many computers and databases have been breached by intruders who successfully guessed a password.

Don't use passwords that are based on information that someone else may know, such as your child's name, your dog's name, your nickname, your license plate, or your birth date.

Creating Complex Passwords

If you've enabled the credit card protection feature in QuickBooks (covered in Chapter 3), you must create a complex password (sometimes called a *strong password*) if you're the Admin or a user who has permission to view customer credit card information. The rules for the complex password are

- A minimum of seven characters
- At least one character must be a number
- At least one letter must be uppercase

However, even if you're not using the credit card protection feature, you should consider using a complex password; after all, if you're going to use passwords you might as well be serious about security.

The longer the password and the more complicated it is, the harder it is to guess. For example, Xyyu86RDa is a great password. The problem with that password is that it's almost as mysterious to the user who created it as it is to anyone attempting to break into the company file. There's nothing logical or memorable about the characters or the order in which they appear, which makes it very difficult to remember. As a result, people who create these well-designed passwords take one of the following actions to make sure they'll be able to enter the password correctly:

- Write the password on a sticky note that's attached to the monitor.
- Write the password on a piece of paper that's on the desk (sometimes tucked under the monitor or keyboard (which are known as popular hiding places so intruders find the password easily).
- Write the password on a piece of paper that's in the top drawer (which is not locked).

Storing Passwords Safely

If you have a password that's difficult to remember or to type (because you have to use the SHIFT key for some letters but not for others), you'll probably need to create a password reference to use when you log in to QuickBooks.

 TIP: When you create a written record of your password, write it backward (and don't forget to read from right to left as you enter the characters in the Login dialog).

The only safe place to store a written reference to a password is a place that nobody but you accesses. This could be a desk drawer that you lock and keep the key to on your person (not on the desk or in another unlocked drawer), or it could be your wallet.

NOTE: Chapter 3 includes more information about ways to store complex passwords safely, including storing passwords within documents.

The QuickBooks Admin

The QuickBooks user named Admin is the administrator of the QuickBooks company file. The administrator is in charge of all QuickBooks users and is the only user who can set up additional users. The person who creates the company file becomes the administrator automatically because he or she is the first person to open the file.

 NOTE: The administrator's privileges in QuickBooks are totally unrelated to your Windows logon name and privileges. Even if you're an ordinary user in Windows and can't install software or manage users on the computer, you can be a QuickBooks administrator.

It is never a good idea to use QuickBooks without the security of having users log in to a company file with a user name and a password. Even if you're the only person who works in QuickBooks, and therefore you're automatically the administrator, be sure the user named Admin has a password.

 NOTE: QuickBooks lets you change the name Admin to any other name, without losing the administrator power. I've never come up with a good reason to do so (not seeing the name Admin in the User List would confuse me), but if you have some compelling reason to take this action, you can.

The way the administrator account is preconfigured, and whether you have to log in to your company file, depends on the way you created your company file. Here's how QuickBooks establishes the administrator account:

- If you use the EasyStep Interview to set up your company file, and you create a password for the administrator account when the wizard offers that option, every time you open the company file you have to log in as Admin and enter the password.
- If you use the EasyStep Interview to set up your company file, and you do *not* create a password for the administrator account when the wizard offers that option, the Admin account is established. However, because there's no password, when you open the company file you don't see a Login dialog.

- If you do not use the EasyStep Interview to set up your company file (you select Skip Interview on the first wizard window), you do not have an opportunity to set up the administrator's password (although the Admin user is created automatically). When you open the company file you don't see a Login dialog.

Adding or Changing the Administrator Password

If you didn't create a password for the user named Admin when you set up the company file, you can create a password at any time. If you did create a password and you think the existing password may have been discovered by someone else, you can create a new password.

To add or change the password for the user named Admin, log in to QuickBooks as Admin and choose Company | Set Up Users And Passwords | Change Your Password to open the Change QuickBooks Password dialog seen in Figure 26-1. If the Admin account is already password-protected, and you're merely changing the password, you have to enter the current password to proceed to this dialog. Enter the new password, enter it again in the Confirm Password field, and select a challenge question (and the answer).

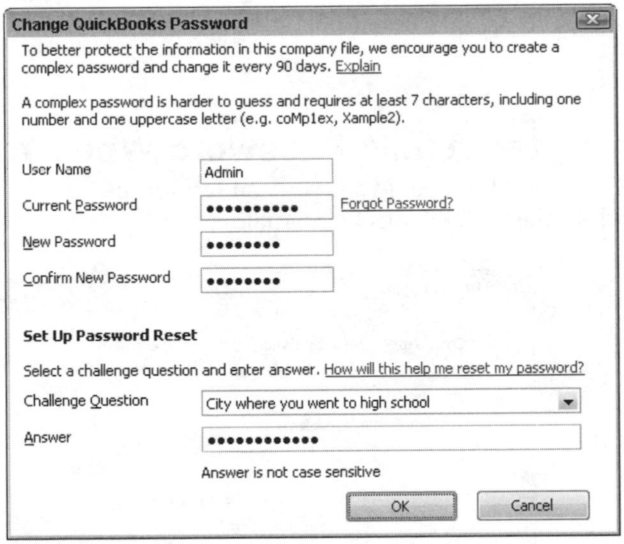

FIGURE 26-1 You can easily add or change an Admin password.

Creating a Challenge Question for the Admin Account

If you don't remember your Admin password, you can't get into your company file. If Admin is the only user, that means you can't use QuickBooks. If there are other users, they can open the company file, but they can't perform administrative tasks in the file (many QuickBooks functions can only be performed by Admin). Essentially, this brings your QuickBooks work to a screeching halt.

QuickBooks offers services to remove an Admin password if you forget it, which lets you start over by creating a new password, but using that service puts your company file out of service until the problem is fixed.

To prevent this inconvenience, QuickBooks offers the Admin user the opportunity to create reminders about the password. This feature is optional, but I can't think of any valid reason to skip it.

Select a question from the drop-down list in the Challenge Question field, and then enter the answer to that question in the Challenge Answer field. Be careful about the answer you enter. You cannot see what you're typing so type carefully (QuickBooks treats this the same way it treats password entry; you see bullet characters instead of the characters you're typing).

In addition, you have to apply some rules about the text you enter for the answer (to make sure you can enter the right text when you need this feature). For example, if I select the question "City where you went to high school," the answer might be Philadelphia, Phila, or Philly. If I decide that I'll use full names for my challenge answers (in this case, Philadelphia), then, if I later change the question to "Name of your oldest niece," I'll know to enter Elizabeth instead of Liz (which is what I call her).

Resetting the Admin Password When You Forget It

If you forget your Admin password you can reset it, using the challenge question you created. In the QuickBooks Login dialog, click Reset Password.

NOTE: If Admin is the only user, the login dialog does not display the User Name field, only the Password field.

In the Reset QuickBooks Administrator Password dialog, the question is displayed. Enter the answer you recorded in the Answer field (this time you can see what you're typing).

> **Reset QuickBooks Administrator Password**   ⊠
>
> Enter the answer to your challenge question. When you answer correctly, you'll be asked to create a new password.
>
> If you are not an administrator, you cannot reset your password. Ask your administrator to reset it for you.
>
> Challenge Question   **City where you went to high school**
>
> Answer   philadelphia
>
>   I can't remember my answer.
>
>   OK   Cancel

When you answer the question correctly, all of your password information is removed from the company file and you can start all over with a new password (and a new challenge question and answer).

> **Password Removed**
>
> Your password and challenge answer and question have been removed, and your company file is no longer password-protected.
>
> When you close this window, you will be asked to create your new password and select and answer your challenge question.
>
>   Close

If you can't remember your challenge question, click the link labeled I Can't Remember My Answer. A QuickBooks Help file opens with a link to a password recovery program you can download. The program removes the password so you can start all over again with a new password. To download the program you have to fill out information about your QuickBooks installation, company file, license information, and other data.

Adding Users

Only the Admin user can add users. To add a new user to your company file, choose Company | Set Up Users And Passwords | Set Up Users. QuickBooks asks you to enter your Admin password to proceed, and then opens the User List dialog. Click Add User to open the Set Up User Password And Access Wizard that assists you in setting up the new user.

Use the following guidelines to create a new user:

- The user name is the name this user must type to log into QuickBooks.
- A password is optional, but it's dangerous to omit passwords. Enter the same password in both password fields. (Later, the user can change the password—see the section "Users Can Change Their Own Passwords.")
- Assign permissions for this user to access QuickBooks features. See "Setting User Permissions" later in this section.

Deleting a User

If you want to remove a user from the User List, select the name and then click the Delete User button. QuickBooks asks you to confirm your decision. You can't delete the Admin.

Editing User Information

You can change the configuration options for any user. Select the user name in the User List window and click Edit User. This launches a wizard similar to the Set Up User Password And Access Wizard, and you can change the user name, password, and permissions.

> **TIP:** Users will come to you because they cannot remember their password. You don't have to store all those passwords; instead, use the Edit User feature to create a new password and tell the user what it is (the user will probably change the password and then forget again).

Setting User Permissions

When you're adding a new user or editing an existing user, the wizard walks you through the steps for configuring the user's permissions. Click Next on each wizard window after you've supplied the necessary information.

The first permissions window asks if you want this user to have access to selected areas of QuickBooks or all areas. If you give the user access to all areas of QuickBooks, or you select the option to make this user an External Accountant, when you click Next you're asked to confirm your decision, and there's no further work to do in the wizard. Click Finish to return to the User List window. (See Chapter 21 to learn about the External Accountant user type.)

If you want to limit the user's access to selected areas of QuickBooks, select that option and click Next. The ensuing wizard windows take you through all the QuickBooks features (Sales and Accounts Receivable, Check Writing, Payroll, and so on) so you can establish permissions on a feature-by-feature basis for this user.

You should configure permissions for every component of QuickBooks. Any component not configured is set as No Access for this user (which means the user cannot work in that part of QuickBooks). For each QuickBooks component, you can select one of the following permission options:

No Access The user is denied permission to open any windows in that section of QuickBooks.

Full Access The user can open all windows and perform all tasks in that section of QuickBooks.

Selective Access The user will be permitted to perform tasks as you see fit.

If you choose to give selective access permissions, you're asked to specify the rights this user should have. Those rights vary slightly from component to component, but generally you're asked to choose one of these permission levels:

- Create transactions only
- Create and print transactions
- Create transactions and create reports

You can select only one of the three levels, so if you need to give the user rights to more than one of these choices, you must select Full Access instead of configuring Selective Access.

Special Permissions Needed for Customer Credit Card Data

If you provide Full Access permissions to a user for the Sales And Accounts Receivable area, by default, the user is not able to view customer credit card data. A separate option for this permission appears on the wizard window.

- If you've enabled the Customer Credit Card Security feature (explained in Chapter 3), the next time this user logs in to the company file, he or she will be asked to create a strong password.

- If you haven't enabled the Customer Credit Card Security feature, this user, and any other user you configure to have access to customer credit card information, does not have to set up a strong password and can view credit card numbers you store in your customers' record.

Letting users without strong passwords view credit card numbers is dangerous. You should be protecting the security of your customer's sensitive data. More important, credit card companies (and some state governments) are becoming fussier about the way businesses store this information and will begin auditing your procedures. As these rules are enforced stringently (and they will be), you might lose your ability to accept credit cards.

Configuring Special Areas of QuickBooks

There are two wizard windows for setting permissions that are not directly related to any specific area of the software: sensitive accounting activities and sensitive accounting reports.

Sensitive accounting activities are those tasks that aren't directly related to QuickBooks transactions, such as:

- Making changes to the chart of accounts
- Manipulating the register for any balance sheet account
- Using online banking
- Transferring funds between banks
- Reconciling bank accounts
- Creating journal entries
- Preparing an accountant's copy
- Working with budgets

Sensitive financial reports are those reports that reveal important financial information about your company, such as:

- Profit & Loss reports
- Balance Sheet reports
- Budget reports
- Cash flow reports
- Income tax reports
- Trial balance reports
- Audit trail reports

Configuring Rights for Existing Transactions

If a user has permissions for certain areas of QuickBooks, you can limit his or her ability to manipulate existing transactions within those areas. This means the user can't change or delete a transaction, even if he or she created it in the first place.

You can also prevent the user from changing transactions that occurred prior to the closing date you set (even if the user knows the password to access transactions that were created before the closing date). See Chapter 24 to learn about setting a closing date and password-protecting access to transactions that predate the closing date.

When you have finished configuring user permissions, the last wizard page presents a list of the permissions you've granted and refused. If everything is correct, click Finish. If there's something you want to change, use the Back button to return to the appropriate page.

Users Can Change Their Own Passwords

Any user can change his or her password by choosing Company | Set Up Users And Passwords | Change Your Password to open the Change QuickBooks Password dialog. The dialog opens with the name of the current logged in user in the User Name field, and that text cannot be changed.

To change the password, the user must enter the old password, and then enter the new password (twice). That's an excellent security device because it prevents other users from changing a user's password (which can happen if a user leaves the computer without logging out of QuickBooks).

Technically, it's a good idea for the QuickBooks administrator to know all user passwords and to ask users to notify the administrator when a password is changed. This is useful when a user forgets his or her password and has to get some work done in QuickBooks.

However, tracking passwords is an annoying responsibility if you have more than a couple of users, and depending on the manner in which you store the information, it could be dangerous. It's perfectly acceptable to decide that you don't want to know user passwords, because if a user forgets a password you can edit the user's record to create a new one (as described earlier in this chapter) and tell the user the new password.

QuickBooks Login Dialogs

The QuickBooks Login dialog appears whenever you open a company file, unless you have not configured any users in addition to the built-in administrator named Admin, and the Admin user has not been assigned a password.

The Login dialog displays the name of the last user who logged in to this company file on this computer. If the same user is opening the file, entering the correct password opens the file.

If a different user is opening the file, replace the text in the User Name field with the login name of the new user, enter the password, and click OK.

Managing Your QuickBooks Files

Chapter 27

In addition to performing bookkeeping chores in QuickBooks, you need to take care of some computer file housekeeping tasks. It's important to keep your software up-to-date and to make sure your data is accurate and available. QuickBooks provides some features to help you accomplish these responsibilities.

Deleting Company Files

Sometimes you have a valid reason to get rid of a company file. Perhaps you created a company to experiment with and you no longer use it, or you sent a copy of the local community association's file to another QuickBooks user who is taking over your job as treasurer.

So, how do you delete a company file? There's no "Delete File" function, which would take care of all the details required to prevent side effects. There's a workaround, of course (I wouldn't mention this topic if I didn't have a workaround to offer), but you must use it carefully and pay attention to the order in which you perform tasks.

You've probably guessed the basic workaround: delete the file from Windows Explorer or My Computer. However, before you click the file's listing and press the DELETE key, read on so you don't encounter a problem when you next open QuickBooks.

How QuickBooks Loads Company Files

QuickBooks automatically opens the company file that was loaded when you last exited the software. If it can't find that file it gets confused, and when software gets confused it sometimes slows down or stops working properly. Even if QuickBooks accepts the fact that the file it's trying to open is missing and displays the No Company Open dialog, it's cleaner to make sure you don't have the about-to-be-deleted company file loaded when you close QuickBooks. To accomplish this, take one of the following actions:

- Choose File | Open Or Restore Company, or File | Open Previous Company to select another company file.
- Choose File | Close Company to close the current file and have no company loaded if you shut down QuickBooks and reopen it. (If you have created additional users for the file, the command is File | Close Company/Logoff.)

I can hear you saying, "Why would I have that file open if I no longer use it?" The answer is, "Because almost every user who has called me for help in this situation opened the file to make sure it didn't contain anything important, closed QuickBooks, and then deleted the file." That last-minute check to make sure it's okay to delete the file is the quicksand many people wander into.

It takes QuickBooks longer to load when it can't find the last-used company file (the one you deleted), and when the No Company Open dialog appears to ask you to select a company file to open, the deleted file is still listed. For some reason, many people select that file (perhaps they're checking to see if they really did delete the file—they did).

QuickBooks displays an error message explaining that the file could not be found, and when you click OK, you're returned to the No Company Open dialog. Open another file to make that file the file that opens when you next launch QuickBooks. To remove the listing in the No Company Open dialog, see the section "Eliminating Deleted Files From the Company File List." (You can also force QuickBooks to open without loading the last-used company file; see the section, "Force QuickBooks to Open with No Company File Loaded.")

Deleting the File

To delete a company file, just navigate to the folder that holds the file and delete the file, which has the format *filename*.QBW. You can also delete any files linked to the company file, which have the same filename, such as with extensions of .ND and .TLG. Just in case, however, copy the file to a "safety folder" that is backed up with your computer. I mention this because I've had quite a bit of mail from readers explaining how they'd set up a "fake" company for training and then deleted it when everyone was comfortable enough to work in the real company file. When they updated QuickBooks to the next version, they wished they hadn't deleted the training file. When you make the safety copy, rename the file as follows: *MyCompany*-DoNotUse.QBW (substitute your own company filename for *MyCompany*, of course).

TIP: I always create a separate folder on my hard drive for my QuickBooks company files. I store all the import and export files I create in that folder, too. Having a discrete folder for my data makes it easy to find files and makes it easy to back up everything by backing up the folder.

Eliminating Deleted Files from the Company File List

QuickBooks tracks the company files you've opened and lists the most recently opened files on the Open Previous Company submenu (under the File menu) to make it easier to move among files. You don't have to open a dialog to select one of those files, you just point to the appropriate listing. The submenu lists the company files you've opened starting with the most recent (it's a duplicate of the listing displayed in the No Company Open dialog).

After you delete a company file, its listing may still appear on the Open Previous Company submenu, or in the No Company Open dialog. A user could inadvertently select it, which produces a delay, followed by an error message, and then followed by a user panic attack.

To eliminate this possibility, open another company file and choose File | Open Previous Company | Set Number Of Previous Companies. Change the data for the number of companies to list from its current setting to 1, and click OK.

This changes the company files that are listed in the Open Previous Company menu and the No Company Open dialog to the current company file only. The next time you open QuickBooks, repeat these steps and change the number back to the number that's efficient (depending on the number of companies you work with). QuickBooks begins tracking your work; as you open different company files it rebuilds the list.

Force QuickBooks to Open with No Company File Loaded

Sometimes you need QuickBooks to open without loading the last-used company file. This helps avoid delays and error messages if you deleted a company and you aren't sure whether it was the company file that was loaded when you last closed QuickBooks.

To force QuickBooks to open without any company file (the software opens with the No Company Open dialog displayed), press and hold the CTRL key and then launch QuickBooks (using your desktop shortcut or the listing on the Programs menu). Continue to hold the CTRL key until QuickBooks opens.

TIP: This trick also avoids delays and error messages when the last-used file is damaged and won't open.

Backing Up and Restoring Files

Backing up your QuickBooks data is an incredibly important task and should be done on a daily basis. Once a week, use removable media to make an extra backup, and take that backup off site. Even better, have removable media available for each day of the week, and take every backup off site. Buying five or seven USB flash drives (labeled for each day of the week), or keeping a plentiful supply of CD/DVDs, is less expensive than losing data.

If you need to use a backup file, you don't open it the way you open a regular company file; instead it has to be restored, using the QuickBooks Restore command. In this section I discuss backing up and restoring company files.

NOTE: New to QuickBooks 2009 is the ability to back up a file that's operating in multi-user mode.

»» FYI

Backing Up a Remote Company File

If you're working on a network, and the company file is on a computer that's acting as a datafile server only (QuickBooks is not installed on the computer; instead, only the QuickBooks database engine is installed), don't use the QuickBooks backup feature when the company file is open on your own computer.

If you back up a remote company file, the backup that's created is not as complete as a backup made when the company file is on the same computer as the QuickBooks user. Some important files are not included in the backup file, and you'll have to restore, rebuild, and reconfigure some of the file.

Instead of creating a backup of the company file using the QuickBooks backup function, back up (copy) the entire folder on the server that holds your company files to a removable drive (flash drive or CD/DVD).

Backing Up

Do this every day! You don't have to create a manual backup, as described here, every day if you set up scheduled backups (covered later in this section); you'll still be making a daily backup, you just won't have to do the work.

 CAUTION: In the sidebar, "Backing Up a Remote Company File," I mention that backing up a file across the network results in a backup that isn't a full backup. Unfortunately, backing up a company file that *is* located on your computer can also result in a backup file that's missing some information, although the problem isn't as severe. If you do payroll in-house, any payroll forms you saved (940, 941, W-2, etc.) are not backed up. Luckily, you can back up those forms separately by copying them to your backup media. Look for a folder named "*<YourCompanyFile>* Tax Forms" in the folder that holds your company files; all the forms you saved are in that folder.

To create a backup of the company currently open in QuickBooks, choose File | Save Copy Or Backup. This opens the Save Copy Or Backup Wizard window seen in Figure 27-1. Select Backup Copy and click Next.

In the next window, choose Local Backup and then click the Options button to set the location of the backup in the Backup Options dialog seen in Figure 27-2. Use the guidelines in the following sections to select options in this dialog.

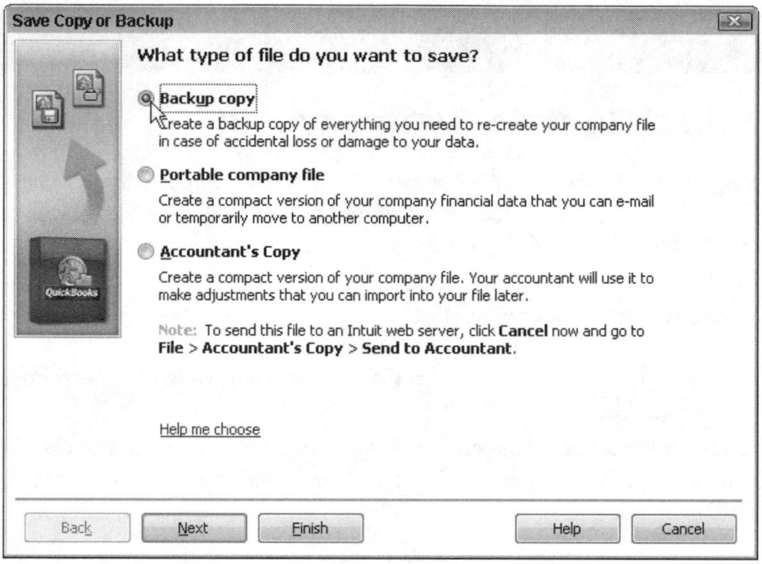

FIGURE 27-1 Select the type of copy you want to create—in this case, it's a backup.

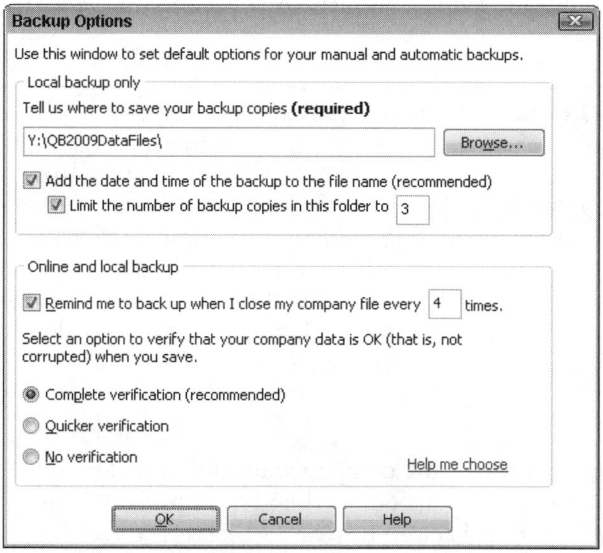

FIGURE 27-2 Configure the options for this backup.

> **NOTE:** If you select the option Online Backup, QuickBooks opens a browser and takes you to a website with information about the QuickBooks online backup service (a fee-based service). You can sign up for the service on the website.

Selecting a Location for the Backup

Click the Browse button to select the location for this backup. The optimum location is a USB drive, a CD/DVD, or a drive on another computer on your network (if you have a network). (The location shown in Figure 27-2 is a standalone network drive attached to a remote computer on the network, and the folders on that drive are burned to CDs and taken offsite every two days.) If you select a local drive, QuickBooks issues a warning message when you click OK.

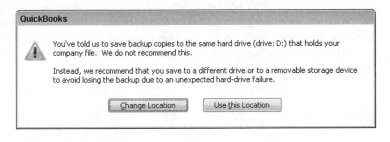

Unless you're saving the file to a folder on this computer that is going to be backed up later in the day or at night, heed the warning. Putting a backup on your hard drive is asking for disaster, because the whole purpose of a backup is to restore data when the hard drive (or the computer) dies—notice I said "when," not "if."

Setting Backup Reminders

You can ask QuickBooks to remind you about backing up when you close a company file by selecting that option and then indicating the frequency. This shouldn't be necessary, because you should be backing up every day; you need to develop a habit, not ask for reminders. However, if you think you won't develop an obsessive compulsion to back up your business data (a very healthy compulsion), use this option to be reminded. In fact, set the frequency to 1 to change the feature from "reminder" to "nagging."

Choosing File Verification Options

If you wish, you can ask QuickBooks to verify the data in your company file before backing up (by selecting either verification option). This can increase the amount of time it takes to complete the backup, so if you're performing a quick backup because you want to make configuration changes in your file, or you're about to perform some other action that makes you think you want a safety backup, select the option No Verification.

You can also verify your data file by selecting File | Utilities | Verify Data. See the section "Verifying and Rebuilding a Company File," later in this chapter, for more information on verification.

Adding Time Stamps to Backup Filenames

You can select the option to append a date/time stamp to the filename, which lets you tell at a glance when the backup file was created. The backup filename has the following format:

```
CompanyFilename(Backup Jun 01,2009 04 36 PM).QBB
```

If you select the time stamp option, you can also create multiple backups in the same location, and you can limit the number of backups you save in a specific location. Multiple backups over continuous days provide an option to restore a backup from two days ago (or longer) if you think the backup you made yesterday may have some corrupted data. During backup, QuickBooks notes the number of backups you opted to keep and when a backup is made that exceeds that number, QuickBooks asks if you want to delete the extra backup (always choosing the oldest backup as the one to delete).

Click OK in the Options dialog to return to the wizard.

Choosing When to Save the Backup

Click Next to choose when to create this backup. You have three choices:

- Save It Now
- Save It Now And Schedule Future Backups
- Only Schedule Future Backups

The second and third choices are concerned with scheduling automatic and unattended backups, a subject that's covered later in this chapter in the section, "Scheduling Backups."

Assuming you're creating a backup now (the option chosen by default), click Next. QuickBooks opens the Save Backup Copy dialog with your location selected, and the backup filename in the File Name field. Click Save.

Backing Up to a CD

If you're using QuickBooks on a computer running Windows XP, Windows 2003 Server, or Windows Vista, you can select your CD drive as the backup target (assuming your CD drive is capable of writing CDs).

QuickBooks actually saves the backup to the default folder on the hard drive that holds files waiting to be written to a CD, and the software displays a message telling you your data has been backed up successfully to that location. When you click OK, QuickBooks displays a dialog in which you can choose to burn the CD using

the Windows CD Wizard (Burn Now) or using your own CD burning software
(Burn Later).

(In fact, you can burn the CD later through the Windows CD Wizard; you don't
have to use CD burning software.)

If you choose Burn Now, QuickBooks creates the backup in the folder Windows
uses to save files for CD transfers (a subfolder in your user profile reserved for this
task). You may see a balloon over the notification area of your taskbar, telling you
that files are waiting to be written to the CD (the standard notification when you
burn CDs in Windows). You don't have to click the balloon to open the folder that
holds the file, because the QuickBooks backup feature automatically opens the
Windows CD Writing Wizard and copies the file to the CD.

If you choose Burn Later, QuickBooks creates the backup file in the folder
Windows uses to save files for CD transfers (look in the folders under your name in
C:\Documents and Settings). You can open your CD burning software and direct it
to that location, or you can use the Windows CD Writing Wizard by following
these steps:

1. Select the CD drive in My Computer, where Windows displays the file(s)
   waiting to be written to the CD.
2. Choose File | Write These Files To CD.
3. When the Windows CD Writing Wizard appears, follow the prompts to move
   your backup file to the CD.

Scheduling Backups

QuickBooks offers both automatic backups and unattended backups (which are
also automatic). You can schedule either or both of these types of backups from the
same wizard that walks you through the backup process (described in the previous

sections). Click through the wizard windows until you get to the window titled Save Backup: When.

- Select Save It Now And Schedule Future Backups if you want to create a manual backup and also set up automatic and/or unattended backups.
- Select Only Schedule Future Backups if you just want to set up automatic and/ or unattended scheduled backups.

Clicking Next after either selection brings you to the wizard window shown in Figure 27-3.

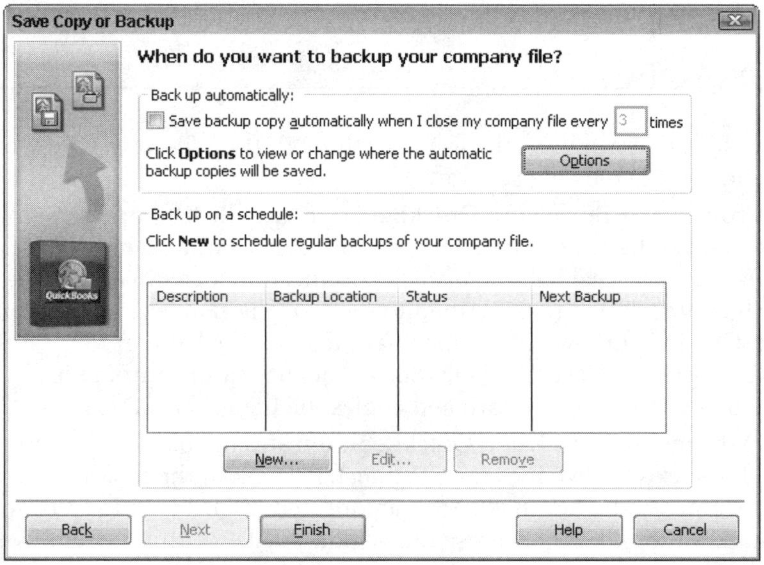

FIGURE 27-3   Set up automatic backup procedures to make sure your data is always safe.

Configuring Automatic Backups

An automatic backup is one that takes place when you close the company file, an action that can take place under any of the following circumstances:

- You open another company file.
- You choose File | Close Company (or File | Close Company/Logoff if you've set up users for the company).
- You close QuickBooks with this company file loaded.

Set the frequency of automatic backups to match the way you use QuickBooks and the way you work in this company file. For example, if you open QuickBooks with this company file loaded in the morning and keep QuickBooks open all day without changing companies, set a frequency of 1 to make sure you have at least one backup each day (and you can also set up another scheduled backup for that evening). The automatic backup is created using the settings, including the location, you configured in the Options dialog.

Configuring Scheduled Backups

You can configure QuickBooks to perform a backup of your company files at any time, even if you're not working at your computer. This is a cool feature, but it doesn't work unless you remember to leave your computer running when you leave the office. Before you leave, make sure QuickBooks is closed so all the files are available for backing up (open files are skipped during a scheduled backup).

To create the configuration for an unattended backup, click New to open the Schedule Backup dialog seen in Figure 27-4.

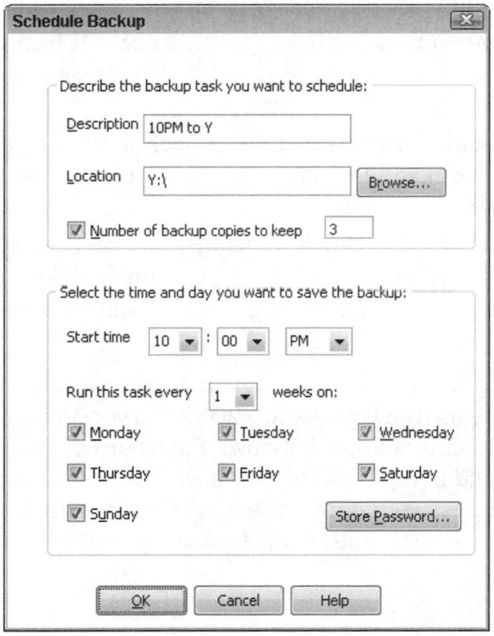

FIGURE 27-4 Configure the specifications for an unattended backup.

You can give the backup a descriptive name (it's optional), but if you're going to create multiple unattended backup configurations, it's a good idea to identify each by name. For example, if you're backing up to a USB stick drive that's had its drive letter assigned as F:, a good description of a backup scheduled for 10 P.M. is "10PM to F."

Enter a location for the backup file. In Figure 27-4, the location is a mapped network drive, but another backup scheduled later at night is sent to a local USB flash drive.

> ($) **C A U T I O N :** Be sure the target drive is available—insert the Zip, USB, or other removable drive before leaving the computer; or be sure the remote network computer you're using for backup storage isn't shut down at night.

If you don't want to overwrite the last backup file every time a new backup file is created, select the option Number Of Backup Copies To Keep, and specify the number. QuickBooks saves as many discrete backup files as you specify, each time replacing the first file with the most recent backup and copying older files to the next highest number in the filename. These backup files are saved with the filename pattern SBU_0_<*CompanyFilename*><Date/Time Stamp>.

If you specify two backup files in the Number Of Backup Copies To Keep field, the second filename starts with SBU_1_. This pattern continues for the number of backups you specified.

Create a schedule for this unattended backup by selecting a time and a frequency. For this example, I created a daily schedule to make sure the backup occurs every night.

If you're on a network, QuickBooks displays the Enter Windows Password dialog. The password in question is not to your QuickBooks user and password configuration; it's your Windows logon name and password.

> ($) **T I P :** If you're using Windows XP/2003 Server/Vista, and you're familiar with the Run As feature, this Enter Windows Password dialog works similarly; you can enter a user name and password that exists on the remote computer (if your own login name and password isn't already on the user list of the remote computer, which is really an easier, better way to manage network access on a peer-to-peer network).

You can create multiple unattended backups and configure them for special circumstances. For instance, in addition to a nightly backup, you may want to configure a backup every four weeks on a Saturday or Sunday (or during your lunch hour on a weekday) to create a backup on a removable drive that is earmarked for off-site storage. Be sure to bring the office backup media to the office on that day and take it back to the off-site location when the backup is finished.

I'm a backup freak (my entire professional life is on my computers), so in addition to the nightly backup that runs at 11:00 P.M., I have a second unattended backup running at 1:00 A.M. to a different mapped drive (on a different network computer). A third backup is configured for Fridays at 3:00 A.M., and its target is a USB flash drive (that's my off-site backup). On Fridays, before I leave the computer, I insert the USB drive into the USB port, confident that all three backups will run while I'm gone. On Monday, I take the removable media off site. In fact, I alternate between two removable media disks, so I'm never backing up over the only existing removable backup.

Mapped drives are unique to your Windows login name. If you log off of Windows before you leave the office (not the same as shutting down the computer, which would prevent the backup from running), you cannot use a mapped drive to create your backup. While it's not common to take the trouble to log off of Windows, if you do normally log off, use the full path to the remote folder you're using as the target location instead of the mapped drive letter. The format of the full path (called *Universal Naming Convention* or *UNC*) is

```
\\ComputerName\ShareName
```

Restoring a Backup

You just turned on your computer and it sounds different—noisier. In fact, there's a grinding noise. You wait and wait, but the usual startup of the operating system fails to appear. Eventually, an error message about a missing boot sector appears (or some other equally chilling message). Your hard drive has gone to hard-drive heaven. You have invoices to send out, checks to write, and tons of things to do, and if you can't accomplish those tasks, your income suffers.

Don't panic; get another hard drive or another computer (the new one will probably cost less than the one that died because computer prices keep dropping). If you buy a new hard drive, it will take some time to install your operating system. If you buy a new computer, it probably comes with an operating system installed.

If you're running on a network (and you were backing up your QuickBooks files to a network drive), create the mapped drive to the shared folder that holds your backup. Then install your QuickBooks software.

Maybe your computer is fine, and it's your QuickBooks file, or your QuickBooks software, that has had a disaster. QuickBooks won't open, or QuickBooks opens but reports a corruption error when it tries to open your file. In this case, you don't have all the work of rebuilding hardware. If QuickBooks won't open or opens with error messages about a software problem, reinstall QuickBooks. If the new installation of QuickBooks opens but your company file won't open, restore your backup.

➡ **FYI**

The QuickBooks Transaction Log and Backups

QuickBooks keeps a transaction log file that tracks changes to the data in your company file data since the last good backup. The filename is *<YourCompanyFilename>*. TLG. The transaction file is in the same folder as your company file (the .QBW file).

(Rumor has it that if you have a company file that becomes corrupt or disappears, Intuit Technical Support can use the log file and your most recent backup to recover data up to the point of the transactions saved at the time of the backup file you supply.)

The TLG file can grow quite large; in fact, it can become larger than your company file. Because the TLG file is active while you're working in QuickBooks, the combination of a large company file and a large TLG file can cause QuickBooks to perform quite slowly.

QuickBooks documentation articles, including the online Knowledge Base, tell you that the TLG file is reset (emptied and then built again from scratch as you work in QuickBooks) each time you successfully do a manual backup in QuickBooks. (Performing automatic backups when you close the file, or performing scheduled backups, does not impact the TLG file.)

The statement regarding manual backups resetting the TLG file is not exactly accurate. The TLG file is reset when you perform a *good backup*, and the definition of a *good backup* is a backup that is performed with the Verify option enabled.

Because the verification process makes the backup process much longer, many users deselect the Verify option when they create a manual backup. The truth is, if you have an apparently successful backup with Verify deselected, you could very well be backing up corrupted data, which won't be a welcome discovery if you have to restore the backup file after your QBW file becomes so corrupted that it won't open or produces errors when you create transactions.

If you don't have the patience to wait for a backup with Verify enabled to complete, compromise; back up manually every three or four days (this is safe as long as you're using automated and/or scheduled backups daily) and enable the Verify option every other time (or, if you're really impatient, every third time). This will prevent the TLG file from growing large enough to impede performance.

It's also a good idea to verify the integrity of your company file periodically by choosing File | Utilities | Verify Data. If everything is fine, then the automatic and scheduled backups you're creating are fine. If QuickBooks finds problems with the data, you can check the QuickBooks support site or call technical support to get information about fixing the problems. However, you still have to perform a verified manual backup periodically to reset the TLG file.

Here's how to restore a backup file:

1. Start QuickBooks. If the opening window tells you there's no company open and suggests you create one (if this is a fresh installation of the software), ignore that message.

2. If you backed up to removable media, put the disk that contains your last backup into its drive. If you backed up to a network share, be sure the remote computer is running. If you purchased the QuickBooks online backup service, be sure you've configured your Internet connection in QuickBooks.

3. Choose File | Open Or Restore Company from the QuickBooks menu bar to start the wizard that walks you through file backups and restores (the same wizard discussed in the previous sections).

4. Choose Restore A Backup Copy and click Next.

5. Select Local Backup if your backup files are on removable media or on a remote computer on the network. Select Online Backup if you subscribe to that QuickBooks service. Then click Next. (If you use the QuickBooks online backup service, at this point follow the prompts to restore your backup.)

6. If you selected Local Backup, the Open Backup Copy dialog appears. Navigate to the folder or drive where your backup is stored.

7. Select the backup file—if you store multiple backups with time stamps embedded in the filename, select the most recent backup.

8. Click Open, and then click Next to continue with the Restore Wizard.

9. In the Save Company File As dialog, select the folder to which you're restoring the file and click Save.

10. If you're restoring to an existing company (because the problem was a corrupt data file), QuickBooks asks if you want to replace the existing file. Click Yes. Then, just to make sure, QuickBooks displays a warning that you're about to overwrite/delete the existing file. That's fine; it's what you want to do, so type Yes in the dialog and click OK.

QuickBooks displays a message that your data files have been restored successfully and opens the file.

> **TIP:** If this backup wasn't saved yesterday, you must re-create every transaction you made between the time of this backup and the last time you used QuickBooks.

The restored file isn't exactly the same as the original file, and you should use My Computer or Windows Explorer to open the folder into which you restored the file.

You'll find a folder named Restored_<*CompanyFilename*>_Files, and the folder contains the following components:

- A folder named Letters_Templates, which contains subfolders for all the letters you can create using the QuickBooks feature called Prepare Letters With Envelopes.
- A folder named Printer_Settings, which contains the files that track your QuickBooks printer configuration settings.
- A folder named Spell_Checker, which contains your spell-check settings and the dictionary (the words added to the spell checker) of the user logged on at the time the backup was created.
- A text file named HowToRestoreExternalFiles.txt. Double-click this file to open it in Notepad. It contains information about the way restored files are saved and how to make sure you can use all the files again.

Testing the Restore Process

It's imperative that you periodically test whether your backup file will restore properly. For all you know, you've been backing up corrupted data, or the drive on which you store your backup file isn't reliable, or <*insert any hardware/software/operating system problem here*>.

You should perform this exercise every two weeks, so if a restore doesn't work, and it's because your backups aren't good files, the quicker you learn this fact the fewer transactions you have to re-create in the restored file you create from the last good backup.

QuickBooks makes it very easy to maintain multiple backup files instead of overwriting each backup with the last backup, with the use of the time-stamp feature, where you can choose the number of backups to keep (and each backup file has its date and time in the filename).

Even better, have separate media (a USB flash drive or a CD/DVD) for each day of the week. Make time-stamped backups onto each media (so your Monday media has three or more backups that were made on successive Mondays). This lets you continue to test restores until you find the last good backup.

A "test" restore should be managed as a laboratory experiment, which means you set up your computer to perform the experiment without touching any real QuickBooks files.

Restore your last backup using the steps explained in the previous section, *except* when you're asked to select a name for the file, enter **TestRestore.QBW** instead of using the company filename for the backup file. You do not want to overwrite your current company file!

When QuickBooks finishes restoring the file, it opens in the usual manner, as long as the backup file was good. Log in (if you log in to QuickBooks) and open a few reports to make sure all the data, as of the date of the backup, is there (the Profit & Loss report is a good candidate for this).

Create a few transactions, and make sure you can perform the tasks your original, real QuickBooks file was set up to do. For instance, if you do payroll in-house, make sure you can create payroll checks without any errors about payroll tables; if you send customer transactions by e-mail transactions, make sure it works properly (send yourself an invoice; don't scare a customer with a phony invoice), and so on.

If everything works, you can close the file and open your real file, then delete the restored file from the TestRestore folder. Remember that the test file will be in the Previous Files list, so use the instructions at the beginning of this chapter to reset that list.

If there are problems, close the file (you'll have no file open in QuickBooks, but you can still access the Restore command) and repeat the test with the backup previous to the backup you just restored. Keep going back until you have a good file that works.

When you've loaded a good file, back it up immediately, even if it's missing a few days of transactions. Open your real file and run the Verify command. If the file passes muster, the problem with your backup may be in the backup media you used (which is why it's a good idea to rotate the media every night). Buy a new flash drive or a new CD/DVD-R, and use it to back up and test the restore.

If QuickBooks encounters a problem during the Verify routine, but you can still work with the file, create reports for the time period that's missing from the last good backup you restored so you can enter those transactions when you restore the good backup over this file. If you have to replace your QuickBooks file you can either restore the good backup to your real QuickBooks folder, or copy the good restored file from the TestRestore folder to your QuickBooks data folder, overwriting the file that didn't verify properly.

Using a Portable Company File

A portable company file is a copy of your QuickBooks company file that has been condensed to save disk space to make it "portable." Portable files are designed to move data between computers (such as your home computer and your office), so you can work at home and then bring the updated file back to the office. You could also send the file to your accountant.

Creating a Portable Company File

To create a portable company file, choose File | Save Copy Or Backup, select Portable Company File, and click Next. In the Save Portable Company File dialog, select a location for the file (by default, QuickBooks selects the Desktop as the location).

If you're taking the file to another computer (perhaps you're taking it home), choose removable media such as a Zip or USB drive, and take the media with you. Or, save the file on your hard drive and then send it to the person who will be working with the file (such as your accountant), either by e-mail or by burning it to a CD and sending the CD to the recipient.

> **CAUTION:** If your company file is very large, the portable file, even though it's condensed, could be too large to e-mail. Many users have size limitations on their mailboxes or have slow connections. In that case, burning and mailing a CD is a better method.

QuickBooks automatically names the file using the following format:

```
CompanyFilename (Portable).QBM
```

Click Save. QuickBooks displays a message telling you it has to close the company file to create the portable file. Click OK.

It takes a while to create the file, and when it's done, QuickBooks issues a success message.

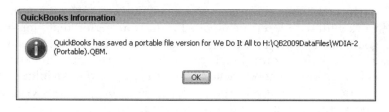

Restoring a Portable Company File

QuickBooks uses the word "restore" for the process of installing a portable company file on a computer. That term is generally reserved for the process of replacing a file with a backed up version of that file, and a portable file is not a backup and isn't usually used for the reasons you use a backup file.

When you restore a backup, it's because you know the original file is either bad or missing. If the file is bad, it's OK to overwrite (delete and replace) the original file with the restored file. In fact, QuickBooks has utilities that can recover lost or damaged data from a backup file, but there are no such utilities available when you install a portable company file.

When you restore a portable company file to a computer that has an existing file for the same company, replacing the existing file may cause you to lose any work you've performed in the existing file. The process of overwriting the existing file with the portable company file deletes the existing file and replaces it with the portable company file.

If you're the only person who works in the company file, and you take a portable file to another computer (such as your home computer), work on the file and bring it back to the office, it's safe to overwrite the office copy with the portable company file. Nobody has created any transactions since you created the portable company file, so deleting the original file doesn't delete any new transactions.

However, if you send a portable company file to someone else, and then continue to work in the original file, you can't restore the portable company file when it's returned unless you're prepared to lose all the work you did in the meantime. You have two ways to avoid this potential disaster:

- Stop working on the file until the portable company file is returned. Then, when you restore the portable company file, you don't lose any data.
- Have the person who performs work in the portable company file send you a list of the transactions that were entered, instead of returning the file, and enter those transactions in the existing company file.
- Restore the file to a different location, or use a different filename (or both). You can open the restored company file and see what's new, then add that data to your real company file.

To restore a portable company file, either on your home computer or on the office computer after you've worked on the file at home and saved it as a portable file, follow these steps to use the wizard that guides you through the process:

1. Choose File | Open Or Restore Company.
2. In the Open Company: Type window, select Restore A Portable File and click Next.
3. In the Open Portable Company File dialog, navigate to the folder or removable media drive that holds the file, select the file, and click Open.
4. In the next window, click Next and then use one of the following guidelines to select a location and filename:

Replacing the Existing Company File with the Portable File   If you're deliberately replacing a company file, select the folder that holds the original company file and use the same filename as your company file. QuickBooks displays a warning that you're about to overwrite the existing file and asks if you want to replace it; click Yes. To make sure you really understand what you're about to do, QuickBooks displays the Delete Entire File dialog and asks you to confirm your action. Type Yes and click OK to continue.

Creating a Different Company File from the Portable File   If you want to create a separate company file to avoid overwriting the work you did in your real company file, change the location or the filename (or both) before you click Save.

After the portable company file is uncompressed, it's loaded in the QuickBooks window so you can work in it.

Verifying and Rebuilding a Company File

QuickBooks includes utilities to verify and rebuild the data in your company file. They're both found on the File | Utilities submenu.

Verifying a company file checks the data and the accuracy of the file's contents. If any problems are found, they're written to a log file named QBWIN.LOG. You can view the contents of the log within QuickBooks by pressing F2 to open the Product Information window, and then pressing F3 to open the QuickBooks Tech Help window. Click the tab named Open File, select QBWIN.LOG, and click Open File.

 NOTE: When you perform a backup with the option to verify the file enabled, any problems QuickBooks finds are also written to the QBWIN.LOG file.

Sometimes the log file has clear, helpful information about the problem and you can remove the troublesome record from the data file. However, it's common to have to call Intuit support for help. If you do, the support technician may ask you to send the log file, along with other files available in the QuickBooks Tech Help window, using the button labeled Send Log Files To Intuit Support on the Open File tab.

Rebuilding a company file that had problems reported during Verify can be a very long, very complicated process that shouldn't be performed unless a QuickBooks support technician asks you to do so.

Cleaning Up Data

QuickBooks provides a feature that enables you to remove certain data in your company file in order to remove elements that you no longer use or need. Using this feature does *not* make your file smaller, but it does get rid of some list items and transaction details you no longer want to wade through as you work in QuickBooks. While this seems to be a handy feature, it carries some significant side effects in the loss of details about transactions.

Understanding the Data Removal Procedure

The data removal process deletes closed transactions and replaces them with a journal entry that shows totals posted to accounts. (If you subscribe to any QuickBooks payroll services, no current year transactions are condensed.) Open transactions (such as unpaid invoices and bills and estimates that are not marked "Closed") are not removed. Before removing the data, QuickBooks creates an archive copy of your company file (which you can open to see the original transactions that were removed).

Choosing a Date

QuickBooks asks you for the date you want to use as the cutoff date. Everything you no longer need before that date is removed, if it can be safely removed without interfering with transactions that remain. No open transactions are removed; only those data items that are completed, finished, and safe to remove are targeted. Also, any transactions before the cutoff date that affect current transactions are kept, so the details are maintained in the file.

Understanding Summary Transactions

The transactions that fall within the parameters of the condensing date are deleted and replaced with summary transactions. Summary transactions are nothing but journal entry transactions that show the totals for the removed transactions, one for each month. The account balances are not changed by removing data, because the summary transactions maintain those totals.

Understanding the Aftereffects

After you clean up the file, you won't be able to run detail reports for those periods before the cutoff date. However, summary reports will be perfectly accurate in their financial totals. You will be able to recognize the summary transactions in the account registers because they will be marked with a transaction type GENJRNL. You can open the archived file if you need to see the original transaction details.

Running the File Cleanup Utility

To run the File Cleanup utility, choose File | Utilities | Clean Up Company Data. The Clean Up Company Data Wizard opens, offering two cleanup methods (see Figure 27-5). You may see a warning about losing your budget data when your file

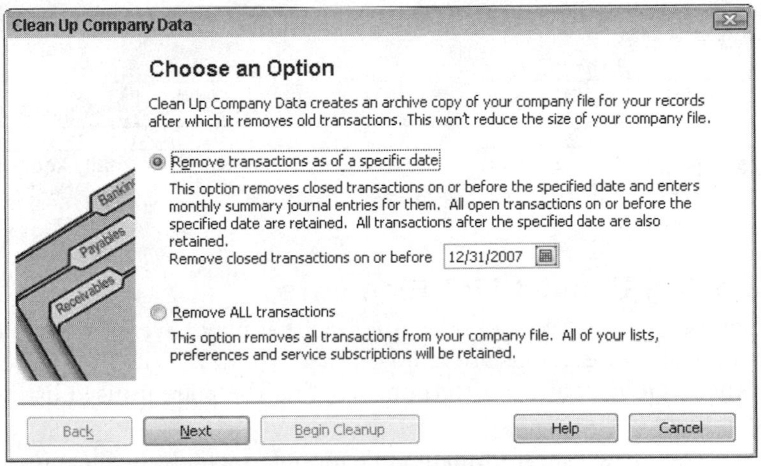

Choose an Option

Clean Up Company Data creates an archive copy of your company file for your records after which it removes old transactions. This won't reduce the size of your company file.

◉ Remove transactions as of a specific date

This option removes closed transactions on or before the specified date and enters monthly summary journal entries for them. All open transactions on or before the specified date are retained. All transactions after the specified date are also retained.
Remove closed transactions on or before [12/31/2007]

○ Remove ALL transactions

This option removes all transactions from your company file. All of your lists, preferences and service subscriptions will be retained.

[Back] [Next] [Begin Cleanup]   [Help] [Cancel]

FIGURE 27-5 You can choose to clean up your file or empty it.

is condensed, because some budgets are based on detailed postings. Click Yes. (Chapter 23 explains how to export your budgets to Excel and import them back into QuickBooks.)

For this discussion, select the option Remove Transactions As Of A Specific Date. (Read "Removing All Transactions with the Cleanup Wizard," later in this section, to learn about that option.) By default, QuickBooks inserts the last day of the previous fiscal year as the date. Usually, it's a good idea to go back a bit more if you've been using QuickBooks for several years For example, I'd choose the last day of 2007 instead of 2008. Click Next when you've entered the cutoff date.

Selecting Additional Transactions to Remove

In the next wizard window, you can select one or more types of existing transactions to remove, even though they wouldn't be removed automatically during a file cleanup process (see Figure 27-6). For example, if you have a transaction marked "To Be Printed" that's more than a year old, you probably aren't planning to print it (and you probably forgot you ever created it). When you've made your selections, click Next.

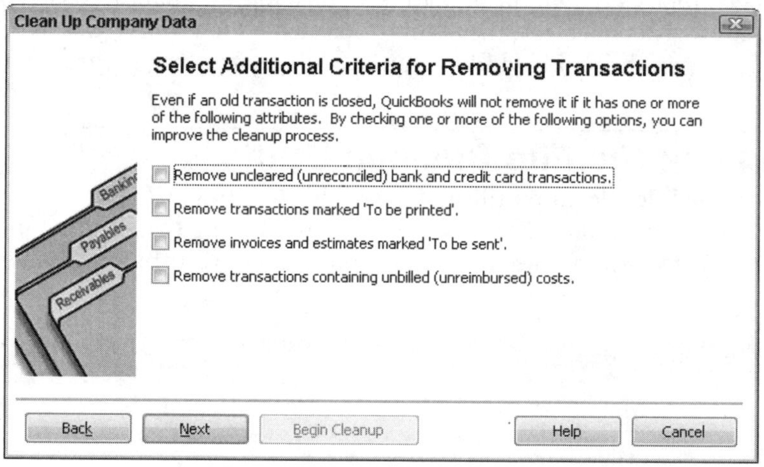

FIGURE 27-6 You can remove transactions that QuickBooks would normally keep, but make these selections thoughtfully.

Removing Unused List Elements

In the next window you can select the lists that may have elements that won't be used after old transactions are removed (see Figure 27-7). Click the list(s) you want QuickBooks to examine to determine whether there are unused listings, and if so, remove them.

Click Next to see an informational window in which the cleanup process is explained. Click Begin Cleanup to start the process. QuickBooks displays a message

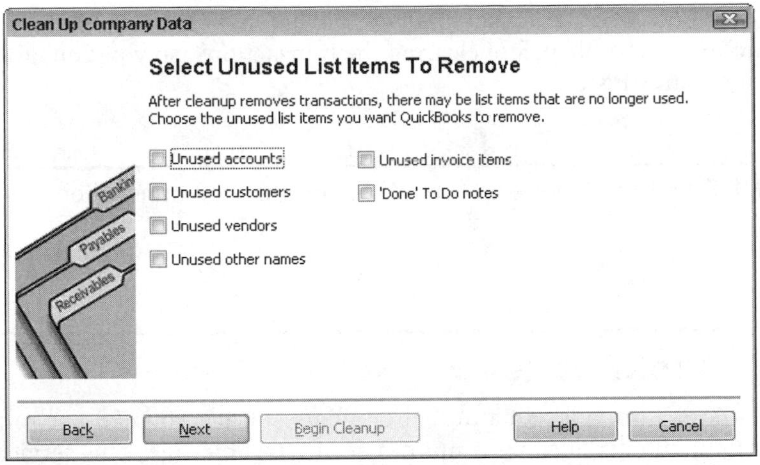

FIGURE 27-7   Empty lists that have elements you created but never use.

telling you that first your data file needs to be backed up. This is not an everyday backup; it's the last backup of a full data file before information is removed. Therefore, add text to the name of the backup file to indicate that it's special (for instance, MyCompanyFile-Cleaned.QBB). Click Save to begin the backup.

As soon as QuickBooks finishes backing up, it starts removing data. You'll see progress bars on your screen as each step completes. When the job is complete, you're given the name of the archive copy of your data file.

The archive copy is intact, just the way your file was before you ran the cleanup feature. This means you can open it if you need to see transaction details the next time a customer or vendor calls to discuss an old, old transaction.

Removing All Transactions with the Cleanup Wizard

The Clean Up Company Data feature offers an option to strip the file of all transactions, leaving behind only the lists and the configuration settings you created for printers and Edit | Preferences categories.

Often, this function is used shortly after you start using QuickBooks as a way to "start all over." Accountants tend to recommend this as a quicker way to straighten out tons of misposted transactions than forming a new company file. Accountants and users have also told me about other reasons they use this tool, including the following:

- Start a new file at the beginning of a new year when the current company file has become so large that working in it is slower than you'd like.
- A company has changed its legal structure (from a proprietorship to a corporation or to an LLC). Payroll, equity accounts, and other elements of the file must be changed to reflect the new organization type.

QuickBooks creates a backup of the file before beginning the process and creates an archive of the file before clearing the transactions, so you don't really wipe out the company's history.

 N O T E : This choice won't run if you have payroll transactions for the current year.

Updating QuickBooks

QuickBooks provides an automatic update service you can use to make sure your QuickBooks software is up-to-date and trouble-free. This service provides you with any maintenance releases of QuickBooks that have been created since you purchased and installed your copy of the software. A maintenance release is distributed when a problem is discovered and fixed, or when a new feature is added to the software.

 N O T E : This service does not provide upgrades to a new version; it just provides updates to your current version.

You can enable automatic updates, which means QuickBooks periodically checks the Intuit update site on the Internet for updates to your version of QuickBooks. If new files exist, they're downloaded to your hard drive. If you turn off automatic updates, you should periodically check for new software files manually. Use the Update Now tab to select and download updated files.

Configuring QuickBooks Update Service

Choose Help | Update QuickBooks and move to the Options tab to configure the Update feature. You can enable or disable the automatic check for updates. If you enable automatic updates, set the download location for storing update files.

If you're using QuickBooks on a network, you can configure the update service to share downloaded files with other users. When this option is enabled, QuickBooks creates a subfolder on the computer that holds the shared QuickBooks data files, and the other computers on the network use that subfolder as the source of updated files (instead of going online and downloading files).

For this to work, every user on the network must open his or her copy of QuickBooks and configure the Update options for Shared Download to reflect the folder location on the host computer. The folder location is displayed on the Options tab when you select the Shared Download option.

Customizing QuickBooks Components

In this chapter:

- Customize settings

- Customize transaction templates

The settings you establish in QuickBooks have a great impact on the way data is kept and reported. It's not uncommon for QuickBooks users to change or tweak these preferences periodically. In fact, the more you use QuickBooks and understand the way it works, the more comfortable you'll be about changing preferences.

In addition, you can customize some of the transaction windows you use, in order to store additional information about those transactions. That information is available in reports, and it means you can get a better picture of your company's financials.

Customizing Settings and Options

Your settings and options for the QuickBooks features are maintained in the Preferences dialogs, which you open by choosing Edit | Preferences from the QuickBooks menu bar.

Each category in the Preferences dialog is accessed by clicking the appropriate icon in the left pane. Every category has two tabs: My Preferences and Company Preferences.

- The My Preferences tab is where you configure your preferences as a QuickBooks user. Each user you create in QuickBooks can set his or her own My Preferences. QuickBooks will apply the correct preferences as each user logs into the company file. (Many categories lack options in this tab.)
- The Company Preferences tab is the place to configure the way the QuickBooks features work for the current company, regardless of which user logs in. Only the Admin can change settings in the Company Preferences tab.

As you configure options and move from one category of the Preferences window to another, you're asked whether you want to save the changes in the section you just left.

In the following sections I'll briefly go over the Preferences categories, so the information is available in one place in this book. Many of the categories, settings, and options are discussed in detail throughout this book, in the appropriate chapters.

Accounting Preferences

Click the Accounting icon on the left pane of the Preferences dialog to open the Accounting preferences (see Figure 28-1). There are only Company Preferences available for this section; the My Preferences tab has no options available.

You can select the option to use account numbers, and if so, you should also select the option Show Lowest Subaccount Only. The latter option is useful because it means that when you see an account number in a drop-down list (in a transaction window), you only see the subaccount. If the option is not selected, you see the parent account followed by the subaccount, and since the field display doesn't show

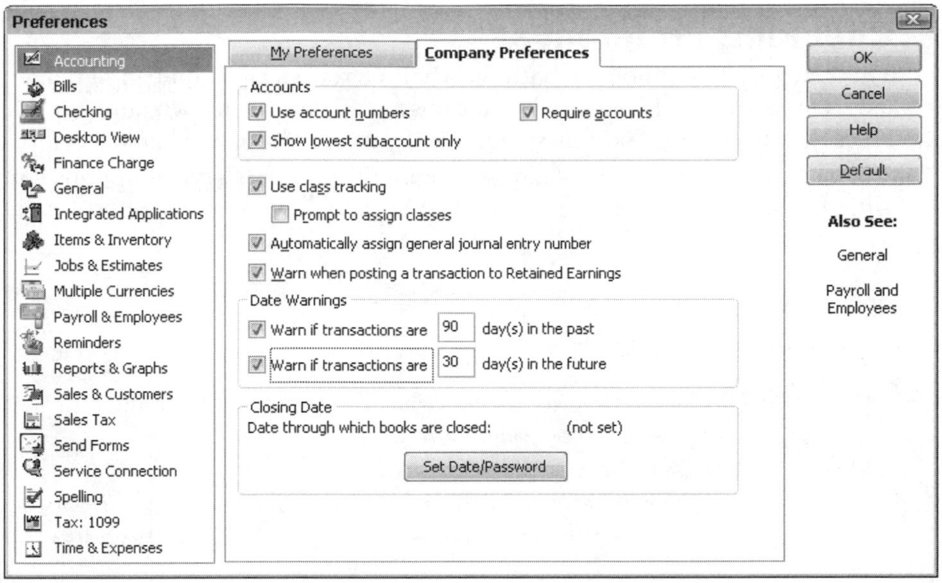

FIGURE 28-1 Configure the way basic accounting functions work.

the entire text unless you scroll through it, it's hard to determine which account has been selected.

The option to require accounts means that every item and transaction you create in QuickBooks has to be assigned to an account. If you disable this option, transaction amounts that aren't manually assigned to an account are posted to Uncategorized Income or Uncategorized Expense, and I don't know any way to produce accurate reports that analyze your business if you don't post transactions to accounts.

You can enable the class feature, which lets you create Profit & Loss reports for divisions, departments, or other categories by which you've decided to analyze your business.

The other options on this dialog are self-explanatory, except for the Closing Date section, which is discussed in Chapter 24.

Bills Preferences

In the Bills category, you have the opportunity to set options for the way you enter and pay vendor bills:

- You can set default terms (QuickBooks sets this at 10 days but you can change this default). When you create terms and link those terms to vendors, QuickBooks ignores this default for any vendor that has terms configured.
- You can tell QuickBooks to take discounts and credits automatically when you're paying vendor bills. Be sure to enter the account in which you post those discounts.

Checking Preferences

This category has options in both the My Preferences and Company Preferences tabs. On the My Preferences tab you can select default bank accounts for different types of transactions. Skip these options if you only have one bank account.

The Company Preferences tab (see Figure 28-2) offers several options concerned with check printing, which are described in the following paragraphs.

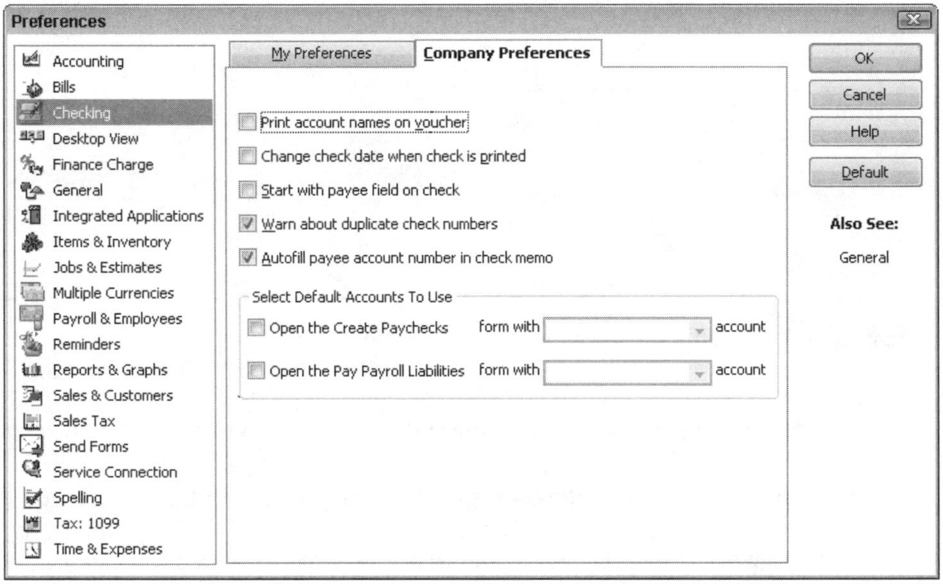

FIGURE 28-2   Select the options you need to make check writing more efficient.

Print Account Names On Voucher

This option is useful only if you print your checks and the check forms you purchase have vouchers (stubs). If so, selecting this option means that the text on the stub will display posting accounts. That information is of no interest to your vendors, so only use this option if you keep and file check vouchers instead of leaving them attached to the check.

Change Check Date When Check Is Printed

Selecting this option means that at the time you print checks, the current date becomes the check date. If you don't select this option, the check date you specified when you filled out the check window is used (even if that date has already passed).

Start With Payee Field On Check

Enabling this option forces your cursor to the Payee field when you first bring up the Write Checks window. If the option is not enabled, the bank account field is the first active field. If you always write checks from the same bank account, enable this option to save yourself the inconvenience of pressing TAB.

Warn About Duplicate Check Numbers

This option means that QuickBooks will warn you if a check number you've used in a check you've created in already exists.

Autofill Payee Account Number In Check Memo

Most vendors maintain an account number for their customers, and your own account number can be automatically printed when you print checks. In order for this to occur, you must fill in your account number in the Vendor card (on the Additional Information tab). The printout appears in the Memo section on the lower-left section of the check.

Select Default Accounts To Use

You can set the default bank accounts for different types of payroll transactions, which is important if you have a separate bank account for payroll. Then, when you create these checks, you don't have to select the bank account from a drop-down list in the transaction window. This avoids the common error of printing the payroll checks on operating account checks, screaming "Eek!", voiding the checks, and starting again with the right account.

Desktop View Preferences

This is where you design the way the QuickBooks window looks and acts. The My Preferences tab (see Figure 28-3) contains basic configuration options.

In the View section, you can specify whether you always want to see one QuickBooks window at a time or view multiple windows.

- Choose One Window to limit the QuickBooks screen to showing one window at a time, even if you have multiple windows open. The windows are stacked atop each other, and only the top window is visible (you cannot resize any window). To switch between multiple windows, use the Window menu.
- Choose Multiple Windows to make it possible to view multiple windows on your screen. Selecting this option activates the arrangement commands on the Windows menu item, which allow you to stack or arrange windows so that more than one window is visible at a time.

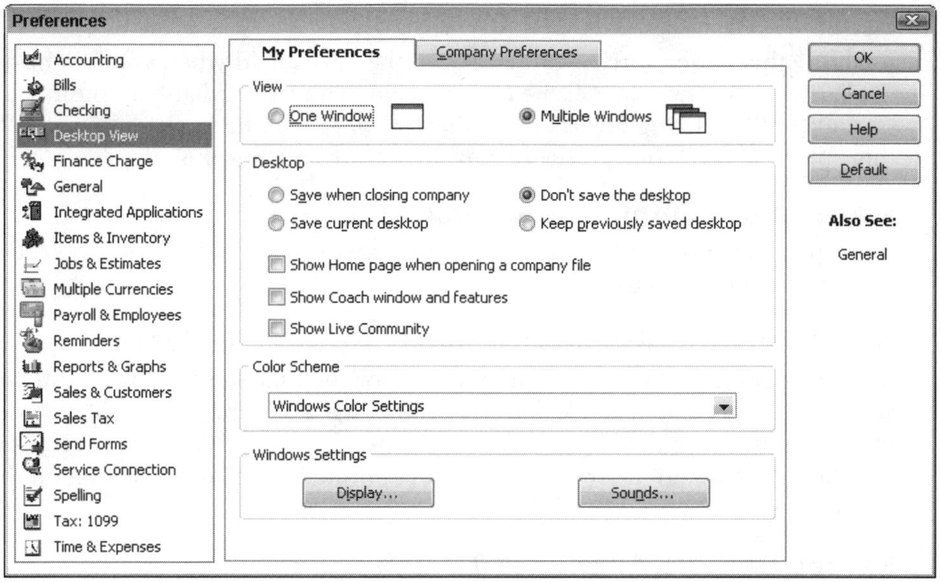

FIGURE 28-3 Configure the look and behavior of the QuickBooks window.

In the Desktop section, you can specify what QuickBooks should do when you exit the software, choosing among the following options:

- **Save When Closing Company**   Means that the state of the desktop is remembered when you close the company (or exit QuickBooks). Whatever QuickBooks windows were open when you left will reappear when you return. You can pick up where you left off. If you select the option Show Home Page When Opening A Company File, that option overrides this option, so if you close the company file after closing the Home page, the Home page appears on top of any open windows when you open the company file.

- **Save Current Desktop**   Displays the desktop as it is at this moment every time you open QuickBooks. Select this option after you've opened or closed the QuickBooks windows you want to see when you start the software. If you select the option Show Home Page When Opening A Company File, that option overrides this option if you close the Home page.

- **Don't Save The Desktop**   Tells QuickBooks to display an empty QuickBooks desktop (unless you enable the Show Home Page When Opening A Company File option) when you open this company file or when you start QuickBooks again after using this company file. The desktop isn't really empty—the menu bar, Icon Bar, and any other navigation bars are on the desktop, but no transaction or list windows are open.

- **Keep Previously Saved Desktop** Available only when you select Save Current Desktop, this option tells QuickBooks to display the desktop as it was the last time you used the Save Current Desktop option.
- **Show Home Page When Opening A Company File** Tells QuickBooks to display the Home page when you open the company file. When this option is selected, the Coach is available.
- **Show Live Community** Tells QuickBooks to open a Help File window with a tab named Live Community whenever you open a company file. The Live Community tab has links to a QuickBooks user forum (see the sidebar on Live Community), and displays forum messages connected to the current open QuickBooks window. You can also open the Live Community window at any time by selecting the Live Community command from the Help menu.

In the Color Scheme section, you can select a scheme from the drop-down list. In addition, buttons are available to configure Windows Settings for Display and Sounds. Clicking either button opens the associated applet in your Windows Control Panel. The display and sounds configuration options you change affect your computer and all your software, not just QuickBooks.

In the Company Preferences tab, you can customize the contents of the Home page. If you want to add an icon on the home page for a particular feature (such as Estimates), this tab shows you whether that feature has been enabled in your company file. If the feature hasn't been enabled, click the feature's name to open its category in the Preferences dialog. Turn the feature on to add its icon to the Home page, and then click the Desktop View icon to return to this window.

▶▶ FYI

QuickBooks Live Community

The QuickBooks Live Community is a user forum where QuickBooks users can ask questions and get answers from other users (and sometimes from Intuit experts). You can read all the questions and answers without joining the community, but if you want to post a question or answer you must join. Joining is free, and all you have to do is provide a user name and your e-mail address.

It's important to be aware that some of the answers and explanations you see may not be accurate; users who provide advice do not necessarily know QuickBooks well (and they sometimes write "guesses" instead of trying their advice by actually performing the tasks they discuss). These users may also lack accounting knowledge. Don't rush to follow advice you find on the forum; instead, check with your accountant or create a test company file to experiment with the advice you find on the forum.

Finance Charge Preferences

In the Company Preferences tab you can turn on, turn off, and configure finance charges. Finance charges can get complicated, so read the complete discussion about this topic in Chapter 10.

General Preferences

This dialog contains options for the way you work in QuickBooks. There are settings on both the My Preferences and Company Preferences tabs.

The My Preferences tab offers a number of options that are designed to let you control the way QuickBooks behaves while you're working in transaction windows.

Pressing Enter Moves Between Fields

This option exists for people who constantly forget that the default (normal, usual) key for moving from field to field in Windows software is the TAB key. Of course, when they press ENTER instead of TAB, the record they're working on is saved even though they haven't finished filling out all the fields. Rather than force you to get used to the way Windows works, QuickBooks lets you change the procedure.

Automatically Open Drop-Down Lists When Typing

This is a handy option that's used when you're making selections from drop-down lists. When you begin typing the first few letters of the listing you need, the drop-down list appears (and you move to the first listing that matches the character you typed).

Beep When Recording A Transaction

If you don't want to hear sound effects as you work in QuickBooks, you can deselect the option. On the other hand, you can use the Windows Sounds and Audio Devices applet in Control Panel to configure the sounds so that some actions produce sound effects and other actions don't. You can even specify which sound you want for the actions that you've configured to play sounds.

Automatically Place Decimal Point

This is a handy feature once you get used to it (I couldn't live without it—and my desk calculator is configured for the same behavior). When you enter currency characters in a field, a decimal point is placed automatically to the left of the last two digits when you enable this feature. Therefore, if you type 5421, when you move to the next field the number changes to 54.21. If you want to type in even dollar amounts, type a period after you enter 54, and QuickBooks will automatically add two zeros to the right of the period (or you can enter the zeros, as in 5400, which automatically becomes 54.00).

Warn When Editing A Transaction

This option, which is selected by default, tells QuickBooks to flash a warning message when you change any transaction and try to close the transaction window without explicitly saving the changed transaction. This means you have a chance to abandon the edits. If you deselect the option, the edited transaction is saved as changed, unless it is linked to other transactions (in which case, the warning message explaining that problem appears).

Bring Back All One-Time Messages

One-time messages are those informational dialogs that include a Don't Show This Message Again option. If you clicked that Don't Show option on any message dialogs, select this check box to see those messages again (and you can once again select the Don't Show option).

Turn Off Pop-Up Messages For Products And Services

Selecting this option stops pop-up messages from QuickBooks that are connected to products and services available from Intuit. For example, when creating checks, Intuit displays a pop-up message explaining that you can buy checks at the Intuit Marketplace.

Show ToolTips For Clipped Text

Enabling this option means that if text in any field is truncated, hovering your mouse over the text displays the entire text. This saves you the trouble of selecting the field and using the arrow keys to read the entire text.

Warn When Deleting A Transaction Or Unused List Item

When selected, this option produces a warning when you delete a transaction or a list entry that has not been used in a transaction—it's a standard message asking you to confirm your action.

If you try to delete an item or a name that has been used in a transaction, QuickBooks won't permit you to complete the deletion.

Automatically Remember Account Or Transaction Information

Enabling this option tells QuickBooks to prefill information in a bill, check, or credit card transaction window, based on previous transactions for the same vendor. If this option is enabled, you can choose either of the suboptions:

- Automatically Recall Last Transaction For This Name, which duplicates the information in the last transaction. This is handy for transactions that don't change (or don't change often), such as the check to your landlord, which is always for the same amount and posted to the same account.
- Pre-Fill Accounts For Vendor Based On Past Entries, which examines the history of transactions for the current vendor. If the same information appears in all or most of the historical transactions, QuickBooks autofills the transaction window (same as the previous option). If historical transactions differ, QuickBooks does not prefill the transaction window, saving you the trouble of removing the data if it doesn't match this transaction.

TIP : In addition to these "memory tricks" that QuickBooks provides for vendor transactions, you can prefill accounts for vendors right in the vendor record, which is a really nifty feature. See Chapter 4 for details.

Default Date To Use For New Transactions

Use this option to tell QuickBooks whether you want the Date field to show the current date or the date of the last transaction you entered, when you open a transaction window. If you frequently enter transactions for the same date over a period of several days (for example, you start preparing invoices on the 27th of the month, but the invoice date is the last day of the month), select the option to use the last entered date so you can just keep going.

Keep Custom Item Information When Changing Item In Transactions

The selection you make for this option determines what QuickBooks does when you change the description text or the price for an item you insert in a sales transaction form, and then change the item. For example, you select an item named Widget, and then in the Description field, you type text to describe this widget, changing the default description that displayed when you selected the item. Or, perhaps the item had no default description, and you entered text to correct that omission. Then, you realize that you didn't really mean to sell the customer a Widget, you meant a Gadget, and the descriptive text you just typed was meant for the item named Gadget (which you thought you'd selected in the Item column). You return to the Item column (on the same line), click the arrow to see your item list, and select Gadget. Now, you think you have to type all that descriptive text again, because Gadget has its own descriptive text, and it will automatically replace your work. This option prevents that work going to waste.

- If you select Always, QuickBooks will keep the descriptive text you wrote, even though you changed the Item. This descriptive text is linked to this different item only for this invoice; no changes are made to any item's record.
- If you select No, QuickBooks just fills in the description that goes with the new item you selected.
- If you select Ask, as soon as you change the item, QuickBooks asks if you want to change only the item and keep your customized description on the invoice. You can answer Yes (or No) and you can also tell QuickBooks to change this Preferences option permanently to match your answer.

The same thing happens if you entered a different price (instead of, or in addition to, the description), and then changed the item.

The Company Preferences tab in the General section has the following options:

Time Format   Select a format for entering time, choosing between decimal (for example, 11.5 hours) or minutes (11:30).

Always Show Years As 4 Digits   If you prefer to display the year with four digits (01/01/2009 instead of 01/01/09), select this option.

Never Update Name Information When Saving Transactions   By default, QuickBooks asks if you want to update the original information for a name when you change it during a transaction entry. For example, if you're entering a sales receipt and you change the customer's address, QuickBooks offers to make that change on the customer's record (you can choose Yes or No when QuickBooks asks). If you don't want to be offered this opportunity and always want the record to remain as is, select this option.

Save Transactions Before Printing   The rule that a transaction must be saved before it's printed is a security device. This thwarts one of the most often used schemes to purloin products (employees create an invoice and packing slip to have products shipped to friends or relatives). Deselect this option at your own peril!

Integrated Applications Preferences

You can let third-party software have access to the data in your QuickBooks files. Click the Integrated Applications icon and move to the Company Preferences tab to specify the way QuickBooks works with other software programs.

When you use a third-party program that links to QuickBooks, you're asked to approve that link. If you say Yes, the information for that program is recorded and appears in this dialog.

Items & Inventory Preferences

Use this dialog to enable the inventory function and set options for processing inventory transactions. Only the Company Preferences tab has options.

Inventory And Purchase Orders Are Active

Select this option to tell QuickBooks that you want to enable the inventory features; the purchase orders are automatically enabled with that action.

Warn About Duplicate Purchase Order Numbers

When this option is enabled, any attempt to issue a purchase order with a PO number that already exists will generate a warning.

Warn If Not Enough Inventory Quantity On Hand (QOH) To Sell

This option turns on the warning feature that is useful during customer invoicing. If you sell ten widgets but your stock of widgets is fewer than ten, QuickBooks displays a message telling you there's insufficient stock to fill the order. You can still complete the invoice; it's just a message, not a functional limitation, but you should order more widgets immediately.

(The option for Units Of Measure is displayed, but the feature is only available in QuickBooks Premier editions.)

Jobs & Estimates Preferences

Use the Company Preferences tab to configure the way your estimates work, as shown in Figure 28-4. The options are self-explanatory. Read Chapter 9 to learn everything about creating estimates and invoices for those estimates.

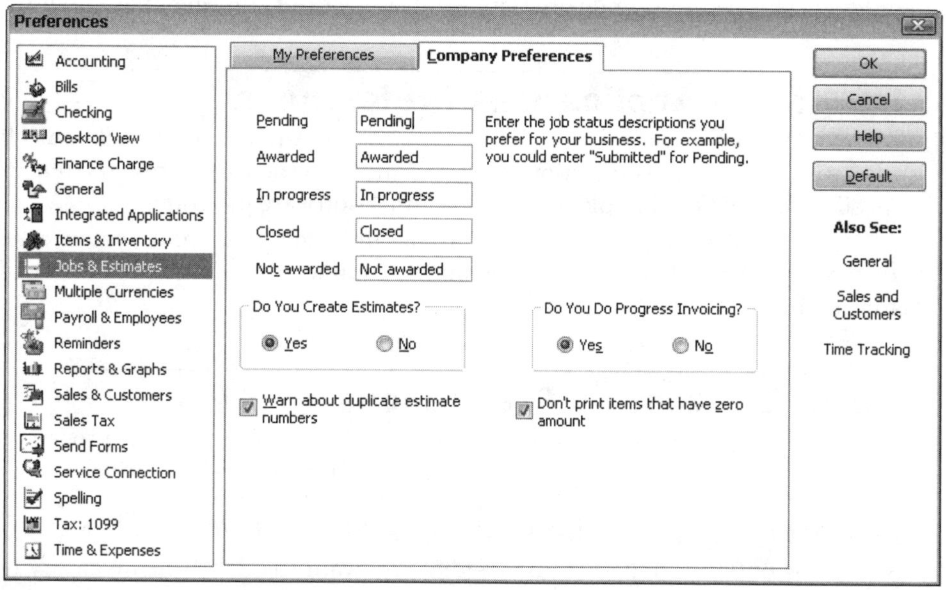

FIGURE 28-4   Set up and configure estimates.

Multicurrency

The Company Preferences tab offers the option to enable the Multicurrency feature, which is described in Appendix A.

Payroll & Employees Preferences

Use the Company Preferences tab of this category to set all the configuration options for payroll. Read Chapter 17 to understand the selections in this window.

Reminders Preferences

The Reminders category of the Preferences dialog has options on both tabs. The My Preferences tab has one option, which enables the display of the Reminders List when you open the company file.

The Company Preferences tab enumerates the available reminders, and you can select the ones you want to use (see Figure 28-5). Of course, these selections are meaningless unless you enabled Reminders in the My Preferences tab.

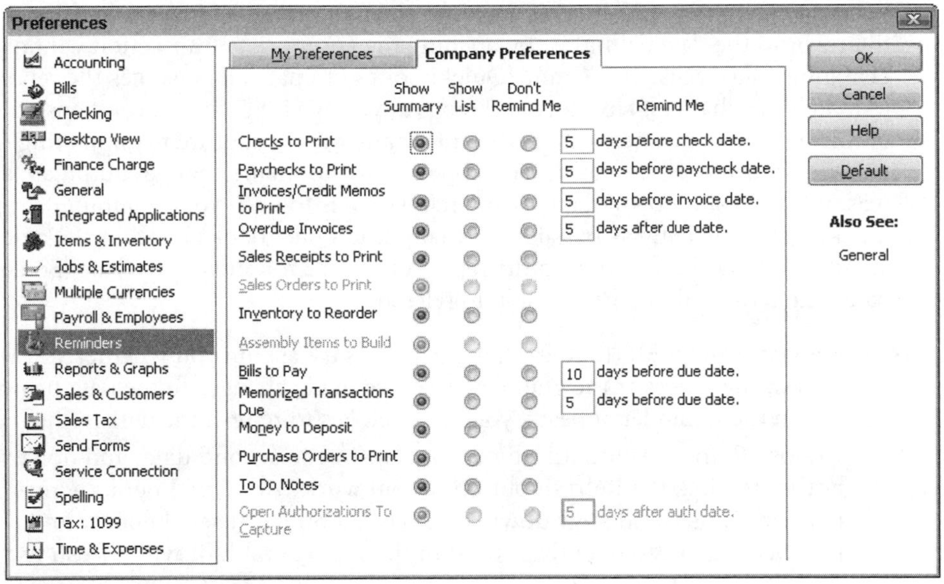

FIGURE 28-5 Decide which tasks you want to be reminded about.

For each item, decide whether you want to see a summary (just a listing and the total amount of money involved), a complete detailed list, or nothing at all. You can also determine the amount of lead time you want for your reminders. (Some of the items are grayed out because they're only available in QuickBooks Premier editions.)

Reports & Graphs Preferences

This is another section of the Preferences window that has choices on both tabs, so you can set your own user preferences and then set those options that affect the current company.

The My Preferences tab configures the following performance issues for reports and graphs.

Prompt Me To Modify Report Options Before Opening A Report

If you find that almost every time you select a report you have to customize it, you can tell QuickBooks to open the Modify Report window whenever a report is brought to the screen. If you find this feature useful, select this option.

Reports And Graphs Settings

While you're viewing a report or a graph, you can make changes to the format, the filters, or to the data behind it (by opening the appropriate transaction window and changing data). Most of the time, QuickBooks automatically changes the report/graph to match the changes. However, if there is anything else going on (perhaps you're also online, or you're in a network environment and other users are manipulating data that's in your report or graph), QuickBooks may not make changes automatically. The reason for the shutdown of automatic refreshing is to keep your computer running as quickly and efficiently as possible. At that point, QuickBooks has to make a decision about when and how to refresh the report or graph. You must give QuickBooks the parameters for making the decision to refresh.

- Choose Prompt Me To Refresh to see a message asking you whether you want to refresh the report or the graph after you've made changes to the data behind it. When the reminder appears, you can click Yes to refresh the data in the report.
- Choose Refresh Automatically if want up-to-the-second data, and don't want to bother to click the Refresh button. If you work with QuickBooks across a network, this could slow down your work a bit because whenever any user makes a change to data that's used in the report/graph, it will refresh itself.
- Choose Don't Refresh if you want to decide for yourself, without any reminder from QuickBooks, when to click the Refresh button on the report window.

Graphs Only

Give QuickBooks instructions about creating your graphs, as follows:

- Choose Draw Graphs In 2D (Faster) to have graphs displayed in two dimensions instead of three. This doesn't impair your ability to see trends at a glance; it's just not as "high-tech." The main reason to consider this option is that the 2-D graph takes less time to draw on your screen.

- Choose Use Patterns to draw the various elements in your graphs with black-and-white patterns instead of colors. For example, one pie wedge may be striped, another speckled. This is handy if you print your graphs to a black-and-white printer.

Move to the Company Preferences tab of the Reports & Graphs category to set company preferences for reports (see Figure 28-6).

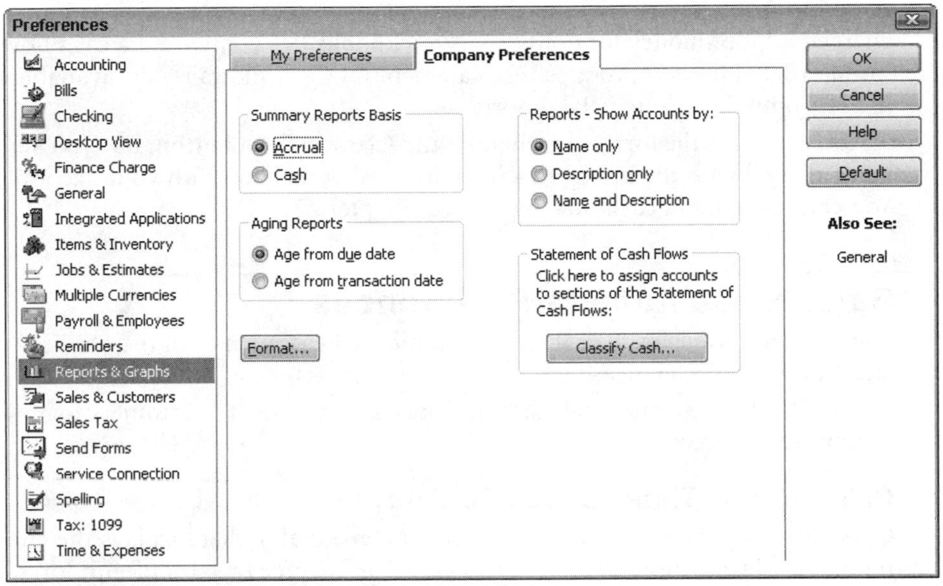

FIGURE 28-6 Set the default options for reports.

Summary Reports Basis

Specify whether you want to see summary reports as accrual-based or cash-based. You're only setting the default specification here, and you can always change the basis in the Modify Report dialog when you actually display the report.

Aging Reports

Specify whether you want to generate A/R and A/P aging reports using the due date or the transaction date.

Reports—Show Accounts By

Specify whether you want reports to display account names, account descriptions, or both. If you enabled account numbers, those numbers are part of the account names.

Setting Report Format Defaults

You can set the default formatting for reports by clicking the Format button and making changes to the default configuration options for parts of reports that aren't data related but instead control the look of the reports. Use this feature if you find yourself making the same modifications to the formats over and over.

Configuring the Cash Flow Report

A cash flow report is really a complicated document, and before the days of accounting software, accountants spent many hours creating such a report (and charged a lot of money for doing so). QuickBooks has configured a cash flow report format that is used to produce the Statement Of Cash Flows report available in the list of Company & Financial reports.

You can view the format by clicking the Classify Cash button, but you shouldn't mess around with the available selections until you check with your accountant. You can learn about cash flow reports in Chapter 23.

Sales & Customers Preferences

You can set options in the Sales & Customers category on both the My Preferences and Company Preferences tabs.

On the My Preferences tab, set the options for invoicing customers for reimbursable expenses and billable time.

Prompt For Time/Costs To Add

Choosing this option tells QuickBooks to open a dialog that displays the current reimbursable expenses whenever you create an invoice or sales receipt for a customer with outstanding reimbursable costs. This is the option to select if you always (or almost always) collect reimbursable costs from customers.

Don't Add Any

Selecting this option prevents the automatic display of any dialogs about reimbursable expenses when you create a sales transaction. Choose this option if you rarely (or never) seek reimbursement from your customers. If you *do* want to collect reimbursable expenses during invoice creation you can click the Add Time/ Costs button on the sales transaction form.

Ask What To Do

Select this option to tell QuickBooks to ask you what you want to do whenever you create a sales transaction for a customer with outstanding reimbursable costs. Depending on your selection in that dialog (discussed in the next section), you can add the costs to the sales transaction or omit them. You can learn how to bill customers for expenses and time in Chapter 9.

On the Company Preferences tab, set the default options for sales transactions.

Usual Shipping Method

Use this to set the default shipping method, if you use the same shipping method most of the time. This saves you the trouble of making a selection from the drop-down list unless you're changing the shipper for a particular invoice.

Usual FOB

Set the FOB language for invoices. FOB (Free On Board) is the location from which shipping is determined to be the customer's responsibility. This means more than just paying for freight; it's a statement that says, "At this point you have become the owner of this product." The side effects include assigning responsibility if goods are lost, damaged, or stolen. FOB settings have no impact on your financial records. (Don't let the size of the text box fool you; you're limited to 13 characters.)

Warn About Duplicate Invoice Numbers

This option tells QuickBooks to warn you if you're creating an invoice with an invoice number that's already in use.

Choose Template For Invoice Packing Slip

Select a default packing slip to use when you print packing slips. If you've created customized packing slips, you can make one of them the default.

Use Price Levels

This option turns on the Price Level feature, which is explained in Chapter 5.

Automatically Apply Payments

This option tells QuickBooks to apply payments automatically to open invoices. If the payment amount is an exact match for an open invoice, it is applied to that invoice. If the payment amount is smaller than any open invoice, QuickBooks applies the payment to the oldest invoice. If the payment amount is larger than any open invoice, QuickBooks applies payments, starting with the oldest invoice, until the payment amount is used up.

Without this option, you must manually apply each payment to an invoice. That's not as onerous as it may sound, and in fact, this is the way I prefer to work, because the customer's check almost always indicates the invoice the customer wants to pay (even if the check doesn't cover the entire amount of that invoice). Sometimes customers don't mark the invoice number on the check and instead enclose a copy of the invoice in the envelope. Read Chapter 10 to learn about receiving and applying customer payments.

Automatically Calculate Payments

When this option is enabled, you can begin selecting invoices to pay in the Receive Payment window before entering the amount of the customer's payment check. When you've finished selecting invoices, either paying them entirely or applying a partial payment, the amounts you've applied should equal the amount of the check you received.

This is efficient if a customer has many invoices (some of which may have credits or may have an amount in dispute) and has attached instructions about the way to apply the checks.

Use Undeposited Funds As A Default Deposit To Account

Selecting this option automates the process of depositing all cash received into the Undeposited Funds account. If the option isn't selected, each cash receipt transaction window (customer payment and sales receipt) offers the choice of depositing the cash into a bank account or into the Undeposited Funds account.

Sales Tax Preferences

If you collect sales tax, you must set your sales tax options. These options are easy to configure because most of the selections are predefined by state tax laws and state tax report rules. Check with your accountant and read the information that came with your state sales tax license. For more information about managing sales taxes (a very complicated issue in many states), see Chapter 6.

Send Forms Preferences

If you send transactions to customers via e-mail, the My Preferences tab offers the opportunity to automatically select the To Be E-Mailed option on a sales transaction if the current customer is configured for e-mail as the preferred send method.

On the Company Preferences tab you can design the message that accompanies the e-mailed transaction, which can be a customer or vendor transaction.

Service Connection Preferences

If you use QuickBooks services on the Internet, use this category to specify the way you want to connect to the Internet for those services.

The My Preferences tab contains options related to online banking if your bank uses the WebConnect method of online access. (Chapter 15 has detailed information about online banking services.)

- **Give Me The Option Of Saving A File Whenever I Download Web Connect Data** Select this option if you want QuickBooks to provide a choice to save Web Connect data for later processing instead of automatically processing the transactions. QuickBooks provides the choice by opening a dialog that lets you choose whether to import the data immediately or save it to a file so you can import it later (you have to supply a filename). The QuickBooks dialog also includes an option to reset this option. This option only works when you select Open on the File Download dialog. If you disable this option, the file is automatically opened and the data is imported into QuickBooks.

- **If QuickBooks Is Run By My Browser, Don't Close It After Web Connect Is Done** Selecting this option means that when QuickBooks is launched automatically when you download Web Connect data from your Financial Institution (after selecting Open on the Download dialog), QuickBooks remains open after you process the data. If you deselect this option, QuickBooks closes automatically as soon as your data is processed.

The following connection options are available on the Company Preferences tab (these options don't apply to payroll services or online banking):

- **Automatically Connect Without Asking For A Password** Lets all users log into the QuickBooks Business Services network automatically.
- **Always Ask For A Password Before Connecting** Forces users to enter a login name and password in order to access QuickBooks Business Services.
- **Allow Background Downloading Of Service Messages** Lets QuickBooks check the Intuit website for updates and information periodically when you're connected to the Internet.

Spelling Preferences

The Spelling section presents options only on the My Preferences tab (see Figure 28-7). This is where you control the way the QuickBooks spell checker works. You can instruct QuickBooks to check spelling automatically before saving or printing any form.

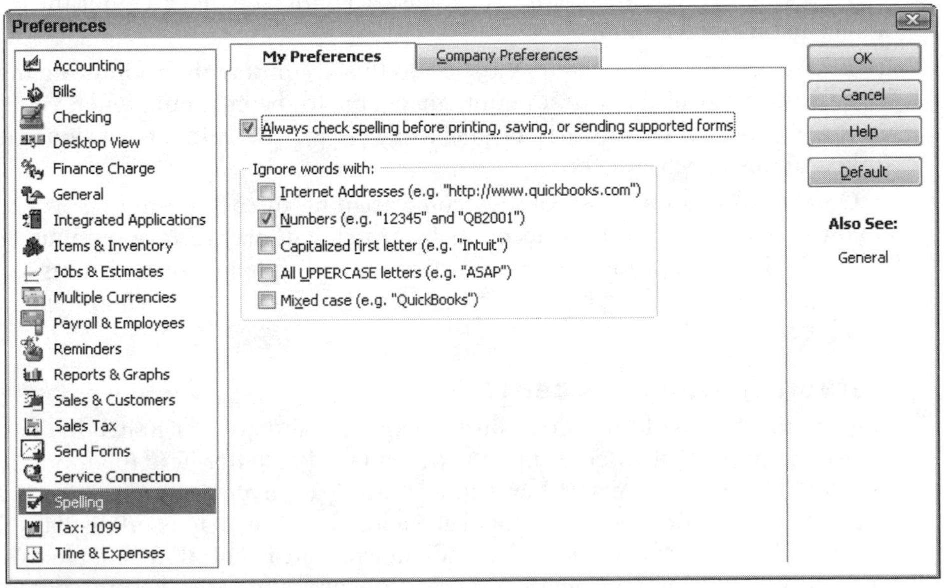

FIGURE 28-7 Set the default options for checking spelling.

In addition, you can specify those words you want the spelling checker to skip, such as Internet addresses, numbers, and solid capital letters that probably indicate an abbreviation.

Tax:1099 Preferences

Use this window to establish the 1099 form options you need. For each type of 1099 payment, you must assign an account from your chart of accounts. See Chapter 24 for detailed information about configuring and issuing 1099 forms.

Time & Expenses Preferences

Use this section in the Company Preferences tab to turn on Time Tracking and to tell QuickBooks the first day of your work week (which becomes the first day listed on your timesheets). Read all about tracking time in Chapter 16.

In addition, you can configure invoicing options, as explained in the following sections.

Track Reimbursed Expenses As Income

Selecting this option changes the way your general ledger handles customer payments for reimbursements. When the option is enabled, the reimbursement is assigned to an income account instead of posting back to the original expense account.

As a result of enabling this option, QuickBooks adds a new field to the dialog you use when you create or edit an expense account, so you can enter the associated income account.

Whenever you post a vendor expense to this account and also indicate that the expense is reimbursable, the amount you charge to the customer when you create an invoice for that customer is automatically posted to the income account that's linked to this expense account.

QuickBooks requires a separate income account for each reimbursable expense. If you have multiple expense accounts for which you may receive reimbursement (a highly likely scenario), you must also create multiple income accounts for accepting reimbursed expenses. See Chapter 11 to learn how to enter expenses as reimbursable.

Default Markup Percentage

You can preset a markup for reimbursed expenses and also for items that have both a cost and price. QuickBooks uses the percentage you enter here to automate the pricing of inventory items. When you're creating an inventory item, as soon as you enter the cost, QuickBooks automatically adds this percentage and displays the result as the price. If your pricing paradigm isn't consistent, don't enable this option; you'll find this automatic process more annoying than helpful, because you'll constantly find yourself re-entering the item's price.

Customizing Transaction Templates

QuickBooks makes it very easy to customize the forms you use to create transactions. (Forms such as invoices, purchase orders, statements, and so on, are called *templates* in QuickBooks.)

You can use an existing template as the basis of a new template, copying what you like, changing what you don't like, and eliminating what you don't need. Templates can be customized in two ways:

- **Basic customization**   Change the appearance by customizing the fonts, colors, and other output settings only—these are minor changes (a form of "window dressing") that can be made to built-in Intuit templates.
- **Additional customization**   Customize the fields and columns that appear on the template—these are major changes and require you to create a new template with a new template name.

Templates that have the word Intuit in the template name are designed to work with preprinted forms you purchase from Intuit (although you can use them with blank paper or letterhead). Except for the Intuit Packing Slip, you can only use basic customization on these templates. To use Intuit templates as the basis of additional customization, you must make a copy of the template and create a new template.

Basic Customization of Templates

To make minor changes to an existing template, select the template from the drop-down list in the Template field at the top right of the transaction window and click the Customize button on the template window toolbar. The Basic Customization dialog opens (see Figure 28-8), offering a number of ways to change the appearance of the template to suit your tastes.

Adding a Logo to a Template

You can add your company logo to a template by selecting the Use Logo check box. Click the Select Logo button to open the Select Image dialog, navigate to the folder that has your logo graphic file, and select the file. Use the following guidelines to add a logo to a template:

- The logo should be a square shape to fit properly on the template.
- QuickBooks accepts all the common graphic formats for your logo. However, the graphic loads when you print the template, and graphic files saved with a BMP format tend to be larger than other formats and may take quite some time to load each time you print. The most efficient format, in terms of size and resolution, is JPG.

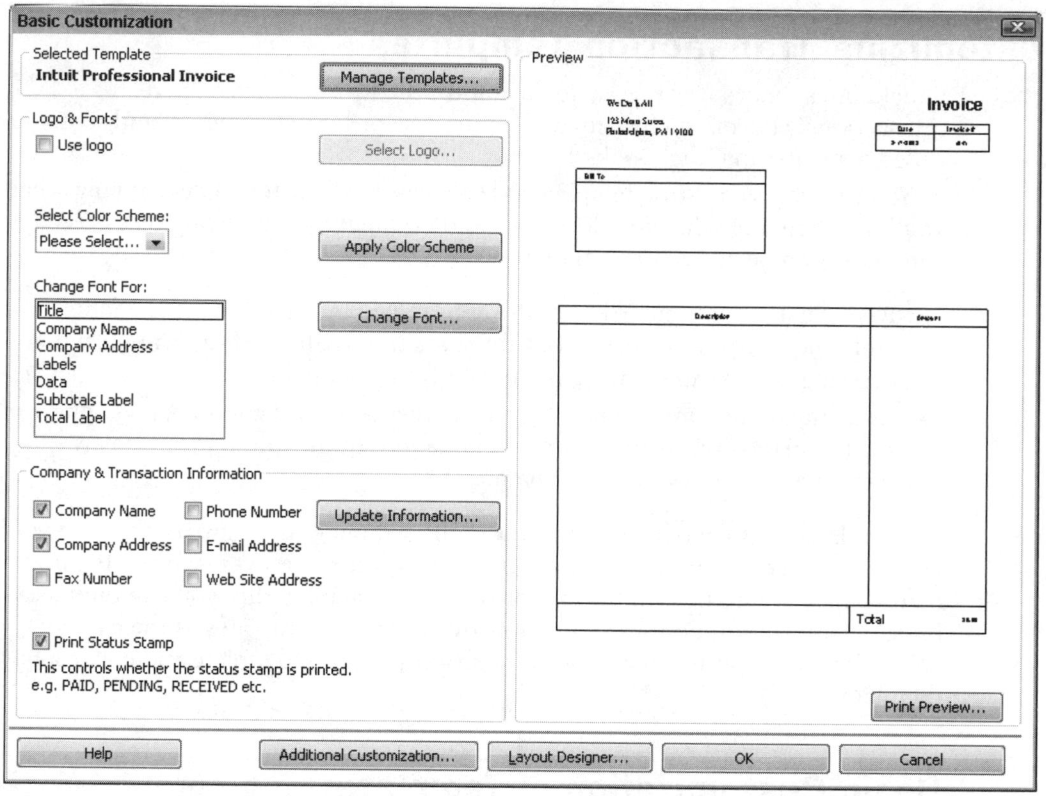

FIGURE 28-8 Change the appearance of a template in the Basic Customization dialog.

- Your logo appears in the upper-left corner of the form, unless you open the Layout Designer (covered later in this chapter) to reposition it.
- You won't see the logo on the screen version of the template.
- If you can't place the logo in the size and position you prefer, consider having stationery printed and using it as the paper source for the template.

Customizing Colors on a Template

You can change the color of the lines that appear on the template by selecting a color scheme from the drop-down list in the Select Color Scheme field. Click Apply Color Scheme to save the change and see its effect in the Preview pane on the right side of the dialog.

You can also change the color of any text that's printed on the form by using the features for changing fonts (covered next) and selecting a color for the font.

Customizing Fonts on a Template

To change the fonts for any elements on the template, select the element in the Change Font For list and click Change Font. Select a font, size, effect (such as bold or italic), or color.

Customizing the Company Information on a Template

You can select and deselect the text that appears in the name and address block of your templates. The data is taken from the Company Information dialog, which you can open by clicking Update Information, to make sure that the data exists.

Printing Status Stamps on Templates

You can select or deselect the option to print the status stamp on a transaction template (PAID, RECEIVED, and so on). The status stamp prints at an angle across the center of the header section of the template. If you deselect the status stamp, you are only removing it from the printed copy of the form; the screen copy always shows the status.

Additional Customization of Templates

You can make major changes in templates to suit your needs as well as your taste. QuickBooks calls this the "additional customization" feature. Start your customization by selecting an existing template on which to base your new template.

Duplicating an Existing Template

The best (and fastest) way to create a new template based on an existing template is to make a copy of the template you want to use as the base, using the following steps:

1. Choose Lists | Templates to open the Templates window, which displays a list of all the available templates.
2. Select the listing of the template you want to use, click the Templates button at the bottom of the window, and choose Duplicate.
3. In the Select Template Type dialog, choose the type of template you're creating (the available types differ depending on the type of template you selected), and click OK.
4. The duplicate appears in the list, with the title Copy Of: *<name of selected template>*.

Double-click the duplicate template you added to the list to open it in the Basic Customization dialog. The first task is to give the template a better name. For example, if you're adding a custom field for customer backorder preferences to the standard Product Invoice you can name the template ProdInv-BOPrefs.

▶▶ FYI

The List of Templates

If you've just started using QuickBooks, the template names you see in the Templates List may confuse you, because you'll notice that several types of templates aren't listed. The templates that appear in the list depend on the preferences you set and the transactions you've created.

By default, QuickBooks installs Invoice templates, a Statement template, and a Packing Slip template. You won't see a Purchase Order template unless you enable Inventory & Purchase Orders (covered earlier in this chapter) and also open the built-in Purchase Order template by choosing Vendors | Create Purchases Orders. As soon as the Create Purchase Orders transaction window opens, the Purchase Order template appears on the list (you can close the transaction window without creating a PO if your only purpose was to add the template to the list). The same paradigm applies to Sales Receipts, Estimates, and other QuickBooks templates.

In addition, you may see templates for transaction types you cannot use in QuickBooks Pro. I've seen QuickBooks Pro installations that displayed Sales Order templates in the list, and sales orders are only available in QuickBooks Premier/Enterprise editions.

Click Manage Templates to open the Manage Templates dialog with your duplicate template selected in the left pane—the Preview pane (on the right) displays a layout of the template as it currently looks and displays the template name at the top.

In the Template Name field at the top of the Preview pane, delete the current name and replace it with the name you want for your new template. Then click OK to return to the Basic Customization dialog.

In the Basic Customization dialog, click Additional Customization to open the dialog seen in Figure 28-9.

Notice that in Figure 28-9, the name I gave this template includes the text "BOPref," which refers to a custom field I created for tracking customer preferences for back orders. You can see that I opted to display this field on the screen version of the template (the field is a guideline for me when filling an order), but not the printed version that is sent to the customer.

Custom fields you create in a Names list appear in the Header section of transaction windows—custom fields you create in the Item List appear in the Columns section of transaction windows.

Customizing the Template Header

The Header section of the Additional Customization dialog includes all the fields that appear above the line items in a transaction form. You can add or remove fields on the screen form, the printed form, or both. The Preview pane on the right is a

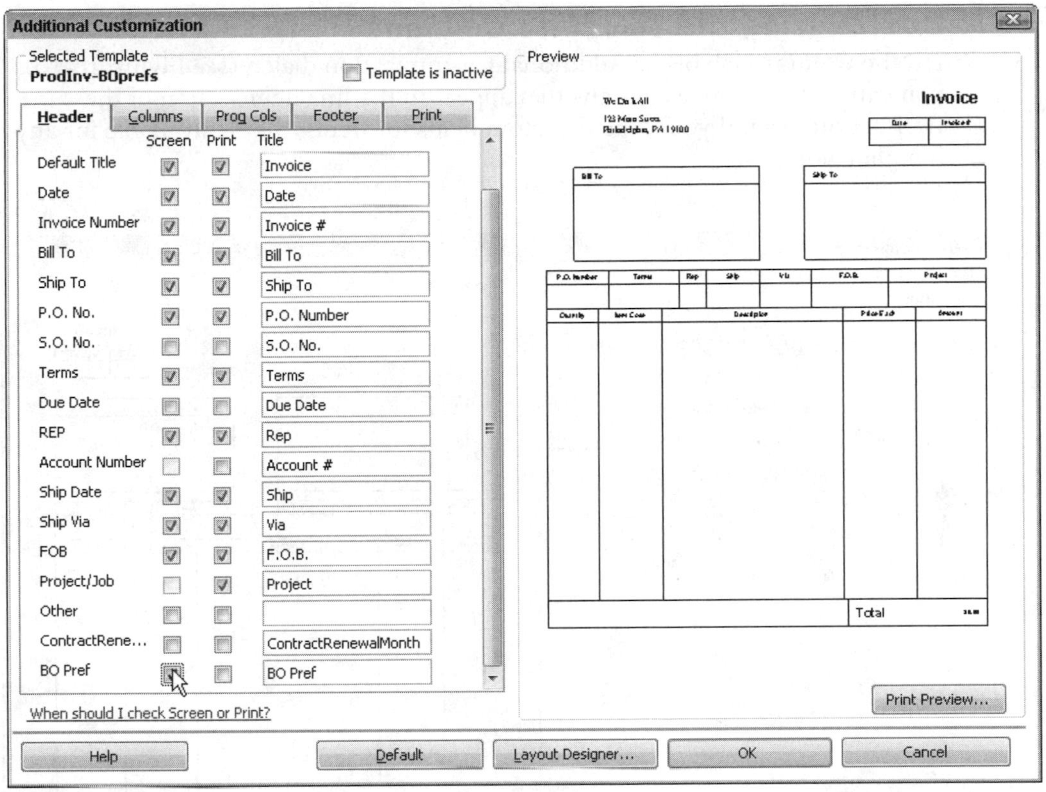

FIGURE 28-9 The Additional Customization dialog lets you point and click to redesign a template.

preview of the printed form, and as you add or remove fields from the printed form you see the changes reflected there.

Following are some changes to the Header section that are often effected by QuickBooks users (the data for the fields is automatically filled in using the data in the customer or vendor record when you use the template to create a transaction):

- If you assign account numbers to your customers, display the Account Number field (only available on the printed version).

- If you use Reps, either as commissioned salespersons or as customer support contacts, add the Rep field to both the screen and printed versions.

- If you're tracking jobs for the majority of your customers, add the job name to the form (only available in the printed version). QuickBooks uses the term "Project" because that's the commonly used term in most businesses (the exception is the construction trade, where "Job" is a common term). If you refer to jobs as "jobs" with your customers, you can change the text.

Customizing the Template Columns

On the Columns tab of the Additional Customization dialog (see Figure 28-10), you can add or remove columns that appear in the line item section of the transaction form. If you created custom fields for items, they're available for any template you design.

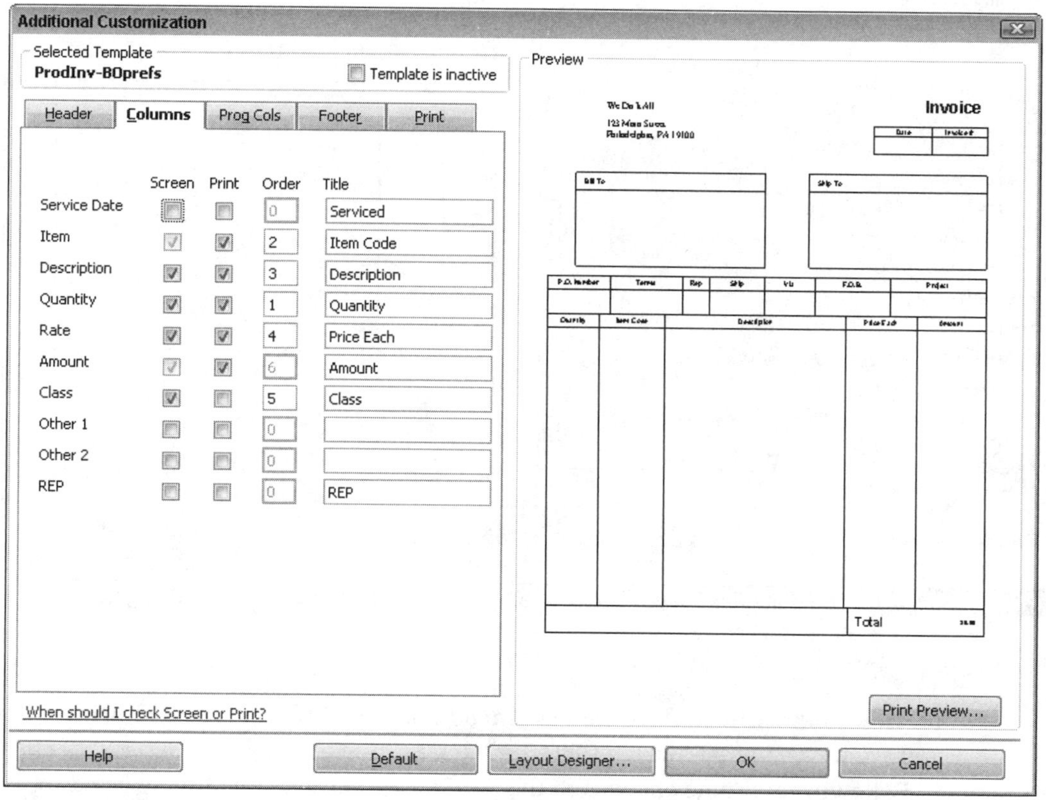

FIGURE 28-10 Add columns to specify details of the items you're including in the transaction.

If progress invoicing is turned on, another columns tab, called Prog Cols, is available for customizing the transaction form you use when you create a progress invoice against an estimate (to learn how to create estimates and progress invoices, read Chapter 9).

Customizing the Template Footer

The Footer tab (see Figure 28-11) contains the elements that appear at the bottom of the transaction form. If you want to add additional fields to this section of the printed transaction form, you'll have to use the Layout Designer to maneuver the positioning, because you don't have a lot of space to work with.

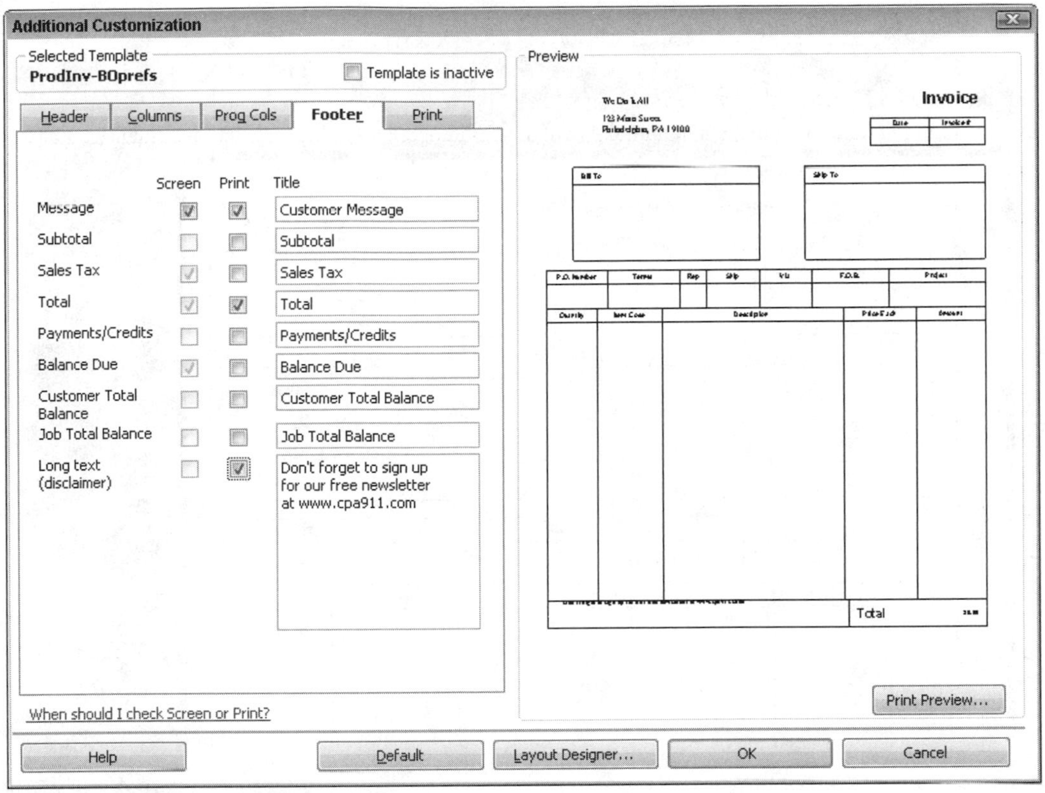

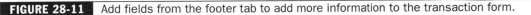

FIGURE 28-11 Add fields from the footer tab to add more information to the transaction form.

Using the Layout Designer

As you customize the printed forms, you can see the effects in the Preview pane. If you notice some overlapping fields, or you think the layout looks too crowded, you can use the Layout Designer to reposition the elements on the form. Click Layout Designer to open your template in the Layout Designer window, as seen in Figure 28-12.

The Layout Designer is a powerful and complicated feature, and it's beyond the scope of this book to go into deep detail about it. However, in this section I'll mention some of the commonly used functions.

If you use window envelopes to mail your invoices, be sure the option Show Envelope Window at the bottom of the Layout Designer is selected before you start. The areas of the form that appear in envelope windows are highlighted in green. This helps you avoid moving any fields into that area.

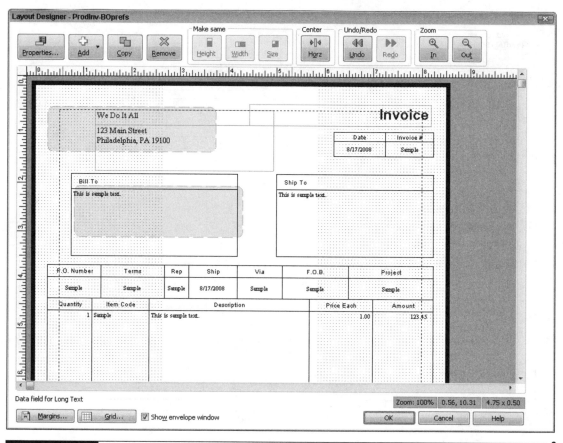

FIGURE 28-12 You can reposition the elements in the form to create your own design.

Select any element to put a frame around it. Now you can perform an action on the frame, as follows:

- To change the size of the element, position your pointer on one of the sizing handles on the frame, then drag the handle to resize the element.
- To move an element, position your pointer inside the frame and, when your pointer turns into a four-headed arrow, drag the frame to a different location on the form.
- Double-click an element's frame to see a Properties dialog (shown next) that permits all sorts of changes for the selected element.

Properties

Data field for Rep

| **Text** | Border | Background |

Justification

Horizontal

○ Left   ☐ Indent First Line of Text

○ Right

● Center

Vertical

○ Top

○ Bottom

● Center

Font...   Color ▮▮▮▮▮

OK   Cancel   Help

- To change the margin measurements, click the Margins button at the bottom of the Layout Designer.
- Click the Grid button to open the Grid And Snap Settings dialog where you can eliminate the dotted line grid, change the spacing between grid lines, or turn off the Snap To Grid option (automatically aligns objects to the nearest point on the grid).
- Use the toolbar buttons to align, resize, and zoom into the selected elements. There's also an Undo/Redo button, thank goodness.

When you finish with the Layout Designer, click OK to move back to the Additional Customization window. If everything is just the way you want it, save your new template by clicking OK. This new template name appears on the drop-down list when you create transaction forms.

 TIP: You can also use this new template as the basis for other customizations.

Appendix

Most computer books have an appendix, because it's a way to provide detailed information about a topic that you may or may not have an interest in.

In Part Five of this book, you'll find an appendix that provides information about using the QuickBooks multicurrency feature. This is a great way to track financial data for foreign customers and vendors; without this feature you'd have to maintain complicated spreadsheets to track exchange rates to figure out what your customers really owe, or what you really owe your vendors.

Multicurrency

I *n this appendix:*

- Set up and configure multicurrency
- Set up and configure customers and vendors for multicurrency
- Create transactions in other currencies
- Run reports

If you do business with customers or vendors in other countries, you can create transactions in their currency. You can track the exchange rate, so you always know what the transactions mean to you in US Dollars. This appendix provides an overview of the Multicurrency feature in QuickBooks.

Setting Up and Configuring Multicurrency

Before you can begin creating transactions in different currencies, you have some configuration and setup tasks to attend to.

It's important to know that unlike most of the configuration preferences available in QuickBooks, once you enable multiple currencies, you can't disable it. If you're already using QuickBooks (either because you updated your company files from a previous version or because you began creating transactions before deciding to use multiple currencies), back up your company file before enabling this feature.

Creating a Special Backup

When you create your backup before turning on multiple currencies, don't use your normal backup routine. Instead, name the backup file differently so you can identify it easily, and also to avoid having the backup file overwritten with "regular" backups.

When you save your backup file change the name of the file from the usual *<CompanyFileName>*.QBB to *<CompanyFileName>*-BeforeMulticurrency.QBB. It's also a good idea to copy the backup file to a CD.

TIP: If you change your mind later and decide not to use multicurrency, and you don't want to restore the backup (because you'd have to re-enter all the transactions you'd created while multicurrency was enabled), it's not harmful to keep using the company file with multicurrency enabled (as long as you use customers, vendors, and accounts that are not linked to another currency). The only side effect you'll experience is that some windows and dialogs have an extra field for currency (printed versions of transaction documents do not have currency information); no financial information is compromised.

Enabling Multicurrency

To enable the Multicurrency feature, choose Edit | Preferences and click the Multiple Currencies category icon in the left pane. In the Company Preferences tab (see Figure A-1), select Yes, I Use More Than One Currency.

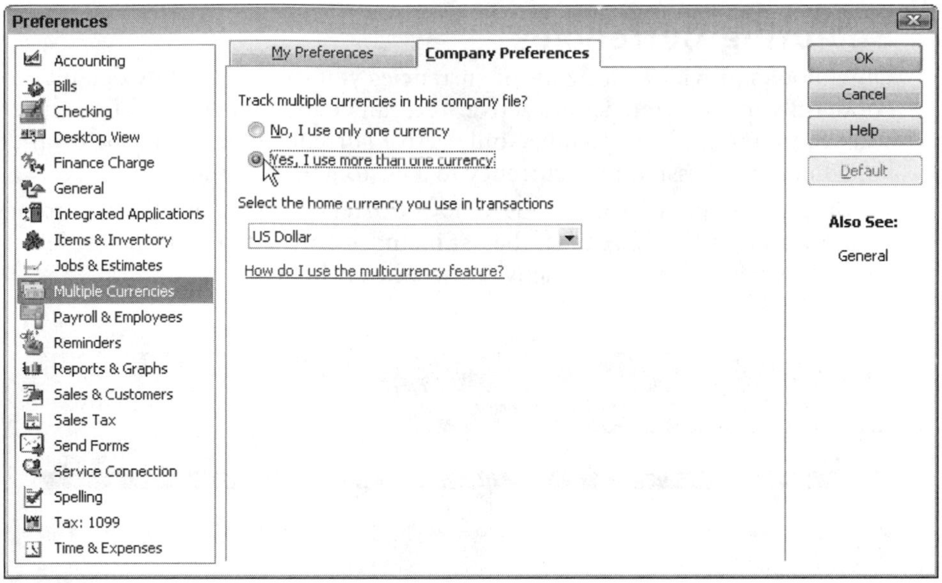

FIGURE A-1 Enable multicurrency and select your home currency.

When you select Yes, QuickBooks displays a warning message.

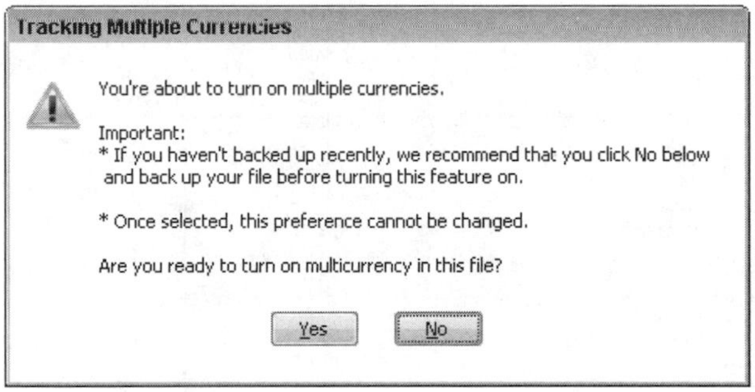

If you've already made a backup, as discussed in the previous section, you can continue. If not, stop the process and create your backup. Then enable multicurrency.

The dialog offers the opportunity to change your home currency from US Dollars to another currency. Changing your home currency is not a good idea, because QuickBooks tracks payroll, sales tax, online banking, and other basic data in US Dollars only.

Selecting Currencies

QuickBooks provides a long list of currencies you can use, but by default only the commonly used currencies are active. You can change the list of active currencies to suit your own needs. Remember, only active currencies appear in the drop-down list when you're assigning a currency to a customer or vendor.

Choose Company | Manage Currency | Currency List to open the Currency List window seen in Figure A-2. (If the list includes only active currencies, select the check box labeled Include Inactive to see the entire list.)

✖	Currency (1 unit)	Code	Exchange Rate (X units)	As of Date
✖	Afghanistan Afghani	AFN		
✖	Albanian Leke	ALL		
✖	Algerian Dinar	DZD		
✖	Angolan Kwanza	AOA		
✖	Argentine Peso	ARS		
✖	Armenian Dram	AMD		
✖	Aruban Florin	AWG		
✖	Australian Dollar	AUD		
✖	Azerbaijanian Manat	AZN		
✖	Bahamian Dollar	BSD		
✖	Bahraini Dinar	BHD		
✖	Bangladesh Taka	BDT		
✖	Barbados Dollar	BBD		
✖	Belarussian Ruble	BYR		
✖	Belize Dollar	BZD		
✖	Bermudian Dollar	BMD		
✖	Bhutan Ngultrum	BTN		
✖	Bolivia Bolivianos	BOB		
✖	Botswana Pula	BWP		
✖	Brazilian Real	BRL		
	British Pound Sterling	GBP	1.95215	08/07/...
✖	Brunei Dollar	BND		
✖	Bulgarian Leva	BGN		
✖	Burundi Franc	BIF		
✖	Cambodian Riel	KHR		
	Canadian Dollar	CAD	0.954335	08/07/...
✖	Cayman Islands Dollar	KYD		
✖	Chilean Peso	CLP		
	Chinese Yuan Renminbi	CNY	0.14562	08/07/...
✖	Columbian Peso	COP		
✖	Costa Rican Colon	CRC		
✖	Croatian Kuna	HRK		
✖	Cuban Peso	CUP		
✖	Cypriot Pound	CYP		
✖	Czech Koruna	CZK		
✖	Danish Krone	DKK		
✖	Dominican Peso	DOP		

Currency ▾   Activities ▾   Reports ▾   ☑ Include inactive

FIGURE A-2   Activate the currencies you need.

To activate an inactive currency, click the X in the leftmost column to remove the X; to make an active currency inactive, click the leftmost column to place an X in the column.

Notice that each currency has a three-letter abbreviation; for example, US Dollar is USD.

You can, if necessary, create a currency if the one you need doesn't appear on the list (a rare occurrence since the list seems very comprehensive to me). With the Currency List window open, press CTRL-N to open the New Currency dialog and configure the currency.

Tracking Exchange Rates

Because QuickBooks tracks both the customer/vendor currency and its worth in your home currency, you need to make sure the exchange rate is accurate. If the exchange rate isn't accurate, your financial reports, which use US Dollars, aren't accurate.

To update the exchange rate for all your active currencies, choose Company | Manage Currency | Download Latest Exchange Rates. QuickBooks travels to the Internet to get the current rates (you don't see an Internet page; all of this is done in the background). When your active currencies have been updated, QuickBooks displays a success message. You can see the updated exchange rates in the Currency List.

Managing Customers and Vendors with Foreign Currencies

You need to identify the currency of every customer and vendor in your company file. QuickBooks automatically assigns your home currency (USD) to all customers and vendors, so you only need to change those that do business in a different currency.

Creating Customers and Vendors with Currency Assignments

When you create customers and vendors who do business in another currency, the basic steps are the same as creating any new customer or vendor in QuickBooks. The only difference is the existence of a Currency Field in the New Customer or New Vendor dialog.

As you can see in Figure A-3, QuickBooks inserts US Dollar in the Currency field, but you can choose another currency from the drop-down list (which displays only those currencies you've marked Active).

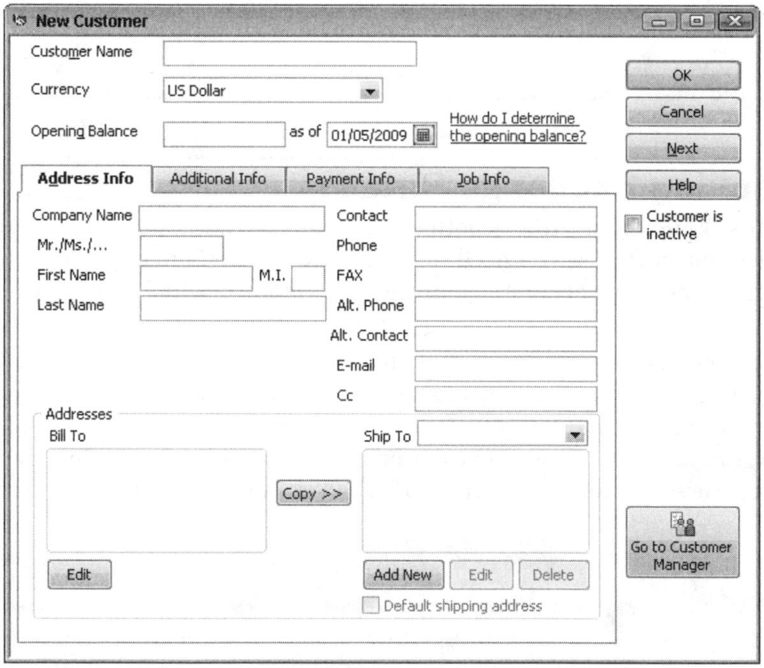

FIGURE A-3   If the new customer or vendor you're creating uses a foreign currency, change the default data by selecting a currency from the drop-down list.

> **$** **NOTE:** If you select a currency other than USD, the Opening Balance field is inaccessible, which is a good thing since you should never use that field when setting up a new customer or vendor. See Chapter 3 for information about creating customers, and Chapter 4 for information about creating vendors.

Changing Currency for Existing Customers and Vendors

You can only change the currency specification for existing customers and vendors that have no transactions. It doesn't matter whether the current open balance is 0.00; the existence of any transaction prevents you from changing the currency. For those customers and vendors, you must create a new entity with the new currency. You cannot merge customers or vendors that have different currencies.

Editing Existing Customers and Vendors

To edit the currency of an existing customer or vendor that has no existing transactions, open the appropriate center, select the customer/vendor, and click the Edit button in the right pane. Select the currency from the drop-down list in the Currency field, and click OK.

Creating New Customers and Vendors for Multicurrency

To create a new customer or vendor for existing accounts with a foreign currency specification, create the new entity using the following guidelines.

In the Name field, use the same name as the existing entity, but add text to make the name unique (QuickBooks does not allow duplicates in the Name field).

It's best to add text after the name, so the customer/vendor appears in the right place in drop-down fields in transaction windows. For example, in Figure A-4, I'm creating a new customer to assign a new currency to an existing customer (you can see the existing customer name in the Customer & Jobs list). I added the three-digit abbreviation for the customer's currency to create a unique name.

Remember that the data in the Name field doesn't appear on transaction documents; instead QuickBooks uses the data in the Company Name and Address fields (and, for Vendors, there's even a field labeled "Print On Check As").

Managing Existing Open Transactions

When you create new customers and vendors, you have to manage existing open transactions using the original customer or vendor. There's no way to accept or make a payment linked to the original entity using the new entity. When the open balance for the original entity becomes zero, you can make the original customer or vendor inactive so the listing doesn't appear in drop-down lists in transaction windows. Use the new (duplicate) entity for all new transactions.

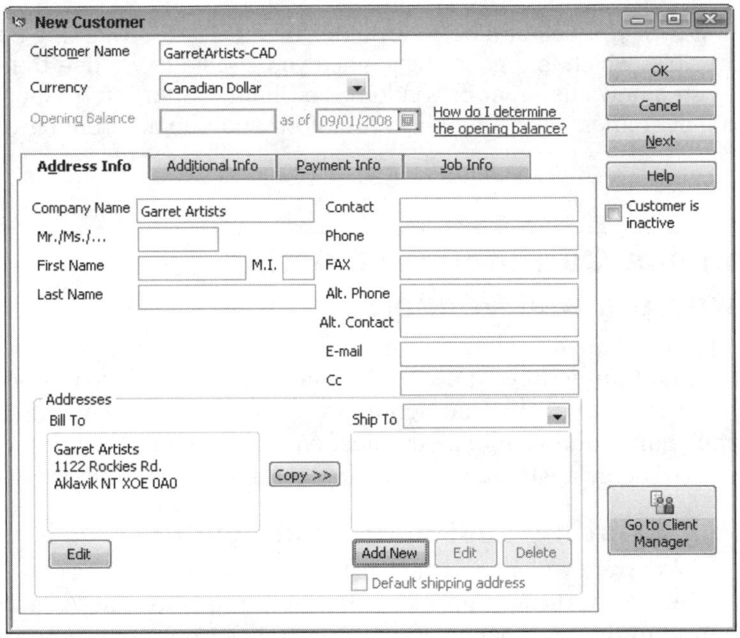

FIGURE A-4 The new customer has the currency appended to the name; everything else is the same as the existing customer.

Currency Data in Customer and Vendor Centers

After you've enabled multicurrency, the Customer Center and Vendor Center display currency information in both panes (see Figure A-5).

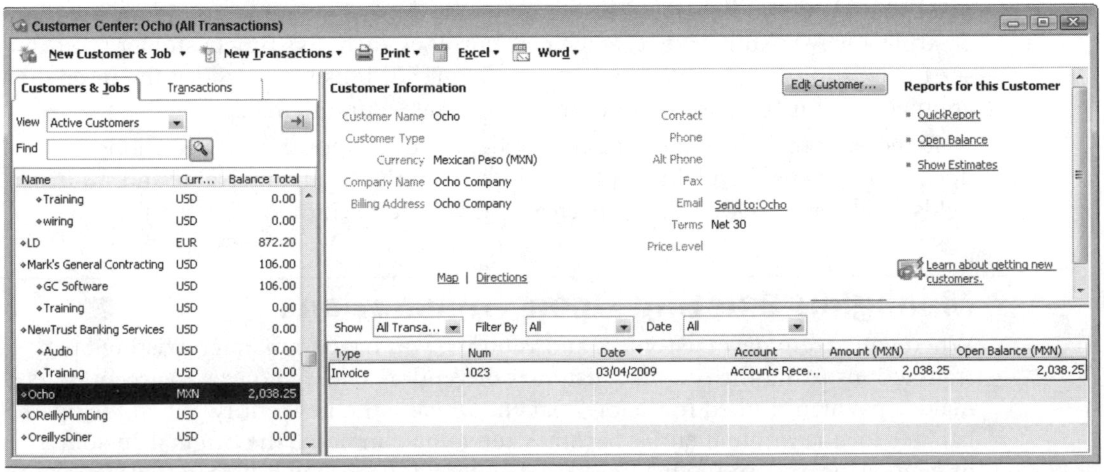

FIGURE A-5 The Customer Center displays information in the customers' currencies.

QuickBooks makes the following changes automatically:

- In the List pane, the currency is noted for each customer/vendor and the current balance total displays using the customer/vendor currency.
- In the Details pane, the Amount and Open Balance columns display amounts in the currency of the customer or vendor.

You can change these default settings to make it easier to understand the data you see in the centers.

Configuring the List Pane

In the List pane you can add the current balance total in USD to save yourself the need to calculate the "real money."

You can either remove the Balance Total column for the foreign currency or display both Balance Total columns. If you frequently talk to vendors or customers about current balances, it's handy to have the foreign currency balance in front of you, so having both amounts display makes sense. However, to save room in the List pane, remove the Currency column.

Configuring the Details Pane

In the Details pane you can add the Home Currency column if it makes you more comfortable.

Chart of Accounts for Multicurrency Transactions

As you create transactions in other currencies QuickBooks adds accounts to your chart of accounts:

- An Accounts Receivable account for each currency
- An Accounts Payable account for each currency

Creating Transactions in Other Currencies

When you open a sales or payment transaction window, QuickBooks automatically takes care of the currency issues by adding fields to the transaction window.

If the customer or vendor currency is USD, you won't see much difference between the transaction window for multicurrency and the same transaction window before you enabled multicurrency. The only real difference is that the text "USD" appears for "Total" amounts.

If the customer or vendor is configured for another currency, the transaction window changes to provide the information you need. For example, Figure A-6 shows an invoice for a customer in Mexico, and Figure A-7 shows a vendor bill for a vendor in the UK who does business in Euros.

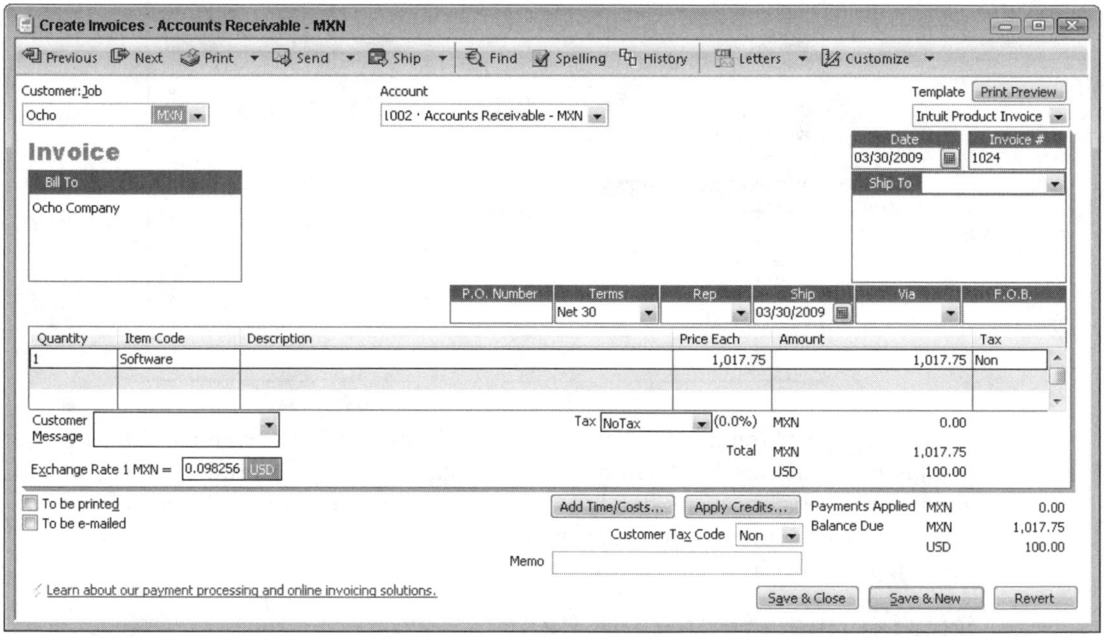

FIGURE A-6   This invoice displays all the data I need to make sense of this transaction.

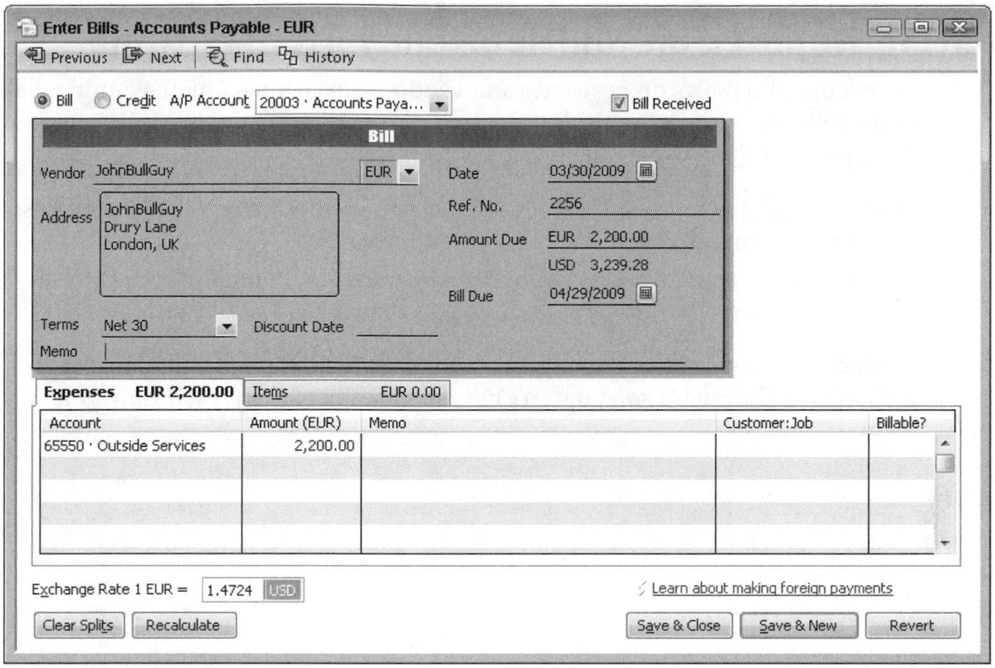

FIGURE A-7 When I enter the amount of the bill in Euros (which is what the bill that arrived showed), QuickBooks also displays the amount in USD.

Notice the following about these transaction windows:

- The A/R or A/P account is specific to the currency.
- The amounts in the line items are displayed in the customer/vendor currency.
- There are two totals: one for the transaction currency and one for USD.
- The Exchange Rate field displays the exchange rate used when this transaction was created.

The printed versions of transactions that are sent to customers (invoices, credits, and so on) and vendors (checks) do not display any fields or data related to USD; those fields only appear on the screen for your convenience.

Be sure to update the exchange rates often. If the exchange rate changes between the day you enter an invoice or bill and the day you receive a payment or make a payment, QuickBooks automatically adds an Other Expense account named Exchange Gain or Loss to track the net amounts that accrue from adjustments in exchange rates for current open balances.

Creating Reports on Multicurrency Transactions

By default, all reports on customer and vendor transactions (such as Aging, Sales, Purchases, and so on) are displayed in your home currency (USD). You can modify the reports so they display the appropriate currencies.

- For Summary reports, click Modify Report, and in the section labeled Display Amounts In, select Transaction Currency.
- For Detail reports, click Modify Report and select Foreign Amount in the Columns list. You may also want to add the Currency column.

Memorize these reports, using a name that reflects the contents (such as Transaction Currency) so you don't have to customize them each time you create them.

Index